Priory Demesne to University Campus

A topographic history of Nottingham University

by Frank Barnes

Frank Barnes
8-XI-93

Published by the University of Nottingham, 1993

ISBN 0 900572 81 7

Printed by Technical Print Services Ltd, Nottingham

DEDICATION

To honour the memory of my two great teachers, Professor Henry Hurd Swinnerton and Professor Kenneth Charles Edwards

FRONT COVER - 'Trent Tower' by M.W.(Bill) Partridge, 1964: Oil on canvas, 30 x 24 inches.
[Maurice William Partridge (1913-1973); Lord Trent Professor of Pharmaceutical Chemistry 1960-1973; Deputy Vice-Chancellor, University of Nottingham 1972-73]

BACK COVER - A fragment of the rental of Lenton Priory's possessions in Lenton and Radford, dated 30 May, 30 Henry VIII (1538). This portion of the 22 feet long parchment roll, which is included among the Middleton collection of manuscripts held in the University's Department of Manuscripts, relates to the priory's demesne or home farm, and includes the University campus as understood in this book, with Trent Wong, now Grove Farm, as the last item. A free transcript appears below as Table 6.

PREFACE

This study of the topographic history and historical geography of the campus of the University of Nottingham and its immediate environs is not to be regarded as a history of the University, which is understood to be in preparation by another author. The central subject of this volume is landscape evolution and not institutional development: indeed the topographic history of each of the individual properties of which the present campus is compounded reaches a natural conclusion upon its becoming part of the University's estate. The final chapter, outlining the physical development by the University of the various constituent estates as parts of a unified campus is of the nature of an appendix, intended to focus attention on the relationship between the new pattern of land use and landscape on the consolidated University estate and the structure that it superseded, pointing out such legacies of the pre-academic landscape as survive, as either active or relict elements, and indicating their place in the present scene.

The University campus, as understood here, is essentially the 'upland' part of the former demesne of Lenton Priory. Except for the site of the Queen's Medical Centre, which is discussed at some length, the history of recent extensions of the University's estate beyond the area allocated for long-term University use by Nottingham city's development plan - and in particular recent residential building in the adjoining part of Beeston and at Bramcote - are not pursued in detail, and the School of Agriculture at Sutton Bonington is totally excluded. No detailed consideration is given to the property in Dunkirk purchased by the University, or to the Department of Adult Education in the city and the surrounding region. On the other hand, that part of Lenton Abbey housing estate north-east of Woodside Road, and Lenton House and its grounds, though not owned by the University, are regarded as parts of the natural geohistorical unit that formed the core of the priory demesne and is now the essential campus of Nottingham University, so they are seen as lacunae within the campus. The low-lying tract of southern Lenton formed by the floor of the Trent vale between University Park and the Beeston Canal finds a place in the earlier discussion as part of the former priory demesne, while Grove Farm, the University playing fields alongside the river Trent, is included because it enjoys much the same sort of relationship to the University campus as it did to the main priory demesne when it was demesne meadow called Trent Wong.

Geographical space and historical time form a continuum, and so do human society and its locale; and the writer believes that the character of neither places nor people can be properly understood either in isolation from each other or without regard to their origins and external relationships. That is why attention is given in this essay to some of the wider family, social and business connections of those who owned and occupied the campus area in the past, and why the physiographic and geological elements that provide the underpinning and the most basic constituents of the physical landscape are set out in some detail and are related where possible to the historical utilization and organization of the land, as well as to their contribution to the present landscape.

This book has its roots in the author's curiosity about his surroundings which increased over the fifty years through which he worked on the campus as student and teacher, for thirty of them living within it, as an undergraduate at Hugh Stewart Hall, a house tutor at Wortley Hall, and from 1962 to 1985 as the founding Warden of Derby Hall, observing at first hand and at close quarters the old landscape giving place to the new, and in some instances playing a minor part in implementing the change. Eventually this led to a wish to record the outcome of a long experience of using the campus as a teaching laboratory for training undergraduate students of geography in field observation and recording, and in inductive and deductive reasoning from their observations, extending from 1948 to 1985 as the University expanded from the original small campus of the University College. Indeed, this experience could be said to have begun as early as 1940-41, when the writer, still an undergraduate, was employed by the University College as Professor Swinnerton's Demonstrator before leaving for war service. Finally, encouragement by University friends and colleagues who also recognize in the campus a rich and convenient field for landscape study, and the interest shown by others associated with the University, provided a persuasive reason for setting down accumulated factual information in a structured form for their use or interest. It is hoped that this book will be a reference source not only for those who may use the 'campus trail' pamphlets planned as adjuncts to this book, but also for those who simply wish to satisfy their curiosity about the nature and history of their immediate environment, whether as resident, neighbour or visitor.

BIBLIOGRAPHIC NOTE

Care has been taken to provide full references, which may lead some readers towards further inquiry or study of primary unpublished data as well as secondary sources. The nature of the source material has required the use of a dual system of reference. For published work, whether books or articles, the Harvard system is adopted, with the author's name and the year of publication (and page number where appropriate) given in parenthesis in the body of the text, and a list of the publications cited provided in alphabetical order of authors' names at the end of the volume. Unpublished manuscript references and brief notes are located by successive superscript numbers in the text referring to a numerical list of notes at the end of each chapter. In the later chapters published Directories are important sources of data, and are referred to by the Harvard system using name of publisher instead of author, with a separate list at the end of the volume. More extensive notes thought to be appropriate and useful, but which might divert the reader from the immediate subject under discussion in the text are relegated as appendices to the end of the volume.

ACKNOWLEDGMENTS

Sincere thanks are due to very many friends and colleagues for their interest in this book, and for the encouragement (not to mention goading) they have given to me in its preparation, but I am especially indebted in this regard to Professors Richard Osborne and John Cole and Dr. Catherine Delano-Smith (Geography) and Professor John Beckett (History) . Expert advice and help have been freely given by Chris Lewis (Chief Cartographer) and Mervyn Evans (Photographer) of the Geography Department in the preparation of the illustrations, and Mr. Lewis drew all the maps. I am grateful, too, for help from Michael Brook, John Briggs and other colleagues in the University's Hallward Library, Special Collections, and from Alan Cameron, Dr. Dorothy Johnston and Linda Shaw of the Department of Manuscripts; John Saunders and David Martin (Directorate of Works); Donald Smith (formerly Deputy Bursar, Administration); and the late Peter Mellors of Messrs. Rotheras (Solicitors). Professor Beckett, Brian Loughbrough (formerly Director of Leisure Services, Nottingham City), Philip Dalling (University Information Officer), Professor Paul Mather (Head of the Department of Geography) and Keith Bradley (Director of Technical Print Services) have been especially helpful with the practical problems of publication, which would not have been possible without the backing of Graham Chandler (Registrar of the University) and generous financial support from the Boots Company plc and Nottingham City Council. Sandra Rose (the Boots Company plc, Corporate Affairs) provided Figure 107 and arranged for Pete Ramskill to design the striking book cover and advise on layout of text. I am also, of course, greatly indebted to the owners and custodians of manuscripts, photographs and prints and to the Ordnance Survey for permission to reproduce their archival and copyright material. I am especially grateful to Lord Middleton for allowing me to use transcripts of many manuscripts from the great corpus of the Middleton Papers held in the University's Department of Manuscripts, and to reproduce part of the Dissolution rental of 1538 on the back cover of this book.

CONTENTS

LIST OF FIGURES

LIST OF TABLES

INTRODUCTORY FOREWORD

In the words of the late Professor K.C.Edwards 'the elegant landscape which forms the University district results from an impressive grouping of natural and man-made features'. The campus occupies a position on the north side of the Trent valley between Lenton and Beeston, and in terms of physical geography its boundaries are the two south-flowing tributaries of the river Trent, the river Leen in the east and the Tottle Brook in the west and south. The northern boundary is the ancient Nottingham to Derby road. The main valley-side rises sharply north-westwards from the edge of the flat floodplain of the Trent to a spine of high ground that runs from Wortley House (formerly Wortley Hall and before that Lenton Firs) southwards to Hugh Stewart Hall (formerly Lenton Hall) and Lenton House. Partly because the land falls to the Leen and the Tottle Brook, flowing some one hundred feet below the level of the ridge-top, and partly for geological reasons, the mile-long valley-side slope above the flat Trent valley floor is steepest in its middle portion, where the Trent Building occupies a commanding position, earlier enjoyed by Highfield House, which now lies behind it.

The particularly extensive outlook from this part of the campus is due in part to the abnormal breadth and flatness of the Trent vale. The present meandering river Trent, which in this reach runs along the southern margin of the vale beneath the high river bluff of Clifton Grove, occupies a valley that was powerfully eroded by the discharge along it during interglacial and early postglacial times of great quantities of ice meltwater which spread a vast sheet of thick gravel over its floor. Subsequent erosion by the meandering river has left some discontinuous terraces of gravel, especially along the sides of the vale, but the lower gravel surface is covered with silt deposited by the Trent in times of flood. The level nature of the valley floor has been exploited by laying out playing fields along University Boulevard, including the University sports grounds, and, indeed, the more recently developed University grounds at Grove Farm alongside the river across the vale. The same circumstance was exploited earlier by establishing large railway sidings and extensive industrial sites, notably by the Boots Company beyond the railway, and this form of development has spread over a greatly increased area during the past two decades.

The view from the Trent building is extended by reason of a wide break in the opposite slope of the vale provided by a tributary valley now drained by the Fairham Brook, but in origin probably an earlier course of the river Trent before its northward diversion as a consequence of glaciation. Thus on a clear day the Wolds of Leicestershire and other distant hills can be seen beyond the vale. On either side of this gap the river valley shows normal development, with the tree-lined Clifton Grove on the one hand and Wilford Hill, crowned by a cemetery on the other - counterparts of the University campus.

The physical compactness of the campus does not derive from the details of configuration, but from recent planning decisions and land acquisition: yet the layout of its physical geography played a part through its influence on the history of the area's utilization over many centuries. The river Leen and the Tottle Brook separate the campus from the built-up areas of Nottingham and Beeston because they formed early administrative and property boundaries, and in particular boundaries of the demesne of Lenton Priory, which experienced a tenurial history quite distinct from those of the adjoining areas, preserving it in a largely undeveloped condition. The lower Leen valley has provided level land for the extensive sites of the Faculties of Science and Engineering, and of Medicine with the University Hospital. The smaller Tottle Brook is now entirely culverted in its lower course along Woodside Road, but reappears in the public University Park close to the lake, though much of its course within the park is artificial.

The alignment of the Trent valley-side governs much of the layout of the original College and University buildings and their surroundings, not only because of their initial planning in close

Figure 1: Aerial view of the University district in 1956

conjunction with the development in the early 1920s of the lake, University Boulevard and the playing fields below as one formal concept, but also, to a degree, on account of previous tenurial history. Buildings and drives on this part of the campus run parallel to the line of the valley side on the one hand, and to that of the old track called Cut Through Lane on the other, to give a formal note to the whole landscape (Figure 1). The larger and newer part of the campus towards Derby Road, however, presents a much more informal scene, with buildings, gardens and clusters of trees less regularly disposed, and strongly influenced by pre-existing features, many of which are incorporated in the University landscape plan.

At first sight the geological composition of the site may appear to be less influential than its geomorphology, but it is certainly of interest, not only because it largely determined the varied nature of the original soils but also because it underlies many of the more prominent, permanent characteristics of the landscape of the campus. The surface outcrops, apart from superficial river deposits, comprise nearly all the formations of the New Red Sandstone (Triassic) series, but none other, although mining in underlying Coal Measures at a shallow depth caused worries about possible subsidence in the post-war period of building development.

Although geological conditions on the campus are discussed in some detail below, two further introductory points can be made. First, much of the campus is occupied by the mainly sandstone rocks now called the Sherwood Forest Sandstone Group (formerly the Bunter), either the red Lenton Sandstone (formerly called the Lower Mottled Sandstone), geomorphologically weak and tending to form low ground, or the more resistant Nottingham Castle formation (formerly the Bunter Pebble Beds), the yellow or buff coloured sandstone so well seen at the Castle Rock in Nottingham. However, the central part of the original campus, and the area containing the chief non-Departmental buildings - the Trent and Portland buildings and the Hallward Library - takes the form of a block of Mercia Mudstones (Keuper Marl) preserved between two normal (inward-sloping) east-west faults about 400 metres apart. Structurally this is a faulted trough (graben), yet it forms part of the highest ground, producing a discordance between geological structure and surface relief. Immediately south of the more southerly of the two faults, below the Great Hall wing of the Trent Building, the general slope ends abruptly in a cliff of Nottingham Castle sandstone which rises to about 40 feet above the edge of the lake, a river cliff similar, on a smaller scale, to the Nottingham Castle rock itself, and containing artificially excavated rock shelters of unknown age.

A second geological point of note is the possible danger to large buildings on account of the instability of the ground, actual or potential. It could be hazardous to build across the faults, even though there is no evidence of any significant earth movement along them. But perhaps more important, especially on the steeper part of the slope formed by Mercia Mudstone rocks, is the danger of slipping of heavy structures. This possibility was foreseen when the Trent Building was constructed in the 1920s, and the 'marl' was stabilized by building massive terraces overlooking the lake on foundations reaching to three feet below the level of the lake bed, backed by a series of concrete buttresses driven into the slope behind. The Trent Building itself was then based on foundations carried down to a depth that allowed them to rest on the stabilized layers. Thus the terraces, besides providing an amenity now sadly neglected, perform a vital engineering function, though they added greatly to the building cost. Less elaborate precautions were taken when the Portland Building was erected.

In many parts of the campus the construction of large buildings, roads and other 'infrastructure' has involved massive earth moving which has raised or lowered appreciable areas of the surface of the campus. For this reason caution is needed when interpreting the forms of the physical landscape as they now appear, and the nature of the underlying rock and the soil upon it. A notable example of large-scale earth sculpture, though not in fact on University property, is the lake in University Park. Well over half a mile long, with a general depth of one and a half metres, it was constructed, together with the park, the lido (now demolished) and University Boulevard during the period 1921 to 1926, and required the removal of 350,000 tons of material, including 240,000 tons of gravel. The first 'fishpond' constructed by the Lowes of Highfield House below the sandstone cliff of the 'staff garden' in about 1830 was fed from the Tottle Brook, but the much extended lake of today was excavated to a depth below the water table of the valley gravels, and is kept at a stable surface level by seepage.

Manifestly the University campus is an area in which the workings of nature and man can be studied in their close interrelationships, and in this respect the rich endowment of mature trees of both native and exotic species is one example, and the houses of those who planted them form another. The campus bears many traces of earlier human occupance over a very long period in the form of house sites, industrial sites, old tracks and the marks of ancient agriculture, all of which are discussed in the pages following. Most of the land that once formed the demesne or home farm of the Cluniac priory of Lenton, situated on the left bank of the river Leen in Old Lenton, remained intact as an agricultural estate from the Dissolution of the priory in 1538 (originally in two Crown leases) until the end of the 18th century, when the major part was sold and broken up. The mansions which still survive in use by the University were built by the substantial citizens who purchased the land of the campus, mostly in 1798. It is of great interest to try to establish a continuity in the evolution of the campus, and by using documentary data in conjunction with material remains to tease out the various historical strands that are woven into the present landscape, and contribute to a coherent topographic history.

Chapter I - THE PHYSICAL ENDOWMENT

ROCKS, LANDFORMS, CLIMATE AND SOILS

Introduction: Past Interpretations

Geological makeup (Figures 2 and 3) is the primary determinant of the physical landscape and through its influence on soils, drainage and water supply, and other attributes that set limits to agriculture and other forms of land use it strongly influences human and historical geography. The larger landforms reflect the unequal erosion of the different geological formations. Since the University area was almost levelled by denudation in the Pleistocene period at a present altitude of about 200 feet (61 m) above sea level - a surface still represented in the highest ground of the campus and of Wollaton Park - further erosion has been guided by the downcutting of the river Leen, the Tottle Brook and the river Trent in response to tectonic uplift or changes of sea level during the Pleistocene period of glacials and interglacials, and these streams have carried away the detritus washed into their beds down the valley-side slopes at varying rates.

The river Leen's broad, shallow 'strike' valley follows the outcrop of the geomorphologically weak Permian Marl, and the Tottle Brook is also a strike stream flowing on soft Coal Measure clays as far south as Derby Road at Lenton Abbey. So too, in essence, is the river Trent itself, persistently adhering to the outcrop of rocks of the Mercia Mudstones Group (formerly called Keuper) over its long course. Only in Nottinghamshire, for about two and a half miles from Florence Boot Hall downstream to Sneinton (with a short break below the Trent and Portland buildings) has the Trent impinged on any other geological formation, here the Sherwood Sandstone group. The influence of these two groups of the New Red Sandstone on the landscape of Nottinghamshire is epitomised within the University campus. The Mercia Mudstone group has its base where predominantly sandy sediments give way upwards to silty and marly beds.

James Shipman's account of the geology of Lenton written over a century ago [Godfrey 1884 408-458] is substantially valid today. Shipman remarked on the great variety of rocks in

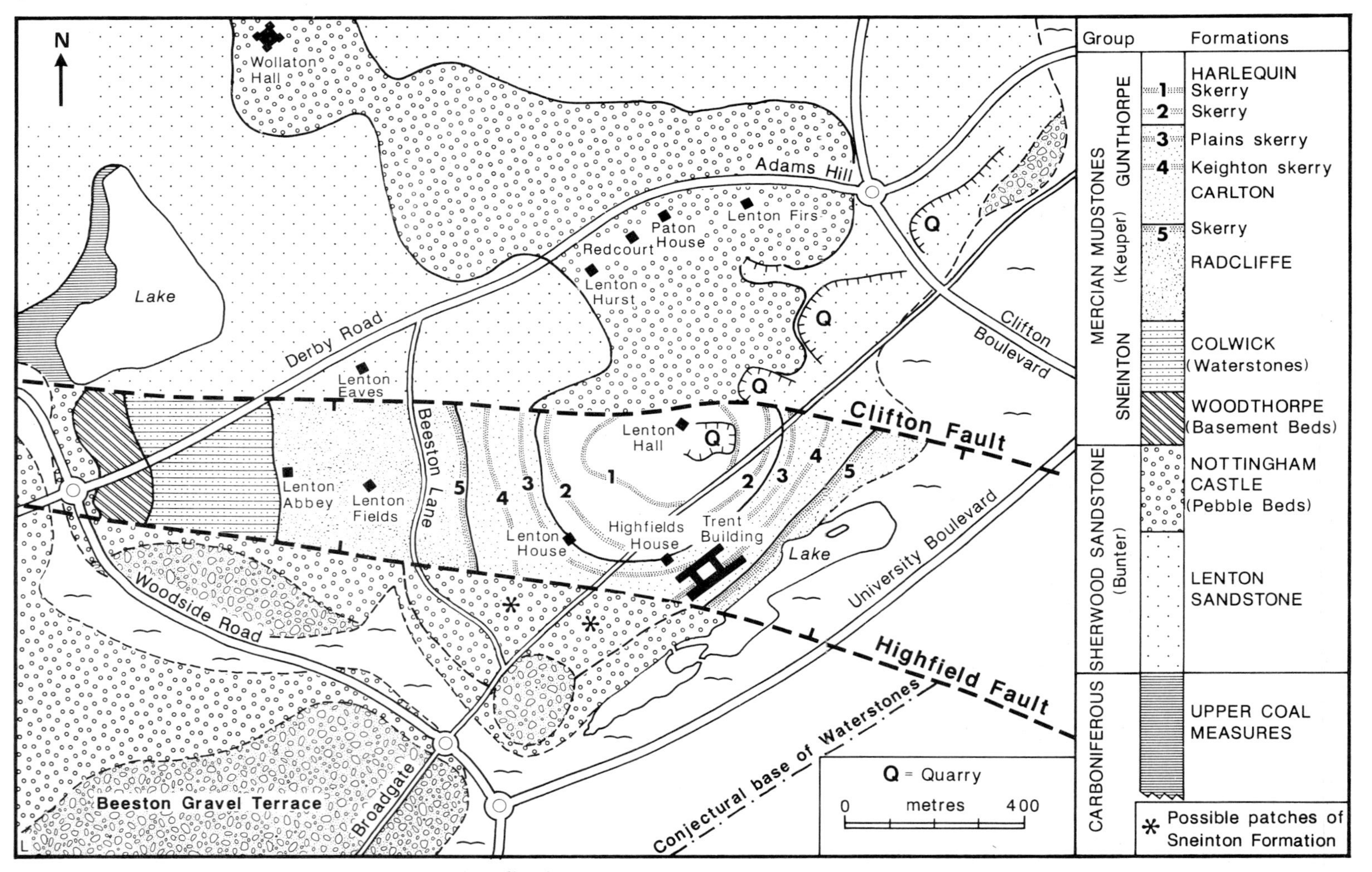

Figure 2: Geological map of the University district

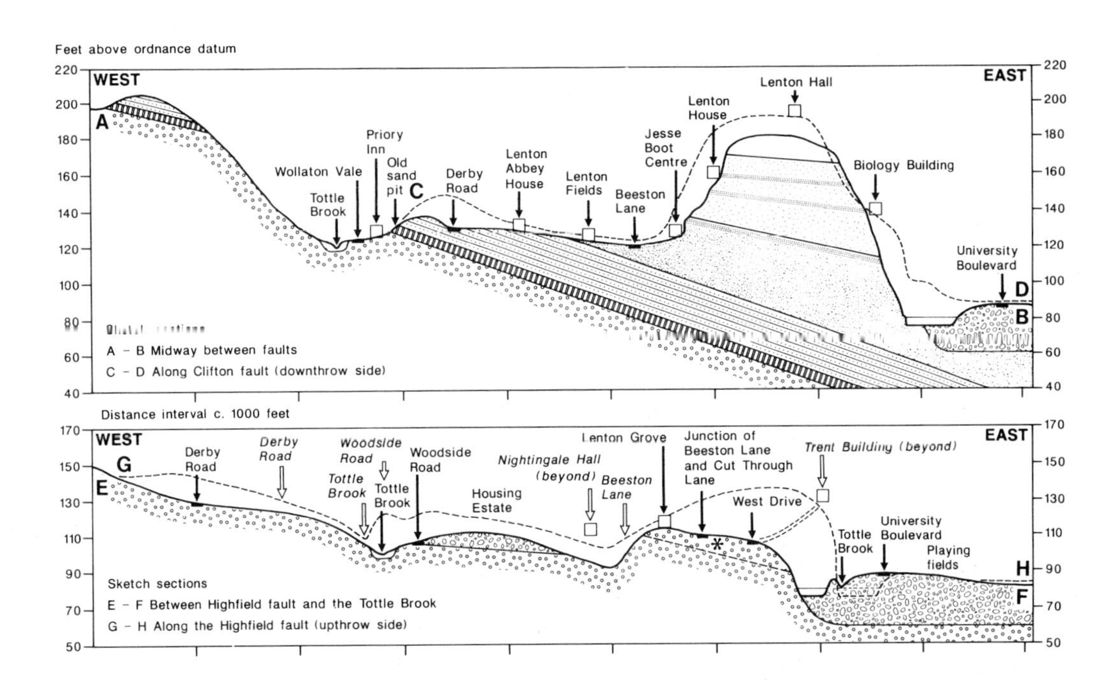

Figure 3: Geological sections across the University area.
For key see Figure 2. Vertical exaggeration x 17.

Lenton and their dislocation by faults in the north-west - the campus area - where they form 'quite a mosaic', although 'all the ground is now....carved into smoothly rounded slopes and hollows'. However, apart from superficial deposits only New Red Sandstone (Triassic) rocks occur on the campus. The Permian system, so prominent in northern England, fades out about a mile to the north, and the underlying Coal Measures rocks, though cropping out only a few hundred yards away in Wollaton Park and Wollaton Vale, nowhere come to the surface on the campus. The New Red Sandstone rocks, displaying depositional cycles on several scales, are so varied lithologically, and their conglomerates, sandstones, siltstones, mudstones and clays so different in their physiographic and pedological implications that the finer stratigraphic variations may be decisive for configuration and for land use. Indeed, it may be suspected that the profusion of 'dislocations' described by Shipman often represent rather the internal complexities of Triassic stratigraphy.

Geologically the campus divides conveniently into northern, central and southern sections, separated by the Clifton and Highfield faults, with superficial deposits associated with the valleys forming a fourth subdivision. North of the Clifton fault (Figure 2) only the two formations of the Sherwood Sandstone Group are found, the Lenton Sandstone overlain by the Nottingham Castle Formation, and in the east both covered by valley gravel and alluvium. In the central section Shipman [1884] and Aveline [1880] identified Keuper Marl (Mercia Mudstones) between the two faults from the edge of the floodplain below the present Trent and Portland buildings westwards almost to Beeston Lane. The underlying Keuper Sandstone [Swinnerton 1948] or Waterstones, (a name dating back at least to the 1860s), later called the Colwick Formation [Warrington et al 1980] and most recently [Charsley et al 1990] the main (upper) part of their Sneinton Formation, were shown coming to the surface beyond, and extending westwards to the Tottle Brook. South of the Highfield fault Waterstones lying above Bunter Pebble Beds (Nottingham Castle Formation) were mapped down to the Tottle Brook.

The Geological Survey's revised one-inch map of 1897 showed Keuper Marl extending much further west between the faults, with a narrower outcrop of Waterstones beyond; but by the 1960s the Geological Survey map at 6 inches to one mile [1] and that of F.Taylor [1965] had Keuper Marl failing to reach Beeston Lane, and then Waterstones extending west almost to the Tottle Brook. Taylor mapped a narrow outcrop of Basement Beds (later called the Woodthorpe Formation) [2] succeeding the Waterstones (Colwick Formation) westwards in Lenton Abbey and Wollaton Park, but the Geological Survey map omitted this. The latest version [Charsley 1990] includes the Woodthorpe with the Colwick Formation in its Sneinton Formation.

South of the Highfield fault the Waterstones, shown in earlier maps overlying the Pebble Beds exposed in the valleyside of the Tottle Brook, have been dropped, and the Geological Survey maps of the 1960s mapped this area as uniformly Nottingham Castle formation, an interpretation also followed by Charsley et al [1990], though there is evidence of younger overlying rocks in places.

Taylor [1965,1966,1968] could refer to R.E.Elliott's detailed study of the stratigraphy of south-east Nottinghamshire published in 1961 [3]. A network of 71 shallow borings ranging from 60 to 300 feet deep made by the Coal Board in the 1950s, supplementing earlier records and existing surface exposures, enabled Elliott to construct a detailed multiple profile of the whole 750-feet sequence of the Mercia Mudstone (Keuper) rocks, chiefly between Ruddington-Clifton in the west, Radcliffe in the north and Bingham-Langar-Colston Bassett in the east. By identifying a large assemblage of small-scale sedimentary structures [4] together with colours and material grade profiles, Elliott was able to collate various borings and demonstrate the persistence of many lithological units in the rhythmic deposits of the Mercia Mudstone Group over a wide area, and to subdivide the Keuper into eight 'formations', to which he gave regional names [Figure 2].

The uppermost six formations of Elliott comprise the Keuper Marl of Swinnerton, and the two lowest the Waterstones (Colwick Formation - Swinnerton's Keuper Sandstone) and the Basement Beds and Keuper Conglomerate of Swinnerton (Woodthorpe formation). Elliott's subdivisions and names were adopted by Warrington et al [1981] but as mentioned above Charsley et al [1990] have combined Colwick and Woodthorpe as their Sneinton formation, and Carlton and Harlequin as their Gunthorpe formation, apparently on the grounds that the subdivisions are unmappable. However, Elliott's original Carlton and Radcliffe subdivisions are retained in the description below because their separate diagnostic characteristics are important in identifying stratigraphical features on the University campus.

Details of the lower part of the succession which applies to the campus area are shown in Figure 7. Elliott was able to place within his formations the main skerry belts (described below) and other landscape forming strata, and to map them. By a judicious westward projection of his findings it is possible to revise and extend earlier stratigraphic descriptions of the campus area, checked by the many exposures revealed through the University's building operations from about 1950 onwards. Elliott's only specific reference to the campus [1961 226] was to '..numerous excavations in the grounds of Nottingham University, where the top of the Keuper Waterstones is thrown approximately against the top of the Lower Mottled Sandstone....'. This can only refer to the vicinity of Rutland Hall as shown on the 6-inch map of the Geological Survey, and more recent exposures throw doubt on this interpretation.

The Northern Campus - north of the Clifton Fault

The arenaceous Sherwood Sandstone group is typically 250 to 300 feet (76-91 m) thick at Nottingham, though its equivalent may be 5,000 feet (1,525 m) thick elsewhere in Britain.

Scattered quartzite pebbles are more numerous and contained in coarser sand than in northern England, but are sparse in the lower Lenton Sandstone. Most deposits are fluviatile, though some are aeolian. Some borings on the Trent valley floor near the University reveal the following thicknesses.

Location of boring (all south of the faults)	Thickness (feet): Lenton Sandst.	Nottm. Castle Sandst.		Total
University playing fields, near railway (1874)	58	170		238
Old Humber Works, Queens Road, Beeston			144	
Boots factory, Beeston, near Beeston Canal			148	
Near Nottingham Rugby Club ground, Beeston	89	140		229
Stony Street, Beeston	93			

Further north the Lenton Sandstone thins from about 100 feet (30m) in the University Science precinct to only 40 feet (12 m) in the west. The overlying Nottingham Castle Formation, everywhere truncated by erosion, is said to be about 35 feet (12 m) thick at Wollaton Hall and Arbour Hill and up to 40 feet on the ridge top between Wortley House (Lenton Firs) and Hugh Stewart Hall, although a recent (1991) exposure of regularly bedded reddish sandstone with few or no pebbles not many feet below the ridge top in front of Cripps Hall suggests transition to Lenton Sandstone. Between the tower block and Wortley House the full thickness of Lenton Sandstone is about 100 feet (30 m).

The Sherwood Sandstone rocks were laid down under a hot and arid 'continental' climate as the wind-worn quartz grains testify. The Nottingham Castle rocks reveal rhythmic deposition from water, with 'current bedding' prominent. The predominant red colour is due to the presence of haematite, with small quantities of goethite, usually forming a pellicle on each grain, its thickness determining the intensity of the body colour. The pale buff colour of the Nottingham Castle beds on the northern part of the campus is less usual than the red colour of the same rocks in central Nottinghamshire.

The Lenton Sandstone Formation

The Lenton Sandstone is the oldest rock exposed at the surface on the campus, and indeed chronologically its lowest part may represent a sandy facies of the Permian Marl, traditionally placed beneath it [Swinnerton 1948]. This remains controversial [5] since the paucity of fossils in the Permo-Trias requires a classification based almost wholly upon lithology, and a recognition of 'rock stratigraphic units' whose actual age may vary from place to place. The type locality of the Lenton Sandstone is 'the north-west side of the Queen's Medical Centre' [Taylor 1988] where the cliff exposure is the abandoned working face of a former moulding sand quarry discussed in a later chapter. There are many other good exposures nearby where the rock has been extensively stripped and modelled in the development of the north-eastern part of the campus, especially in public and private road construction. The outcrop of the Lenton Sandstone is extensive on the western part of the 'downland' above Derby Hall and in Wollaton Park opposite, where the thinning sandstone rests directly upon Coal Measures, the Permian Magnesian Limestone (Bulwell stone) and Permian Marl which intervene at Bulwell having feathered out at Radford. A basal breccia about three feet thick, with many angular fragments has been encountered in a borehole near the tower block on the campus.

Though very coarse locally the bright to dark red sandstone is typically fine to medium-grained, and is soft, friable and 'marly', with thin clay layers. It seldom contains pebbles, but is mainly water-deposited and in places clearly current-bedded (as can be seen in the exposure near the entrance to the University's District Heating centre) though some larger structures may be of dune origin. Its red colour is often varied by patches, lenses, seams and streaks of yellow-green or yellowish sandstone of similar consistency, and especially in its lower strata it usually contains seams of 'marl' about one-fifth of an inch thick, and finely disseminated red clay. Occasional light-coloured patches of more indurated rock contain a high proportion of dolomite crystals in place of quartz, but otherwise it is mostly sparsely cemented and friable.

Because of its weak cementation the Lenton Sandstone yields readily to erosion, and mostly forms low ground and gentle or concave slopes where the overlying, more resistant Nottingham Castle beds have been removed. For the same reason it carried easily worked, warm, medium-light loamy soils suited to arable cultivation by medieval farmers as will be shown later. It forms the low ground in Wollaton Park between the lake and the ridge on which Wollaton Hall stands, and extends across Derby Road below Lenton Hurst into the area of Derby and Sherwood Halls. It underlies the gently rolling slopes north and north-east of the Social Science building and Cripps Hall, and extends across the North Entrance to the campus and the upper part of Clifton Boulevard through the Wollaton Park housing estate and the northern part of the Q.M.C. site to the gravels and alluvium of the Leen valley. Where a dry valley followed by Cripps Hill road runs down to the Trent floodplain a finger of Lenton Sandstone extends up it to a height of about 160 feet (49 m) OD between spurs still capped by rock of the Nottingham Castle Formation. North of Derby Road, and on some spurs, the overlying Nottingham Castle beds form the surface down to as low as 135 feet (41 m) OD. Lenton Sandstone nowhere surfaces in the southern part of the campus, south of a line from the former Lido to Rutland Hall to Lenton Lodge.

Exposures of the Lenton Sandstone

Until they were virtually wiped out by myxomatosis some years ago burrowing rabbits betrayed the areas with Lenton Sandstone at the surface. The rock has been widely extracted on both domestic and commercial scales. In the 18th and early 19th centuries, as shown later, it was often dug by individuals for private uses, especially along Spring Close and Derby Road; but more permanent marks have been left by quarrying, especially in three localities (Figure 2). Shipman [1884] described the rock 'on the east side of the ridge between Lenton Firs and Spring Close, where it breaks out into low cliffs, the bright crimson colour of which forms a pretty contrast with the dark green vegetation around'. But over the last century the low cliff alongside Spring Close has been quarried back, working westwards, to leave a higher quarry face where extraction ended higher up the valleyside slope at the garden boundaries of houses along Derby Road. The progress of this working, which produced a quarry floor now occupied by hospital buildings and roads is outlined in a later chapter. The final phase of quarrying here was mainly for moulding sand used in the iron and bell founding industries because its fine grain resulted in a fairly smooth surface for cast products, minimizing finishing time, while the marl content served to bind the grains well enough to make moulds without recourse to adhesives. In these lower beds of the Lenton Sandstone Formation finely disseminated red clay may form up to 10 per cent of the rock. With the sand grain size about 0.1 mm., and clay present, the deposit here is very suitable for use as moulding sand.

Another accessible exposure of the Lenton Sandstone is the cliff north of the Mathematics-Physics building (Figure 4). Here the rock appears to be similar in its lower part, but harder bands towards the top suggest an upward passage into Nottingham Castle beds, although the colour is still reddish and no pebbles are seen. Some of these hard bands may be similar to those near the base of the old quarry face on the Q.M.C. site, which Swinnerton [1948 55] found to be cemented with dolomite crystals. This is clearly not an abandoned moulding sand quarry, but neither is it a natural feature. Shipman [1884] described how 'the line of escarpment takes a sudden bend to the north for three or four hundred yards and sweeps round so as to form a

Figure 4: Quarry (of 1838) in the Lenton Sandstone Formation.
The quarry floor is now occupied by buildings of the Science Faculty. The post and wire fence marked the boundary between land of the Lenton Hall (left) and Lenton Firs estates. [Photos by H. Cartwright, May 1958]

small bay, ending at the back in a low cliff of the crimson Lower Mottled Sandstone' with 'young trees that cluster its brow....This hollow, now smoothly grass-grown, and with little to indicate how it got formed, was probably scooped out by a sharp bend in the course of the Trent at this spot, at a time when it flowed at a slightly higher level than now .... and when its course lay along this side of the valley'. To the geomorphologist's eye, however, it would seem impossible for a river as large as the Trent to directly cut such a cliff in such a sharply restricted embayment, and it is apparent that the present cliff is man-made. In fact it had been formed by quarrying only 45 years before Shipman wrote.

Sanderson's map of 1835 [6] does not show this cliff feature, but the Middleton estate map of 1863 [7] does. The property boundary between Lenton Hall and Lenton Firs land was marked, before its destruction in the development of the Science precinct, by a straight post and wire fence, on the Lenton Hall side of which a straight slope, steep though low, ran from the north-east end of the sandstone bluff to the intersection of Sandy Lane (Clifton Boulevard) and Cut Through Lane (Figure 4). From the other end of the cliff a similar steep slope diverged, and the flat area between indicates the removal of a very large quantity of the soft sandstone from a considerable area of Lenton Hall land in front of the cliff and down to Cut Through Lane, now occupied by Science Faculty buildings. This whole feature was formerly matched by a very similar one running down from another abandoned quarry face in front of the former Lenton Hall Farm (later called Lenton Firs Farm) to Cut Through Lane, which then ran alongside the site of the present Biology building (Figure 5) . A hedge and a path ran along the bank on the northern side of the now infilled quarry where the footpath from between Cripps and Hugh Stewart Halls to the Science Library now runs, and the former quarry face coincided with the present path along the north-western boundary of the Social Science car park.

There is neither tradition nor documentary evidence that these artificial features were moulding sand quarries, and Robert Mellors remarked in his booklet entitled 'Lenton: Then and Now' [1912 2] that 'the exposure of the rock in the fields east of the [Lenton] Hall was occasioned by excavations for the Midland Railway'. Since this cannot refer to prospecting for a line of construction it must imply that the Lenton Sandstone outcrop here was used as a convenient source of material for the construction of the railway embankment at Dunkirk, mainly in 1838, and this is confirmed by contemporary evidence which is discussed more fully in Chapter XIII.

The quarry floor below Lenton Hall Farm was limited south-west by the Clifton fault which formed the boundary of the Lenton Sandstone outcrop. It is now buried beneath many feet of fill, partly covered by the Social Science car park, but extending down to the original Cut Through Lane alongside the Biology building and the power house. Until it was buried the quarry floor was cultivated by Mr. Bill Barsby, tenant of Lenton Firs Farm, usually under root crops, probably favoured by the effective rise in the water table through the lowering of the surface by quarrying (Figure 5). Clearly major new buildings are unlikely to be constructed in this now unstable area in the near future, but the 1838 quarry further east, which also left an extensive, level, solid floor, proved to be a suitable site for large buildings of the Science Faculty.

Shipman referred in 1884 to a small cliff of Lower Mottled Sandstone (Lenton Sandstone) 'formerly' exposed in Cut Through Lane, 'a curious example of the striped and mottled colouring of this formation ....but it has now been spoiled by the building of a boundary wall in front of it'. The 'small cliff' was east of the northern end of the University road called Keighton Hill, where a boss of relatively resistant pebble-free sandstone surviving from quarrying and recent roadmaking is partly hidden by gorse bushes, and is unfortunately visibly wasting. The boundary wall obscuring it in 1884 must have been the lower end of the retaining wall of Bulwell stone shown in well known postcard photographs of Cut Through Lane in the early years of this century (see Chapter XIII, Figure 93). Much of the wall masked rocks of

Figure 5: Quarry (of 1838) below Lenton Firs Farm
Above: *from a painting by A.E. Schofield of Dunkirk, 1947 [Courtesy of Mr. B.W. Barsby]*
Below: *Infilling of the quarry proceeding in 1960. The head of the quarry ran along the line of the ha ha wall above the Social Science car park, and the line of the footpath (right) and some of the trees survive. The cereal crop may be 'artists' licence' - root crops were usually grown on the sandy quarry floor.*

the Mercia Mudstone Group discussed below.

The Nottingham Castle Formation

The Nottingham Castle (Bunter Pebble Beds) rocks are medium to coarse-grained current-bedded sandstones containing some conglomeratic lenses, and well-rounded, mainly quartzite pebbles varying from about 1/4 inch to about 9 inches or more in diameter, either scattered sparingly or forming bands or lenticular masses. There are occasional marl beds. The usual colour in Nottinghamshire is red-brown, as in the staff garden south of the Highfields fault, but the much paler buff colour of the Nottingham Castle rock itself, the 'type locality', is seen also in the old quarried face below the Lenton Firs summerhouse. The formation is up to 1,000 feet (305m) thick in the Cheshire basin, but only 100 to 200 feet (30-60 m) in the Nottingham area, thickening north-eastwards, and thinning southwards. With its regional equivalents it is much more extensive than the Lenton Sandstone and its equivalents of the former Lower Mottled Sandstone.

The lightening colour and coarsening texture in passing upwards from Lenton Sandstone is nowhere very sudden or marked, but an approximate line of separation can be drawn where the ground slope steepens as Nottingham Castle beds come in. For example on Derby Road the soft red Lenton sandstone at the ring road underpass by the North entrance passes steadily, as the slope steepens up Adams Hill, into a harder, though still sparsely cemented sandrock of a buff or straw colour. Aveline [1880 25] noted its 'massive consolidation', with few lines of bedding or joints, which favoured the excavation of large, unsupported 'chambered caverns' in it, and the excellent dry cellars of Lenton Firs house provide a good example. Smith [1913] emphasized the 'long preservation of its surface under ordinary weathering'. Below Lenton Firs summerhouse, where this rock has been quarried on a small scale, probably for landscaping purposes, it has proved coherent enough to maintain a clean vertical face after many years of exposure to weathering, despite its sparse cement and slight pebble content. This contrasts with the smooth roundness of the very steep slope opposite, below the drive to the Cripps Health Centre, where Lenton Sandstone appears to have been dug at some time. The junction mentioned on Adams Hill follows approximately the road from the North entrance into the campus. On a broader scale the Nottingham Castle outcrop forms a conspicuous feature northwards through Sherwood Forest from the crag of Nottingham Castle.

The outcrop of the base of the Nottingham Castle formation is mapped at about 175 feet (53 m) OD near to Wollaton Hall, and it caps the ridge that extends from the Hall south-east and east to Lenton Firs and then south to Hugh Stewart Hall, its base falling to below 150 feet (46 m) OD and its surviving thickness increasing to 40 to 50 feet. This is only a quarter of the 180 feet (55 m) thickness revealed by the nineteenth century exploratory borings on the University playing fields and at Clifton Colliery. The buttress upon which Nottingham Castle stands - part of a river cliff line that is traced at intervals along the length of Castle Boulevard - is 133 feet (40 m) high, and thus represents more than two-thirds of the total thickness. Broadly, only part of the lower half of the Castle exposure occurs on the northern campus. The formation thickens north and north-eastwards, and is 600 feet (183 m) thick at Mansfield.

Swinnerton [1910, 1914] described a pebble layer containing many dreikanters at the upper surface of the Nottingham Castle beds, a widely distributed residual deposit formed by deflation under arid conditions. This is not seen on the campus. In any area of pebbly rock a pebbly surface layer may form as the residue of current wasting involving the action of worms, burrowing animals and plant roots with rain and slope wash. This can be seen around a few mature beech trees on the campus and is not to be confused with Swinnerton's conglomerate which is found at the base of the succeeding Woodthorpe Formation.

The Clifton and Highfields Faults

The high central area of the campus is formed mainly of those rocks of the Mercia Mudstones Group formerly called Keuper Marl, which, together with the underlying Sneinton formation rocks that emerge from beneath them westwards in the Lenton Abbey area have been let down between Sherwood Sandstone Group rocks on both north and south by two almost parallel, steep, 'normal' east-west faults, and thereby preserved from erosion. This belt of newer rocks is about 500 yards (457 m) wide in the east, narrowing to about 300 yards (275 m) in the west at the Tottle Brook and Lenton Abbey. Shipman wrote that 'Along a tolerably straight line drawn from the south side of the pond in Wollaton Park through Lenton Hall to the Trent alluvium, the Lower Mottled Sandstone is cut off in its extension southwards at the surface by a great fault [the Clifton fault] which throws the rocks down nearly 300 feet on the south, and lets in a broad wedge of Keuper Marl alongside. Of course the Lower Mottled Sandstone continues on underneath these Keuper rocks in its natural position, except that it lies something like 270 feet lower on the south side of the fault'.

The Clifton fault was encountered in Clifton Colliery (sunk 1867-72, closed 1968) with a downthrow to the south of about 285 feet (87 m) (93 yards according to Carr [1896 25] who called it the Bramcote fault). Near to Hugh Stewart Hall the throw in the Triassic rocks is thought to be 240-270 feet. Carr [1896] had seen the Bramcote fault in only one place - in Cut Through Lane - 'but the section is very obscure now'. Shipman [1884] had also seen it in Cut Through Lane, where a wall later obscured it, and 'a wedge of Bunter Sandstone, shattered and tilted, may still be seen dovetailed between Upper Keuper on the south-west side and Lower Mottled Sandstone on the north-east'.

The Clifton fault has been re-exposed on both sides of Cut Through Lane during the last forty years, first in levelling the Biology building site in 1950-51 and then during the widening and diversion of Cut Through Lane in 1959-60 where Shipman and Carr had seen it, on the north-west side of the Lane opposite to the end of Keighton Hill road (constructed later) (Figure 6). On the Biology site observations suggested that the fault might be double, or even multiple, and subsequently small sections of the fault could be seen in cuttings made into the steep faultline scarp south of the finished building, but now removed by excavation for further building.

Two large excavations made in early 1989 between the Biology building and the Keighton Hill road uncovered the fault again. In one excavation there was an indication of a minor fault step some 30 yards south of the fault within the Mercia Mudstone rocks, while in the more easterly exposure fragments of pale, coarse sandstone with small quartzite pebbles just north of the fault suggest material brought down from near the base of the Nottingham Castle Formation. In 1952 ground works near the south-west corner of the Biology building exposed an almost vertical wall-like bed of quartzite pebbles in an extremely hard matrix (probably of a dolomitic cement) on or very near the fault. It was 1 to 2 feet thick, and was destroyed by the University gardening staff only with difficulty, though unfortunately before it could be photographed. Since it is unlikely in that location to have been conglomerate from the base of the Lenton Sandstone it may have been Nottingham Castle formation material brought down along the fault, and the same feature as the 'wedge of Bunter sandstone' described by Shipman 200 yards further north and mentioned above. The exposure of the fault in February 1989 revealed a wet, blue-grey 'reducing layer' one to two feet thick within the Mercia Mudstones along the fault surface.

Although considerable lateral movement probably took place along the Clifton fault the only clear evidence for it is attenuation. The Colwick Formation (Waterstones) thins rapidly westwards. South of the Highfield fault discussed below it is over 100 feet (30 m) thick at the Boots borehole, with an outcrop 1,000 yards (910 m) wide, the base located beneath the gravels south-west of the University sports pavilion. Projected westwards the base would be about

Figure 6: The Clifton Fault and part of its scarp in 1960.
The fault was exposed below the site of the Social Science building opposite to the (later) Keighton Hill road during the widening of Cut Through Lane. Left - Mercia Mudstones: Right - Lenton Sandstone. Note that Lenton Firs farm has gone and infilling of the quarry is proceeding (right).

50 feet (15 m) higher south of the Trent Building and would pass well above the Lenton Abbey area. Between the faults the formation is little more than 30 feet (9 m) thick, which suggests a considerable west to east displacement there.

The line of the Clifton fault can be traced on the ground in the eastern part of the campus by its fault-line scarp, determined by resistant skerry bands in the Mercia Mudstone measures which steeply overlook the Lenton Sandstone westwards from the Biology building past the Social Sciences building until the scarp fades at Hugh Stewart Hall as the Nottingham Castle beds take over from the Lenton Sandstone at the higher level of the summit surface. Further west the faultline scarp reappears as the slope at the head of the 'downland' running down towards Rutland Hall, as Lenton Sandstone replaces the more resistant Nottingham Castle beds north of the fault. The summit surface on which Hugh Stewart Hall stands, which planes across Mercia Mudstones and Sherwood Sandstones alike, rises slightly from about 195 feet (59 m) OD at the Hall to near 200 feet (61 m) at Derby Road at the top of Adams Hill, and a little above 200 feet at the high points in Wollaton Park, Arbour Hill and the site of Wollaton Hall.

The Clifton fault appears to change direction at Hugh Stewart Hall to pass immediately north of the original Lenton Hall, probably associated with a change in the hade of the fault. Aveline [1880] deduced that because the well at Lenton Hall (which he wrongly called Lenton House) passed through 114 feet (35m) of Keuper (Mercia Mudstone) rocks the fault must be either very steep or reversed. It is certainly steep where seen exposed further east; and since the O.S. 1:500 plan of Lenton Hall dated 1881 [8] shows the well within a few feet of the northern corner of the house the fault must be almost vertical there, if not reversed. Pipe laying in Beeston Lane in about 1880 showed that the Clifton fault crossed the lane about 150 yards (137m) from its former northern end, and continuing westwards to the boathouse at the southern corner of Wollaton Park lake it crosses the junction of Parkside and Wollaton Vale and extends on towards Bramcote, but here with Upper Coal Measures on its north side and Nottingham Castle rocks on the south side. Where Colwick formation beds are brought down level with the bottom beds of the Lenton Sandstone formation the displacement can hardly be less than 250 feet.

The Highfield fault, the first of three within a mile south of the Clifton fault [Carr 1896] is approximately parallel to the latter but has a throw at least 100 feet smaller, which is why the rocks seen at the surface in the southern part of the campus are younger than those in the north at similar levels. The Highfield fault can be identified near the steps at the eastern end of the Staff Garden, where chocolate coloured soil containing many brittle 'marl' (mudstone) fragments gives way within a few yards to a vertical sandstone cliff. From this point the fault, passing west of Highfield House, runs through the Lenton House estate and immediately south of Nightingale Hall to cross Woodside Road a little south of its intersection with Derby Road, and then on, parallel to Derby Road, to Bramcote.

Like the Clifton fault the Highfield fault is 'normal' (that is, it hades towards the downthrow side) and so, as mentioned earlier, the structure is that of a graben, or 'rift valley'; but the relief is discordant because the skerries of the down-faulted Mercia Mudstones are more resistant to erosion than the Lenton Sandstone rocks and so stand above them. The Highfield fault, too, is steep, since a well at Highfield House, quite close to the fault, passes through 98 feet (30 m) of Mercia Mudstone rocks. The estimated throw is about 140-150 feet (44 m) in the University central area, but it decreases gradually westwards like that of the Clifton fault. The top of the Lenton Sandstone north of the Clifton fault is at about 150 feet (46m) OD, while the top of the Nottingham Castle Formation is at about 120 feet south of the Highfield fault. Being about 100 feet thick its base is at about 20 feet O.D., or about 130 feet (44 m) lower than north of the Clifton fault, suggesting that the Highfield fault, by subtraction has a throw of about 145 feet (44 m). Between the two main faults are minor faults striking in other directions. Such features are seen in photographs and in such observations as the steep (35 degree) westerly dip in the exposed face in Bath Hill Plantation below the Portland Building compared with the near-horizontal bedding at the lake-shore nearby.

The central campus and the Mercia Mudstones group

The lowest rocks of the Mercia Mudstones group between the faults are of the Sneinton formation [Charsley et al. 1990]. Above them come the lowest three formations of the former Upper Keuper Marl, named (upwards) the Radcliffe, Carlton and Harlequin Formations, of which the Carlton and Harlequin are now grouped by Charsley et al. [1990] as the Gunthorpe formation. It will be convenient to describe first the formations of the former Keuper Marl, since some recent exposures in it have clarified the stratigraphy in the central area, and are important for the interpretation of the lower formations. In their fullest development the formations are up to 6,500 feet (1,980 m) thick, and are predominantly red or red-brown (less commonly green and grey) mudstones and subordinate silt-stones, with thick halite-bearing units in basinal areas, laid down mainly in a playa or sabkha environment, with an arid climate and much windblown dust. Sandstones, often dolomitic, are subordinate to 'marls'. They are dated on microspore evidence as Scythian to Norian. The full succession is at most 600 to 650 feet (200 m) thick in Nottinghamshire.

The red 'marls' always contain very fine sand grains, with hard siltstones or coarser beds at various horizons, but gypsum and other evaporites are present in commercially significant proportions only in the higher horizons not represented on the campus. The so-called 'marls' of the Mercia Mudstones are only slightly calcareous, and consist largely of clay minerals mixed with a high proportion of quartz dust of aeolian type together with minute crystals of dolomite and aggregates of gypsum. Some marls have a bi-modal grain size distribution, suggesting that both wind and water have been transporting agents, while others are well sorted and very fine grained - probably wind-blown deposition in intermittent lakes. Taylor [1963 74] suggested that banded material represents dust blown into standing water, while the 'blocky unstratified material may be the result of dust deposition on dry or nearly dry ground'.

Skerry bands

The sandstones of the Mercia Mudstones above the Colwick Formation (Waterstones) are always thin, flaggy, very compact, fine-grained and hard, and usually of a pale bluish or cream colour, though sometimes pinkish. Known as skerries or skerry bands, they often occur in groups called skerry belts, usually about six feet thick, and comprising an alternation of micaceous sandstone, shale and 'marl'. Only exceptionally are individual sandstones as much as a metre thick, and they vary down to a centimetre or less, with the thicker beds often split up by sandy shales. Skerry belts are unexpectedly persistent, though individual beds thin out or thicken. Low in the succession the skerries are pale sandstones cemented by calcium and magnesium carbonates, but higher the pale, flaggy sandstones contain more silica, and there are coarse sandstones with larger, rounded grains, mostly siliceous. The skerries of the campus are mainly of the first type. Despite their thinness the skerries are important in shaping the landscape, and 'in the relatively flat topography to which the Keuper Marl gives rise almost every hilly feature is the expression of these relatively resistant sandstones.... As a whole the Upper Keuper almost invariably forms a bold physical feature, with a steeper slope marking where it comes in above the Lower Keuper' [Hains and Horton 1969, 1975].

Comparison of the details of Elliott's [1961] slightly generalized section of the lower Keuper Marl in south Nottinghamshire (see Figure 7) with those of exposures seen on the University campus indicates that the skerry at the top of Keighton Hill is the Plains skerry, one of the most extensive, which controls relief and caps the high ground of Mapperley Plains

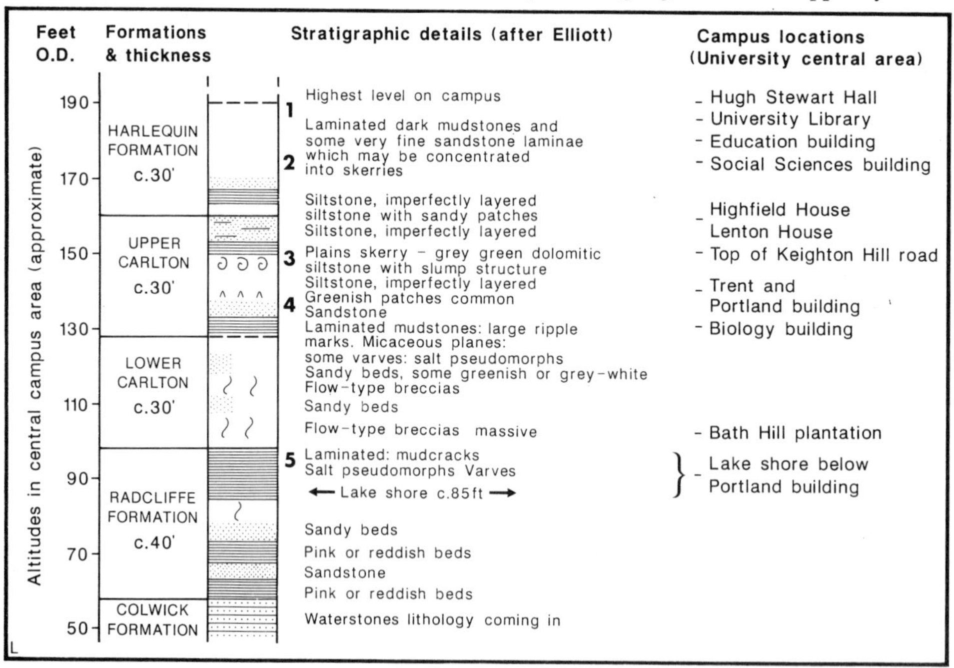

Figure 7: Details of the stratigraphy of part of the Mercia Mudstone Group of rocks occurring on the University campus.
[Modified after Elliott (1961)] Heights and thicknesses refer to the University campus.

[B.Smith 1913 222]. It occurs at Nottingham about 90 feet above the base of the Keuper Marl.

Large and miniature ripple marks and salt pseudomorphs are diagnostic, and can be found on skerry contained in the ha ha wall of Hugh Stewart Hall which probably came from the adjoining old marl pit, now occupied by tennis courts. An unusually thick skerry band seen south of the present Social Sciences building when Cut Through Lane was being widened is thought to belong to the same formation. Impersistent green beds below the skerry in the more westerly of the two excavations at the district heating centre opposite in early 1989 tend to confirm this identification. In the more easterly excavation a strongly developed skerry belt was revealed immediately south of the middle corner of the Biology building. This 'Keighton skerry', mainly of hard siltstone bands, but with one extremely compact pale, hard sandstone two or three inches thick (Figure 8) is identified as a formation recorded by Elliott [1961] 10 to 15 feet below the Plains skerry, near the middle of his Carlton Formation

Some 30 feet below the Keighton skerry is the top of a thick sequence of laminated beds, including sandstones, which are exposed at the lake shore below the Portland Building in an artificial cliff formed when the lake was excavated in 1923-24. These beds are thought to lie in the uppermost 15 feet of the Radcliffe Formation, which extends down to some 40 feet (12 m) below lake level before the top of the Waterstones is encountered. At the top of the Carlton Formation - about 10 feet above the Plains skerry - we pass upwards into the thicker Harlequin Formation, which occupies the highest ground of the central campus. Its colour is relatively dark and purplish, in contrast to the bright red colour in the Carlton Formation, and there are coarse siltstone or fine sandstone laminae that sometimes concentrate to form thin skerries.

Thus, in each of these three formations, Radcliffe, Carlton and Harlequin, potentially significant landscape-forming elements occur. The top of the Radcliffe Formation may be responsible for the lessening slope passing down the lawn in front of the Trent Building, at around 100 feet OD. The Plains skerry probably underlies the upper part of the site of Keighton village, and determines the top of the Keighton Hill road, the car park of the Portland Building, Highfield House and Lenton House, all at 150 to 155 feet (45-47 m) OD. Below, at about 135 feet OD, the Keighton skerry may determine the sites of the Trent and Portland buildings; and above, at about 185 feet OD there is a shelving feature upon which stand the Education building and the present Social Sciences building. Still higher is the surface plateau, with Lenton Hall, Lenton Mount and the Hallward Library, at about 195 feet (60 m) OD. Above about 165 feet (60 m) OD the Harlequin Formation, of which a maximum thickness of about 30 feet has survived erosion, contains the thin skerries and siltstones in the laminated beds that dominate towards the bottom of that formation. On the campus, in the words of Elliott [1961 219] the groups of thin skerries in the lower Harlequin Formation 'may form slight but distinct surface features'.

The artificial cliff at the back of the Trent Building site in 1922 (Figure 9) [9] displayed a marked south-westward dip in the upper Carlton Formation; but this direction depends in part on the alignment of the face, and the true dip here is probably more nearly southwards or south-south-eastwards. The Plains skerry around Nottingham dips generally south-eastwards, declining from the Mapperley Plains at about 350 feet (91.5 m) OD to the river bed near Radcliffe-on-Trent with an average slope of just over 1 degree, and from the University campus to Clifton Bridge at a slightly lower angle. A similar inclination in the campus central area westwards from the Portland Building to north of Lenton House would raise the level of the skerry's outcrop by about 13 feet, to about 165 feet (50 m) OD, disregarding possible minor dislocations.

The steep slope below the woodland west of The Orchard, on former Lenton House land now owned by the University, probably includes the Plains skerry 'scarp', and a grassy hollow there suggests extraction in past times of either 'marl' or skerry sandstone. The Keighton skerry should crop out some 15 feet below this, at about 145 feet (44 m) OD, and is probably

Figure 8: The Keighton Skerry exposed near the Biology building in February 1989.
This belt of laminated mudstones and siltstones is about 5 feet thick. A thin, pale band of resistant fine sandstone occurs near the base.

Figure 9: The Plains Skerry in the Carlton Formation beds exposed behind the Trent Building site, 14 May 1924.
The garden of Highfield House is above, left. [NUMD Acc. 423, No. 18]

represented by the shelf on which Boots' glasshouses stand. A little lower, towards Beeston Lane, hard siltstones were visible recently on the steep artificial slope behind the Jesse Boot Conference Centre, where the lowest, bright red beds will belong to the upper Radcliffe Formation. There remains at least 30 feet (9 m) of the Radcliffe Formation to be accommodated before the underlying Colwick (Waterstones) beds are encountered, and a simple geological section suggests that the area westwards from the Jesse Boot Centre to Lenton Abbey house is underlain by Radcliffe Formation rocks - a conclusion not invalidated by the labelling of this tract on the Geological Survey map of 1962 as 'Red Clay Soil'.

Bernard Smith [1910], identifying two skerry belts about 50 and 100 feet above the Waterstones as important for scenery north of the Trent, was probably referring to the uppermost Radcliffe Formation and the Plains skerry respectively. If the identifications made above are correct the Carlton Formation, including the Plains skerry, is about 60 feet (18 m) thick on the campus, compared with the 70 feet (22 m) average thickness found in borings south-east of the Trent. Some of its stratigraphical features listed by Elliott (Figure 7) are readily identified in the exposures on the campus [10]. Although clay from the lower Carlton beds was used in medieval tile kilns near the Biology building, the marlpit and quarry now occupied by Hugh Stewart Hall tennis courts exploited beds of the lower Harlequin Formation, but may have been deep enough to reach the Plains skerry. The permeable layers associated with the Plains skerry, and below it Lenton Sandstone beneath the Clifton fault, together largely explain why the old marlpit is dry, though lacking a surface drainage outlet.

The Woodthorpe and Colwick Formations, combined as the Sneinton Formation

These lowest of the Mercia Mudstones formations, emerging from beneath the Radcliffe Formation westward to outcrop in the Lenton Abbey area, occupy most of Thompson's Wood inside Wollaton Park before the ground level falls to expose the underlying Nottingham Castle pebbly sandstone alongside the Tottle Brook. Swinnerton called the 'passage beds' of the Woodthorpe Formation 'Keuper Basement Beds' and mapped them in an outcrop about 15 feet thick running south from Oxton through Ramsdale, Arnold and Woodthorpe to Sneinton, deducing that the shore of the sea in which they were deposited was near, and ran through the University area. The beds thicken eastwards from about 12 feet at Nottingham - sometimes only a hard pebbly rib of rock less than a metre thick - to over 40 feet a few miles east, and merge with a micaceous gritty or sandy deposit resembling Nottingham Castle beds in all but its dead white colour when dry [Shipman 1884]. Further east - and further offshore - there are at least six rhythmic alternations, each up to 10 feet thick, of buff and yellow-green sands and red mudstones. West of Nottingham the distribution of a problematical thin deposit will be patchy on an irregularly eroded surface produced in a long erosional episode, though Shipman identified these beds in blocks of calcareous quartzose conglomerate behind the present Priory Inn [Shipman in Godfrey 1884 435].

Charsley et al [1990] subsumed the Woodthorpe with the Colwick Formation in their Sneinton Formation, described as interbedded fine to medium grade sandstone, siltstone and mudstone, mainly red-brown and with micaceous laminae, ripple marks and cross-lamination common throughout. These rocks generally give rise to an undulating incised surface on which the more resistant sandstone bands locally produce marked surface features where not covered by Trent alluvium. In the Nottingham area the Sneinton Formation ranges in thickness from 24 to 50 m. (80-160 feet). On weathering it produces a characteristic silty, often sandy loam soil. It has been used on a small scale as a building stone, and some pieces can be seen in the Lenton Hall ha ha wall.

This description is, of course, essentially that of the Colwick Formation, formerly called 'Waterstones', 100 feet thick in southern Nottinghamshire and best seen at Colwick Wood as alternating beds of greyish, yellowish or brownish soft micaceous, fine-grained sands and red marl - 'siltstones separated by red mudstone layers with mica-laden bedding planes'. A well-known and accessible exposure of Waterstones alongside Derby Road at the southern corner of Wollaton Park wall shows well-cemented brown sandstone in several beds two or three feet thick, and these rocks were formerly identified also in the wood along the south side of Wollaton Park lake [Shipman 1884]. Typically they have alternating light to medium brown mudstone laminae with thinly bedded yellow, green-grey, finegrained sandstone and some thicker sandstone beds. Other diagnostic features are parallel bedding, ripple marks on slabs of the sandstone, mud cracks, salt pseudomorphs, mudstone clasts and organic indications that include reptilian footprints and fish remains. Mica fragments which cover marl surfaces and give the rock a 'watery' sheen that explains its traditional name, are characteristic but not diagnostic since they are seen also in the lower formations of the upper Mercia Mudstones: but unlike these higher beds the Waterstones contain no gypsum while the higher formations contain none of the thickish beds of brown or greenish, soft sandstone typical of the Waterstones, and their sand beds are generally pale bluish dolomitic siltstones.

The Colwick Formation and upper Mercia Mudstone rocks above it both consist of interbedded sandstone and red clay or shale, and the division between them is determined only by the relative prominence of sandstone and marl. The conventional upper limit of the Waterstones is the last fine-grained brown sandstone in the sequence, and the lower limit of the Radcliffe formation is the lowest skerry belt, with the practical boundary drawn between. In fact the lowest Mercia Mudstones of the eastern part of southern Nottinghamshire may well be contemporaneous with the highest Sherwood Sandstone beds of the west, separated by the shoreline feature described by Swinnerton [1918]. Microspore evidence suggests that the base of the Mercia Mudstones should be assigned to the Scythian (Lower Trias); but there are marked differences between the 'Bunter' and 'Keuper' facies [11]. The overlap of Keuper over Bunter may be apparent rather than real because it suggests a transition between land and water depositional environments. The nearshore Woodthorpe formation thickens to 85 feet twelve miles to the east where it was an open water deposit. It is more like the Sherwood Sandstone (Bunter) in the west and like the Mercia Mudstones (Keuper) in the east.

The southern campus

The Mercia Mudstones in southern Nottinghamshire, up to and including the Harlequin Formation, decrease westwards in thickness from about 390 feet (119 m) to about 340 feet (104 m) over 8 miles, with the westward attentuation mostly in the lower formations. South of the Highfield fault no beds of the former Upper Keuper are seen, for although their base crops out below the floodplain gravels less than a mile to the south-east its north-westward projection would carry these rocks well above the present surface of the southern campus. This area, then, is dominated by beds lower in the succession, and the different interpretations seen in published geological maps arise because of the problems of transition from the mainly arenaceous Sherwood Forest Sandstone Group to the mainly argillaceous Mercia Mudstone Group, exacerbated by lateral changes in lithology not yet fully clarified.

Modern geological maps show Nottingham Castle Sandstone occupying the entire area of the campus south of the Highfield fault, although Sneinton Formation rocks have been mapped there by others. The 6-inch Geological Survey map of 1962-63 shows Waterstones about 150 feet (45 m) thick beneath the valley gravels south-east of the campus, but they attenuate rapidly westwards, and at Dale, beyond the Erewash, are present only as a thin, impersistent deposit resting on Sherwood Sandstone rocks. However various exposures suggest their presence, if only thin and discontinuous, on the southern campus.

Shipman [1884] described near the south-west corner of the present Trent Building six feet of 'thin alternations of white and greenish grey compact grit with one or two seams of hard, cemented quartzite conglomerate....resting in a cavity worn out of the underlying Bunter on the north-east side of the Bunter cliff in Highfield park overlooking the lake'. Even then part of the exposure had been covered with earth for tree planting, and the rest was inaccessible and overgrown. Subsequent landscaping has obliterated it, but Shipman's description suggests Woodthorpe beds [12] .

In about 1880 E.J.Lowe of Highfield House had a series of holes dug for Shipman down the slope among the trees between Cut Through Lane and the drive to Highfield House, and Shipman described there alternating buff or yellow friable sandstones with occasional small, flattened pebbles and thin red marls - a description that may fit Colwick Formation (Waterstone) beds. More recently F.M. Taylor [1965] has described the rocks seen in the same area in a temporary trench running from Highfield House to Florence Boot Hall as alternating layers of red marl and fine, buff coloured sandstones, poorly consolidated and infrequently containing small angular pebbles, each layer about $3\frac{1}{2}$ feet thick. Alongside Beeston Lane at Florence Boot Hall it was thought that the junction of Woodthorpe formation beds with Nottingham Castle rocks was seen - a $3\frac{1}{2}$ feet thick bed of 'Bunter' quartzite pebbles overlain by 3 feet of red marl although there was no sign of the Keuper conglomerate described by Swinnerton.

It is unwise to be unequivocal about identification of the surface rocks of the eastern part of the southern campus. The descriptions of beds thought to be younger than the Nottingham Castle Formation are insufficient for mapping purposes, but the soils generally are of much better quality than might be anticipated if formed from the coarse sandy parent material of the typical Nottingham Castle sandstone. Again, recent exposures of beds taken to belong to the Nottingham Castle formation - for example immediately south-east of Cripps Hall - suggest very considerable lithological variation within that formation. The supposed top of the Nottingham Castle beds near Florence Boot Hall lies at about 100-110 feet (30-34 m) OD, and this formation is seen again in the river cliff in the Staff Garden, rising from about 80 feet to about 100 feet OD. At the Highfield fault below Highfield House the total thickness of supposed Sneinton Formation beds may be 30 to 40 feet, with an eroded surface, and these rocks may occupy ground below both Highfield House and Lenton House, and even extend across Beeston Lane to the west of Lenton Grove towards the Tottle Brook where undoubted Nottingham Castle beds occur. They form the sub-gravel surface bed at the Highfields borehole on the University playing fields, though only about 8 feet thick there, and they are even thinner at the former Humber works on Queens Road; but this is due to river erosion when the vale was formed. They are not found beneath the gravels of the Beeston terrace at about 75 feet (23 m) OD.

Assuming the dip of the strata on the southern campus to be of the order of 1.5 to 2 degrees, as between the faults, and taking account of a westward attenuation, it is apparent that while lower Mercia Mudstone beds may be exposed east of Nightingale Hall the surface rocks further west , through Lenton Abbey housing estate and beneath the gravels above Woodside Road must be Nottingham Castle beds.

Finally, the natural river cliff overlooking the lake below the south-west end of the Trent Building, where the pebbly sandstone of the cliff lies against Mercia Mudstone rocks at the Highfield fault, is probably the best and most accessible outcrop of the Nottingham Castle Formation in Lenton (Figure 10). The cliff face here, especially where hollowed into rock shelters, admirably displays the typical quartzite pebbles, scattered or in skeins or seams that highlight the current and false bedding, or 'oblique lamination', which in the Nottingham area is sloping mainly from the north-west, the general direction of the source of the materials. Whether the rock shelters are partly or wholly artificial is, like their age, unknown; but it is suspected that they have been modelled in view of the raised rock terrace feature fronting them. In their present form they were features of the 19th century pleasure grounds of Highfield House, looking over the small lake formed in about 1839, but they may have been excavated much earlier, and could have been incorporated in an ancient dwelling in view of

Figure 10: The river cliff of Nottingham Castle Sandstone and a rock shelter in the Staff Garden, 1987

the name 'Stonehouse Wong' attached to the adjoining land in medieval times.

Exploitation of the rocks

Two of the New Red Sandstone rocks occurring on the campus have been dug or quarried over a long period - the Lenton Sandstone and the upper Mercia Mudstones (Keuper Marl). Apart from the brief episode of railway embankment construction in 1838 the former has been used for various domestic purposes, such as floor sanding, and dug mainly from the sides of the public roads, Derby Road and Spring Close. It was used in small quantities in the Keighton kilns discussed in Chapter II. On a commercial scale the moulding sand quarry at Spring Close was important, and will be discussed later.

Mercia Mudstones have been exploited for three main purposes, and the medieval marl pit in the grounds of Hugh Stewart Hall probably served all three. First, marl was dug, probably for several centuries, to spread over the nearby open arable fields on sandy soils to confer 'body'. Second, the same material - 'clay' of the Harlequin formation - may have been carried in the opposite direction down a graded hollow-way to tile and pottery kilns on and near the site of the Biology building, which also used similar material from the Carlton Formation exposed on the Clifton fault-line scarp nearby [13]. Shipman took 'the usual hummocks' on the slope between the present Portland and Biology buildings to mark places where clay had been worked, but later evidence shows this to be doubtful. A small quarry in the Carlton Formation in Bath Hill Plantation below the Portland Building was probably still worked for clay from time to time as late as the early 19th century. Third, the skerries were formerly important sources of building material.

Bernard Smith [1910] wrote: 'Nearly every church in the Keuper area has some skerry sandstone in its fabric', and the Trent bridge at Newark, the front elevation of Newark Castle and the old Bishop's Palace at Southwell were built of skerry. On the campus 'the boundary wall of Highfield Park in Cut Through Lane is almost entirely composed of the hard, thin bedded, light grey and bluish white stone drawn from this formation' [Shipman 1884 439] and the remains of the lower courses of this destroyed wall can still be seen in places towards the Beeston end of Cut Through. The ha ha walls at Highfield House and Lenton Hall were largely composed of skerry, much of which survives, and it may have been still extracted from the Lenton Hall marl pit into the 19th century when they were constructed. Even some of the houses of the lost medieval village of Keighton were found to have been paved with skerry, (see Chapter II) though some paving there may have been skerry beds in situ.

The valley floors

The level low-lying land on the valley floors of the river Leen and the Tottle Brook and in the vale of Trent, which made up a substantial proportion of the Lenton Priory demesne, has only young superficial deposits at the surface - gravels and alluvium - lying above extensions of some of the outcrops of the rocks discussed earlier.

The differential erosion of the various rock formations of the campus, which has largely determined the salient features of its physical landscape, took place during the Pleistocene period. First, a marine regression from the ultimate strand line at about 700 feet (213 m) OD, was punctuated by intermittent still-stands of sea level which led to a successive development of wide, flattish valley floors by the proto-Trent and its larger tributaries, the lowest perhaps at 200 to 250 feet (60-76 m) OD in the middle Trent area. The upper levels of the campus and Wollaton Park at around 200 feet OD are relics of these surfaces. The subsequent deepening of the valleys and deposition of sediments in them took place under the influence of large climatic fluctuations between severe glacial conditions and more genial interludes in the later Pleistocene and through to recent times. The process still continues.

The boundary between surfaces of erosion and deposition are usually clear-cut unless artificially disturbed. Godfrey wrote, in respect of the campus area 'That portion of the northern escarpment or natural boundary of the alluvial plain of the Trent which comes within the parish boundary is marked by a steep grassy bank or cliff which runs through the middle of Highfield park and round by Spring Close, where it is broken by the gap through which the Leen enters the valley of the Trent' [Godfrey 1884 4]. Little of this feature remains in its natural form after the construction of the University Park and lake, quarrying, road making and extensive building construction.

The superficial deposits

Most of the superficial deposits in Lenton are river deposits of gravel, sand, silt and clay, which occur on the margins of the main campus, but some of those on higher ground are probably thin glacial drifts or boulder clays, fragmentary remains of the 'Older Drift' partly destroyed in the Last (Ipswichian) Interglacial period [Straw 1963]. In some places on lower slopes the surface deposit may be interpreted as 'head' - material, including drift, redistributed under periglacial conditions. There is a patch of glacial drift on Catstone Hill, south-east of Strelley Hall, and another gravel deposit on Wilford Hill. Shipman described what he took to be glacial drift in the patchy mantle of clay, sand or gravel - loamy sheets of pebbly sand or mottled clay that might easily be mistaken for ordinary surface soil developed in situ from the country rock. He identified this 'drift', for example, along the foot of the south wall of Wollaton Park, containing material that could have come only from the north - a dull, red loamy sand containing some clay and a few scattered pebbles [Shipman 1884 445] and thus very similar to the material it is said to overlie - the lowest beds of the Lenton Sandstone Formation. W.T.Aveline [1880 24] complained that 'The lower ground of Wollaton Park is covered by a clay-drift which rendered the determination of the nature of the underlying rocks difficult'.

'In the low ground attached to Lenton Hall on the east side of Beeston Lane [around Sherwood and Derby Halls today] there is a red loamy sand without pebbles, while further south it is a mixture of clay and sand and pebbles' [Shipman in Godfrey 1884 445]. Trenches dug between Beeston Lane and the Jesse Boot Centre, inspected by the writer in 1984 and 1989, and along Beeston Lane in 1992, revealed apparently unconsolidated, unstratified silty sand or silt with occasional quite large rounded quartzite pebbles. These descriptions probably refer to periglacial solifluction material (head), but it must not be overlooked that the lower area of Wollaton Park (the former Sixty Acres open field), and land on either side of Beeston Lane was mostly arable land in the later medieval period, and for several centuries will have received dressings of Mercia Mudstone material (for example, from the marl pit at Hugh Stewart Hall) intended to affect the character of the surface soil. Within the campus area deposition from glaciers has left, at most, only patchy and very superficial traces. The influence of glaciation is much clearer in the valley deposits from water, which are best understood in the context of glacial history (Figure 11).

On the floor of the main Trent valley thick gravels veneered with silt and clay completely hide the solid rocks, and end abruptly at the valley margin. Typical thicknesses of gravel and sand are 25 feet at the former Clifton colliery, 22 feet at the boring on the University playing fields on University Boulevard, and some 16 feet at Chilwell, nearer to the valley side. The horizontally bedded gravel contains well rounded pebbles of quartz and quartzite from the Sherwood Sandstone rocks, less well rolled pebbles of chert, Millstone Grit, Coal Measure and Keuper (Colwick Formation) sandstone, flint and other materials mixed with a coarse red sand. In places sand, silt or tough clay (called brickearth by the earlier geologists) of varying colour, including some blackened by peat, cover the gravel. They contain few pebbles, as may be seen in the side of the Tottle Brook in University Park: and where the brook enters the Trent valley a deep deposit of faintly banded clay occurs. In the lower Leen valley are 6 to 8 feet of gravel with a very pebbly surface - pebbles of varied character that cannot derive

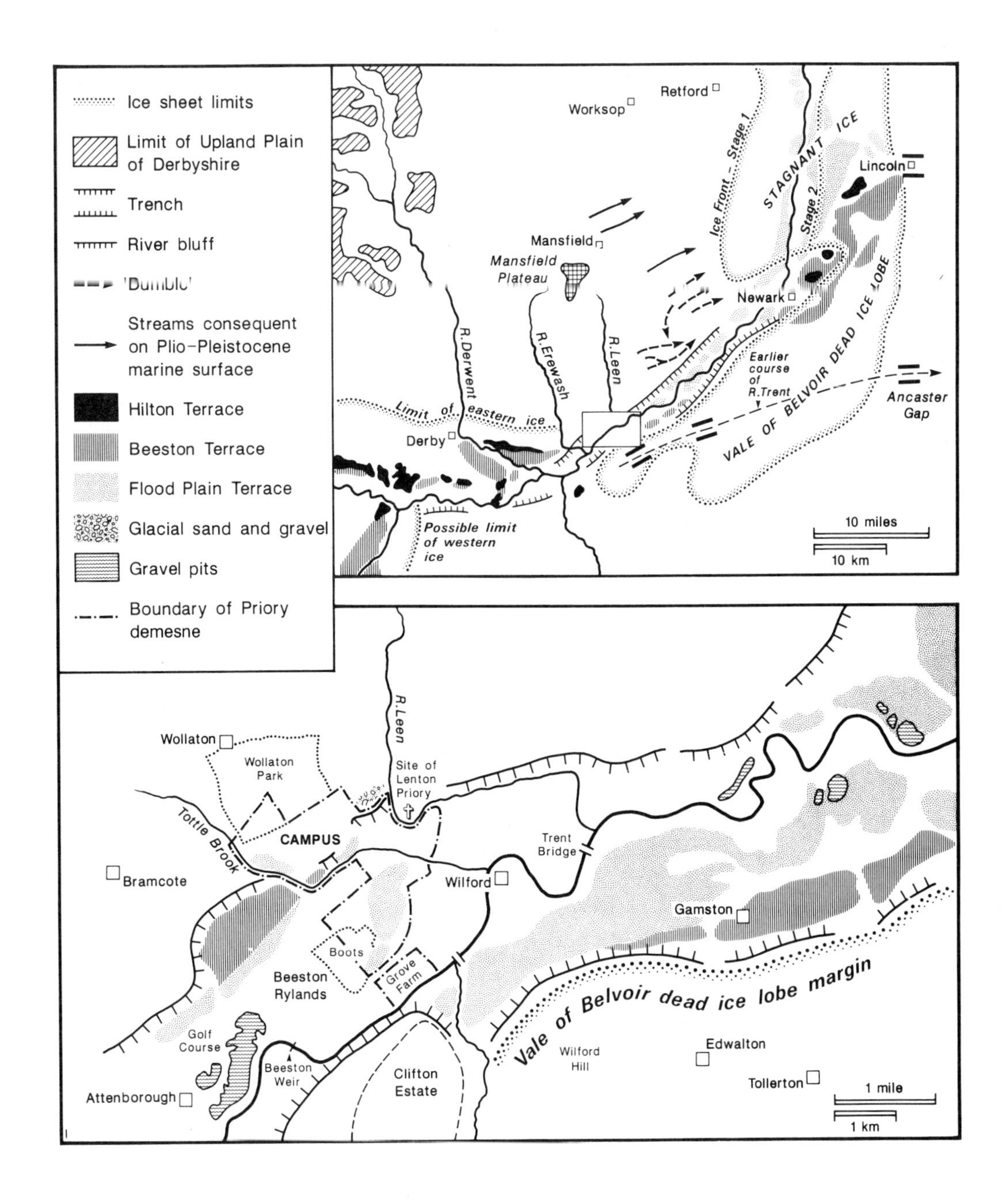

Figure 11: The chief valley gravel terraces in the Nottingham area.
Upper, regional map mainly after C.A.M. King [1966]

from the Lenton Sandstone through which the valley is cut, and which must come mostly from the Nottingham Castle sandstone, though some are far-travelled. The river Leen wanders through a valley floor varying in width from a few yards to a quarter mile, and beneath is a deep channel filled with glacial drift material much older than the post-glacial torrential gravel that overlies it.

Most of the thick valley floor deposits were laid down by the river Trent during periods of ice melt. In times of low base level (usually low sea level) there was down-cutting by the river, with 'knickpoints' working back upstream at the head of newly incised sections of the rejuvenated valley. In this way valley-side and 'island' terraces of gravel have been left by the Trent and some of its tributaries standing above the newly levelled parts of the valley floor which themselves have been subject to further alternation of deposition and erosion. These events can be closely tied in with episodes of ice advance and retreat during the Pleistocene period, and are as much products of glaciation as the drifts on higher ground. Their occurrence and disposition can be explained and understood only in the context of glaciation [14].

The second major ice advance over England, the Gipping, the last advance of the 'Older Drift' period, brought nearly all the glacial till found in the Nottingham area from the north-north-east, a clayey till with a large Mercia Mudstones content and a reddish colour to the south and east of Nottingham. To the south of Nottingham the 'Eastern ice', identifiable by its flint erratics carried from the chalklands of eastern England, at one stage pushed west as far as Abbots Bromley. The final advance, the major advance of the 'Newer Drift' ice sheet in the Last Glaciation, did not cover the Nottingham region, but had important effects on the landscape nearby, scouring the soft rocks of the Vale of Belvoir for example, and leaving thick deposits in the Soar valley and deep till forming the South Notts Wolds.

In the retreat of the Eastern ice a dead ice lobe in the Vale of Belvoir cut off the Trent's earlier outlet through the Ancaster Gap and directed meltwater carrying a heavy bed load of coarse gravel and sand northwards along its western edge (Figure 11). This initiated the anomalous Trent trench from Nottingham to Newark, broad, straight, two miles wide, with a flat floor and with bluffs on the south-east side reaching 200 feet (61 m) OD. Gravels laid down from this water form the older Hilton terrace as far downstream as Long Eaton, and reappear between Newark and the Lincoln Gap, through which water escaped eastwards because it was still blocked to the north by stagnant ice. Flints in these gravels show them to be younger than the Gipping ice advance which brought in material from the chalk areas of Lincolnshire and Yorkshire. Swinnerton [1948] regarded them as glacifluvial, and, unlike Clayton [1953] not as river terraces. During the Last Interglacial period there was relatively little erosion in the Vale of Belvoir and the lower Trent area, already lowered by glacial erosion, but elsewhere there was lowering and incision of streams. This period is especially significant for the campus and its vicinity, where two distinct terraces well below the level of the Hilton terrace are prominent - the Beeston terrace and the Floodplain terrace.

The Beeston terrace can be traced far upstream from Beeston, forming a wide ledge between Rugeley and Burton, and in the Dove valley and along the Trent valley south-east of Derby. At Beeston it stands about 30 feet above the recent alluvium, and provides the site for the town. Relics of it appear downstream on the south side of the Trent vale, extending east from just west of Melton Road in West Bridgford through Gamston, Bassingfield - where it is half a mile wide - and Holme. On the north-west side of the Trent vale the last remnants downstream are the small patch on which Florence Boot Hall stands, separated from the main terrace at Beeston by the Tottle Brook, and a fragment now removed by quarrying and site works that lay on a ledge of Lenton Sandstone at Spring Close, about 25 to 30 feet above the river Leen, and varying in thickness from 10 to 12 feet down to nothing towards the Leen and Trent [15]. The latter contained quartz pebbles and flints, with other travelled rocks, as well as clays and sands. Shipman provided a drawing dated 1879 which showed contortions in the top two or three feet attributed to intense freezing under periglacial conditions during later glacial periods which themselves left no deposits. Shipman also described the makeup of the Florence Boot Hall deposit - dull brown sand and pebbles, with about 5 feet of banded red and yellow sand below, with occasional thin partings of drab clay resting on gravel. The gravel of the main terrace has been seen in a pit north of Beeston village to a depth of 12 to 15 feet, resting on Nottingham Castle sandstone, with its surface up to 30 feet above the alluvium [Aveline 1880]. Downstream of Florence Boot Hall the river Trent has impinged again on the 'solid' valleyside, leaving cliffs in the Staff Garden, along Castle Boulevard and beyond, and removing all traces of the Beeston terrace.

Among the dates suggested for the deposition of the Beeston terrace gravels the most likely is the early part of the Last Interglacial period or the waning phases of the last ice advance that directly affected the area the Weichsel. The most favoured view is that they were laid down because the eastern ice of the Newer Drift period blocked both the Humber and Fenland outlets of the Trent and impounded a lake that spread as far upstream as Nottingham, with a water level of about 100 feet OD at the maximum extent of the ice sheet. Outwash gravels fed into the upper Trent valley were carried down the trench. The Beeston gravels were aggraded progressively towards the Lincoln Gap, and eventually through it as the level of the lake slowly fell. When the ice withdrew from the Humber the Trent reverted to its former course. Much erosion of the Beeston gravels then occurred due to rejuvenation working up-valley while sea level was still low after the ice retreat, with downcutting of as much as 50 feet at Bassingfield, before a slight readvance of the ice partially blocked the northern outlet of the Trent. The Floodplain Terrace gravels now standing at 7 to 10 feet above the level of the alluvium were laid down in Late Glacial times during this second phase of impeded drainage. They have themselves been incised and eroded by the river Trent flowing into the dry North Sea basin after the final post-glacial ice retreat, but before the North Sea basin was re-flooded.

The knick point marking the head of this phase of downcutting by the rejuvenated Trent has worked back up the river as far as the Wilford shoals, which formerly allowed the Trent to be forded on the route now served by Clifton Bridge. It is now fixed by Beeston weir, above which the Floodplain Terrace gravels are still spread across the whole valley floor, while below the weir they have been cut and planed away from considerable stretches of the valley floor by migrating river meanders. The remnants form 'islands' of gravel standing above the alluvium, and providing flood-free sites for valley villages from Wilford downstream through West Bridgford, Adbolton, Holme Pierrepont, Colwick and on to Newark, as well as offering well-drained loamy soils for their arable fields and good water from shallow wells. Such valley-floor villages are not found upstream of Beeston weir, and the Floodplain Terrace 'islands' furthest upstream, and most recently formed, are those in Lenton lying alongside and north-west of the Beeston canal, and formerly within the demesne of Lenton Priory. The canal mainly follows the line of the old Blotoff Dyke, possibly an abandoned channel of part of a meander or a distributory of the Trent, which was a string of pools and marsh in late medieval times when known as The Rounds. The smaller gravel island now lies partly within the Boots factory site: the larger probably provided arable land for the pre-Norman settlement called Morton, and was partly worked for gravel in recent decades (Figure 12). Much is now covered by extending industrial building.

In addition to these two patches, a narrow terrace of Floodplain gravel lay at the foot of the slope below the present Portland Building, but most of it was excavated when the eastern reach of the University Park lake was formed, although a little remains around and north of the Lake Pavilion. The gravel terrace along Woodside Road, now largely built over west of Ancaster Hall, should probably be assigned to the Beeston Terrace. The lower part of the original village of Beeston round Nether Street and up to the parish church appears to have occupied a fringing strip of Floodplain Terrace gravel, since there is a clear rise in level up to

Figure 12: Aerial view of the campus from the south, with an 'island' terrace of Floodplain Gravel in the foreground, 1963.
The view extends north across the campus and Wollaton Park to Catstone Hill and Strelley and beyond. [Photo. courtesy Mr. Beric Tempest]

the High Road on the surface of the main Beeston Terrace.

The Trent valley gravels are widely extracted for industrial use today. The significance of the gravel terraces for land use, settlement sites and road patterns in the past will be discussed in later chapters.

CLIMATE: RECORDS AND LOCAL CHARACTERISTICS

The climate of the Nottingham area, including the University campus, has been described in some detail in a volume prepared for the Nottingham meeting of the British Association for the Advancement of Science in 1966 [Barnes in Edwards (ed) 1966 60-102 and 521-527 (Appendix 1)] where it is summarized as follows. The Nottingham area 'forms part of the very extensive Midland plain, which exhibits considerable uniformity of climate .... relatively dry with a rather variable annual rainfall. It is characterized by a comparatively large seasonal and diurnal range of temperature and a moderate amount of sunshine. Apart from occasional late killing frosts the growing season is adequate for the satisfactory cultivation of almost any crop grown in Britain. Indeed, one of its chief advantages is that it favours agricultural diversity, providing adequate sunshine, warmth and rainfall to sustain a good growth of grass throughout normal summers, and to bring cereal and root crops to a rewarding harvest, subject always, of course, to the suitability of soils. In human terms, by British standards, it is a moderately rigorous but distinctly invigorating climate'.

From the viewpoint of topographic history, local climatic variations with implications for land use and settlement are of interest, especially those resulting from configuration, and relating particularly to temperature and insolation. The former is manifest especially in night and early morning temperature differences as between summit levels, valley slopes and valley bottoms, expressed in a corresponding variation of frost frequency and severity, including the risk of killing frosts which damage fruit blossom in late spring. Compared with higher ground valley bottom sites record mean temperatures reduced by 0.5 to 1.0 Celsius degrees in every month; reductions by 2 to 3 C deg. in the monthly averages of the lowest minimum temperatures; and on individual nights air temperature reductions in the valley bottoms by the order of 5.5 C deg.. The greater prevalence of fog over valleys and low ground might be a factor in the choice of settlement sites, including villages and individual houses.

Variations of insolation in a rolling countryside such as that of the University campus, with relief of the order of 100 feet, are determined by aspect and angle of slope, with moderate south to west facing slopes the sunniest and warmest - an important consideration in the siting and design of houses in rural settings until quite recent times. Plans of the old houses on the campus show that such factors also influenced the siting of the glasshouses which were associated with all of them in the 19th century. However, because arable agriculture on the campus was almost entirely confined to times before the middle of the 16th century, ease of cultivation under medieval technology, and the choice of some of the lighter soils for it, meant that considerations of soil quality, drainage and water supply over-rode those of temperature peculiarities and aspect in determining traditional patterns of agrarian land use.

Records

Unfortunately most of the weather records kept on the campus during the past 180 years were maintained for only short periods, and the exact sites of some of the stations are not known. More were of rainfall than of temperatures, and temperature data survive generally in the form of averages, with few records of daily figures from which local temperature variations could be demonstrated. The earliest known observer on the campus was Matthew Needham of Lenton House (see Chapter VIII) whose readings began before 1809 and continued until his death in 1840. Some fragments of his record were printed in the local press at the time, but otherwise the only survival is in the form of values incorporated in the 10-year temperature means of 1810 to 1840 derived by A.S.H.Lowe and E.J.Lowe in 1853. Taking account of a north-wall exposure these figures are remarkably consistent with modern averages for stations on comparable 'warm' sites on upper slopes. Needham recorded air temperature at 11 p.m. and 8 a.m., and night minimum temperature, to which he added maximum temperature from 1820.

E.J.Lowe regarded Needham's record as virtually homogeneous with that of his father and himself at nearby Highfield House on a very similar upper-slope site, which extended from 1840 to 1881. Unfortunately Lowe's observations at his house called The Observatory on Broadgate, Beeston (now occupied by the University Air Squadron) which began in about 1851, and which would have provided an interesting comparison, are not known to have survived. No observations are known to have been made on the campus between 1881 and 1912, when rainfall readings at Lenton Hall began, presumably by or for Charles Hingston, the owner, but these were published in summary in volumes of 'British Rainfall' only until 1915.

Lenton Fields had a station recording a range of elements from 1920 to at least 1927, with summaries of temperature published in the Monthly Weather Report of the Meteorological Office, and although the original records are lost the summaries are useful because of the character of the site, on relatively low ground. At Lenton Grove rainfall was measured by an old tipping rain gauge during Sir Louis Pearson's time, but whether the readings were systematic and continuous, and whether any were published is not known. The gauge was still in place when Lenton Grove was taken over by the University. It will be seen that most of the few climatic records of the early enthusiasts which survive are of little value for the small-scale climatology which is relevant in the present context.

Observations by the Zoology Department on a sloping site near the western end of the present Portland Building car park (near to the Department in the Trent Building at that time) began in 1936 and continued until 1944. Subsequently the Department of Geography took a full range of daily observations on three different sites near to successive post-war locations of the Department because they were used primarily for teaching purposes. The first station (from 1951 to 1957, when the Department was in the 'Cowsheds') was located immediately west of the present Social Sciences building, between Hugh Stewart Hall tennis courts and Cut Through Lane. A second station situated between the present Education building and the boundary fence of Lenton House grounds was operated from 1960 to 1967, and a third between the present Social Sciences building and Hugh Stewart Hall, at the western end of the car park, from 1967 to 1980, when observations were abandoned because of the difficulties of sustaining a continuous service of volunteer observers. At the same time the Lenton Experimental Station of Messrs. Boots alongside Lenton House recorded a full range of observations from 1952 until its closure, very close to Matthew Needham's original station of 150 years earlier. Unfortunately all its records were destroyed immediately the research station ceased to operate, and only the summary figures published in the Monthly Weather Report by the Meteorological Office survive.

All these more modern stations were on 'warm' sites on high ground or upper slopes in and near the University's central area, so the degree of influence of site on local temperature variation cannot be demonstrated directly from numerical data collected on the campus itself, with the exception of the brief record at Lenton Fields: but the order of values involved can be deduced from comparisons with records from nearby places. These show that a place in the Trent vale, such as Attenborough, experiences much lower temperatures on still, clear 'radiation' nights than places on ridge-tops or upper slopes such as Nottingham Castle or the central area of the University campus, and that this tendency operates at all seasons, and has a noticeable effect even on mean daily and monthly and thus on annual minimum temperatures.

Comparisons between air temperatures at stations on 'warm' and 'cold' sites for various periods, but adjusted to the 30 years 1921-50 (Table 1) show a reduction of the monthly mean temperatures at the colder, lower sites of the order of 0.5 to 1 C deg., and of the average of the lowest monthly minimum temperatures of 2 to 3 C deg.. The mean minimum temperatures (1926-50) of local stations include : Nottingham Castle 6.1 deg. C, Chilwell 5.4 deg. C, and Attenborough 4.9 deg. C. The monthly difference between Nottingham Castle and Attenborough is 2 C deg. in September. On individual clear calm nights low level stations are of the order of 5.5 C deg. colder than high level stations, and Mr.A.B.Tinn showed that this degree of difference between Woodthorpe and Mapperley, some 195 feet higher, could be reached within two hours after sunset. This effect is more than sufficient to be strongly felt when walking down the paths across the 'downland' on a clear, still summer or autumn evening.

Cold air drainage does not necessarily reduce the effective growing season in low-lying areas, especially since daytime warming by insolation may more than nullify its effects, but it may reduce growth rates at night, and can have a crucial effect from time to time on the risk of frost damage to plants. In general the lower temperature at night on low ground is reflected in an increased number of both air frosts and ground frosts. Lenton Fields is markedly more susceptible to frost than the University central area, or the vicinity of Lenton House, where Boots' experimental station did not experience a serious late frost in 20 years of recording. Site differences have the most marked effect on frost occurrence and abnormally low minimum temperature in April and May, which is the most critical period for danger to plants. The seriousness of a 'killing frost' is increased if vegetative growth and flowering have been advanced in spring by unseasonably genial weather, but in normal seasons the critical screen temperature averages about -3.3 deg. C in April, -2.2 deg. C in May and -0.5 deg. C in June, with the May figure usually the most important in respect of damage to fruit blossom.

While the temperature on still cold nights at Lenton Fields may be 5 C deg. or more lower than at Highfield House, the grass minimum temperature very near the ground may be 5.5 C deg. lower than the screen minimum temperature (read in the Stevenson screen at 4 feet above the ground). Although variations of this magnitude occur only under very suitable meteorological conditions, and killing frosts are only occasional, even unusual phenomena, the same effect in less extreme form tends to occur on every clear, calm night throughout the year, and shows up in mean temperature values. It therefore might be expected to be a factor, together with aspect, in the choice of sites for settlement and for cultivation of vulnerable crops such as orchard fruit, and this can be demonstrated in some degree on the campus by the location of orchards, though choice was obviously limited on the small estates, and availability of well water and ground water for cultivation may have overridden considerations of local temperature climate. Clearly the moderately steep south-east facing slope of the site of the medieval village of Keighton (Chapter II) was favourable for insolation and for drainage, well above the cold valley floor, and well water nearby at no great depth in the Lenton Sandstone was an added amenity. However, although a coldness map of the campus can be drawn in qualitative terms it is uncertain to what extent such considerations influenced actual practical decisions about settlement siting and cultivation.

Table 1
Some local temperature variations in the Nottingham area

	Jan.	Feb.	Mar.	Apr.	May	Jun.	Jul.	Aug.	Sep.	Oct.	Nov.	Dec.
Mean temperatures (deg.C) at four local stations, adjusted to 1921-50												
Nottingham Castle (1921-50)	3.9	4.1	6.0	8.5	11.5	14.7	16.8	16.3	14.0	10.2	6.4	4.4
Burford Rd. (1919-34)	3.7	3.9	6.0	8.7	11.8	15.1	17.0	16.2	13.8	10.1	6.1	4.
Attenborough (1928-38)	3.5	3.8	5.7	8.0	11.2	14.4	16.6	16.0	13.5	9.8	5.9	4.0
Lenton Fields	3.2	3.5	5.6	7.9	10.8	14.0	16.2	15.4	13.2	9.3	5.5	3.7

Table 1 (Continued)
Some local temperature variations in the Nottingham area

	Jan.	Feb.	Mar.	Apr.	May	Jun.	Jul.	Aug.	Sep.	Oct.	Nov.	Dec.
Averages of lowest minimum temperature, monthly												
Nottingham Castle	-5.3	-4.3	-3.1	-0.6	1.1	5.4	7.6	6.8	3.8	-0.6	-2.1	-3.8
Burford Rd.	-5.2	-4.4	-2.3	-0.4	1.7	5.7	8.4	8.0	4.6	-0.2	-2.0	-3.7
Attenborough	-6.9	-6.2	-5.4	-3.1	-1.1	-2.8	5.1	5.0	0.9	-2.7	-3.9	-5.7
Lenton Fields	-7.3	-5.5	-4.5	-2.2	0	3.4	5.8	4.7	2.2	-2.6	-3.9	-6.1

Examples of potential killing frosts - minimum temperatures

	9 May 1926	30 April 1927
Nottingham Castle	-1.1	-1.7
Lenton Fields	-2.8	-5.0
Killing temperatures	May -2.2	April -3.3

DRAINAGE AND WATER FEATURES (Figure 13)

The dry grassland that encourages unrestricted walking over much of the University campus is an attractive amenity. The total absence of surface drainage features from the campus contrasts with their prominence, especially in the past, on the level floor of the Trent vale, with its high watertable. There the sluggish flow was collected by a rectilinear network of field ditches, often regularized from natural streamlets. Small relief features control the direction of drainage in detail, and it is often directed away from the main river, to be collected by lateral tributaries of the river Trent running along the margin of the vale - the Tottle Brook and the river Leen - and delivered by them to the main river downstream. The same system of channels in the past distributed flood water from the river over the vale, which was thereby veneered with alluvium. Such floods irrigated water meadow and wet cattle pasture. The slightly higher patches of the floodplain gravel terrace introduced irregularities in the drainage pattern and acted as subsidiary interfluves.

All the water features of the University area are closely related to the geology. The campus above the flood plain drains very freely, is dry underfoot, and devoid of streams and drainage ditches, and in these respects it resembles the adjoining Wollaton Park because both are underlain by highly permeable rocks, predominantly sandstones, and have a rolling surface with moderate slopes. Even the Mercia Mudstone rocks between the Clifton and Highfield faults contain enough permeable strata to ensure generally free drainage. The campus includes several well-developed dry valleys, shallow and open, as south of Cripps Hall, or more narrowly incised, as along Cripps Hill. These have the appearance of stream valleys, although only where Mercia Mudstone rocks are crossed and there are occasional flash floods do they ever contain surface water. They may have been shaped and graded wholly or partially under periglacial conditions in the late Pleistocene period. Although it is not visible there must be, today, a substantial subsurface flow of water by convergent seepage down these valleys.

In the medieval period stagnant water lay in parts of the Trent vale which remained unreclaimed for agriculture, for example in 'The Rounds' described in Chapter III, and along Blotoff Dyke, now followed by the Beeston canal. But any body of standing water in the University district at present or in the recent past is of 'artificial' origin, whether canal, lake, pond, mill pool or gravel pit. The only surface water feature on the campus itself today (apart from 'architectural' pools within new building complexes) is a small, circular dew-pond, located on the high ground between the Education building and Lenton House (Figure 14). The water must be retained in the pond by an impermeable layer in the Mercia Mudstones, probably

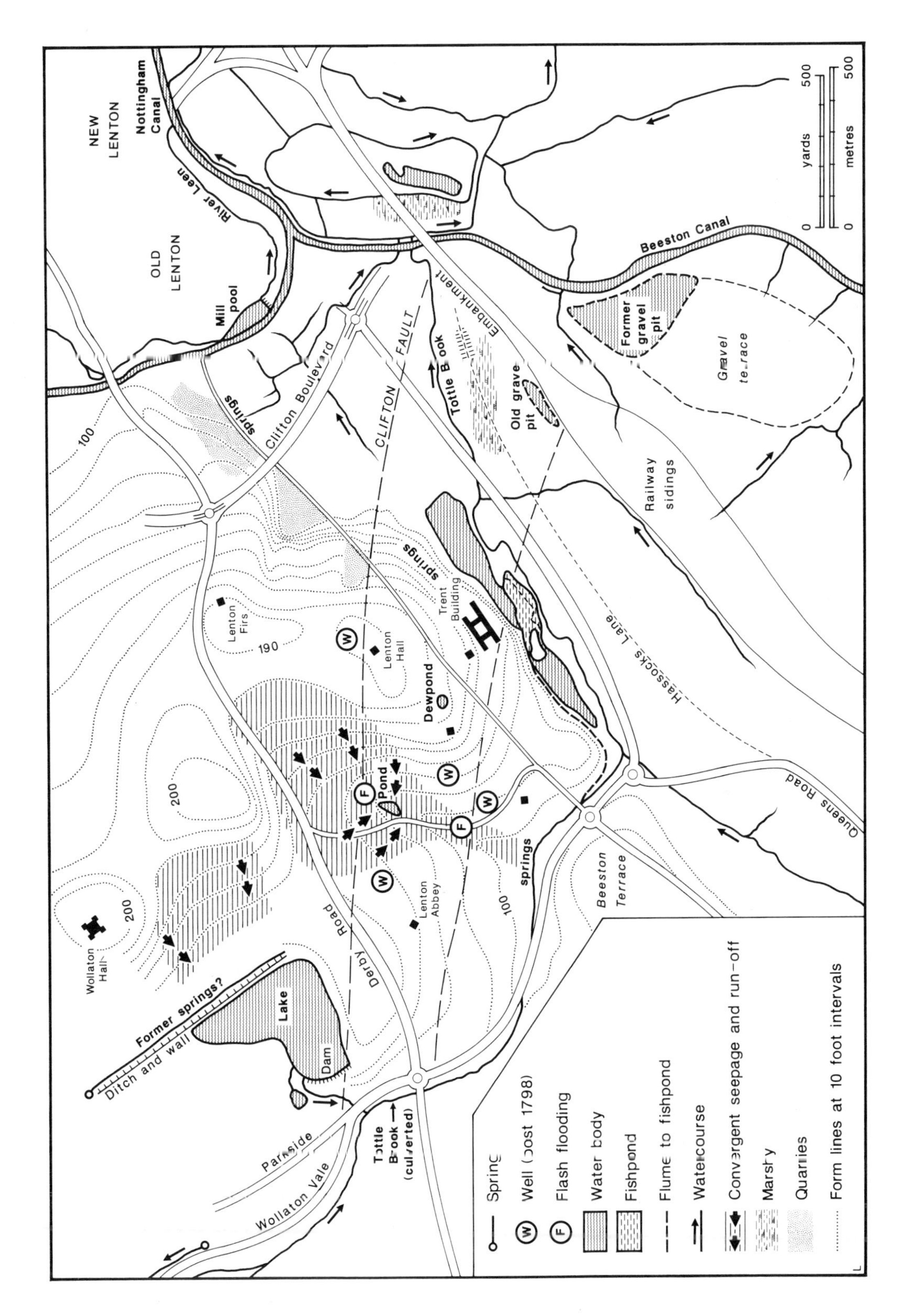

Figure 13: Some drainage and water features of the University district. (not synoptic)

Figure 14: The dew pond west of the Education building.
Above: *Fencing round the pond is seen (right) in a grass field being ploughed up for wartime cropping in October 1939 by Mr. J.W. Steeples senior of Chilwell Hall Farm. This land had been purchased by John Boot of Lenton House from W.G. Player of Lenton Hurst in 1930, and was exchanged to the University for a strip of the 'downland' in 1959. [Photographer unknown. Courtesy of Mrs. M. Pykett].*
Below: *The dew pond in 1991.*

near the top of the Carlton Formation. The age and origins of the pond are unknown. It is prominently shown on the large-scale O.S. maps of about 1850, and on the Sturgess survey of Lord Middleton's Lenton estate in 1863, but earlier maps of the area are on too small a scale to include it. It is most probable that it was dug originally to provide drinking water for stock, especially cattle, grazing these pastures distant from the Tottle Brook or other surface water, and it could be of almost any age. Subsequently it has been treated as an ornamental feature, and paved and planted round its margin, probably early in the present century when it was included in the grounds of Lenton House.

The former pond near Beeston Lane, now infilled as Rutland Hall car park, was a much larger feature, alongside which Lenton Hurst Farm was built. Its water was retained on account of impermeable strata of the Mercia Mudstones and excavation to below a high water table fed by seepage from the 'downland'. This pool was certainly present in the early 1830s (Sanderson 1835, Carey 1831), but again earlier data are lacking and its origins are speculative. It is unlikely that such a 'wet' excavation could have been a medieval marl pit, and it is more likely to have been formed by quarrying for road metal, either for maintaining the Sawley turnpike in the latter part of the 18th century, or for constructing the new section of the turnpike from the pool to Derby Road when the line was diverted in about 1805 (see Chapter XIII). However it originated the pond must have been used for watering stock. It was located on the floor of the dry valley that runs south-south-west from above Lenton Hurst down to the Tottle Brook in front of Cavendish Hall, where springs formerly discharged into the brook (Figure 13). It will be seen that downslope seepage normal to the contours converges beneath the floor of this dry valley, and water would be supplied in quantity from the Lenton Sandstone to the pool on the Mercia Mudstone outcrop south of the Clifton fault. In the earlier 19th century a much smaller pool existed a little further south on the Lenton House estate near to Derby Road, probably an excavated 'waterhole'. It is not surprising that even today the places on the campus most susceptible to flooding after heavy rain (apart from the west entrance above the culverted Tottle Brook) are across the downland path north-east of Rutland Hall, and Beeston Lane opposite to the entrance to Nightingale Hall, each on the Mercia Mudstone outcrop between the Clifton and Highfield faults (Figure 13).

The convergent flow of water by seepage, for example on the 'downland' above Derby and Rutland Halls and in Wollaton Park opposite (Figure 13) may be part of the reason why medieval arable cultivation could be maintained in these areas, and especially on the steeply sloping and very permeable Lenton Sandstones of the former, where 'ridge and furrow' survives, and where marling helped to retard soil water loss. There is, however, no spring or stream within the campus substantial enough to have attracted early village settlement, a circumstance that might support the view that the medieval village of Keighton (see Chapter II) was an estate village of the 11th century, and not a Saxon settlement. Keighton village, in common with the farmsteads and houses of the 18th and 19th centuries, obtained water from wells. The well at Keighton, described in Chapter II, was sunk through a layer of Mercia Mudstone rocks above the Clifton fault plane and into Lenton Sandstone to a depth of about 40 feet below the surface, and it maintained a water depth of about 10 feet. Wells on the higher ground, however, needed to be deep to reach the permanent water table, and would have been impracticable much before the end of the 18th century. The well at Lenton Hall, at about 190 feet OD, passed through 114 feet of Mercia Mudstone rocks before reaching the underlying sandstone from which the water was drawn. The well at Highfield House at about 160 feet OD passed through 98 feet of Mercia Mudstone rocks. The water table at these two points would be at about 70 and 60 feet OD respectively.

In general the water table sloped down westwards and southwards to the Tottle Brook and eastwards to the river Leen, and springs discharged into the stream beds. However, in the varied lithology of the Mercia Mudstones impermeable beds alternating with more permeable layers resulted in the occurrence of small and inconstant springs on the valley side, for example, one below the Portland Building which proved troublesome during construction of the crypt chapel in the Portland Building itself. Whether Keighton village was partly supplied with water from such sources is not known. Further north-east other springs emerged at valley-floor level at Spring Close, including one which was the locating factor for a bleach works in the early 19th century (see Chapter XIV). Some of these springs were ephemeral, and well water at an accessible depth was available only on the lower ground, so that dew ponds such as that described above would have been essential if cattle in any numbers were to grazed on the present campus, and the area was clearly more favourable for sheep than for cattle keeping for this, as well as for other reasons.

Two lakes, in Wollaton Park and University Park, the major water bodies of the district, were both formed 'artificially', but under two - indeed three - different principles of water engineering. Wollaton Park lake was formed by building a substantial earth dam, faced with stone, across the lower end of a small valley tributary to the Tottle Brook. The valley is here floored by clays and shales of the Upper Coal Measures, exposed by stripping of the thin Lenton Sandstone cover, and weakly resistant to erosion but largely impermeable. It seems probable that the present lake bed was originally drained by a stream or streams fed by springs emerging at the base of the Lenton Sandstone at the foot of the slope from Wollaton Hall. Today slope wash and seepage is intercepted by a ditch, which also carries water collected from the slopes further north. The lake, which stands some 20 feet above the Tottle Brook, overflows from its northern side to empty into the brook, now culverted, after passing beneath Wollaton Vale road. The dam has recently undergone a major renovation, and large quantities of silt have been removed from the northern end of the lake. The date of construction of the lake is not known, but it may have been at the time of the establishment of the New Park immediately following the purchase of the Sixty Acres from John Sherwin in 1698 (see Chapter IV). Reasons for its construction would include amenity (landscape), fishing, boating and fowling as well as watering cattle, and perhaps deer. It should not be confused in documentary references with the Fishpond in the Old Park, north of Wollaton village.

University Park lake was constructed in the early 1920s, partly as a decorative landscape feature and leisure amenity for the public, especially for boating, but also to provide material for the construction of University Boulevard (see Chapter XVI). It replaced an earlier, smaller pool known as the Fishpond, which was formed in about 1830 as part of the 'pleasure grounds' of Highfield House (see Chapter VI: Figures 37 and 44). The Fishpond was probably developed from a small peaty pool of natural origin. It was impounded by a small dam with a sluice which could be opened to drain the pool and allow the removal of weeds. It was not simply an expanded part of the Tottle Brook, into which it emptied, and which ran along its south-east side, but was fed at its western end at a higher level with water taken from the brook near its crossing of Beeston Lane, and carried along a flume round the contour. Part of the south side of the Fishpond was filled in when the present lake was formed, to provide the wide terrace and steps down to the lake near to the central entrance to the park. The present lake cannot be controlled in the same way as the Fishpond, for although it is partly supplied with surface water by the Tottle Brook it is maintained mainly from the valley gravels around, having been excavated to below the water table.

Apart from the lake in University Park the chief open water features in the Trent vale have been 'wet' gravel pits from which commercial extraction of gravel extended to below the water table. In particular the former Chaunters Close, on a patch of Floodplain terrace, was worked in the inter-war period, being conveniently located alongside the Beeston Canal (Figure 12) but fortunately southern Lenton has escaped the total devastation inflicted upon Attenborough, and the limited working has not obstructed the development of the valley floor as sites for industry made possible by land fill and the successful regional flood prevention scheme for the river Trent. The old mill pools on the river Leen, impounded by mill dams, have long since disappeared, and, indeed, the river itself has been diverted to make use of the channel of the Nottingham Canal south of Derby Road.

Finally, inadvertent obstruction of the natural drainage, especially by the construction of embankments to carry railways, roads or canals, has been a problem on the level valley floor, especially in Dunkirk. Such impedance leads progressively to waterlogging and dereliction. One example is the north-eastern portion of the tract of playing fields alongside University Boulevard, where by the 1930s an extensive area was shown as marshy on O.S. maps, and the waterlogged area extended south-westwards during the 1950s and 1960s. The problem here must have originated in the 19th century. The situation has been remedied through drainage work associated with the construction of the Highfields Science Park and the new tennis centre. Poor surface drainage also affects some areas on the campus where earth sculpture has changed surface levels. For example, the grassland below the Social Science car park, though steep, is ill-drained because it is formed of dumped, mainly impermeable material, and after thirty years is still to a degree unconsolidated. The Beeston Lane playing fields levelled in the 1960s, and provided with a system of field drains, still tend to become muddy in wet weather because of the very slight fall in surface level across them, and the nature of the Mercia Mudstones that underlie them.

SOILS [16]

For those who lived and worked on the campus before the late 18th century the most important physical resource was the soil. This varied considerably over the area because the parent material varied widely in texture, composition, slope and drainage characteristics, even within the small compass of the University estate. But given reasonable drainage, which prevails except in the valley bottoms, the sands and sandstones, marls and shales (mudstones and siltstones) clays, glacial drifts and gravels all tend to develop soils of the Brown Earth type - free-draining and leached of calcium carbonate but with no breakdown of clay minerals, and no very clear horizon development. On the coarsest sandy parent material, however, podzols could form under suitable natural heath or coniferous vegetation and favourable site, and the Brown Earth soils may themselves vary much in texture and fertility in accordance with local variations in lithology which are numerous in the New Red Sandstone rocks. Apart from this variability further reservations are necessary to any assumption that the characteristic 'natural' soils developed on the major rock formations will be those found today, because of possible superficial drift deposits - for example, round the northern end of Beeston Lane - and the spreading of 'marl' over some soils in the past, and because of widespread removal or addition of surface material, including soil, by working and filling quarries, grading roads, levelling building sites and playing fields, and by landscaping for ease of maintenance or aesthetic effect. Such operations have altered the level, drainage and soils of much of the campus not covered by buildings or roads.

With these reservations it is useful to review briefly the general characteristics of the soils developed normally on the chief types of geological parent material, as likely to be nearer to those of past times than most of the present surface soils. The Nottingham Castle sandstone typically carries light, loose, coarse sandy soils, varying from thin sandy loam to blowing sand. Sometimes pebbly, with excessively free drainage, they are 'hungry' soils in cultivation, demanding supplementary water and organic fertiliser. Their natural flora is heath and gorse, with oak, birch and coniferous open woodland, readily invaded by bracken. In cultivation this land used to be known as 'sheep and arable' country, healthy for animals but unable to maintain turf for satisfactory permanent pasture, and so unsuitable for cattle keeping. Most was traditionally under the plough, and in the 18th and 19th centuries often in a 4-course rotation with oats and rye the favoured cereal crops, and barley a cash crop, because the soil was not strong enough to grow wheat satisfactorily. Root crops and peas were also grown.

The dryness of the ground on the Nottingham Castle Formation rocks is very apparent on the campus in the higher area around Wortley House, Cripps Hall, the new buildings of Hugh Stewart Hall and Lenton and Wortley Hall. Puddles are rarely seen after rain and the ground remains firm. Most of the soils developed naturally on these beds will have been of the 'sandy Brown Earth' type, also called 'sols bruns acides' [Duchaufour 1958] which are acid but without clay mineral breakdown and impoverishment. Where the proportion of fractions finer than fine sand increases such soils may be well cultivated permeable, quick-warming, 'early' soils giving moderate crops. But because of their vulnerability to drought, with rapid percolation and leaching and quick loss of added soil nutrients, they need continuously building up with organic manures. In medieval times, with no root fodder crops for folding sheep, such soil could not sustain adequate production of field crops, even with marling, and much was left in its natural state and used as rabbit warren. Although the woodland around this part of the campus is so well grown as to indicate that the most sterile soils are not found there, much of the area was rabbit warren - perhaps all of it at times - though parts of the warren were cultivated when economic conditions were favourable.

The Lenton Sandstone, less coarse and containing more of the finer fractions - silts and clays - gives rise mainly to a sandy loam; light, easily worked, permeable and generally well cultivated soil which extended over the lower parts of Wollaton Park and much of the northern half of the campus. Such soils were more suitable for growing barley than wheat, and with their free drainage and lack of 'lushness' provided healthy grazing, more suitable for sheep than cattle. The Abbey Fields (see Figure 21), described later, which show the marks of ridge and furrow, and which were strengthened by marling, were cultivated as open arable land up to the early 16th century, with the sheep of Lenton Priory grazing the stubble, but after the Dissolution they were 'dry pasture grounds', very different from the pastures of the Trent valley floor. Parts of the Colwick and Woodthorpe Formation rocks will have carried similar Sandy Brown Earth soils, also rewarding to cultivate.

Soils formed on rocks of the Mercia Mudstone Group are variable, and generally of only moderate fertility, though usually suitable for wheat growing. Characteristically the clay loams are 'sols bruns lessives' - Brown Earth soils with well differentiated horizons, decalcified, with an acid mull humus, generally well incorporated in the mineral soil through cultivation, and with clay moving down to a clay-enriched B-horizon. Though heavy, the stiff, dark red or chocolate-brown soil, generally free of stones and described as a dolomitic, sometimes calcareous clay marl, works fairly freely. Physically it behaves like a heavy clay, often becoming plastic when wet and forming hard clods when dry, but with a high fraction of very fine sand it is a good plant medium, especially for grass and grain. The fine silt fraction is especially significant in determining overall texture, and there are more loamy belts where the skerries, with their siltstone beds, occupy the surface. The Colwick and Woodthorpe Formations give more variable and more freely draining soils, the former carrying generally loamy, deep, medium to light soils of moderate productivity, but with patches of heavier land - among the best arable land in Nottinghamshire.

The utilization and value of the alluvial soils of the valley floors depend very much on their drainage characteristics. The reddish Trent valley alluvium is rather similar as a soil forming medium to the Mercia Mudstone formations. The thick gravel of the Flood Plain terrace, of varied mineral composition, protrudes in patches above the recent alluvium. The alluvium produces a clay loam or silty clay loam soil, and with the water table near the surface gleying often develops, and the land is better used for grazing or meadow than for arable cropping. The soil developed on the gravel patches is coarser in texture, loamy where well drained, and of Brown Earth type - a sandy clay loam containing many rounded stones, chiefly of quartzite or flint. It is much more often ploughed than the alluvium, and in the medieval period and later often carried the open arable fields of the valley villages. Field names in the priory demesne and elsewhere in southern Lenton, for example in the 16th century, show the distinction very clearly, as will appear below (see Figures 17 and 21). River gravel soils with 45 to 50 per cent of coarse sand, much fine sand and only 1 to 2 per cent of clay are clearly distinguished in properties and utilization from recent alluvium, which varies from free-working loams where drainage is good to medium to heavy clays, the latter usually at the foot of slopes with a downwash of fine particles, where waterlogging may lead to peat formation, The meadow land along the Tottle Brook, which was excavated to form the lake in University Park, was of this type. Ribbons of peaty soil also occurred in the past along the sluggish streams such as Blotoff Dyke. Drainage ditches are vitally important in such places.

Finally, it must be re-emphasized that the 'natural' or original types of soil described above are not necessarily to be found anywhere on the University campus today. Much surface soil and subsoil has been moved about the campus in the course of building site preparation, garden creation, infilling and levelling, for example of quarries, sports fields and car parks, cut and fill in grading new roads, extensive cutting and laying of turf and in other ways, so that a large proportion of the campus has an 'artificial' surface, even where it appears to be 'natural'. 'Natural' or near-natural soils are to be sought only in certain places such as residual high woodland, or around mature forest trees. Even the open 'downland', carefully preserved, has been subjected to marling in the past, and turf stripping recently, modifying the nature of the surface soil.

NOTES

1. Geological Survey of Great Britain, Solid and Drift, *Sheet 125* (1972) 1:50,000. Originally surveyed 1855-78: surveyed at 6-inch scale 1902-07: re-surveyed at 6-inch scale 1960-66. *Sheet 126* (1972) (for eastern part of campus) - surveyed at 6-inch scale 1903-05: published with drift 1908: reprinted 1959: reprinted at 1:50,000 1972.
2. G.Warrington et al., *A correlation of Triassic rocks in the British Isles* Geol. Soc. London, Special Report No. 13 (1980). This publication radically reviewed and revised the nomenclature of the New Red Sandstone and suggested new names, mainly with regional connotations, which are being slowly adopted. Frank Taylor has recently codified the new nomenclature with references to earlier names and workers in his valuable publication *ALexiconofNewRed Sandstone stratigraphy* (Jan. 1988), published as two parts of *The Mercian Geologist* 11, parts 1 and 2.
3. R.E.Elliott, 'The Keuper Series in southern Nottinghamshire'. *Proc. Yorkshire Geol. Soc.* 33 (1961) 197-234. Warrington et al [1980] accepted Elliott's formation names and their vertical distribution in the Keuper succession.
4. The details of the stratigraphy are described by Elliott [1961] in pp. 199 to 209 of his paper, and illustrated in his Figures 2, 3 and 4.
5. B. Hains and A. Horton, *Central England* (H.M.S.O., 1969 and 1975) p. 64. Sherlock and Wills held different views, both at variance with those of the Geological Survey. F.M.Taylor [1966] 26-27 discusses the problems of the age of the Bunter series.
6. 'Thirty miles around Mansfield'. Map by George Sanderson at 2 inches to 1 mile, published 1835.
7. N.U.M.D., Mi P 5 (1863). Plans of Lord Middleton's estate by Sturgess: Plan No. 2. The reference book for the maps is N.U.M.D., Mi 2 S 3.
8. O.S. map at scale 10.56 feet to the statute mile, or 1 inch to 41.66 feet (1:500). For Lenton Hall, Sheet XLII.5.21 (1881). Notts. Archives Office holds copies of maps at this scale.
9. N.U.M.D., Accession 423. A collection of photographs from Mr. H. Stafford, item 18 (1924).
10. Only a few of the more obvious characteristics are incorporated in Figure 7, derived from Elliott [1961] Figures 2, 3 and 4 with the accompanying text., Table 1, and the table in p. 218 describing the upper Carlton Formation.
11. Elliott [1961] 210-11 and Figure 5, p. 213. The level of gamma ray activity, as seen on seventeen Schlumberger gamma ray logs is distinctly higher in the Keuper (Mercia Mudstones) than in the Bunter (Sherwood Forest Formation), a difference equivalent to about 2 microgrammes of radium per ton of rock. Elliott remarked (pp. 213-14) that '....the correlation of 18 gamma ray logs between Ruddington Hall on the west and Bingham oil boring on the east does suggest a thickening eastwards of the basal Keuper from 15 to 85 feet, though this may in part be at the expense of the highest Bunter'.
12. See also E. Wilson and J. Shipman, 'On the occurrence of Keuper Basement Beds in the neighbourhood of Nottingham'.

Geol. Mag. 1879, 532.

13. J.T.Godfrey [1884 17] wrote: 'In excavating for clay on the side of Bath Hill at Highfield, a short distance to the eastward of the spot where what is believed to have been the remains of a Roman habitation were found, large quantities of broken pottery were met with about eight years ago'. This refers to the same location, and shows, incidentally, that Keighton village and its kilns, described in Chapter II, were known a century before their recent rediscovery.

14. Relevant papers include those by Swinnerton [1935, 1948], Clayton [1953, 1955, 1957], Posnansky [1960], King [1966, 1972] and Straw [1963].

15. Described by J. Shipman in Godfrey [1884 447-48] quoting his paper in the *Midland Naturalist* 6 (1883) 264.

16. Useful references include Avery [1956], Bridges [1962 1966], Edwards [1944] and Goodwin [undated].

CHAPTER II

THE UNIVERSITY CAMPUS IN PRE-REFORMATION TIMES

The pre-medieval period

J.T.Godfrey wrote in 1884 that 'the early antiquities of this [Lenton] parish are exceedingly meagre', and little is known of the area occupied by the University campus before the Domesday survey of 1086. There are scattered references to chance finds of artefacts of various pre-medieval dates, but no coherent picture emerges of any pattern of human occupance in the university district. Probably the oldest objects discovered with an historical significance are the Palaeolithic implements found in the Stoney Street, Beeston gravel pit by F.W.G.Davey, dated late Acheulian and described in the Nottinghamshire Weekly Guardian of 16 August 1928 and in the Antiquaries' Journal of January 1928. Seven of the implements are in the British Museum. Late Neolithic axes have been found in Beeston, and a perforated stone axe of similar date was picked up on the 'sand hills' in Wollaton Park, on the borders of Lenton parish, 'some years' before Godfrey [1884 11] described and illustrated it.

Godfrey reported that Alfred Lowe of Highfield House had had in his possession several antiquities, chiefly of the 'Celtic period', found at various times in Lenton parish. They included 'a good socketed bronze celt of the ordinary type, three small arrowheads of iron .... a bronze key and several bronze ornaments'. Also, in the possession of Edward Joseph Lowe of Shirenewton Hall, Monmouthshire, Alfred Lowe's son, was a bronze sword two feet long with a riveted bone or wooden handle and a 19½ inch leaf-shaped blade, found by workmen employed in enlarging the lake below Highfield House in about the year 1830, and according to Godfrey 'evidently of the Roman period' [1]. The sword, later in the Castle Museum, lay near the remains of a human skeleton preserved in peat, the bones of which 'quickly perished on being exposed to the atmosphere'. Several other articles discovered with it, but stolen by the workmen, included a small, silver bell-shaped vessel, sold for a trifling sum and melted down. The peat bog was the central part of the present University Park lake through which the Tottle

Brook ran.

Noting only 'some traces of Roman occupation', Godfrey [1884] described how 'about 50 years ago', that is, in about 1820-30, 'a portion of the foundations of the walls of what would appear to be a *villa urbana* was discovered on the Bath Hill near Highfield House, but these remains were unfortunately never investigated'. Several fragments of tiles and pottery were found on the spot, together with some small bronze ornaments, 'the latter of which are of undoubted Roman origin' and had fortunately been preserved, being in the possession of E.J.Lowe. They included the figure of a dolphin about 2½ inches long; a cock; and some kind of fish or serpent. Unfortunately nothing more is known of the place of discovery or the present whereabouts of this reputed find. However, allowing for the Victorian tendency to attribute puzzling archaeological finds to the Roman period, it is likely that the 'villa' was one of the houses of the medieval village of Keighton, discussed later. Confirmation is provided by the large quantities of broken pottery found in 1876, indicating the proximity of a kiln, 'a short distance to the eastward of the spot where what is believed to have been the remains of a Roman habitation were found', and thus in the area of kilns found more recently near the south-west corner of the Biology building.

A small defaced bronze coin of Constantine II (340 A.D.) was dug up in the garden of Highfield House in the 1870s [Godfrey 1884], but this does not confirm Roman-period occupation of the campus area. Finds made during excavations on the site of Keighton village are suggestive, but no more. Romano-British sherds lying above late medieval material, suggest that earth from a nearby site, occupied in the Roman period, had been spread over demolished houses, perhaps with a view to levelling the site of Keighton village after its abandonment, probably in the later 15th century; but there is no indication as to where the Romano-British material came from. Godfrey's reference to the discovery in the early 19th century of 'a tessellated pavement' in 'one of the Keighton meadows' just beyond Bath Hill seems to relate to encaustic tile kiln waste rather than to any 'Roman' building or settlement. As Fyfe wrote [1856] nothing found of Roman provenance 'constitutes a claim to settlement'.

Godfrey [1884 15-16] described how 'the old inhabitants of Lenton had a tradition, now nearly forgotten, that a fierce battle was fought between the Britons and the Romans in the valley to the south-west of Lenton, and that the former were victorious, although they suffered heavy losses'. Skulls of horses as well as human remains occasionally turned up in the Keighton meadows were thought to confirm the tradition, but it is more likely that the finds gave rise to the 'tradition'. If such human burials were thought to be associated with an early church foundation at Keighton, such as 'Kirketon', a common early version of the name might suggest, it should be said that no archaeological or documentary evidence has been found to confirm it. Yet the presence of Romano-British pottery sherds on the site of Keighton village, though unstratified, is unexplained, and counsels caution before completely ruling out pre-Saxon settlement.

While the main University campus has yielded little of pre-Medieval provenance, there have been several finds indicating early settlement in the locality. Although the University sports grounds at Grove Farm were uninhabited meadow (Trent Wong) through the medieval period, the southern end on the banks of the river Trent was the site of a very early settlement of pile dwellings, which yielded artefacts indicating pre-Roman occupancy perhaps as early as 400 B.C.. The site was occupied at least periodically by a community or family of fishermen, probably for several hundred years.

The settlement was revealed in early 1938 through dredging of the river by the Trent Navigation Company in the reach between Clifton and Wilford where gravel deposition results in the shoaling of the river, and provided a ford that was important for many centuries, and is now represented by Clifton Bridge. A gravel deposit on the Lenton side was found to be underlain by a number of wooden piles set in rows forming squares. The piles were four feet apart and extended onshore beneath the river bank. While they could have been part of a fish trap the finds associated with the piles strongly suggest a settlement. A number of human skulls, a few deer antlers, two querns, a crucible and at least six bronze spearheads were regarded as 'contemporary with 400 B.C.'. The spearheads were all of different dates in the late Bronze Age, including an early bronze rapier blade, and one dredged from the river that was probably of Irish origin. Found with the spearheads, some of which may have been fish harpoons, was a beehive quern of Roman to late Anglo-Saxon date, and a crucible for copper of the late Bronze Age. On 13 May 1938 two dugout canoes were found associated with the numerous wooden piles. They were about 27 feet long and 2½ feet wide, each weighing two tons. After drying they were moved to the Castle Museum. They are dated to about 100 B.C.. Drawings of the artefacts from this site were published by Campion [1939 21,23], but no further published discussion of the nature or significance of this pile settlement has been seen by the writer. Its location at the junction of Beeston, Lenton, Clifton and Wilford parishes and at an important river crossing is noteworthy.

The second site of interest was at Broxtowe, where in early 1937 Broxtowe Hall, within three miles of the University campus, was demolished by Nottingham Corporation. In June 1937 a Roman coin hoard was found on the estate, and then a large 'camp' with many remains of Roman date. A plan of the station and drawings of the finds were published in the Third Annual Report (for 1938) of the Thoroton Society, Excavation Section.

Other discoveries, described in unpublished notes by Arthur Cossons intended for a history of Beeston, included sites at Barton-in-Fabis and Thrumpton, south-west of Clifton. At Barton the many finds of Roman date were probably relics of a farmstead or 'villa'. Although little in the way of foundations were found in situ, a fragmentary tesselated pavement was removed 'some years ago' to Nottingham public reference library, and loose tesserae of the same or a similar pavement were found scattered over the site at Glebe Farm, marked on the O.D. 1-inch map as 'Roman Villa (site of)'. Surface finds of broken pottery point to a long occupancy and several successive sets of buildings. Other remains of Roman date were found near Thrumpton where another 'Roman Villa (site of)' is shown on the O.S. 1-inch map very near to the river Soar a few hundred yards above its junction with the river Trent. They were placed in Long Eaton public library.

The Domesday Survey and the manors of Morton and Lenton

The medieval settlements of Keighton and Morton, lying west and south of the river Leen in Lenton parish, have names that appear to have an Anglian (Early English) origin like Lenton's and Beeston's with their '-tun' (farmstead) element, but this is no sure indication that as settlements they date from the 6th to the 8th century prior to the Danish occupation. Although the Anglo-Saxon Chronicle under 868 AD described the Danish host wintering at Nottingham, the Mercian king secured the town in 922, and there are relatively few '-thorpe and '-by' place names in Nottinghamshire though many Danish personal names with the English '-tun'. This seems to indicate that the population was mainly English, though from the time of Ethelred II paying 'danegeld' as a bribe to the Norse invaders.

Medieval documents refer to Keighton and Radford as hamlets of Lenton, which gave its name to the parish. For example, the accounts of Lenton Priory demesne in 1297 include receipt of tallage from 'Lenton cum hamelettis' [Stitt 1959 13]. The Domesday survey of 1086[2] did not mention Keighton by name, from which Godfrey [1884] deduced that Keighton 'apparently had no manorial rights attached to it'. It suggests, at least, the subordinate status of the inhabitants of Keighton, if, indeed, it then existed. It was certainly present in about 1108, when it figured in the foundation charter of Lenton Priory [3]. The manor of Morton, by contrast, seemed to Godfrey, 'to have been of superior importance and value to the manor of Lenton at the time when the Domesday survey was taken'. Yet some 200 years later Morton was never mentioned and was lost as a territorial entity, while Keighton ranked with Lenton in population and importance. This problem must be clarified if the social and economic history of Lenton and the University campus in the medieval period is to be understood.

That 'Morton' may be descriptive of a farm on or near a moor - the level 'waste' of the Holmes perhaps - is supported by field name evidence. Keighton was never mentioned by that name before the foundation of Lenton Priory, but its alternative spelling, Kirketon, cannot signify ownership by the priory since it was named in the priory's foundation charter. Godfrey suggested that the manor of Morton 'extended over the more southern portion of the parish' on the evidence of 'some meadows yet known as The Mortons lying near the Dunkirk bridge over the canal, midway between the old village of Lenton and the river Trent', and that 'the village was conjectured to have been situated somewhere near where Dunkirk Farm now stands'. Whether Morton was ever a nucleated village is not known, but is unlikely. However, the site proposed by Godfrey is certainly plausible as a settlement site, lying at the margin of the most extensive area of Flood Plain terrace in the district. Many villages downstream along the Trent vale occupy such situations, standing generally above the flood level, and surrounded by tractable loamy soils. In this instance 16th century field names such as Wheatcroft and Great and Little Ryecroft point to former arable cultivation of the gravel patches in the vicinity.

In 1538 Edmondson's Close was among the supposed village lands later attached to Keighton (see Chapter III) and not part of the priory demesne in its narrowest sense. A survey-rental of the demesne in about 1554 refers to 'one close called Morton, otherwise Edmondson's Close, cont[aining] vi acres', which was meadow. References much later to Morton Nook Meadow, adjoining Edmondson's Close, tend to confirm the location. This meadow was enclosed in 1769 with the rest of the Holmes, and eventually acquired by John Wright of Lenton Hall (see Chapter V). But 'it would appear that from an early period it [Morton] became absorbed in the manor of Lenton, as it yet remains' - a half-truth at best as will appear. Godfrey [1884] here follows Thoroton [1677/1790] who wrote that Morton 'is now lost in Lenton, and so is Kighton, saving one place which is still called Kigh. closes'.

Evidence as to the nature and locations of Morton and Keighton will be examined later, but considerations of physical geography, and notably soils and drainage, as well as later history, suggest that the territory of Morton, as described in Domesday, must have extended westward from Blotoff or Blotah Dyke in the Trent vale on to the higher ground later identified as Keighton, and this whole area became the demesne of Lenton Priory, clearly and permanently distinct from the Crown manor of Lenton. Both Keighton and Morton were named as parts of the original endowment of the priory in its foundation charter only some 20 years after Domesday.

While a minor portion of the land of Lenton township was in the hands of the king in 1086, most had been added to the great possessions of William Peverel, the first Norman lord of Lenton, who also had Morton. The holdings at Domesday are transcribed as follows:

The king's lands

Soke : In Lenton 4 oxgangs [bovates] of land to be taxed [to the Danegeld]: Soke in Arnold to be taxed. It is waste.

William Peverel's lands

Soke : In Lenton 2 carucates of land to be taxed (as certified before the Conquest)
Soke in Newbold. Land to 2 ploughs.
4 sokemen and 4 bordars have there 2 ploughs and a mill.

Manor: In Lenton Unlof [before the Conquest] had 4 oxgangs of land to be taxed. Land to half a plough. It is now in the wardship of William [Peverel].
The same Unlof had there one plough and one villane and one bordar having one plough, and one mill of 10 shillings, and 10 acres of meadow and 10 acres of coppice (small) wood.
Value in King Edward's time [the Confessor] 10 shillings, now 15 shillings.

Manor: In Morton Boui [before the Conquest] had a manor with one carucate and a half of land to be taxed. Land to 12 oxen. William [Peverel] has there one plough and a half and 5 sokemen who hold 3 oxgangs of this land, and 12 villanes and one bordar, having 9 ploughs and a half.
Value in King Edward's time and now 20 shillings.

The pattern of a substantial demesne with various classes of tenant can be seen, although in view of the details discussed below of the economy of the area over 200 years later, towards the end of the 13th century, it would be rash to identify the sokemen and villani as forebears in title of the free and bond tenants of later times. However, the Domesday distinction between villani and the more exiguously landed bordarii may reflect the division apparent in the 13th century between bovators and cottarii [Stitt 1959], and, broadly, the sokemen may represent Morton and the villeins Keighton.

In 1086 there were 24 villani on William Peverel's estates in Lenton, Radford and Morton, and of these half were in Morton: but these soon 'disappeared'. On the other hand Keighton, not mentioned in Domesday, had bond bovates in 1297 in numbers similar to those in Lenton and Radford, and probably about the same number of tenants as Morton had in Domesday, two centuries earlier, in addition to its cottarii. This tends to confirm the equivalence of Morton with Keighton as one territorial unit, though possibly with an internal shift of population following the establishment of the priory and the development of its demesne. Such a transfer of population might be expected if a village agrarian structure was converted into an estate structure of the kind that would be required to support a substantial religious community, integrated in its operation with the priory's possessions elsewhere, as, for example in the annual receipt of tithe lambs from Derbyshire. There are, however, many possible scenarios. For example, the 12 villeins of Morton described in 1086 might be equivalent to the 14 'bovators' of Keighton two centuries later, in 1296-98, living in dispersed homesteads, or even in Lenton village, and distinct from a dozen cottagers in Keighton village, established by William Peverel, or even by the priory itself as an estate or colonizing village. Keighton and Morton were 'manors', not townships.

William Peverel was reputedly a natural son of the Conqueror, given charge of the newly-built Nottingham castle in 1068 when very young, and lord of 162 manors in England at the Domesday survey. In Nottingham alone he possessed at Domesday 48 merchants' houses, 13 knights' houses and 8 bondmen's houses in addition to land granted to make a wall round the town, and the churches of St. Mary, St. Peter and St. Nicholas. The castles and vast landed possessions constituting the Fee of Peverel eventually reverted to the Crown, and were bestowed in 1174 by Henry II on his son John, on whose accession the Honour of Peverel became annexed to the Crown, and remained so thereafter. The origins of William Peverel, however, are obscure. He was not mentioned in the chronicles of Normandy during the 30 years preceding the Conquest, and from the date of his death in about 1113 he could have been no more than 24 or 25 when given such immense possessions and power. Probably this gave rise to suggestions of nepotism. One story supposes that his mother, a daughter of an Anglo-Saxon thane, Ingelric, was given in marriage to one Ranulph Peverel, a Norman knight whose name William Peverel took [4].

According to the register of the Priory of St. James, Northampton, William Peverel died on the fifth of the kalends of February 1113 [Godfrey 1884 22]. He founded Lenton Priory, probably in 1108 [5], and bestowed on it his whole manor of Lenton except for four mills, two in his own demesne, one held by his wife Adelina and a fourth by his knight Herbert. The remaining seven mills in Lenton and Radford were granted to the priory. At least three of them were on the section of the river Leen bordering the east side of the present University campus. William also endowed the priory with all his lands in Keighton, Morton, Radford and many other townships and manors [6]. The chief manor of Lenton remained in the hands of the prior and monks of Lenton until the final suppression of religious houses in the time of Henry VIII. Many of William Peverel's homagers or feodaries bestowed further property on the new priory, among them Robertus de Mortuein, whose grandson Eustachius de Moreton, lord of Wollaton, confirmed the grant. Robert de Moreton, in lieu of a portion of the tithes of his demesne, gave the priory an annual rent of 10 shillings for ever. Robert held Wollaton, together with part of Cossall under William Peverel, and was an ancestor of a family which remained seated at Wollaton until the early 14th century when their lands were acquired by the Willoughby family, through marriage and by purchase.

Lenton Priory and its demesne

The Cluniac priory of Lenton was one among 150 religious houses that were established during the 35-year reign of Henry I, testimony to the energy and resources expended by the Anglo-Normans on their passion for building and architecture. The Cluniac order was a reformed congregation following the Benedictine rule as revised by Odo of Cluny about 912. The parent house was at Cluny in Burgundy, and the first priory of the order in England was established at Lewes in 1077. William Peverel no doubt chose the Cluniac order for his foundation because its style and character was attractive to men in his position, with a 'high profile' life-style that was signified by its striking dress - a black frock, a pelisse, a hood of lamb's wool, red hose, a white woollen tunic and black scapular, and, in choir, copes of linen and occasionally a pelisse, a frock and a cowl of scarlet cloth.

The perceived luxurious life-style led to a revulsion that ended in the establishment of the Cistercian reform, and the foreign affiliation of Cluniac houses led to repeated difficulties of a political nature. Lenton Priory suffered in this way despite the importance and wealth of its priors, who entertained royal visitors - for example, Edward I in April 1302 and April 1303, and Edward II in 1307. The situation depended closely on the relations between the king of England and his French counterpart, and in 1346 it was ordered that all foreign monks quit the realm. Lenton Priory, the only monastery in Nottinghamshire subject to foreign jurisdiction, was placed under sequestration, which was lifted only in 16 Richard II (1393) when the monks obtained denizenship, and the tie with Cluny was cut.

As consciousness of the national identity of England became stronger, and the French connection faded, the foreign base of the Cluniac order caused the priory embarrassment and financial loss on many occasions. The immediate significance of this problem in the present context is that when the priory was taken over for periods and run by the Crown, the accounts could be expected to pass into the national records, and this allows us to analyse in detail the economy of the priory and its possessions in the late 13th century [Stitt 1959]. These particular accounts date from 230 years after the Conquest, 210 years after Domesday, 190 years after the founding of the priory and 240 years before its suppression - a 'snapshot' of conditions about midway through the 432 years of the priory's existence.

The priory was built at the southern end of Lenton village inside the bend of the river Leen

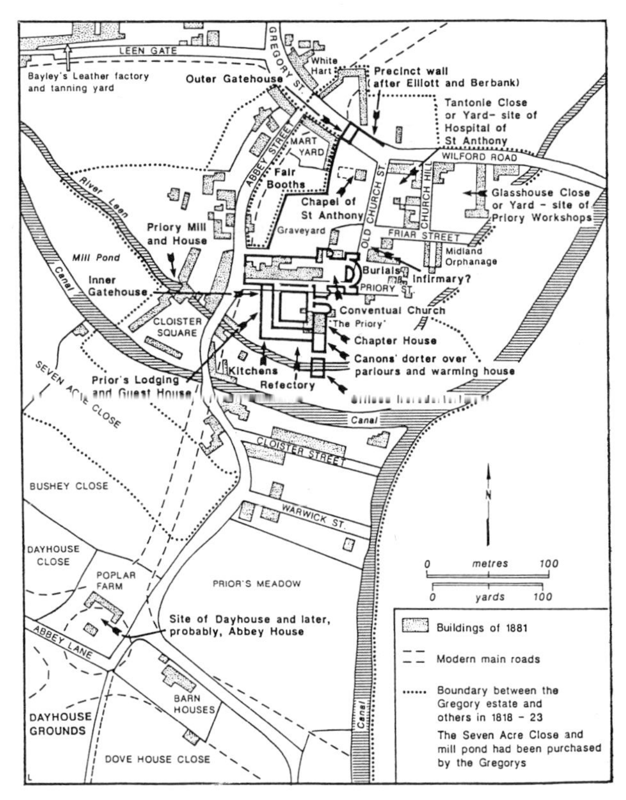

Figure 15: Conjectural plan of Lenton Priory
[From F.A. Barnes (1987)]

in Old Lenton (Figure 15). Cluniac churches were noted for their magnificence, and that of Lenton was no exception. It was larger than Southwell Minster, with a width of nave and aisles of 80 feet (over transepts 150 feet) compared with Southwell's 72 feet (and 135 feet). All Cluniac churches in England are now ruined. All other priory buildings at Lenton have also disappeared, though the chapel of St. Anthony's Hospital which stood within the northern part of the court or curia of the priory was rebuilt to become the old parish church. Apart from this chapel and the conventual church the layout of the priory and the location of its buildings are still subjects for speculation [Barnes 1987].

The priory's 'temporalities', or lay properties in Lenton and Radford outside the precinct of the priory itself were of two main types - tenements, which included enclosed and open-field land and grazing rights, the rents for which provided cash income for the priory, and the priory's demesne, or home farm, run by the priory itself to provide produce for the community. The former occupied most of Lenton and Radford north and east of the river Leen, while the demesne proper was confined to the area south and west of the Leen.

The household or community of Lenton Priory normally consisted of 25 to 30 monks together with a number of lay persons (conversi) and collodors or corrodions [7]. Its requirements dominated the economic and social life of Lenton, and the priory controlled trading at the important seven-day Lenton fair. The University campus, excluding the northern fringe of the Medical School and University Hospital site, forming part of the priory demesne, or home farm, was cultivated with the main object of feeding the priory community. It comprised several large open arable fields and a dairy or stock farm, as well as a rabbit warren and some patchy woodland, water meadow and feeding pastures for cattle. These are shown in Figure 17. The priory also owned much of the cultivated land in Lenton north and east of the river Leen,

Figure 16: Aerial views of the site of Keighton
Above: *View looking north-west from above the Lake Pavilion. The areas disturbed by the excavations of Kerridge and Coppack are clearly seen. The well was situated just outside the right hand margin of the picture.*
Below: *View looking north-west from above the Social Sciences building car park before the Keighton Hill road was constructed.*

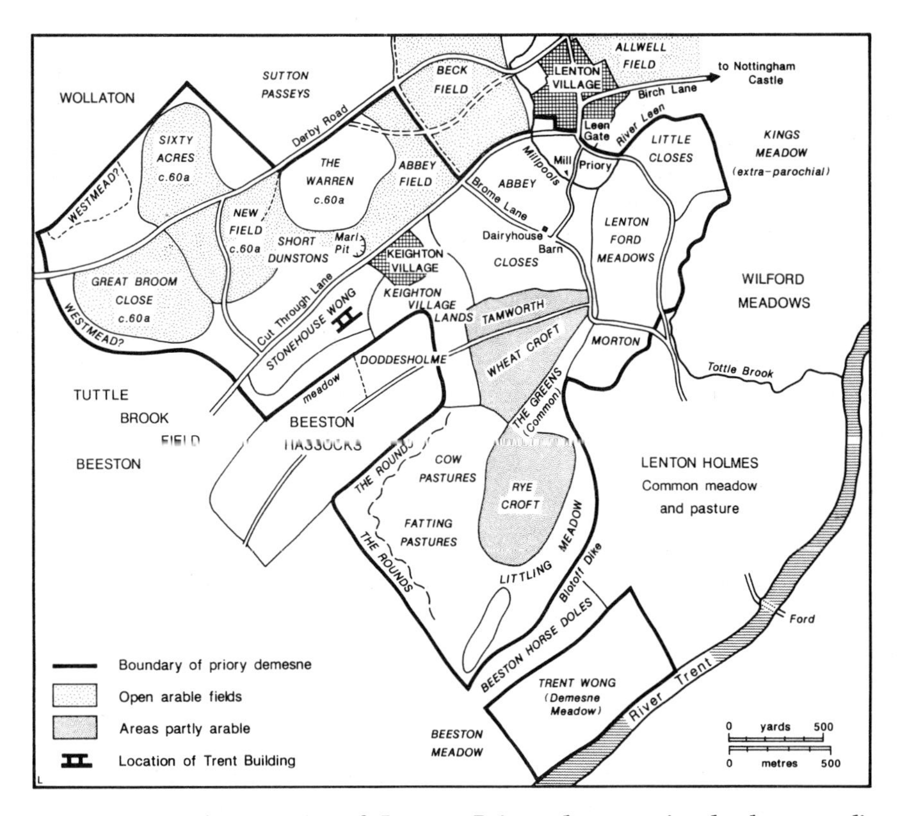

Figure 17: Some land use units of Lenton Priory demesne in the later medieval period

including that in the open common arable fields, and similar, though less extensive land in Radford. While these lands were mainly let for rent to tenants who lived in Lenton and Radford villages, and who cultivated them on their own account, there is evidence that some of the selions in the open fields were owned by and cultivated for the priory. Initially the demesne proper must have been cultivated by the labour of tenants of the priory, particularly by that of the people of Keighton. Later it appears that the agricultural work was done increasingly by hired labour, doubtless drawn from several nearby parishes, including Beeston, Lenton and Radford, especially after the village of Keighton was abandoned. In addition to the labour dues, tithes and other obligations were important elements in the economy of the priory. Indeed, its income from spiritualities exceeded that from temporalities, and at the Taxation of Norwich in 1291 temporalities produced only £147.15s.8½d. of the annual income of £339 1s.2½d..

Further discussion of Lenton Priory as an institution would be inappropriate, except incidentally, and what follows will be restricted largely to matters of rural economy and settlement on the former demesne of the priory west and south of the Leen and north-west of Blotoff Dyke, together with Trent Wong.

Agrarian economy in the late 13th century

In the first half of the 13th century there was much building at Lenton Priory; in the second half, perhaps partly on account of this, there was chronic indebtedness, exacerbated by seizures of the priory's property by the Crown in order to recover unpaid tax debts. In 1276, when a visitation from Cluny took place, the priory owed 1,080 marks, a burden from which it was never freed for the rest of the century, and which made it difficult for the priory to pay fines imposed upon it [8]. In 1287 Thomas de Normanville, escheator beyond the Trent, was to 'take into the hand of the king all the lands and tenements belonging to the Priory of Lenton, vacant through the resignation of Brother Reginald de Jora, until lately prior of the same'. Towards the end of the century, when relations between the kings of England and France were bad, Edward I regarded the monks of Lenton Priory, subordinate to Cluny Abbey - a subject of the king of France - as enemy aliens, and like his successors extracted considerable profit from it by imposing restrictions, and raising them only on payment of fines and rents. One series of restrictions was imposed in 1295, and in mid-November the monks of Lenton were ordered to Dunston, Derbyshire and their estates seized by the Crown, being restored by the end of December subject to an agreed fine of 200 marks. This had not been paid by Michaelmas 1296, and by the end of the year the king had again seized the priory's estates, this time to administer them for profit to raise the unpaid fine. Administration of the estate by Crown representatives led to their accounts being deposited in the Exchequer, and in abbreviated form on the Pipe Roll, thus preserving the only detailed data in existence on the operation of the priory demesne in the medieval period. The accounts cover 21 months, from the end of December 1296 to Michaelmas 1298. A similar seizure has left a similar, though more abbreviated record for the period from October 1324 to Michaelmas 1325 [9].

The P.R.O. documents that provide the data on which the following account is based give a picture of the priory's estates under somewhat abnormal conditions, with the monks subsisting on a pension and the estates run for profit; but there is no reason to suppose that royal custody brought any drastic alteration to the structure of the estate and its management. However, the husbandry of the demesne lands - with which we are mainly concerned here - may well have been distorted, and this difficulty must be addressed in any interpretation of the data. The records have been transcribed and analysed in great detail by F.B.Stitt, and the following account is based heavily on extracts from his paper of 1959. However, he had nothing to say about locations, boundaries or distributions, and seems not to have identified even the area covered by the priory demesne, much less its geographical differentiation.

The priory estates were centred on the manor of Lenton, which comprehended administration of the priory's property within Lenton itself, Radford and Keighton. The organization of the 'manor of the priory' followed the traditional pattern of a home farm or demesne, together with groups of free and villein tenants, the former with conditions of tenure protected by the royal courts, and the latter subject to the custom of the manor. It should be noted that although sokemen in Morton were mentioned in Domesday, no freeholders were recorded in Keighton in 1296-98.

The annual area normally sown in demesne by the priory in the late 13th century was more - perhaps much more - than 400 acres; but whether there was a biennial or triennial rotation of crops, and thus whether this represented one half or two-thirds of the total arable area in demesne is not clear. There was no indication in the accounts of the distribution of the land sown, and no contemporary evidence to show whether it was consolidated in large areas, whether enclosed or not, or lay scattered widely in open fields. These questions will arise again in connection with conditions at the Dissolution, but it seems likely that most of the arable land of the priory occurred in large open fields in Keighton, though some lay scattered as selions or groups of selions in the common open arable fields of Lenton and Radford [10]. In round figures it appears that at Domesday there were some 180 acres of cultivated demesne in Keighton, 240 acres in Radford, but comparatively little in Lenton. Although there is a suggestion that the arable area in Keighton had increased from the Domesday figure, perhaps substantially by the late 13th century, it seems likely that the crop rotation used was triennial. However, with no root crops or other sown fodder crops, a triennial rotation would have little practical advantage over a biennial one. It will be shown later that peas were a crop of considerable importance in the 1290s, though no ley legumes were then grown, and it is possible that the introduction of peas was associated with an expanded arable area.

In considering the extent of the priory demesne, the area of arable land that it contained, and the medieval system of agriculture - notably the question of whether a 3-field or a 2-field arable system was practised - the starting point must be reference to later, more precise data than were available for the medieval period. In 1798 the area of the Milward estate was about 615 acres, plus 96 acres for Trent Wong, a total of some 711 acres, including the lands in the partly abortive auction of December 1797 (see Chapter V). To this must be added about 8 acres for the Hill Closes, 4 acres for Far Field Close, about 12 acres for Broom Close (Lenton Grove), about 90 acres for the Sixty Acres field (now in Wollaton Park) sold in 1698, and 4 acres for Jervis Close, sold to Thomas Charlton in 1670, together with the 140 acres (by the 1725 terrier) of the Gregory estate south and west of the river Leen, a total area for the demesne of about 970 acres. In 1684 the area was given, in round figures, as 400 acres of arable, 200 acres of meadow, 100 acres of pasture and 200 acres of furze and heath, a total 900 acres, which, with the addition of the Gregory estate lands and other minor adjustments gives a total area of about 1035 acres. In respect of arable land, however, it is clear that much ill-drained ground on the valley floor, and certain sterile land on the higher ground could never have been used as ploughland.

The 1387 survey (Appendix 1) described 3 carucates (about 360 acres) and 3 neglected carucates as arable land, totalling about 720 acres at most; and this is almost certainly too high, with the carucate usually below 120 acres, its nominal value. On physical and other grounds arable land south of the river Leen might extend to about 305 acres north of Cut Through Lane, 70 acres south of Cut Through Lane on the higher ground, and 100 acres on the Flood Plain terrace gravels of the valley floor, a total of 475 acres at a maximum. When 457 acres were cropped in 1297 and 539 acres in the exceptionally expanded cropping of 1298, it is apparent that some of the arable land must have lain in the open fields of Lenton and Radford, where, on other grounds - notably the difference between the areas at inclosure and the tithable lands in these fields - there was probably some 110 acres of demesne arable, to give a reasonable total of about 585 acres of arable in demesne. If, as seems likely, about 400 acres were normally sown annually in the years about 1300, and 380 acres were cropped in 1324-35, the system could not have been 2-field, and was probably 3-field.

Tenants and their dues

No customal or formal rent roll of the manor is available earlier than that of 1538, the year of the priory's suppression, and the information in the account rolls is incomplete and unsystematic. Thus any description of rents and services must be incomplete, although most of the tenants' obligations can be identified. A list of the free tenants' names is given in the accounts, with their rents and the areas of their holdings. However, areas were quoted mainly in bovates, a unit of uncertain extent in Lenton, and stated by Gray [1915] to vary between 8 and 14 acres in 1605 [11]. It is clear from the Domesday entries that there were 8 oxgangs or bovates to the carucate of about 120 acres, so that the average bovate area, though varying in fact, would in theory be about 15 statute acres. The holdings also had grazing or pasture rights. Fifteen free tenant holdings at Lenton are shown in the 1298 account, with seven tenants holding land in terms of bovates, with a total area of the order of 160 acres. In Radford six free tenants held about 35 acres of land. No freehold land was recorded for Keighton, although at Domesday there were five men in Morton who held 3 oxgangs in socage. It is not known whether the free tenants of the priory's manor had any share in the obligations of boon works on the demesne, though it is clear that those at harvest times came mainly from bond tenants [Stitt 1959].

Bond tenants in the late 13th century were in two major classes - those whose holdings were called bovates and those called cottarii. The distinction was between those with, say, 10 to 15 acres of arable land in their holding, and those with only an acre or two plus rights in common meadow or common pasture. This difference was prominent centuries later, and is very clear in rentals of the 16th century [12]. The former class, bovators, could be regarded as independent small farmers, but the latter class, the cottarii depended crucially for subsistence on the sale of their labour. The numbers of the two classes of holdings in 1298 were:

	Bond bovates	Cottarii
Lenton	24	21
Radford	23	5½
Keighton	22	11½

This does not mean, as the halves must confirm, that the number of bond tenant farmers was in like proportion, for one man might hold more than one bovate, perhaps even in different villages. Probably more Keighton bovators lived in Lenton than in Keighton.

The 'bovators' were further subdivided into two classes of tenancy, 'mollands' and others. Mollands, held by 'molmen', included all the bond bovates in Lenton and Radford and six of those in Keighton. For the mollands labour services had been effectively commuted for higher money rents, on a basis permanent enough to be recognized as the custom of the manor. The remaining 16 bovates in Keighton, apparently held by 8 tenants, paid a 'corn rent'. This was a money payment based on the price of malt, although the account of 1324-25 stated that in that year the corn was received in kind and sold at about 3s. 6½d. a quarter. It was worth less than the rent from the other bovates, but those tenants provided much more in the way of labour services, commuted only casually. All bovators, like the cottarii, were subject to 'tallage' - 3s.4d. for the bovate, 2d. for a horse or ox, and ¼d for a sheep or pig.

The mollands each paid an annual rent of about 3s.0d., the total amounting to £3.12s.10d. at Lenton from 24 mollands, £3.5s.10d. at Radford from 23, and 19s. 1d. at Keighton from six. The remaining 16 Keighton bovates, held by 8 tenants, paid half a quarter of malt, or about 1s. 6d.. 'Et de 28s. 4d. de 8 qu. brasei ordei molliti de redditibus natiuorum de Kyketon ...'. Also due from the Keighton tenants were 123 hens in 1298 (though reported as 223 in 1324-25); but whether they were required from all the bovates is not known. Stitt wondered whether the large provision of hens by Keighton implied that the priory kept few poultry other than geese.

The labour supply

Medieval labour services included a given number of days per week for the whole or part of the year, called 'weekworks' or 'harvest works', and 'boons' due at harvest, ploughing or seed time, when the demand for labour was particularly heavy. In the 1290s weekworks outside harvest times, as distinct from boons, were due only from the 16 Keighton tenancies (with 8 tenants) that paid corn rent and not, apparently, from the other 53 bond bovates in Lenton manor: but the extent to which these were performed or charged in the late 13th century is uncertain. For example, the number of plough hands on the permanent staff of the home farm of the priory suggests that these 'famuli' rather than labour services were relied upon for ploughing the demesne. Many tasks often performed by week works, such as threshing, hoeing and mowing, were probably handed over to hired labour at Lenton, and plough boons were used little and irregularly.

The 16 Keighton bovates with 8 tenants owed three mornings' work weekly per pair (a week's work being valued at one penny) from October to early February, in May and June, and perhaps some in other months; but during the 13 weeks covering the harvest each pair probably owed 60 works, that is, nearly every weekday. On this basis the demesne would have available from the 16 bovates at least 480 day works in harvest, and certainly 576, but perhaps as many as 900 during the rest of the year. Again it is not clear how many were actually used on the demesne at the end of the 13th century.

The mollands paid higher rents than the 16 Keighton bovates, doubtless in lieu of some commuted labour service, for they performed no week works in 1297 or 1298, even in the busy period from July to October. But in money plus work plus produce (hens) the cost of his tenement to the molman was no more than two-thirds that of the works group, if all the works were sold to him during the year. The 'works group' of eight Keighton tenants was probably the older tenure, surviving from a more general system of the same type: but nothing is known of how the mollands originated or of how many of the 53 molland bovates had been created out of demesne or waste in the 12th and 13th centuries - the comparatively recent past - since only 24 villani were recorded by Domesday. The corn rent of the 16 Keighton bovates suggests a long-standing if not archaic service structure: but the average two bovates per tenant may have been confined to Keighton and of recent origin. If most molland bovates and the cottarii originally owed week works there would have been an ample supply of labour for the lord of the manor of Lenton, and for the early priory; but by the end of the 13th century the services of the mollands were tenuous for much of the year. By 1324-25, though expenses in respect of the performance of Keighton week works were listed, none were mentioned for 53 of the 69 bond bovates, and the 8 Keighton cottagers alone worked on the demesne as rent, the remaining work being done by hired labour. Table 2 for harvest labour and Table 5 for famuli give details of work arrangements that lead to this conclusion.

Table 2 .
Harvest labour on Lenton Priory demesne in 1297 and 1298

1297 (451½ acres)						1298 (539 acres)					
						Man-days					
Week ends	Hired Men	Days	Man-days	Boon works	Approx total	Week ends	Hired Men	Days	Man-days	Boon works	Total
22/7	-	-	-	-	-	21/7	40	x 4	= 160	180	340
29/7	30	x 3	= 90	(180)	270	28/7	50	x 4		120	340
							40	x ½	= 220		
5/8	40	x 5½	= 220	(120)	340	4/8	50	x 4	= 200	80	280
12/8	60	x 3½	= 210	(80)	290	11/8	60	x 2½	= 150	60	210
19/8	80	x 3				18/8	40	x 3	= 120	30	150
	55	x 2½	= 377½	(60)	437½						
26/8	80	x 2		(30)	263	25/8	-	-	-	-	-
	36										
	37		= 233								
Day works			320								
Total			1,130½	(470)	1,920½				850	470	1,320

The boon works of 1297 are the 1298 figures for the corresponding weeks of the harvest, which was very wet in 1297, and the wet weather extended into August, delaying harvest work.. In the weekly figures no day works, the dies feriales of the 16 Keighton bovates, were mentioned, but a total of 320 were apparently called on in 1297. No famuli labour is included in the figures above.
Data from Stitt (1959)

The cottagers' dues are less well documented. Their average rent was about 2s. 0½d. in Lenton, about 2s. 9d. in Radford and about 1s. 4d. in Keighton, substantially lower than the rest. They were probably now largely free of labour services in view of their comparatively high rents.

In both 1297 and 1298 some 470 harvest boons were employed, while a similar number may have been sold. In addition at least 480 works from the 16 Keighton bovates were available, and of these 320 were used in 1297. Outside the harvest period 168 plough boons were used in 1298 when the cultivated area had been expanded; but the demand for them was irregular, for they were not mentioned in 1297 and only 54 were used in 1324-25. Thus the Keighton week works were not all sold. Especially outside the harvest period the demesne relied on hired labour, whether famuli, the manorial staff engaged for a year, or day to day casual task labour. During the period of royal control the famuli increased in number from 18 to 26, mainly because more ploughmen were required for the expanded crop area of 1297-98. The composition of the famuli is shown in Table 5, and the types and amounts of labour used in the harvests of 1297 and 1298 in Table 2.

Crops and livestock

Some figures of cropping are given in Table 3. In considering these it should be noted that when the sheriff took over the management of the estates the winter corn for the year 1296-97 had already been sown, but in other respects the most important normal objective of the home farm - to feed the priory and its animals - was almost irrelevant. The changes in grain production were far from negligible, and part of the system of animal husbandry was completely disrupted.

Table 3.
Corn sown and reaped on Lenton Priory demesne in 1296-98

	1296-97			1297-98		1297 tithe receipts		
	Sown		Reaped	Sown		Quarters from		
	Acres	Q'ters	Q'ters	Acres	Q'ters	Lenton	Beeston	Nottm.St.Mary's
Wheat	80		114	62	23	6	-	10
Rye	126		222	89	33½	10	42	23
Oats	77	30¼	95¾	183	183	10	24	-
Barley	101½	57	190	101	54	15	25	60
Peas	68	17¾	32	104	26	-	-	-
Total	451½		653¾	539	319½	41	91	93

If the figures for 1324-25 are taken along with those of 1297-98 it is seen that the annual acreage normally sown was about 400, but in 1297-98 an additional 90 acres were sown. This is too large to have been simply an imbalance in the area available year by year under open field rotation, and it was almost certainly achieved in part by 'inhoking', or sowing land due to be fallowed, to reap an immediate profit at the expense of soil exhaustion. If the 380 acres sown in 1324-25 were to represent a stage in the contraction of cultivation, then 450 acres in 1296-97 may have been characteristic of that time - the area of corn that was hoed by 40 men in 1297. The cultivated area declined further to only 3 carucates, say 360 acres, in 1387, perhaps areflection of the epidemic diseases which led to population decline in the 14th century.

From 1296 to 1298 the number of ploughmen among the famuli increased from 8 to 12. Perhaps because the produce of the demesne was not intended to feed the priory, the area sown to bread grains, wheat and rye, fell by 25 per cent, while peas, and especially oats greatly increased. Perhaps the price for oats was high at the time, but the large area under peas, 15 per cent of the total sown area in 1296-97, may be an indication of a growing interest in leguminous crops which became more general by the middle of the 14th century. The early cultivation of peas was a feature of parts of the East Midlands, and is reflected in the village name of Barton-in-Fabis, in use by the end of the 14th century [Stitt 1959 xl]. In 1324-25, when peas and beans covered 10 per cent of the cultivated priory demesne, over one-third of the arable land of Barton-in-Fabis was sown with them. There was the usual large area of barley for malt. The importance of rye as a bread crop is to be expected, since in medieval times rye was a more reliable cropper than wheat, and more suitable than either wheat or barley for use on newly cultivated arable land.

Table 4 shows the structure of the priory's livestock enterprise during 1296-98. The takeover of the demesne appears to have completely disrupted the animal husbandry, not only of the Lenton demesne but also of the priory's Blackwell grange in the Peak district, which normally operated in association with Lenton. Draught animals, predictably, were least affected, and the 37 oxen and 24 horses remained as ample provision for the priory's ploughs. But the herd of young cattle was dispersed, and sheep husbandry was much affected. It should be recognized, however, that the seasonal movements of sheep, the response of husbandry to a varying economic situation and the prices obtainable for wool and other sheep products, together with the extremely severe effects of diseases, must have involved rapid changes in sheep numbers even in normal times.

Table 4 .
Lenton Priory demesne livestock in 1296-98

	Dec. 1296	May 1297	July 1297	Sept. 1298
Oxen	37	30	30	34
Bulls	2	2	2	1
Young bull	1	sold	-	-
Cows	14	14	10	11
Steers	10	sold	-	9 (one died)
Calves	15	sold	10	10
Ewes	97	sold	-	-
Lambs	-	-	120	101 (from tithes)
Tegs	-	-	-	96 (24 died)
Wethers	-	-	-	-
Boars	3	3	3	1
Sows	12	12	12	7
Porkers	1	1	1	- (25 sold)
Young pigs	87	45	45	113
Sucking pigs	3	-	22	40
Draught horses	24	24	24	21
Mares	1	1	1	1
Foals	3	3	3	3

Stitt showed the importance of lambs given as tithes in the sheep rearing district of Derbyshire, which were driven to Lenton for feeding on the stubble of the arable fields and on the drier grazing of the priory demesne, such as the warren, before being sold off. There were no wethers at Lenton, but many on the upland grazings of Blackwell, with which the connection was one-way. In the spring of 1297 all the sheep were sold, not only the 100 at Lenton but also 500 at Blackwell. However, the accounts reveal also how rapidly the flock could be rebuilt. By July 1297 the Lenton flock had been re-established by a transfer of 120 tithe lambs from the Peak district, of which 96 survived the hazards of murrain and were alive in September 1298. In the spring of 1298 the flock was augmented by 62 lambs from the tithe of Nottingham St. Mary, and 40 of the 160 handed over in the Peak district were transferred to Lenton. Thus in 15 months, without any purchases, and despite the sale of the St. Mary's tithe lambs in 1297, the priory flock at Lenton had increased to over 300. But in 1324-25 events were dramatic.

In October 1324 the priory owned over 1,000 sheep - 800 at Blackwell, where the wethers were based, 60 at Horsley, and 120 at Lenton - but in the next 11 months over one-third of them died. Just over 100 lambs were received from tithes and 200 were produced by the priory's ewes, but no fewer than 66 died, probably those born on the priory's estate, and the bailiff accounted for 422 sheep pelts. Yet the priory's flock decreased by barely 100 because the tithe lambs were kept in hand.

Small livestock such as poultry and beehives do not appear in the accounts, and probably were left in the hands of the priory, although a deleted entry suggests that at least 20 geese were kept. The priory's livestock will be referred to again below in discussion of land use.

As to equipment for the home farm, eight ploughs were available from May 1297, and there were plough hands among the famuli sufficient to manage four, and later six ploughs at Lenton. There were six carts of the type called carecte in 1298, and seven called plaustra, probably a variety of sideless float. Both types were wheeled. The carpenter built them, but many parts were bought in, along with various other materials such as ropes, grease, mercury to treat sheep, iron, timber, charcoal, wheels, axles, locks, and farming equipment such as forks, scythes, barrels and sheep hurdles, as well as nails and laths for buildings, though mud for daub and straw for thatch would be at hand. Millstones were bought for the mills on the river Leen.

The composition of the famuli at Lenton is shown in Table 5. In the winter of 1296-97 the shepherds were probably at Blackwell, since there were then only 97 ewes at Lenton in December, and these were all sold before May. As was normal the famuli received wages in both cash and grain, except for the carpenter in 1298, and he was probably a craftsman under contract. Ploughmen and carters received 3s. 6d. per annum; teamsters, cowmen, shepherds and blacksmiths 2s. 6d.. Each man received a quarter of corn every three weeks for bread making, mainly rye, but with some oats and peas, which over the year were worth at least £2. There is no evidence for provision of lodging in common, and the famuli were probably cottagers living in the village of Lenton or Keighton. Cottagers described in Lenton at the Dissolution [13] had a small garden and perhaps a small paddock attached to their cottage, but even with grazing rights would have been unable through poverty to take full advantage of them, and must have subsisted mainly through work for payment in cash and kind. The corn payments to famuli suggest that they had no stake in the open arable fields of Lenton or Keighton. Much additional casual or task labour was required for operations such as harrowing, threshing and harvesting as described earlier.

Table 5.
Composition of the famuli of Lenton Priory in 1296-98

	Dec.-May 1296-97	May-July 1297	July-Sept. 1297	Oct. 1297- Sept. 1298
Ploughmen	8	9	12	12
Carters	4	5	6	6
Oxherds	1	-	-	-
Cowmen	1	1	1	1
Swineherds	1	1	1	1
Shepherds	3	-	1	1
Blacksmiths	-	1	1	1
Gardeners	-	1	1	1
Carpenters	-	-	-	1
Reeve or Messor	-	1	1	2

The shepherds in the winter of 1296-97 were probably at Blackwell, Derbyshire, since the 97 ewes at Lenton were sold before May.

Tithes and granges

The importance of tithes as a major part of the priory's income has been mentioned above, for example in connectiomn with the maintenance of sheep numbers, and figures for tithes of corn from Lenton, Beeston and Nottingham St. Mary's for 1297 have been given in Table 3. The accounts offer much information about both collection and disposal of tithes. Grain tithes were collected in sheaf form, and presumably were threshed at the grange to which the sheaves were taken. In 1297 93 quarters of corn were collected from St. Mary's Nottingham by seven men at a cost of £2, and in 1298 eight men were needed. At Beeston in 1297 115 quarters of corn were received, and it took six men five weeks and an expenditure of 35s.10d. to collect them. In 1298 six men, with a carter and a rickman were employed for four weeks at a cost of 33s. 6d.. At Lenton itself in 1297 tithe corn from the non-demesne lands amounted to 41 quarters, and it took six men five weeks to collect the sheaves, while in 1298 six collectors took four weeks. Tithe barns or granges acted as depots for the collection, sale and distribution of tithe corn, and doubtless stored supplies in normal times.

The location of Lenton Priory's granges and tithe barns is not accurately known, though the accounts of the priory refer to their maintenance. For example, wood was bought for replastering Beeston grange, at which the Beeston tithe corn would be collected and stored, but its location is not known. There was thatching at the grange in Nottingham where the St. Mary's tithes would be collected. In Lenton there was prolonged repair work on three barns, and these are thought to have been located as follows. A tithe barn of seven bays of building was situated within the precincts of the priory, and after the Dissolution was let with the tithe. An even larger barn, of nine bays, probably associated with a dovecote, is thought to have been converted into dwellings called the Barn Houses, in Dunkirk, in the late 17th century. The existence of a third barn is less well authenticated, but is suggested by the field name Barn Close, south of the site of Morton, with indications of the site seen on aerial photographs near the centre of the 'island' gravel terrace. But this would have been an unsuitable site for a tithe barn, and the structure was probably much more recent than medieval.

There is a tradition that the present Lenton Abbey house, towards the boundary with Beeston, was built on the site of, and partly incorporated a grange of the priory, but this seems very unlikely. It would have been pointless to build a tithe barn in that location since Keighton, as priory demesne, yielded no tithes, and it is too distant from the priory itself and from its mills to be a credible site for an ordinary storage barn. Furthermore, had a grange existed at Lenton Abbey it must have been mentioned in some of the rentals, surveys and accounts over the centuries, and it was not. It will be shown later that it is likely that a farmstead was built at Lenton Abbey between 1725 and 1738, but there is no earlier mention of buildings there in the documentary records.

The ratio between the area cropped and the grain harvested in the demesne, when applied to the tithe returns, gives a rough estimate that in Lenton some 250 acres were subject to tithes. The accounts do not mention Radford tithes; but even so there were 62 bovates of free and bond tenanted land in Lenton and Keighton.

The pattern of land use in the medieval period (Figure 17)

Stitt remarked that there was no indication in the priory accounts for 1296-98 of the distribution of the land growing the crops described. However, it is possible to establish the broad pattern of land use in the late 13th century by inference from geographical considerations and surviving relics in the landscape, particularly 'ridge and furrow' and from old field names. The pattern, shown in Figure 17, will be imprecise, but substantially true. The 1½ carucates of arable land held in Morton by its Saxon lord before the Conquest were, by Domesday, shared between the manor of William Peveril, and five sokemen holding together about 45 acres (3 bovates). The manor's share (and later the priory's) some 130 to 150 acres, formed the arable land of the home farm of the priory. However, the priory also owned selions in the six open fields of Lenton and Radford. It is probable that arable land of the priory in Keighton-Morton was partly located on patches of gravel on the Trent valley floor, and partly on the higher ground of the present campus area. There is good evidence that this arable area expanded considerably over nearly two centuries to the 1290s, perhaps to as much as three carucates or about 360 acres in Keighton. This expansion was almost entirely on the higher ground of the present campus area, including parts of the former warren, and the open field called the New Field (see Figure 17). The period down to about 1300 A.D., plus or minus 10 or 20 years, is thought to have been very favourable climatically for agriculture, but was followed by a decline associated with a deteriorating climate, and exacerbated by disease, high mortality and population decrease.

At its maximum the arable land of Keighton will have included the areas where 'ridge-and-furrow' can still be seen, for example on the New Field, often now called 'the downland', above Derby and Sherwood Halls, and on the nearby lower part of Wollaton Park, then called the Sixty Acres (Figure 17). By the mid-16th century, as will be shown, such areas were pasture, 'formerly arable', and the decline seems to have begun as early as the 14th century. In 1387 there were said to be six carucates of arable land in the Lenton demesne, but three of them were neglected, and worth only half as much as the others [14] . The neglect of cultivation was almost certainly a consequence, direct or indirect, of the high mortality from the Black Death, decimating the labour force over a period of years. If three carucates of demesne arable land (using the word demesne in its broader sense) - about 360 acres - were in the open fields of Radford and Lenton, while the tithe data indicate some 250 acres subject to tithes as tenanted land, the total area of the six open fields of Lenton and Radford would be about 610 acres. The total area calculated from the enclosure data of 1768, supported by rentals of the Gregory estate, was about 630 acres, and the figures seem consistent. The open field areas estimated from the 1768 data are:

Alwell Field - 86 a.: Beck Field - 146 a.: Sand Field - 163 a.:
Church Field - 64 a.: Red and Moor Fields together - 160 a.;
Total area 629 acres

That part of the priory's arable land in the University campus area lay mostly north of Cut Through Lane (Figure 17), and most of it was known collectively after the Dissolution as the Abbey Fields. Except for grazing of the stubble, the farm animals occupied distinct and different areas, including grass closes, especially for the dairy herd, feeding or fatting pastures, and meadows where the aftermath was grazed. There were also crofts and tofts, with small enclosures attached to the cottages of the farm workers - in the present context notably those of Keighton village. These categories of land use are shown in Figure 17, which incorporates some information from the map produced in 1632 by Richard Smythe (Figure 24, Ch. IV), showing the boundaries of several areas of distinctive forms of occupance or usage [15] . Abbey Field is shown, lying north-west of Cut Through Lane and south-west of Beck Field, one of the Lenton open arable fields, from which it was separated by Sandy Lane.

South of Abbey Field on Smythe's map were the Keighton Closes, the area that had earlier contained the cottages, gardens and crofts of Keighton village, together with its meadow. All this land remained down to the present century tenurially distinct from the areas around it, as will be shown later, and its distinctiveness lay in its status as village land. East of the Keighton Closes Smythe mapped 'Abbey Closes Lenton together'. This was the livestock farm of the priory, with the Dayhouse (dairy house), and south of it the 'Dayhouse grounds' of the Sherwood Forest map of 1609 in the area of the Dunkirk housing estate west of Montpelier Road. The Abbey Closes also included to the south the area around the former Dunkirk Farm south of the Tottle Brook, associated with Morton, which had become the fields called Tamworth and Wheatcroft by the 16th century, and probably much earlier. East of the

Abbey Closes were mapped 'Lenton Ford meadows together'. Unfortunately Smythe's map is very distorted, but it is probable that these meadows were separated from the Abbey Closes by The Greens, originally common land extending north as far as the Tottle Brook along Blotoff Dyke, and they included such later meadows as Ledgett Wong, Mortons Meadow and Great Moor Close. These meadows were bounded southwards and eastwards by the Holmes, and the boundary can be established by studying the inclosure award of 1768. Smythe's map unfortunately omitted the southern portion of the priory demesne, which included some arable land on the gravel terrace, with meadow to the east and feeding pastures to the west and south, interspersed with strips of marsh and alder thicket. Trent Wong, about 100 acres of meadow alongside the river Trent, was separated from this last area by the narrow Horse Doles in Beeston parish along Blotoff Dyke. The individuality of these different environments persisted for centuries through periods of economic and tenurial change, and will be further examined in succeeding chapters.

Keighton village

The site of Keighton village is clearly visible on aerial photographs (Figure 16). Godfrey [1884 16] suggested that Keighton or Kirketon 'appears to have occupied the site between Spring Close and Highfield Park, on the slope of the hill on the south side of the footroad to Beeston [called] Cut-throat Lane'. He was essentially correct, while Arthur Cossons' belief that Keighton village had a cruciform plan centred on the junction between the present Clifton Boulevard and the former Cut Through Lane-Spring Close [Cossons 1929] has no basis in historical fact. He may have been misled by Godfrey's [1884] incorrect reference to 'The Keightons' being situated near the point where Spring Close merges with Cut Through Lane, and it 'could mark the site of the village'. But Cossons' hypotheses were advanced largely on a morphological basis without consideration of documentary evidence (which may have been unavailable to him) of the use and affiliations of the land involved. Godfrey wrote: 'The meadows on the hill side still known as The Keightons present extraordinary and unnatural undulations, the origin of which has been the subject of considerable conjecture'. Lawson Lowe, who assisted Godfrey with his 1884 book, had earlier used almost identical words, but referred to 'various unsatisfactory conjectures' [Lowe 1876 136].

Much more recently two lines of enquiry have been directed to archaeological remains in this area. First, Miss Alice Selby of the Department of Classics, discovered wasted encaustic tiles and kiln rubble while digging her wartime allotment in Keighton Close in 1940, and this led to Professor H.H.Swinnerton's excavation of several kilns and waste heaps near the southern end of the present Biology building in the early 1950s [Swinnerton et al. 1955]. Second, road construction east of the Portland Building (Portland Hill) exposed an intersecting track, and a platform suspected of being a house site on the undulating area to the west [Kerridge 1954] (called Site II by Coppack [1971]). The track was excavated by D.H.Kerridge and others in the first half of 1953, when the question of the village site was still unresolved. These excavations proved the existence of a medieval settlement, and through the artefacts uncovered pointed to dates of occupation and abandonment. Subsequently G. Coppack was invited to undertake further excavation to test Kerridge's findings and prepare a report on all excavations on the site. With a main objective to establish the date of abandonment of Keighton village Coppack chose for excavation nearly 1,200 square feet well away from the site of the kilns near the Biology building and west of the Kerridge site, and found evidence of three buildings there to add to those uncovered by Kerridge. The excavations are discussed below with special reference to dating (Figure 18), and then the kilns and other associated features nearby are described.

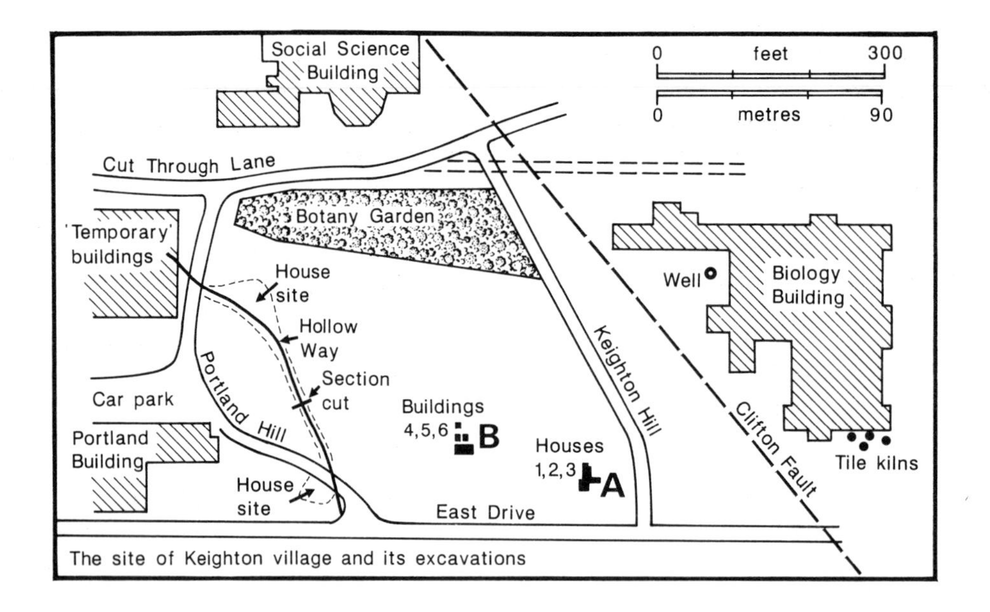

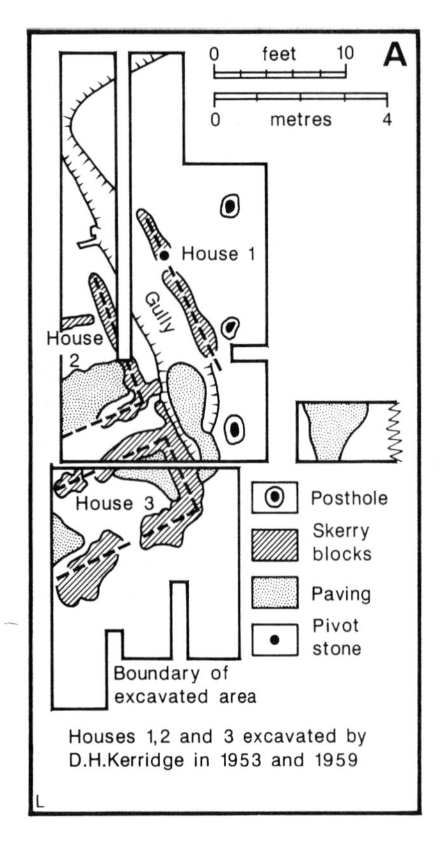

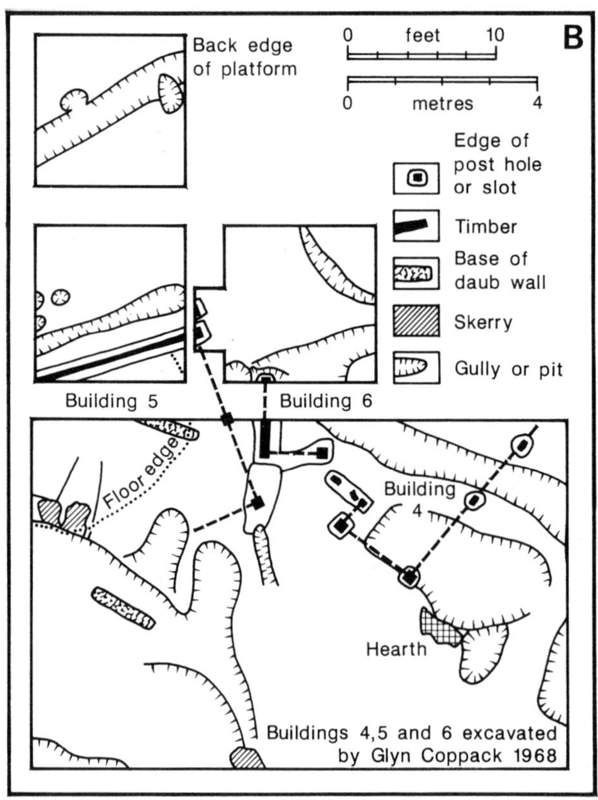

Figure 18: Excavations of Keighton village
Above: *Site of the village with well, kilns and hollow way.*
Below: *Plans of excavations of house sites at Keighton.*

Keighton village buildings

The ledges or platforms standing out from the Mercia Mudstones slope at Keighton have no ready 'natural' explanation. They could have been sites of houses or other buildings, or they could have been produced simply by small scale clay digging - as some almost certainly were. Swinnerton suggested originally that clay digging could explain adequately the occurrence and form of the platforms, but excavation showed that if some did originate in that way they were adapted subsequently as house sites. The marl cut from the upslope side was deposited down-slope, and at least one site had a level surface too large to have been simply the result of clay digging.

Coppack [1971] wrote that 'some years ago it was speculated that an undulating area to the west of "Keit'n Closes"....was in point of fact the area of settlement', and not the Keighton Closes referred to by Thoroton, and taken by Cossons to be the site of the lost village. But 'this area was suspected to have been the site of clay-diggings, and because of this the suggested identification was regarded with suspicion'. Coppack's own excavations, and his review of the slightly earlier work in the vicinity, together established the area between the Biology and Portland buildings as the actual village site, part of the field called Little Keightons. Aerial photography suggests, probably wrongly, that village plots occupied the site of the Portland Building and the temporary buildings behind it, but there are no indications of any former buildings or other structures there.

The areas excavated by both Kerridge and Coppack were found to contain house sites productive in dateable finds (Figure 18). The Kerridge site, the largest platform on the field, located immediately west of the junction of the new road, Keighton Hill, with the East Drive, and said to have been used as a masons' yard during the construction of the Trent building, was excavated between June 1953 and 1959. About one-third of its area of 70 feet by 50 feet was stripped to reveal traces of three buildings. Typically a gully cut along the upper (northern) margin took water draining from the impermeable marl slope above, with another gully running north to the main gully to drain off the surface water. Both gullies were clearly visible on the surface before excavation. They probably belonged to the mid-13th century, and on the evidence of pottery remained in use until the mid-14th century. The main gully, though silted, was in use well into the 15th century, but part of the smaller gully was filled in and paved over the southern end in the mid-14th century. Part of the filling was silt containing mid-13th century pottery and a coin of Richard I of a type that was withdrawn in 1238. Kerridge suggested that this little-worn silver 'cut halfpenny' was probably brought in with the soil used to fill in the ditch and therefore indicates when that went out of use. Three post holes 8 feet apart were sealed beneath later occupation layers. When the smaller gully had gone out of use two buildings, called Houses 2 and 3 in Figure 18 were erected west of it, their end walls following its edge.

House 1 was represented by only a west end-wall and an occupation scatter that sealed the post-hole structure. It was dated to the middle of the 14th century, and debris from it was traced above the skerry sandstone footings of House 2. The lack of building debris on the floor suggests that House 1 was probably the last house built on this site, with its last occupation dated by pottery as late as the third quarter of the 15th century. An unpaved floor, a width of about 13 feet and a suggested length of 40 feet were similar to the description of House 2, which had a similar plan. A pivot stone - a circular recess three inches in diameter in a footing skerry - marked the north jamb of a door in the middle of the west wall of House 1.

House 2, on the evidence of only the footings of the east end- wall, probably measured internally about 12 feet by 36 feet. A break in the footings at the northern end of the east wall suggested the position of a door. The stone footings, intended to protect the timber frame resting on them from decay, were needed only on two opposite sides. The lack of side-wall footings suggests a timber framed structure that depended on the strength of its end frames, and footings were slight in each building on this site. The floor of House 2 had a heavy scatter of charcoal and potsherds which pointed to a beginning of occupation in the second quarter of the 14th century, with the house remaining in use into the early 15th century.

House 3, south of House 2 and aligned with it, was probably contemporaneous, with more substantial footings traced on three sides. Most of the floor paving of skerry slabs had been removed. This was a very small building, perhaps only six feet wide and 14 feet long, with a gap in the large skerry blocks of the south wall footings indicating adoor. It may have had a timber bay without footings, or alternatively it may have been an outbuilding. Kerridge seems to have thought it possible that Houses 2 and 3 were parts of a building of two bays.

These three buildings were all standing at the same time. Kerridge thought that the pottery suggested the remains of a medieval cottage. He had thought that this part of the village might be connected with the nearby kilns, but failed to understand the significance of the late pottery, which was very like that from Professor Swinnerton's kilns, but in the absence of waster material was probably occupation debris, and not spread from the kiln site. The pottery fragments were of cooking vessels and skillets, many with traces of soot indicating that they were utensils in domestic use. Fragments of small 'breaster' jugs and large strap-handled pitchers were sometimes green glazed, and occasionally had a yellow or brown glaze obtained by adding iron, copper or manganese salts to the lead oxide base of the glaze. Smaller finds included several iron nails, presumed to be from the timber structure of the buildings.

The pottery excavated by Kerridge and his colleagues has been reassessed by Coppack [1968] in the light of his own subsequent studies of the local ware, and has been dated securely to the third quarter of the 15th century. Until this was established it had been assumed that the village of Keighton was deserted about 1387 or soon afterwards, because at a valuation of that year a jury 'being asked if any waste was made in any houses belonging to the said priory or not, say upon oath that there were five cottages belonging to the said priory in Kyrkton, as much in want of repairs as of tenants, which in the time of the present prior, who holds the same in fee farm, fell into ruins to the detriment of the lord the king and of the said priory, to the amount of ten marcs', although within the priory itself every building was well maintained [16]. This statement does not, however, necessarily imply that there were no houses at Keighton in 1387 other than those in ruins.

Although the name Keighton has remained in use in field names continuously down to the present day, this reference of 1387 is the last known documentary mention of the village. This had been taken to indicate actual or imminent desertion in 1387, which would not be surprising in an agrarian settlement in the years after the Black Death and its aftermath, and was supported by the circumstantial evidence in the same 1387 document of a serious decline in arable farming on the priory demesne. The jury, giving evidence on oath, stated that half the arable land of the demesne was uncultivated. But whatever the state of the rural economy and agriculture the village was either only partially abandoned, or it revived when the population recovered from the disastrous epidemics of the 14th century; or it was partly reoccupied by labourers or artisans engaged in tile and pottery production nearby, not necessarily as permanent dwellings. As suggested above, the cultivation of the demesne could certainly have continued without the cottagers of Keighton. Although the archaeological evidence tends to refute the desertion of Keighton village before about 1460-70 there remains half a century before the Dissolution during which it was almost certainly abandoned, and it had become overgrown by the mid-1550s (see Chapter III).

Glyn Coppack's work followed because the excavations by Kerridge and the University Archaeological Society in the 1950s yielded no firm date for the desertion of Keighton. He began in April 1968 with a proton magnetometer survey to locate a site likely to be productive, and described the site chosen, called Site III, as 'an area of occupation' (Figure 18). The shallow terraces on this site, built up on the slope, were generally blanketed in a 6-inch layer of loam, with turf and humus of the period of occupation. Here, near the middle of the slope,

1,187 square feet were stripped to the natural surface, revealing traces of occupation that were interpreted as indications of timber buildings set upon shallow terraces formed in the same manner as the platform excavated by Kerridge . A section cut into one such terrace proved the method of construction, but provided no date. Since the earliest occupation on the terraces was dated to the middle 12th century the terraces themselves were probably not much older.

Coppack located three separate buildings by post-holes or timber slots, and they are numbered 4, 5 and 6 following the numbering of the earlier excavation (Figure 18). Most of the filling was homogeneous, but the pottery remains could be separated into dated groups, giving some indication of stratigraphy.

Building 4, an early structure dating from about 1150, was only six feet wide, but at least 12 feet long, with a porch, the north side of which was cut away by a later drainage gully on the west side of the southern bay. Though badly disturbed its structure did not involve stone footings, but one double and four single post holes, two stone-packed. No door was found, but most of the west wall was unrepresented. The building was demolished for redevelopment, certainly by the end of the 13th century.

Building 5, the major structure encountered, began as a building like Building 4, but was represented as such only by a length of daub walling. A 6-inch deep L-shaped footing trench indicated a rebuilding just before the beginning of the 13th century. Most of the footing had been removed in a second rebuilding, but several scraps of pottery from this footing trench attest to a mid-13th century date. Footings of stone were found only in the later buildings at Keighton. These two early phases were superseded near the close of the 13th century by a large building parallel to the back edge of the terrace, where the north wall was defined by a single beam slot and associated eaves-drip gully. The rest was defined by post holes, though the cut-away south wall may have had a beam slot. Up to 8 inches of floor deposit in the northern half of the building was well stratified, with much bone, pottery and metal work. The animal bones were mainly of sheep, goats and pigs, with an occasional cow or ox bone. There was part of a sickle blade and an assemblage of early 14th century pottery. In the mid-14th century it appears that Building 5 was dismantled and a new terrace cut into its south side to form the site of a new wattle and daub building represented by only one identifiable wall, with associated later 14th century pottery. One sherd found here was a variant of Nottingham ware featuring a technique of random glazing generally thought to have gone out of use by 1230, but the fabric was of late 14th century type. The area that had been occupied by Building 5 was drained by gullies cut into the terrace.

Building 6 lay east of Building 5. In an area disturbed by pits and gullies there were traces of a corner of a timber structure contemporaneous with the final stage of Building 5. An early 14th century gully cutting across it and across Building 4 shows that it went out of use soon after 1300. In the latest of a series of pits cut into the western end of this gully was pottery of the mid-14th century. The drainage gully silted up only in the first half of the 15th century, its upper filling containing much pottery similar to late material from the Kerridge site, all seemingly domestic rubbish with no waster material. Unfortunately no late structures were found on this site, but a small part of a sunken area south of the gully yielded almost two stones weight of iron slag. It showed signs of heavy burning, with slag and deep deposits of charcoal, and was very probably a blacksmith's workshop, or at least a place of customary metal working. A few sherds from this area suggest an early 14th century date. The hollow was cut into a rubbish pit containing much charcoal, pottery and tile fragments of the immediately preceding period.

Excavation of this whole site of Coppack's was very difficult, for some of the post holes that represented the buildings could be located only when the site was wet, while the timber buildings were without stone footings. Indeed little stone was found on this site. However it did yield large quantities of pottery dating from the mid-12th century to the late 15th century, and a number of metal items together with some large, unstratified Roman grey-ware sherds of the late 2nd century A.D. or later, discussed further below. 'On the whole the material from Site III [Buildings 4 to 6] argues for a desertion date some time in the third quarter of the 15th century'; but it is not known, of course, how protracted was the process of desertion, or whether other sites, if excavated, might have yielded material of a still later date.

Coppack's conclusions [1971] reaffirmed that there was little to suggest that Keighton village was established much before Lenton Priory (c.1108), since no stratified pottery dating from before the 12th century was found; and this may be significant in view of the fact that Keighton was not mentioned in Domesday. The pottery scatter on the natural Mercia Mudstones surface and its stratification shows an unbroken sequence from at least as early as the middle of the 12th century to the third quarter of the 15th century, with no evidence for abandonment in the later 14th century. The interpretation of the pottery is crucial to dating,, and will be referred to again later in discussion of the kilns at Keighton, but some further points may be mentioned here.

The supposedly 15th century pottery excavated at Keighton village was described by Coppack as of 'Nottingham ware' type, the dating of which derived from the kiln excavations of Swinnerton and others. While little work has been done on pottery of the 'Nottingham school', and its dating may need revision in the future, Nottingham itself has yielded no evidence for the production of pottery after the late 14th century. However, Godfrey described loaded kilns containing both pottery and tiles found at Keighton during clay digging according to Coppack [1971 51] ; and Swinnerton's report [1955], although it did not deal with the great quantity of pottery, much of it wasted, found in his excavation, did point to the presence of a pottery in the near vicinity, operating at the same time as the tile kilns, with waste pots finding their way into the tilery waste heaps. It was this circumstance that made possible the dating of the pottery, since, as will be shown, the approximate date of the tile making is known. A description of the more substantial pottery finds from the excavation of the Keighton house sites, all of which are illustrated, is given by Coppack [1968 51-58], with notes and illustrations of other small finds. The dates given come from an unpublished survey of Nottingham ware carried out by Coppack since 1968.

Before discussing the tile kilns of Keighton, two other features of the village will be examined - a sunken way on the west side of the village site, and a well on the east side.

The Keighton village sunken way

In February 1953 preparatory work for the construction of the road now called Portland Hill, linking Cut Through Lane with the East Drive, exposed in section a hollow way that was crossed obliquely by the new road cutting. When the exposed sections were cut back to give true cross-sections the nature of the feature was revealed as a gully running through the small plantation, part of which survived the road building. It was crossed by the Portland Hill road in two places, giving four sections. In one section a crescentic band of dark soil was noticed. An emergency excavation was organized in February-March 1953 by the University Archaeological Society.

On inspection of the surface a shallow gully could be traced for a distance of 112 yards, but neither end could be seen. At the higher north-west end it looked as if the gully had joined Cut Through Lane, though any junction was lost, presumed destroyed beneath the temporary buildings then occupied by the Geography Department, and later by the Buildings Department. At the lower south-east end it must have been buried beneath a deep deposit laid above it when the East Drive was graded in the 1920s as a terrace feature, below which superficial material can be seen to spread down the grassy slope towards the lake. A fifth section was made by cutting a trench across the gully about halfway along it, here in sandy material of the Mercia Mudstones. Three sections across the gully are reproduced in the paper by Coppack [1971 44] which re-states the description of the feature given by D.J.Kerridge [1954 45-47].

The gully was cut into the hillside to a depth, where possible, at which layers of hard grey-green skerry sandstone of the Plains and Keighton skerries occur. A track at the bottom of the gully, was metalled with gravel and pebbles where skerry *in situ* did not form its surface, but it was not proved whether the grading of the track was intentional or caused by attrition and downwash to the skerry level. In places the metalling was embedded in a layer of dark brown clay. The track ascended the slope at a fairly constant gradient of one in seven, and because the natural upper surface was convex the sunken way varied in depth from about one foot in the south-east to 18 feet in the north-west, but met Cut Through Lane at a point where before its conversion into a University road it too ran in a gully up to 10 feet deep. The floor of the Keighton gully was about 5 feet wide, and the metalled surface varied in width from 2½ to 5 feet.

There were few finds by which the gully could be dated, but two small pottery fragments of a coarse, orange sandy ware with soot traces on the outside were tentatively dated by J.G.Hurst to the late 13th or early 14th century. Several fragments of bone and teeth of sheep and pigs were found. At some stage the gully had been filled to some depth with a heavy light-brown clay, too substantial to have been weathered material from the sides of the gully itself. Indeed disturbed, unweathered 'marl' in the filling suggests that it was filled by hand. It seems probable that material from the site of the Trent Building was dumped there in the 1920s. Above this marl were several relatively modern layers of brick rubble and other waste containing several old turf lines. The writer recalls the use of the lower section of the gully in the 1930s and 1940s as a repository for gardeners' rubbish.

Associated with the trackway were two flat areas thought to be house platforms (Figure 18). Only the edge of the more southerly platform lying near the junction of Portland Hill and East Drive could be examined, and this was found to be cut into sandy marl immediately south-west of the track. No traces of building were found in the very small area excavated, but there were several pieces of green glazed pottery, dated to the late 13th and early 14th centuries [Coppack 1971 45: Kerridge 1954 47]. In the brown clay covering was found a fine mortar of Millstone Grit, about 9 inches square and 4 inches high, each corner decorated with a column formed by two vertical recesses, and in the centre a hollow about 8 inches in diameter worn smooth by use. The more northerly platform, on the opposite side of the track near the top, was not investigated for lack of time.

Despite the extensive building operations immediately west of the trackway at Portland Hill (formerly called Bath Hill) no medieval pottery or buildings have been discovered there, and this led Coppack to suggest that the sunken track might mark the western boundary of the village. This is supported by the fact that it was part of the western boundary of the Keighton Closes down to recent times. An aerial photograph of the 1930s appears to show that the site of the Portland Building and the temporary buildings behind it was once subdivided into small rectangular enclosures and it is tempting to suppose that these may have been crofts occupied by Keighton villagers, and the area part of the village in a wider sense: but imperfect photography is a likelier explanation. A complete plan of the village may never be possible, since an unknown area has been destroyed, and even in the small areas excavated most structures were incomplete, and not amenable to further reconstruction.

The Keighton well

In May 1952, during site preparation for the new Biology building, an area forming part of the old Keighton Close and impinging in places on the Clifton fault was levelled by machine, uncovering what was clearly a well. Professor Swinnerton was informed and with the help of Mr. (later Professor) Merrick Posnansky and the University Archaeological Society the well was excavated to a depth of about 22 feet below the scraped sandstone surface, where the water table was reached. Because pumping was inadequate this excavation had to be abandoned, but a decade later, in 1963, after heavy pumping in the locality had lowered the water table, R.C.Alvey was able to reopen the well and excavate the remainder of the filling. He obtained organic material from the bottom, and identified carbonized grains and grain impressions [Coppack 1968 51, 56].

J.T.Godfrey was probably describing this well when he wrote in 1884 that 'near to one of these hollows' (the undulations of the sloping site of Keighton village) 'there was within the memory of man a subterranean passage hewn out of sandstone rock, the entrance to which was sheltered by an old thorn bush' - doubtless one of a group of which several survived until 1990 on the east side of the new road called Keighton Hill. There was a tradition amongst the villagers of Lenton that this 'passage' had originally led to Lenton Priory: and although there were many such improbable traditions, 'of the existence of this particular passage there can be no doubt whatever, but its alleged connection with Lenton Priory must obviously be fallacious'. The passage undoubtedly ran for some little distance underground, but 'owing to the dangerous entrance and the presence of water it was never thoroughly explored', and Godfrey concluded that it was filled up 'some years ago, and the old thorn bush has since disappeared, but the entrance is still plainly indicated by a visible depression in the bank, and by the difference in the vegetation growing upon the spot' [Godfrey 1884 17]. It is clear that Godfrey was describing the excavated well; that the bank was the Clifton fault line scarp; and that the upper part of the well, destroyed by the earth-moving machines, was dug as an incline into the scarp.

As excavated the Keighton well was a vertical, circular shaft, 3 feet 6 inches in diameter, sunk from the medieval land surface to a depth of about 40 feet. By the time the writer saw the well the ground surface was of Lenton Sandstone, but at the original excavation it was found that the top 9½ feet was cut through Mercia Mudstone (Keuper Marl) beds, and the rest through fairly soft red sandstone (of the Lenton Sandstone formation). The top section cut through 'marl' above the Clifton fault surface was lined with roughly squared blocks of skerry by the constructors of the well, but most had collapsed into the well, especially since the upper part was cut away by the earth-moving machine before any feature was noticed. Rough foot holds in the sandstone, on average 16 inches apart and 6 inches deep were cut into the north and south sides of the well down to the bottom. Between 12 and 15 feet from the top a door-shaped opening was cut into the west side of the shaft, but only 4 inches deep and with chamfered edges. It was measured by Alvey at 3 feet 7 inches high and 2 feet 4 inches wide at its widest. It use was not suggested by the excavators, though it could have been associated with some device for drawing up water. The bottom of the shaft was dished, and still bore tool marks, as did the sides. Just above the bottom a hole 6 inches in diameter was cut into the north side of the shaft, and at the time of excavation water poured out of this hole at an estimated rate of 9 gallons per minute. A water depth of 10 feet was maintained. A section of the well filling, and illustrations and descriptions of the pottery contained in it, can be found in Coppack [1968] pages 52 53 and 54-55 respectively.

Most finds in the well may be expected to have dated from times after it went out of use, but it began to silt up from the beginning with fine clayey material from the Lenton Sandstone carried in by the water, and in this early deposit were sherds of pottery from green-glazed jugs, three with sagging bases and six with flat bases. A date of late 13th century to early 14th century was suggested, though some sherds demonstrated mid-14th century traits. Small finds of organic material from below the water table included a blackthorn (sloe) stone, half a carbonized grain of barley, grains of barley and oats and skeletons of rat, mouse and shrew. Once the silting had reached up to the water table the well would have gone out of use. Part of the lining was allowed to collapse, and thereafter the well became nothing more than a rubbish tip. The rubbish could be dated to the second and third quarters of the 15th century, and was interstratified with layers of skerry that had fallen from the shaft lining. The pottery from this rubbish deposit was contemporaneous with that from the kiln waste heaps excavated by Swinnerton in 1951, and was made locally, though probably not in the same kilns as the tiles. Coppack noted that potsherds uncovered by Swinnerton - several of them wasted and none abraded - were sealed in the tile kiln waste heaps dated to about 1457 [Swinnerton et al. 1955 93]. This later pottery from the well deposit included 9 pancheons, thought by Coppack to have been produced in kilns at Keighton, and five cooking pots.

Coppack stated that after its period of use as a rubbish tip the well was left until the late 18th century when Joseph Lowe built Highfield House, and the well, still 16½ feet deep and unsafe, was filled in with local material containing no medieval pottery. Presumably the depth was estimated from the excavation stratification, because the implication that the well was filled in by Joseph Lowe appears to be incorrect since the Lowe family never owned or rented this land which had been in the Gregory estate for centuries and remained so until after the first world war.

The kilns at Keighton

The probability that there were kilns in the vicinity of Keighton village was suggested by J.T.Godfrey [1884 17]. 'In excavating for clay on the side of Bath Hill at Highfield, a short distance to the eastward of the spot where what is believed to have been the remains of a Roman habitation were found, large quantities of broken pottery were met with about eight years ago. These were all of the earlier medieval type, and from the fact that most of the pieces were evidently the fragments of utensils which had been distorted or otherwise damaged in the process of baking, it seems evident that there must have been a kiln near here, probably belonging to the monks of Lenton, and that these were the damaged articles which had been discarded as worthless'. Subsequently the first direct evidence of kilns here was Miss Selby's turning up of fragments of overburnt bricks and glazed tiles, one with traces of a pattern, in 1940.

It was suspected that the tiles used for paving the floor of the chancel in the priory church were made locally, and in the autumn of 1949 a diligent search resulted in the discovery of a kiln. Systematic excavation brought to light other kiln sites [Swinnerton et al. 1955 84-85] but building operations stopped the work, and the excavated area lies buried beneath the south walls of the Biology building and the asphalted area fronting it (Figure 18). The excavation required heavy work by staff and students of the Classics Department, laboratory staff of the Geology Department and various local archaeologists. Teams organized by W.R.Chalmers and G.R.Watson worked through the summer vacation of 1950, and the Peverel Archaeological Group led by H.O.Houldsworth extended the trench system and dug deep exploratory holes through skerry waste and overburden down to the natural soil surface. They were rewarded when at the end of September E.J.Langley and W.B.Baguley struck the extreme fringe of what became known as Site II (Figure 19). In the autumn of 1951 the student Archaeological Society formed by Merrick Posnansky and Helen Boulton excavated a third site and several subsidiary sites. This third site included the remains of a kiln half destroyed by a drain trench .

Kiln site I lay in a slight hollow of the natural surface lined with broken and spoiled roofing tiles laid on each other to a depth of about six inches and bonded with red clay. The tiles covered about 3 square yards. On this foundation was three square yards of red clay, six inches thick. Part of the south-east rim, faced with half-baked bricks, overlooked a shallow channel floored with small inward-facing skerry slabs, probably part of a flue. South-westwards a scatter of bricks disappeared beneath a deep overburden of skerry waste (Figure 19) [17] . No burnt ashes were found in the original excavation, but two years later, when a bulldozer had destroyed the site and removed part of the dump of skerry, black ashes were seen exposed only three feet from the clay platform, six inches deep in a hollow excavated in the original soil surface, and bounded on the west by a vertical face one foot high. Half a metre from the edge of this step

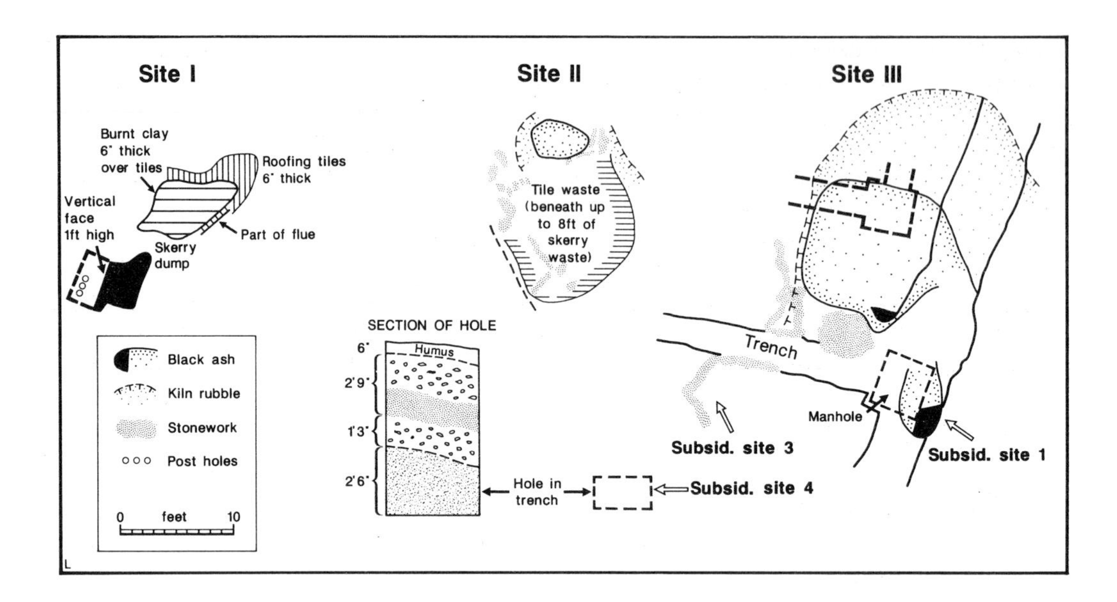

Figure 19: Excavations of kilns at Keighton
[Redrawn after Swinnerton, Chalmers and Posnansky (1955)]

were three post holes, less than a foot apart. The ash was buried beneath a maximum of half a metre of chocolate coloured soil which yielded the base of a medieval pot, and was in turn covered by black soil from a grassy turf, suggesting a lengthy period between the abandonment of the kiln and the deposition of the waste.

The bricks suggested a late 16th century date for the kiln, that is, half a century after the Dissolution. This dating, made by Professor E.M.Jope (who visited the kiln excavation twice in August 1956 and helped with the digging) has no direct documentary support from 16th century rentals in which there was no reference to brick making. Fragments of late 15th century encaustic tiles from the subsoil round the foundation of roofing tiles (among which no encaustic tiles were found) suggests that the production of coloured tiles had ceased when this kiln was in use, and supports a late date for it. Jope, in fact, thought that other and older kilns must be nearby. Several weeks later the fringe of the second kiln site was found.

Kiln site II was almost completely buried under overburden up to 8 feet deep, comprising an upper, thicker layer of skerry waste, and a lower, thinner layer of dark material including much kiln waste or rubble of overburnt bricks and parts of broken tiles. No superstructures were found, but abundant kiln rubble suggests that a simple ad hoc erection, perhaps of beehive type, was constructed for each firing. Probably the tiles made here were produced specifically for reflooring the chancel of the conventual church.

The ash deposit on the north side indicates a hearth. It thickened to one foot deep along the southern margin, where it was banked against a crude barrier, 8 feet long, of stones and fragments of burnt brick. At the eastern margin a rough pavement of small skerry slabs was baked red, and this was the place where traces of this kiln were first found. South of the barrier was a waste heap 20 square yards in area and up to three feet deep, banked against a barrier and a short stone wall. The waste was clay, bright red to pinkish white in colour, in which were embedded innumerable fragments of encaustic tiles spoiled in firing or glazing. Under the waste heap a level platform passed under deep overburden, but was defined on the east by a low step, six inches above the natural surface, formed of very dark soil, six feet wide, with a boundary of bricks on the south, and on the north dry stone walling three feet long and three feet high, containing 8 courses of flat skerry blocks. At one end this merged into a barrier of brick fragments, and at the other end it passed into a series of much larger stones lying at the same level as the ash deposit.

Kiln site III was examined when the deep overburden of skerry waste had been removed by bulldozer down to a level just above the kiln relics. Here stonework was much more extensive. A side trench just missed destroying it. The site is best described in two entities.

a. Close to the present manhole was a shallow hollow about one foot deep, dug in the original soil, and on the floor of the hollow pieces of stone partially supporting well-made paving of large skerry slabs whose natural grey colour proved that this was not a hearth. Above was a discoloured occupation earth, banked on the north side against a crude two-feet high stone barrier. This earth had a thin sooty cover passing west under two large blocks of skerry.

b. Two to three feet from these blocks was stone walling of regularly placed slabs of skerry, with an irregular triangular area bounded by pieces of skerry, and north of this four feet of narrow skerry paving which was seen again in the sides of a foundation trench eight feet further on. Kiln deposits of sooty ash were buried under a layer of dark soil and kiln rubble., The ash covered about 20 square yards, to a depth of 9 inches along the southern margin where it overlapped on to the stonework of (a) above. Tile waste on the opposite side of the trench suggests that a waste heap had been there, but had been removed by the bulldozer.

A brief mention of the findings at four subsidiary sites may be added.

1. A main drainage trench revealed south of the manhole an area of black ash covering less than 9 square yards, but about 15 inches thick near its southern margin. This lay on a foundation of skerry waste, so it was perhaps slightly later than sites II and III, both on natural soil; and again the ash was covered by dark soil containing kiln rubble.
2. Twelve yards north of the manhole there were traces of another kiln site. A feebly developed black layer yielded pieces of coal of poor quality, and several fragments of pottery.
3. South of the side trench and west of the kiln was a straight series of regularly placed pieces of skerry, 4½ feet long, running north-east to south-west; and at each end similar, shorter series diverging from each other eastwards. There was sooty soil round the western and southern courses, and pure black ash exposed in the side of the trench, banked against the end of the other course.
4. A deep hole made by the Peverel Group provided a section that showed an accumulation of skerry slabs suggesting deliberate arrangement such as that in the stone walling.

The excavation of kiln sites I, II and III showed that each had ash, kiln rubble, barrier, stone walling and waste heap, arranged in the same general way. A prominent feature of the sites was the large quantity of skerry waste, which led Swinnerton to believe that 'for a long time after the kilns had ceased to be worked the clay must still have been excavated and transported elsewhere', and this might explain the name in the 16th century of Quarrel Close, adjoining Keighton Close on the south-east. The clay for these kilns must have come from the Mercia Mudstones very near to the new exposure of the Keighton skerry shown in Figure 8, and below it to the south-east. The bands of interbedded, unwanted skerry sandstone and siltstone produced much waste, which was dumped below the clay working and almost buried the kiln sites under an overburden six feet or more in thickness. It was this mass of skerry waste that made locating the kilns so difficult and arduous. It also proves that the main clay supply was obtained from the Carlton Formation beds on the spot, for it is very unlikely that skerry waste would have been carted from other quarries or marl pits at a distance, such as that in the grounds of Hugh Stewart Hall.

From Swinnerton's records Coppack suggested that he did not, in fact, locate a tile kiln, though the kilns he found lay very near to one, and were overlain by deep heaps of tile wasters and kiln rubble. Coppack also suggested that Swinnerton's kiln No. I was almost certainly a tile or brick kiln of the late 16th century, as Professor Jope speculated. The kilns found later, badly mutilated, were probably pottery kilns, almost certainly dating from the 15th century since they were associated with the waste tips of tile kilns which were producing tiles for the choir of the conventual church to replace those made in the 14th century, one actually marked with the date 36 Henry VI (1457-8). After the bulldozers had levelled and destroyed the first two kiln sites they excavated two deep drainage trenches in the levelled surface - the main and side trenches in Figure 19 - bringing to light the third and most extensive kiln site with the subsidiary sites. It is very likely, therefore, that other kilns were never exposed or disturbed by the building operations, and thus not surprising that the Biology building site failed to produce an unquestioned pottery kiln. The erection of the building destroyed the Swinnerton kilns, and no further excavation was possible. Trial holes revealed a complex stratigraphy, but the work could not be followed up for lack of time.

Location factors for the choice of site for the Keighton kilns, given that the priory itself was the immediate market for their products, included the Clifton fault, which brings down Mercian Mudstones on the south side against Lenton Sandstone on the north. The former provided clay, conveniently exposed on the fault-line scarp slope, avoiding the drainage problems of clay holes. The latter provided pebble-free sand for mixing with the clay, easily dug and of suitably fine grade with its clay fraction. Swinnerton wrote that 'north of the field' (Keighton Close) 'there still exists an old grass-grown quarry in this sandstone', but it is not clear whether he was referring to one of the two '1838 quarries' or to a probable earlier quarry below the drive up to the Cripps Health Centre from the present Cripps Hill. Water was obtainable from a streamlet that flowed across the field, or, in copious supply from the nearby well. The sandstone offered a dry working site, and the skerry bands of the Mercia Mudstones supplied sandstone for construction purposes. Wood for charcoal was available within the priory's estate, and there is evidence to suggest that coal was brought from the shallow pits being worked in the Wollaton area along a suitably graded route by packhorse. A fragment of this track that survives on the ridge south of the Cripps Health Centre is discussed in Chapter XIII below. The use of coal as well as wood for firing the kilns is proved by the composition of the excavated ash layers.

The tiles

Swinnerton's attention was focussed sharply on tiles, but a considerable body of pottery was found in association with the kilns, and is described below. The profuse tile fragments included roofing tiles, floor tiles both plain and decorated, and some decorated panel tiles. The foundation material for all was the 'marl' of the Mercia Mudstones, and suitable sand was present nearby. A mixture of marly clay and fine sand was used for the roofing and plain floor tiles, but for decorated tiles a white clay, probably from the local Coal Measures, was added to the red mixture of clay and sand, resulting in a range of pinks from dark to light. Broken surfaces often show fine streaks of red and white due to imperfect mixing. By analogy with later methods as described by Lloyd Haberley [1937 44] and quoted by Swinnerton et al. [1955 91] clay was pressed into shallow wooden moulds, the moulds for roofing tiles 10½ by 7 to 7½ inches and ½ to ¾ inch deep; those for flooring tiles 5½ inches square and about 1 inch deep; and those for panel tiles about 8 by 6 inches. Except for roofing tiles the sides of the moulds sloped outwards and upwards, so the top surface of the tile was larger than the bottom, easing the drop-out of the partially dry tiles being turned. The bottom of the mould was sprinkled with coarse sand from the Nottingham Castle Sandstone formation. The top edges of the tiles were sharp, projecting clay having been scraped off with a strip of wood. Triangular tiles were produced by deeply incising the clay in the mould before glazing and firing. Of the thousands of fragments found not one was without glaze: so the glazing material was applied to the air dried tiles, and the clay fired and the glaze melted in one operation. The tiles were stacked for final air drying, and in the kilns plain glazed tiles were stacked criss-cross on their edges, but the decorated tiles were laid flat with a half-inch layer of sand between them.

Much attention has been given to the patterns of decoration on the encaustic tiles. These were impressed by wooden dies dipped in white slurry and then gently pressed on to the tile, usually leaving only a very shallow impression on the clay, with slight excesses of slurry sometimes blurring the edge of the design. Reconstructions have been made of many of the patterns produced on the Keighton tiles. They were all counterparts of those on tiles made at Malvern Priory. The patterns of 10 floor tiles and 4 panel tiles found in the kiln waste tips at Keighton were reproduced and described by Swinnerton and others [1955 95-97]. The panel tiles were similar to four of five found in a panel at Malvern, and a complete example of a top or canopy tile from Malvern bears an inscription which fixes the first date of the design as 1457-58. Fragments at Lenton showed parts of the same inscription, so the Keighton tile works were in operation shortly after this date, and were of 'the Malvern School'. The date corresponds approximately with that of the 'desertion' of Keighton village as indicated by pottery finds. Tiles with similar patterns have been found at Dale Abbey and Beauvale Priory, suggesting that peripatetic bands of tile makers set up kilns for a period near to a building being refloored, although Kerridge suggested that the Keighton kilns may have supplied Dale and Beauvale as well as Lenton Priory.

Because the site of Lenton Priory itself has been built over there has been little systematic excavation on it during the past century. Relatively few tiles have been found, and these usually fragmentary. Many were certainly lost in the early 19th century when William Stretton, the builder and architect, built his own house called The Priory on the site (see Appendix 21) and 'from his own statement it is known that....he took up thousands of monastic tiles' [Robertson ed. (Stretton) 1910 172]. The fate of most is not known, though Godfrey [1884] illustrated a selection of 11 floor tiles and three very small tiles that were presented by William Stretton's son to Sir Henry Dryden in 1848 and by him to Nottingham Corporation in 1881. Only one of these floor tiles has the same design as one of the group illustrated by Swinnerton. According to Parker [1932 and 1936] the fragments found on the site of the priory represented 24 different designs, all except two belonging to a period preceding the middle of the 15th century; and the two exceptions, larger and more complex patterns about 5½ inches square and over an inch thick, are precisely the same as Types 1 and 10 among Swinnerton's 14 types [Swinnerton et al. 1955 95]. This strengthens the view that some of the priory tiles were made at Keighton - 'a practical certainty when, on comparing the samples of type 10 from both priory site and kiln site it was found that both were printed by the same die, which happened to have a crack running from the margin towards and across the crown, a feature absent from the corresponding Malvern tiles. Many tile fragments from the priory site have had their patterns almost or completely worn away by prolonged traffic over them, showing that a little after the middle of the 15th century the paving of the chancel needed renewal, and was therefore taken up, and parts buried under structural alterations. The Keighton tile kilns were established at this time, to provide new tiles for the renovations, presumably under the direction of Malvern craftsmen aided by local labour.

The pottery

Because his published report was focussed on tiles and the priory Swinnerton did not mention the quantities of medieval pottery recovered from the tile kiln waste at Keighton, though he did leave ample notes which were used by Coppack [1971]. Since the tile kilns could be accurately dated to 1457-58 or shortly thereafter, unabraded pottery sealed in their waste heaps can be assumed to have the same date, and as none of the several wasters found there were abraded a pottery kiln must have been nearby - unless the pottery was fired in the tile kilns. Because little pottery was found in association with kilns producing encaustic tiles Coppack deduced that the pottery was produced in another kiln and the waster sherds spread over a fairly limited area. Swinnerton was unable to cover the area that was in use as a pottery in the 15th century because his excavations were of a 'rescue' character.

It is fairly certain that a distinctive form of pancheon was made at Keighton in the 15th century, and that cooking pots were also produced there. Pancheons of a remarkably similar form and fabric were found in the filling of the Keighton well, and a waster was also found there. Cooking pots from the well found in association with pancheon rims must also be dated to the third quarter of the 15th century, and one certain waster was recovered. The cooking pots were all of one pattern, and for that reason probably a local product, though this is unproven. Pancheons from the well were probably contemporary with pottery from the tile kiln sites, and in Coppack's opinion must constitute an important and closely dated local group.

An archaeological enigma

Before leaving this review of the archaeology of medieval Keighton village we should return to an archaeological enigma which poses interesting questions in respect of the agrarian history of the campus. Scattered through the subsoil on both house sites II and III were adventitious large sherds of Roman period grey ware pottery of late second century A.D. or later. These were not stratified in relation to the pre-Conquest Saxo-Norman sherds found, but all lay above the later medieval pottery and all were abraded, presumably by ploughing. No other evidence found here pointed to a Roman period or pre-Conquest settlement on the site, and it is difficult to understand how this unstratified ancient pottery came to be present, lying above later material. To suggest that it was brought to the village area from somewhere nearby would of itself be no answer to the problem.

An aerial photograph of the village site in the 1930s appears to show up-and-down slope ridge and furrow traces very similar to those that are found today on the 'downland', and with a similar orientation, though nothing of it can be seen on the ground. Whether these possible marks of former arable cultivation would date from before the establishment of Keighton village - for example, as part of Morton's arable land - or from the brief period after the presumed abandonment of the village in 1460-70 but before the Dissolution of 1538 cannot be suggested. However, if the supposed ridge and furrow were to date from the latter period it could explain an import of soil containing the Roman period sherds in process of levelling the more irregular parts of the former village site to make it suitable for ploughing. By 1538 all the lands that could have been Keighton village lands were in closes let to various individuals (see Chapter III) and some were described as 'land' - meaning arable land [18]. But arable cultivation of the demesne was in severe decline by the early 16th century. Furthermore, there was little incentive for the priory to convert a village site into arable land. The ascetic life was no longer admired or practised, and the number of monks at Lenton had probably decreased by half and they were mostly aged by the Dissolution. Their life at that time was described by Trevelyan as 'easy, sauntering comfort, without grave offence but without marked benefit to the world around them'. They still fed the poor, but the smaller community will have relied more on its rent and tithe income, and less on vigorous cultivation of its demesne than in earlier times. There is also the possibility that the supposed ridge-and-furrow at Keighton, uncorroborated, may be no more than an accident of photographic processing.

NOTES

1. Cossons referred to a bronze sword dredged 'some years ago' from the lake in Highfields Park, and 'now in the Castle museum'. It is not clear whether this refers to the same find or to one dating from the lake excavation of 1921-25. The latter is unlikely since Robert Mellors in 1916 referred to the presentation by Hugh Lowe to Nottingham Castle museum of 'the Ancient British sword found in the lake of Highfield House'.
2. *Domesday Book,* 4 volumes, 1783. Many partial transcripts exist: for example, in Robert Thoroton, *The Antiquities of Nottinghamshire* with additions by John Throsby, 3 volumes, 1797. A recent publication is John Morris (ed) from Celia Parker and Sara Wood, *Domesday Book 28, Nottinghamshire,* Phillimore, Chichester, 1977.
3. Sir William Dugdale, *Monasticon Anglicanum* [1846 edn.] Six volumes: Vol. 5, 113: '....William lentonae cum omnibus pertinentiis suis, exceptis quatuor molendinis....similiter Radford, Morthonam, Kichthonam cum omnibus pertinentiis carum....'. This comes from an Inspeximus Charter of king Edward II, where the foundation charter is recited, apparently verbatim . Printed in Godfrey [1884] 63-66, together with the confirming charter of king Henry I. See also V.C.H. Notts. II, 91, and Thoroton [1797] II 201
4. Godfrey [1884] 19-22. Godfrey mentioned several theories and discussed William's pedigree and his posterity with their chequered history and intrigues [pp. 22-27].
5. Matilda, daughter of king Henry I was mentioned in the charter. She was born in 1108. Gerard, Archbishop of York, a witness, died in 1108, but another witness, an abbot of Cluny, was not elected until 1109. The date is probably 1108.
6. The details are set out in Godfrey [1884] 62-63, with a transcript [63-65] and the confirming charter of Henry I [65-66]. The endowments are described in detail on pp. 666 et seq.
7. Colladors (literally 'contributors') were persons provided with board and accommodation by the priory in return for a cash payment. Lenton Priory, heavily in debt, mainly on account of litigation, collected a number of them, and paid heavily for the arrangement. The most damaging litigation related to a long-running dispute with the Chapter of Lichfield.
   Some estimates of the size of the priory community were:
   1262 - 27 monks, 2 conversi
   1276 - 27 monks, 4 conversi
   1279 - 25 monks, 'as customary'
   1296 - 25 monks, 4 conversi
   1324 - 21 monks, 20 corrodions
   1405 - 32, 'a full complement'.
8. The debt was quoted by Godfrey [1884 129] from the Cluny Mss., Bibl. Nat., Paris.
9. Several seizures by the Crown in the reigns of Edward II and Edward III have left Extents among the Exchequer records [P.R.O., E 106/8/3, 9/5, 9/9 and 11/8] but these are less detailed and instructive than those for the 21 months in 1296-98. There are accounts for the period October 1324 to Michaelmas 1325 which are useful, and are discussed by Stitt [1959].
10. N.U.M.D., Mi 1/38/39 (i) to (iv) undated.
11. These figures were derived by Gray from a selection of the holdings in Lenton and Radford recorded in P.R.O., Misc. Books (Land Revenue) 211, ff. 105 et seq., 5 James I. The 'bovates' of 1605 may have been much changed since the 1290s in the course of land transactions over many generations.
12. These rentals are discussed in Chapter III below. See particularly N.U.M.D., Mi 1/38/31 [1538] and Mi 1/38/33 [about 1554]. The accounts of the 1290s give no information about possible sub-letting, and whether any holders of free land were villeins in law - a not infrequent situation by the late 13th century.
13. N.U.M.D., Mi 1/38/31 [1538]
14. P.R.O., Add. Mss. 6164. f. 502. See Godfrey [1884 151]. This statement does not,in fact, preclude the possibility that other houses at Keighton survived.
15. N.A.O., RD 3 L, 'A mappe of ye Lordshippe of Lenton and Radford taken the tenthe day of Julye anno 1632 by me, Richard Smythe, Surveyor'. The map is partly covered in thick, opaque green paint, but most of the larger captions can be read with difficulty.
16. P.R.O., Add. Mss. 6164, 202. [Godfrey 1884 151-53].
17. The plans of the three kiln sites in this Figure are adapted from Plate I of Swinnerton et al. [1955].
18. N.U.M.D., Mi 1/38/31 (30 May 1538).

CHAPTER III

THE PRIORY DEMESNE LANDS IN THE SIXTEENTH CENTURY

The early sixteenth century
The Dissolution and the rental of 1538
The Stanhopes and their leases
The village lands of Keighton
Crown leases and tenant farmers
The fields and closes of Lenton Priory demesne
The construction of a map of field names
Agrarian landscape and land use in the mid-sixteenth century
The rental or survey of about 1554
'Concealed lands'
Field pattern and land use on the Trent valley floor
The valley-side and 'upland' parts of the former demesne
The marl pit
The Abbey Fields and the Sixty Acres
Conversion of arable land to sheep walk
The surviving marks of arable cultivation
The later sixteenth century and the Harrington lease

The early sixteenth century

The valuation of Lenton Priory in 1387 (Appendix 1) which described the dereliction and abandonment of five cottages at Keighton, also indicated by implication a marked decline in agricultural activity on the priory demesne [1]. Three of the six carucates of arable land in the priory's estate in Lenton, Radford and Keighton were uncultivated and neglected, and presumably turned over to grazing at half rent. This decline may have been associated with a marked deterioration of the climate from the end of the 13th century onwards, itself not unconnected with the decimation of the labour force by the Black Death and other epidemic diseases of the middle and later 14th century. It may have been foreshadowed in the decline of the area of demesne sown to crops from 451 acres in 1296-97 to 380 acres in 1324-25 (disregarding the abnormal peak of 539 acres in 1297-98). It is not known where the deterioration in cultivation mainly took place, but it is probable that the demesne arable land in the six open fields of Lenton and Radford was progressively let to 'tenants at will', while the priory's own crop production was more and more concentrated on the home farm - that is, on Keighton, including the present University campus - and even here was substantially reduced.

Since a survey-rental of the priory's possessions in Lenton and Radford in 1538 (Lenton here including Keighton) was dated only weeks after the execution of the last prior, it is better regarded as a picture of the final condition in the pre-Dissolution period than of the post-Dissolution situation. All the priory's land east and north of the river Leen was tenanted except for the site and precincts of the priory itself, but the area now occupied by the campus and the valley floor lands below it was still administered as a single unit, and called demesne, a word not used elsewhere in Lenton and Radford.

Through the 15th and early 16th centuries the decay of the agrarian economy of Lenton and its hamlets characteristic of the 14th century was arrested if not reversed. The open field arable land in the present campus area was still cropped. Names such as New Wheat Close,

Table 6.
Free transcript of a fragment of the terrier or rental of the demesne of Lenton Priory in 1538
[Extract from N.U.M.D., Mi 1/38/31 - see back cover of this book]

The items are listed on separate lines although in the document they run on..

Demesne land

Michael Stanopp, armiger, for farm of the site of the former Priory
aforesaid, and all barns, dovecotes, fisheries, gardens, orchards,
waters, vineyards, land etc. within the site of the former Priory.
a water mill
a close called Neweheate Close [New Wheatclose]
3 pastures called the Feedings and Cow Pastures
Another pasture called Ryecrofte
a close called Wheyt Close [Wheatclose]
a close called Lytle Brome Close
a pasture called Ryecrofte Leys
a pasture called The Ley Close
a closure called Tamworth
a closure called the Calf Close
a closure called the Dayhouse Close
a closure called Aspley Wood and a messuage
a meadow called Stonehouse Meadow
a meadow called Lytlyng
a meadow and a pighcell [pingle] called Prior's Meadow
a ploughed meadow
a ploughed orchard
a parcel of land called Stonehouse Wong with
a close called Kighton
a parcel of land called Merpitt right up against New Field [Marlpit]
a parcel of arable land lying in the field called the New Close,
right up to The Warren
an open field called the Sixty Acres
an open field called The Warren
a close of land called Leget Wong, upper end
besides 15 acres of meadow lying in Carleholmes and
one pasture in Carleholme

with all and singular appurtenances, to pay per annum at the feast
of the Annunciation of the Blessed Virgin Mary and St. Michael the
Archangel in equal parts - £ 38. 19s. 9d.

Held by the same the farm of a meadow called Trent Wong, paying at
the feasts aforesaid - £8.

and New Close - the so-called 'downland' of today - called 'campo' in 1538, suggest that new land had been brought into cultivation or returned to it. Most of the land on the Trent valley floor was in 1538 described as meadow or pasture, but otherwise the land was partly in closes and partly in open field. It will be shown later that much of the demesne on the higher ground was under arable cultivation in the early 16th century and the site of Keighton village was enclosed, and may even have been cultivated. The situation changed drastically with the Dissolution of the priory.

The Dissolution and the rental of 1538

Early in 1534 Parliament severed all ties with Rome, and in November annexed the first-fruits and tenths permanently to the Crown, with the promulgation of a new oath of supremacy.

In 1535 clergy refusing to take the oath were hanged for high treason, and commissioners were appointed to investigate the religious, and to enforce the oath. In 1536 insurrection at Louth and in Yorkshire - the 'Pilgrimage of Grace' - led to further hangings, and subsequently lesser religious houses were dissolved by Act 27, Henry VIII c.20, and greater houses by Act 31 Henry VIII c.13 of May 1539. Lenton Priory was dissolved and its possessions confiscated by the Crown in 1538. Its last prior, Nicholas Heath, was executed in April 1538 and his Inquisition Postmortem was dated 3rd September 1538. A 24-feet long parchment roll contains a rental or survey of the priory's confiscated property in Lenton and Radford dated 30 May 1538 [2], and records the rents that produced about 20 per cent of the priory's income.

The items of land listed in the 1538 rental for Lenton were grouped under four heads, which can be summarized thus:

	Rent yield	No. of houses or cottages
Rent assize of free holdings	£ 1. 7s. 6d.	6
Copyhold rents	10.17s. 3d.	6
Rents of tenants at will	54.19s. 0d.	59
Property farmed (leased)	62.13s. 0d.	

Most of the last item is accounted for by £ 38.19s. 0d. for demesne land held as one unit by Michael Stanhope, together with £8 for the meadow called Trent Wong (now Grove Farm, a University playing fields area). This land had been the home farm of the priory, and lay entirely west and south of the river Leen. It included the University campus in Lenton . The first item above showed a considerble reduction from the rent of assize of freehold land in 1297. The houses and cottages would have been concentrated in Lenton village.

Godfrey [1884] stated that the site and demesne of the priory were granted in 1539 to Michael Stanhope for a term of 40 years at an annual rent of £38. 13s. 0d.; but he failed to add that this lease for years was changed to a term of 'life in survivorship' to Sir Michael and his wife in 1549, and this omission has led to a wrong conclusion that the lease was forfeit when Sir Michael Stanhope was executed in 1552 [Cameron 1975]. The 1538 rental shows Stanhope already holding the priory site and demesne lands, Trent Wong and Lenton fair (for £ 26.13s. 4d) [3], although his Crown lease was dated 1539; but nothing further is known of this interim arrangement.

The Stanhopes and their leases

Sir Michael Stanhope of Shelford was the second son of Sir Edward Stanhope of Rampton and East Markham by his first wife Adeline, daughter of Sir Gervase Clifton of Clifton. The Stanhopes, later earls of Chesterfield, came to Nottinghamshire from Northumberland in the 14th century when John Stanhope married the heiress of manors that included Rampton, and they became landed gentry. Sir Richard Stanhope was M.P. for Nottinghamshire in the first quarter of the 14th century, and his grandson John for most of the period 1449 to 1473. This John's grandson, Sir Edward, was a commander for Henry VII at the battle of East Stoke in 1485. He died in 1511. By his second wife Elizabeth, daughter of Lord Fitzwaren, he had a daughter, Anna - half-sister to Sir Michael who obtained Lenton Priory - and she married Edward Seymour, the Duke of Somerset. Edward's eldest son, Richard Stanhope of Rampton, died without male issue in 1528-29, and although his only daughter Sanchia took Rampton to the Babington family by marriage, Michael Stanhope succeeded to the rest of the family estates.

Sir Edward had been a courtier and servant of Cromwell, and was Governor of Hull during part of Henry VIII's reign. Sir Michael was chief gentleman of the privy chamber, and served on many of the commissions of the 1530s, including the Commission of Peace for Nottinghamshire in 1537 [4]. In favour with the king, Sir Michael obtained a 60-year lease on the site and demesne of the small Augustinian priory of Shelford founded in the reign of Henry II when it was dissolved in 1536, and having got the lease extended to include his heirs in 1538 he established his family home there [5]. In 1539 he obtained both the lease of Lenton Priory site and demesne, and appointment as bailiff of the Crown's other estate in Lenton.

The later career of Sir Michael was chequered. After the death of Henry VIII he remained in favour, and at the succession of Edward VI became deputy to the Lord Protector, Somerset, who had married his half-sister Anna. With such a powerful relative and friend at Court Michael Stanhope was knighted, made chief gentleman of the Privy Chamber to Edward VI, and remained in high esteem at court until Somerset's troubles began. Becoming involved in political intrigue Stanhope shared in both the rise and the swift descent of the fortunes of his relative, which ended in his disgrace and imprisonment in 1551, and his subsequent execution at Tower Hill in 1552. After Somerset was constrained to resign the Protectorate he retained his popularity, and the Duke of Northumberland, regarding him as the chief obstacle to power, engineered his downfall by claiming a conspiracy against his life. Sir Michael remained loyal to Somerset, and on the day after Somerset was arrested, 16 October 1551, the Duchess, with Stanhope and Sir Miles Partridge were imprisoned. Somerset was executed on 22 January 1552, and Sir Michael, with several others, shared his fate.

Before returning to topographic matters it may be appropriate to point out that Lady Anne Stanhope, who was daughter of Nicholas Pawson of Essex, survived her husband for some 35 years until 1587-88, and continued to enjoy the estate of the Lenton Priory demesne for that whole period. Since her lease was not for three lives, as shown wrongly in the survey-rental of about 1554 (discussed later) but expired with her death, the Stanhope interest in the estate ended in 1588. But the reversion of the lease was granted as early as 1563 to John Harrington, a courtier of Queen Elizabeth. Not only were the main leases at Shelford and Lenton retained, but even the minor lease of the 'Alexander Wright closes', discussed later, which was for 21 years from 1540, was re-granted to Anne Stanhope within months of her husband's execution, which appears to have been no handicap whatever to the careers of their children, recorded on Lady Anne's tombstone.

Sir Thomas Stanhope of Shelford, Knight of the Shire in 28 Elizabeth (1586)
Elinor, married Thomas Cooper of Thurgarton
Edward Stanhope Esq., one of Her Majesty's Council in the North Parts of England, Knight of the Shire in 1571 and 1572
Julia, married John Hotham of Scoreborough, Lincolnshire
John Stanhope Esq., a Gentleman of the Chamber to Queen Elizabeth
Jane, married Sir Roger Townshend of Eyam, Norfolk
Edward Stanhope, Doctor of Civil Law, High Court of Chancery
Michael Stanhope Esq., one of the Privy Chamber to Queen Elizabeth
(Margaret, William and Edward died in infancy)

Lady Anne 'lived in great repute for her piety and virtue'. Her tomb at Shelford also tells that during her 35 years of widowhood she 'brought up all her younger children in virtue and learning, whereby they were preferred to the marriages and callings before recited in her lifetime. She kept continually a worshipful House, relieved the poor daily, gave good countenance and comfort to the Preachers of God's word, spent most of the time of her latter daies in Prayer and using the church where God's word was preached; she .....died 20th Day of February Anno 1587, the thirtieth year of the Reign aforesaid... ' [6]. The succeeding generation included Philip, great-grandson of Sir Michael and Dame Anne Stanhope, who in 1616 paid £10,000 for the honour of becoming Baron Stanhope of Shelford, and in 1628 became Earl Chesterfield. It was he who in 1642 raised a regiment and fortified Shelford for the king. His eighth son Philip was killed in the siege there in 1645. Thereafter the family seat was at Bretby, Derbyshire.

The brief inventory of the priory demesne lands transcribed in Table 6 and reproduced on the back cover of this volume is an extract from the long and detailed rental of 1538 mentioned above. It will be seen to include Aspley Wood and a messuage there that was presumably Aspley Hall. This house, about two miles north of the demesne proper, was regarded as part of it, and was the 'retreat of the prior of Lenton' [Barnes 1987, Barley 1987]. Trent Wong is present as an item separate from the demesne but immediately following it. A close called Kighton (Keighton) is included, but a number of closes that later became parts of the University campus are not, and they are found among the 'tenants at will', let separately to various individuals. While clearly not parts of the demesne lands as defined in the rental they differed from the remaining items in the 'tenants at will' group in several respects. Most of the latter were small holdings, each with a cottage or farmhouse, a toft, arable strips in the common fields of Lenton and defined grazing rights. The other holdings, grouped at the end of the list of tenancies at will, were closes without dwellings, having neither grazing rights nor common arable land attached to them; and, unlike all the cottage holdings, they were named. They all lay west or south of the river Leen. Their late and consecutive placing in the tenants-at-will rental is significant, and so is the fact that they were granted as a single unit to Sir Michael Stanhope in a separate Crown lease in 1540 [7] .

The lands in question, in Sir Michael Stanhope's second lease, are listed in Table 7. Their annual rent, totalling £14.13s.8d. included £2. 0s. 8d. for meadow called Leggett Wong, which in 1538 appeared as copyhold land held by four tenants (called 'late occupiers' in the lease of 1540) - William Mason, John Standley, Thomas Mason's widow and John Delapeze, all Lenton tenants. These 'Alexander Wright Closes', though incorporated in the body of the priory demesne, were clearly distinct from it tenurially well before the Dissolution. Alexander Wright obtained them from Anne Stanhope by assignment in 1552, immediately she had recovered them after her husband's execution, and he was granted Letters Patent of Philip and Mary, probably in 1553-54 [8] . In later lists of former priory lands they remained separate under the sub-heading 'Sanders (or Saunders) Wryght closes' [9] . They remained distinct down to the present century, finding their way into the Gregory estate in the early 17th century after a period in the hands of the Hanmers of Radford. They were included in William Gregory's rental at Michaelmas 1631, immediately after he bought the Manor of Lenton in November 1630, and in 1663 were still known as 'Mr. Hanmer's lease' [10] .

The reason why these particular closes, varying in physical character, should have become tenurially distinct from the land around them in the 16th century probably lies much further back in time than the Dissolution. They are almost certainly the village lands of Keighton, the tenants of which from the 12th century onwards at least provided the labour for the cultivation of the priory demesne lands as rent for their own land holdings. When Keighton village was finally abandoned, probably piecemeal, and probably in the later 15th century (see Chapter II) the village lands were not absorbed into the structure and organization of the demesne, but were let for rent by the prior. The rents are quoted in the 1538 rental. 'Little Kightons' was probably the tofts of the village, appropriately descriptive of the land division, and located in the right place. An old footpath running south from Cut Through Lane near to the present Science Library gave access from Lenton village to all the Keighton closes, and remained a right of way until the late 19th century. It crossed Keighton Close, ran along the boundary between Bacon Close and Quarrel Close and down the west side of Ley Close, Great Mare Close and Little Mare Close. Whether it was linked to the sunken way described in

Table 7.
The village lands of Keighton and Morton

[Extracted from N.U.M.D., Mi 1/38/31 - the rental of the priory's estate in Lenton and Radford in 1538]

The items listed come from near the end of the schedule of 'Tenants at will' in Lenton. Of the preceding 69 entries under this head nearly all included a cottage or house. The items below appear consecutively in the document. None of them included a dwelling or garden.

Robert Chapman	2 closes		Land	3s. 0d.
John Jepson	Lytle Kyghton, 2 closes.	8 ac.	Land	26s. 8d.
do.	Greatmare Close	6 ac.	Pasture	20s. 0d.
John Willoughby, milit.	Willo[w]holme closure		Meadow	30s. 0d.
Edmund Landisdale	Bacon Close and Quarrell Close		Land	66s. 8d.
John Thorne	Lytle Mare Close	3 ac.	Pasture	10s. 0d.
Richard Butler	Gervis Close	3 ac.	Meadow	13s. 4d.
Wm. Edmondson	Edmondson's Close	6 ac.	Meadow	33s. 4d.
Robert Jackman	Great Bolymire and 3 ac. with 1 parcel		Land	14s. 0d.
		1½ ac.	Meadow	
Vicar of Lenton	Brome Close and parcel adjoining	8 ac.	Meadow	26s. 8d.
John Hanford	Under walls of monastery	2½ ac.	Meadow	10s. 0d.

Notes

These lands were leased to Michael Stanhope by the Crown separately from the major part of the demesne, and after his execution in 1552 were recovered by his widow, Dame Anne Stanhope, who leased them in about 1554 to Alexander Wright. They have been described in later documents as the 'Alexander Wright Closes'. After a period in the hands of the Hanmers of Radford they were purchased by William Gregory of Nottingham in about 1628, and remained in the Gregory [Pearson-Gregory] estate until the 1920s. The Crown lease also included Trent Wong and a close of pasture called Plumptre Orchard in Radford.

Edmondson's Close was elsewhere called Morton.

Gervis or Jervis Close was sold to Nicholas Charlton of Chilwell in 1690.

John Jepson was a Radford copyholder, holding a messuage with 3 bovates of land, and a second messuage with 2 bovates, rent 46s. 0d..

John Thorne was also a Radford copyholder with a cottage and 2 bovates held for a rent of 18s. 8d..

Chapter II is not known. The close called Edmondson's Close, occupied by William Edmondson in 1538, was in other rentals of the early 17th century called Morton, and it adjoined common land enclosed in 1768 and called Morton Nook Meadow. Bullmires or Bolymire Close and Brome Close were nearby. Whether these Morton lands were later part of the village lands of Keighton cannot be determined, but it seems likely.

Crown leases and tenant farmers

A distinction has to be made between the Crown lessees of the possessions of the dissolved priory and the tenant farmers who actually worked the land. Although the priory demesne itself was granted by Letters Patent only after the Dissolution, various groups of holdings in Lenton and Radford had been leased out by the prior of Lenton at earlier dates to persons such as John Delapeze, William Courtnall, John Collingwood, John Salt and John Cockeram, who retained their leases after the Dissolution up to their normal expiry dates. Details are given in the rental of c. 1554 though not in that of 1538. Later, parts of the demesne were sub-leased by the Stanhopes to Agnes Allen and others, and the lease to Alexander Wright has been mentioned above. These arrangements were distinct from the annual letting of holdings by the Crown Steward or Bailiff directly to the small peasant farmers. The fact that no tenants were named in 1538 for the demesne lands (excluding the Alexander Wright Closes) is taken to imply that the demesne remained under cultivation by and for the priory community down to the Dissolution, though perhaps less intensively than earlier.

Little is known precisely about the land of the demesne in the 1540s and to 1554, although it is clear that the northern part of the present campus, occupied before the Dissolution mainly by the open arable fields of the home farm, was quickly converted into sheep walk, which was rented from Sir Michael Stanhope by the Willoughbys of Wollaton. A lease by Anne Stanhope to George Madeley (discussed further below) was of 'All her grounds and closes of pasture lying in the parish of Lenton called ye feeding pastures or fatt pastures with the roundabout of the same' - which were demesne lands on the Trent valley floor, between the railway and Beeston canal of today - and 'other grounds and closes of pasture there (called the Abbey Fields, the Conyngre and Syxtye Acres) upon which grounds and closes and pastures the flocke of sheep of Wollaton of late belonging to Mr. Henry Willoughby deceased is at this present day kept and pastured, and is and at this day remaineth under the guydyng and order of Henry Avery, nowe shepherd there. And together with fre warren and connies of and in the same ....' [11]. Henry Willoughby had the Willoughby estate in Wollaton only from 1548 to 1549, being killed at Norwich in Kitt's rebellion against enclosure when his sons were children.

The fields and closes of Lenton Priory demesne

It is proposed to examine now the rental or survey of the former demesne made in about 1554; to describe the landscape and land use of that time; and to indicate some changes that had taken place since the terrier of 1538. In order to do so, however, it is necessary to provide a map on which closes, parcels of land and open fields can be located, by the names given in surveys and rentals down to the end of the 18th century. Without such a location map no sensible use can be made of such documentary material as is available, no view taken of the structure of farm holdings or estates, and no comparison made between the tenurial and agrarian patterns at different dates. Reference has already been made above to some details from a field names map without explaining their origins.

No map of Lenton parish dating from earlier than the 19th century is known, with the single exception of the 'Mappe of ye Lordshippe of Lenton and Radford taken the tenthe day of Julye: anno 1632: by me, Richard Smythe surveyor' [12], and unfortunately even this is of very limited value. The map of Sherwood Forest which includes part of Lenton, dated 1609, covers very little of the area of the demesne, and is so damaged as to be virtually illegible in that area [13]. Smythe's map omits most of the priory demesne, is grossly distorted, gives few land names, and has been damaged by an application of thick green opaque paint which seriously obscures the annotation, and makes it impossible to discern detail clearly on a photocopy though most can be made out by eye on the original.

No estate map or cadastral map of any description showing field patterns or names in any part of the campus is known before about 1809, by which time the area had been almost totally remodelled. There is no tithe map or commutation schedule to refer to because the priory demesne was not subject to tithes. No enclosure map for Lenton survives, and in fact the former demesne lands were not involved in the inclosure of the parish. By the time that Ordnance Survey maps and estate maps became available in the 19th century very little

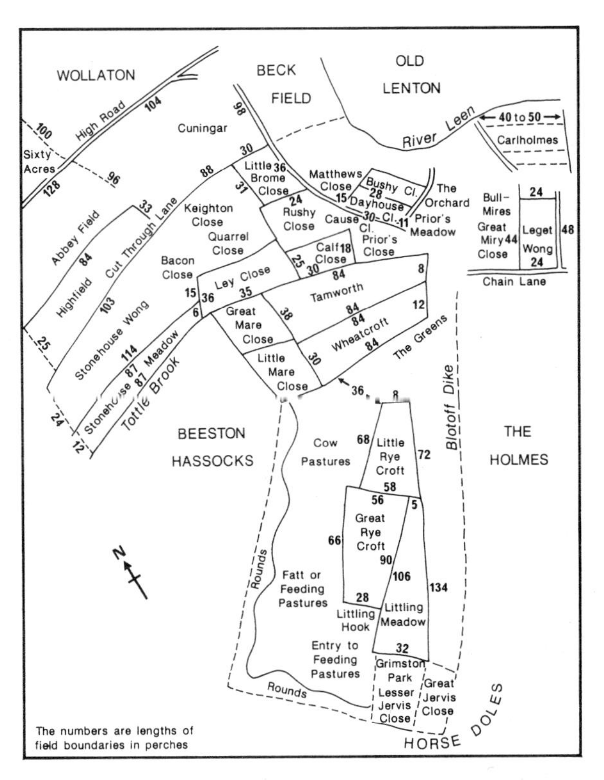

Figure 20: Sketch-map showing relative locations of fields and closes of the former priory demesne in the 16th-early 17th century
Compounded from documentary sources discussed in the text.

remained of the old order in the former demesne lands except on the farm lands of the Trent vale. A plan of the Lenton Abbey estate in the north-west of the campus, dating from about 1809 [14] (Figure 74) already shows field names different from those used in the survey of 1798, and this in perhaps the least altered part of the campus area. Later estate maps such as that of Lord Middleton's estate in Lenton in 1863 [15] , covering most of the northern part of the campus, and those associated with the sale particulars for the Highfield estate in 1881, 1893 and 1900 [16] , contain no field names surviving from even the 18th century. A map of the Gregory estate in Lenton by H.M.Wood, surveyed in 1818-23 [17] provides outline detail for that estate only, and no key to field numbers has been located; and it includes no detail for the areas not in the Gregory estate.

The construction of a map of old field names

Reconstruction of the landscape of the University campus at any date before 1800 is hampered by the lack of the kind of precise information on location that is provided by maps and gives meaning to the details recorded in rentals and surveys. Uncertainties about the location of fields and other parcels of land make it impossible to interpret terriers in terms of farm holdings, and changes in the names of fields as well as in their areas exacerbate the difficulties. A first and absolutely essential task therefore is to construct a map of field names, however imperfect, to which other forms of land data can be referred, and to do so from non-cartographic sources.

Fortunately the problem can be addressed and partially solved by making use of two quite early documents, both undated but certainly of the period between 1550 and 1610, corroborated where possible by other, scattered references to location. The later and more important source is no more than a number of scraps of folded paper carrying rough calculations in shorthand form of the areas of a number of fields derived from some sort of survey measurements [18]. No units are given and dimensions are not always easy to establish, especially where gores are involved, but useful indications of the general shape of fields can be deduced. Most useful are the names given of adjoining closes or other land units to north, south, east and west, and these crude data can be used to build up rough patterns of groups of closes which can then be fitted into the area within the boundaries of the demesne by reference to other data, including physical geography - an exercise similar to that of a jigsaw puzzle.

The second, earlier document is a description of the so-called 'concealed lands' in part of the Trent valley portion of the demesne, probably dating from fairly soon after the middle of the 16th century. This gives useful information on the names, adjoining closes and relative locations of fields, and helps in the interpretation of the other, later document by confirmation and elimination [19]. Where fields are mentioned in both documents the details are not identical. A few of the land units named are known only because they are described as adjoining others being described, and there are some names of closes not mentioned by these two sources, either because field names change, sometimes more than once over a century or two, or because new fields are formed and other joined or absorbed from time to time. The use of the tenant's name can be temporary and misleading, and a number of closes are known to have been called by personal names - for example Bacon Close, Matthews Close, and Edmondson's Close.

A summary in tabular form of the details found in these two documentary sources is given in Appendix 3. Because of the uncertainties about field boundaries and the changes in them over time, it has been thought prudent in constructing the map of field names (Figure 21) to show the old names in their approximate positions superimposed on later boundaries, on the understanding that the boundaries shown are included for identification purposes, and are not necessarily the boundaries of the fields named at any particular juncture. Figure 20 is a sketch map or cartogram which has been included to illustrate the intermediate stage in transferring the documentary data into map form.

Agrarian landscape and land use in the mid-sixteenth century

The rental or survey dated about 1554 provides a list of the lands of the former priory demesne held in the Crown lease by Anne Stanhope, together with details of land use and an inventory of trees growing on the estate. Unfortunately it reveals little about the way in which the estate was sub-let. The details are given in Appendix 6, and Table 8 is a transcript of an extract from the document. When the items are mapped it appears that some parts of the demesne are not represented, notably a tract north-west of Cut Through Lane that includes the present Lenton House estate and a number of closes in the Dunkirk area. Perhaps a folio is missing from the original rental. However, some points of note arise from the schedule.

Pasture and meadow were in about 1554 wholly predominant, with only one close - Marlpitt - described wholly as arable land. There are definite statements indicating the conversion of former open arable fields and arable closes into pasture - wholesale conversion in the case of the open fields called the Sixty Acres, the Warren, New Close and Short Dunstons, and Great Broom Close, which were later called collectively the Abbey Fields, and partial conversion in the case of Stonehouse Wong, Wheatcroft Leys and Ryecroft. The Abbey Fields had become one extensive sheep walk, as mentioned above. The change elsewhere reflected the fact that former demesne closes were now tenanted individually by farmers as outlying land at a distance from their holdings, especially in Lenton village. These farmers were involved in the cultivation of the open arable fields of their village, and valued the additional land chiefly as supplementary meadow or pasture.

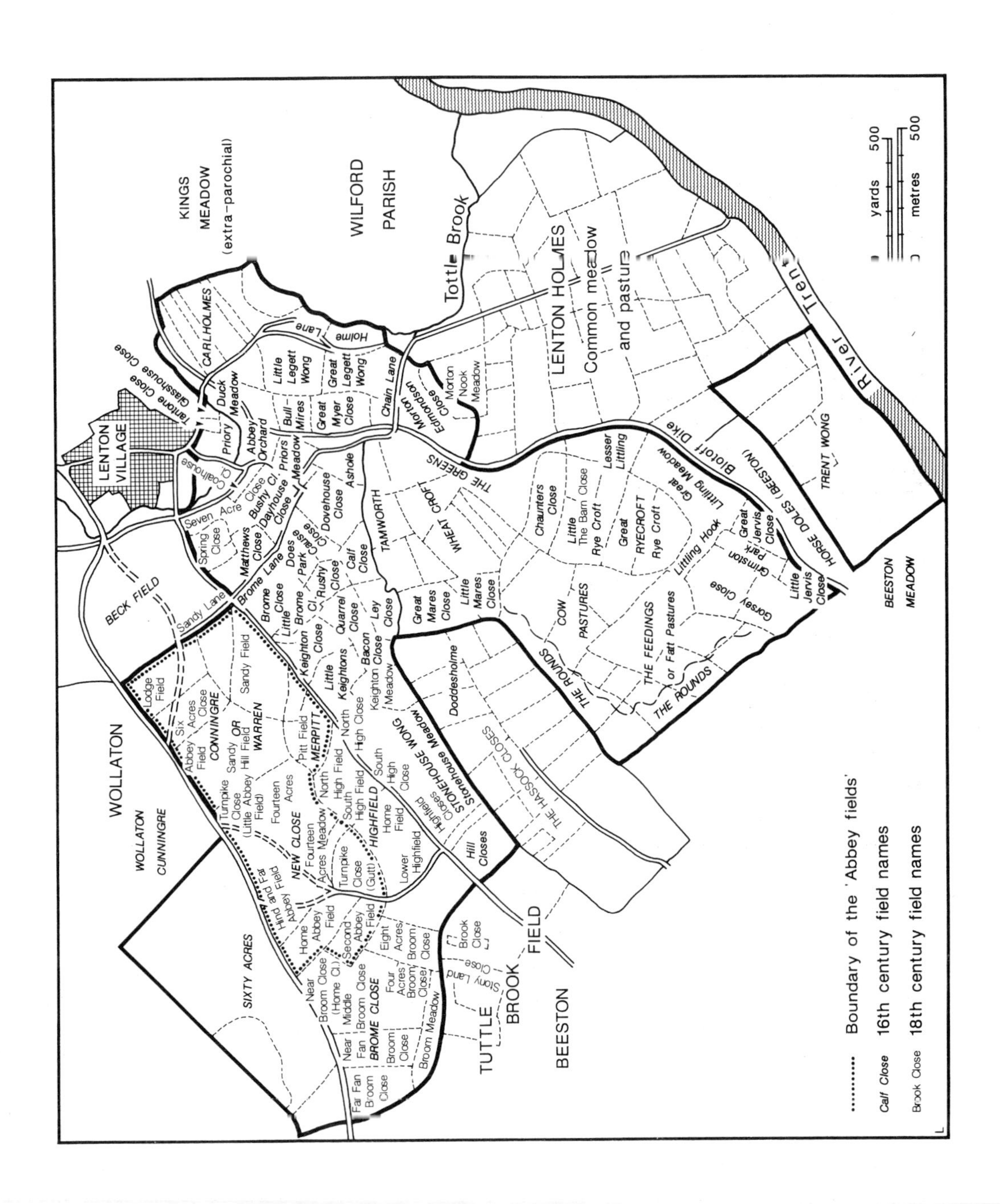

Figure 21: Some old field names of the former priory demesne

Table 8 .
Extract from 'Lenton Monastery - Rental' of about 1554

[Each item is placed on a separate line: the Latin text of the original runs on.]

Dame Anna Stannop for the Priory and site with all gardens, orchards,
dovecotes, barns, waters, vineyards and other buildings and lands within the said circuit of the said Priory, with:

a water mill
a close called Newe Wheatclose
three pastures called the Feedings and Cowe Pastures
a pasture called Ryecroft
another close called Wheatclose
and another close Lytle Brome Close
another pasture called Ryecroft Lees
another pasture called The Ley Close
another close called Tamworth
another close called Calf Close
another close called Dayhouse Close
another close called Assheple Wood Close with a messuage there
a meadow called Stonehouse Medowe
another meadow called Lytleynge
a meadow and for a le pighell called The Prior's Mede
a meadow ploughed, The Orchard
a parcel of land called Stonehouse Wong
a close called Kighton
a parcel of land called Le Merlepit near the Newe F[i]eld
for parcels of land from the said field [campus] called The Newe Close
as far as the Conyngrye
another field [campo] called the Sextye Acres
for Warren
for a close of land called Leget Wonge Upper Ende
15 acres of meadow in Carleholme and
a pasture in Carleholme.

with all and singular ....
leased by Letters Patent etc. for a term of lived or years and
renders annually to the Crown until the end of the same
£ 38. 13s. 9d.

The tree census arose from a suspicion by the Crown agent that Anne Stanhope was about to fell and sell all the timber on the estate [20] . The number of hedgerow trees was probably insufficient to qualify the landscape as 'bocage', but it was far from bare. Woodland, as distinct from trees, was limited, but trees in numbers within some of the closes is probably an indication that they had remained unploughed for many years. Grimston Park was a plantation of some 200 young ash trees in the valley south of the Rye Close and the Littling. The Rounds, poorly drained ribbons in the valley floor, carried about 200 trees of indifferent quality, probably mainly alder, with willow and sallow. On the higher ground were Keighton Close, Little Keightons and the Bacon and Quarrel Closes, containing 60, 60 and 30 trees respectively. These may have been 'self-set' trees on land not cultivated by the priory before the Dissolution, and probably their use as farm land was hampered by the remains of Keighton village and the Keighton tile and pottery kilns, waste tips and associated clay workings. The Sixty Acres, now part of Wollaton Park and containing part of Thompson's Wood and other woodland, contained only ten trees on its 90 acres in about 1554.

'Concealed lands'

The rentals of the 16th century did not account for the total area of Crown land, for they omitted lands regarded as waste, usually on account of poor drainage. These were unusable for normal farming under the conditions of the time although they might have some value for other purposes, including hunting, and might carry useful woodland. Such land was specifically excluded from Crown leases, and a considerable area of it lay on the Trent valley floor. Sir Michael Stanhope's 21 year lease of the Alexander Wright closes in 1540 [21] was of 'divers parcels of land, meadow and pasture within our lordship or manor of Lenton....except and always reserved to us and our heirs all and any woods, underwood, marshes, of mynes and quarrells and all other royalties whatsoever that be to the premises above said or to any of these pertaining or belonging....'. The low-lying waste of the demesne was called 'concealed lands' because it was being exploited piecemeal in the 16th century, the woodland felled and the better-drained areas converted into farm closes, and illegally incorporated into their estates by the holders of the Crown leases. Those concealed lands in the priory demesne are described in an undated document mentioned above [22] , probably dating from the later decades of the 16th century since it is grouped with a rental of John Harrington. It gives illuminating detail of the condition of the valley lands at that time.

The document was entitled 'A copie of particulars for concealed landes in Notts.'. It stated that none of the premises was ever in the record (of the estate) but 'pcell of theme claimed by the inhabitants and occupiers as there inheritance, other parcels by the occupiers by other colours withheld from the prince without answering to the Queene any rents for the same. The parcels above named or [are ?] found out by the trava[i]ls of the procurer hereof who will answer for theme the rente above said, and will defende the Queen's title if it will please your honors to grant him a lease of the premises'. The 'valuation' appears to be a personal estimate by a candidate for a lease. A transcription of the document is given as Appendix 4. Its content provides a convenient starting point for a more detailed review of the landscape and land use of the whole former priory demesne in the second half of the 16th century, in which a description of the fields and land use of the valley floor area is followed by an account of the valleyside and 'upland' parts of the demesne.

Field pattern and land use on the Trent valley floor

The description provided by the late 16th century terrier of 'concealed lands' is of a low-lying, almost level area of gravel patches, most of which were already cultivated in enclosed fields and included in the rentals. The higher parts, on the Floodplain Terrace gravels, had been in arable cultivation, and the remainder were meadow or pasture land. These areas were interlaced with ribbons of alluvium along sluggish minor streams, too persistently wet even for water meadow, but which were themselves varied by small, unreclaimed patches of slightly higher ground called pinghills. Much of the lowest area was left in natural woodland, probably mainly marshy alder thicket, but some of this was being felled and cleared for use as seasonal grazing and for tree planting. For example, Grimston Park in the south, near to Beeston Horse Doles, was a parcel of wooded land, 'lately waste', called 'of old and still Grimston Park', bounded east by Great Jervis Close, south by Lesser Jervis Close, westwards by the entry to the Feeding Pastures and northwards by Littling Meadow, and containing 2 acres of measured woodland. The suggested rent was 16d.. 'The said lytle pece of grounde called Grimstone Park was wood grounde, the timber and wood felled and soulde' [23] .

The 'concealed lands' became absorbed into the Crown leasehold, for in 1573 Dame Anne Stanhope leased to John Cleveland of Lowdham for 21 years the mill adjoining the priory, and the mansion house, and gardens, orchards and other greens and grounds adjoining, together with the Prior's Meadow and also 'all that her kylne house, Kylne house yard, the yarde called Little Pond Yard and one lytle pyngle called the pynfolde' which were 'concealed lands'[24]. In 1609 Sir Michael Hicks, then owner of the estate, leased the same property with its 10 acres, all described as meadow, for 31 years to Sir Percival Willoughby for £12 yearly, £5 more than in 1573 [25] .

The survey of 'concealed lands' had its starting point precisely located at the 'southern angle of the Little Maire Close' (see Figure 21). The area covered was bounded on the east by a sluggish tributary of the Tottle Brook called Blotoff Dike, part of which was known as Littling Ditch. Its line is thought to be followed fairly closely by the Beeston Canal as far north as its crossing by Chain Lane. Cossons stated that the canal is merely the result of widening and deepening a pre-existing dyke, probably itself partly artificial, called, at least at its Lenton end, the Blotah Dyke - the spelling used in the 1794 Act authorizing the construction of the canal, and also on the map which accompanied the earlier Trent Navigation Act of 1785 - but also known in the form Blotoff. Eastwards of the Blotoff line was the common meadow and pasture land of Lenton township called The Holmes, the boundaries of which are easily established by studying the schedule of awards at Lenton's inclosure of 1768 [26] . In the south Blotoff Dyke separated the lands of the priory demesne from the Horse Doles of Beeston, and beyond the Horse Doles lay Trent Wong, nearly 100 acres of meadow extending to the river Trent.

Southwards from the angle of Little Mare Close, and following what became railway land bordering Beeston Hassocks, was a poorly drained finger of alluvium known as the Roundabout Water or The Rounds, extending south-west to the angle of the parish boundary and then south-east along the boundary with Beeston parish as far as the Gorsey Close, including three wooded areas called The Rounds. This ill-drained, partly wooded land extended south-east as far as Blotoff Dyke, which flowed so sluggishly that it could be described as 'a strip of marsh, either stagnant or with running water'.

Northwards from the Rounds at the boundary of Lenton with Beeston parish there were three distinct environments, each with its distinctive land use. An extensive, slightly elevated, oval-shaped patch or 'island' of Floodplain Terrace gravel (see Figure 12) was certainly cultivated as arable land when it was part of the priory's farm, as indicated by the 16th century field names of Ryecroft, and Great and Lesser Rye Closes, although by the mid-16th century it was already mainly pasture [27] . Because of its comparatively good drainage, though with a high water table, this land provided sites much later for the farmsteads from which the valley land was worked in the later 18th and the 19th centuries. Secondly, east of the Ryecroft was the lower-lying strip of alluvial land associated with Blotoff Dyke, extending northwards as the Littling meadows, where Blotoff was called Littling Ditch. Thirdly, to the west of Ryecroft, and extending to the Hassocks where the Rounds did not intervene, was an extensive belt of grassland, reasonably well drained except in times of high flood, called the Cow Pastures in the north, and the Feeding Pastures or Great and Little Fat Pastures in the south.

These three belts converged and narrowed northwards to The Greens (Figure 21) - open grassland of which at least part was used as common pasture over which ran a public way [28] . The Greens in turn narrowed northwards alongside Blotoff Dyke to its crossing by Chain Lane, an old road that was possibly part of the route from Morton (near to the later Dunkirk Farm house) towards St. Wilfred's church, Wilford, across the Trent. Around Dunkirk Farm was more former arable land in Wheatcroft, and probably in Tamworth, extending north to the Tottle Brook, and now at least partly pasture. Both the names and specific reference to former arable use in the rental of about 1554 testify to the earlier status of such land, while the rental described the lower-lying closes simply as meadow or pasture. The rental also shows that these land units were enclosed fields bounded by hedgerows in which there were numbers of trees[29]. In the alluvial 'Rounds' however the 200 trees were 'good indifferent timber', presumably mainly alder, reserved to the Crown. Grimstone Park, near the boundary with Beeston, was also not in the Crown rental proper, but described in the tree inventory in the 1554 rental thus: 'Item ther ys a pece of Severall ground inclosyd callyd Grymston P[ar]ke wherin ar growinge in yonge spyers some bigger some lesser asshies, 200'.

North of the Tottle brook were the Keighton Closes named by Smythe in his map of 1632, comprising Keighton Meadow, Little Keightons, Keighton Close, Bacon Close and Quarrell Close, Ley Close and Great and Little Mare Closes, most of which had been leased in 1554 to Alexander Wright and later became part of the Gregory estate. The more southerly closes were on the valley floor. Bacon was a personal name [30] but Quarrel Close, very near to, if not containing the Keighton kilns, probably owed its name to the clay working discussed in Chapter II. Between the Keighton Closes and the Leen, and between Beck Field and the northern part of Blotoff Dyke were the closes of the dairy farm of the priory, all meadow or pasture.

Not all the identifications on the map of field names are certain, partly because of alternative or altered names as irregular areas of usable land extended with drainage improvements, and the field pattern became more regular. East of the Ley Close was Calf Close, upper and lower , and Ashole, also called Great Doars (or Does) Park, with Rushy Close north of Calf Close and east of Quarrel Close, and Brome Close probably north of Rushy Close in the angle formed by Cut Through lane with Brome Lane, later called Abbey Lane and now Clifton Boulevard. There were other Brome Closes in the demesne [31] . Further north-east were the Prior's Meadow alongside the present canal, Dovehouse Close, Dayhouse Close (adjoining the dairy house), Bushey or Lane Close, Matthews Close, Seven Acre Close, Five Acre Close, Spring Close and Snodon Close, together called The Abbey Closes by Smythe in 1632.

Before the Dissolution this lowland part of the demesne of the priory in southern Lenton was therefore mainly - but originally by no means exclusively - concerned with stock farming for cattle, dairy farming in the north around the Dayhouse , with Feeding Pastures and Cow Pastures in the south for meat animals, dry cows and young stock. It included much meadow land which yielded the hay crops which formed their almost exclusive winter fodder at that time.

The valley-side and 'upland' parts of the former priory demesne

The valleyside slope fronting the main University campus on the south-east, overlooking the lake and University Park, was occupied in the east by the Keighton closes, while at the western end, where Florence Boot Hall stands on a fragment of the Beeston terrace, were the Hill Closes and Far Field Close. Between, and forming the slope on which the Trent Building and Highfield House now stand was the land called Stonehouse Wong in the 16th century, with Stonehouse Meadow lying south of it and now largely occupied by the western reach of the University Park lake. The name was sometimes written Stanhouse Wong [32] , but if Stonehouse was the true name it might refer to the rock shelters in the sandstone cliff in the Staff Garden below Highfield House. The name is not known to have survived beyond the early 17th century, and it was certainly not in use in 1684 for either wong or meadow [33] . It seems to have been replaced by variations on the name Highfields. Although called 'Wong' in the rental of about 1554 the land was not innocent of the plough, for the rental of 1538 [34] includes, among the demesne lands farmed to Michael Stanhope:

> 'One parcel of land called Stonehouse Wong with a close called
> Keighton: and a meadow called Stonehouse Meadow.'

The term 'land' in this context means arable land.

The position of Stonehouse Wong in the rental points to a location on the higher ground, and the entry immediately precedes 'Merpitt' (later called Marlpit), identified as the quarry in the gardens of Hugh Stewart Hall, on the other side of Cut Through Lane. Evidently Stonehouse Wong and Keighton were contiguous. In the rental of about 1554 [35] the entry was similar, but 'with' was omitted, and again no area was given in the main rental. However, the separate tree survey in the same document described Stonehouse Wong as a close containing

40 acres, sometime arable, now pasture, with 30 trees growing in its hedgerows. An undated terrier [36] headed 'The names of all such houses lands tenements closes and pastures as are granted to Mr. Harrington within the town of Lenton' includes:

'One parcel of land called Stonehouse Wong and
One close called Keighton, cont. by estimation 36 acres of land'

Earlier in the schedule is:

'One meadow called Stonehouse Medowe 8 acres of meadow'

Evidence from later centuries confirms the identification of Stonehouse Wong as the land that later formed most of the western half of the original campus of the University College at Highfields. In 1608 [37] it was subdivided into three closes:

'One closure of arable land called Stanhouse Wong, now in the occupation of Emery Waplington, containing...6 acres [38]
One other closure called Stanhouse Wong, now in the occupation of William Kirke, containing.....10 acres
One other closure called Stanhouse Wong, now in the occupation of the said William, cont. ...'(included above)

This area of 16 acres is somewhat larger than that arrived at in the undated survey notes of the early 17th century, which was 13a.0.35 but also in three closes [39] . As a whole Stonehouse Wong was elongated, with ends measuring 15 and 24 perches, and the sides 114 and 103 perches (see Figure 20). One end was called the Beeston end and the longer side was 'next ye medo'. Stonehouse Meadow was also very elongated, with ends of 6 and 12 perches, and both sides of 87 perches, giving an area of about 4a.3.23 according to the survey notes. It is now mainly occupied by the western reach of the University Park lake.

If Stonehouse Wong with Keighton extended to 36 acres in about 1600, the latter would appear to have had an area of more than 20 acres, exclusive of Little Keightons [40] , and so must have included Bacon Close and Quarrel Close. Stonehouse Wong did not figure under that name later in the 17th century, and it is thought that the name Highfield or Highfields, originally attached to land north of Cut Through Lane and now in the Lenton House estate, was at some stage extended south to at least part of Stonehouse Wong.

Rose Parker held a 21-year lease from Lady Day 1681 on three closes at a yearly rent of £ 16.10s. 0d.. They were described as 'Part of Highfield Closes', and consisted of about 28 acres, thus:

'Part of a field or close of pasture....the Highfield Close 16 acres [41]
Piece or parcel of the Highfield Close next the Field 12 acres'.

In 1731 [42] the same land was part of Dame Sarah Winford's jointure and was described as:

'Part of Highfields Pasture 16 acres
Part of Highfields Close next the Field 12 acres.'

'The Field' here must mean the Abbey Field, the next item :

'Abbey Fields, pastures 200 acres'

It is almost certain, therefore, that this pair of closes later formed the land of Lenton House, with the 12-acre field, called the Grass Field in the early 19th century, on the north-west side where the East Midland (Jesse Boot) Conference Centre now stands. The survey notes of the early 17th century include (preceding Stonehouse Wong) Highfield 'next to ye Abbey field' on one side, and with its ends next to 'ye lane' and 'Cidgie' (which may represent Cun[nin]gre, the handwriting being very poor and many words abbreviated). The area was 15a.3.05, but in view of the description of the location it should probably be equated with the 12-acre field called The Grass Field rather than the field of 16 acres.

There were two other closes called Highfield Close in 1684 [43]. They were:

'A piece of meadow ground being the nether part of the Highfield
Close next Beeston, occupied by Thomas Henson 10 acres
A piece of pasture ground, part of the Highfield Close,
occupied by William Smith or his assigns 10 acres

Thomas Henson also occupied a close or piece of pasture ground called Hilley Close, of 7 acres, which is probably to be identified as the later Hill Closes, on part of which Florence Boot Hall now stands, and which bordered on Beeston. Thomas Henson's 10 acres of meadow may have been part of the former Stonehouse Wong and Stonehouse Meadow, although it might have been the land on the west side of Beeston Lane which eventually became part of the Lenton Grove estate and on which Cavendish and Willoughby Halls are now built.

When offered for sale in 1901 the Highfield estate included about 59 acres on the valley side, of which North Park (17 a.) and South Park (c. 26 a.) made up 43 acres [44]. This would be about the combined area of Stonehouse Wong, a Keighton close held with it, and Stonehouse Meadow. Reference to Smythe's map of 1632 [45] suggests that land south-east of the Portland Building originally formed one of the Keighton closes, though by 1798 it had long been in the Milward estate.

Marl Pit

The palpably artificial hollow of which Hugh Stewart Hall tennis courts now make use, and which was an attractive feature of the grounds of Lenton Hall in the early 19th century, originated as a marl pit. In the 1538 rental [46] we find (in translation) 'A parcel of land called Merpitt up to the New Field'. This item immediately follows Keighton in the document, and is followed by the New Close, extending to the Warren. Reference to the map of field names (Figure 21) indicates the location of Merpitt as the high ground in the vicinity of Hugh Stewart Hall. The rental of about 1554 includes the same items in the same order, and here the entry reads: 'One parcel of land called le merle pitt as far as the New Field' [47]. An undated document of the later 16th century headed 'The names of the pclls of all such houses land closes and pastures as are granted to Mr. Harrington within the towne of Lenton ....' [48] includes 'All the parcel of land called Marlepytt butting the Newe field cont. by estimation 36 acres of land'. Although apparently referring to the same land the considerable area suggests that it extended at least as far west as the vicinity of Lenton House, and it may have included part of the Lenton House estate land. A second mention in the 1554 document describing land use and trees field by field indicated that 'The feyld callyd Marlpit' was arable land, and contained no trees. As will be shown the name Marlpit had been lost from the rentals by 1608.

The marly soils of the Harlequin Formation (see Chapter I) would be productive arable land, especially suitable for growing wheat. The marl pit, at almost the highest point of the outcrop, was ideally placed to supply marl for spreading on the light land in the vicinity, and in particular on to the open New Field, the present 'downland'. It was nearby, and transport would be downslope in all directions. The geological circumstances, with the Clifton fault at the surface within 50 metres, and permeable sandstone beneath the quarry, ensured a dry floor - an important practical advantage. It is supposed that the demand for marl as a soil improver greatly declined when the light-soil arable land of the Abbey Fields - discussed next - was converted to dry pasture at the Dissolution or a little earlier, as made explicit by the wording of the rental of about 1554. Thus the marlpit will have ceased to function as such as early as 1538 except perhaps irregularly on a small scale, although later working for clay for the Keighton kilns is possible but unlikely. Much skerry sandstone incorporated in Lenton Hall haha wall probably came from this quarry as it was tidied up to prepare for the planting of trees as part of the pleasure grounds of the new Lenton Hall in the early 19th century.

The Abbey Fields and the Sixty Acres

The northern side of the present University campus extends for over a mile along Derby Road, which divides it from that part of the former priory demesne north of the road, now the south-west segment of Wollaton Park. These mainly dry, waterless lands with mostly light soils developed on sandstone rocks are of special interest because of their very rapid, even sudden conversion from extensive open field arable cultivation before the suppression of the priory to open grassland particularly suitable for sheep, and managed on a ranching scale. Much of this tract became known collectively as 'the Abbey Fields'. The name Abbey Fields did not occur in the detailed rental of 1538, and neither did it appear in the rental made in about 1554 [49] ; but it was used in 1556 in 'My Lady Stanhope's lease of Lenton Groundes to George Madeley of Taltey, Essex', mentioned earlier [50]. The lease was for 21 years, fine £ 40, annual rent £27.

Included in the demesne land farmed to Michael Stanhope, armiger, but given no areas, rents or valuations in 1538, were the Sixty Acres and the War[r]en, both called 'campo', together with Merpitt (Marlpit) lying alongside the New Field. The New Field appears to have been subdivided, one campo called the New Close running up to the Conyngrye (warren). In the 1554 rental the Warren (Conyngrye) and the Sixty Acres were named, but not the Abbey Fields, which were represented by the lands called the New Field and the New Close, 'formerly Short Dunston' [51] , together with the Great Brome Close of 50 acres. The 1556 lease by Anne Stanhope to George Madeley included 'grounds and closes of pasture' called The Abbey Fields, the Conyngre and Sixty Acres, 'upon which grounds and closes and pastures the flock of sheepe of Wollaton....is kept and pastured'....'And also that part of Avery Walker's close which before time did belong and was pcell of the said Connygre or warren' [52] . It appears that the Willoughbys of Wollaton rented this extensive sheep grazing in the 1540s from Sir Michael Stanhope, and their interest in this tract of land continued at intervals until 1869. Although Henry Willoughby died in 1549 when his sons were children, and the Willoughbys then left Wollaton, the lease of this land in 1556 was to George Madeley or Medeley, who from 1550 to 1558 was guardian to Francis and Margaret Willoughby, and probably leased the land on behalf of the young Thomas, the elder brother who died in 1558 aged 15: so in 1568 his widow assigned the lands to Francis Willoughby when he attained his majority.

Of the £27 annual rent quoted in Madeley's lease of 1556, £12 was for 'the pastures called the Abbey Fields, the Connyngar, The 60 Acres and the aforesaid part of Avery Walker's close, warren and connies'. This land extended south-east from Derby Road to Cut Through Lane in the east, though not in the west, and it included also land in Wollaton Park westwards from the present Lenton Hurst. The total area was about 270-280 acres according to the field areas given on modern Ordnance Survey 25-inch maps, and it could be regarded as a single sheep walk, with Henry Avery (possibly Avery Walker's son) in 1566 looking after 418 sheep and 149 lambs [53] .

It is not immediately apparent which parts of the area carried the name Abbey Fields, and where exactly the Sixty Acres and the Warren of the 16th and 17th century rentals and terriers were located. Comprehensive remodelling of the demesne lands in the first years of the 19th century, converting fields into parkland and destroying former field boundaries, with no known cartographic record of the earlier patterns, raises difficulties in establishing precise locations on the ground.

The rental of about 1554 covering the whole of Lenton and Radford included the outline of the demesne land held by Anne Stanhope transcribed in Table 8. This included open fields (campo) called the Sixty Acres, the Warren and the New Field, with New Close. A parcel of land called the Marl Pit adjoined the New Field. The 'rental' includes a second schedule of part of the estate recording the number of trees growing in the fields and hedgerows, with some interesting marginal notes on land use history. It makes clear that the New Field included a close called New Close of 30 acres, which had formerly been called Short Dunston [54], and extended as far as the Coningry, and the Great Brome Close containing 50 acres. It is thought that the Great Brome Close - in the early 17th century subdivided into five closes, each including 'Brome' in its name [55] - was essentially the area that later became Lenton Abbey Farm, and the Short Dunston was the area now commonly called 'the downland' between the former Great Brome Close and The Warren. The Warren was an area of irregular shape determined essentially by geology, occupying the higher ground of the outcrop of the Nottingham Castle Formation (Bunter Pebble Beds) between Lenton Hurst, Lenton Firs and Hugh Stewart Hall.

The lands in the northern parts of the campus are discussed again later, but it may be appropriate to confirm here their locations based on later data. An undated late 16th century terrier from between 1587 and 1603 [56] gives the following areas:

'A parcel of land called le Merlepitt abutting the New Field	36 acres
Two pcls of land from the field called the New Close abutting (or extending to) the Conygre	79 acres
One close called the 60 acres	60 acres
One field called the Warren	60 acres'

These areas total some 235 acres, but it will be shown later that the Sixty Acres had an additional 30 acres of probably uncultivable land associated with it. The Great Brome Close is not, apparently, included here. Since Smythe's map of 1632 named Abbey Field at the eastern end, in the angle between Cut Through Lane and Sandy Lane [57], and the Warren would be expected to occupy the pebbly, dry and sometimes barren soils on the higher ground, the old name Sixty Acres might be looked for in the west, possibly in the area of Lenton Abbey farm. The survey notes of the early 17th century [58] include some describing the Sixty Acres which mention a side 'towards Lenton', with 'the other [side] cutting on ye towne field and Cow Close', while the larger end abutted on Wollaton Cunningar. The Town Field mentioned cannot be Beck Field, which could not be on 'the side away from Lenton', and it is impossible to find a location for the Sixty Acres on the eastern side of the demesne, with the Abbey Closes lying south of Beck Field and Abbey Field shown west of it on Smythe's map. However, reference to a Wollaton rental of the later 16th century [59] (before the present Wollaton Park was formed) shows that the Town Field and Cow Close were important areas in Wollaton, and suggests that if the Sixty Acres had one side towards Lenton it probably had three towards Wollaton, and therefore must have lain within the present Wollaton Park. Other documentary evidence confirms this, and the Sixty Acres must be represented on later O.S. maps by the salient of Lenton parish into Wollaton Park, although the boundaries must have been regularized.

A document dated 1575, quoted by J.T.Godfrey in another context [60] sets out the boundary of the manor of Lenton, part of which is described as follows:

> '....leaving the Horse Doles towards a close in the aforesaid Manor of Lenton called [word illegible] Terry's Close and from thence by the Exterior Hedge of a certain Close called the Rounds and then following the Hedge towards [word omitted] called Tuttleberry Gate and from thence by the hedge of a certain close within the aforesaid Manor of Lenton called Broom Close towards....Gate [Derby-gate] and thus by the Hedge of a certain Field belonging to Francis Willougbie Knight of Woollaton....called the Fat Field and so by the Hedge surrounding a Field called the Sixty Acres to the Gate [called] Derby Gate and from the said Gate by the Hedge belonging to our Lady the Queen round one side of the Fields of Lenton towards a wood called Aspley Wood...'

This describes the western boundary of Lenton parish followed northwards from the salient of Beeston parish into Lenton called the Horse Doles between Trent Wong (now Grove Farm) and the Beeston Canal, along the parish boundary past Jervis Close (probably Great Jervis

Close) - not 'Terry's Close' as transcribed by Godfrey - round the Hassocks (now the University Boulevard playing fields) and along the Tottle Brook to the west entrance to the University campus, where Beeston Lane (then Tuttleberry or Tuttle Brook Gate) crosses the now culverted brook; then along the brook (approximately along Woodside Road) to Derby Road near the Priory Hotel. The boundary continued past the hotel - the Fat Field was in Wollaton [61] - and turning east and north-east through the now flooded valley (Wollaton Park lake) to a boundary stone on the golf course just south-east of Wollaton Hall haha wall, it then doubled back to meet Derby Road again at right angles opposite to Lenton Hurst, then continuing north-east along Derby Road, and along the old parish boundary to Aspley. This description precisely fixes the location of the Sixty Acres.

The area of the salient of Lenton parish into Wollaton was about 90 acres, despite its name of Sixty Acres, which referred only to the arable part of it. The survey notes of the early 17th century are puzzling, however, because they show two calculations, one arriving at an area of 53a.3.15 and the second at 71a.2.08 [62] . It is presumed that these two areas were the original arable field and the whole salient including rough, gorsy and wooded land, especially in the areas now occupied by Thompson's Wood and Arbour Hill Wood, and that the boundary formed by the hedge was irregular, and the area changed when the park was formed, the boundary hedge removed and the boundary straightened between boundary stones. . A valuation of the Wollaton estate in 1809 by Jonathan Teal [63] gave the area as about 85 acres (58a. pasture, 27a. wood and pond), while the map by Thomas Sturgess in 1863 [64] showed some 94 acres, comprising Thompson's Wood with 17a.0.24, part of Arbour Hill Wood with 2a.2.17, part of the lake 11a.3.13 and pasture 63a.0.15. The grassland on which ridge and furrow can be seen today, will have been the original open arable field. Sturgess's land area was about 83 acres.

Since the Sixty Acres lay entirely within the present Wollaton Park it follows that the Abbey Fields and the Warren did not together occupy the whole tract between Derby Road and Cut Through Lane from Beck Field to the Tottle Brook, an area of well over 270 acres. The early 17th century survey notes on the Cunningre [65] , about 60 acres in area, indicated that one side, the longest dimension of a quadrilateral, was 'next Wollaton', and one end was 'at ye Corne', which is unidentified. The side was 104 perches long - about 570 yards - so it must have extended along Derby Road from the vicinity of Lenton Hurst north-eastwards to the top of the present Adams Hill, and straight on along the old line of road towards the present entrance to Wollaton Park from Middleton Boulevard. The Warren narrowed southwards [66] , as did the outcrop of the Nottingham Castle pebbly sandstone, the coarse, thin acid soils of which are much less suitable for either arable cultivation or grassland than the soils developed on the lower land of the Lenton Sandstone outcrop. Thus the Warren may have reached as far south-east as Cut Through Lane near the Social Sciences building. The shepherd's small holding taken out of the Warren was said to 'cut on' the Quarrel Close, with a boundary of about 135 yards, while the head, about 90 yards long, cut on 'Keightons' [67] . This would be impossible if the Quarrel Close mentioned here was that identified south-east of Keighton Close, near the tile kilns, and it is possible that the Quarrel Close here refers to the marl quarry in the gardens of Hugh Stewart Hall, In that case the shepherd's smallholding must have been in the vicinity of the Social Science building and its car park.

The early 17th century reference to 'The Abbey Field with ye conygre' [68] suggests that these were contiguous, though possibly with an irregular boundary between them, and not necessarily separated by fencing. Together, and excluding the Sixty Acres, they covered about 200 acres, and after the name 'Warren' disappeared from the records they can be treated as one unit - The Abbey Fields. They extended south-westwards from Sandy Lane (Clifton-Middleton Boulevard) between the old Derby Road and Cut Through Lane about as far as the Clifton fault and Lenton Hall; but the boundary then turned from Cut Through Lane to round the site of Lenton Hall (Marlpit) before running south-westwards again to Beeston Lane and the Tottle Brook, leaving the later Lenton House estate and Lenton Grove estate south-east of it. One of the early 17th century surveys [69] giving the area of 'Highfield' as 15a.3.05, added that one side was 'next th'abby field', and the two ends 'next ye lane' and 'next cidgie' respectively: so this Highfield must have been on the north-west side of Cut Through Lane. The Abbey Field, given an area of only 64a.2.28 in the early 17th century survey notes was said to have a side of 124 perches (660 yards) on the Sixty Acres, and the calculation therefore must relate to land extending south-eastwards from Derby Road between Lenton Hurst and Lenton Abbey as far as the upper part of the slope towards Hugh Stewart Hall and the Education building. The late 16th century terrier mentioned earlier, referring to two parcels from the New Field, together 79 acres, probably included this area with a further, smaller part of the Abbey Fields east of the Warren

There is corroborative evidence that the lands around the later Lenton Abbey farm, west of Beeston Lane, had also been known as part of the Abbey Fields from the later 17th century [Godfrey 1884 209] and their full extent can be calculated from the schedule of lands involved in the sale of 1798 [70]. In the early 17th century this was almost certainly another open field called Great Broom Close. In 1822 [71] Samuel Brownlow aged 77, the oldest person found who knew the priory demesne estate 70 years earlier - in about 1750 - said that the land along Derby Road 'was formerly in two large closes called the Near Abbey Field and the Far Abbey Field'. He testified that 'the Abbey Fields were larger formerly they are now' [in 1822] 'but have since been divided into less inclosures....'. Those inclosures, said to have been in 1684 parts of the Far and Near Abbey Fields were at the 1798 sale:

The Abbey Field next Turnpike Close (2 parts)	13a.0.01
The Abbey Field or Sandy Field (2 parts)	22a.2.20
The Lodge Field (agst. Derby Road)	17a.2.10
The Sand Hill or Sand Hill Field (2 parts)	19a.2.22
The Pitt Field (2 parts)	11a.0.00
Six Acres Close	6a.2.17
Home Abbey Field	11a.1.09
Second Abbey Field	12a.1.18
Hind and Far Abbey Fields	17a.2.12
Turnpike Close or Little Abbey Field	6a.2.24
Total	138a.1.13

If to this area is added about 59 acres for the remainder of Lenton Abbey farm - the closes with names including 'Broom' - the figure is raised to 197a.1.13, or a round figure of 200 acres, which probably represents the full extent of the lands called the Abbey Fields, including the Warren. Of the above list the Lodge Field, running up to the gate to Wollaton Park, with its lodge situated approximately where the park gate from Middleton Boulevard is now located, was mostly incorporated into Wollaton Park in 1822, while much of the Sand Hill was quarried away in 1838, providing the level site for the buildings of the Pure Science Faculty.

To summarize, it would be expected that under conditions of late medieval agrarian technology in the mid-16th century land use would be closely related to physical geography, and especially to drainage, steepness of slope and soil texture and fertility, and documentary evidence confirms this expectation. For example, the Floodplain terrace gravels, secure from frequent flooding, formed traditional arable land, as suggested by such field names as Great and Little Ryecroft, and Wheatcroft, and confirmed by the rental-terrier of c. 1554. They were marked out by field boundaries that could almost double as physiographic boundaries between the gravels and the alluvium a few feet lower, and used as meadow and seasonal grazings - the Cow Pastures and the Feeding or Fatting Pastures and the Littling Meadow, in some parts subject to seasonal flooding. The still lower alluvial ribbons followed by sluggish drainage channels, with the water table near to or at the surface for much of the year, were left in semi-natural low marshy woodland of alder and willow, as in The Rounds, which were later among the so-called 'concealed lands' because they were not included in the rentals, and though reserved to the Crown by the terms of the Crown leases were often regarded by lessees as waste within their own lands.

On the higher ground there was a noteworthy correlation between the large open arable fields of the priory demesne - some with names suggesting 12th or 13th century origins - and the outcrop of the Lenton Sandstone with its open, easily worked soils, more cohesive and retentive than the coarser sandy soils of the Nottingham Castle formation, which was mostly rabbit warren after the Conquest, though amenable in parts to 'strengthening' by dressings of 'marl'. The contrast between the relatively healthy sheep walks established on these dry lands of short turf after their abandonment for arable cropping in the earlier 16th century, and the wetter, lusher cattle lands and meadow of the Trent valley floor, with coarser grasses and the danger to sheep of liver fluke infestation, has been mentioned earlier, and was recognized in the wording of the 16th century leases.

The conversion of arable land to pasture

The marginal notes of the 1554 rental or survey show that although the whole of the northern part of the campus (except 'Marlepitt') was by that time pasture, the conversion of much of it from arable use had taken place relatively recently, and certainly within living memory, and it must have been a consequence of the Dissolution of the priory in 1538, sixteen years earlier. The usual description of such changes of land use in the 1554 rental was (in translation) 'formerly arable, now pasture', or 'sometime arable, now pasture'. For example, the Sixty Acres was 'qoudm arrabil et modo pastur' and the Warren was 'aliqd arr modo pastur'. While no date was given or implied for the change in land use, the use of the term 'terre' in the rental of 1538 implies that the land was then arable land, so that the change must have occurred at about the time of the Dissolution, if not exactly then. It may be recalled that land on the Floodplain terrace gravels of the Trent vale, with names such as Wheatcroft and Ryecroft, as well as Stonehouse Wong on the valley side were also 'formerly' arable land according to this survey. The name New Field including Short Dunston, and the Great Brome Close suggest an extension of arable cultivation into those areas, but at what stage in the development of the priory demesne is difficult to suggest.

On the University campus the 'downland' is one of the least disturbed areas, and displays under suitable conditions of observation a clear and regular pattern of 'ridge and furrow', produced by the medieval system of ploughing strips in open field and surviving from its use as open arable land for several centuries (Figure 22). Similar features are seen even more clearly in Wollaton Park opposite, on the former Sixty Acres. The ridge and furrow on the downland can be seen only under special conditions of two kinds. For a short time after the sun has risen above the horizon between Cripps and Hugh Stewart Halls in midsummer it shines across the downland almost parallel to the ground, and parallel to the line of the slope, so that ground features normally imperceptible become visible by the contrast of light and shade. Though clear enough to the eye when viewed from Derby Hall, the ridge and furrow is too faintly lit by the low sun to make very clear photography of the phenomenon possible, and in such conditions it is not possible to take measurements on the ground. However, in certain conditions of melting light snow cover, as seen in Figure 22, measurements are possible, and show that although individual ridge-furrow widths vary between extremes of 15 and 24 metres the majority are 20 to 22 metres in 'wavelength'. They are clearly plough acres, and they date

Figure 22: Medieval ridge-and-furrow on the 'downland' above Derby Hall picked out by melting light snow cover in 1986
Last ploughed in the early 16th century these particular plough acres were called 'Short Dunstans' and formed part of the New Field. Up-and-down-slope alignment indicates ploughing by oxen. [From a colour photo. by Dr. Duncan Martin]

from the early 16th century at the latest, were probably formed over the several preceding centuries, and have been fading ever since.

The later sixteenth century and the Harrington lease

Although the reversion of the main Crown lease of the former priory demesne (which included Trent Wong and Aspley Hall but excluded the 'Alexander Wright closes') was granted to John Harrington for three lives in 1563, Anne Stanhope continued to enjoy it for a further 24 years. The lease of much of the demesne that she granted to George Madeley for 21 years from 1556, mentioned above [72], was held by Madeley virtually in trust for the under-age Willoughby heirs, and the deed is endorsed to the effect that Mary Madeley, widow of George, assigned the lands to Francis Willoughby Esq. on 22 December 1568. George Madeley had been from 1550 to 1558 the 'guardian' of Francis and Margaret Willoughby after their father's death, and received funds for their board, clothing, education and other needs [73]. Francis Willoughby inherited the Wollaton estate on the death of his elder brother in 1558 while still a minor.

Certain parts of the 'site and demesne' were leased separately from the main grazing lands. Thus in 1573 Anne Stanhope granted a 21-year lease to John Cleveland of Lowdham of parts of the precincts of the former priory that included the mill adjoining the priory site, and the Prior's Meadow [74]. Anne was not, however, appointed bailiff of the Crown's village lands in Lenton in succession to her executed husband in 1552, and it appears that this role passed to Edward Southworth, gent., called 'surveyor of the Queen's lands in Nottinghamshire' [75]. In this position Southworth would have administered the Crown 'Manor of Lenton', including the former estate of the priory in the open fields and village of Lenton east and north of the river

Leen, and he appears to have done so from Aspley Hall, where he was tenant of the 'arbage and pannage' at Aspley Wood in about 1554 [76]. The house itself, perhaps unused since the Dissolution, was decayed, but Southworth probably restored it, and in doing so acted in a high-handed manner by closing the road through Radford that linked it to the former priory [77]. Southworth died in 1573 or soon afterwards [78] and he was certainly not the Crown bailiff in 1581, when on 12 December 24 Elizabeth, James Leycester, as 'bailiff of the manors of Lenton' received chief rents from Sir Francis Willoughby for freehold land owned by him in Lenton [79].

The lease granted to John Harrington for three lives (with his wife Isobel and son John) could not begin before the death of Dame Anne Stanhope in 1589. Unfortunately rentals of the late 16th century which mention 'Mr. Harrington' are undated, and it is not known whether the John Harrington who took possession of the estate in 1589 was father or son, though the latter is more likely. Sir John Harrington was already in 1563 a favourite of the Queen and a powerful figure at Court,, and he would almost certainly have been referred to as Sir John later in the century. One document records 'The names of the parcels of all such houses, lands, tenements, closes and pastures as are granted to Mr. Harrington within the town of Lenton....' [80] and may have been compiled in connection with the younger John Harrington's succession to the Crown lease of the estate.

Associated with this manuscript under the title 'A copy of ye particulars for concealed lands in Notts.' is a second undated document headed 'A note of such conce[a]led land as Ed Stanhope hath gotten from Mr. Har[r]ington' [81]. Edward Stanhope, the second son of Sir Michael and Lady Anne Stanhope, was one of the Commissioners concerned with a perambulation of the Manor of Lenton in 1575, of which Godfrey [1884] published an account in transcript entitled 'Inquisition indented and taken at the Castle of Nottingham ... the 3rd day of October ... 17 Elizabeth ...' [82]. Stanhope may have taken over the grazing lands of the present campus when Francis Willoughby's lease expired in 1577. There is an interesting note in the Willoughby accounts for February 1572-73: 'The same day [26 February] in reward to Mr. Stanhope his connye keeper for taking connyes for my Mr. 3s. 4d.'. The Wollaton and Lenton warrens were adjoining across Derby Road: but this was still during Sir Francis's tenure of Anne Stanhope's lease, and Edward Stanhope's involvement with Lenton both before and after 1577 is not clear. He may have acted as agent for his elderly mother, Dame Anne, in connection with her priory demesne estate.

Although Sir Francis Willoughby had what appears to have been a loan from Harrington in the early 1590s [83] (he had completed the building of Wollaton Hall in 1588) and may have held priory demesne lands then, no deed of lease is known, and there is no sign of the property in the Wollaton estate rental for 1597 [84], the year after Sir Francis died. Sir Francis may have occupied the property on an annual basis, down to his death, and indeed it is known that about 1600 the northern parts of the present campus were occupied by others, for example William Foster and others, followed by John Needham.

The Alexander Wright Closes were not, of course, involved in these arrangements. Immediately Lady Anne Stanhope recovered the Crown lease of them in 1552 she released them to Alexander Wright, who obtained a regular Crown lease in his own name shortly afterwards [85]. In 1583 they were leased by the Crown to Humphrey Hanmer of Radford [86] and in 1588 this lease was renewed for the lives of Hanmer's wife Winifred (widow of Edward Southworth) and sons Philip and Thomas Hanmer [87]. In 1601 the property was leased again by the Crown to Thomas Cowper and Philip and Thomas Hanmer [88] before being purchased from the Crown by William Gregory of Nottingham in 1628 or thereabouts [89].

Despite the changes of ownership there is no evidence that the forms of occupation and use of the former priory demesne, except for the precincts of the priory itself, changed in any significant way during the latter part of the 16th century from those established in mid-century after the Dissolution and the destruction of the priory. The Harrington lease was surrendered in 1603 or 1604 [90] , presumably on the accession of King James I. The site and demesne of the priory were granted by king James in fee farm to Sir Michael Hicks and his heirs on 20 June 1604 [91] , and this marked the beginning of a new chapter in the history of the estate.

NOTES

1. P.R.O. Add. Mss. 6164, f.202. Transcribed in J.T.Godfrey [1884] 151-3
2. N.U.M.D., Mi 1/38/31 [1538]. Cottages, lands etc. in Lenton and Radford, 30 May 30 Henry VIII. Parchment roll, Latin. This document shows Michael Stanhope in possession of the priory demesne lands in the year before he was granted the Crown lease. The rental refers to the 'former priory'.
Only 39 per cent of Lenton Priory's income was yielded by its temporalities, and of these Nottinghamshire accounted for 53 per cent, or 23 per cent of the total income, with Lenton and Radford the chief source and with small contributions from Basford, Awsworth and Newthorpe.
3. N.U.M.D., Mi 1/38/31. Under the heading of 'Terr Dmcal', Michael Stanhope, armiger, for farm of the site of the former priory aforesaid and all barns, dovecotes, gardens, orchards, vineries .... etc. .... £ 38.19s.. The same tenant for farm of one meadow called Trent Wong ... £ 8.
4. For a biographical account of Sir Michael Stanhope see Cornelius Brown [1882] 108-09.
5. The lease was to Michael Stanhope and his wife and their heirs male [Bailey 1853, 401]. Shelford House was destroyed in the Civil War, and its storming, with great loss of life, on 27 October 1645, and the surrounding circumstances are described in detail by J.B.Firth [1916 105-113]. The Stanhope family buried its dead in the Stanhope chapel of Shelford church for a further two centuries.
6. For a photograph of Anne Stanhope's monument at Shelford (opposite p. 46) and notes on the Stanhope family see *Trans. Thoroton Soc.* 7 [1903] 55-62
7. N.U.M.D., Mi 1/38/2, 2 H 8. 'Ye King grants to Mic Stanhope several lands for 21 yeares forfeited by ye treason of Nic Heath, Prior. The grant of Michael Stannop knyght for dyvers lands medowes and parcells of pasture late of ye Monasty of Lenton Henry ye VIIIth ... have granted gyffen and to farm letten and by these presents ... to Michael Stannop esquire ... divers parcels of land meadow and pasture within our lordship or manor of Lenton ...'. It is presumed that 2 H 8 is a copyist's error for 32 H 8, though the document ends 'Witnessed myself at Westminster 11 day of May in the 2nd year of our reynge'. The correct year is almost certainly 1540.
8. N.U.M.D., Mi 1/38/33, which is a copy of part of P.R.O., Rentals and Surveys, Portfolio 24, No. 12 : 'Lenton Monastery - Rental (Eliz. ?)' undated.
9. For example, N.U.M.D., Mi 1/38/41(iii), probably of the early 17th century.
10. L.A.O., 1 PG 6/2 (1631) and L.A.O., 1 PG 3/3/1/3 - 'A rental of Lenton made upon my marriage 1663'.
11. N.U.M.D., Mi 1/38/4. 'My Lady Stanhope's lease of Lenton Groundes to George Madeley for 21 years, fine £ 40, paying £ 27 yearly: 2-3 Ph and Mary, 1 April'.
12. N.A.O., RD 3 L (1632))
13. P.R.O., MR 1142. Photograph in N.A.O., XF 1/1 to 6.
14. N.A.O., BE 2 S undated. N.U.M.D., Mi 3 E 4.
15. N.U.M.D., Mi P 6 (map) and Mi 2 S 3 (schedule) 1863
16. N.U.M.D., Accession 795/2 (1881), 650 (1893) and 23 (1901).
17. N.A.O., RD 4 L.
18. N.U.M.D., Mi 1/38/41 (i) to (vii) undated
19. N.U.M.D., Mi 1/38/40 undated (Elizabeth)
20. P.R.O. Rentals and Surveys, Portfolio 24, No. 12, p. 13 undated, circa 1554.
21. N.U.M.D., Mi 1/38/2, 2 H 8. (Date thought to be 32 H 8 - 1540)
22. N.U.M.D., Mi 1/38/40(ii) undated. 'A copy of particulars for concealed lands in Notts.'.
23. ibid.
24. N.U.M.D., Mi 1/38/14 Quitclaim Widdoson to Stanhope. The document records the release by Gabriell Wydoson, gent. of Nottingham to Lady Anne Stanhope of the lease she had demised to John Cleveland, deceased, for 21 years at £ 7 a year in 1573.
25. N.U.M.D., Mi 1/38/18(i) (1609)
26. Reprinted in Godfrey [1884] 316-326
27. P.R.O., Rentals and Surveys, Portfolio 24, No. 12 (c. 1554)
28. N.U.M.D., Mi 1/38/40(ii) undated
29. P.R.O., Rentals and Surveys, Portfolio 24, No. 12 (c. 1554)
30. In the 1640s Richard Bacon rented a cottage in Lenton - see L.A.O., 2 PG 3/1/9. He was named in the Protestation Returns of 1642.

31. Great Broom Close, later subdivided, formed the western end of the Abbey Fields, and much later most of the land of Lenton Abbey farm. The Far Broom Close later formed the nucleus of the Lenton Grove estate.
32. See, for example, the Crown Lands survey of 1608 - P.R.O., Misc. Books, Land Revenue 2/211 CP 2940 ff. 105 to end for Lenton and Radford: 'Survey of the manor', 5 James I.
33. N.U.M.D., Mi 3 E 4 (1867) and N.U.M.D., Wadsworth 50.
34. N.U.M.D., Mi 1/38/31 (1538)
35. P.R.O., Rentals and Surveys, Portfolio 24, No. 12 (c. 1554)
36. N.U.M.D., Mi 1/38/40(i) undated
37. P.R.O., Misc. Books, Land Revenue 2/211 CP 2940
38. N.U.M.D., Mi 1/38/31 (1538)
39. N.U.M.D., Mi 1/38/41(iv) undated
40. Stonehouse Wong is given 13 - 14 acres in the survey notes (ibid.), which by subtraction gives about 22 acres for Keighton.
41. N.U.M.D., Wadsworth 50. N.U.M.D., Mi 3 E 4 (1867) Abstract of title.
42. N.U.M.D., Wadsworth 51 (1830) 'Copy parcels in the deed of 14th April 1731....'.
43. N.U.M.D., Wadsworth 50 and Mi 3 E 4.
44. N.U.M.D., Accession 23 (1901). Map and schedule of the Highfield estate, to be sold by auction.
45. N.A.O., RD 3 L. Richard Smythe's map of the lordship of Lenton and Radford, 10 July 1632
46. N.U.M.D., Mi 1/38/31 (1538)
47. P.R.O., Rentals and Surveys, Portfolio 24, No. 12 (c. 1554)
48. N.U.M.D., Mi 1/38/40(i) undated
49. N.U.M.D., Mi 1/38/31 (1538), Rental of Lenton, taken May 1538. N.U.M.D., Mi 1/38/33 undated (c.1554): 'Rental of lands belonging to ye Monastery ...' - dated from internal evidence in the original document of which this is a partial copy (P.R.O., Rentals and Surveys 24/12)
50. N.U.M.D., Mi 1/38/4 (1556)
51. The origins and meaning of the name Short Dunstons is not known. It may have been connected in some way with Dunston, Derbyshire, to which the monks were moved on occasions when the demesne was taken over by the Crown (see Chapter II). Tithe lambs from Dunston may have grazed the stubble on these lands, which were 'short acres'.
52. N.U.M.D., Mi 1/38/4 (1556). Avery Walker was one of the first pair of churchwardens at Lenton, whose names were recorded in 1552.
53. *Historical Manuscripts Commission, Report on the Middleton Papers* [1911] 418
54. P.R.O., Rentals and Surveys, Portfolio 24, No.12 (c.1554)
55. N.U.M.D., Mi 1/38/41 undated (early 17th century). Survey notes.
N.U.M.D., Wadsworth 52 - copy of the survey of 1798
56. N.U.M.D., Mi 1/38/35 undated (c. 1600): 'Coppy of the Rentall of Lenton Abbey', pp. 7 and 8. On p. 7 'The rentall of the demesne of Lenton Abbey by Mr. Jo. Harrington: ho: thereof and then by quartr and yeare lett so ...'. On internal evidence the date is probably between 1597 and 1603. An identical copy (N.U.M.D., Mi F 10/5) is given an index date of 1636, but on the evidence of tenants' names it appears to be much earlier.
57. N.A.O., RD 3 L. 'A mappe of ye Lordshippe of Lenton and Radford taken the tenthe day of Julye anno 1632 by me, Richard Smythe, surveyor'. (With a scale of perches).
58. N.U.M.D., Mi 1/38/41(i).
59. N.U.M.D., Mi F 10/5 undated (probably late 16th or early 17th century. The Wollaton rental is on p. 9.
60. J.T.Godfrey [1884]27-31, quoting Mon. Ang.v.110: 'Inquisitio tangems divisiones manerii de Lenton per metas et Bundas a manerio de Wilford. Mich. Eliz. ro.381. The document is from the King's Remembrancer's office in the Exchequer: 'Inquisition indented and taken at the Castle of Nottingham in the County aforesaid the 3rd day of October in the 17th year of the reign of our Lady Elizabeth ...'.
61. N.U.M.D., Mi F 10/5
62. N.U.M.D., Mi 1/38/41
63. N.U.M.D., Mi S 3 (1809). 'A valuation of the estates ... of Henry, Lord Middleton ... in 1809 ... by Jonathan Teal'.
64. N.U.M.D., Mi P 6 (1863)
65. N.U.M.D., Mi 1/38/41
66. N.U.M.D., Mi 1/38/41
67. ibid. See also Mi 1/38/4
68. ibid.
69. N.U.M.D., Mi 1/38/41(iv)
70. N.U.M.D., Wadsworth 52
71. N.U.M.D., Mi 1/16/1a (1823). Since the case was intended for the Lent Assizes it is assumed that evidence was collected mainly in 1822.

72. N.U.M.D., Mi 1/38/4 , 'My Lady Stanhope's lease of Lenton Groundes to George Madeley for 21 years, fine £40, paying £27 yearly, 2-3 Ph and Mary, 1 April'. It included the valley floor pastures (£15) and 'other grounds and closes of pasture called the Abbey Field, the Conungree and Syxt(y)e Acres (£ 12).

73. *Historical Manuscripts Commission, Report on the Middleton Papers* [1911] 46.

74. N.U.M.D., Mi 1/38/14

75. Cameron [1975] followed Godfrey [1884] in supposing that the demesne estate was forfeit with the execution of Sir Michael Stanhope in 1552, and that Edward Southworth was thereafter responsible for administering the demesne lands as well as the rest of the Crown's estate in Lenton, citing in support Mi 1/38/5 and Mi 1/13/5, documents relating to the farming of the tithes and Edward Southworth's will respectively. But Sir Michael had changed the terms of his lease long before his execution, and his widow continued to enjoy the estate [Barnes 1987].

76. P.R.O., 24/12 (c. 1554) p. 20.

77. N.U.M.D., Mi 1/38/10, 23 April 12 Elizabeth (1569). The sayings of divers witnesses for the proof of the usage of an higheway through the myddle of the towne of Radforthe ... leading by the house of Mr. Edward Southworthe the Queen's surveyor, and now by him enclosed to the great annoyance of the said town and countrie thereabouts'. N.U.M.D., Mi 1/38/6, 5 Eliz., records the lease of a cottage belonging to the monastery of Lenton' to William Houtton by Edward Southworth 'of Aspley near Radford'.

78. Southworth's will was dated 25 June 1573. N.U.M.D., Mi 1/13/5

79. N.U.M.D., Mi 5/169/103/5. As early as 1571 (13 Elizabeth) Francis Willoughby paid chief rents due to the Crown to Mr. Brodbent and not to Southworth. N.U.M.D., Mi 1/38/36.

80. N.U.M.D., Mi 1/38/40(i) undated, gives the names of the properties granted to Harrington, and they are those of the main demesne together with Trent Wong, which in c. 1554 had been held with the Alexander Wright Closes.

81. N.U.M.D., Mi 1/38/40(ii)

82. Inquisitio tangens divisiones manerii de Lenton per metas at Bundas a manerio de Wilford. Mich. Eliz. ro.381: Mon. Ang. v.110.

83. N.U.M.D., Mi E 1/3 - a notebook on Wollaton estate matters - contains notes such as: 'Nov. 1st. Mr. Harrington 1591 550'; and 'Michaelmas: to Mr. Harrington # 550. Quer if this may be continued ?'
This may relate to a loan associated with the building of Wollaton Hall, or Sir Francis's industrial speculations, and seems to be too large to represent accumulated arrears on land rents.

84. N.U.M.D., Mi R 145 (1597). By this time others probably leased the former demesne lands after the death of Sir Francis, who certainly held Trent Wong in 1586, just before Lady Anne Stanhope's death, and his 1556 lease may have been extended beyond 1577. N.U.M.D., MI A 60/5

85.. P.R.O., Rentals and Surveys 24/12, p.13. The lease was for 21 years.

86. L.A.O., 2 PG 1/7/2/5 records the grant of this lease on the occasion of its surrender. It was dated 15 March 3(0) Elizabeth.

87. L.A.O., 2 PG 1/7/2/3: Letters Patent, lease for 3 lives from Queen Elizabeth to Winifred Hanmer, widow, Philip Hanmer and Thomas Hanmer her sons ... Fine of £ 20 and surrender of former lease.

88. Lease dated 24 July, 43 Elizabeth (1601) from the Crown to Thomas Cowper, Philip Hanmer and Thomas Hanmer, gents.. Quoted in an inspeximus of Letters Patent, L.A.O., 1 PG 2/8/1/1, 20 May 4 Charles (1628).

89. The closes are listed with their individual tenants and rents in William Gregory's rental of 1631 - L.A.O., 1 PG 6/2. The inspeximus of the previous note may have been associated with their acquisition by Gregory.

90. Godfrey [1884] gave the date as 1604, but without a supporting reference.

91. Lawson Lowe [1871 12] stated that '... King James the First on 20th June 1604 granted the site and demesne of Lenton Priory to William Hicks Esq., a descendant of Sir Ellis Hicks'. This incorrect. The grant was to William's father.

CHAPTER IV

THE SEVENTEENTH CENTURY

Sir Michael Hicks' purchase of 1604

The death of Queen Elizabeth, the last of the Tudors, brought a new dynasty, the Stuarts, to the throne of England, and a new owner to the estate of the priory demesne. Sir Michael Hicks, a son of Robert Hicks, a wealthy London mercer descended from a Gloucestershire family was granted the priory site and demesne in fee farm in 1604. A London barrister and mercer, he had purchased the estate of Ruckeholte Manor near Leyton, Essex, which he made his home, and also bought Beverston Castle, Gloucestershire, which later became the chief seat of the Hicks family. He was the elder brother of Sir Baptist Hicks, knighted by King James and raised to the peerage as Baron Hicks and Viscount Camden in 1629. Sir Michael himself was Secretary to Lord Burghley, the Lord High Treasurer, to whom he was mainly indebted for his advancement, and who was godfather to Sir Michael's eldest son, William. Sir Michael died at Ruckeholte Hall in 1612, aged 69. For seven years after his death, until William came of age, Sir Michael's widow, Dame Elizabeth, as his guardian, was effectively the owner of the estate of Lenton priory demesne, and received the rents. She died in 1634, and was buried alongside her husband at Leyton.

While Sir Michael held the estate for only 8 years, his son ,Sir William Hicks 'the elder' had it for 68, until his death in 1680, aged 84. He was created baronet in 1619 on reaching his majority, and in 1625 married at Drayton, Middlesex, Margaret, the eldest daughter of Lord Paget of Beaudesert. She was interred in Henry VII's Chapel, Westminster Abbey in 1652. Sir William the elder was followed by Sir William Hicks 'the younger', his son, who, it is said, was knighted by King Charles II when he was being entertained at Ruckeholte after hunting in Epping Forest. He married Marthagues, eldest daughter and co-heiress of Sir Henry Coningsby of North Mimms, Hertfordshire, and they had 13 children. Both father and son suffered for their devotion to the Royalist cause, especially in the Civil War, and were compelled to alienate much of their estates. Although the elder Sir William died still owning the Lenton priory demesne estate, four years later in 1684 Sir William Hicks the younger and Dame Marthagues sold to Thomas Winford in two parts 'the manor of the priory demesne, with the site, circuit and precinct of the dissolved priory of Lenton, and 2 messuages, 3 cottages, 2 tofts, a water mill, 400 acres of arable land, 200 acres of meadow, 100 acres of pasture and 200 acres of furze and heath ... in Lenton and Radford' for £ 9,650. This area, of the order of 900 acres in total, is excessive when compared with the aggregated areas given in the actual survey for the sale [1], but it is not known whether any land in Radford itself was included.

The Crown lands survey of 1608

A description of the estate derived from the survey made for the sale of 1684 forms part of the closing section of this chapter, and is the starting point from which to follow the devolution of ownership and tenancy and the evolution of the landscape of the estate through the 18th century and into modern times. But a picture of the estate as it was when it came into the possession of the Hicks family is best obtained from the nationwide survey of Crown lands made in 1608 [2]. This survey in Lenton and Radford was comprehensive, for the Crown owned as chief lord not only the demesne of the former priory in its narrower sense, but also the priory's other lands let and leased to the villagers of Lenton and Radford and surrendered as escheat to the Crown at the Dissolution, as well as the lesser area in Lenton that had remained in the hands of the king when William Peverel was granted the property with which he endowed the new priory in the early 12th century. The Crown survey and rental of 1608 is therefore useful in tracing the residences and other property of those who rented parts of the former demesne south and west of the river Leen, including the present University campus (Tables 9 and 10 and Figure 23).

It is disappointing to find that two early 17th century maps including Lenton, which might have been expected to add significantly to an interpretation of the survey data of 1608 are of only very limited value. The earlier map of the two, of 'Sherwood Forest', which extended into Lenton, omits all detail west of the river Leen, to which, apparently, the Forest did not extend. Further, in the area it covers the map has a severely cracked surface, with parts of the parchment surface missing altogether through flaking, so that it is legible only in parts and with difficulty [3]. This is especially tantalizing since its date, 1609, would have made it a valuable adjunct to the 1608 survey - though not, it is true, in respect of most of the University campus, to which it did not extend. The second map is that of the Lordship of Lenton and Radford by Richard Smythe dated 1632 [4] (Figure 24). Unfortunately this, too, fails to include much of the area of the present campus, and it has been mutilated by a partial covering of heavy, opaque green paint which makes reading of the annotation difficult on the original, and virtually impossible on a photocopy. The Smythe map, though crudely drawn and with much distortion, is nevertheless useful in outlining the boundaries of such areas as those named as Keighton Closes, Abbey Closes and Lentonford Meadows accurately enough to be transposed on to modern maps.

The Crown lands survey, with the formal date of 28 September 1608, was made four years after Sir Michael Hicks purchased the estate of the priory demesne. Although in 1608 there were numerous Crown leases of land, farms and houses in Lenton township east and north of the river Leen, and including the village of Lenton, the former priory demesne continued to be held in only two leases, as immediately after the Dissolution, a tenurial division that persisted down to the 20th century. The holdings of Sir Michael Hicks, headed 'Lenton demesnes', are listed in Appendix 8 and summarized in Table 9. The 'Alexander Wright closes' described in the previous chapter, also figured as one group in the 1608 survey, which showed that Philip Hanmer, gen., held them by Letters Patent dated 24 July, 43 Elizabeth (1601) [5], together with a mansion house and a number of houses and tenements in Lenton and Radford occupied by various sub-tenants. The eleven closes and two parcels of land together called the Alexander Wright closes are listed in Table 10. Unlike almost all other land holdings included in the 1608 survey none of these have a named occupier, and it is therefore supposed that Philip Hanmer let the closes individually for annual or even shorter terms.

Philip Hanmer also held in 1608 six houses and tenements in Lenton by virtue of a Crown lease for 41 years granted to his mother, Winifred Hanmer on 1 October 37 Elizabeth (1595). Philip was the elder of the two surviving sons of Humphrey Hanmer of Radford by his wife

Table 9 .
Sir Michael Hicks' tenants in Lenton in 1608

Lands of the former Lenton Priory demesne occupied by the 17 tenants of Sir Michael Hicks in 1608, with areas in acres and roods.

Tenant / Land	Area
Jervase Eyre	
Site of 'manor'	4.
Mansion house	
Brickhouse cottages	
Dayhouse Close	2. 2
Dayhouse	
Lea Closes	4.
Gorsey Close	26.
Alderman Richard Hurte of Nottingham	
Great Ledgett Wong	15. 1
Little Tamworth	6.
Abbey Pinfold	1 perch
Robert Nixe	
Cow Close	30.
Rye Close	30.
Little ...[Littling ?]	28.
Doe Park	1. 1
Ashoult	1. 1
Blotoft Pool (water)	
Trent Wong	100.
Robert Nixe with Richard Johnson	
Great Jervis Close	6.
Jacob Leicester	
Littling Hook	2.
Ludovic Oxley	
Carleholme	7.
Carleholme	5.
Emery Waplington	
Stanhouse Wong	6.
Sarah Foster	
Rushy Close	6.
William Stamp	
Mill (adjoining priory site)	
Mill house	
Kiln Yard	1. 2
Prior's Meadow	2. 1
Roger Howton	
Abbey Field and Conygre	80.
Rye Close	12.
Tamworth Close	16.
Widow Brockett	
Sixty Acres Close	60.
Roland Dan	
Brome Close	20.
William Kirk	
Stanhouse Wong in 2 parts	10.
Thomas Markham	
Little Brome Close	8.
Calf Close	
Christopher Sprintall	
Dovecote and barn, 9 bays	
Wheat Croft	20.
Highfield	20.
Richard Cawton	
Great Fatt Pasture	35.
The Rounds adjoining	
Little Fatt Pasture	16.
The Rounds adjoining	
Alice Sturton and William Davye	
The Greens	4.

Gorsey Close, named under Jervase Eyre above, was allowed by Sir Michael Hicks in 1609 to Mr. Palmer of London, his agent and courier.

Winifred, earlier the wife of Edward Southworth discussed in Chapter III above. Winifred received all Southworth's lands in Lenton and Radford (except Willowholme Close) for life after his death in 1573, together with the house where he lived, most probably Aspley Hall. Winifred survived Humphrey, and her will of 31 October 1604 named her stepdaughter, Ann Southworth, as well as her own five daughters and two sons, Philip and Thomas Hanmer, who were placed under the care of Sir William Hanmer of Flintshire [Godfrey 1884 277].

Although part of the main demesne estate appears to be missing from the Crown survey schedule of 1608, the existing data are sufficient to indicate an incoherent pattern of land holding by the sub-tenants of Sir Michael Hicks, as well as by those with Hanmer's Alexander

Table 10.
Philip Hanmer's lands on the former priory demesne in 1608

The 'Alexander Wright Closes' listed among the lands of Philip Hanmer of Radford in the survey of Crown lands in 1608.

	Area	Rent	Value
A close of meadow called Leget Wong	8a.	40s.8d	£5. 6s 8d
A close of pasture called Cook Close	4a.		2. 0s 0d
A close of pasture called Glasshouse Close	4a.	26s.8d	2. 0s 0d
A close of pasture called Little Kightons	8a.	26s.8d	4. 0s 0d
A close of pasture called Great Mare Close	6a.	20s.0d	3. 0s 0d
A close of pasture called Bacon Close	4a.	66s.0d	2. 0s 0d
A close of pasture called Quarrel Close	1a.2r.		15s 0d
A close of pasture called Little Mair Close	3a.	10s.0d	1.10s 0d
A close of pasture called Jervis Close	3a.	13s.4d	1.10s 0d
A close of pasture and meadow called Edmunds Close	6a.	33s.4d	4. 0s 0d
A close of pasture called Great Bulmer Close	3a.		1.10s 0d
Meadow in Lenton	4a.	14s.0d	2. 0s 0d
Parcel of meadow adjoining	1a.		13s 4d

Notes on the above schedule

Unlike almost all other land holdings included in the survey of 1608 none of these closes had a named occupier. It is therefore presumed that Philip Hanmer let the closes individually for annual or even shorter terms.

The Glasshouse Close (or Yard) and probably the Cook Close were parts of the site of the former priory, north of the Leen.

The five closes from Little Keightons to Little Mare Close were in-cluded in William Gregory's rental of 1631 as 'My owne Rent for Kightons and other land £1.12s. 0d.' (half year).

Jervis (or Blotoff) Close occupied by Nicholas (1631) and Thomas Charlton of Chilwell (1651,1657,1662,1664) was purchased by Thomas Charlton in about 1670. [L.A.O., 1 PG 3/3/1/5 - Deed of revocation]

Edmunds or Edmondson's Closes were called 'The Mortons' in 3 closes in 1664 and 'Morton Closes' in 1684. They were occupied by Philip Willoughby in 1631, by John Wood, gent. in 1651 (when in 4 closes 'lying between Lenton Meadows and the Cheaney Lane') 1662 and 1664.

Great Bulmer Close lay 'between the river Leen and the Legett Wong',and was held with Plumtre Orchard. It was shared between William Towle and William Leicester in 1631, held by Francis Mathews, the vicar in 1651, shared between Richard Goodwin and Widow H....son in 1657 and held by Barnaby Wartnaby, gent. in 1664.

The 1-acre parcel of meadow that joined 'to the monastery wall on the north, Duck Meadow to the south' was also called Stonewall Close. It was held by Francis Mathews in 1631 and by Richard Smith in 1657.

Jervis or Gervas Close lay 'on the far side of the Abbe grounds joining to Littling Ditch on the east (Blotoff Dyke) and Great Jervis Close on the north'.

Wright closes (Figure 23). The tenancies, with one possible exception, did not represent viable farm units, but parcels of land let to farmers holding other land and living elsewhere. The traditional English nucleated village containing all the farmsteads of the township's yeomen, as well as the cottages and crofts of the labourers and artisans, with shares in the surrounding open arable fields and meadows and on the common grazings, remained as the dominant form of rural organization until the 18th century, when general inclosure began. It is true that the mansions of landowners were often set in parks adjoining the village, and in Lenton the priory and its demesne were their equivalent: but here the landowners were absentees from the Dissolution through the 16th, 17th and 18th centuries after the destruction of the priory community in 1538. For at least two centuries there was no ready form of land organization to replace that of the priory, and to Michael Hicks and Philip Hanmer and their successors the estate represented simply a source of investment income, essentially unmanaged and to be exploited. As might be expected from its earlier tenurial history the whole area west and south of the river Leen to the boundary between Lenton and Beeston parishes was virtually uninhabited. The Dayhouse was probably the only permanent dwelling there, for the house and cottages held by Jervase Eyre were on the site of the former priory across the river, and the 'Barn Houses' were not formed by conversion until almost a century later.

Some landholders of 1608

Some of Sir Michael Hicks' tenants in 1608 clearly did not themselves farm the land that they held, but sub-let further to under-tenants. Among these tenants were Jervase Eyre and Richard Hurte. Jervase (or Gervase) Eyre, called 'gent', was probably one of the Rampton Eyres, a military family originally from Derbyshire, which acquired Rampton because Sir Gervase Eyre married a co-heiress of John Babington. Rampton Manor had been held by the Malovels, and then by the Stanhopes, and the Babingtons had it through the marriage of Sir Michael Stanhope's eldest sister, Rampton having been the Stanhopes' base before the Dissolution [Jacks 1881 103-07: Train 1969/1973]. Sir Gervase of Rampton was killed at the siege of Newark in 1644. A record of the marriage of Jervase Eare to Isabella Bell at Lenton on 21 April 1585 is unlikely to refer to the same person, but might refer to the Jervase Eyre of the 1608 survey. Alderman Richard Hurte of Nottingham who held over 20 acres from Hicks, was particularly interested in mills. He held the tithes of 'Dalies mill', the malt mill, and also held Kirkmill and land in Radford [7]. 'Hurte's Mill' on the river Leen, just north of the Derby Road bridge at Hillside, later called Ingram's Mill, is marked and named on the Sherwood Forest map of 1609.

Robert Nixe of Nottingham was a substantial property owner, but probably farmed his land on the floor of the Trent vale from Wilford, especially since he was the tenant of Trent Wong. He is discussed further below. James Leicester had property in Lenton through Crown leases of 1588 and 1589 [8] - a house occupied by himself and five other houses, four of them occupied, respectively by Thomas Worthington (with a bovate of arable land and common grazing rights), Thomas Smedley, Thomas Bosworth and Thomas Windley. Nixe also held by a 'charter' of 1583 a house, with land in the common fields, occupied by Matthew Greene, and further tofts or parcels of land acquired by Letters Patent of 1607, and occupied by others.

Francis Matthews, vicar of Lenton, in 1609 held 14 acres of meadow, arable and pasture land, and 16 acres of arable land distributed among all six of the open arable fields of Lenton and Radford, as well as other land near the vicarage, and including Launder Green, Le Kitchen 'in the same place', and 'Beadhouse ground' [9], all parts of the former priory precinct. The vicar also held various lands by Letters Patent, and a large house of seven bays of building, with a barn, a cowhouse and other buildings and associated common meadow and arable land in all six open arable fields of Lenton and Radford by an indenture granted by the Prior of Lenton before the Dissolution. He figured in Sir Percival Willoughby's rental discussed below, holding lands that had been tenanted in 1608 by Ludivic Oxley, who himself occupied a 'mansion house' in Lenton village., with a barn, a stable and other buildings, and with enclosed farm land and pasturage rights.

Roger Howton in 1608 occupied over 200 acres of former priory demesne land, including much of the northern part of the present University campus. Also, by Letters Patent of 1607, he had his own house and farm buildings in Lenton village, with nearby arable land and with pasturage rights, together with another house, a 'workhouse' and a barn, with common pasturage rights, occupied by John Reason. Howton was also the tenant of a cottage, barn and associated buildings, with pasturage rights for three plough oxen and one horse in Lenton Holmes, and for 15 sheep on the common arable fields, through Letters Patent granted to William Stevenson, also in 1607. These and other examples show that the former priory demesne lands in 1608 were chiefly, in effect, extensions of the farms of the more prosperous yeomen of Lenton village, and were used chiefly as peripheral grazing and meadow land.

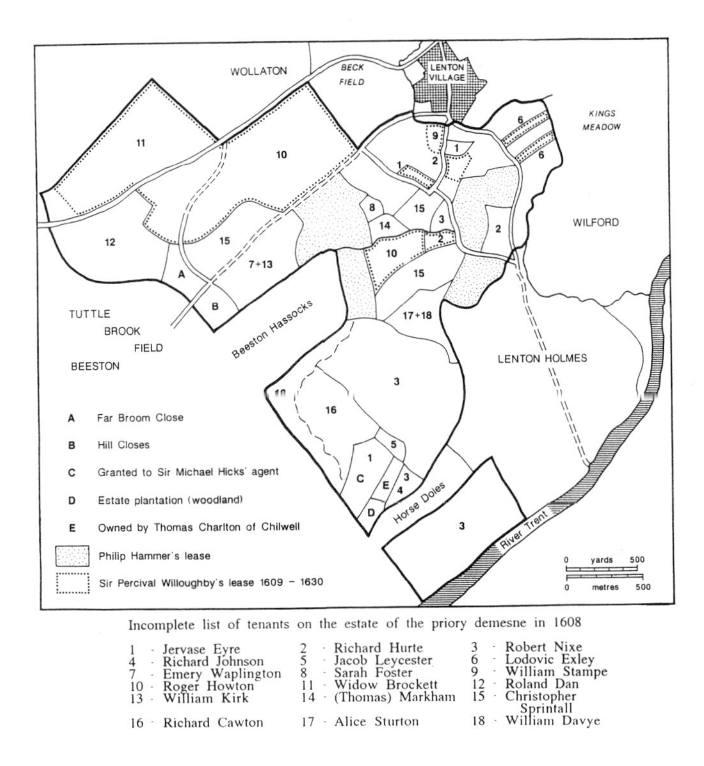

Figure 23: Tenants of land on the former priory demesne in 1608

The records of the burleymen discussed below, show that in the early 17th century there were 60 to 65 'farmers', large and small, in Lenton. An undated rental, probably of about 1600 [10] , relating to the estate of John Harrington - the former priory demesne - excluding 'Mr. Stanhope's concealment' and Aspley Hall, named 46 persons paying rent. In 1608 the survey named only 19 holders or tenants of the demesne lands, and two were only co-tenants. Whether or not Harrington let land directly to farmers while Hicks often did not, it is clear that the 1608 survey does not provide a full picture of the degree of fragmentation involved in the use of the former demesne. This is well demonstrated in the case of the lands held by Jervase Eyre in 1608, which when leased by Sir Percival Willoughby were in 1630 divided among several occupiers who actually cultivated the 28 acres [11] .

The total area of Sir Michael Hicks' Lenton estate according to a summation of the areas given in the 1608 survey was about 566 acres, including the 100 acres of Trent Wong. At the sale of 1684 discussed below the total area was just over 800 acres, and the terrier of 1731 gave 710 acres, excluding the 90 acres (the Sixty Acres) sold in 1698. The shortfall of over 230 acres in the 1608 figures probably has several causes. One was the exclusion of 'waste' land, for example in 'the Rounds' - which was named but no area given - and 'the Greens', and land around the Sixty Acres. There was also a general under-estimation of areas, especially of the larger units. The greatest uncertainty however relates to the Abbey Fields, in which the Great Broom Close is certainly not fully represented, while the 'Abbey Field and Conygre', given 80 acres, is greatly under-estimated. This may involve each of the reasons already suggested, but the discrepancy may also involve transcription error. The figure given was four score, which would be written CC/iiii; but CC/viii (or 160 acres) or CC/ix (180 acres) would be more realistic. For such reasons any map of landholding in 1608 based on presently available evidence, has to be interpreted with very great reserve.

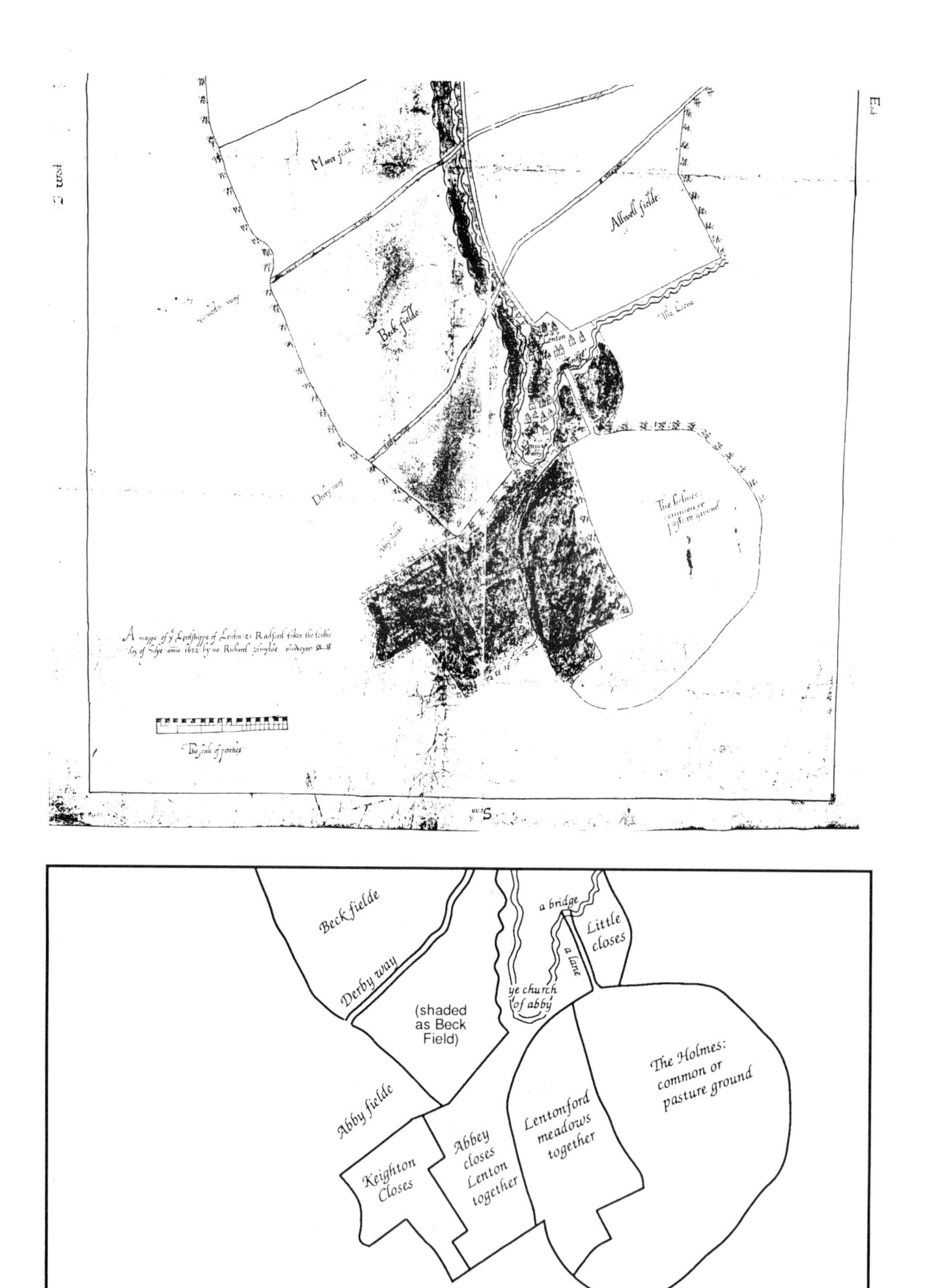

Figure 24: Part of Richard Smythe's map of the Lordship of Lenton and Radford, 1632

Reduced. Some writing is illegible when copied. (Courtesy of Notts. Archives Office [RD 3 L])

Sir Percival Willoughby's lease, 1609-1630

Around 1600, under John Harrington, William Foster occupied the 'Conigree' (Warren) and the Sixty Acres for an annual rent of £ 23, while Richard Hill and Anthony Trueman shared the Abbey Fields equally, with a combined rent of £ 15.10s. 0d., a total of £38.10s.0d. for the three items. Later, under the new owner Sir Michael Hicks, John Needham was the tenant, but it is not known who, if anyone were his 'assigns' or sub-tenants who actually farmed the land, though it was probably, as at the 1608 survey, Widow Brockett (Sixty Acres) and Roger Howton (Abbey Fields and Conygree). It was in 1608 that this tract of former open field land again came under the influence of the Wollaton family.

Two Middleton estate documents, identical in content, one dated 14th March 1608 [12] and the other endorsed 'Bargain with Sir Mic. Hicks for the 60 Akers and other grounds' [13] show that 'Sir Percival Willoughby Kt. hath compounded for an estate for 21 years in those drie pasture grounds late in the occupation of John Needham or his assigns, known by the names of the Conigrey, the Abbey Field and the Sixtie Acres ... conteyning 280 acres or thereabouts at a yerelie rent of £45 and in 'certain messuages or tenements and lands in graunte to Gervase Eyre gent.' together with the Priory mill and its lands occupied by William Stampe.

Sir Percival Willoughby, Kt. (d. 1643) of the house of Eresby in Lincolnshire, but resident in Kent, in 1583 married Bridget (d. 1629) eldest daughter of Sir Francis Willoughby by his first wife Elizabeth (d. 1595), daughter of Sir John Littleton. Portraits of Sir Percival and Lady Bridget, both by C. Janssen, are reproduced in Smith [1988]. The estates of Sir Francis Willoughby passed to them on his death in 1596. They were in financial difficulties from the outset, for Sir Percival, knighted at Worksop in 1603, inherited from his own father estates that were similarly deeply in debt. Sir Percival's difficulties were exacerbated by his extravagant style of living, and he was imprisoned in the Fleet for debt from January to November 1606 [Strauss 1978 21-22]. The 1608 survey shows that Sir Francis Willoughby's second wife, Dorothy, daughter of Thomas Coleby of Grays Inn and widow of John Tamworth, who after the death of Sir Francis married Philip, Lord Wharton, retained much property in Lenton and Radford, probably under a marriage settlement with Sir Francis. None of this is directly involved in this discussion, but Dorothy's portion may have weakened the residual Wollaton estate and thus had some effect on the solvency of Bridget and Percy.

The actual lease to Sir Percival, dated 6/7 June 1609 [14] involved some redistribution of the lands in the tenancies of 1608, including those held in 1608 by Roger Howton and Widow Brockett; some of those held by Jervase Eyre; and the dovecote and barn that had been in the tenure of Rowland Dan and Christopher Sprintall - the northern and north-eastern parts of the University campus - but also some land in the Trent vale, to a total area of 320 acres. Gorsey Close, 26 acres also held by Gervase Eyre, was from 1608 reserved for a Mr. Palmer of London, who acted as a courier for Sir Michael Hicks [15] .

So far as is known the various parts of the estate of the priory demesne remained in the same occupation after Sir Michael Hicks bought it, and the subtenants involved in Sir Percival Willoughby's leaseholding from Hicks in 1609 were also unchanged except that the dovecote was let to William Nixe instead of Rowland Danne. Roger Howton, who leased or rented the Abbey Field and Conygrey in 1608, seems to have remained in occupation for many years, for in 1621, when Sir Percival demised for five years to his 'servant' Bartholomew Pearson, a yeoman of Beeston, 'all those two severall closes, inclosures or parcels of land commonly called the Conygrey and Abbey Field, lying in Lenton ...', they had been 'late in the tenure or occupation of Roger Hooghton' [16] , and Pearson paid the same rent, £ 45, as Hooghton (Howton). Only later in his leaseholding is there an indication that Sir Percival retained the Sixty Acres in hand for his own use, foreshadowing its eventual incorporation into the new Wollaton Park. The vouchers for receipt of rent payments between 1609 and 1630 include some from 'Mr. Martin and Mr. William Nixe for the Abbey ffeilde ... £27', and for 'the Sixty Akers' £14, a total of £41 [17]. Trent Wong remained in the hands of Robert Nixe for many years.

Yet the sub-leases were short, mainly for 5 or 7 years. For example, for the priory mill William Stamp's lease was apparently regranted for 7 years in 1608/9; then in 1615 granted to John Richards for 7 years at £16; then to George Bond, and then to Francis Matthews, the vicar, in 1628 for £12 rent. There was a hierarchy of landlords, with Hicks holding of the Crown, Willoughby of Hicks, Matthews of Willoughby, and the miller of Matthews [18]. Like all the owners of the priory demesne lands after the Dissolution until the end of the 18th century Sir Michael Hicks was an absentee landlord with little interest in the estate beyond the rent return on his investment. In the early years of his ownership he appears to have relied on Sir Percival Willoughby to perform the functions of a local agent in conjunction with the courier, Mr. Palmer from London, who was given tenure of Gorsey Close which he would no doubt re-let at a profit to himself.

In a letter of 20 July 1609, a fortnight after the indenture of Sir Percival's own lease was sealed, Sir Michael was asking Sir Percival to deal with the leases on other parts of the estate [19]. There was an interesting suggestion in Sir Michael's letter that Sir Percival may have wished to be granted leases on some or all of this other property: but this was long before 'My Ladye Hicks', his widow, was experiencing difficulty in collecting from Sir Percival his own rent [20]. Sir Michael's letter read, in part:

> 'I am now to entreat you according to my former request that you will please to take the payne and care for me to see all the counterparts of the several leases, signed and sealed by the several tenants, and according to your good discretion (as if the case were your owne) to take bond of them severally for payment of their rents. A form of bond Mr. Palmer shall deliver you together with the leases, and will himself be a witness unto them, and bring them all back agayn (to me) at his return. I pray you to give them charge to look well to ye grounds in husbanding them according to their covenant. If hereafter I sell it to you you shall find it the better for your self'.

The letter went on to give instructions about matters relating to Robert Nixe, another large tenant of Sir Michael on the valley floor lands; arrangements for payment of Hicks' fee farm rent to 'his Majesty's Receiver of them' by Rowland Dan; his wish for any trees to be marked and the name of the tenant recorded; and a request that Willoughby would receive from each leaseholder fees for Mr. Dod for engrossing and drawing, and for 'his clerk that wrote them', to be carried to London by Mr. Palmer. It was signed 'Your assured lovinge friend, Mich Hicks'.

Whether Sir Percival discharged the services asked of him is not known. Receipts for his half-yearly rent of £42.10s. (£36 for land and £6 for the mill on which he had a 31-year lease) were signed by Sir Michael Hicks from 1610 to June 1612 [21] and the remittances delivered in London by Robert Nixe [22] or Edward Willoughby were signed by Elizabeth Hicks, his widow, from 1612 to 24 May 1615, after Henry Benny, 'servant to the Ladye Hicke' had written on 20 May that she 'doth comende her verye kyndlye unto you and she doth much marvayle she cannott here from you touchinge certayne rent long since due unto her. I have bene here three tymes to have spoken with you as afforesayd I pray you lett my Ladye here shortelye from you'. Henry Benny continued to sign receipts on behalf of Lady Hicks and Mr. William Hicks until 1620, when William had become knight and baronet. In the 1620s payments were often for irregular amounts, usually in arrears. In 1627 Mr. Nixe was still the messenger. The last Lady Day payment was made on 2 April 1630, and the rental of 1630 noted that the lease ended on 26 March 1630 [23].

It is not surprising to find Sir William Hicks, dissatisfied with the irregular payment of Sir Percival Willoughby's rent writing to him on 19 April 1629 in polite but threatening terms[24]:

> 'I have many tymes, long since, written divers letters to you concerning your not paiment of your Rents. As yet I never receaved any answere by letter but faire promises from you by my tennant Ro. Nixe, and as small performance. I have all this while forborne to take any rigorous course with you, still thinking you would out of your noble disposition have taken some order for those my ...(word missing) which have been long due unto me. But I see now my gentleness hath caused all this trouble to me. I should be very sorry you should as yett drive me to use any extremity , especially with a gentleman of your quallity whome I so much honor and respect. I should not have written so hastily at this tyme, but yt I have occation to use my monyes; and besides the tearme of your lease is neere at an end, and I know you expect a new lease from me.'

Sir Percival did not get a new lease in 1630, even though Hicks, 'your assured friend to command', promised that if the arrears were paid 'noe man shall have your lease from you'. Although the 1609 lease expired on 26 March 1630 there is a schedule dated 10 April 1630 of 'Rents ... uppon Sir Percival Willoughby of those grounds he holds in Lenton under Sir William Hicks' [25] , which may indicate a short extension of the lease - possibly to give Sir Percival an opportunity to clear his arrears. A possible reason why Sir Percival did not renew his lease is suggested in Chapter XIII below.

The final rental of Sir Percival in 1630 is summarized in Table 11. It reveals the status of the lands involved, although it is ambiguous in one respect - namely whether the Sixty Acres was sub-let or not. The final regular rental itemizes the Sixty Acres without naming a tenant, but in what appears to be an extension lease it is included with Abbey Field [26] . The first rental of William Gregory, discussed later, was for 1631 [27] and the names of his tenants reveal that Sir Percival let his leased land mainly to Lenton people. Francis Matthews, the vicar, had considerable property in Lenton from Gregory's estate - a tenement (rent 7s. 6d.), a cottage (4s. 0d.), another tenement (£1.15s. 0d.) and Bullmires and other land, part of the Alexander Wright closes. Marjorie Steeples (widow or mother of Rowland Steeples) had a cottage (5s. 0d.), and Richard Ward a tenement (7s. 6d.) and two cottages (6s. 0d.). John Leeming held a cottage, probably on freehold land since it was subject to a chief rent at Michaelmas, and William Nixe also had property subject to 5s. 0d. chief rent [28] .

Table 11.
Sir Percival Willoughby's sub-tenants in 1629-30 at the end of his lease

Rental of Lenton lands held from Sir William Hicks - the lease ending 26 March 1630 [N.U.M.D., Mi 1/38/37(i)]		Rents 10 April 1630 [N.U.M.D., Mi 1/38/37(ii)]	
Ffrancis Mathew for Carleholmes	£2.10s 0d	Carleholmes	10s 0d
Rowland Steeples for Churchyard Close	4.13s 4d	Churchyard Close	£1. 6s 8d
Mr. Mastin for Tomworth	9. 0s 0d	Tamworth	10s 0d
Richard Ward for two closes neare to Tomworth (Lea or Ley closes)	6. 0s 0d	Ward's two closes	1. 0s 0d

John Leemin[g]e for Dayhouse Close	4. 0s 0d	Dayhouse Close	1. 0s 0d
Ffrancis Mathew for the Millnes	12. 0s 0d	The Mills	4. 0s 0d
John Leemine for Abbey Orchard	3. 0s 0d	Abbey Orcharde	1. 0s 0d
The Brickhouse cottages and gardens	1.16s 7d	The bricke house and cottages	5s 0d
Mr. Martin and Mr. William Nixe for the Abbey Field	27. 0s 0d	Abbey Field and Sixtie Akers	9. 0s 0d

'The dovecote cost at the first £5 to repayre it and was never worthe in pidgeon, but is and hath been for the most parte in olde Mr. Nixe's hande, the profitt beinge not answerable to the charge of repayers'. 'Old Mr. Nixe' was Mr. Robert Nixe.

In these rentals the name Abbey Field must have applied to the whole tract south-east of Derby Road from the Tottle Brook in the west to Sandy Lane (Clifton Boulevard today) in the east, including the Coningre (Warren), New Field and Brome Close.

For the Brickhouse cottages, remnants of the priory buildings, see F. A. Barnes [1987].

Little is known of the operation of the Hicks' estate over the next half-century, including the lands that had been in Sir Percival's lease, because they were not now in the hands of the Willoughbys, and are not, therefore, represented among the Middleton documents [29]. The Alexander Wright closes however are well represented among the properties of the Gregory estate, about which much is known in the middle 17th century, and is discussed below. First the commoning arrangements in Lenton parish (which directly affected the former priory land only through the use of Trent Wong) are examined, and then the history of the Gregory family, which acquired most of the territory of Lenton that was not part of the priory demesne.

The burleymen of Lenton and the common use of Trent Wong

The former priory demesne lands had no traditional grazing or commoning rights attached to them. The common use of the open arable fields of Lenton and Radford for grazing of the stubble and fallow was associated with the land of the manor of Lenton, east and north of the river Leen, and was regulated by allocations incorporated in the rentals as intrinsic parts of the properties. Regulation of the common 'wastes' or pastures and the common meadows was a separate arrangement outside the rentals, and charges were levied on the cottagers and tenant farmers.

A Middleton estate document of 1545 [30] sets out the arrangements for commoning in Lenton and Radford in the form of an indenture recording the 'award' of commons by Henry Willoughby and Sir Hugh Willoughby to 'the husbandmen and cottagers of Lenton and Radford, with their consent and agreement' (Appendix 7). Sir Henry Willoughby held much land in Lenton and Radford in 1544, purchased from John Waplington, John Hare and Richard Burton [31]. However, it is presumed that the two Willoughbys gained their authority as bailiffs of the Honour of Peverel, a Crown appointment held by the Willoughby family. The system was operated by the burleymen (or barleymen, or burlimen) who were two husbandmen and one cottager 'wyche shall be elected by the homage of the township' [32].

Although the former priory demesne as such was outside the system, part of its land, Trent Wong, became involved in the arrangements, while the commoning did involve the various Lenton residents who rented and worked former demesne land. Later, the Lenton burleymen assisted the constable at the court leet, and their special duties were said to be to act as referees when damage, trespass, encroachment etc. were being assessed [33] . There are records of the Lenton burleymen from 1718 to 1769 when one, or, more commonly, two burleymen were appointed. Details of the arrangements in the 16th and early 17th centuries are given in the discussion of Trent Wong in Chapter XV below. In essence only landholders of Lenton and Radford and their own beasts were included in the system of commoning, husbandmen being awarded three beast pastures free for every oxgang of their land, for which they discharged customary duties in the maintenance of bridges, causeways and highways by carrying and loading stone, gravel and timber. The cottagers shared 120 beast pastures or 'gates', but paid for them by head of stock, the burleymen collecting the money to pay chief rents and lords rents for the land commoned, with the balance used in maintenance work, which included scouring ditches.

The accounts of the burleymen for 'Lenton pastures' in 1622 [34] , almost 80 years after the award document cited above, show that all landholders paid by a cessment made on 16 May, for the burleymen to pay for 'all those beast pastures that are wantinge for ye fraughtinge of the pasture of the parte of everye beast 5d. and every horse, mare and ox 2d., that are put downe between Lammas and Michaelmas into the pasture or meadows made by the Jurye ...'. Other accounts for the same year show that the maintenance work was now done by paid employees [35], and presumably the charges on the husbandmen meant that they were no longer required to take part in the work. Among the 63 contributors to the levy in 1622 were three men who held land from Sir Percival Willoughby in 1630, namely Francis Matthews the vicar (7 beasts, 2s. 9d.), John Leeminge (3 beasts) and Richard Ward (5 beasts, 2s. 1d.).

The receipts for the 'Lammas Stage' in 1622 [36] distinguished for each person their total number of beast gates, and how many were free gates and how many 'taking gates'. Charges were specifically made for Trent Wong and for Ditch Silver in addition to the Stage charges. Ditch Silver has not been identified, but it was probably land in private ownership along a dyke. Later 'Littling Ditch' was commoned, and this would be along the Blotoff Dyke between Ryecroft and The Holmes, privately owned meadow like Trent Wong. In 1693 [37] the burleymen paid a yearly rent of 13s. 4d. for 'commons in the cow pasture etc.'. Evidently the pressure on the common pastures at some times of year was so heavy that The Holmes and other traditional common pastures could not meet the demand. Among additional grazing lands rented by the burleymen from its tenants was Trent Wong. A second levy was made on 15 June and another on 1 December 1622. In 1539 Trent Wong was described as 'lett among ye tenants there', but it is clear that in 1622 it was opened for common grazing of the aftermath only at Lammas (1 August) after meadow hay had been taken.

The accounts of the Lenton burleymen show that their income was much greater than the rent they paid for the commons, and one important item of their expenditure was the salary of the 'Great herdsman'. In 1744, when Richard Burton was appointed to this position, his duties were clearly set out - 'to look after and attend ye beasts, horses and sheep during their abode and continuance upon ye comons thereunto belonging, every sort of cattell in their season, and yt he shall pay pinship for every sort of cattell trespassing in ye day time, and yt he shall take and care to drive and attend every commoners beasts to ye Forrest every year whilst he continues in his place, beginning about ye tenth of March if ye weather be seasonable, and from thence to continue so doing till ye comon pasture be broken; and also yt he shall take care yt ye quicksett be weeded yearly whilst it needs yt; is now sett ... yt he shall doe his whole business upon ye same salary yt belonges to ye place'. The signatories were nine well-known Lenton men - John Chamberlain, John Clarke, William Dickenson, Thomas Wood, Samuel Keetley, Thomas Roughton, Robert Cassells, William Norris and Humphrey Hopkins; and Robert Burton made his mark.

The Gregory family and the Manor of Lenton

Most of the University campus that was not included in the Hicks estate was, from about 1630, in the Gregory estate. The rise to prominence of the Gregorys in Lenton was a feature particularly of the second quarter of the 17th century, when William Gregory, an alderman of Nottingham, bought the Crown lease of the 'Alexander Wright closes' in 1628 or thereabouts from the Hanmers of Radford [38] , and in 1630 purchased the Crown Manor of Lenton [Throsby 1790/1972 II 203]. From then onwards the two estates, of the manor and the demesne, dominated Lenton, with virtually no exchange of property between them for 300 years. The following brief account of the Gregory family has been carried down to the present century at this point for convenience in Appendix 9.

For almost 100 years, from the Dissolution of the priory, the Crown retained possession and control of the whole of Lenton and Radford, directly or indirectly. The priory demesne was leased to the Stanhopes and their successors, while to the Crown's property remaining in Lenton and Radford townships after the grant to William Peverel in the later 11th century (with which he later endowed the priory) was added the much more extensive possessions of the priory now confiscated to the Crown. Many farm and cottage holdings with dwellings in Lenton village, arable land dispersed in strips, usually in several of the six open fields of Lenton and Radford, and associated meadow land provided the priory with a substantial rent income. This Manor of Lenton was retained by the Crown until the early part of the reign of Charles I, when in 1625 it was granted to the Corporation of the City of London [Godfrey 1884 31].

In 1628 the manor of Lenton, together with its ancient fair, all royalties, privileges, rents and services belonging, was granted in fee farm by Letters Patent of 9 September to Edward Ditchfield, salter, John Highlord, skinner, Humphrey Clarke, dyer, and Francis Mosse, scrivenor, all citizens of London, who were constituted commissioners and duly 'authorized and empowered by the Lord Mayor, Aldermen and Commoners of the said city to sell and dispose of such manors etc.' as had been granted to the city by King Charles I. By their indenture of 6 November 1630 these four men sold to William Gregory, an alderman of Nottingham, and his heirs, for £2,500 paid to Robert Bateman, then Chamberlain of London, the manor of Lenton with all due appurtenances excepting an annual fee farm rent of £94. 5s. 0d. which had been reserved to the Crown [Throsby 1790/1972 II 203-04]. William Gregory also held the lease of Lenton fair for the usual rent of £26.13s. 0d., and subsequently that part of the priory site where the fair was held became the property of the Gregory estate [Barnes 1987]. There is a surviving copy of the rental of William Gregory for the half-year at Michaelmas 1631 [39] which lists the properties and their tenants, though unfortunately parts of it are illegible.

William Gregory was descended from 'a younger branch of an ancient and opulent Lancashire family' [Lowe 1871 15]. The pedigree of the Gregory family obtained by J.T.Godfrey 'from Major Lawson Lowe's MS. collections' [40] begins with Nottinghamshire yeomen in the 16th century - Hugh Gregory; his son Thomas Gregory, a small farmer and grazier of Broughton Sulney, Nottinghamshire, whose wife Dorothy came from Beeston; and their son John Gregory of Broughton Sulney (Figure 25). The son of this John Gregory and his wife Alice was the William Gregory who bought Lenton Manor, and who had 'gained a considerable estate by agricultural pursuits'. William made his fortune from 'grazing'. Godfrey suggested that the register records of the baptism of his sons reveal that he was 'following no higher a calling than that of a butcher', failing to recognize that in the 17th century grazier and butcher were virtually synonymous terms, and that the grazier was the larger, market oriented farmer of that time. Thoroton stated that the family was 'raised to opulence' from very humble beginnings 'through the pursuit of what would then appear to have been a new industrial occupation, the grazing and fattening of cattle expressly for the markets' [Bailey 1853 469].

William Gregory married Anne Jackson of Nottingham (1583/4-1664/5) and became prominent in local government in Nottingham - which is not surprising if, as the pedigrees

WILLIAM GREGORY of High Hurst, Lancashire
HUGH GREGORY, William's younger son
THOMAS GREGORY of Broughton Sulney, Notts. = Dorothy ... of Beeston
son of Hugh Gregory, farmer and grazier

JOHN GREGORY of Broughton Sulney, yeoman = Alice ...
Mayor of Nottingham 1571 and 1586

Ald. WILLIAM GREGORY = Ann Jackson of Nottm. JOHN EDWARD HENRY
d.1650 Sheriff 1618 1583/4-1664/5 Settled at Boston
Mayor 1632, 1639. New England

JOHN GREGORY gent. of = Elizabeth Alton FRANCIS GREGORY gent.= Ann ...
Nottm. 1605/6-1654/5 d.1681 of Nottm. 1608-1664/5
one daughter

WILLIAM G. JOHN G. GEORGE GREGORY I =Susanna Lister of
1631-1637/8 1633-33 of Nottm. 1638-88 of Thorpe Arnold
Sheriff 1666. Leics.
Rebuilt Pelham St.
mansion 1674

- Elizabeth
- PHILIP
- FRANCIS 1643-
- EDWARD
- Ann
- Winifred

Susanna WILLIAM G. MARTIN G. GEORGE GREGORY II=Susanna
1667/8- 1668/9- 1669/70-1746 Williams of
1667/8 died un- MP Nottm. 1702 Rempstone
married and 1714-27 Hall
Sheriff 1694 d. 1756

- JOHN
- Elizabeth
- RICHARD
- WILLIAM
- ROBERT
- Mary
- THEOPHILOUS
- Barbara=George Needham 3 daus (one married John Sherwin)

WILLIAM G. GEORGE GREGORY III=Anne Orton
1694-1726/7 of Rempstone Hall d.1758
and later of Harlaxton Manor inherited
1697-1758 Harlaxton

- JOHN G. 1698-98
- RICHARD
- EDWARD
- THEOPHILOUS
- Susannah 1704-81

GEORGE DE LIGNE GREGORY of Harlaxton Manor 1732-1822 Died unmarried
WILLIAM GREGORY [WILLIAMS] 1742-1814 = (1783) Olivia Preston of Flasby Yorks.
EDWARD GREGORY 1744-1824 Vicar of Langar. Died unmarried

GREGORY WILLIAMS [GREGORY] of Rempstone & from 1851 Harlaxton d.1854 unmarried
Ann died unmarried
CAPT. DANIEL GREGORY=Catherine Beckingham

GEORGE GREGORY of Harlaxton 1775-1860 died unmarried
EDWARD GREGORY died unmarried

JOHN SHERWIN SHERWIN [GREGORY] inherited: died without issue in 1869.

Figure 25: Selective pedigree of the Gregorys 'of Lenton'

indicate, his father, yeoman John Gregory, was Mayor of Nottingham in 1571 and 1586. William is said to have been Sheriff in 1618 and Mayor in 1632 and 1639. Thomas Bailey described Alderman William Gregory, M.P., as 'a great Parliamentarian', meaning 'an ardent partisan of the Parliamentary faction in the Civil Wars' [Lowe 1871 15], and he was one of the Commissioners appointed by Parliament to collect the weekly assignment on the town for the payment of the Army and other public expenses [Bailey 1853 766]. By his will, made shortly before his death in August 1650, William devised certain property to his eldest grandson, George Gregory (1638-1688) and his heirs in tail, and the residue to his own son John Gregory (1605/6-1654-5) who survived him by less than five years, but who had 'added to his fortune by marrying Elizabeth, a daughter and co-heiress of George Alton, gent. of Nottingham, and Mary (nee Kyme) his wife'.

A few months after the death of his father, John Gregory bought for £1,460 from James Stuart, Duke of Lennox and Richmond, to whom it had been granted by Letters Patent on 16 December 1638, the fee farm reserved rent of the Manor of Lenton, the indenture of 20 February 1650-51 being in the names of John and his eldest surviving son George, then aged 12 years [Throsby 1790/1972 204]. George had just received the bequest from his grandfather of 3 water corn mills, with 2 houses, 8 crofts, tofts, closes or pingles and 11 acres of land belonging to the same mills in Lenton and Radford, and all his tithe of hay in Lenton and Radford. John's wife, Elizabeth Alton, married in 1629/30 had brought property that included the mansion at the top of Swine Hill (Pelham Street) Nottingham, owned and inhabited by Dr. Alton, Elizabeth's father, and attractively described by Thomas Bailey [1853 III 955].

By his will of 1654/5 John Gregory, who had nine children, devised his Manor of Lenton with his lands in Lenton and Radford to his eldest daughter Elizabeth (two older sons having died in childhood) until George Gregory reached the age of 21, in 1659. In 1663 George obtained Letters Patent for a second 7-day fair at Lenton (having failed to obtain confirmation of the legal protection that had traditionally protected Lenton fair against competitive trading at Nottingham [Barnes 1987]). He was High Sheriff of the county in 1666, and died in 1688, aged 50. Like his forbears and successors who owned Lenton Manor estate George Gregory never lived at Lenton, but in Nottingham, first in the house inherited from his father in 1654/5, described in a rental of 1663 made in connection with a post-nuptial marriage settlement with Susannah Lister and dated 21 April 16 Car. 2 as 'my dwelling house in Nottingham', with an annual rent value of £40. Later he lived in the old, large Alton mansion that was largely rebuilt by him in 1674 [41] . The rebuilt Alton mansion was shown in Thoroton's 'North-east Prospect of Nottingham', and in an engraving called East Prospect of Nottingham made by Thomas Sandby in about 1750. Part of the site of this house was later occupied by Messrs. Wrights' bank. George Gregory and his wife Susannah, daughter of Sir Martin Lister of Thorpe Arnold, Leicestershire, had at least twelve children, including Barbara, who will be mentioned later in connection with the eventual succession to the Gregory estate. [See Appendix 9]

This first George Gregory was followed directly by three others, and later a fifth. His third son, the second George Gregory (1669/70-1746) was High Sheriff for the county in 1694 and M.P. for the borough of Nottingham in 1702, 1714 and 1722, and for Boroughbridge in 1734. He was a commissioner for the sale of rebels' estates after the 1715 rising, and held the office of Storekeeper of the Ordnance. He was married in about 1694 to Susanna (d. 1756), daughter and co-heiress with her brother John of William Williams of Rempstone Hall, a wealthy London merchant and the younger son of John Williams of Denton, Lincolnshire. Although the second George was living with his mother in the house on Swine Hill in December 1693, just before his marriage, he later removed to Rempstone Hall.

Like his father and grandfather, the second George Gregory, who married Susanna Williams of Rempstone Hall, had many children. His eldest son, William (1694-1726/7) died before his father, who was succeeded in ownership of the estate by his second son, the third

George Gregory (1697-1758). George Gregory III lived first at Rempstone Hall. He was the Nottingham lawyer who in 1732 informed Anne Orton, living in London, that she had inherited Harlaxton Manor near Grantham, which later became the principal Gregory home. In about 1736 he married Anne . She was the daughter and sole heiress of John Orton of London by Elizabeth, daughter and eventual heiress of Daniel Tyrwhitt, son and heir of Scope Tyrwhitt, whose wife Elizabeth was the eldest daughter and co-heiress of Sir Daniel de Ligne of Harlaxton Manor. The de Lignes had acquired the estate in 1619, and the male line ended in 1731. George Gregory III and Anne moved in about 1748 from Rempstone to Harlaxton, where George was buried in 1755 and Anne in 1758.

The later history of the Gregory family and the eventual devolution of their estates are outlined in Appendix 9. These Harlaxton Gregorys must be carefully distinguished from a second prominent Lenton family of Gregorys, wharfingers of Leenside, which was notable for its output of distinguished clerics

The Gregory estate in Lenton

The Gregorys 'of Lenton' never lived in Lenton, and even left Nottingham in the 1690s after the marriage of the second George Gregory. The acquisition of the Harlaxton estate in the mid-18th century moved the centre of the Gregory landed interests even further eastwards from Lenton, and it is not surprising that the 2,000 acres of the Lenton estate were later progressively disposed of to finance, for example the building of the new Harlaxton Hall in the 1830s (Appendix 9).

The Gregory estate contributed two areas to the present University campus. The first of these was part of the tract called the Keighton Closes by Smythe in 1632, a group of the Alexander Wright closes discussed earlier, and purchased by William Gregory in 1628. The second contribution is part of the site of the Queen's Medical Centre, which includes the southernmost part of the former open common arable field called Beck Field, allotted to the Gregory estate at the inclosure of 1768, and a few of the 'Abbey closes' (Smythe's name) adjoining it to the south, some of which were purchased by the estate in the early 19th century. These are discussed in more detail later, and are to be seen on the map of the estate of Gregory Gregory surveyed in 1818-23 by H.M.Wood [42] .

While few details of the main priory demesne estate are available from between 1608-09 (the Crown survey and Sir Percival Willoughby's lease) and the year 1684 when the estate was sold - that is, for most of the Hicks' tenure of the Crown lease - much is known about the Gregory estate in Lenton in the mid-17th century. Indeed, there are schedules of burleymen's receipts for as early as 1622 (discussed briefly above and again in Chapter XV below) which provide a full list of names of the 63 occupiers of land in Lenton manor and a rough indication of the size of their holdings by the numbers of their beast gates. A rental of William Gregory's newly acquired estate in 1631 [43] with about the same number of items and with some indication of the nature of the holdings, the names of the land holders and their rents, and a few field names, does not in some cases give the names of the occupiers and is imperfect in other ways. There is a copy of the burleymen's accounts for 1643 [44] which can be compared with the Protestation Returns for 1642 [Webster 1980] to provide the names of the adult inhabitants of the parish.

A survey and rental for 1651-52 [45] provides a much fuller description of the holdings of the Gregory estate and their make-up, occupiers and rents, and this is followed by a 'cessment' or levy in 1657 on 98 persons called 'the inhabitants of Lenton', intended to raise a sum 'towards the relief of the poore' and 'for a convenient stocke to sett the poore to worke and to putt poor ... children apprentice' [46]. The rate was three pence in the pound. While some land names are given in this document, including some Alexander Wright closes, there is unfortunately only one single figure for 'Sir William Hickes for the Abbie lands', namely £7. 14s. 4d. out of a parish total of £18. 9s. 0d.. In 1662 there is a terrier of the jointure of Elizabeth

Gregory [47] , and in 1663 a rental of George Gregory associated with his post-nuptial marriage settlement, which gives no names or rents. However, a detailed schedule of the jointure lands in 1664 [48] shows how the Alexander Wright closes were incorporated into the farm holdings of Lenton village. An extract from this manuscript is tabulated in Table 12.

Most of these data relate to Lenton east and north of the river Leen, and are therefore not directly relevant to this account of the history of the priory demesne and University campus. Since the former demesne was virtually uninhabited the value of the rentals and other schedules at this stage is limited, but it is of interest to note that the Alexander Wright closes on the present University campus were occupied in the mid-17th century by half a dozen of the leading farmers in Lenton village (Table 12). The other closes, in the Dunkirk area, were held by several persons described as 'gent', including Nicholas Charlton of Chilwell, William Derry and Francis Smith of Nottingham. Five farmers shared the Keighton closes - John Fairbrother, Henry Fairbrother, Christopher Stocks, Richard Dawson and Francis Revell, but John Garland of the Hall then had only Willowholme (12 acres), outside the campus. The complicated make-up of their holdings can be appreciated from Table 12. The five large farmers mentioned above all held arable selions in each of the six common arable fields of Lenton and Radford, scattered stints of meadow, commons (gates) for grazing animals in several places and a number of closes. They would gain access to their Keighton lands via Leengate, Spring Close and Cut Through Lane, from which a bridle path took off southwards through the Keighton closes at a point clearly seen on even modern maps published before 1950.

It is interesting to find that Francis Revell, who rented the Quarrel Close (that is, Quarry Close) of 4 acres had two cottages in Lenton village with adjoining meadow and a little croft, and common gates for 6 beasts, 2 horses and 30 sheep, but had no arable land whatever. Swinnerton believed that clay was extracted for working elsewhere long after the Keighton kilns ceased operations, and it seems possible that Francis Revell may have been involved in clay working in Quarrel Close in the mid-17th century, and could afford to purchase his grain.

The sale of 1684 and the pattern of land holding and land use

In 1684 Sir William Hicks sold his Lenton estate to Thomas Winford (with the trustees of his marriage settlement). Thomas, son of Sir John Winford, the royalist, was Second Prothonotary of the Court of Common Pleas. The transaction was in two parts, by indentures dated 25/26 January and 27/28 January 1684. The first transaction was effected by indentures of Lease and Release between 'Sir William Hickes of Ruckholts, Essex, Knight and Bart., and Dame Marthagnes his wife', and Thomas Winford Esq. of Lincolns Inn, with Richard, Lord Gorges, Baron of Dundalk, Peter Barwicke, Dr. in Physic, Robert Winford and William Winford, gents, of Holborn as second parties. The price was £6,000 for a total area of about 531 acres. Sir William Hicks covenanted that he was 'lawfully seized and had good right to convey free from incumbrances' except for leases described in a schedule annexed to the indenture [49] . The purchase was made in pursuit of the articles of 7 July 1684 between Thomas Winford, Michael Pearce, an apothecary of Drury Lane, Westminster and Sarah his daughter and sole heiress, and the four parties of the second part named above, who were trustees of the marriage settlement of Thomas Winford and Sarah Pearce. They were to lay out £6,000 'in a purchase of lands and hereditaments of the yearly value of £300 at least' [50] . A document of 5/6 March 1684 records that Thomas Winford was to lay out £6,000 in trust to purchase lands and hereditaments 'not being Fenlands nor houses in a city or borough town'. Thomas Winford and Michael Pearce, Sarah's father, had each paid £3,000 to the trustees. A schedule of the lands involved, which must have been based on an up-to-date survey, is found copied in Wadsworth Ms. 50 (N.U.M.D.) and also on the dorse of an abstract of title of Lord Middleton made in 1867 [51] . Nearly 50 years later, in 1731, this major part of the estate was still Dame Sarah Winford's jointure.

Table 12.
Seven holdings in Elizabeth Gregory's jointure estate in Lenton in 1664, including Keighton Closes and other 'Alexander Wright' closes

Extracted from L.A.O., 1 PG 3/3/1/1

Tenant	Buildings	Attached land	Area of selions in arable fields Beck	Alwell	Sand	Red	Church	Moor	Common meadow
Henry Fairbrother	House etc	Close 1a backside	5a	2a	6a	5a	1a.1r	1½a	Thackholme 1a,4x1r,2x 2r,3x1r,5x 1r = 5a.
Richard Dawson	House etc 1 cott.	Croft: arab.2a	5a	7a	5a	5a	1a	4a	1a,3a,1a 1a,1r.
John Hawton (or Houghton)	House		9½a	2a	12a	8a	2½a	3a3r	Thackholme 2x2r 4x2r, 12x1r,2x1r 1x2r.
Christopher Stocks	House 2 cotts.	3 oxgangs orchard with cotts	7½a	12a	7½a	6a1r	2a1r	3½a	8x2r,1a,2r 4x2r,3x1r.
John Garland	Capital messuage [The Hall] 2 cotts. pulled down		11½a	9a	6½a	10a3r	1a3r	6a3r	14x1r,1a, ½a,3a,2x2r 2a,3x2r
Francis Revell	2 cotts backside little croft	Orchard				2a.			
John Fairbrother	House 2 cotts	2 orchards backside	10a	8a	5a3r	9a	2a	8a	Thackholme 1a,2a,1a, 3x2r,2a,3r 3x1r

Tenant	Beast gates Horse	Beast	Sheep	Closes	Areas acres	Farm area acres	Rent £ s. d.
Henry Fairbrother	5	9	60	Leen Bridge Close Bacon Closes (2) Mill Close Hannibles	2 6 2 2	38¾	20. 5. 0
Richard Dawson	6	12	90	Carleholme Great Bacon (adjng Keightons)	1 6	42¼	18.10. 0
John Hawton	5	14	?	Below Buttery Mill Meadow Close	4 11	61¾	32.15. 0
Christopher Stocks		9		Little Reedy Close Barnard's Close Snoton Close Kightons Maire Closes	 1 1½ 9 7	65¾+	35.10. 0
John Garland	11 =9+2	21 =15+6	105 =165 +30	Saffron Close Great Reedy Close Little Reedy Close Willowholme	5 5 1 12	81¾	47.10. 0
Francis Revell	2	6	30	Quarrel Close	4	c. 6½	9. 0. 0
John Fairbrother	10	18	180	Townend Close Leene Close Fframford Lane End Kightons Maire Close	1 1½ 2 8 5	70	34.10. 0

The second transaction was a direct sale by indenture of Lease and Release between Sir William Hicks and his wife and Thomas Winford, of 'The scite, circuit and precinct of the late dissolved Priory of Lenton and several closes, parcel of the said Priory', for £3,650. The property involved is detailed in the abstract of title of 1867 (though not in the Wadsworth manuscript) and comprised about 270 acres, including the 100 acres of Trent Wong, bringing the total area of the estate to just over 800 acres.

Appendix 11 is a schedule of the land holdings on the estate of the priory demesne derived from the data of the survey of 1684. The fragmented nature of the geographical pattern of land holding adds to the difficulty of mapping it, and there is a limit to what can be accomplished in constructing historical maps of tenure and land use from disordered contemporary data. Further, individual closes change over time in name as well as in area, ownership, tenancy and usage. About a dozen of the smaller closes included in the 1684 terrier cannot be located with confidence, but all except one were described as meadow, and they all lay in the area formerly known as the 'Priory Closes', south and south-west of Lenton village. One particular problem in identification arises from the practice of using the name of the current tenant to name a close, so that names of earlier and later dates cannot be readily matched. For example, in 1684 Barley's Close, six acres of meadow, was occupied by Robert Barley, Clarke's Close by Widow Clarke of Beeston, and Pares Close by William Pare. Other closes called by the names of earlier tenants were Greason's Close, Ward's Close, and probably Partable Close. For these reasons Figure 26 is necessarily incomplete.

The details of the Alexander Wright closes nearest in date to 1684 are contained in a Gregory estate rental of 1664, almost a generation earlier, but they, too, serve to illustrate the chaotic nature of the pattern of land holding on the former demesne generally, despite the large individual holdings of John Scattergood and Robert Alcock, of Christopher Hall, and of John Garland, the largest holder of Gregory estate land in Lenton. It is not known whether some or all of the larger holders of land sub-let portions to others, which would add to the very large number of actual occupiers.

In 1684 there were as many as 35 different occupiers of that part of the priory demesne included in Sir William Hicks' estate, while in 1664 the Gregory estate's Keighton Closes were shared among a further 8 occupiers [52]. Keighton Close was divided between John Fairbrother (8a.) Christopher Stocks (9a.) and Margaret Wallis; Bacon Close between Richard Dawson and Henry Fairbrother; Mares Close by John Fairbrother and Christopher Stocks; and Quarrel Close was occupied by Francis Revell. Such fragmentation was in no way unusual within a system in which the arable land of even the largest farmers was widely dispersed in several open arable fields, often in selions of one rood or less in area.

The largest holding of former demesne land in 1684 was that of the graziers Scattergood and Alcock, with their lease of the 200 acres of the Abbey Fields, and the addition of 5 acres of The Greens and Little Broom Close. Scattergood himself also had the Oxhouse Close (3a.). This holding therefore dominated the area of the present campus. It was probably farmed from premises later called Abbey House on the site of the priory's Dayhouse, adjoining the Oxhouse Close, as it was a century later. It might thus be seen as the precursor of Stevenson's farm of the later 18th century discussed in the next chapter, and of the Lenton Hall estate in the 19th century.

The only other very large holding of former demesne land was the 147 acres occupied by Christopher Hall, but his land was all on the alluvium and gravels of the level Trent valley floor, and included the Rye Close, Cow Close and the Littling Meadow. Like Scattergood and Alcock's holding it could be seen as a precursor, this time of the Dunkirk Farm. Otherwise, excluding Trent Wong, which was occupied by John Garland together with the Great Broom Close of 20 acres, and the Sixty Acres of John Sherwin (to be alienated by him in 1698, and now part of Wollaton Park) the largest holdings of demesne land were those of

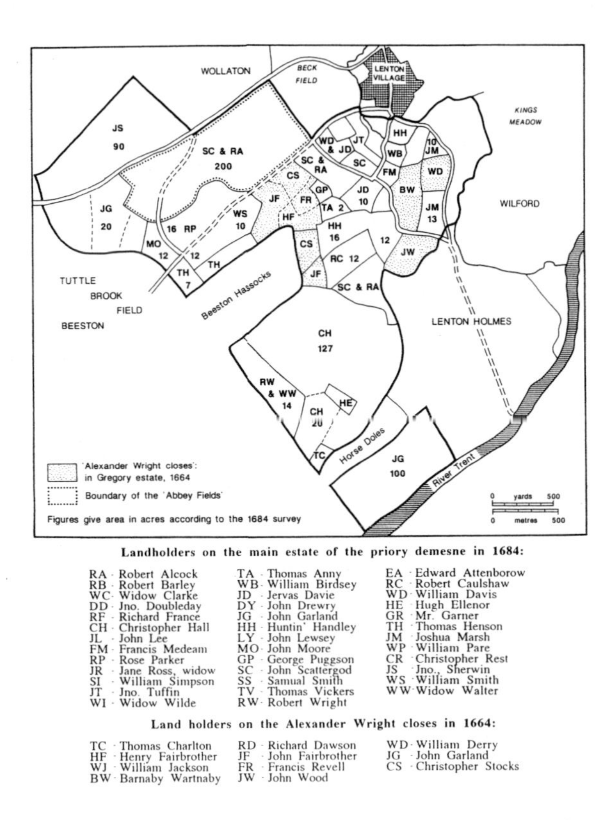

Figure 26: Some tenants of land on the former priory demesne in 1684 and 1664

Huntin' Handley of Wilford (33 acres, all in the Trent vale); Rose Parker, probably the widow of Robert Parker, named in the 1674 Hearth Tax schedule for Lenton, with Highfield Close (28 acres); and Joseph Marsh (23a.) also of Lenton, whose land comprised the Broom Close of 10 acres, 'next Abbey Lane and Carlholme', and Ledgett Wong of 13 acres [53].

When the survey of 1684 is inspected for evidence of land use, as classified at that time, towards the end of the 17th century, it is found that not a single acre of the former priory demesne was regarded as arable land. This is striking, but not surprising, given the persistence of the medieval system of farming, with arable cropping and ploughing confined to the common open fields. Additional arable land had suddenly entered the local system with the extinction of the priory, but the system, through its inertia, could not yet accommodate individual field cropping. There was, indeed, no incentive to do so, at a time when profitable commercial farming was overwhelmingly concerned with animal products, while absentee landlords were interested in little more than collecting their rents, and in no position to take any action to maximize the agricultural output from their estates. The 'privatization' brought by the Dissolution was ineffectual and premature as far as the inhabitants of Lenton were concerned.

There were some 291 acres of meadow and 496 acres of pasture on Sir William Hicks' estate as described in 1684. However, Trent Wong was called pasture, whereas in earlier times it had been meadow, though grazed in the aftermath, and later, in 1731, it was called 'meadow or pasture'. Most of the parcels called meadow ground were, in fact, grazed after hay crops had been taken, and if Trent Wong was classified as meadow the figures for 1684 would become 391 acres of meadow and 396 acres of pasture. So-called meadow ground may not have been cut for hay every year, but meadow and pasture were not generally interchangeable, and there is no doubt that much the greater part of the present University campus was pasture rather than meadow on the lighter, freely draining soils of the sandstones, with meadow in the lower areas such as much of the site of the Queen's Medical Centre and alongside the Tottle Brook.

All landholders kept animals for draught, dairy produce, meat or wool, and the problem of winter fodder was always a serious constraint on animal husbandry before the introduction of root crops and rotational farming. But summer grazing was also prized, so that the attachment to their holdings of meadow and pasture closes such as those available for rent on the former demesne was much sought after by farmers, and it was mainly the larger and more prosperous farmers who could afford it. The problems of stock feed can be seen from the entries (for 1680) in the 'Park Book' of Wollaton [54], (probably relating to the 'old park' north of Wollaton village) which show that pigs were brought to Wollaton Park to feed, no doubt on acorns, beech mast and whatever they could find, from considerable distances, though some familiar Lenton names can be recognized among their owners. In 1680 the book recorded about 115 pigs and 49 owners, paying from 1s. 0d. to 2s. 6d. (for sows) per animal. There were 17 farmers (31 pigs) from Lenton, 6 (10 pigs) from Radford, 3 (25-30 pigs, mostly from one man) from Nottingham, 10 (14 pigs) from Chilwell, 5 (6 pigs) from Wollaton, and others from Wilford, Beeston, Long Eaton, Stapleford, Toton, Bobbers Mill, and an unfortunate man from West Hallam, whose 'swine ran away'.

Unfortunately no rental or survey of the Gregory estate in Lenton is known between the terriers of 1664 and 1725 [55] , respectively 20 years before and 41 years after the survey of the Hicks estate in 1684, a gap of 61 years and two or three generations. Therefore it is not possible to demonstrate fully how the lands of the main estate of the demesne fitted into the agrarian economy of the parish as a whole towards the end of the 17th century. Before moving forward into the 18th century, however, it is appropriate to describe the alienation from the demesne estate of the Sixty Acres, the wedge of Lenton parish land north of the Nottingham to Derby road, and now in Wollaton Park.

Wollaton Park and the alienation of the Sixty Acres in 1698

By the 1680s the Warren was generally understood to be part of the Abbey Fields, and so was Great Broom Close, but the remaining open arable land of the priory, the Sixty Acres, remained separate and under different tenure. In 1684 we find 'All those fields or pcls of Pasture ground ... called The Abbey Fields, containing by estimation 200 acres' included in the first sale indenture. The second indenture includes the 'Parcel of pasture ground, the Sixty Acres' occupied by Jno. Sherwin, and extending to an estimated 90 acres [56] .

It was shown in Chapter III that the Willoughbys of Wollaton occupied the Lenton lands on both sides of Derby Road at least as early as the 1540s, and, including Madeley's lease, remained in occupation until 1577. They held them again probably from 1588 to 1596, perhaps year by year; and then by Sir Percival Willoughby's 21-year lease from 1609 to 1630. The indications that during Sir Percival's lease the Sixty Acres was mostly, if not totally kept 'in hand' by him seem to foreshadow its eventual purchase and its incorporation into the 'new' Wollaton Park being developed around the 'new' Wollaton Hall. It will be suggested in Chapter XIII that an important reason why the Willoughbys leased the northern part of the campus was to ensure passage for their coal from the Wollaton pits en route for the river Trent at Wilford ford, a traffic that ended by the mid-17th century. A sub-lease by Sir Percival to Bartholomew Pearson, a Beeston yeoman who was involved with the Wollaton coal mines was for five years from 1621 [57] and of the Conygrey and Abbey Field only.

Although no documentary evidence can be quoted to show that the Willoughbys occupied the Sixty Acres in the 1650s and 1660s it must be presumed that they did. Much development of the new Wollaton Park was taking place, with palings erected, a stone dam to the pool in the park made, and trees planted. For example, in 1660 acorns were planted along the great walk to the lake from the house, and oaks and ashes planted along the great walk from the house at Wollaton village. In 1665 the Lower Conygree (of Wollaton) was subdivided by planting quicksets and young oaks [58] . It is probable that although the Willoughbys had no lease from Sir William Hicks they occupied the Sixty Acres by a sub-lease or by renting from John Sherwin, who had it from Hicks. The Wollaton rentals of the middle and later 17th century (for example, that of 1671 [59]) referred under Lenton only to the Lenton burleymen, because the salient into their territory formed by the Sixty Acres would be held by the Willoughbys for their own use as grazing or parkland.

The Sixty Acres was finally sold in 1698-99 by John Sherwin and his wife Anne to Sir Thomas Willoughby. Sherwin was a prominent citizen of Nottingham, Sheriff in 1680 and Mayor in 1687, whose house at the top of Pilcher-gate, probably built shortly after the middle of the 17th century, 'had in front a fine garden, afterwards made into a paddock occupying all the ground between Halifax Lane and St. Mary's-place as far as the theatre ...'. The indenture of lease and release forming the Middleton documents Mi 1/3/1-2 of 6/7 July 1698 read in summary: 'John Sherwin, in consideration of the sum of £700 ... hath granted, bargained and sold, aliened released and confirmed ... for one year (etc,.) ... all that piece or parcel of pasture ground commonly called or known by the name of the Sixty Acres, containing by estimation 90 acres ... now in the tenure or occupation of the said John Sherwin ... and situate in Lenton ... or in the ffields or precincts thereof ... to have and to hold the said land, close, lands and premises with the appurtenances ... in fee simple...'. The final concord [60] made in the third week after Trinity, 10 William III concerning the '90 acres of pasture in Lenton with appurtenances' noted that 'for this recognition, remission, quitclaim, warrant, fine and concord the said Thomas gave to the said John and Anne £120 sterling'. The Willoughbys clearly wanted the Sixty Acres very badly to secure the integrity of the new Wollaton Park.

A schedule of areas and rents called 'An Account of Wollaton taken in the year 1701' includes a number of entries described as 'now Parke' or 'New Parke' [61] . No areas were given for these eleven items, but their total rent value was as much as £65.2s.0d. The Sixty Acres, being in Lenton, was not included in this account, but in view of the transaction of two years earlier it, too, was doubtless 'now Parke'. Its original boundaries were lost in the course of early 18th century landscaping. The acquisition of the Sixty Acres, to complete the new Wollaton Park, made possible the building of Wollaton Park wall, said to date from the 1720s. John Sleight of Wollaton, aged 78 in 1823, after over 54 years as park-keeper to Lord Middleton, had heard very old workmen of Lord Middleton saying (in about 1770) that they remembered - presumably from about 50 years earlier, in about 1720 - the deer being driven from the old park (north of Wollaton village) to the new one [62] . This seems to corroborate, at least approximately, the dating of the wall.

NOTES

1. N.U.M.D., Mi 3 E 4 and N.U.M.D., Wadsworth 50
2. P.R.O., SC 12/24/12 6591, Exchequer Queen's Remembrancer. P.R.O. L.R. 2/211 CP 2940, ff. 106-158
3. N.A.O., XF/1/4/R (photocopy): Map of Sherwood Forest, 1609
4. N.A.O., RD 3 L : 'A mappe of ye Lordshippe of Lenton and Radford taken the tenthe day of Julye anno 1632 by me Richard Smythe surveyor.
5. L.A.O.,1 PG 2/8/1 : Lease of 1601 to Cooper, Hanmer et al. in Radford and Lenton.
6. N.U.M.D., Mi 1/38/18(i) (1609)
7. P.R.O., L.R. 2/211 CP 2940, ff. 106-158
8. ibid.
9. Landers or Launders Green was probably within the outer court of Lenton Priory on the evidence of an item in the rental of c. 1554 - 'The Bo(o)thes of the fare within the outer court conteyn ii acres with Landers Grene also called the lether fare ...'. 'Le Kitchen' also suggests a former priory building. The vicarage would probably be near to the rebuilt church within the priory court, and Beadhouse ground was churchyard, but not necessarily burial ground.

10. N.U.M.D., Mi F 10/5 undated. 'The Rental of the demesnes of Lenton Abbey by Mr. Jo. Harrington: Lo. thereof and then by quarter and yeare lett so'. It is thought that the date was towards the end of Harrington's lease.
11. N.U.M.D., Mi 1/38/37(i) (1630).
12. N.U.M.D., Mi 1/38/17(i) 'For Sir Michael Hicks, Lenton Abbey', 14 March 1608 (6 Jac.)
13. N.U.M.D., Mi 1/38/17(ii) 'Bargain with Sir Mic. Hicks for the 60 Akers and other grounds'.
14. N.U.M.D., Mi 1/38/19(i) and (ii), 1/2 June 17609 (for the mill and its lands): Mi 1/38/18(ii) 6 June 1609 (for the rest of the property).
15. N.U.M.D., Mi 1/38/17(i) 14 March 1608. Sir Percival Willoughby was to have property then 'in graunte to Gervase Eyre, gent., excepted always unto Sir Michael Hicks one olde house ... and one grounde called the Gorsey Close conteyning 26 acres, which is reserved for Mr. Palmer of London and is valued to be worth #10 ...'. Palmer is mentioned in Sir Michael's letter to Sir Percival.
16. N.U.M.D., Mi 1/38/26 19 December 1621
17. N.U.M.D., Mi 1/38/37(i) to (xxx) (1609-1630)
18. The lease of the mill was separate from that of the rest of the property leased by Sir Percival Willoughby. N.U.M.D., Mi 1/38/19(i) and (ii): Mi 1/38/25 (16 October 1615): Mi 1/38/27 (4 Oct. 1628) - the mill 'late in the occupation of George Bond and now in the occupation of the said Francis Matthews or his assigns'.
19. N.U.M.D., Mi 1/38/20
20. N.U.M.D., Mi 1/38/37(xix) 20 May 1615
21. ibid. (i) to (xxx) (1609-1630)
22. ibid. (viii) 14 April 1627
23. ibid. (i) (1630)
24. N.U.M.D. Mi 1/38/28 19 April 1629. 'To his worthy and much respected friend Sir Percevall Willowby, knight, at his house in Nottingamshr 5 Car I ffrom Sir W. Hicks: about renewing his lease'.
25. N.U.M.D., Mi 1/38/37(i)
26. N.U.M.D., Mi 1/38/37(ii)
27. L.A.O., 1 PG 6/2 (1631)
28. William was a son of Robert Nixe of Wilford, who held nearly 200 acres of former priory demesne land in the Trent vale, including Trent Wong in 1608 and later years. It was probably Robert who had the former priory dovecote for most of Sir Percival Willoughby's lease. N.U.M.D., Mi 1/38/37(i) (1630)
29. Even the levy made on 1 May 1657 for the relief of the poor in Lenton, although it comprised almost a hundred items, made no differentiation within the former demesne lands, with Sir William Hicks alone answering for all the 'Abbie lands'. L.A.O. 2 PG 13/6 1st May 1657.
30. N.U.M.D., Mi 1/38/3 1 March 1545. 'Award of commons in Lenton ...' 1 March 36 Henry VIII.
31. N.U.M.D., Mi 1/38/32 'My brother Henry Willoughbye, rental of his lands in Lenton and Radford, 35 H 8'. 'The rental of Sir Henry Willoughby esq. of all the lands and tenements in Lenton and Radford ... sent the 14th day of March in the 35th year of the reign of ... Henry VIII ... '.
32. N.U.M.D., Mi 1/38/3 (1545)
33. Lenton Local History Group, Broadsheet No. 20, April 1981.
34. L.A.O., 2 PG 13/5 'Account of the burlimen of Lenton for Lenton pastures 1622'. Accounts are given in detail for a cessment made on 16 May 1622 - receipts for the Lammas stage, Trent Wong and Ditche Silver; 'a second Levye or Cessment made the 15th day of June 1622'; and receipts of a cessment made 1 December 1622.
35. L.A.,O., 2 PG 13/6 Burlimen Accounts. This document details payments made to individuals for work done on roads, water control etc., out of the money collected from parishioners by the burleymen.
36. L.A.O., 2 PG 13/5 (1622)
37. L.A.O., 1 PG 3/3/1/13 Surrender of jointure
38. The Alexander Wright closes' were in the 1631 rental of William Gregory - L.A.O., 1 PG 6/2. An inspeximus of Letters Patent (L.A.O., 1 PG 2/8/Bundle 1/1), a decayed and fragmentary document which recites the Crown lease of these lands dated 24 July 43 Elizabeth (1601), is itself dated 20 May 4 Charles (1628), and may record the assignment of the lease to William Gregory from the Hanmers and their associates.
39. L.A.O., 1 PG 6/2 (1631). Half year rent at Michaelmas 1631.
40. A Gregory pedigree is printed in Godfrey [1884] opposite page 201. It was compiled from 'Major Lawson Lowe's manuscript collections'. Most of Godfrey's information is printed in Lowe's 'History of the Hundred of Broxtowe', part 1, prefaced in 1871, pp. 15-16. For Lawson Lowe as a genealogist see Chapter VI below.
41. L.A.O., 1 PG 3/3/1/3/ endorsed 21 April 16 Car 2.
42. N.A.O., RD 3 L, 'A mappe of ye Lordshippe of Lenton and Radford taken the tenthe day of Julye anno 1632 by me Richard Smythe surveyor'.
43. L.A.O., 1 PG 6/2 (1631)
44. L.A.O., 2 PG 13/6 (1643)
45. L.A.O., 2 PG 3/1/9 (1651-52)

46. L.A.O., 2 PG 13/6 (1657)
47. L.A.O., 1 PG 3/3/1/3 (1662 and 1663)
48. L.A.O., 1 PG 3/3/1/1 (1664)
49. N.U.M.D., Mi 3 E 4 'Abstract of title of Henry, Lord Middleton and Hon. Digby W. B. Willoughby to a freehold estate called Lenton Abbey, 1684-1867. Notes and opinion by C. Butler'. For details of the indenture of 25/26 January 1684 only see N.U.M.D., Wadsworth 50, which carries the marginal note: 'It is the earliest of all the deeds in the bundle sent by Mr. Pares, but evidently there are others somewhere'. For both indentures see Mi 3 E 4 dorse.
50. N.U.M.D., Wadsworth 50
51. N.U.M.D., Mi 3 E 4 (1867)
52. L.A.O., 1 PG 3/3/1/1, 20 January 15 Car. 2. 'Settlement previously to the marr(iag)e of George Gregory Esq. with Susanna Lister'. Includes a terrier of lands devised by George Gregory to his mother, Elizabeth, and by her redeemed to George Gregory at the rent of £ 100 per an .... The schedule of the jointure lands. (Repeated in L.A.O., 1 PG 3/3/1/3, a document in a better condition.)
53. This will be that part of Ledgett Wong not among the Alexander Wright closes.
54. N.U.M.D., Mi R 316(b) N 92 - 1680 Park Book
55. L.A.O., 2 PG 3/1/8 (also 10). Terrier of George Gregory's estate in Lenton and Radford, 1725.
56. N.U.M.D., Mi 3 E 4, 1684-1867, Abstract of title of Henry, Lord Middleton and Hon. Digby W. B. Willoughby to a freehold estate called Lenton Abbey (dorse).
57. N.U.M.D., Mi 1/38/26 Indenture, 19 Dec. 18 Jac. (1621): Percival Willoughby of Wollaton/Bartholomew Peereson (Pearson) of Beeston, yeoman, now servant of Sir Percival.
58. N.U.M.D., Mi F 12 - Rev. Kellar's remarks, 1654, 1660, 1664, 1665. N.U.M.D., Mi R 170-173 Rental books, Lady Day and Michaelmas, 1661-1668.
59. N.U.M.D., Mi R 43/1 Rentals 1671-73.
60. N.U.M.D., Mi I 5/169/49(i) and (ii), Trinity Term 10 William III (1698).
61. 'An accompte of Wolloton taken in ye yeer 1701'
62. See N.U.M.D., Mi 1/16/1a to 1d (1823) and Chapter XIII

CHAPTER V

THE EIGHTEENTH AND EARLY NINETEENTH CENTURY

Introduction

The 17th century, discussed in Chapter IV, the age of the Stuarts, was an eventful and disturbed, even revolutionary period in British history, the first half shared by the reigns of the first Stuarts, James I (1603-25) and Charles I (1625-49), and after a decade of Cromwell's Commonwealth (1649-60) the Restoration, with the Plague and Great Fire of London (1665-66) followed by the 'Glorious Revolution' of 1688, the Bill of Rights (1689) and the reign of William III and Mary (1689-1702). The Civil War, beginning in 1642, punctuated the long conflict between Parliamentary power, merchant wealth and Puritanism, and the 'divine right' of kings and bishops, including the power to raise money without the authority of Parliament. There was conflict, too, between the developing scientific view of the world and the theological. By contrast the history of the campus in the 17th century was uneventful, even uninteresting, essentially because it was virtually uninhabited, was marginal, stagnant and exploitive in agrarian economy, and owned by a distant absentee landlord. The 18th century was different, and instead of political, intellectual and social tensions it was economic forces in industry, transport and trade that prompted changes in the countryside. On the campus a slow reorganization in the use of the land culminated in a rapid, major transformation of the area about the end of the century.

In the following paragraphs the organization and landscape of the area in the first half of the 18th century (1730-40) is compared with that in the last decades of the century, revealing the progress made from Stuart times - little different from the mid-16th century - towards the redevelopment and resettlement of the former priory demesne, and after its sale, breakup and entry upon a quite new and different stage of occupance about the end of the 18th century.

The former priory demesne in the earlier 18th century

Two particular events in the earlier 18th century gave rise to surveys of the major part of the former priory demesne in 1731 and 1743, both associated with transference of the estate to

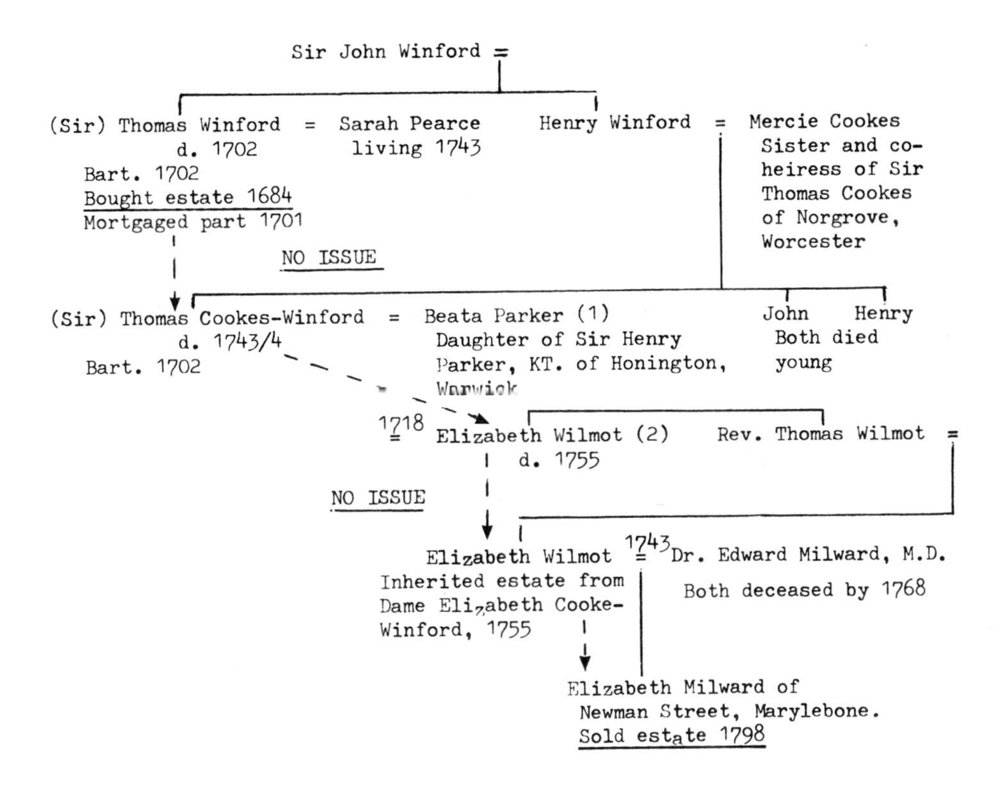

Figure 27: The Winford-Milward succession to the estate of the priory demesne

trustees.These surveys, in combination with evidence from terriers of the Gregory estate for 1725 and 1738 [1] make possible a reconstruction of the tenurial pattern of the campus area at that time.

Thomas Winford, who had purchased the estate in 1684, seems to have owned also the manor and estate of Ruddington, later acquired by Sir Thomas Parkyns of Bunny [Bailey 1853 1190]. Winford was created baronet in 1702, with limitation to the heirs of his younger brother, and he died about two months later. An indenture of 22 May 1701 [2] shows that Thomas and Sarah Winford mortgaged part of their estate to secure £2,000, and the mortgage was discharged on 25 February 1707. The will of Sir Thomas Winford, dated 18 October 1701 (proved 28 September 1702) devised all his property in Nottinghamshire to his nephew Thomas Cookes-Winford for life, with his brothers John and Harry in tail, and Thomas took possession at Sir Thomas' death in 1702 (Figure 27).

Thomas Cookes-Winford's first wife, Beata Parker, died without issue, and in 1718 he married Elizabeth Wilmot. Her marriage settlement provided for lands and tenements yielding an annual income of £400. The 1731 terrier of the estate was made when Sir Thomas Cookes-Winford and his wife transferred to trustees all their premises in Lenton, described as 'The site of the late priory, with appurtenances, 2 messuages, 3 cottages, 2 tofts, 1 water mill, 400 acres of land, 200 acres of meadow, 100 acres of pasture and 200 acres of furze and heath'. These are very round figures, for the total of 900 acres in this description is almost 200 acres more than the total area of land included in the terrier [3] (Table 13).

Sir Thomas Cookes-Winford died in 1743 without issue like his predecessor. The Lenton and Radford property, including the jointure lands of Dame Sarah, Sir Thomas Winford's widow, passed to Cookes-Winford's widow, Dame Elizabeth Winford, by devise, and this was the occasion for the terrier or rental of 1743 [4] (Table 14). Sir Thomas Cookes-Winford's brothers John and

Table 13.
Terrier of the estate of the priory demesne, 1731

N.U.M.D., Wadsworth W (23a) 51 (1830): 'Copy parcels in the deed of 14 April 1731, lately of Priory of Lenton'

All those several closes or parcels of arable, meadow and pasture ground ....in Lenton and Radford ....known as:	
The Rey [Rye] Close, the Cow Close and Littling estimated	127 acres
The Broom Close Pasture	12
Ledgett Wong Meadow	13
Part of Highfields Pasture	16
Part of Rushy Close Meadow	3
Pryor Meadow	5
Nether Wheatcroft Meadow	12
Geeson's Meadow	4
Ward's Meadow	4
Doe Park Meadow	1
Part of Temes Close Meadow	4
Hilley Close Pasture	7
Tamworth Pasture	16
Part of The Rounds Pasture	14
Barley's Meadow	6
Part of High Fields Pasture	10
Clarkes Meadow	6
Pores Meadow	4
Part of Partable Meadow	5
Gorsey Pasture	20
Dovecote Pasture and Salters Pasture, together	10
Little Broom Meadow	9
Part of Rushey Meadow	4
Nether part of Highfields Meadow, next Beeston	10
Part of Highfield Close next the Field	12
The Abbey Fields Pastures	200
The Abbey Orchard	3
All which premises are now held by Dame Sarah Winford, widow, relict of the said Sir Thomas Winford for life for her jointure.	
And also all that scite, circuit and precinct of the late dissolved Priory of Lenton .... and that	
Piece or parcel of meadow or pasture ground called Trent Wong 100 ac. now or late in the tenure or occupation of Benjamin Deverall, his assigns or undertenants, by him rented at £61 per annum.	
All that Paper Mill and yard belonging	1 acre
All those closes or parcels of meadow ground and pasture called:	
Oxhouse Meadow	3
Dancy [Davey ?] Meadow	2
Tame Meadow	3
Part of Duck Meadow, the Littling Meadow	3
Cats [Calf ?] Meadow	2
Five Acres Meadow, Great Broom Meadow	20
Broom Meadow next the Abbey Lane and Carlho[l]me, together	10
Over Whreat Croft Meadow	12
Seven Acres Meadow	7
Greens Pasture	5
Churchyard Meadow	5
2 messuages or tenements with the gardens belonging	

Harry having died young, the nearest relative in succession was the niece of his wife, also named Elizabeth, the daughter of her brother Rev. Thomas Wilmot, and Dame Elizabeth bequeathed the property to her. In 1743, before Sir Thomas' death, a marriage settlement was arranged for young Elizabeth Wilmot, the heiress presumptive, to secure an annuity of £200 a year for her and her intended husband, Edward Milward, Doctor in Physic, while Dame Elizabeth Cookes-Winford had the rest of the estate, with certain exceptions, for life. It was the transfer of this settled property to trustees that required the survey of 1743, which recorded details of tenants and their rents, but not the areas (which fortunately the 1731 terrier provided). The 1731 document (Table 13) shows that most of the estate was held in that year by Dame Sarah Winford, widow of Sir Thomas, as her jointure, and that she held this for life. Only Trent Wong and the Abbey closes were not included in the jointure estate. A second Elizabeth Milward, only child of Edward Milward and Elizabeth (Wilmot) inherited the estate from her parents, and, as described later, it was she who sold the estate in 1798.

The campus in 1725-43

The condition of the present University campus in the second quarter of the 18th century can be described in respect of agrarian status, settlement and tenurial pattern from data extracted from four particular sources - the rentals or terriers of the demesne estate in the years 1731 and 1743, and of the Gregory estate in 1725 and 1738. The demesne estate schedules are set out in Tables 13 and 14, the former listing closes or parcels of land with their areas in 1731, and the latter the lands held by named tenants together with their rents. Appendix 12 combines the data of the Winford/Milward estate with those of the Gregory estate to show the relationships between the farm holdings of the two estates, tenants of the Gregory estate being included only if they occupied Gregory estate land within the present campus, or if they also occupied land of the Milward estate.

In addition to the three cottages at the end of the schedule of properties in Table 14, three houses are mentioned in 1743, one being associated with the paper mill on the river Leen, the successor of the house attached to the priory's corn mill of the 16th and 17th centuries. The other two were farmhouses, which were not mentioned in the terrier of 1731, although the two messuages at the end of the 1731 schedule would be former 'Brickhouse' cottages [Barnes 1987]. The first farmhouse, associated with Broom Closes and Meadow occupied by Hugh Standley, must have been the old farmstead named on Chapman's map surveyed in 1774 as The Odd House [5], possibly a barn conversion. This was on the site of the present Lenton Abbey house, and is discussed further in Chapter X (on Lenton Abbey). The other farmhouse was also marked and named on Chapman's map, and was a house, with barn and garden called the Abbey House, occupied by the tenant of the Abbey Fields and other land, and located near the junction of Abbey Street with Clifton Boulevard, on or near the site of the later Poplar Farm and now beneath road works. It was later occupied by Thomas Stevenson, who farmed broadly the same land as that held by Francis Allgood. This house, too, may have been a conversion, incorporating the old Dayhouse (dairyhouse) of the priory.

The near-contemporaneous data on the Gregory estate, including land within the present University campus, are derived from two sources. The first is a terrier and rental of 1725 [6] which provides full details of the tenants and their holdings, with the area and rent charged for each close or parcel, and the total area held by each tenant in each of the open arable fields together with the rent; but no details are given of the complicated makeup of their lands in the various individual open fields. The second source is a rental or terrier of Gregory lands dated 1738, to be found among the Middleton papers [7], though this gives no information about holdings in the open arable fields, and only a collective area for the enclosed land of each holding. The first dozen items in this document are repeated without names of tenants in a Pearson-Gregory document of the same year [8] which relates to a mortgage and quotes the marriage settlement of George Gregory the younger and Ann Orton.

Appendix 12 indicates the makeup of the holdings of individual farmers in both Winford

Table 14.
Rental of the estate of the priory demesne, 1743

N.U.M.D., Wadsworth W 21 (1743): 'Copy of the premises at Lenton mentioned in deeds of 5 and 6 August 1743'

All the site, circuit and precinct of the late dissolved Priory of Lenton...and also...the closes, lands, tenements and farms in Lenton and Radford as the same are now known...and now are or late were in the several tenants' possessions...under the yearly rents:

Trent Wong occ. by Mr Benjamin Deverall	£61. 0s.
Messuage or tenement and Middle Broom Close, Next Broom Close and Broom Meadow occ. by Hugh Standley	24.10s.
Messuage or tenement and paper mill, and 2 pond yards, the Five Acre Close and David Close, occ. Mr. Field	23.13s.
Duck Meadow, occ. Thomas Trigg	3s.4d.
The Near Broom Close, Dayhouse Close and Ox Close occ. by Mr. Lowe	14. 5s.
The Hill Close, Hill Close Gutt, Little Tims Close, the other Little Tims Close, Churchyard Close and Round Close, occ. William Morris	23. 0s.
Carleholme occ. by Francis Roberts	2. 0s.
The Seven Acres meadow occ. by Thomas Wood	6.10s.
The Cow Close, The Gossy Close, Upper Wheatcroft and Little Littling, occ. by Thomas Partridge	54.10s.
The Near Abbey Fields, the Far Abbey Fields, the Higher Hill Close, the Lower Hill Close, the Abbey Orchard, the Little Broom Close and the Dovecote Close	82. 5s.
together with Wards Close with a house, barn and garden both occ. by Mr. Francis Allgood	9. 0s.
The Rye Close, Great and Middle Littling, Rounds Close and 2 Highfields Closes, occ. by Mr. Jno. Chamberlain	76. 0s.
The Leggit Wong and The Greens, occ. by Mr. Beardsley	21.10s.
Pryers Meadow, occ. by Mr. Hawkesley	5. 5s.
Tamworth, Nether Tamworth and Nether Wheatcroft, occ. by Mr. John Devrall and Mr. Handley	23.10s.
The Lower Highfield Close, Nether Highfield Close and the Great Rounds Close, occ. by Thomas Hanson	25.10s.
Rushey Close, occ. by Bridgett Hooley	3.14s.
The Less[er] Rushey Close, occ. by Thomas Newham	3.10s.
The Calf Close occ. by William Commins	4. 0s
The Far Broom Close and the Rounds Close occ. John Moore	12.10s
A Rounds close, occ. Edward Attenborow	4. 0s
Doe Park, occ. William Black	2. 0s.
Great Tims, occ. Matthew Welsh	4. 0s.
A messuage or cott. and garden, occ. William Shelton	10s.
A cott and garden occ. Edward Crowcroft	8s.
A cott and garden occ. Jno. Alling	8s.

Total rents, excluding Trent Wong, £426.11s.4d.

(Milward) and Gregory estates in the 1730s/1740s, the latter including the former Alexander Wright closes. Virtually all the former demesne land of the priory is accounted for in this schedule, which emphasizes the fragmentation of occupance in the earlier 18th century. Indeed, when an attempt is made to map the land holdings the incoherence of the farm pattern is revealed, and the map adds little to the conclusions that can be drawn from the Table (Figure 28). Nevertheless there had been, by 1743, a significant reduction in the degree of fragmentation of land holding during the preceding 60 years.

In the 1684 survey of the priory estate three cottages were described - probably the old Brickhouse cottages on the priory site beyond the river Leen - but no farmstead was mentioned on the former demesne, which appears to have been totally uninhabited, although it is believed that the Abbey House on the Dayhouse site was occupied then. Yet there were 35 different occupiers of the demesne land, excluding those occupying Alexander Wright closes. By 1743 they had been reduced to 22, and in addition to the three cottages and the mill house on the Leen two farmsteads were included, though neither figured in the 1731 terrier - the farmstead of Hugh Standley on what was later called Lenton Abbey farm (the Odd House), and the Abbey House, discussed above, occupied by Francis Allgood, the farmer of the Abbey Fields. Land that had remained unploughed since before the middle of the 16th century was being returned to arable cultivation in a system of convertible husbandry under the stimulus of the stirrings of the Industrial Revolution and its population growth. A beginning was being made on the estate in replacement of subletting in small units, as appendages to farms outside, by the formation of self-contained farm holdings. Subsequently the extensive grazing lands of the Abbey Fields on the 'upland' and the cow pastures and feeding pastures of the valley floor were subdivided into closes of manageable size.

We can discern through the 18th century a halting but considerable reorganization of the estate, in the process of which the former demesne lands were being 're-colonized', especially later in the century as revealed by new houses mentioned in the 1798 survey. By the 1780s the pattern of holding and occupation had become more stable, as longer leases were granted by the estate owner, and in 1780 the number of tenants had decreased to only 12 (Figure 29) although a similar number still shared the campus lands not then in the Milward estate - most of them 'Keighton Closes'. Only 6 of the 12 paid land tax of more than £1.10s. 0d. a year, the others holding only a small field or two. Even in 1743 we can discern incipient self-contained farm holdings, and in the lands of Hugh Standley, Francis Allgood, Thomas Hanson, Thomas Partridge and Jno. Chamberlin a foreshadowing of the shape of the tenurial pattern that persisted into the present century. The process of reorganization was punctuated by the grant to David Drake in 1782 of a lease of over one-third of the entire former demesne, out of which a rationalization of the valley-floor Dunkirk lands arose, notably in the subdivision of the farms occupied in the 1790s by James White and William Wigley [9], where 174 acres was divided exactly into two, to leave each half with a fair share of land of varying quality. By the end of the century there was a farmhouse on each Dunkirk farm.

While there are signs in the 1730s of the beginnings of reorganization on the main part of the demesne estate, the Keighton Closes, in the Gregory estate, remained unchanged in character and function. Distinct from the rest of the demesne in tenurial status before the Dissolution, they were never used together as part of a single farm, but were held individually by various Lenton farmers as separate fields isolated from their farmsteads, though hardly more isolated than their strips of arable and hay land dispersed in the common fields of Lenton and Radford. Their function was very much the same as that of the closes of the main demesne estate, and it was common to find farmers holding closes from both estates. This is well seen in Appendix 13.

Inclosure

As mentioned earlier, the inclosure of the common fields was a major event in the social and economic history of rural areas, and in Lenton it took place in 1768-69. It liberated landowners and farmers alike to improve the organization and productivity of their lands, not least by permitting the

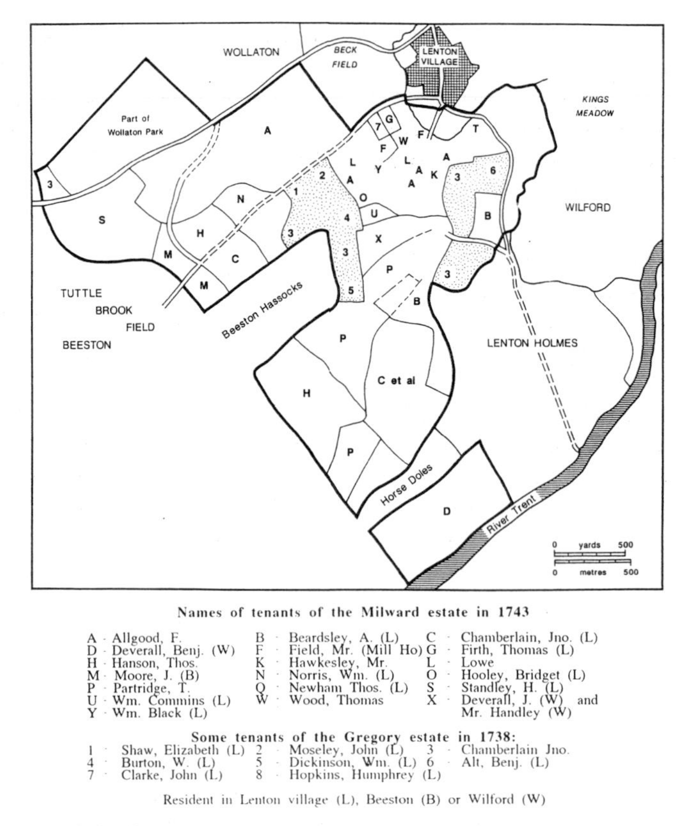

Figure 28: Tenants of the former priory demesne in about 1740

consolidation of highly fragmented holdings, and the building of farmhouses and other farm buildings conveniently located within the consolidated farms. There were, necessarily, serious social consequences for the cottagers who relied on their shares of common grazing, including that on the open arable fields after harvest. This hardly concerned the priory demesne estate since it was virtually uninhabited; but there was a more fundamental and very important reason. On account of its monastic origins and private status as the priory's farm the whole demesne enjoyed freedom from tithes, but had no common grazing rights for its tenants; and these two features together meant that it had no claim on the fruits of inclosure. The only part of the University campus in Lenton (Beeston was a different matter) that was involved directly in the inclosure was a strip of land on the north-west side of the site of the Queen's Medical Centre, where the land between the present Clifton Boulevard and Hillside, including the houses and gardens of Derby Road, the perimeter road of the Q.M.C., and the north-western part of the Q.M.C. buildings was outside the demesne and formed the south-eastern end of the Beck Field, which was involved in the inclosure.

The common Beck Field extended south from Ilkeston Road to Spring Close, on the margin of the flood plain, bounded west by Wollaton Park and separated from the river Leen to the east, north of the old Derby Road, by Thackholme, a common meadow. The Gregory estate gained very greatly from the inclosure of 1768, and was awarded most of Beck Field. Not only was George de Ligne Gregory 'the owner and proprietor of the greatest part of the lands' but he was also the 'lord of the manors of Lenton and Radford and owner and proprietor of all the impropriate tythes of corn and hay': and he was heavily rewarded for each. The owner of the estate of the priory demesne, by contrast, received no allocation of land whatsoever since the former demesne was not 'tytheable', and it had no attached common grazing rights or beast gates in either the six open arable fields or in the common meadows and pastures of Lenton parish, including The Holmes.

The Inclosure Award of 1768 [10] gave Gregory 572 out of the 665 acres allotted to the six landowners of Lenton (excluding the former demesne), as follows.

Gregory, George de Ligne	572a.2.30
Brentnall, G.and Garland R.	40a.3.35
Middleton, Lord	25a.2.08
Wayte, George, vicar of Lenton (glebe)	23a.3.36
Thane, James	1a.1.26
Webb, John	3.02
Total	665a.1.17

Although no enclosure map, or a copy of one is known to exist, it is not difficult to reconstruct a map from the details given in the text of the award. Gregory received two substantial blocks of Beck Field - 91a.2.36 in the north, which included part of Thackholme Meadow, and 54a.3.05 to the south - the part of Beck Field south of the old Nottingham to Derby turnpike [11]. Lord Middleton later acquired the first of these blocks of land and included it in his park, and he subsequently bought the northern part of the second allotment for the same purpose when he diverted Derby Road to the present line of Adams Hill in 1822, as recounted in Chapter XIII below. The tract between the present Derby Road and the former Spring Close was retained in the Gregory estate. The Gregory estate map compiled between 1818 and 1823 [12] shows that by that time the estate included also much of the remainder of the site of the Q.M.C., fields called Abbey Closes in the 17th century, which had been acquired by purchase [13].

The Milward estate in the later 18th century

Landholdings in 1770-1780

The inclosure of 1768 had little direct effect on the area of the present campus, but had an indirect effect in so far as the lands held from the Gregory estate were occupied by tenants whose main holdings were transformed by the consolidation effected by enclosure of the arable fields and related exchanges of land. In the absence of an enclosure map the Gregory estate rentals of 1768 and 1769 are useful because they record the land holdings and rents applying immediately after the enclosure [14]. However, while they include land in the Gregory estate such as the Keighton Closes they do not indicate the affiliations of Milward estate land.

There is no terrier of the Milward estate between the initial one of 1743 [15] and the final one of 1798 [16], but Land Tax assessments that are available annually from 1780 onwards record owners and occupiers of parcels of land without naming them, and offer useful evidence of the pattern of land holding year by year from 1780. The Land Tax returns are in the form of an annual schedule of taxes demanded from individual occupiers of land in order to raise a fixed annual sum from the parish - in the case of Lenton a total of £292.17s. 4d.. This was itself a proportion of a larger, global sum, and was apportioned on the basis of actual or supposed rent value of each piece of land, whether occupied by owner or tenant. The schedule was drawn up and approved by assessors from the parish in May or June for the year ending Lady Day (25 March) in the following year, and thus the situation reflected in the schedules was that existing in May or June. This detail is of some importance in times of rapid changes of ownership and tenancy such as 1798 to 1800 on the former priory demesne. The annual assessments of Land Tax were recorded as quarterly values from 1780 to 1795, and thereafter as annual sums. In this discussion all quarterly values have been expressed as equivalent annual amounts. Copies of the Lenton Land Tax schedules can be found in the Nottinghamshire Archives Office.

It is immediately apparent from the Land Tax returns which occupiers held land of more than one proprietor, and in particular which occupiers of Gregory estate farms also held Milward estate land. The details of areas and rents of individual houses, closes and parcels of land in the 1768 and 1769 Gregory estate rentals clearly show the consolidation of holdings of land as a consequence of the consolidation of ownership of formerly tiny, widely scattered strips in the open arable fields to form closes of considerable size, made possible by the near-monopoly of the Gregory estate. What is not seen, however, is a consolidation of actual farm units as distinct from land ownership within the individual former open fields. This was a matter of estate management outside the remit of the Inclosure Commissioners, and had not yet been tackled. It is therefore not surprising to find that Gregory estate lands in the campus area were still isolated units attached to usually quite large farm holdings.

Such dispersion was less apparent in the Milward estate. The great fragmentation of tenancy seen in the former demesne lands in 1684 [17] had been substantially reduced by 1743 [18], the 33 tenants (plus 3 cottagers) of 1684 having fallen to 22 tenants (plus 3 cottagers). By 1780 there were only 12 tenants [19], though the number increased again towards the end of the century. This increase was an industrial rather than an agrarian phenomenon, being attributable to the appearance of several small land holdings in the vicinity of the river Leen and the new Nottingham Canal. The process can be followed through the Land Tax assessments. Land taxes for 1780 on lands in the Milward estate and the Gregory estate that are now in the University campus are included in Appendix 13, which gives details of Gregory estate farms in 1768-69.

Tenurial devolution 1780-98: Land Tax evidence

The tenurial devolution of the twelve properties of the Milward estate from 1780 down to 1798 is shown in Figure 29, based mainly on annual Land Tax schedules, and notes on the changes shown are given in Appendix 14. But beginning in late 1797, and mainly in 1798, the history of the 'upland' part of the demesne as a tract of farm land was suddenly and permanently ended by the sale of the whole Milward estate, and the conversion of much of it into residential parkland.

The sale was precipitated by the private financial problems of Miss Milward, the owner, and not by any local pressure for development, but the timing was such that the campus area was sold very speedily to five chief purchasers, joined shortly afterwards by a sixth. The details of the transactions are discussed later, but the attractions can be readily appreciated. They included the rural setting and pleasant contours, and the location on the west side, and within commuting distance of the city of Nottingham at a time when a wealthy middle class were seeking more salubrious settings for their homes away from the increasing congestion and pollution and adjoining squalor of the city. The subsequent residential development of The Park estate, and, after the inclosure of Nottingham, of areas such as Sherwood, were urban or suburban in character, but the developments on the former priory demesne were of a rural, 'country-house' nature, with the houses set in small parks rather than large gardens. It is interesting to speculate as to whether the long delay in enclosing Nottingham's open fields ultimately helped to preserve the campus for its present function.

It is sometimes implied that those who purchased parts of the present campus, and built houses on them 190 years ago were all escaping from the city environment. But of the six early builders Matthew Needham (Lenton House) moved from Wilford, and James Green (Lenton Abbey) from Wollaton, while Francis Evans (Lenton Grove), who moved from Thurland Hall, had bought much of his land, including the site of his house, in 1791 for a quite different purpose (see Chapter XI). Joseph Lowe (Highfield House) did move from Nottingham Market Place, and John Wright (Lenton Hall) from Low Pavement, Nottingham. The previous residence of Thomas Watson (Lenton Firs) is not known.

The farm holdings of the Milward estate before the sale of 1798

It is possible to identify most of the closes and parcels of former demesne land listed in the 1798 survey in the terrier of 1684, over a century earlier. In that interval, however, changes in

1780 (10 May)	Property and changes of occupier	1797 (1 June)	1798 (11 June)
Miss Milward's estate			
Thomas Wright 8s. 0d.	Little Rushy Park = Doe Park	Thomas Wright 8s. 0d. Auctioned December 1797	Thomas Wright 8s. 0d. GREGORY
Widow Welsh £ 1. 8s. 0d.	Seven-acres Close Thomas Rowe 1783	Killingley and Green £ 1. 8s. 0d. Bleach yard 1797	J.W.Killingley £ 1. 5s. 1d LOCK
Mrs. Wood 18s. 8d.	1792 Miss Hannah Wood 1795 Execs. Mrs. Wood		
Messrs. Roberts of Nottingham £ 3.14s. 8d.	Leather mills Ellis, Roberts and Co. 1794 lease 1797	Ellis, Roberts and Co. £ 3.14s. 8d.	Ellis, Roberts and Co. £ 1. 2s. 0d. PAGET
Thomas Stevenson £ 15. 7s. 4d (£ 14.11.4 and for the Greens 16s. 0d.)	Abbey House and farm	Thomas Stevenson £ 15. 7s. 4d	Thomas Stevenson JOHN WRIGHT £ 18.18s. 0d.
William Norris £ 4.19s. 0d. (£ 4. 3s. 0d. and for Cummins Close 16s. 0d.)	1789-90 £ 4.9s.0d. → 1794 Wm. Wigley £25.8s.8d.		Joseph Lowe £ 4. 6s. 5d. JOSEPH LOWE
David Drake £ 32. 6s. 4d. (£ 1. 0s. 0d. and late Deverals £ 4. 7s. 8d Nether grounds £23. 5s.4d. The Rounds 12s.0d. Ledgett Wong £ 3. 1s.4d.)	1782 lease → 1794 Wm. Wigley £25.8s.8d. 1783 James White £12.4s.8d. 'Half the Nether grounds'	William Wigley £25. 8s. 8d. James White £12. 4s. 8d.	William Wigley £13.12s. 3d. PAGET James White £ 9.11s. 4d PAGET
Joseph Newton 8s. 0d	1782 8s.0d.		
Mr. Wilkinson £ 5. 7s. 8d.	Odd House and farm 1790 John Clayton	John Clayton £ 5. 7s. 8d.	James Green £ 8.10s. 4d. JAMES GREEN
Mr. Hall £ 10.16s.8d.	Trent Wong 1787 Abel Smith 1796 Robert Smith	Samuel Smith £10.16s. 8d.	Samuel Smith £12. 1s. 2d. SAMUEL SMITH
Joseph Black of Nottingham 12s. 8d.	Five Acres Close 1783 William Black	William Black 12s. 8d.	William Black £ 1. 4s. 6d. WILLIAM BLACK
Messrs Hague and James £ 4.18s. 8d.	Cottage farm on Beeston Lane 1782 Messrs. Hopkin and Hooton	Hopkin and Hooton £4.18s.8d.	Hopkin and Hooton £8.11s.7d. HOPKIN AND HOOTON
			Francis Evans £ 1. 8s. 3d. FRANCIS EVANS
Other land			
John Moore £ 2. 9s. 4d.	Attenborough Francis Evans 1791 £1.10s.0d. Lenton Grove land	Francis Evans £ 1.10s.0d.	Francis Evans £ 1.10s. 0d. FRANCIS EVANS
William Hodges 18s. 0d.	Hill Closes Attenborough and Hodges	Attenborough and Hodges 18s. 0d.	Unchanged
William Lowe 10s. 0d.	Far Field Close	William Lowe 10s. 0d.	Unchanged
Widow Welsh £ 1. 1s. 4d GREGORY ESTATE	Thomas Rowe 1783	Thomas Rowe £ 1. 1s. 4d.	Unchanged

Figure 29: Land tax of Miss Milward's estate and some adjoining property, 1780-1798
Notes in extension of these data form Appendix 14.

tenancy and some little remodelling of field boundaries, inevitably led to changes of area and of name. It is no surprise, therefore, to encounter difficulties in definitely identifying in 1798 successive closes in the 1684 terrier called Clarke's Close (6a.) and Pares Close (4a.), occupied by Widow Clarke and William Pare respectively. 'A close, piece or parcel of meadow ground' called Barley's Close (6a.) was occupied in 1684 by Robert Barley or his assigns. In 1798 it had alternative names - Rounds Close or Rounds (8a.0.13): but the Rounds were irregular, discontinuous and virtually impossible to map, like The Greens, so identification of this land is uncertain. Examination of the 1684 terrier shows that some of the references in the 1798 document are not found there, and must come from the terrier of 1731 or the rental of 1743. For example, the Fourteen Acres, and Fourteen Acres Meadow (14a.3.3a and 14a.0.29 respectively) are indicated as having been the High Hill Close and Lower Hill Close, of 29 acres together (now usually called the downland). This reference must come from the 1743 rental, since the names do not occur in 1684. These particular names in 1743 are found in the lands occupied by Mr. Francis Allgood, together with the Near Abbey Field, the Far Abbey Field and other closes. In 1731, when they were not named, the Abbey Fields pastures were given 200 acres. In 1798 land identified as belonging to the Near or Far Abbey Fields in 1684 totalled only about 167 acres, and it is fairly certain that the Fourteen Acres and Fourteen Acres Meadow (the Higher and Lower Hill Closes) were in 1684 parts of the Abbey Fields. There is also some doubt about the exact identification of the various High Fields and High Closes, North and South, Upper and Lower.

For such reasons the map of the campus area in 1798 (Figure 30) as well as those of 1684 and 1730-40 may be subject to revision if actual field boundaries are drawn. The boundaries used are those of the first edition O.S. six-inch map, modified by the evidence of earlier maps such as the Gregory estate map of 1818-23, and the Lenton Abbey farm map of about 1816. The details of the farm map (Figure 30) will be discussed further later, though it may be pointed out here that most of the former demesne, including the area of the University campus was now, for the first time, divided into coherent, consolidated farm holdings.

The sale and breakup of the Milward estate, 1797-1800

The halting agrarian development of the demesne estate in the later 18th century continued on the Trent valley floor in the 19th century, but the area that has become the University campus underwent a sharp change about the turn of the century, when the farming population was replaced by a very different group of residents. The new settlers immediately set about radically reshaping the landscape to serve their different purposes. A succession of absentee landlords and their tenants, whose interest in the land had been materialistic, if not exploitive, was replaced by a group of wealthy, middle-class, educated people of some culture and taste, who, with their employees constructed over a century or more what the late Professor K. C. Edwards called 'the elegant landscape of the University district'. Their own farming activities were subsidiary to the main purpose of creating and maintaining a residential environment of beauty and privacy. In describing this landscape revolution physical determinism is irrelevant compared with the outlook and motivation of the new landowners, and the outcome of their taste and vision is still prominent in the older buildings and gardens, and the woodland, copses and vistas that the University eventually inherited.

The sale of the Milward estate in Lenton in 1798, which was followed immediately by its dismemberment and partitioning, was thus the event that set in train the great changes in land use and landscape which effectively determined the present character of much of the campus, surviving through later changes of ownership and usage. The circumstances that led to the sale of the estate by Miss Milward on Old Lady Day 1798 can be discovered especially from the abstract of title to Lord Middleton's part of the estate that was prepared for its sale in 1867 [20].

As shown above, Elizabeth (nee Wilmot), wife of Dr. Edward Milward, was a niece of Dame Elizabeth Cookes-Winford, from whom she inherited the estate, and Miss Elizabeth Milward, the

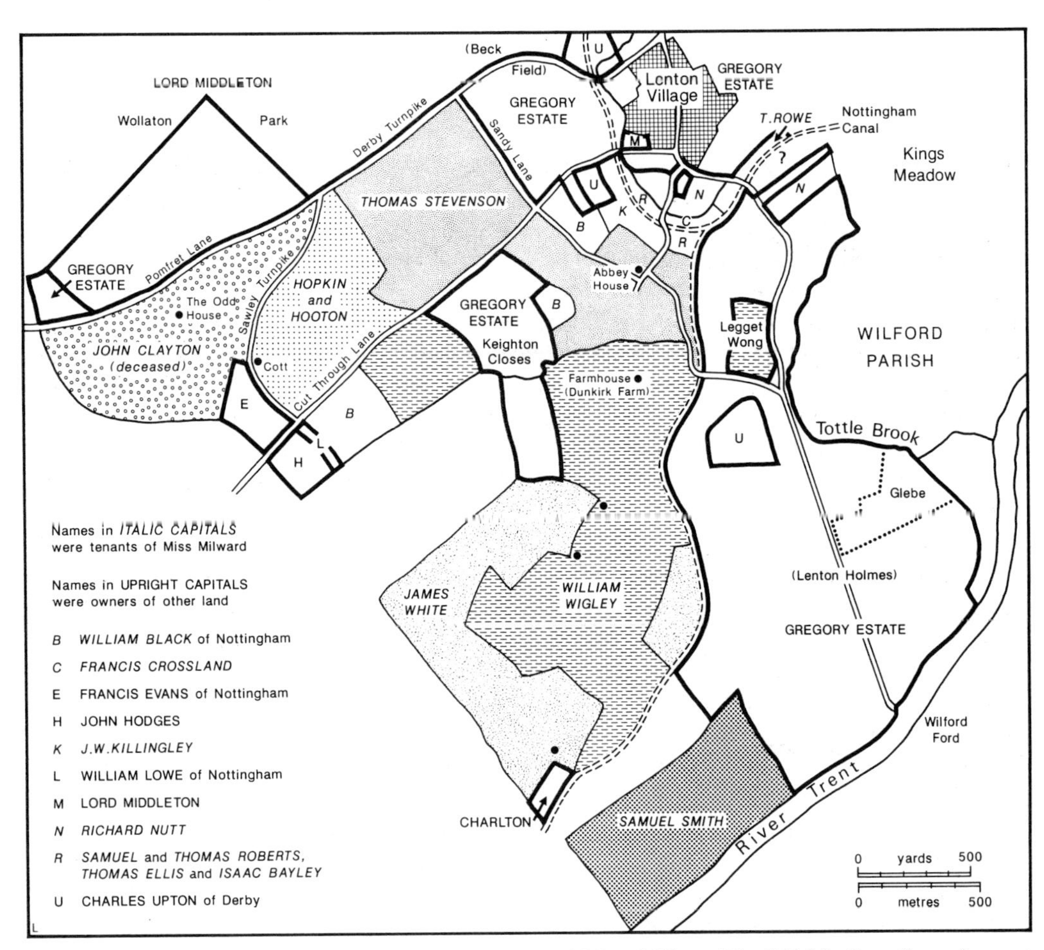

Figure 30: Tenants' land holdings on the estate of Miss Milward in 1798 before the sale

vendor of 1798, inherited it from her mother. In 1752 Dame Elizabeth had mortgaged the 'site and lands' (of the former priory) to Thomas Brotherton for £1,800. Complications arose because Brotherton was declared a lunatic in 1755, when, at the request of Mrs. Elizabeth Milward, then the owner, Thomas Wyld advanced £2,200 in trust to Brotherton to clear up Dame Elizabeth's will and debts. It appears that by 1768 Miss Milward's parents were both dead. When she inherited the estate from her mother the mortgage was transferred to Joseph Hewitt, and it was increased by £800 in 1785. But in 1797 Hewitt asked Elizabeth Milward to pay off the £3,000. She was unable to do so, but James Graham took over the mortgage by indentures of 7 and 8 December 1797, and it was later in that month that the Odd House (Lenton Abbey) farm of about 100 acres, and three closes near to Lenton village were put up for auction, evidently with a view to paying off this debt and extinguishing the mortgage.

The auction was first announced in the Nottingham Journal of 9 December 1797, the day after the premises were 'sold' to James Graham of Lincolns Inn, and was to be on 27 December at the Blackamoor's Head, Nottingham. The advertisement was repeated on 16 and 23 December. Although it seems that the auction was held, and at least one of the three closes up for sale was sold, the farm at Lenton Abbey was not, but formed part of the comprehensive transaction whereby the whole estate, with the exception of Trent Wong, was sold as from Old Lady Day, 29 March 1798 to Thomas Pares the younger of Leicester, and Thomas Paget of Scraptoft, Leicester, an absolute purchase in fee simple, free from all encumbrances, for £34,000 [21]. The £3,000 owed to James Graham was discharged by Miss Milward asking him to join her in the conveyance, and he was paid from the purchase money - at least that was the effect of the legal devices used in the transaction. Trent Wong, detached from the main estate, was sold separately to Samuel Smith for an unknown sum. By deed poll of 29 March 1798, the same day as the sale of the main estate, we learn of an interest in the purchase being conveyed to John Pares, and also the exception from the sale of 'certain hereditaments ... sold and conveyed or assigned to the use of Samuel Smith, his heirs and assigns ... '.

Samuel Smith was a banker, and so were Thomas Pares and Thomas Paget. Smith had his home at Wilford, and in the discussion of Trent Wong in Chapter XV it will be pointed out that the Smiths who remained at Wilford also remained owners of nearby Trent Wong throughout the 19th century. Thomas Paget was a member of the Leicester banking house of Pares, Pares, Paget and Heygate, and when he ceased to be a member of the partnership he set up a bank on his own account early in 1825 in the High Street at Leicester. Pares and Pares would be Thomas and John Pares. John Pares, a brother of Thomas, was also a Leicester hosier. Unlike Smith's purchase it is clear that in buying the estate Pares and Paget were investing their clients' funds and obtaining a substantial profit by immediately selling off the estate in portions. The re-sale was expertly organized and carried through, as would be expected of successful, business men and bankers. They lost no time in finding wealthy purchasers wishing to build houses for their own occupation, and some of the transactions were so expeditious as to suggest that they had been negotiated well in advance. Within a few days, on 4/5 April 1798, much of Lenton Abbey farm (as it became known), most of which is now occupied by Council and private housing, was sold for £4,780 to James Green of Wollaton, with a minor share adjoining his own land to Francis Evans of Nottingham [22]. They built, respectively, the existing Lenton Abbey House, and Lenton Grove. Lenton Grove was built on land that was not part of the Milward estate, but had been acquired by Evans in 1791 (see Chapter XI).

By the time that the land tax assessments for 1798-99 were approved, on 11 June 1798, John Wright, another banker, had purchased the farm occupied by Thomas Stevenson, which then included the land of Lenton Firs and most of what became Lenton Hall park, and he later built Lenton Hall on the ridge-top. Joseph Lowe had bought most of the 'upland' part of what became the Highfield estate; and Messrs. Hooton and Hopkin had acquired the land that later included the Lenton House estate, which they already occupied as tenants, together with an adjoining tract of land immediately to the north called the Fourteen Acres and Fourteen Acres Meadow, extending as far as the old line of the Sawley turnpike between the present Lenton Hurst and Rutland Hall. There were other, minor sales; for example a Mr. Lock acquired the Seven Acres Meadow occupied by J.W.Killingley, who had a bleachyard there. At this stage, only two months after their purchase of the Milward estate, Pares and Paget retained unsold only the Abbey Orchard and Mill Close alongside the river Leen and the industrial site of Ellis, Roberts and Company nearby, together with the farms of Dunkirk in the Trent valley between the Tottle Brook and the Beeston Canal, occupied by William Wigley and James White (Figure 31). This is evident because Paget was shown as the owner of the farms in the land tax assessment of 1798, although this is not to say that sales documents for these properties were not already in preparation in this flurry of legal activity .

One year later the land tax assessment dated 27 June 1799 showed that the only parts of the former estate remaining in the ownership of Pares and Paget were the site of Ellis, Roberts and Co., and the Abbey Orchard with Mill Close (Figure 31). The former remained in their hands for many years; the latter was soon sold. John Wright had bought the valley farms of Wigley and White, and on Lady Day 1799 had taken in hand the farm occupied by Thomas Stevenson, who in 1823 described how he was allowed to remain in his 25-year-long tenancy for the first year of John Wright's ownership, with additional land, but was given notice to quit on Lady day 1799 [23]. Most of his farm was about to be converted into parkland, but the north-east corner of it was sold to Thomas W. Watson, a Nottingham hosier, who built on it the house later called Lenton Firs. Lenton Firs was probably built in 1799-1800, since Watson first appeared in the land tax assessments in 1800. The house was greatly extended in the 1860s (see Chapter IX). Matthew Needham purchased from Messrs. Hooton and Hopkin some land on which Lenton House was built for him. The tax on this land was assessed at 18s. 8d., and it was probably the Home Field or House Close near the hill top where the house stands.

11 June 1798	Land Tax		1799	Land Tax		1800	Land Tax	Property
Thomas Wright GREGORY	8s. 0d.		Thomas Wright GREGORY	8s. 0d.				Little Rushy Park
J.W.Killingley MR. LOCK	£1.5s. 1d.		J.W.Killingley MR. LOCK	£1.5s. 7d.		J.W.Killingley MR LOCK	£1.5s. 7d.	Seven Acre Cl. Bleach Yard
Richard Nutt RICHARD NUTT	4s. 8d		Richard Nutt RICHARD NUTT	4s. 8d		Richard Nutt RICHARD NUTT	4s. 8d	Priory Orchard
Paget & Pare PAGET & PARE	14s. 9d.		William Stretton PAGET & PARE	15s. 0d.		William Stretton PAGET & PARE	15s. 0d.	Mill Close etc.
Ellis, Roberts and Co. PAGET & PARE	£1.2s. 0d.		Ellis, Roberts and Co. PAGET & PARE	£1.2s. 5d.		Ellis, Roberts and Co. PAGET & PARE	£1.2s. 6d.	Leather mill etc.
Thomas Stevenson JOHN WRIGHT	£19.4s. 9d.		John Wright JOHN WRIGHT	£19.4s. 9d.	A→ B→	T.W.Watson T.W.WATSON	£4.2s. 0d.	Lenton Firs
				£1.5s. 0d.	C→	John Wright JOHN WRIGHT	£15.2s. 9d £ 5.0s. 0d.	Lenton Hall Park
Joseph Lowe JOSEPH LOWE	£4.6s. 5d.		Joseph Lowe JOSEPH LOWE	£4.8s. 0d.		Joseph Lowe JOSEPH LOWE	£4.8s. 0d.	Highfield House
Willm. Wigley PAGET & PARE	£13.12s.3d.		William Wigley JOHN WRIGHT	£13.17s.1d.		Willm. Wigley JOHN WRIGHT	£13.17s.1d.	Dunkirk Farm
James White PAGET & PARE	£9.11s.4d.		James White JOHN WRIGHT	£9.14s.9d.	D	John Wright JOHN WRIGHT	£9.14s.9d.	A Dunkirk farm
James Green JAMES GREEN	£8.10s.4d.		James Green JAMES GREEN	£8.13s.0d.		James Green JAMES GREEN	£8.12s.2d.	Lenton Abbey
Samuel Smith SAMUEL SMITH	£12.1s.2d.		Samuel Smith SAMUEL SMITH	£10.16s.8d.		Samuel Smith SAMUEL SMITH	£10.16s.8d.	Trent Wong
William Black WILLIAM BLACK	£1.4s.6d.		William Black WILLIAM BLACK	£1. 5s.0d.		William Black WILLIAM BLACK	£1. 5s.0d.	Five Acre Close
Messrs Hopkin and Hooton HOPKIN AND HOOTON	£8.11s.7d.	E→	Hopkin and Hooton OR SUCCESSORS	£7.16s.0d.		-------		Beeston Lane Farm
Francis Evans FRANCIS EVANS	£1. 8s.3d. (plus £1.10s.0d.)		Francis Evans FRANCIS EVANS	£1. 8s.8d. (plus £1.10s.0d.)		Francis Evans FRANCIS EVANS	£1. 8s.8d. (plus £1.10s.0d.)	Lenton Grove
		F→	Matthew Needham MATTHEW NEEDHAM	18s.8d.	G→	Matthew Needham MATTHEW NEEDHAM	£3.14s.8d	Lenton House

Notes: A - Part sold to T.W.Watson included an area later (1822) incorporated into Wollaton Park.
B - Remainder formed major part of Lenton Hall park.
C - Addition to Wright's land, not identified.
D - Purchase of the south-west part of the 'downland' - the Fourteen Acre Close and the Fourteen Acre Meadow.
E - Matthew Needham's initial purchase of land on which to site Lenton House.
F - Matthew Needham's second purchase to complete the Lenton House estate.

The only change identified in the Land Tax schedules from 1800 to 1801 was the sale by Matthew Needham to John Wright of a strip of land which became an orchard, dividing the Lenton House estate from the present 'downland'. This transaction increased Wright's land tax on Lenton Hall park by 1s.8d. and reduced Needham's tax by the same amount, from £3.14s.8d. to £3.13s.0d..

Owners are shown in capitals, occupiers in lower case.

Figure 31: Completion of the sale of Miss Milward's estate as shown by land tax charges on the occupiers and owners of the new estates, 1798-1801

Over the next year, to June 1800, there were further developments. Hopkin and Hooton sold the remainder of their land purchase to Matthew Needham and John Wright. The former transaction was in respect of the greater part of the Lenton House estate, taxed at £3.14s. 8d., and comprising the Lower Highfield and the Grass Close. It was described in the tax schedule entry following that for John Wright as 'Mr. Needham's proportion of do. (that is, of £5) £3.14s. 8d.. The 1800 assessment was dated 22 May. John Wright's portion must have been the Fourteen Acres Close and Fourteen Acres Meadow of the 1798 estate survey, the present 'downland' running down from the Lenton House boundary towards the present Derby and Sherwood Halls, though not extending beyond the line of the old Sawley turnpike. Taxed at £1. 5s. 0d. it was added to the Lenton Hall park occupied by John Wright himself in 1799, and described in the land tax assessment as 'John Wright's proportion of the late Hopkins and Co., £5. 0s. 0d'. John Wright had also himself become the occupier of James White's farm, which he had bought the previous year, and he in fact continued to operate it, presumably through a bailiff, until 1809 or 1810, when Robert Cheetham took it until 1812, followed by Alice Wood. Joseph Lowe of Highfield House suffered an increase in his land tax assessment from £4. 6s. 5d. to £4. 8s. 0d., but it is not known whether this followed a small land purchase, or was the kind of minor change that would be produced by reassessment after large changes in ownership and occupance such as those of these few years. It is possible that the changed assessment marks the purchase by Lowe of Keighton Meadow (see Chapter VI).

The new land owners of the campus very soon made their presence felt in the parish. Godfrey [1884 259] described public criticism of the overseers, Gervas Boot and Mr. Chamberlin. 'At a vestry meeting held this 31st day of August 1798 in the parish church of Lenton, pursuant to a notice for making a rate for the relief of the poor of the said parish; It appeareth that the Church and Poor rates of this parish are assessed with much inequality. Resolved that the churchwardens and overseers are instructed to obtain a proper valuation of the parish in order to make an equal Rate, and they are requested for that purpose to take the advice and assistance of Mr. John Bayley, or, if he shall refuse or not be able to attend, some other competent surveyor'. The resolution was signed by W.Gill on behalf of the vicar: by J. Stubbins on behalf of G. de L. Gregory; and by T. Paget and Thomas Pares junior (the first purchasers of the Milward estate), Samuel Smith (purchaser of Trent Wong), Francis Evans (Lenton Grove), Joseph Lowe (Highfield), William Wigley and James White (occupiers of the lowland (Dunkirk) farms soon to be bought by John Wright).

By 1802 the new pattern of land ownership on the former Milward estate had been largely stabilized (Figure 32). Changes over the previous two years had been few. The land tax assessment dated 15 June 1802 shows that Mrs. Elizabeth Watson had succeeded to her husband's property (Lenton Firs) on his early death. William Stretton, the architect and builder of Lenton Hall, had acquired the last property remaining in the hands of of Pares and Paget apart from the industrial premises of Ellis and Roberts, and he subsequently built the house called The Priory on it. Finally, a transfer from Matthew Needham to John Wright of 1s. 8d. tax on land formerly owned by Hopkin and Hooton probably represents the sale to Wright of the crescentic strip of land along the northern boundary of the Lenton House estate which became an orchard, and has now reverted to University ownership after having been returned by exchange to the Lenton House estate in the 1950s (see Chapter XVI)

Redemption of their land tax by some of the new owners during the next few years robs us of further information about possible changes in land affiliation from that source, but any change is likely to have been small. Francis Evans, Samuel Smith, William Stretton, Joseph Lowe and James Lock redeemed their tax in 1803, and Matthew Needham followed in 1805. However, all change did not cease, and while further details are discussed later, particularly in connection with the devolution of ownership and occupation of the individual new estates, some of the earlier changes should be mentioned here, at risk of repetition, if only to emphasize that total stability of land tenure is never achieved while an area is owned by a number of different landlords.

Changes of land ownership and occupation, 1802-1832

Land tax returns continue to provide information, though in decreasing detail, until 1832, and Appendix 16 offers a summary of changes, mainly from this source. In addition there are some details of acquisitions of other land in Lenton, especially by John Wright, and of exchanges that involved Lenton land in the enclosure award of Beeston in 1809; and these merit some additional discussion.

John Wright of Lenton Hall, the principal purchaser of the Milward estate land, owned more than half of it by 1800. He paid £44.1s.7d. in land tax in 1799 out of a total of £84.4s.8d. for the whole estate, and his share soon increased further. It included Lenton Hall park as originally formed after the sale of Lenton Firs land, to which was then added the 'downland' and two Dunkirk farms, as well as Abbey Field Close, allocated in the Beeston enclosure award. In addition John Wright purchased land called in 1803 'late Longdon's', and then in 1804 land called 'lately Upton's', and although neither affected the campus directly the latter is of considerable interest in respect of developments in Lenton. Longdon's land was taxed at £1.8s.8d. in the assessment of 12 May 1803, and it was added to William Wigley's farm. John Longdon, who built Bramcote House in the early years of the 19th century, inherited the property from his uncle, John Sherwin, by his will of 14 March 1800, he having inherited it from his father, also John Sherwin, by his will of 17 March 1755 [24] (see Appendix 17); so John Longdon's ownership was brief. The land was occupied by Widow Buck in 1780, and she remained the tenant until John Wright bought it.

The 1804 increment of tax on John Wright's estate was for land called 'lately Upton's' occupied by Richard Price, and, although the tax was redeemed, earlier data show it to have been £5.16s.0d. a year (in 1799 and 1800 when owned by Upton). In 1798 it had been owned by Mr. Brentnall, and taxed similarly. The 1804 purchase was of some 23 acres of land at the lower, western end of the former open Alwell or Allen Field, awarded in the Lenton inclosure award of 1768 to Rebecca Garland and George Brentnall (see Appendix 18). The boundaries of the allotment, made in exchange for field land together with land dispersed in Alwell Field, were described in the award (Godfrey 1884 319-26) and are clearly discernible in the Gregory estate map of 1818-23 [25]. Richard Price farmed the land from 1784 onwards.

In 1794 Brentnall granted to Charles Upton shares - held as an undivided moiety - in his estate in Lenton for £2,000. There were three parts: the 23 acres of the former Alwell Field; 8 acres occupied by Elias Roberts and divided by the Nottingham Canal north of the Derby Road-river Leen crossing at Hillside; and 12 acres in The Holmes called Morton Nook Meadow. Upton subsequently acquired the whole before selling to Wright in 1804 the first and largest of these areas. In 1819 this was occupied by J.B.Milne and I.Armitage, and though land tax was redeemed in 1820 it is clear that there were several occupiers in 1822. In fact John Wright had sold 15 acres of the land for building development, and it became the original core of New Lenton. Godfrey [1884 after Bailey 1853 555] wrote : 'It is stated that 16 acres of land purchased at this time by [John Wright] were re-sold in the year 1815 at a rate of £1,000 per acre - at least ten times the amount which had been given for it only about 15 years previously. The village of New Lenton now (1884) occupies the whole of this'. It was already laid out and partly built over by 1824 [26]. The remainder of the 23 acres became the site of the new parish church, presented to the parish by John Wright's son Francis in about 1842; the adjoining recreation ground; and the sites of the house of John Wright's three unmarried daughters and the schools they established.

The 8 acres near Derby Road were purchased by Samuel Goodacre, who owned and operated the nearby mill on the river Leen. Later developments on this land included the Rose and Crown Inn. Morton Nook Meadow, 12 acres called 'late Charlton's', and according to the land tax assessments occupied in 1814-18 by Thomas Shepherd junior, and in 1819-27 by Thomas Shepherd senior (probably the same person) lay adjacent to the Edmondson's Closes, otherwise called The Mortons, and presumed to have been on or near the site of the primary holding of the lost medieval township of Morton. It was bought by John Wright in 1812. Meanwhile the inclosure of Beeston affected the land holdings in Lenton of John Wright and some others.

The effect of the Beeston inclosure of 1809

The Private Act for the inclosure of Beeston was dated 1806 [27] and the Final Award was made in 1809. The sponsoring landowners were Henry, Lord Middleton, Thomas Charlton, John Longdon, John Fellows and Francis Evans esquires, with John Burton, John Deverill, John Cheetham and others. The leading spirit in the pressure for inclosure many years earlier was the attorney and speculator Francis Evans who later built Lenton Grove, and who, having bought land speculatively in Beeston in 1791 was anxious to make the best use of his investment (see Chapter XI). It was he who took the first steps in December 1796 [28]. The Inclosure Commissioners made arrangements that recognized that some owners of land in Lenton also owned land, and were entitled to allotments, in Beeston, and they took the opportunity to tidy up the map, partly by exchanges and partly by awarding allotments in Beeston contiguous with the Lenton lands of the owners concerned [29]. The outcome was an orderly arrangement of property in both parishes. An example of the process is seen in the award to Francis Evans (Lenton Grove) of a tract of the Tuttle Brook Field in Beeston south-west of the brook and adjoining his existing land in Lenton across the brook, extending west to Salthouse Lane north-west of Broadgate, and for a corresponding distance on the opposite side of Broadgate. This allocation eventually led to development problems because the Lenton Grove estate remained in trust for over a century. E.J.Lowe, in the mid-19th century, could not build his 'Observatory' (Broadgate House) any nearer to Highfields, and in the mid-20th century the extension of Woodside Road to link with University Boulevard was impeded until after the second world war. A happy outcome for the University has been the preservation of a green area in front of Willoughby and Cavendish Halls on one side of Woodside Road and of an undeveloped site for building student flats on the other. Further land to the north-west was allocated to Francis Evans by allotting it to John Wright, and then effecting an exchange (Figure 32).

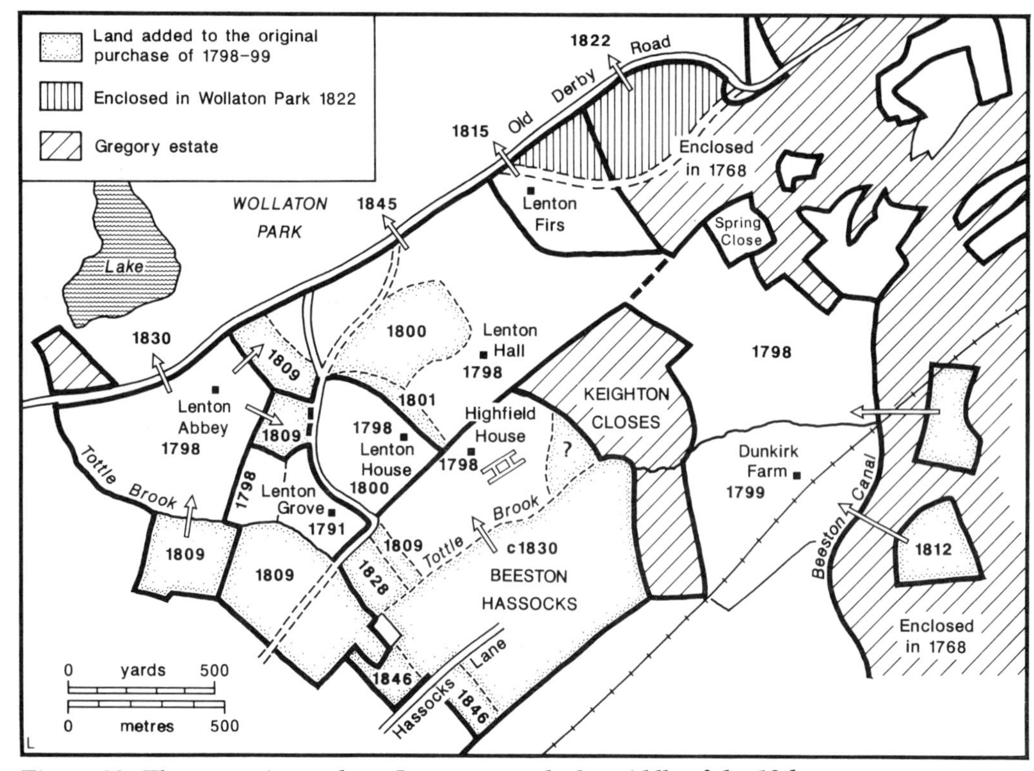

Figure 32: The estates in southern Lenton towards the middle of the 19th century
Dates of acquisition of additional land are shown

The end of the south-facing slope of Highfields running down to the Beeston boundary at the Tottle Brook west of the Beeston Lane entrance to the Highfield House estate and the original College campus, was not a part of the Milward estate at the end of the 18th century [30]. The level fragment of gravel terrace now occupied by Florence Boot Hall and its grounds, together with part of the field that separates the Hall from University Boulevard, (as far as the brook, now culverted) was held in part jointly in trust by John Hodges and Mr. Attenborough, and in part by William Lowe of Nottingham, a Beeston landowner. Lowe was the owner of the Beeston silk mill later destroyed by the Reform Bill rioters, and is not to be confused with the Lowes of Highfield House.

At the inclosure of Beeston Hodges owned the four Hill Closes - the Enclosure Commissioners having agreed to divide the moiety - with a combined area of 8a.1.38, and William Lowe owned the Far Field Close containing 3a.3.2. Both were allotted land in the Far Field of Beeston, near the junction between the present Wollaton Road and Derby Road. Joseph Lowe of Highfield House was awarded land in the same area, and this was immediately exchanged, by agreement, to William Lowe for the Far Field Close, which was added to the adjoining Highfield estate. Far Field Close does not figure in the land tax records because Joseph Lowe had redeemed his tax in 1803, and presumably did the same for the close. The Hill Closes were added to the Highfield estate by purchase only in about 1828. From 1828 to 1832 the 'redeemed lands' of the Highfield estate were not mentioned in land tax assessments, but Alfred Lowe paid tax of 19s.0d. on land occupied by himself. This was probably for the Hill Closes, which were earlier taxed at 19s.4d. Their acquisition made it possible for Alfred Lowe to construct a conduit to carry water from the Tottle Brook at its bridge on Beeston Lane (by the present west entrance to the campus) to feed the extended lake (see Chapter VI). The separation of the Hill Closes from the Lenton Grove land across Beeston Lane, purchased by Francis Evans in 1791, is discussed in Chapter XI.

The allotments made in Beeston to John Wright of Lenton Hall could not, of course, adjoin the main body of his land in Lenton except for those in Beeston Hassocks. Wright was allotted about 57 acres in Beeston, in 15 parcels of open and enclosed land, in compensation for loss of rights of common and five Thorndike Closes exchanged to P.S.Broughton. But Wright also had an old enclosure of about 4 acres called Brook Close adjoining the Tottle Brook in Tuttle Brook Field, facing, across the brook, Broom Meadow in Lenton belonging to James Green of Lenton Abbey. The purchase of Brook Close, with 'other premises in Beeston' by John Wright from John Sherwin and others on 13/14 April 1807, for £3,500, can be seen as preparation for the transfer to Wright of Abbey Field Close (now part of the sports ground in front of the Indoor Sports Centre) by exchange with James Green in the enclosure award. The Commissioners allotted about 7 acres of open field land in Tuttle Brook Field adjoining Brook Close to John Wright, and then exchanged this land, together with the Brook Close for about the same area on the north-east side of James Green's Lenton Abbey, lying west of the new northern section of the Sawley turnpike (Beeston Lane) [31]. The Beeston enclosure map confirms that the Sawley turnpike had already been diverted by 1809 (see Chapter XIII).

The land tax assessments for Lenton indicate that this exchange between Wright and Green had already taken place *de facto* by 1808, when Green's assessment in Lenton fell from £8.12s.2d. to £6.17s.3d., that is, by £1.14s.11d.. However, only £1.4s.5½d. was added to John Wright's account, and the balance of 10s.4½d. was charged to Matthew Needham of Lenton House (which he redeemed in 1810). This was for Lenton Field, upon which the house called Lenton Fields was built by Needham for Mrs. Catherine Turner and her school in about 1835 (see Chapter VIII). It is interesting to find that this house, which cannot be grouped by age or style with any other on the campus, owed its existence to some degree to a chance event in the process of the inclosure of Beeston. The area of Abbey Field Close was 10a.2.17, and of Lenton Field about 6.3 acres.

P.S.Broughton's Rounds Close of 8a.3.18, allotted to John Wright because he now owned virtually the whole valley tract north-east from the Beeston boundary to the Leen, was almost certainly Gervas Close, rented and then bought in 1670 by Thomas Charlton of Chilwell [32]. In 1812 its tax was 16s.0d. 'for land late Charlton's', occupied by Wright; but in 1814 to 1826 it was let to Thomas Shepherd. Except for the athletics track and the 1st XV Rugby ground [33] the University and public playing fields extending north-east to the Tottle Brook between University Boulevard and the railway, now including the tennis centre, formed part of the Highfield estate when Sir Jesse Boot acquired them in 1920, but they had been allotted in the Beeston inclosure award of 1809 (as Beeston Hassocks) to John Wright of Lenton Hall as a block of twelve of the Hassock closes that formed a salient of Beeston parish into Lenton. All were allotted through exchanges. They were purchased for the Highfield estate by Alfred Lowe in about 1830.

Most of the parkland formed in the early 19th century, ornamental though it may have been as a landscape, continued to be farmed in one way or another, partly by the new owners who established small farmsteads by their houses (though Lenton House took over the cottage farm on Beeston Lane, recently demolished), sometimes employing bailiffs, but partly by commercial farmers from outside. For example, the land tax schedules show that part of Lenton Hall park was let in this way, doubtless with limitations on acceptable forms of enterprise in order to preserve the parkland 'prospects' from the Hall. Grazing was the most acceptable form of land use.

The area east of the northern end of Beeston Lane, with the 'downland' above it, had before 1798 been called the Fourteen Acres and Fourteen Acres Meadow, part of the Abbey Fields, and formed part of a holding leased from Miss Milward by Messrs. Hague and James, and after 1782 by Messrs. Hopkin and Hooton (Figures 29 and 30), farmed from the Beeston Lane farmstead. After adding it to his earlier purchase in 1799 (Figure 31) John Wright occupied the land himself until 1815, but from 1816 to 1825 the occupier was Francis Cheetham, and from 1826 to 1832 and later it was S. Cheetham. Cheethams were part-occupiers of James White's former farm in the valley, while others farmed part of Lenton Abbey, and it is not known from where the 'downland' was farmed; but the system continued through the 19th century, and it is interesting to note that in the early 20th century this land formed the main body of Lenton Hurst Farm when sold by Henry Smith Wright to William Goodacre Player.

The periodic changes in land ownership through the 19th and early 20th centuries will not be pursued further here, but will arise in the historical accounts of the various small estates into which the campus had become divided. These accounts will reveal how Lord Middleton, whose forebears had incorporated the Sixty Acres field into Wollaton Park in 1698, purchased in turn Lenton Firs, Lenton Abbey and in 1844 Lenton Hall to complete his acquisition of the whole Derby Road frontage of the present campus, which remained in the Wollaton estate until 1868-69, when the sitting tenants of Lenton Abbey and Lenton Firs were able to purchase them, and Lenton Hall was bought by a member of a branch of the Wright family, the original owners. Sale of peripheral land for building purposes began, giving rise to a second generation of houses on the campus, all of which fortunately survive.

To conclude, briefly, the outstanding feature of the history of the campus in the early years of the 19th century was its change of status from rural agricultural to residential, in two major respects. First, the sale of the Milward estate led to its division into large units, with houses built on them by prominent and wealthy citizens of Nottingham and district well before the inclosure of Nottingham (1865) and before the residential development of Nottingham Park estate, mainly after 1854. Second, by contrast, at the eastern end of the campus, near the river Leen and stimulated by the opening of the Nottingham canal, industrial developments led to construction of working class housing nearby, including Hillside and Spring Close, both now demolished and part of the Q.M.,C. site. These developments - mentioned only in passing above, but discussed in some detail in Chapter XIV - were virtually contemporaneous with the development of the mansions and their gardens and small parks. The line of Sandy Lane-Abbey Lane, now Clifton Boulevard, was the boundary between two very contrasting types of contemporary landscape change.

The Milward estate detailed in the survey or terrier of 1798 extended to some 620 acres, of which more than 550 acres were occupied by five substantial farm holdings, the culmination of the

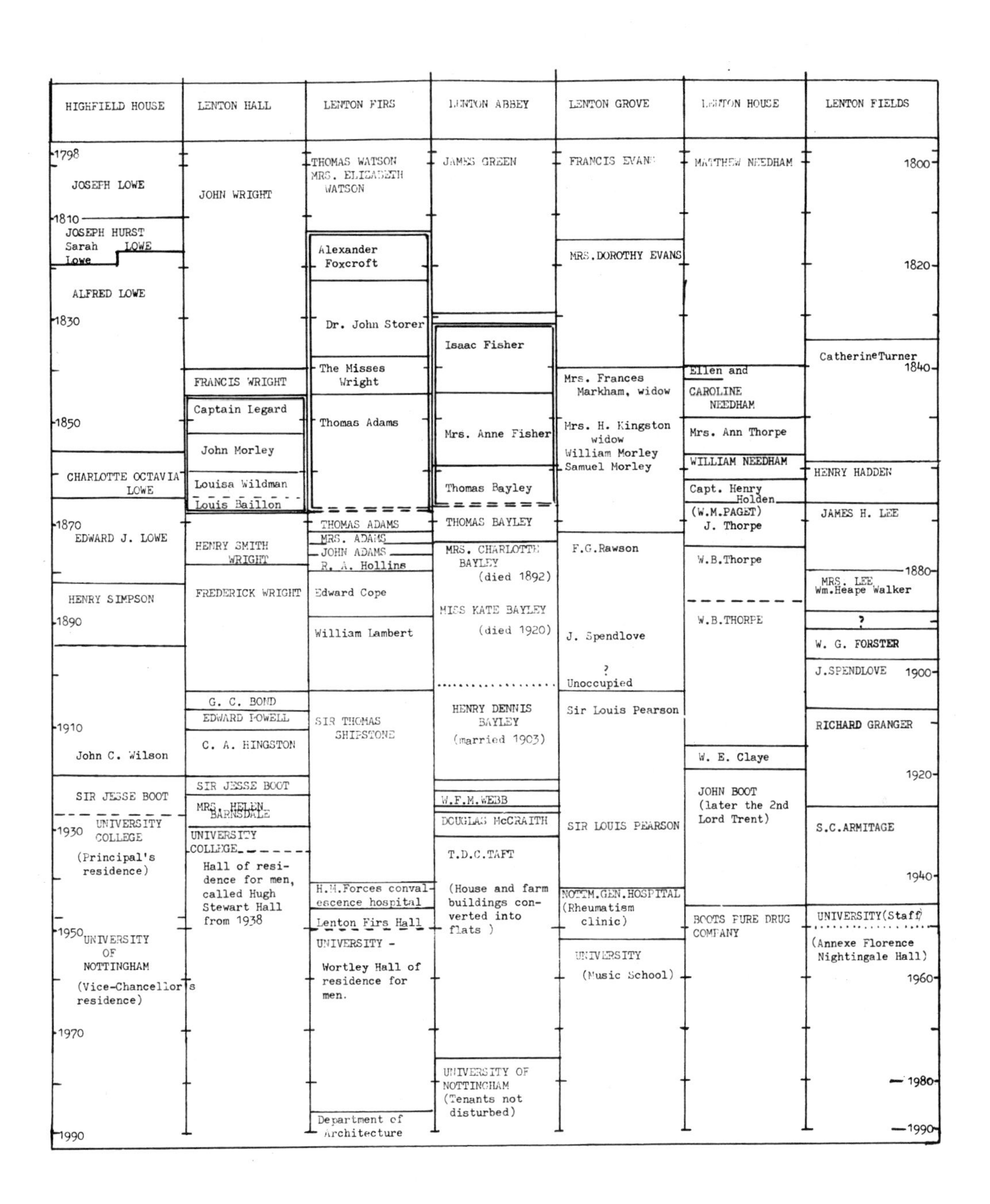

Figure 33: Owners and occupiers of the 'Georgian' houses on the University campus, 1798-1990

Owners are named in capitals, tenants in lower case. Double enclosure lines indicate Lord Middleton's property. Broken lines indicate purchase by sitting tenants. Lenton Fields is included although it was not built until the year before Queen Victoria's accession.

agrarian consolidation tendencies of the preceding century. They were occupied by William Wigley (166 acres) and James White (87 acres) in Dunkirk, the late John Clayton (100 acres) at the Odd House (Lenton Abbey), Thomas Stevenson (130 acres) at Abbey House, and Messrs. Hopkin and Hooton (75 acres) at Beeston Lane farm. The first two were in the Trent valley section between the Tottle Brook, the Beeston Canal and Beeston. The last three formed the basis of the Lenton Abbey, Lenton Hall and Lenton House estates respectively. The individual histories of these and later houses and estates are pursued in Chapters VI to XII which follow, and the owners and occupiers of the Georgian houses are summarized in Figure 33.

NOTES

1. L.A.O., 2 PG 3/1/10 (1725). N.U.M.D., Mi 1/39/4 (1738)
2. N.U.M.D., Mi 3 E 4 (1867): Abstract of title of Henry, Lord Middleton and the Hon. Digby W.B.Willoughby to a freehold estate called Lenton Abbey (with notes and opinion by C. Butler). Most of the details of the devolution of the Winford/Milward estate derive from this document, including details of mortgage transactions mentioned below.
3. N.U.M.D., Wadsworth W (23a) 51 (1830): Copy parcels in the deed of April 14th 1731, lately of the priory of Lenton.
4. N.U.M.D., Wadsworth 21 : Copy of the premises at Lenton mentioned in the deeds of 54 and 6 August 1743.
5. John Chapman, 'Map of Nottinghamshire', scale 1 inch to 1 mile. Surveyed in 1774, printed in 1785 for W. Faden.
6. L.A.O.. 2 PG 3/1/10 (1725)
7. N.U.M.D., Mi 1/39/4 (1738)
8. L.A.O., PG 3/3/5/2 (1738)
9. N.U.M.D., Mi 3 E 4 (1867): Abstract of title ...(1684-1867)
10. Lenton Inclosure Act 1767, Award 1768. The Award, in so far as it relates to Lenton, is reprinted in J.T.Godfrey (1884) 319-326
11. Extract from Lenton and Radford Inclosure Award 1768: 'To the said George de Ligne Gregory ... One piece, plot or parcel of land in a field called Beck Field, containing 54a.3.5 or thereabouts, bounded by the said river Leen, by old inclosed lands belonging to him, the said George de Ligne Gregory, by other old inclosed lands called the Abbey Field and by the Turnpike Road leading from Nottingham to Derby'.
12. Map of the estate of Gregory Gregory Esq., in the Lordships of Lenton and Radford ... Surveyed by H.M.Wood in the years 1818 to 1823. N.A.O., RD 4 L.
13. For example: The Five Acres Close, six acres of meadow in the survey of the Milward estate in 1798, occupied by William Black of Nottingham, was bought by Black in 1798: sold by Mrs. Black to William Surplice in 1805: and transferred to George de L. Gregory on 21 February 1821 in exchange for two other closes
14. L.A.O., 2 PG 3/1/1 and 2. L.A.O., PG 3/2/6 and 7.
15. N.U.M.D., Wadsworth 21
16. N.U.M.D.,. Mi 3 E 4 (1867)
17. N.U.M.D., Wadsworth 50 (partial) and N.U.M.D., Mi 3 E 4 (complete)
18. N.U.M.D. Wadsworth 21
19. N.A.O., Land Tax Assessment (Lenton) for 1780 : 10 May 1780
20. N.U.M.D., Mi 3 E 4 (1867): Abstract of title, 1684-1867.
21. N.U.M.D., Mi 3 E 4, 28 and 29 March 1798: Indentures of lease and release (1) James Graham of Lincolns Inn (2) Elizabeth Milward, spinster (3) Thomas Pares the younger of Leicester, and Thomas Paget of Scraptoft.
22. N.U.M.D., Mi 3 E 4, 4 and 5 April 1798, by indenture of lease and release tripartite between (1) Pares and Paget (2) James Green of Wollaton, gent. (3) Francis Evans of Nottingham, gent.. The connection between Green and Evans, in the building of the Nottingham Canal, is discussed in Chapter XIII.
23. N.U.M.D., Mi1/16/1a-1d (1823)
24. N.U.M.D., Wadsworth 49, relating to property in Beeston, Chilwell, Lenton etc..
25. H.M.Wood (surveyor), 'Map of the estate of Gregory Gregory Esq., in the Lordships of Lenton and Radford in the county of Nottingham'. 1818-23. N.A.O., MP Acc. No. 1167.
26. ibid.
27. Act to enclose lands (Beeston), 46 Geo. III C 52 (Private) 1806. Award 11 November 1809.
28. Nottingham Journal, 7 January 1797. 'Notice to proprietors', dated 24 December 1796

29. The original map was entitled : 'Survey and map of lands to be inclosed and of present inclosed lands to be made tithe-free by John Brown of Nottingham, Land Surveyor'.A copy by E.A.Bush, Surveyor, Beeston, of the inclosure map of Beeston, 'attached to the award made in 1809' entitled 'Plan of the parish of Beeston in the County of Nottingham, 1809' is in the Notts. Archives Office together with a typed copy of the Award, which explains the reasoning of the Commissioners in their awards of allotments, and arranging exchanges.

30. N.A.O., Land tax assessment for 1780 (10 May 1780)

31. N.U.M.D., Wadsworth 49. N.A.O., Beeston Inclosure Award and map, 1809, Allotment No 236. The area of Abbey Field Close was 10a.2.17. In 1798 it was called Home Abbey Field.

32. L.A.O. 1 PG 3/3/1/5 (1670)., Deed of revocation of use by George Gregory...to sell or exchange with Thomas Charlton'.

33. This land was part of Beeston Hassocks, but was allotted not to John Wright but to Francis Evans of Lenton Grove because it adjoined other land awarded to him. It was eventually purchased, with the rest of the Lenton Grove estate west of the Tottle Brook, by Nottingham Corporation for the extension of Woodside Road and is still leased by the University from the Corporation.

CHAPTER VI

HIGHFIELD HOUSE AND ITS ESTATE

Introduction

The pedigree of the Lowes of Highfields printed in Godfrey's History of the Parish and Priory of Lenton [1884 201] indicates that Joseph Lowe 'purchased the Highfield estate and built Highfield House circa 1797'. However, it is clear that the land was bought from Thomas Pares and Thomas Paget after their purchase of the whole Milward estate in April 1798 as in the case of all the other portions upon which houses were built, although this does not rule out the possibility of a slightly earlier informal arrangement. Godfrey also suggested that 'previous to the purchase of the Highfield estate Mr. Lowe appears to have held the tenancy of some portion of the priory demesne at Lenton'; but there is no indication of this in the survey for the sale of 1798, in which field names including 'Highfield' were attached to land tenanted by Messrs. Hopkin and Hooton and by William Black of Nottingham [1]. Although it is possible that Joseph Lowe could have been a sub-tenant it would be difficult to suggest why he should have been, and a more likely reason for Godfrey's statement is that he was misled by the fact that William Lowe, not of the same family, owned the Far Field Close lying immediately north-east of the present Florence Boot Hall between the two entrance lodges and the present University Park lake until it was assigned to Joseph Lowe through the arrangements made for exchanges in the inclosure of Beeston in 1809. The Far Field Close was not part of the Milward estate in 1798. The land tax assessments for Lenton from 1780 to 1798 do not mention Joseph Lowe as either land owner or tenant.

Highfield House, 'a plain substantial mansion' according to Godfrey [1884] and 'a plain Georgian mansion' according to Lawson Lowe [1876] who lived there, must have been built almost immediately after the purchase of the land. The architect was a Mr. Wilkins, 'father of the late Venerable Archdeacon Wilkins' and architect to the Duke of Newcastle's estate [2]. A recent brief description of the house [Notts. C.C. 1972 13] is 'Early/mid 19th century, 2-storeyed stuccoed villa: 4 windows and 3 windows plus 3 added at left-hand rear. Arched openings. Cornice and blocking to hipped slate roof'. The house was altered internally in 1928 to become the residence of the Principal of the University College and subsequently of the Vice-Chancellor of the University, and its grounds formed the basis of the original campus of the University College and the adjoining public University Park. The Lowe family occupied the house and estate for over 80 years, and effectively owned them for over 120 years. Their antecedents are therefore of some interest.

Origins of the Lowe family of Highfield House

Perhaps the first link of the Lowes with Nottingham was the appointment of Lawrence Lowe as Recorder of the Borough in about 1480, and it is thought that later connections of the family with southern Derbyshire and thence with Nottingham were foreshadowed as the Manor of Denby came to Lawrence Lowe through his first marriage to an heiress of the Rossell family of Derby [3]. The later family history, however, begins with John Lowe (b. 1565) a yeoman of Hartford, Cheshire, who married Elline, daughter of William Rowe of Hartford Hall in 1595, and three of their sons from whom sprang three branches of the family (Figure 34). George, the eldest son, was ancestor of the senior branch of the family, and Braunsdorff [1895 10-14] discusses his descendants. Robert, the fifth child, was ancestor of the Lowes of Newton Hall near Middlewich. The ancient seat of the Lowe family was near Witton in the parish of Great Budworth, Cheshire, and was known as La Lowe, but early in the 16th century some Lowes removed to The Hulse in the same parish, and through this branch Joseph Lowe of Highfield House was descended. The family still possessed landed property in Great Budworth parish in the 19th century. By coincidence Lenton Priory received £30 per annum from Middlewich in tithes and other profits, and after the Dissolution the impropriate rectory was vested in the Crown, from which it passed in about 1579 to the Breretons of Brereton. In 1663 William, Lord Brereton, sold the advowson and most of the tithes to Robert Lowe of Newton Hall, elder brother of John Lowe, direct ancestor of Alderman Joseph Lowe, so that the Lowes were connected with the Lenton Priory estate earlier than any other Lenton family except the Gregorys.

John Lowe, the sixth child of John and Elline Lowe, originated the Lowes of The Hulse, Lostock Gralam township, and later of Highfields and Shirenewton. John and his wife Ursula had an only son, William Lowe, born in 1640/1. William's only son, Joshua (b. 1662) was also of The Hulse. Joshua Lowe and his wife Joane had eight sons, of which the five eldest died without issue. The sixth son, Daniel, had three daughters and four sons, and the line continued through him, though the eighth and youngest son, Joseph Lowe (b. 1699) inherited The Hulse on the death of his mother in 1744.

Rev. Daniel Lowe, born at The Hulse in 1698/9, graduated M.A. Glasgow in 1723 and settled at Duffield Hall, Derbyshire in 1727 as domestic chaplain to the family of Henry Coape. He stayed there for nine years, and married Elizabeth Mather, whose family were frequent visitors at Duffield. Daniel and Elizabeth were the parents of Joseph Lowe, the builder of Highfield House. After eight years as a Presbyterian minister at Loscoe, near Heanor (1736-44) Daniel became domestic chaplain to a close University friend, Joseph Offley, who inherited Norton Hall in 1727; and though Offley died in 1751 Daniel remained there for 32 years, until his death, teaching many private pupils , including some of the Wrights of Nottingham. In later life he enjoyed a considerable income, having inherited his father's estate. His wife inherited from her father, Joseph Mather, the family estate at Marehay, and with it a large old mansion on the Market Place at Nottingham, later to become an important Lowe residence. Elizabeth Lowe died in January 1775, and like Daniel, who died at Norton a year later, on 2 January 1776, was buried in Heanor church. Braunsdorff [1896] described the severe weather, when the hearse bringing Daniel's body from Norton to Heanor was buried for three days in a snowdrift near the Cat and Fiddle Inn.

None of Daniel Lowe's writings were published, but he had become relatively wealthy. He had five older brothers, two younger brothers and two sisters. All five older brothers had died without issue by 1770, and the younger brothers by 1772. Daniel's father, Joshua Lowe (1662-1729), who married an heiress, and his grandfather William Lowe (1640/1-1697/8)

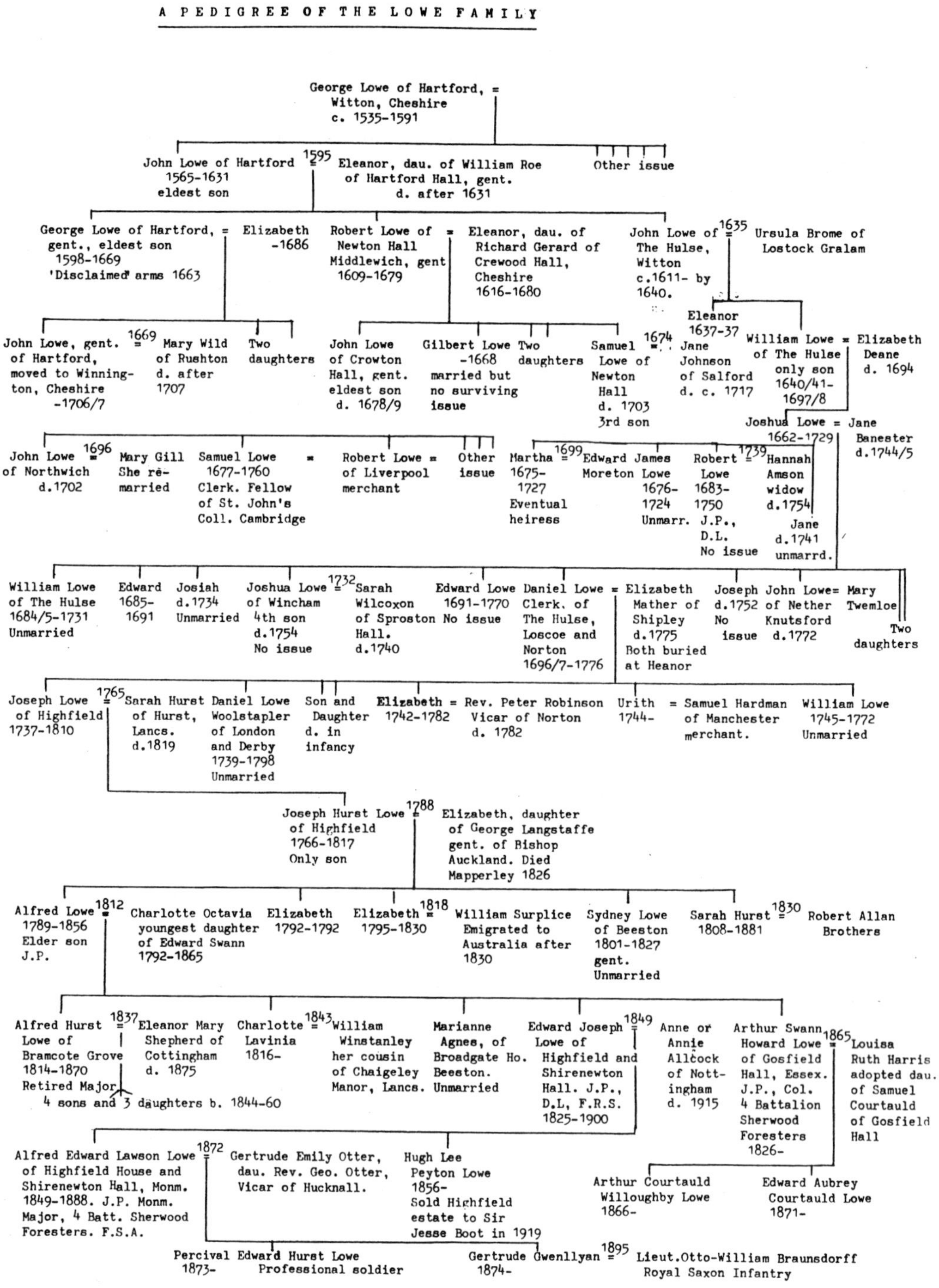

A PEDIGREE OF THE LOWE FAMILY

George Lowe of Hartford, = Witton, Cheshire c. 1535-1591

John Lowe of Hartford 1565-1631 eldest son =1595 Eleanor, dau. of William Roe of Hartford Hall, gent. d. after 1631
Other issue

George Lowe of Hartford, gent., eldest son 1598-1669 'Disclaimed' arms 1663 = Elizabeth -1686
Robert Lowe of Newton Hall Middlewich, gent 1609-1679 = Eleanor, dau. of Richard Gerard of Crewood Hall, Cheshire 1616-1680
John Lowe of The Hulse, Witton c.1611- by 1640. =1635 Ursula Brome of Lostock Gralam

John Lowe, gent. of Hartford, moved to Winnington, Cheshire -1706/7 =1669 Mary Wild of Rushton d. after 1707
Two daughters
John Lowe of Crowton Hall, gent. eldest son d. 1678/9
Gilbert Lowe -1668 married but no surviving issue
Two daughters
Samuel Lowe of Newton Hall d. 1703 3rd son =1674 Jane Johnson of Salford d. c. 1717
Eleanor 1637-37
William Lowe of The Hulse only son 1640/41-1697/8 = Elizabeth Deane d. 1694

John Lowe of Northwich d.1702 =1696 Mary Gill She re-married
Samuel Lowe 1677-1760 Clerk. Fellow of St. John's Coll. Cambridge =
Robert Lowe = of Liverpool merchant
Other issue
Joshua Lowe 1662-1729 = Jane Banester d.1744/5
Martha 1675-1727 Eventual heiress =1699 Edward Moreton
James Lowe 1676-1724 Unmarr.
Robert Lowe 1683-1750 J.P., D.L. No issue =1739 Hannah Amson widow d.1754
Jane d.1741 unmarrd.

William Lowe of The Hulse 1684/5-1731 Unmarried
Edward 1685-1691
Josiah d.1734 Unmarried
Joshua Lowe of Wincham 4th son d.1754 No issue =1732 Sarah Wilcoxon of Sproston Hall. d.1740
Edward Lowe 1691-1770 No issue
Daniel Lowe Clerk. of The Hulse, Loscoe and Norton 1696/7-1776 = Elizabeth Mather of Shipley d.1775 Both buried at Heanor
Joseph d.1752 No issue
John Lowe of Nether Knutsford d.1772 = Mary Twemloe
Two daughters

Joseph Lowe of Highfield 1737-1810 =1765 Sarah Hurst of Hurst, Lancs. d.1819
Daniel Lowe Woolstapler of London and Derby 1739-1798 Unmarried
Son and Daughter d. in infancy
Elizabeth 1742-1782 = Rev. Peter Robinson Vicar of Norton d. 1782
Urith 1744- = Samuel Hardman of Manchester merchant.
William Lowe 1745-1772 Unmarried

Joseph Hurst Lowe of Highfield 1766-1817 Only son =1788 Elizabeth, daughter of George Langstaffe gent. of Bishop Auckland. Died Mapperley 1826

Alfred Lowe 1789-1856 Elder son J.P. =1812 Charlotte Octavia youngest daughter of Edward Swann 1792-1865
Elizabeth 1792-1792
Elizabeth 1795-1830 =1818 William Surplice Emigrated to Australia after 1830
Sydney Lowe of Beeston 1801-1827 gent. Unmarried
Sarah Hurst 1808-1881 =1830 Robert Allan Brothers

Alfred Hurst Lowe of Bramcote Grove 1814-1870 Retired Major =1837 Eleanor Mary Shepherd of Cottingham d. 1875
4 sons and 3 daughters b. 1844-60
Charlotte Lavinia 1816- =1843 William Winstanley her cousin of Chaigeley Manor, Lancs.
Marianne Agnes, of Broadgate Ho. Beeston. Unmarried
Edward Joseph Lowe of Highfield and Shirenewton Hall. J.P., D.L, F.R.S. 1825-1900 =1849 Anne or Annie Allcock of Nottingham d. 1915
Arthur Swann Howard Lowe of Gosfield Hall, Essex. J.P., Col. 4 Battalion Sherwood Foresters 1826- =1865 Louisa Ruth Harris adopted dau. of Samuel Courtauld of Gosfield Hall

Alfred Edward Lawson Lowe of Highfield House and Shirenewton Hall, Monm. 1849-1888. J.P. Monm. Major, 4 Batt. Sherwood Foresters. F.S.A. =1872 Gertrude Emily Otter, dau. Rev. Geo. Otter, Vicar of Hucknall.
Hugh Lee Peyton Lowe 1856- Sold Highfield estate to Sir Jesse Boot in 1919
Arthur Courtauld Willoughby Lowe 1866-
Edward Aubrey Courtauld Lowe 1871-

Percival Edward Hurst Lowe 1873- Professional soldier
Gertrude Gwenllyan 1874- =1895 Lieut.Otto-William Braunsdorff Royal Saxon Infantry

Figure 34: Selective pedigree of the Lowes of Highfield House

were both only sons: so much property came the way of Joseph Lowe from his father. After leaving portions of over £5,000 to his younger children by his will of 22 February 1775, Daniel Lowe devised all his landed property to his eldest son, Joseph (born 14 August 1737). Apart from the twins Hannah and Joshua, who died in infancy, the younger children were Daniel (b. 1739) and William (b. 1745) who died in 1772 unmarried, and who were merchants in partnership on Friars Gate, Derby; Elizabeth (b. 1742) married to Rev. Peter Robinson, vicar of Norton, with two sons; and Urith (b. 1754) married in 1771 to Samuel Hardman of Manchester, with four daughters and a son.

Joseph Lowe (1737-1810), who built Highfield House

Joseph Lowe was educated by his father, Daniel Lowe, up to the age of 17, and was then placed with a linen merchant in London. In about 1758, at the age of 21, he decided to settle in Nottingham, where for some years he traded as a mercer on Bridlesmith Gate. This business was sold, and his premises in later years, and down to his death, were on Long Row [Holden 1805, 1809, 1811] where he ran his business as a 'Woollen and Linen Draper' [Willoughby 1799], or, according to Bailey's Directory of Nottingham for 1783 and 1784, as 'linen draper and haberdasher'. Thus Joseph Lowe of Highfield House was not simply a landed proprietor, but retained business interests in the town that had begun 40 years earlier, and it was through this that he - and later members of his family - qualified for their municipal honours in Nottingham. Nottingham burgesses (called freemen after 1835) were elected through notoriously easy qualifications, and enjoyed considerable financial privileges, especially in connection with common rights and powers. Election to public office was not a sign of public distinction before the Municipal Corporations Act of 1835, but rather a manifestation of nepotism and the political influence of wealth. Too much should not, therefore, be read into the fact that by 1759 Joseph Lowe's name was on the burgess roll, and in 1762 he was a chamberlain and in 1763 Sheriff, all before reaching the age of 26. On 16 May 1777 he was elected a member of the Senior Council in the Corporation of Nottingham.

At 28, already prominent in public life, Joseph Lowe married at Manchester on 15 October 1765 Sarah (b. 1743) the only daughter and sole heiress of James Hurst of Hurst, Lancashire, a name that recurs as a Christian name in later generations of the Lowes. Having about this time sold his business on Bridlesmith Gate to Edward Willoughby, a younger son of Edward Francis Willoughby of Aspley Hall, he moved into the large old house on Long Row that had belonged to his mother's family (the Mathers) and had been recently devised to her by her father [Braunsdorff 1896 43]. Braunsdorff wrote of the house on Long Row :'This house is still standing, and is now divided into two shops; the large garden behind it has been entirely built over, and the arched gateway leading to it now forms the entrance to a small street known as Greyhound Yard'.

On 31 July 1787 Joseph Lowe was elected Alderman for the North Ward of Nottingham in place of the deceased Alderman Thomas Oldknow (who had married Lowe's mother's eldest sister) and the bells of St. Mary's church were rung in his honour on the following day. A fortnight later he was nominated Mayor for the ensuing year, and he entered the Mayoralty on Michaelmas Day. Braunsdorff [1896 44-45] gives an account of Lowe's activities as Mayor in 1787-88, some of which Sutton [1852] also recorded - the colourful ceremony of his inauguration; the riot of framework knitters on 26 October, when Lowe swore in special constables and distributed handbills; his Christmas Eve distribution of penny loaves to 500 poor people and coal to all almshouses, poorhouses and the gaol; his active advocacy of efforts to end the slave trade, with a public meeting at the Guildhall on 11 February 1788; his promotion of the first social club in Nottingham - the Coffee Club, meeting at the Exchange; the riot of 12 March about the price of meat; a great banquet at Thurland Hall on 17 July at the end of the Quarter Sessions; and other events. An important achievement of Joseph Lowe during his term of office as Mayor was the appointment of a Steward of the Corporation's estates, which had been neglected.

A Whig of the old school, Joseph Lowe is said to have been outspoken in support of his own strong views, but he was by no means a political radical. Although no portrait of him is known to exist he was described as a handsome man of fresh complexion, fairly tall and broad. His attributes, physical and intellectual, combined with a strong character to make him one of the outstanding personalities of his time in Nottingham. He was Mayor of Nottingham for a second time in 1797-98, a year in which he was active in forming companies of militia against the threat of invasion from France, and he personally provided muskets, one of which, bearing his name, was long preserved at Highfield House. In this year of office he was, in his private capacity, disposing of his wife's property from her mother's family; receiving the Cheshire estate from his brother Daniel, who died on 16 July 1798; and purchasing the land that formed the nucleus of the Highfield estate and arranging for the building of Highfield House upon it. Details of this purchase are discussed below.

By the time that he acquired the land at Highfields and built his house, Joseph Lowe was aged 60, and long established as a prominent personality and political leader in the town. When he took up residence at Highfield House his only son, Joseph Hurst Lowe (b. 1766), who had married in 1788, went to live in the house on Long Row. Joseph remained active in public life for a few more years, and the parish books of 1803 show that he offered, in the event of invasion, to furnish two waggons, six horses and two drivers. He became Mayor for a third time in 1807-08, but after this he took little further interest in practical public affairs, and the last two or three years of his life were devoted almost entirely to the improvement of his Highfield estate. 'The natural beauty of the situation was not a little enhanced by the extensive and judicious plantations which he made' [Braunsdorff 1896 46]. Some years ago the present writer counted annual growth rings of two beech trees felled by gales, one near the western end of Cut Through Lane, which would have been planted for Joseph Lowe, and both indicated an approximate germination date of 1800-1805.

Probably the most important original attraction that determined the site of Highfield House was the aesthetic quality of its setting and outlook, although other factors such as the dry and gently sloping surface formed by the Plains skerry would also have been important. Joseph Lowe's great, great grandson, the young Lawson Lowe, in 1871 described it thus in his clear Victorian prose . 'Its situation is singularly beautiful. Standing as it does upon a considerable elevation above the valley of the Trent the view obtained is one of the most extensive in the vicinity. To the south-west Breedon bulwarks and church are plainly visible, together with the wooded eminence in Donington Park, whilst more to the south the long, bleak range of Charnwood Forest forms a striking feature in the landscape. Beyond Clifton Grove the woods in Bunny Park appear, backed by the Willoughby Wolds and by the far-distant Leicestershire hills, and to the east the landscape stretches away beyond Belvoir Castle into Lincolnshire ... Upon a clear day the steeples of more than 30 churches can be seen from the terrace walk in front of Highfield House'. It is not easy to visualize these extensive open vistas now that trees planted by Joseph Lowe himself and his descendants, and large buildings obstruct them in all directions except to the south-west. But the attraction of a firm, level, dry site, for which the Mapperley Plains skerry was responsible (see Chapter I) and accessible well water must have been important locating factors of a more practical kind.

On his death at Highfield House on 20 March 1810 Joseph Lowe was buried, in the presence of Nottingham's civic dignitaries, in a vault with a square tomb above it near the eastern end of the chancel of Sneinton church, a family vault that was made for an infant grandchild of Joseph's (Elizabeth) in 1792, and was used for the interment of Joseph's wife's mother and of seven other members of the family after Joseph [Braunsdorff 1896 46]. These included Joseph Hurst Lowe and his wife, and their other children Alfred (d. 1856), Elizabeth

(Surplice) of Lenton (d. 1830) and Sydney Lowe of Beeston (d. 1827). It might be suspected that Joseph Lowe had lived at Sneinton or had worshipped there, especially since his only son was baptised there as early as 1766; but Braunsdorff [1896] suggested otherwise. Sneinton, then a country village, was probably selected for its picturesque situation, for in a letter to his sister, Mrs. Hardman, Joseph mentioned his repugnance to the idea of being buried in a town, and it was believed that Sneinton church bore some fancied resemblance to one Joseph had known earlier in life - though which of three successive Sneinton churches is not suggested. A new church replacing an earlier one at Sneinton was opened in 1790, and a third in October 1810, to replace a building 'demolished a few years back' [Sutton 1852 288]. This church, built in brick, was replaced in 1839 by a larger church on the same site, and only in the early years of the present century was the existing church at Sneinton built around its predecessor before that was demolished [Truman 1946, Ablitt 1980/1986].

Joseph Lowe bequeathed all his property ultimately to his only son Joseph Hurst Lowe and his heirs, but left his wife a life interest in the Highfield estate and in some other estates. His property was considerable, since a large part of the Lowe family's possessions had come into his hands, and by the turn of the century he could be regarded as a landed proprietor rather than a man of commerce or industry. His widow Sarah, or 'Old Madam Lowe' as she was commonly called, died at Highfield House on 30 March 1819 and was buried in the family vault in Sneinton church.

Composition of the Highfield estate

Recognition of the 18th century identity of the lands of the Highfield estate which formed the historical nucleus of the University campus is hampered because none of the original deeds relating to the property are available for consultation. This may arise in part from the removal of the Lowe family to Monmouthshire over a century ago, but also, perhaps, because A.E.Lawson Lowe, living at Shirenewton Hall by 1888 when he died, passed on the family papers to his son-in-law, Otto-William Braunsdorff, who was similarly interested in genealogy and could be regarded as Lawson Lowe's literary executor. Braunsdorff used the papers to compile the history of the Lowe family that he published in Dresden in 1896. Whether the Lowe papers survive in Germany or elsewhere is not known.

The earliest map of the Highfield estate known to the writer is one produced for its sale in 1881 [4]. This shows the estate extending to an area of 151a.2.36, of which 57a.0.27 lay in Lenton parish, including part of the lake (before its enlargement in the 1920s), and the remaining 94 acres in Beeston parish, south-east of the Tottle Brook. The Beeston part comprised almost entirely the former Hassocks Closes, which by allotment and exchanges effected by the Beeston Inclosure Commissioners came into the hands of John Wright of Lenton Hall in 1809 and were later sold to Alfred Lowe [5], who was thereby enabled to form the 'Fishpond' which was the precursor of the University Park lake by damming the Tottle Brook (Figure 37).

The Lenton part of the Highfield estate of 1881 was made up mainly of land of the Milward estate purchased by Joseph Lowe in 1798, but with three later additions. The land bought in 1798 was:

North Highfield, 7a.3.25 in 1798

This included the site of Highfield House and its gardens (5a.0.36 in 1881) with, to the east, a paddock called North Highfield and another called Upper Orchard, each of about 1 acre - a total of 7a.1.34.

South Highfield, 7a.2.31 in 1798

This was 'adjoining Home Field' - presumed to be the Home Field of the Lenton House estate. Part of the South Park of 1881.

These two areas together were called the Lower Highfield Park in 1684. In 1798 they had been occupied for many years by Messrs. Hopkin and Hooton (and were farmed from the recently demolished Beeston Lane farm) but were not purchased by them.

Two High Field Closes, together 13a.1.15 in 1798.

Highfield Meadow, two parts, together 3a.0.02 in 1798

These lay south-east of North and South Highfield, and both were occupied in early 1798 by William Black of Nottingham. They are now mainly covered by the western reach of University Park lake.

Rushy Meadow, 4a.1.24 in 1798

This was also occupied by William Black

This was probably the full extent of Joseph Lowe's original purchase, for which he was taxed at £4.8s.0d. a year. The tax was redeemed by Lowe in 1803. The area was in total about 36½ acres, which leaves some 21 acres still to be accounted for north of the Tottle Brook.

Land at both ends of the hillside was later acquired by the Lowes. The land west of the entrance lodges on Beeston Lane down to the Tottle Brook to the south and west was not part of the Milward estate at the end of the 18th century. This area of gravel terrace, now occupied by Florence Boot Hall and its grounds, and part of the field on the west side of the Hall, was owned by Mr. William Lowe and Mr. John Hodges. Hodges owned the four Hill Closes, with a combined area of 8a.1.38, and William Lowe had the Far Field Close of 3a.3.21. As shown in Chapter V, Joseph Lowe exchanged land of his in Beeston to William Lowe for the Far Field Close. The Hill Closes were acquired for the Highfield estate later, probably purchased by either Joseph Hurst Lowe or his son Alfred - most probably the latter - respectively son and grandson of Joseph Lowe, though the transaction would not be revealed by the land tax assessments because the tax on this land had been redeemed. Adding the combined area of these two acquisitions reduces the shortfall of area compared with that of 1881 to about 9 acres.

Godfrey [1884 199], probably following Lawson Lowe, stated that Joseph Hurst Lowe bought adjoining lands from the Gregory family. Lowe [1871] had stated that Joseph Lowe 'increased his estate by various purchases of land from the Gregorys and others' but gave no details. Any land bought from the Gregorys must have been at the eastern end of Highfields, because the valley floor lands added to the estate later had been owned by John Wright of Lenton Hall. The Gregory land added to the Highfield estate was probably Keighton Meadow. Rentals of the Gregory estate in the 18th century included Keighton Meadow, but it is missing later [6]. Comparison of later maps with that of Smythe [1632] [7] suggests that an area at the eastern end of the Highfield estate had been transferred to it from the Keighton Closes, and the Gregory estate map of 1818-23 shows that this took place before that map was completed. The land in question is marked off on 19th century maps by a line of elm trees running approximately north-south diagonally down the slope from the position of the eastern end of the Portland Building to the lakeside terrace below the Trent Building. Keighton Meadow was given areas ranging from about 8 acres to over 9 acres in the Gregory estate rentals and terriers. Much of it is now submerged beneath the eastern reach of the University Park lake.

If this land is allowed an area of 9 acres it accounts for the balance of area required to equate the Lenton part of the Highfield estate in 1881 with the land purchased in 1798 and later. Since Joseph Hurst Lowe is said to have built a bath-house in the vicinity of the Bath Hill plantation (below the Portland Building) before he inherited the estate and took up residence there it is likely that the purchase of Keighton Meadow was made by Joseph Lowe. Joseph's land tax for Lenton increased from £4.6s.5d. in 1798 to £4.8s.0d. in 1799, and remained at that figure until 1828, long after the death of Joseph Hurst Lowe in 1817. An increase of 19s.0d. a year in the land tax paid by Alfred Lowe, his son, from 1828 must relate to his purchase of the land of Beeston Hassocks and, in Lenton, of the Hill Closes which enabled him to enlarge the lake and take water to supply it from the Tottle Brook where it crossed Beeston Lane.

In his decade of residence at his new Highfield House Joseph Lowe began the landscaping and planting around the house, and a small ornamental pool that he had excavated below the sandstone cliff forming part of the extended gardens or 'pleasure grounds' of Highfield House, as well as alongside his drive and Cut Through Lane, which still contribute powerfully to the essential landscape character of the central part of the University campus. Godfrey [1884 198-99] wrote: 'The natural beauty of the situation [of Highfield House] was greatly enhanced by the number of trees which he planted, and the delightfully sylvan aspect yet retained [in 1884] in this part of the parish is mainly due to Mr. Lowe and to those who subsequently followed his example'. They had their difficulties, and Godfrey describes how damage to the young plantations by local youths led the Vicar of Beeston, the Rev. Thomas Bigsby, to preach a sermon on the subject, but 'with what effect we know not'! It was Joseph Lowe's grandson Alfred who later extended the pool to form the 'Fishpond'.

Joseph Hurst Lowe and his children

Joseph Hurst Lowe, the only son of Joseph and Sarah Lowe, born 31 August 1766, baptized at the Presbyterian Meeting House at Nottingham on 21 September 1766, married 1788 and died 1817, owned Highfield House (subject to the life interest of his mother in the estate - and she, in fact, survived him) for only seven years after the death of his father. Soon after being enrolled freeman (burgess) at the age of 21 in 1787 he became a member of Nottingham Corporation, and was elected to the Senior Council in February 1805. He was sheriff in 1789, a year after his father had been Mayor for the first time. Again it should be emphasized that local public office did not always imply personal distinction, because until the reform of the 1830s the Corporation was a self-perpetuating oligarchy, its members elected for life. Joseph Hurst Lowe was married on 5 March 1788 at Auckland, County Durham, to Elizabeth, eldest daughter and eventual co-heiress of George Landstaffe, a merchant of Bishop Auckland. Braunsdorff [1896] printed the Landstaffe pedigree, with a portrait of George Landstaffe opposite, and on the following page miniature portraits of Elizabeth Lowe, Joseph Hurst Lowe, and two of their children, Alfred and Sydney, unfortunately of very poor quality. Elizabeth, who was born in 1770, died at Mapperley on 13 February 1826, and like her husband and his parents was buried at Sneinton.

These bare facts tell little of the man. After the completion of Highfield House Joseph Hurst Lowe and his family were able to move into the old house on the Market Place at Nottingham vacated by his parents. Although he was a Senior Councillor for thirty years chronic ill-health must have been a great handicap in public life. 'It was his custom during the greater part of the year, whenever his health permitted, to walk from Nottingham to Highfields every morning and bathe in a spring in Highfield Park, where he had built a small bath-house, from which the present Bath Hill Plantation takes its name' [Braunsdorff 1896]. A rectilinear feature, possibly wall foundations, shown within Bath Hill Plantation on the O.S. large-scale (50 foot series) map of 1881, might indicate a former building, possibly a bath-house. Bath Hill Plantation, now near the lake shore, would have been in Keighton Meadow, on the steep valleyside slope some distance from Highfield House. The stratigraphy of the Mercia Mudstones would favour springs on the lower slope, and the plantation covers an embayment in the valley side which could have been produced by spring sapping, with or without marl digging: but it seems an unlikely location for a bathing pool. Lawson Lowe, Joseph Hurst Lowe's great grandson, suggested by implication a different location [1871]. 'The site of the ancient battlefield already referred to [Keighton] extends into the North Park adjoining this mansion [Highfield House] and near here is a remarkably fine group of old elms, beneath which was a spring (now exhausted) supposed to have possessed medicinal qualities'. This may refer to the site of Joseph Hurst Lowe's bathing place, and it might possibly have been the spring that revived to cause serious difficulties in the building of the crypt chapel in the Portland Building.

The ill-health, which appears to have been asthma to which Joseph Hurst Lowe finally succumbed, was supposedly brought on by an illness, probably pneumonia, suffered as an infant. Braunsdorff [1896 53] recounted the interesting, but hardly convincing story of the negligent misdemeanour of the nurse-maid following her soldier friend in inclement weather which was believed by the Lowe family to have caused the illness. It limited Joseph Hurst Lowe's participation and effectiveness in public affairs, and he was chiefly occupied in outdoor pursuits. He was especially fond of and knowledgeable about horses, like his son Sydney.

J.H.Lowe had five children. Alfred was his elder son, and he owned the estate for 40 years following his father. The younger children were two daughters, both called Elizabeth, a son Sydney, and a third daughter, Sarah. The elder Elizabeth, born in 1792, three years after Alfred, died in infancy and was buried at Sneinton (where the registers wrongly named her Mary) - the first interment in what became the family vault. The second Elizabeth, born at Nottingham on 17 March 1795, and also named for her mother - a common custom in those times of high infant mortality - was baptized at the Presbyterian Meeting House on 16 May 1795. She married William Surplice, later of Woodville, Nottinghamshire, at the old parish church of Lenton on 12 May 1818, and they had 'numerous issue'. She died on 18 October 1830 aged 35, and was buried in a vault adjoining that of the Lowes at Sneinton. Shortly after her death her husband settled in Australia, and died there at Brisbane. Although a Thomas Surplice figured in the land tax assessments for Lenton from 1783 onwards, holding lands of the Gregory estate, William Surplice appeared first in 1806, as owner and occupier of land earlier owned and occupied by Mr. William Black (mentioned earlier in this chapter). He remained in the tax schedules until 1831, when 'Widow Surplice', presumably his mother, replaced him because he had emigrated.

Sydney Lowe of Beeston, younger son of J.H.Lowe, was born at Nottingham on 9 February 1801. He went to live at Beeston soon after reaching his majority in 1822, (by which time his father and grandmother had died and his brother Alfred had taken over Highfield House) and he remained at Beeston for the rest of his short life. At one time he occupied an old house in the Robinet belonging to the Charlton family, but afterwards lived in a house that was later converted into the Commercial Inn on what was then called Cow-gate (later Butchers Lane and now Wollaton Road) almost opposite to the entrance to Sainsbury's store car park today. He was lavishly hospitable, and very popular in the village. At wakes he always gave a barrel of ale for the public, and liked to promote 'all kinds of old English sports and games on such occasions, giving prizes of hats and waistcoats to the men and "smocks" to the women who won foot races'. Racing, indeed, seems to have been his chief pastime, if not occupation, and he owned several good race horses. Sydney Lowe never married. He died at Beeston on 29 June 1827 aged 26, and was buried in the Sneinton vault on 6 July 1827. It cannot be claimed that he was more than an undistinguished, though amiable and sociable scion of the Lowe family.

Alfred Lowe (1789-1856) : musician, scientist and art collector

Joseph Hurst Lowe's elder son Alfred (Figure 35) was born on 1 August 1789, and educated at the old Nottingham Academy on Parliament Street, 'then one of the principal schools in the neighbourhood', where for a time from 1798 Lord Byron was among his schoolfellows. In 1815 he was described as 'Draper, Long Row'. He moved to Highfield House in 1817, aged 28, on the death of his father, and remained there as head of the family until his own death in 1856. Besides the Highfield estate he inherited much landed property, was Lord of the Manor of Stanton-on-the-Wolds, which he purchased, and was the owner of other property in Nottinghamshire as well as estates in Cheshire, Lancashire and Derbyshire. He was able to devote time to a very active public life as well as following his own intellectual pursuits, artistic and scientific. He became Chamberlain in 1811 with Edward Swann junior,

Figure 35: Alfred Lowe (1789-1856)
[From Braunsdorff (1896); courtesy of Notts. County Library Service]

and they became sheriffs in the following year, when Edward Swann senior, Alderman and 'Grocer, Long Row', was re-elected Mayor, and Alfred Lowe married his youngest daughter, Charlotte Octavia. Appointed to the Commission of the Peace for the county in 1825 and later a Justice of the Peace for the county and town, and described in 1848 as Commissioner of the Property and Land Taxes for Nottinghamshire [Lascelles and Hagar 1848], his chief interests nevertheless lay in the cultural and scientific fields rather than in the local government matters that had occupied his grandfather. But only death deprived him of appointment as Deputy Lieutenant.

An obituary memoir in the Journal of the Royal Meteorological Society noted that as 'a lover of the Arts and Sciences he mainly contributed to the establishment of amateur musical societies in Nottingham', and was a zealous supporter of the daily and Sunday school attached to the Nottingham Unitarian Chapel (High Pavement Chapel) that he attended. In 1846 he was teaching the vocal music class at the new Mechanics Institution, from which sprang the Sacred Harmonic Society, which is still thriving. As early as January 1816 his musical advice was sought, for with Mr. J.M.Fellows the donor he delivered an account for the purchase and fixing of the organ at High Pavement Chapel, and 'thanks were given for their services'.

Alfred Lowe was a discerning collector of paintings, and formed a well-known collection at Highfield House that was eventually removed to Shirenewton Hall, Monmouthshire by his son Edward J. Lowe in 1882 [8]. Lawson Lowe in 1876 observed that Highfield House contained a fine collection of pictures, chiefly paintings by 'the ancient masters', and in 1871 [p. 25] he gave a selective list, among which the following are noteworthy.

Gainsborough - Portraits of the Spencer family:
Watteau - Snatching a kiss: Murillo - St. Aloysius Gonzago:

Kard du Jardin - Venus and Adonis: Naysmith - Landscape:
John Wycke - Battle of the Boyne: Moreland - Gipsies:
Ostade - Frozen Ferry: Decker and Hondekoerer - Farm:
Ruysdaal - Rapids: Guido - Infant Jesus:
Andrea del Sarto - Holy Family: Carlo Dolce - Head of Christ:
Correggio - Finding of Moses: Danby - Sunset:
Carlo Cignani - Joseph and Potiphar's wife:
Claude - Landing Stairs: Rottennamer - The Last Judgment.

Many societies and organizations in the Nottingham area can trace their beginnings to the old Mechanics Institution, among them University College, and thus the University of Nottingham, Wollaton Hall Natural History Museum, Nottingham Operatic Society and Photographic Society. Alfred Lowe was a founder and an original trustee of the Institution. The first move to establish it was diverted into the formation of an Artisans' Library (see Chapter IX) but interest was renewed at a meeting in early 1837 led by John Smith Wright (1774-1848) of Rempstone Hall, the banker cousin of John Wright of Lenton Hall. The actual resolution to establish the 'Mechanics' was adopted at a meeting on 30 October 1837 chaired by the Mayor of Nottingham, Richard Morley, and John Smith Wright's benefaction ensured its permanence. Its original rented premises were at No. 17 St. James' Street. Alfred Lowe carried through two 'Mechanics Exhibitions', the first in the Exchange Rooms in 1840, to provide the basis of a fund to enable the Institution to move into new, purpose built accommodation. The second exhibition promoted by Alfred Lowe was in 1850, with his son Arthur as secretary and chief organizer, and it attracted over 62,000 visitors between August 1850 and January 1851. The fund provided by the first exhibition was augmented by John Smith Wright, who also presented half the site for the new building on Milton and Burton Streets, opened in January 1845.

Alfred Lowe was Vice-President of the Mechanics Institution from 1842 to 1847, and its Treasurer from 1848 until his death in 1856. Incidentally, his son, Edward Lowe, was Treasurer in 1858 and 1859 and Vice-President from 1860 to 1880, overlapping with terms of office of his neighbours at Lenton Hall - Henry Smith Wright, Treasurer 1868-78 and his brother Frederick for many years from 1878. The Annual Report of the Institution, referring to Alfred Lowe's death, recorded that 'from the Commencement of the Institution he has been connected with its management, and on every occasion to require it manifested the greatest interest in its welfare, an interest which continued unabated to the close of his life. The labours of our deceased Treasurer and his hearty devotion to the Institution are well known to all who have been identified with him in the management of its affairs.' The Report might have added that he had been an early and inspirational teacher in it. Unfortunately his activities in his later years were restricted by the heart disease from which he died, aged 67, on 10 August 1856. He was buried at Sneinton.

Astronomy and meteorology were the areas of Alfred Lowe's chief scientific interests. He established a meteorological station at Highfield House and operated it jointly with his better-known son Edward. They took weather observations from at least as early as 1840, when the meteorological record at nearby Lenton House ceased with the death of Matthew Needham [9], until 31 July 1856, only ten days before his death, and the recordings were continued by Edward Lowe for a further 25 years. Alfred was a founder member of the (Royal) Meteorological Society, but also 'took much delight in astronomy'. Not only did he have a powerful telescope mounted on the roof of Highfield House, but he also had built an observatory at Beeston Rylands, a pointed building on Meadow Road known locally as 'The Rylands Lighthouse', and 'Pepper Box Hall' and 'The Beeston Fogworks'. The reason for its location is not known. With eight openings in an octagonal roof it was clearly designed for astronomical and not meteorological purposes, and served the interests of Alfred rather than those of his son Edward [10] . It was reported in 1866 that all the instruments were transferred from the tower to Highfield House, which would clearly be related to the removal of Edward Lowe from 'The Observatory' (Broadgate House) to Highfield House after the death of his mother on 26 April 1865. Thereafter the octagonal tower became in turn a storehouse, dovecote and home for wild birds and bats, and on 10 January 1963 it was demolished to make way for housing.

The best known achievement of Alfred Lowe in the musical world developed from the infant Mechanics Institution where 'there are several music students who are instructed gratuitously by Alfred Lowe Esq. of Highfields' [11] . Dr. E. Becket [1928 20] tells how, in 1846, he conceived the idea of uniting the casual elements of local musical life, and formed, and for a time conducted a small choir for the cultivation of musical knowledge in general, and the practice of madrigal and part-song in particular. The singing class, or choral society supported by the Mechanics Institution, was eventually known as the Mechanics Institution Vocal Music Class, the members of which at the end of 1856, the year of Alfred's death, inaugurated the Sacred Harmonic Society; and in 1887 J.A.H.Green could write: 'To the efforts and enterprise of this Society, sometimes under very discouraging circumstances and at considerable pecuniary risk, the present high standard of musical taste in Nottingham is mainly due' [12] .

Alfred Lowe was described as 'a man of wide culture and an enthusiast in everything calculated to improve the conditions of daily life', a judgment that is not belied by his appearance. Copies of what at first appear to be two different portraits suggest by their almost identical likeness that they depict his appearance accurately, but closer examination reveals that they are almost certainly touched-up versions of the same portrait (Figure 35). They are probably copies of a presentation portrait by Gilpin that hung in the Mechanics Institution until the building burned down in 1867. The Institution was rebuilt in 1867-68 to the design of T. Simpson, and reopened in 1869; and it was at a meeting to discuss rebuilding that a University College was first mentioned publicly when the secretary spoke of an idea in the mind of Alderman Heymann - that the Mechanics Institution should become the future University [13]

On 30 October 1812 at St. Mary's church, Nottingham, Alfred Lowe married Charlotte Octavia Swann, youngest daughter of Alderman Edward Swann, who was twice Mayor of Nottingham and was sheriff in 1784 [14] . Edward Lowe was probably named for his grandfather Swann. The Lowes' household seems always to have been on a more modest scale than those of other families living on the campus in the 19th century, perhaps limited by the modest size of the house. In 1841 [15] Alfred and Charlotte, with their daughters Charlotte Lavinia, aged 25, and Marianne (or Mary Ann) Agnes, and their sons Edward Joseph (15) and Arthur (14) were served by four house servants, Emily Glover (35), Elizabeth Jenkinson (30), Eliza Robinson (20) and William Cooper (15). In addition there was a coachman, William Lewis (25), who lived with his wife Elizabeth and their son and daughter at the lodge, which stood where the drive from Highfield House joined Beeston Lane, and more precisely exactly where the entrance gate to the new University College was placed between the two new lodges built in 1924-25 (Figure 45). William and Elizabeth Lewis were still at the lodge forty years later.

The three sons and two daughters of Alfred and Charlotte Lowe all survived them. Their eldest son was Alfred Hurst Lowe (1814-1870), (Figure 36) but he did not succeed Alfred at Highfield House. Having married Eleanor Mary, third daughter of Joseph Shepherd of Cottingham in November 1837, at the Census of 1841 he was living at Bramcote Grove, which had been recently purchased by his father together with the adjoining estate. He was there only briefly however, for by 1844 [Curtis 1844] Bramcote Grove was owned and occupied by Laurence Hall. For some years Alfred Hurst Lowe practised as an attorney in Nottingham; 'but having relinquished the legal profession he quitted Bramcote Grove and lived for several years upon the continent', his eldest children being born in Italy and France in 1844 and 1847. In 1848 he was gazetted Lieutenant in the Royal Sherwood Foresters (or Notts. Regiment of Militia), was promoted Captain in 1853 and was at least Acting Major at his death in 1870. He

Figure 36: Alfred Hurst Lowe (1814-1870) and Arthur Swann Howard Lowe (b. 1826), eldest and third sons of Alfred Lowe.
[From Braunsdorff (1896); courtesy NCLS]

served through five 'embodiments', including those of the Crimean War and the Indian Mutiny, and throughout the second was in command of the depot at Newark, where his youngest child was born. He was especially interested in musketry, in which he was an instructor, and he acted for a time as adjutant at the School of Musketry at Fleetwood. He was allowed to retire in March 1870 with the honorary rank of Major, awarded for long service, but he died after a long lung illness at Merton, Surrey on 27 March 1870 before his award could be gazetted. He was buried at Mitcham. His wife Eleanor Mary died on 1 May 1875, and was buried at the same place. They had four sons and three daughters born between 1844 and 1860, and brief details of them are given in a footnote from which the movements of this peripatetic family can be traced [16].

Alfred Hurst Lowe's elder sister Charlotte Lavinia, born on 14 February 1816 and baptized on 21 July 1817, was married on 14 September 1844 to William Winstanley of Preston, her second cousin once removed, the only son of William and Elizabeth Winstanley of Chargeley Manor and Wootton Lodge in Lancashire. Elizabeth was the daughter and co-heiress of Samuel Hardman by Urith, daughter of Rev. Daniel Lowe of Norton and sister of Joseph Lowe.

The second daughter of Alfred Lowe, Marianne Agnes, remained unmarried, and lived for many years at Broadgate House, Beeston (The Observatory) after Edward Lowe moved into Highfield House. She is mentioned again below.

Leaving aside for the moment the second son, Edward J. Lowe, the family of Alfred Lowe was completed by the youngest son, Arthur Swann Howard Lowe (Figure 36) who was born at Highfield House on 4 December 1826, and remained there until his marriage in 1865, the year of his mother's death, to Louisa Ruth Harris, adopted daughter and testamentary co-heiress of Samuel Courtauld of Gosfield Hall near Halstead, Essex, which then became his

Figure 37: The Fishpond in the late 19th century
[From Braunsdorff (1896) Courtesy of NCLS]

home. He was commissioned in the Sherwood Foresters based at Newark, and served in Ireland in 1852. A captain in the Militia in 1861, he later became Colonel commanding the 4th Battalion The Sherwood Foresters. Arthur Lowe appears to have shared some of the artistic abilities of his father. He was mentioned in the History of the Nottingham Sacred Harmonic Society as having 'occasionally officiated as leader of the band at concerts given between 1845 and 1855'. He was a competent draughtsman, and made the engravings for his brother Edward's book 'The Conchology of Nottingham', published in 1853 from drawings by F.E.Swann. In 1887 he lived at Gosfield Hall when included in the electoral roll of Rushcliffe Division, for which he qualified by owning The Observatory (Broadgate House), Beeston.

The gardens and pleasure grounds of Highfields in the mid-19th century

Before proceeding to outline the career and contributions of Alfred Lowe's second son, and his successor at Highfield House, Edward Joseph Lowe, the influence of Alfred on the park at Highfields and the traces of his hand in the landscape of the present University campus should be recognized. Alfred seems to have added to the earlier planting round Highfield House, for in 1856 [Fyfe 1856] 'we with surprise saw the transformation which thirty years of successful arboriculture had effected on the face of that little landscape ... We beheld the huge stem of the Himalayan deodara already towering to the skies, and all the most splendid trees of the coniferous tribe recently imported into our climate springing up side by side - the most magnificent specimen of the *Cupressus excelsa* of ten or eleven years growth, the *Cryptomeria japonica*, the Scotch pine, the English yew and the oriental cypress in unrivalled profusion and of remarkable growth, including, amongst those of recent introduction, the superb *Araucaria imbricata* and the glittering golden yew ... all planted ... and with judicious care within and during the past thirty years by Mr. Lowe'.

Some of the forest trees planted and cultivated by Alfred Lowe still survive, but others have gone. The shrubbery avenue from Highfield House to the steps leading down to the lake shore below the sandstone cliff in the 'staff garden' - where a number of exotic tree species remain - disappeared when the College was built in the 1920s. The 'pleasure grounds' were part of the landscaping scheme that involved the enlargement of the early small pool into a small lake - the 'fishpond' - in about 1830, associated with Alfred Lowe's purchase from John Wright of the Hassock Closes, now occupied by public park and playing fields. The Sanderson maps of 1834-35 and 1835-36 show the lake as it remained until the 1920s, but the Teesdale and Cary maps of 1830 and 1831 indicate only a small pond, while the Beeston enclosure map shows no pool at all. The appearance of the 'fishpond' as it was formed for Alfred Lowe is seen in Figure 37.

Fyfe [1856] described the pleasure grounds incorporating the 'fishpond' in the curious fulsome prose of the mid-Victorian topographer.

> '... The grounds, where they descend from the summit plaform... by a romantic walk, turning the corner of the sandstone bluffs ... reach their extremity'. 'At the bottom of the high cliffs the sward has been lowered and levelled, and stretches a short distance onwards to a walk or road which skirts the margin of a wild and beautiful lake of about five acres in area, encompassed by a long walk, and diversified by clumps of trees, coppice and underwood, scattered in great profusion and with considerable attention to the picturesque, around its sides, or at some points, deeply indenting its bosom. Swans sail statelily over the waters, fed from a neighbouring source and artificially collected; and the elegant swan-goose forms an imposing tribe of aquatic tenants to enliven the surface, which is, however, almost sufficiently clothed in many parts with aquatic plants of rapid and extending growth - but these the owner can at any time (and probably shortly will) clear away by running off the water, and drawing away the superfluous masses of stranded vegetation in carts to top-dress the neighbouring pastures. ... Grottoes of shells or spar in secluded spots around the border of the lake, take the visitor by surprise. And here also, in clumps, are various nurseries for indigenous ferns. But the finest part of the whole of this secluded piece of scenery is undoubtedly the face of the sandstone rock here turned towards the lake. From sixty to eighty feet in altitude, tufted aloft by fine trees and with ferns and creeping plants peering forth from its crevices, the abraded front of the cliff rises perpendicularly from a pure sward of vivid dark green. In its face, but only towards the eastern extremity, are sundry caverns, of great capacity, which the proprietor has lately had cleared ...'. 'Mounting the brow of the rocks by the steep acclivity at their eastern extremity, the wooded path along the verge repeats all the enchantments of the plateau prospect at Highfield'.

In Braunsdorff's summary [1896 55] Alfred Lowe's estate 'in every part displayed the refined taste which he possessed and exercised in bringing it to its state of beauty and perfection. The grounds in which were placed numerous most rare and exotic plants showed that no expense had been spared to make it one of the most delightful and picturesque domains in the neighbourhood'.

When the achievements of Edward Lowe are outlined below it will be apparent how obviously his range of work and interests were rooted in those of his father. It is clear, too, that Edward's botanical interests were cultivated and encouraged at Highfield House, where, in Fyfe's words of 1856 'the vineries, stove and greenhouse are pretty extensive', containing grapes, an orange tree, cacti, orchids and other exotic plants, 'victorious in all the neighbouring floral exhibitions of Nottingham'; and also there were 'at least 600 ferns in additional greenhouses, and one house exclusively for *Lycopodiums*'. The extent of the sheltered walled gardens and glasshouses at Highfield House can be seen on the O.S. 'Fifty Foot' series (1:500) plan of the house and grounds in 1881 (Figure 41).

Finally, Alfred Lowe, like so many other leading Nottingham personalities including Matthew Needham, his neighbour at Lenton House, was a member of the congregation of High Pavement Chapel. His children were sent to the school kept by Rev. Benjamin Carter, pastor at High Pavement Chapel from 1831 until his death in 1860 (in succession to Rev. James Taylor, whose daughter Emily he married). The school was kept in a house west of 'Fellows Vista' on the south side of High Pavement, but moved later to St. James Street. Carter gave it up in 1835. Among the fellow pupils of the Lowe children were Kirk Swann, Richard Enfield, Philip James Bailey (author of 'Festus'), Robert Gregory, afterwards Dean of St. Pauls, and Samuel Hollins. It can be presumed that Edward Lowe, F.R.S., received a sound basic education there, for 'The class of work in the school was of a high order'.

Edward Joseph Lowe, F.R.S. (1825-1900), who left Highfield House

Born on 11 November 1825, Edward Lowe (Figure 38) married on 2 January 1849 at St. Mary's church, Nottingham, Anne, eldest daughter of George Allcock of Nottingham, who was a son of William Allcock of Trowell and his wife Sarah, daughter of Samuel Pinckney of Trowell. On their marriage Edward and Anne took up residence at Beeston Lodge, a substantial house in a large garden on Beeston High Road (then called The Turnpike), opposite to Beeston silk mill and adjoining Beeston Square. The garden, which now has a National Westminster Bank branch on it at the corner of Beeston High Road and Wollaton Road, had a frontage on the High Road extending from this corner to Villa Street, and along Wollaton Road for about the same distance. The property, which later became the Conservative Club, remained largely unaltered until the turn of the century, but before the first world war, although

Figure 38: Edward Joseph Lowe, FRS (1825-1900) second son of Alfred Lowe
[From Braunsdorff (1896) Courtesy NCLS]

the house retained a High Road frontage, the garden was built over by shops and other premises. The fabric may still be incorporated in part in the existing buildings there.

The Lowes did not stay long at Beeston Lodge, although their elder son, Lawson Lowe, was born there, but moved in late 1851 or in 1852 to Broadgate House, built to Edward Lowe's specifications and then called The Observatory. At that time The Observatory was the most easterly house on the south side of Broadgate, its grounds bounded to the north-east by land of the Lenton Grove estate which extended to the Tottle Brook and the boundary of the Highfield estate, and which was in trust to support the unmarried daughter of Francis Evans of Lenton Grove. The house is not identifiable in the Census Enumerators' Books for 1851 [17], but it may have been the house reported to have been in process of being built on Broadgate. Hugh Lee Peyton Lowe, the younger son of Edward and Anne, was born at The Observatory on 27 October 1856. It was he who ultimately sold the Highfield estate to Sir Jesse Boot in 1919-20. The subsequent history of Broadgate House and its connection with the University College and the University is outlined in the closing paragraphs of this chapter.

With no University or other formal type of higher education, but with a sound basic schooling and an intellectually brilliant father, Edward Lowe became the typical mid-Victorian scientific amateur, acutely observant and insatiably curious about natural phenomena, as well as appreciative of the Arts. Born and privately baptized at Highfield House, he evidently showed early signs of a latent scientific bent, doubtless under the close and continuinmg influence of his father, for he began his daily weather observations at Highfield House under Alfred's supervision in 1840, at the age of 14. This work continued without a break until his removal to Shirenewton Hall near Chepstowe, Monmouthshire in 1882 - perhaps a token of the patience and perseverance of the dedicated scientist. Beginning with a minimum thermometer his recordings extended to include rainfall in 1843, when he contributed a letter to the Nottingham Mercury on meteorological phenomena, and was already, at the age of 17, one of the nation-wide team of 50 pioneer observers taking twice-daily readings for the Royal Agricultural Society.

Edward Lowe contributed daily weather observations to The Times from 1845, and in 1846 at the age of 21 he published his first book, 'A Treatise on Atmospheric Phenomena', a volume of nearly 440 pages. Two years later he was engaged on meteor observations for the British Association with Professor Baden Powell, and became a Fellow of the Royal Astronomical Society. He contributed articles to the Transactions of the Royal Astronomical Society every year for a decade after 1848 on a variety of topics, including meteors, sunspots and zodiacal light, and he was one of the observers who, within a few minutes of each other, discovered the great comet of 1854. He is said to have been the first to point out 'the convergence of meteors to a point in the heavens' [Godfrey 1884 200]. What part the assistance and advice of his father played in this astronomical work is not known, but it is safe to assume that it was considerable.

Meantime, in 1849 Edward Lowe published 'Prognostications of the weather', a short work that was dedicated to Henry Lawson of Bath, who is discussed further below. In 1850 he was a founding member, with his father, of the Meteorological Society, and served on its Council until he retired by rotation in 1854, still aged only 29. His early work in meteorology and astronomy must have been in some sense an extension of his father's interests, but his own catholic scientific enquiries had already broadened into biology before his father's death. In 1853 he became a Fellow of the Royal Geographical Society and published two works on local topics - 'The Climate of Nottingham' and 'The Conchology of Nottinghamshire'. The former is mainly a discussion of the weather observations made at Highfield House in 1852, produced in collaboration with his younger brother, A.S.H.Lowe, also a member of the Meteorological Society. The latter work contains many references to the Highfield House estate and its lake. At the same time the first parts of Lowe's 'A Natural History of British and Exotic Ferns' were appearing, and he was assisting in the compilation of 'British Mollusca' edited by Professor Edward Forbes. In 1857 Lowe became a Fellow of the Linnaean Society, and there followed publications entitled 'British Grasses' (1858), 'Beautiful leaved plants' (1861), 'New and Rare ferns' (1862) and 'Chronology of the Seasons' (1862).

Edward Lowe's work was practical as well as literary. In addition to his long series of weather observations - he was one of the first to send daily telegrams to the Meteorological Office established by Admiral Fitzroy from January 1846 - he was a member of the government party that visited Spain for the solar eclipse of 1860, being in charge of the meteorological work in the Santander district. He conducted many experiments and trials on observation of weather, such as investigating the significance of rain gauges and thermometers exposed at different heights above the ground. He was the inventor of the 'dry-powder' tests for ozone in balloon ascents; was the discoverer of a new British species of worm (*Megascolex rigida* (Baird)); and was the first person to successfully hybridize two British ferns, having formed at Highfield House perhaps the most comprehensive collection of living ferns in existence.

The ferns were grown both outdoors in a 'chasm' at Highfield House, and in glass houses there. An extensive list of species in both collections was given by Lowe himself in an article on the 'Collection of ferns grown at Highfield House' in a 'Handbook to Nottingham' [Allen 1866 34-39], which also contained an article by him entitled 'Nottinghamshire ferns' [p. 26 et seq.]. The species list of 'Exotic ferns in the Highfield House collection', of which there were over 300, was 'arranged according to Mr. J. Smith, late Curator of the Royal Gardens, Kew'. According to Fyfe [1856 169] 'The collection comprises we believe every British fern ... The way into the walled gardens is over a bridge of one arch thrown across the artificial chasm of rocks that shelter the ferns ...The vineries, stove and greenhouses are pretty extensive .... By far the most superb portion of the exotic collection is, however, the unrivalled assemblage of ferns, British, foreign and exotic ... There are said to be collected at least six hundred specimens of ferns in Mr. Lowe's greenhouses'.

The meteorological and astronomical instruments in use at Highfield House and The Observatory in 1856 were described in detail by Fyfe [1856 184-210]. Briefly, they included, at Highfield House, a telescope on the roof, a Newman's barometer, radiation thermometers, wet and dry bulb and maximum and minimum thermometers, rain gauges at different levels, a wind vane (marked on the O.S. 1:500 map of 1881) 54 feet above the ground, a Lind's anemometer and an 'ozonometer'. But 'recently the chief labours of Mr. Lowe's son, the observer [that is, Edward Lowe] have been conducted at Beeston Observatory, his own residence ... Mr. Lowe working both observatories'. The published meteorological record was throughout provided by the instruments at Highfield House, and the equipment at Broadgate House was concerned with experimental rather than routine recording. At Broadgate House was the collection of pioneering astronomical and meteorological instruments which Edward Lowe obtained from Henry Lawson of Bath. A scheme for building an observatory north of the town of Nottingham by public subscription to house Lawson's instruments had been initiated in 1851, but fell through in 1854, and the instruments were then presented to Edward Lowe and installed at Broadgate House in 1855, to make the Beeston Observatory 'one of the most complete meteorological observatories in Great Britain'. Further details of these events are given in Appendix 20.

Edward Lowe was an indefatigable writer and lecturer. Fyfe [1856 185-198] in his 'Rambles round Nottingham' listed numerous papers published by him down to 1856. Other, later works included [Braunsdorff 1896 58-59]:

A Natural History of new and rare ferns [1862, 1868, 1871]
The earthquake of 6 October 1863
Our native ferns. Two volumes. [1874 1880]
The coming drought or the Cycle of the Seasons [1880]

British ferns and where found [1891] Young Collectors Series
Magazine of Natural Phenomena
Barometric Tables of Corrections
Meteorology of Morton's Farming Calendar
Practical Meteorology [1860] (with Scofferon): Orr's Circle of the Sciences.

In addition Lowe delivered papers on various subjects to a variety of learned societies and to the British Association for the Advancement of Science, and he gave occasional lectures on scientific subjects over many years. His Fellowships of the Royal Astronomical Society (1848), Geological Society (1853), Linnaean Society, Zoological Society, Meteorological Society (1850) and Royal Horticultural Society, and his membership of the Geological Society of Edinburgh and the British Natural History Society, and Honorary membership of the Natural History Societies of Dublin, Penzance and Orkney testify to the catholicity of his scientific interests as well as to his country-wide reputation.

In the local area Edward Lowe's interests included the Mechanics Institution, of which he was Vice-President for many years in succession to his father; long service as a magistrate; and the Nottingham Literary and Philosophical Society, of which he became President in 1868. He was also Worshipful Master of the Royal Sussex Lodge of Freemasons, and an honorary member of Nottingham Ancient Order of Oddfellows, being Acting Grand Master of England in 1866. Later appointments include those of Hon. Secretary of the British Association at the Nottingham meeting of 1866, for which he wrote the Report of the Botany section; Fellow of the Royal Society (1867); and Hon. Secretary of the Royal Horticultural Society at the Nottingham meeting of 1872, when he was made Honorary Life Fellow. He was Deputy Lieutenant for Nottinghamshire, and later for Monmouthshire.

It appears that in his later years Edward Lowe's interests moved towards the Arts, but in the 1890s, after moving to Shirenewton, he remained very active in the field of scientific horticulture. In 1890 he won a silver cup presented by the Royal Horticultural Society for the best collection of British ferns, and in 1892 he won 22 of the 29 medals offered by the same Society for varieties of British ferns. It must be presumed that when he moved from Highfield House to Shirenewton Hall in 1882 he took with him his collection of ferns as well as the Old Masters collected by his father. In 1895 he published his last printed work - 'Fern growing, or fifty years experience in their cultivation, with an account of the discovery of multiple parents; dividing and cultivating divided prothalli; showing that more than one plant can be grown from a prothallus; detecting a new fungus on ferns (*Milesia polapodii*); and that the skipjack (*Podura plombea*) conveys sperms of ferns and is thus able to impregnate them'. In 1896 he read a paper to the Linnaean Society 'showing apospory in divided prothalli and an entirely new growth of the prothallus with reproductive organs on both the upper and the lower surface of the prothallus' [Braunsdorff 1896 59]. He was then 71 years old. He died in 1900. It seems very appropriate that the family home of this eminent Victorian polymath and his forbears should have become the residence of the Vice-Chancellor of the University.

Cornelius Brown [1882 375], writing as Edward Lowe left Nottingham for Monmouthshire, could state that 'Mr. Lowe has won a world-wide reputation as an astronomer, meteorologist and botanist. He is the author of numerous works on his favourite subjects of study, the best known being his "Natural History of British and Exotic Ferns", and his "British Grasses"'. But it is difficult, over a century later, to evaluate with confidence the intellectual power of E.J.Lowe and the calibre of his scientific and scholarly achievements. His portrait (Figure 38) certainly conveys an impression of a man of forceful personality and of driving energy, as his multifarious activities must confirm, perhaps more concerned with intellectual challenges than with his house and estate. As a young man he seems to have been something of a self-publicist, possibly in reaction to his private, informal education and lack of any known connection with a University or College. The title page of his book 'The

Conchology of Nottingham' (1853) lists at length his books and papers to date, and his Society memberships. But even then, a passage from the conclusion to that work reveals a surprisingly humble response to his intellectual confrontation with the principles of science and natural order some years before Darwin published his Origin of Species. 'How wonderful must be this law of nature, when we reflect that each species produces shells always so exactly alike as to be at once recognized, and when we further consider the endless diversity of form and colour, it is in the highest degree exalting to ponder on the wisdom therein displayed of an all-wise creator'. Lowe was just 27 years old, and not surprisingly the interest in meteorology and astronomy instilled by his father later took second place to work in botany, and particularly on grasses and ferns, in which he found his deepest intellectual challenge and satisfaction, and for which he received the greatest recognition and respect.

Returning to domestic matters, Charlotte Octavia, the widow of Alfred Lowe, remained at Highfield House after his death in 1856 until at least 1864, and probably until her death in 1865 at the age of 73. At the 1851 census Marianne and Arthur were living at Highfield House with their parents, Alfred and Charlotte, and house servants Emily Glover, Ann Bexon (29) and Edward Beresford (18). In 1861 [18] Marianne and Arthur were still living with their mother, with a domestic staff consisting of Emily Glover, now called housekeeper, Emma Preston (16) a general servant, and a butler, John Murden. William and Elizabeth Lewis with sons William (16) and Thomas (12) were still living at the lodge. Edward Lowe, then aged 35 and described by the Census Enumerator as 'Astronomer etc.', remained with his wife Annie and their sons Alfred Edward Lawson (11) and Hugh Lee Peyton (4) at The Observatory (Broadgate House) with a cook, Jane Williamson (29) and a 21-year-old housemaid. According to White's Directory for 1864 Edward and Annie Lowe were still there, while at Highfield House Charlotte was enumerated together with 'Alfred Lowe' [19] , presumably Alfred Hurst Lowe, her peripatetic eldest son on a visit to her. In 1866 the local Directories recorded Edward Lowe living at Highfield House, while his unmarried sister Marianne had exchanged homes with him, and was living at Broadgate House, where she remained until at least 1887 [Wright 1886, Kelly 1887]. Highfield House, with its scientific equipment and installations, was willed to Edward Lowe by his father, who shared his interests and intellectual powers, and it is assumed that Edward's elder brother Alfred Hurst Lowe received estate elsewhere.

At the census of 1871, then, [20] , Edward Lowe, aged 45, lived at Highfield House with Annie and their sons Lawson, now 21 and a captain in the Sherwood Foresters, and Hugh aged 14, attended by a modest domestic staff of three - Susanna Rowston (32) and Harriett B. Lackbourne (26), both from Ruskington, Lincolnshire, and Henry Smith, a butler aged 30. William and Elizabeth Lewis were still at the lodge with their son William, a gardener and now a widower with a three year old son, Frank William.

Although Braunsdorff [1896] indicated that he had removed to Shirenewton Hall in 1880, Edward Lowe was still enumerated at Highfield House at the 1881 census, with his 24-year old son Hugh, Edward being described as drawing his 'income from land' and Hugh as of 'no profession' [21] . Edward's wife Anne was not mentioned, and she may have been already at Shirenewton - or on holiday - since only one servant was at Highfield House - Beeston born Martha Ann Walker (22), 'cook and domestic servant'. Remarkably, in 1881 William Lewis the coachman and his wife were still at Highfield Lodge, an example of unusually long service with one family. Details of the 'sale' of the Highfield estate to Henry Simpson are discussed later.

Lawson Lowe (1849-1888), genealogist

Alfred Edward Lawson Lowe (Figure 39) the elder son of Edward J. Lowe, died before his father. He was for some time educated at the private school of Rev. Dr. May near Nottingham, but on account of his delicate health he was removed from the school to be tutored

Figure 39: Alfred Edward Lawson Lowe (1849-1888), elder son of E.J. Lowe
[Both portraits from Braunsdorff (1896) Courtesy NCLS]

privately by the Vicar of Beeston, Rev. T.J.Oldrini [22] under whose care 'the boy soon attained proficiency and imbibed a taste for literary and scientific pursuits, more especially genealogy and archaeology, which developed early in life [Braunsdorff 1896 59]. He became known later as a trustworthy man with strong views on integrity and a careful regard for the truth. He delighted in the military life, and served several periods of duty with line regiments. He joined the Sherwood Foresters in 1866, became Captain in 1868, Major in 1880 and Lieutenant Colonel in 1886. Though offered command of his regiment in 1888 he was then too ill to accept it, but was allowed to retain rank in recognition of his long service. Advised to seek a warm climate he stayed at San Remo, but without advantage, and was returning to England when he died at Boulogne on 29 May 1888. He was buried at Shirenewton, which was his home after Highfield House was sold. He had married in 1872 at St. George's, Hanover Square, Gertrude Emily Otter, only daughter of Rev. George Otter, Vicar of Hucknall Torkard, by whom he had a son and a daughter, both born at Highfield House.

Described by Mellors as a diligent and accomplished scholar and an able antiquarian, Lawson Lowe was elected F.S.A. in 1878, and was a member of various antiquarian societies. His first known publication, in 1872, was an Historical Record of the Royal Sherwood Foresters. He edited Black's Guide to Nottinghamshire, published in 1876, a well written and well arranged volume full of useful historical and topographical information. A paper on Wollaton and the Willoughby monuments in 1877 was followed by a privately printed 'Pedigree of the family of Otter of Welham in the County of Nottingham and elsewhere' (his wife's family) in 1880, with special reference to Dr. William Otter, D.D. (1768-1840) who was in 1830 the first Principal of King's College, London, and in 1836 became Bishop of Chichester. To Briscoe's 'Old Nottinghamshire' in 1881 he contributed four short papers, including one on the

East Bridgford family of Hacker, and in the second series [1884] one on the Byron vault at Hucknall Torkard. The Nottinghamshire Guardian of 19 April 1882 printed an article by Lawson Lowe on 'The Strelley monuments in Strelley church'. Cornelius Brown [1882] acknowledged the help of 'Major A.E.Lawson Lowe, F.S.A., who is second to none in his knowledge of our county families [and] has very kindly and willingly furnished me with many genealogical and historical facts and useful references and additions'. Lowe certainly helped J.T.Godfrey with his well-known history of Lenton [1884] and had himself embarked upon a history of the Hundred of Broxtowe, of which only a preliminary number is known to have been published [23] .

Lawson Lowe's writings were sparser than those of his father, and his achievements, though in a totally different field, are overshadowed by those of Edward Lowe; but such publications as survive show him to have been meticulous and scholarly, and he was certainly recognized in his time to be the genealogical expert of the area. It is interesting to find that Rev. Samuel Kirk Swann bequeathed to him the remains of Lenton Priory and some adjacent property in 1886 [Godfrey and Ward 1908 106-7] and that Lawson Lowe's son, Major P.H.Lowe of Hedingham, Essex, presented artefacts from the priory site to the University College museum, and made possible the excavations on the priory site directed by Herbert Green in 1935-36.

After his marriage in 1872 Lawson Lowe remained at Highfield House with his parents, and was recorded there in 1876 by Kelly's Post Office Directory. He moved with them to Shirenewton Hall in 1882 or thereabouts. His son, Percival Edward Hurst Lowe, mentioned above, was born at Highfield House on 28 July 1873. He became a professional soldier, perhaps living out his father's enthusiasm. Educated at Cheltenham and Sandhurst, Percy Lowe was gazetted to the 2nd Battalion, West Yorkshire Regiment in 1894, becoming Lieutenant in 1895. In 1895-96 he served in the expedition to Ashanti. His sister, Gertrude Gwenllyan Lowe, born at Highfield House on 14 August 1874, was married on 2 January 1895 at St. Mary's church, Bryanston Square, London, to Otto-William Braunsdorff, Lieutenant in the 6th (King William II of Wurttemberg's Own) Regiment of the Royal Saxon Infantry, whose pedigree is set out in his own book based on the Lowe family papers left by Lawson Lowe, published at Dresden in 1896, and drawn upon heavily in this account.

Highfield House and its estate from 1881 to 1920

After four generations Highfield House passed out of the ownership of the Lowe family. E.J.Lowe sold the estate in 1881-82 to Henry Simpson, a Nottingham lace manufacturer. Lowe put the property up for sale through his solicitors, Freeth, Rawson and Cartwright, with auctioneer John Eddison. An abstract was to be sent to the purchaser on or before 30 July 1881, and the purchase was to be completed on 24 December 1881. Conveyance of the main estate was complicated by the inclusion of three portions added after 1800. These portions were about 4 acres from the Beeston inclosure award of 11 December 1809; Hassock Close Pasture of 5a.2.17 conveyed to Alfred Lowe on 6 April 1846; and the 6-acre field called Wylde's Hassock Close (which involved an indenture dated 26 January 1825 made between Rev. Charles Wylde and his wife Esther, and William Wylde and Clinton James Fynes Clinton), both additions to the Hassocks lands bought earlier by Alfred Lowe from John Wright of Lenton Hall. The actual indenture of conveyance to Simpson was therefore completed only on 20 March 1883 [24] .

Henry Simpson and Co., manufacturers of silk and cotton lace, were in 1871 located in Sims' factory and Whitehalls' factory, but by 1882 were of 18 Stoney Street, with their factory at High Church Street, New Basford, and with London premises [Wright 1871 and 1882]. Simpson was living at Highfield House in 1883, and remained there until 1895 [Wright 1883, 1895], but thereafter it is less clear who occupied the house. A succession of Directories after the turn of the century do not mention Highfield House, which suggests that it may have been vacant. Kelly's Directory for 1900 and 1904 included Henry Simpson 'of Highfield House' among the landowners of Beeston, while Beeston and District Local History Society's Newsletter No. 11 of 1974 stated that Simpson was at Highfield House in 1904 and 1908, without giving a source reference. It seems unlikely. In 1897 [Wright 1897] a Henry Simpson was said to be living at Emerald Bank, Gregory Boulevard, and he was not mentioned under Beeston, while Wright's Directory of 1900 included a Henry Simpson as a director of E.G.Simpson and Co. of 4 High Pavement, living at 2, Gill Street. It is not known whether either was the same person, and in 1905 the only Henry Simpson mentioned in Wright's Directory was a Radford window cleaner.

It is supposed that Simpson left Highfield House in the mid-1890s after meeting sudden financial difficulties. In 1891 he was contributing funds for scholarships at the University College [Wright 1891], but in 1893 either he or the Lowes (from whom Simpson had a mortgage) was attempting to sell the estate through solicitors Wells and Hind of Nottingham and Hind and Robinson of London [25]. 'Messrs. Mabbott and Edge' (London auctioneers) 'have received instructions to offer this property for sale by auction at the George Hotel, Nottingham, on Wednesday, the 17th day of May 1893 ... first as a whole, and if not sold in that manner, then in two Lots'. It was described as the 'valuable freehold residential, mineral and building estate ... the whole extending to about 153 acres, and forming not only a very charming Residential Property, but possessing great value as a Mineral and Building estate'. Simpson (or Lowe) envisaged that the Hassocks (Lot 2) offered, in the words of the sale brochure 'one of the finest speculations to any capitalist seeking to employ his money with a prospect of a very large profit in the near future', not to mention that acquiring coal mining leases on the surrounding lands would 'enable the valuable mineral resources to be worked with advantage', favoured by the large local market, and with railway sidings 'practically on the property'.

Although Hassocks Farm was in disrepair 'very great value attaches to this Lot for building purposes', comprising as it did nearly all the land 'uncovered' between Lenton and rapidly-growing Beeston. It 'may therefore be regarded as Ripe for Immediate Development'. 'A fact that would tend greatly to open up this building land is that if a road were made along the northern boundary of the Lot, and the narrow strip of land connecting it with the Beeston and Nottingham road [Beeston Lane] the traffic would be diverted through the estate, as such road would give direct, level communication from Sandiacre through Beeston to Nottingham, thus avoiding the necessity of using the existing road with its many steep gradients' [26]. As an alternative the proposed road could be continued westward direct from the point marked A on the plan [27]. 'It may be mentioned that the Corporation of Nottingham have laid their gas mains through the estate adjacent to the northern boundary of this Lot', evidently anticipating its early development.'A purchaser of this Lot will be entitled to a right of road, 40 feet wide, over the strip 17A' - which ran south from Beeston Lane just east of the Tottle Brook bridge, beneath the present Florence Boot Hall, to the present University Boulevard near the paddling pool. It will be recognized that these suggestions for road developments are almost identical with those adopted under Sir Jesse Boot's scheme thirty years later.

These carefully marshalled and, it must be admitted, sound arguments proved to be unpersuasive, for at the end of the century the whole estate was still for sale. Nottingham Borough Records include a note dated 10 September 1900 that a communication from the Royal Agricultural Society had been received stating that London had been chosen as the place for their permanent show ground. The Council had been prepared to buy the Highfields estate for the purpose, and were thanked for their help and interest [28]. Then, in the following year, shortly after the death of Edward Lowe, through the same solicitors, Messrs. Freeth, Rawson and Cartwright of 13 Low Pavement, the estate was again presented for sale by auction by Messrs. Morris and Place of Nottingham on 10 July 1901 [29]. Again there was no sale. This time the would-be vendors were certainly the Lowes, and it is apparent that Henry Simpson's mortgage from the Lowes had been 'called in'.

The 1901 sale brochure emphasized advantages similar to those pressed in 1893, notably potentialities for residential development and mineral exploitation. 'As a compact country residence enjoying the advantages of thorough seclusion although within easy distance of the centre of Nottingham, the property has scarcely its equal; and in addition it offers to the speculator a splendid opportunity from its great adaptability for sites for villa residences, some of which, for beauty of position and surrounding scenery can scarcely be equalled in the Midland Counties'. Minerals, essentially coal seams, 'exceedingly important', were included in the sale. 'In the year 1874 trial borings upon the estate were executed under the superintendence of eminent mining engineers'. The main boring was on the present University sports fields, and in the Coal Measures, reached at 85 yards deep, were several thin beds of coal until at 186 yards deep good quality coal 3ft.10in. thick was encountered. A further 17 yards down (203 yards below the surface) another coal bed estimated at 6ft.2 in. thick was reached. These seams were thought to correspond to the Deep Soft and Deep Hard coals 'so extensively worked in the Erewash valley'.

It is not known who, if anyone, lived at Highfield House during the following decade: whether, indeed, Henry Simpson did not stay on there for some time. The next known resident was John Croshaw Wilson, managing director of James Wilson and Son (Nottingham 1914 Ltd.), hosiery manufacturers of 66 Carlton Road and Dakeyne Street. He occupied the house from 1913 to 1920, having lived at West Bridgford in 1900, at 2 Park Terrace in 1904 and 1908, and at 7 Park Valley in 1908 and 1912. He was a tenant, and as late as 31 March 1920 a plan forming part of a deed conveying 48 acres immediately adjoining the Highfield estate on the north-east (including the Keighton Closes) from T.S.Pearson-Gregory to Frederick Mitchell showed Highfields belonging to 'Lowes representatives' [30] ; and it was from 'the Lowes' that Sir Jesse Boot purchased the Highfield estate in 1919-20. Wilson was then still in residence.

These seemingly contradictory facts are somewhat clarified by deeds held in the Bursar's Department of the University. A conveyance dated 19 November 1919 for the sale of the Highfield estate in fee simple to Sir Jesse Boot by the surviving younger son of E.J.Lowe, Hugh Lee Peyton Lowe (Figure 40) of Blagden House, Stoke Bishop in the City of Bristol, refers to an Indenture of Mortgage dated 21 March 1883, made between Henry Simpson and Edward Joseph Lowe, whereby the estate was 'conveyed by the said Henry Simpson to the said Edward Joseph Lowe in fee simple by way of Mortgage for securing payment to the said Edward Joseph Lowe on a day therein mentioned and since passed of the principal sum of £35,000 with interest thereon ...'. The fact that Simpson or Lowe put up the estate for auction in May 1893 suggests that the mortgage was for a ten year term, especially since 'Edward Joseph Lowe as Mortgagee went into possession of the said hereditaments ... and possession thereof has ever since been retained by the said Edward Joseph Lowe and the persons deriving title through him' (E.J.Lowe having died in October 1900) tends to confirm that foreclosure took place in 1893 or 1894, and that Simpson, if he remained, did so as a rent-paying tenant.

The executors of E.J.Lowe were his widow Anne, and his younger son Hugh (Figure 40), Lawson Lowe having died in 1888, when the will was made. Anne Lowe died on 10 March 1915, leaving Hugh as the sole surviving executor and beneficiary, and it was Hugh, therefore, who in 1919 agreed to sell the estate to Sir Jesse Boot at a price of £32,254.3s.4d. - below the price of 1881 - subject to a mining lease and an easement [31] . The plan and schedule annexed to the conveyance were virtually the same as those for the sale brochure of 1901, and little different from those of 1893 and 1881.

Highfield House: the buildings and garden

The Ordnance Survey 1:500 plan of 1881 (Figure 41) shows the house and grounds as E.J.Lowe left them, with stables and coachhouses around an enclosed stable yard through

Figure 40: Hugh Lee Paton Lowe, E.J. Lowe's second son, born 1856
[He sold the Highfield estate to Sir Jesse Boot in 1919 [From Braunsdorff (1896) Courtesy NCLS]

which the present main entrance to the house is approached, and a farmyard where the car park now lies nearer to Cut Through Lane. A gate at the southern corner of the farmyard gave access to the drive running from the stable yard to Beeston Lane, and another gate at the northern corner to a drive or track running north-east alongside Cut Through Lane and then south-east to the fields outside the ha ha wall, approximately along the line of the present Cherry Tree Hill. A separate branch from the main drive led to the main entrance door, with its porch, and this formal entrance to the house was served by a carriage turning circle visible in the contemporary engravings of the house as viewed from the south (Figure 42). A path lined by trees and shrubs, already shown on Sanderson's map of 1835, ran from the lawn south of the house to the western end of the now neglected pleasure grounds above and below the sandstone cliff and alongside the lake.

The sales brochures of the later 19th century (in 1881, 1893 and 1901) each distinguished the 65-acre 'residential estate' from the pasture closes of the Hassocks on the Trent valley floor, and all emphasized the commanding site of Highfield House and the beauty of its surroundings. The 1893 brochure described the 'moderate sized mansion', 'standing high, with south aspect, in a finely timbered park ... and surrounded by most charming pleasure grounds containing some very fine specimen trees and shrubs, and sloping to a beautiful ornamental lake of considerable extent [32] (Figures 42 to 44). The gardens and grounds are of unusual beauty ... very pretty pleasure grounds surrounding the house, with lawns, flowerbeds, shrubberies etc., adorned by a quantity of choice timber, including many fine upright oaks and a golden yew, one of the finest 'out of doors' yews in England'. A ha ha fence divided the pleasure grounds from the park, through which 'shrubbery walks and numerous rustic steps and slopes' led to the lake 'with islands and boathouse, surrounded by pretty and extensive

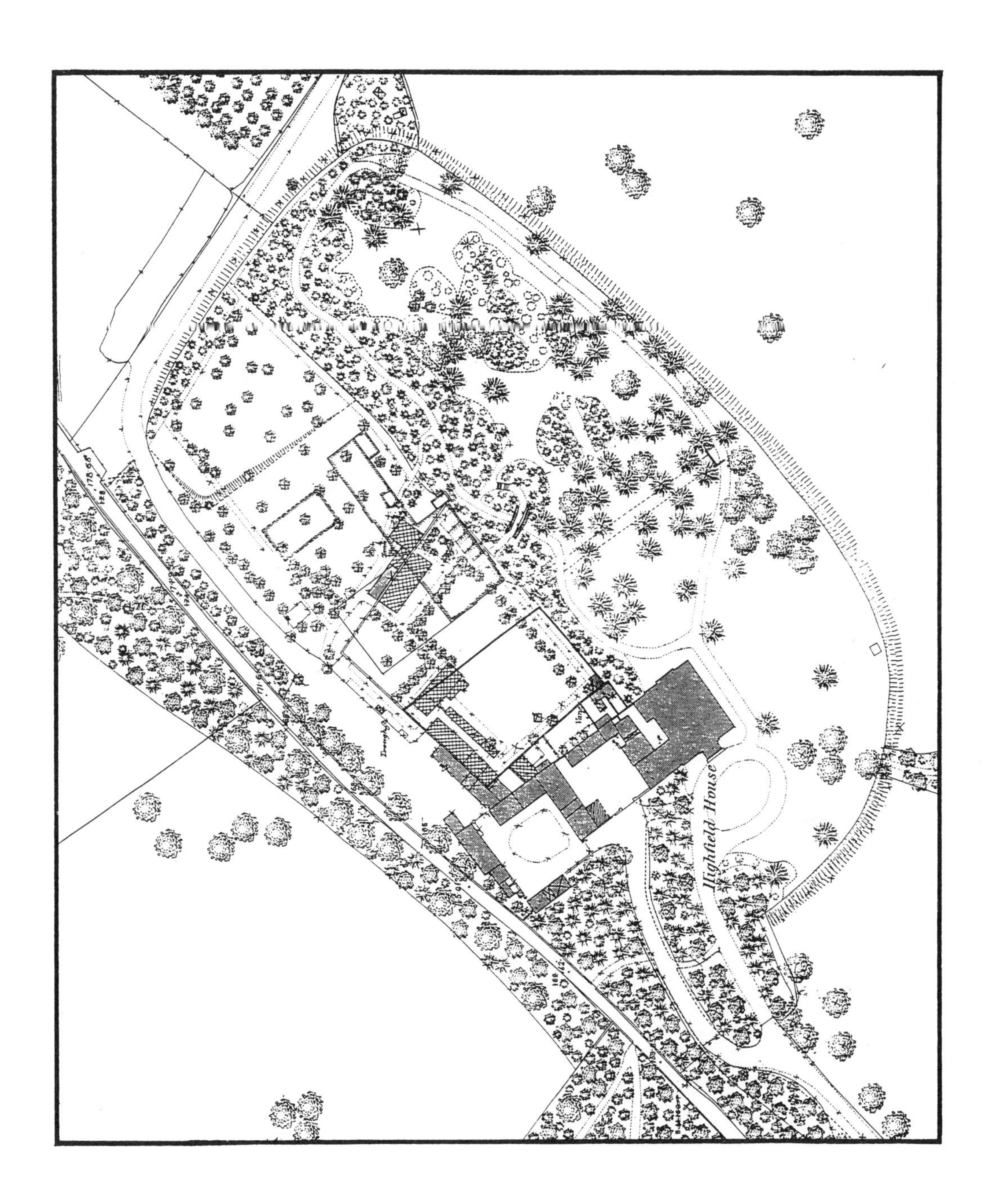

Figure 41: Plan of Highfield House and gardens, 1881
[Reduced from the O.S. 1:500 map, of 1881: Nottingham sheet XLII 5 21] Note the location of the wind vane, the bridge over the 'chasm', and the extensive glasshouses. Superimposed on this map are the outlines of contractors' buildings of the early 1920s, and of the reduced walled garden of the same date.

Figure 42: Highfield House viewed from the west in about 1890 and 1950
Above: *from Braunsdorff (1896) [Courtesy NCLS], probably engraved from an original in the sale brochure of 1881]. For a slightly different viewpoint see Lawson Lowe [1871].*
Below: *photo. of about 1950.*

Figure 43: Two views of Highfield park, 1881
Above: *View across the Fishpond towards the site of the present Lower (lakeside) Terrace. Highfield House is visible near top right; the Staff Garden left. A scar of a possible slip of Mercia Mudstones is visible.*
Below: *Looking east from below Highfield House towards Dunkirk across Keighton Meadow.*
[Both views from the sale brochure of 1881].

woodland walks'. The 'massive rocks' - the cliff overlooking the lake - of course formed 'a novel feature of the place'. Also on the estate 'there is a good rabbit warren affording excellent shooting' (though its location is not known) and there was coarse fishing at the lake. The 1901 brochure mentioned rookeries.

The 'capital walled garden', then over twice its present size, was an important feature. The 1893 brochure referred to 'an excellent double vinery, store, fernhouse, six other glasshouses, forcing pits etc.'. A somewhat unexpected feature was the substantial farmstead associated with the house, between the stable yard and Cut Through Lane (Figure 41). The range of brick and tiled farm buildings comprised six large loose boxes, open cart and implement sheds, a large cowshed with room for about 25 cows (which had been built by Henry Simpson - see Figure 44), three calf pens and a range of five piggeries, with large lofts above them. In addition, around the farmyard, were a large storehouse, a further cowshed for six cows, and two stalls for carthorses. Only a few of these former farm buildings survive today, and the northern range and the large cowshed nearby have gone. The latter, which was not present in 1881, may indicate Henry Simpson's expansion of farming operations on the estate from Highfield House while Hassocks Farm was allowed to fall into disuse and disrepair.

Distinct from the farmyard and other farm buildings were the stables and coachhouses, which were not associated with farming. 'The excellent stabling, conveniently near the house and surrounding a spacious yard, consists of three stalls, a coachhouse for six carriages, a harness room, matchboarded and with a fireplace, and a washing shed'. Over the coachhouse were a corn store, a straw loft, a large lumber room and a potato and fruit room. There was also a fowlhouse, a wood and potting shed, and drying ground. Adjoining the house itself was the servants' yard, now partly incorporated within the house. In it in 1893 were a fitted dairy, coal and lumber sheds, a water closet and a bottle store.

The arrangements were substantially changed after 1919. Those buildings nearest to Cut Through Lane have been demolished. Large glasshouses, mostly within the original walled garden have also gone. During the construction of the Trent building in the early 1920s a wide path was cut through the walled garden to give access from the main building site to the contractors' building north-east of Highfield House. This is shown on a partial revision of the 1881 O.S. 1:500 plan dating from the mid-1920s [33]. The garden wall facing the University museum is therefore modern, although it may be built of re-used bricks. Some of the contractors' buildings, later converted for use by Engineering Departments, are now occupied mainly by the University Works Department. Photographs of the 1920s [34] show that the original ha ha wall south-east of Highfield House gardens and shrubberies was cut away in the excavation needed to level the back (northern) part of the Trent building site before construction began. The cliff so formed is now clad in concrete alongside the rear service road of the Trent building.

The cement-rendered, brick-built mansion was entered through a porch on the south-west side (Figure 42). In 1893 the ground floor rooms, 10 feet 6 inches high, comprised an entrance hall, out of which opened the library, with a black marble mantelpiece and casement windows to the garden, and the drawing room, 22 by 16 feet, which overlooked the lake and had a handsome white marble mantelpiece; the morning room looking over the garden, also with a white marble mantelpiece; and the dining room, 23 by 14 feet, with two fireplaces (the other rooms were heated by 'Register stoves'), used in 1893 as a billiards room. The 'domestic offices', shut off from the rest of the house, included a butler's pantry, with fireplace, hot and cold water and room for a bed: a store room: a large paved kitchen, larder and scullery, a servants' hall and cellarage for wine, beer and wood. The upper floor, served by principal and secondary staircases contained five bedrooms in 'the house' and three in the servants' wing, two with fireplaces. Of the former, two 16-feet-square rooms with fireplaces were linked by a fitted bathroom, and a third led to a smaller room overlooking the lake, either a dressing room

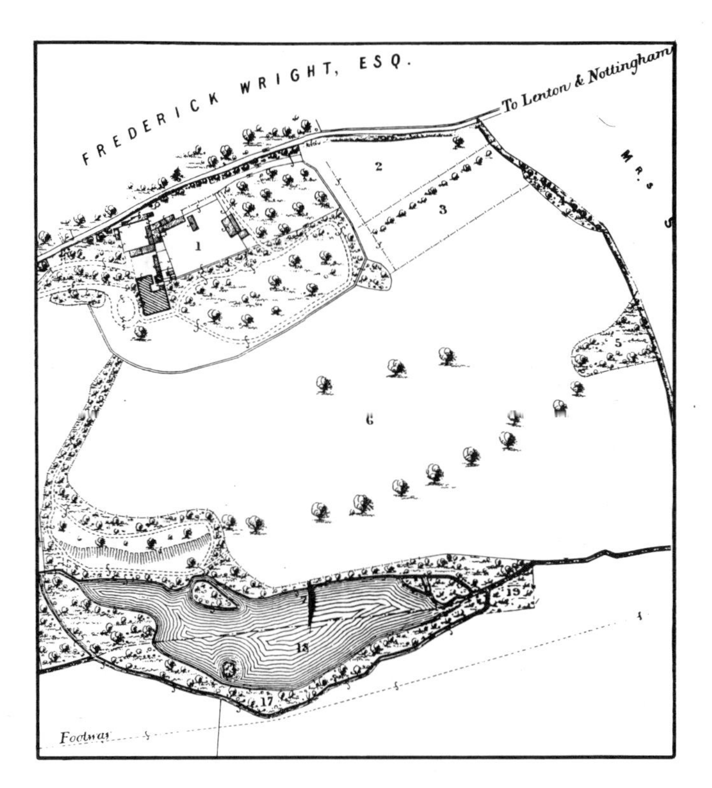

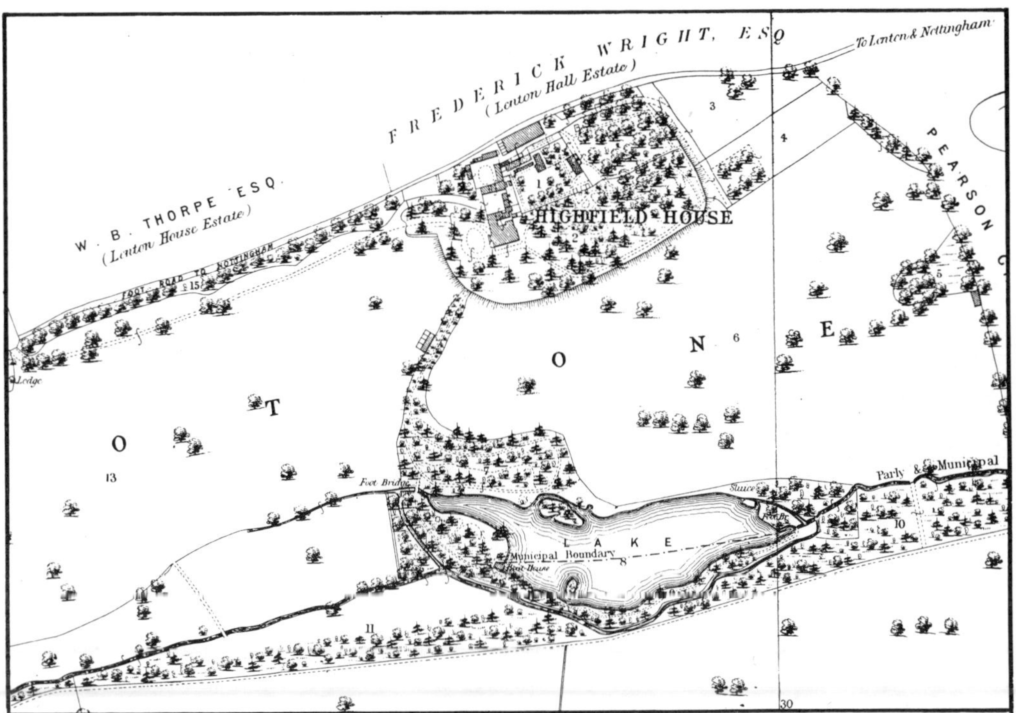

Figure 44: Parts of the Highfield estate in 1881 and 1893
[From the sale brochures] Note the addition by 1893 of a large cowshed north of the house, bordering on Cut Through Lane.

or another bedroom. A fourth bedroom, looking east, had a dressing room, and a fifth had a Register stove in a marble fireplace.

The house will have remained essentially unaltered from 1881 until after 1920, apart from the probable temporary conversion of E.J.Lowe's study into a butler's pantry, and a change of name from Smoking Room to Morning Room, though the introduction of an 'en suite' bathroom was at the expense of one of the principal bedrooms. However, alterations were made in the preparation of the house as the Principal's residence in the 1920s. The porch and main entrance door on the south-west side were replaced by a french window (Figure 42 lower) and the main entrance transferred to a door in the former stable yard, where stables and coachhouses had become redundant. The carriageway to the former main entrance therefore disappeared. The transfer meant that the original entrance hall could be combined with the rooms on either side of it to form the present spacious drawing room, and the stubs of the walls removed are positive features of this attractive room. The new main entrance now leads into a flagged hallway which in 1881 appeared as an unroofed light well.

The changes in the Highfield estate arising from its sale to Sir Jesse Boot in 1919-20 are outlined in Chapter XVI, an obvious one being the demolition of the original entrance lodge of 1799 in 1925 (Figure 45). One part of the estate has suffered from unwarranted neglect and deterioration. The former pleasure grounds of the Lowes above and below the sandstone cliff by the lake, later a promenade for University College staff (and occasional students) have been for many years virtually inaccessible, ignored and unkempt. Yet these now abbreviated 'sylvan walks' remain delightful, and it is to be hoped that the University will soon find resources to give them restorative treatment, to care for the fine flights of steps descending to near lake level, with their old cast iron hand rails, and the interesting trees planted so long ago. This would involve taking serious steps, probably in collaboration with the City Parks authority to secure the area from the ravages of youthful vandals entering from the public park through damaged railings to pursue their destructive activities undisturbed, and action is needed to 'turn around'

Figure 45: Highfield House lodge, between the two new College entrance lodges in 1925, just before its demolition

The original entrance gate was at the left of the photograph where vehicle tracks can be seen. [NUMD Acc. 423]

the area by improving access from the direction of the Trent building. For a University striving to please paying guests, especially in summer, this part of its heritage from the 19th century should be a potentially valuable amenity, well worth preserving and restoring before it is destroyed.

Hassocks Farm

The valley-floor half of the Highfield estate, a salient of Beeston parish, the former Hassocks, now used as University and public playing fields and that part of the public University Park south of the Tottle Brook, has always been distinct and separate from Highfields park. As common pasture the Hassocks contained no farmstead before the Beeston inclosure of 1809, but Hassocks Farm was marked on Sanderson's map surveyed in the early 1830s [35] (see also Figure 105). It was probably built after 1828 when Alfred Lowe bought most of the Hassocks from John Wright of Lenton Hall. Its farmhouse was small and its farm buildings not extensive. It was situated just south of the present University sports pavilion, off the former Hassocks Lane of which a fragment remains alongside the tennis courts. Its land seems to have comprised only grass closes, and its chief enterprise throughout must have been small-scale dairying.

At the 1861 census Hassocks Farm was occupied by Francis Holmes, aged 78, who was said to farm 32 acres - that is, only half of the valley land of the Highfield estate [36]. With him lived his farmer son, William Holmes (47) and his wife Elizabeth and their six children, ranging in age from William (20) and Elizabeth (18) (who was a silk mill worker like her younger sister Anne) to a 10-month old baby. Young Elizabeth was born at Clipstone, as was her father, but the four youngest children were born at Beeston, and since Anne was aged 15 in 1861 this suggests that the family were at Hassocks Farm by 1846. Francis Holmes may have been there even earlier, but other tenants may have preceded him. He was still mentioned in Wright's Directories of 1862, 1866, 1879 and 1881, when he would have been 98 years old. Not surprisingly his name was absent from the 1891 Directory, when a William Holmes, described as a cottager and cowkeeper, lived on City Road, Beeston. Francis's son William would by then have been 77 years old, so this is more likely to have been his grandson, aged 50. Wright's Directory of 1879 named William Holmes as a farmer at Dunkirk, Old Lenton, and he may have farmed the Hassocks with other land, for the farmstead there was not even mentioned in the 1881 sale brochure, and in 1893 it was described as being in disrepair.

Henry Simpson doubtless used some of the Hassocks land in extending farming operations in the 1880s from Highfield House where a cowshed to hold 25 cows was built adjoining Cut Through Lane between 1881 and 1893. The engraving of the park in the 1881 sale brochure indicates that cows grazed the park at that time. It is doubtful whether Hassocks Farm was ever renovated, though its buildings may have remained in farming use down to the 1920s, when they were demolished.

Broadgate House

Broadgate House, Broadgate, Beeston has been closely associated with Highfields through most of its history, and it seems appropriate to review briefly its origin and successive owners and occupiers at this point rather than to group it with the newer houses on the campus. It is situated on former open arable field land enclosed in 1809. Broadgate House and several other houses south-west of it are on the allotment in the Tuttle Brook Field made to Richard Sheldon. The land of the Lenton Grove estate between the Sheldon allotment and the Tottle Brook was in trust, and thus effectively sterilized against sale for development for much of the 19th century.

'The Observatory' - its original name - was built for Edward Lowe in about 1850, and he moved into it with his wife and infant son from Beeston Lodge in 1851. They remained there for some 15 years. The house was 'purposely erected for an observatory' [Fyfe 1856 200] and when first built, unscreened by trees, it was a prominent feature in the view looking west from the Beeston Lane end of Cut Through Lane. 'Suddenly the beautiful lane extending from Lenton to Highfield House terminates, and the rambler perceives that the high road to Beeston [that is, Beeston Lane] sweeps past with a curve and is lost in the ascent of an eminence in front [the main Beeston terrace] forming the commanding site of an observatory'. There were then no intervening houses, and no University Boulevard or Woodside Road.

Fyfe devoted a whole chapter to a description of a visit to Beeston Observatory in 1855 or 1856, and though a considerable part of it was devoted to eulogies of E.J.Lowe and his achievements to date, there followed an exhaustive description of the instruments in use and their mode of operation, including those presented by Henry Lawson of Bath (see Appendix 20) which had just been installed. Instruments seem to have been installed all over the house, including the roof, and there was a specially built Transit Room for Lowe's 4-inch telescope. Over thirty thermometers 'of different construction, each devoted to a particular purpose' were in use. After his father's death in 1856 Edward Lowe cared for the meteorological installations at both The Observatory and Highfield House. Upon his mother's death in 1865 he immediately moved into Highfield House, while his unmarried sister Marianne Agnes took up residence at The Observatory - an exchange of homes that seems to have been satisfactory to both.

Miss Lowe, as she was named in the Directories, was recorded as of Broad Gate or Broadgate, together with increasing numbers of other householders through the 1870s and 1880s, but the house was called Broadgate House (no longer an observatory) at least as early as 1869 (by Morris's Directory) only four years after Edward Lowe left it. Miss Lowe was still there in 1887 [Wright 1887], some years after the family had gone from Highfield House. Her household was certainly elderly, for even at the 1881 census, when she was 63, her housekeeper Emily Glover was 74, her general servant Harriett Middleton 81, and her gardener Charles Braylar was 67. Emily Glover had come with Marianne in 1865 from Highfield House, where she had been housekeeper in 1861 and a house servant in 1851, thirty years earlier. How long Marianne Lowe remained at Broadgate House is not known, though it is thought she probably died in 1887, the year in which Marianne's younger brother Arthur, of Gosfield Hall, qualified for inclusion in the electoral roll of the Rushcliffe Division by owning Broadgate House. In 1903 Walter George Vincent was said to have occupied Broadgate House 'for many years past' [37]. Vincent probably rented the house from Arthur Lowe until on 11 July 1898 he raised a mortgage on it of £ 1,050 from Henry Wing of Nottingham, presumably on the death of Arthur, then aged 72, with two sons aged 32 and 27 . Vincent's mortgage was apparently for five years, with a provision for recovery on repayment. Although the interest was paid the capital was still owing at the end of the term, Wing foreclosed, and on 5 August 1903 Vincent sold Broadgate House to Margaret Armitage for £2,100, half of it paid to Henry Wing [38].

Margaret Armitage and her husband Stephen had lived at 56 Burns Street, Nottingham in 1895, at 13 Gedling Grove in 1897, and then at Epperstone [Wright 1900, Allen 1901, 1902] before moving into Broadgate House in 1903 [Kelly 1904]. Stephen was one of the three directors of Armitage Brothers Limited, grocers and cafe proprietors of Victoria Street, Nottingham, and according to Mellors it was he who had largely developed the cafe business[39]. An active and capable business man, who cared for the welfare of his employees and was much respected by them, he devoted most of his leisure time to 'works of charity and philanthropy' in connection with the Women's Hospital, Children's Hospital, Eye Infirmary, District Nursing Association, the Midland Orphanage for Girls at Lenton, and other bodies on which he 'brought to bear his business abilities to their advantage'. He was a pioneer motorist, and in 1903 registered from Broadgate House a five horsepower steam car with a green-painted dog-cart body, built by the Locomobile Company, one of the earliest cars in the Nottingham area [40] . Stephen Armitage died at Broadgate House after a very brief illness in February 1915, aged 50. Margaret remained there until 1920 [Wright 1920].

Soon after they bought Broadgate House Margaret and Stephen Armitage (not to be confused with S.C.Armitage who bought Lenton Fields) obtained a mortgage of £1,400 from Robert Wilkinson Smith of Bunny Hall on the security of Broadgate House, and a map attached to the indenture shows the two cottages in the grounds together with a glasshouse on the Broadgate frontage east of the entrance gate [41] . R.W.Smith died on 20 December 1907, the mortgage being transferred to his trustees; and on 16 December 1910, by indenture, Samuel Herrick Sands of Eastbourne (formerly of West Hill House - now Paton House and chairman of Nottingham Joint Stock Bank) and Edward Parry of London, surviving executors of R.W.Smith, were joined as mortgagees by C.W.Birkin of Nottingham Park, F.N.Ellis of Mansfield and Harold Sands of Eastbourne (also formerly of West Hill House). S.H.Sands and Edward Parry both died in August 1920, so the discharge of the mortgage by repayment of the capital sum, and the recovery of the property by Margaret Armitage on 1 July 1921 was to Col. C.W.Birkin, F.N.Ellis and Harold Sands. This was in preparation for the conveyance of Broadgate House on 7 July 1921 by Margaret, then of 41 Compton Road, Nottingham, for £2,500 to J.H.Linday, apparently already in residence.

It appears that Kellys' Directory in 1912 confused Stephen Armitage with Stephen Cecil Armitage (later Sir Cecil Armitage), recording the former at No. 46 Broadgate and the latter at Broadgate House. S.C.Armitage was a solicitor with E. King, Morris and Armitage of Caulton Chambers, Long Row, Nottingham. In 1928 he bought and moved to Lenton Fields after living at Cavendish Crescent in The Park, and he retained Lenton Fields after he had purchased Hawkesworth Manor from Sir Alexander Russell Birkin, and moved there. By 1950 he was C.B.E., J.P., and by 1956 it was Sir Cecil Armitage, C.B.E., D.L., J.P. Chairman of Armitage Brothers.

In 1921 the Broadgate property still comprised the house, two cottages, a stable, carriage house (probably by now a garage) and outbuildings with 4a.2.10 of land [42] . John Howard Linday, the purchaser of 1921 with his wife Amy Elizabeth, was a soap manufacturer. The Lindays lived at Broadgate House for nine years. On 5 July 1930 they sold the house and two-thirds of the grounds to the Sir Jesse Boot Property and Investment Company Limited (Sir Jesse Boot's instrument for carrying out his Highfields scheme - see Chapter XVI) for £2,900. The 2.955 acres in this transaction were 'the north-westerly portion of a larger piece of land containing 4a.2.10' conveyed to the Lindays. Margaret Armitage still retained the mineral rights below 200 feet deep.

Sir Jesse's Company bought Broadgate House on behalf of, and at the specific request of the University College to act as an annexe to the new Florence Boot Hall for women. An agreement between the Company and the College was dated 9 December 1930 and headed 'Agreement relative to the purchase and equipment as a hostel of Broadgate House, Beeston, Notts.' [43] . The arrangement was that the Company would render an account to the College for the purchase, alteration and furnishing of the house - a total estimated on 1 January 1932 at £5,847.7s.9d., including about £1,581 for reconstruction and alteration and £1,296 for furniture and equipment, covering renewed electrical wiring, installing central heating, providing two more bathrooms, ten washbasins, a complete new hot and cold water supply system, new drains and complete redecoration. The College was to have Broadgate House free of rent and interest for five years, and make repayment within that period. In the event the actual sum paid by the College was £3,923 on 28 April,1932. Twenty women occupied five large study-bedrooms (approved by the Board of Education for only temporary use) from Autumn 1930 until summer 1933.

The number of students in the University College decreased from 1932, and with the pressure on residential places easing Florence Boot Hall was able to dispense with its annexe. Broadgate House then became the home of Mrs. Margaret Massey-Stewart, widow of Principal Hugh Stewart, who married her as his third wife in 1930 and who died in 1934. She remained at Broadgate House for some years, but in 1941, when the University Air Squadron (which catered also for Loughborough College) was expanding, Broadgate House was let to the Air Ministry as the Squadron's Headquarters: and so it remains after half a century. Mrs. Massey-Stewart, who retained an interest in and connection with Hugh Stewart Hall for the rest of her life, died in 1988 aged 91. She occupied Broadgate House from 1935 to 1941.

NOTES

1. N.U.M.D., Wadsworth 52. 'Copy of the Parcels in the conveyance from Miss Milward to Messrs. Pares and Paget dated 28 and 29 March 1798'. Messrs. Hopkin and Hooton occupied Lower High Field, South High Field and North High Field. William Black of Nottingham had two Highfield Closes and Highfield Meadow. He was a hosier, of Fisher-gate, Nottingham. Hopkin and Hooton were innkeepers in Lenton and Nottingham respectively.
2. Otto-William Braunsdorff, *Some account of the Family of Lowe* 'compiled from the papers left by the late Lieut.Col. Edward Lawson Lowe of Highfield and subsequently of Shirenewton Hall, F.S.A. etc., and from other authentic records'. Dresden, 1886. See p. 45.
   William Wilkins was architect to the Newcastle estate: see the *Lenton Listener* (Lenton Local History Society) No. 35 (Aug.-Sept. 1985). He was the architect of Donington Park, built mainly in 1793 for the second Earl of Moira, a house described by Humphrey Repton, the great landscape gardener, as one of the 'most correct specimens of true Gothic recently built' - a commendation that might have been relevant to Lenton Hall but not to Highfield House. William Wilkins the elder was from about 1780 agent to the first Viscount Newark of Thoresby Hall, later Earl Manvers [Brand 1988]. Archdeacon Wilkins, D.D., had the living of St. Mary's Nottingham, which he vacated in the 1840s [White 1865].
3. In Braunsdorff [1896 7] the Lowe pedigrees have been traced back to brothers William del Lowe and Thomas del Lowe, who died, respectively, between 1392 and 1398 and in 1415.
4. N.U.M.D., Accession 795/2 (1881)
5. Inclosure of Beeston parish, 1809. A copy of the map and a typed schedule of allotments are held in Notts. Archives Office.
6. L.A.O., 2PG 3/1/10, a terrier of 1725, shows John Chamberlane renting Keeton Meadow, 8a.3.31, for £13: and in 1768 [L.A.O. 2PG 3/1/10] Mr. Chamberlain held Keetons Meadow, 9a.0.16 for £10.10s.0d. a year. When Keighton Closes were sold in 1920 [L.A.O., 4PG 108] Keighton Meadow was not included, presumably because it was already part of the Highfield estate.
7. N.A.O., RD 3 L, 'A mappe of ye Lordshippe of Lenton and Radford ...' (1632).
8. Lawson Lowe [1876] gave a selective list (p.25), and the Lowe paintings were described by Joseph Roberts in *Allen's Illustrated Handbook and Guide to ... Nottingham and its environs* (1866), but the most complete description is that by Fyfe [1856 173 et seq.].
9. See *Nottingham and its Region* ed. K.C.Edwards, 1966, Ch.III (F.A.Barnes) pp. 60-102 and Appendix I, pp. 521-527.
10. Beeston and District Local History Society, Newsletter, 14 November 1974, contains a useful account of the observatory at Beeston Rylands, but is inaccurate in stating that it was built by Joseph Lowe, who died in1810.
11. *The Stranger's Guide* (1849). See also R.Iliffe and W.Baguley, *Victorian Nottingham* 14 (1975) 14.
12. Dr. Becket's account comes mainly from Arthur Johnson, *The Nottingham Sacred Harmonic Society, a Retrospect* (1905) 13, and J.A.H.Green et al. [1887 11].
13. 'Nottingham Journal', 23 August 1867
14. The Lowes and the Swanns were near neighbours on Long Row, Nottingham, and close associates in municipal office. It was Alderman Swann who bought the meagre ruins of Lenton Priory in order to preserve them, and his son who willed them to Lawson Lowe.
15. Census of 1841, Enumerators Books, H.O. 107/858
16. The children of Alfred Hurst Lowe were:
   Eleanor Mary Charlotte, b. 5 November 1844 at Pisa, Italy: died an infant 4 December 1844.
   Alfred Joseph, b. 15 May 1847 at Boulogne: married 13 August 1881 at Covent Garden to Maria, younger daughter of W.H.Oakes of Wimbledon.
   Edward Robert, A.J.'s twin, for a time held a mercantile appointment on the west coast of Africa. He died of fever on board the SS. Biafra a few hours after embarking for England on 7 April 1869 and was buried at Lagos.
   Louisa Agnes, b. 12 November 1849 at Worthing, married 9 December 1879 at Streatham to Charles Havey Malim of London. They had two sons and three daughters.

Arthur William, b. 16 February 1852 at Braders, Sussex. He eventually settled in Australia and married Ellen Smith of Brisbane on 9 November 1879.

Augusta Eleanor, b. 10 October 1854 at Ockbrook, Derbyshire: died unmarried 5 October 1886 at Balham, Surrey, and buried at Norwood.

Sydney Armerin, b. 10 February 1860 at Newark-upon-Trent. Admitted solicitor in 1884 and married in the same year.

17. Census of 1851, Enumerators' Books. For Lenton 2129 pp 4-143, 178-181 and 2130 pp. 4-35.

18 Census of 1861, Enumerators' Books. For Lenton RG 9/2947

19. Reference to Alfred Lowe at Highfield House with Charlotte in 1864 [White 1864] must relate to her eldest son, Alfred Hurst Lowe, who was still an officer in the local militia - unless it was an error for Arthur, who did not marry until a few weeks before his mother's death in 1865. In Wright's 1862 Directory Highfield House was recorded in the names of Mrs. Lowe and E.J.Lowe, but on 14 April 1864 Edward Lowe, giving evidence to the House of Commons Select Committee on Private Bills, which was considering the Nottingham Gas Bill, in answer to the question 'Do you live at Highbridge (sic) House near Nottingham ?' replied 'At Beeston Observatory I live'.

20. Census of 1871, Enumerators' Books. For Lenton 3499 and 3500 (4-32 and 52-63).

21. Census of 1881, Enumerators' Books. For Lenton 3340 and 3341.

22. Rev. T.J.Oldrini, Vicar of Beeston from 1854 to 1885, when he died, was the author of 'Gleanings about Beeston' (1873), No. 8 (Vol. 2) of Nottinghamshire Historical Tracts. A photograph of him appears in Robert Mellor's *Nottinghamshire Villages - Beeston* (1916) 45.

23. *The genealogical and topographical history of the Hundred of Broxtowe* (Richard Allen, Nottingham) is not what its title promises. Lowe planned a history of Broxtowe to be published in about 15 monthly parts, each of about 40 pages, as the first section of a proposed history of Nottinghamshire. In the event only this first part of 40 pages relating to Lenton was published. The foreword is dated as early as 25 January 1871. In his will Lawson Lowe left the manuscript to his friend Thomas Charlton, son of T.B.Charlton of Chilwell Hall, but no further publication is known to the writer.

24. N.U.M.D., Accession 795/2. Sale brochure of the Highfield estate, 1881. For the conveyance of 1883 see N.U.M.D., (part of) Accession 23, Box 4.

25. N.U.M.D., Accession 650. Sale brochure, Highfield estate, 1893.

26. This road built 30 years later was called University Boulevard. The 'existing road' mentioned here is Derby Road into Nottingham.

27. Point A was near the present University Boulevard - Queens Road traffic island, and Queens Road is the realization of the road suggested, though not perhaps exactly on the line envisaged in 1893.

28. *Records of the Borough of Nottingham* p. 409, 10 September 1900. Presumably the Highfield estate was already on the market again in the summer of 1900, after the death of Edward Lowe.

29. N.U.M.D., Accession 23 (1901)

30. L.A.O., Pearson-Gregory of Harlaxton Papers, 4PG 108, 31 March 1920.

31. The mining lease, to mine the Deep Hard Coal, was granted to the Clifton Colliery Company only two days before the conveyance to Sir Jesse Boot. It was surrendered to Sir Jesse on 9 August 1922. The easement was in respect of the Corporation of Nottingham's gas mains which crossed the western end of the estate.

32 N.U.M.D., Accession 650. Highfield estate sale brochure 1893.

33. O.S. 1:500 plan ('Ten-foot series') 1881, revised manually in 1925-26. Sheet XLII 5/21. N.A.O..

34. N.U.M.D., Accession 423.

35. George Sanderson, 'Thirty miles around Mansfield': map at 2¼ inches to 1 mile (1835). Surveyed 1830-34.

36. Census of 1861, Enumerators' Books: Beeston parish 2440 fol. 51.

37. N.U.M.D., U.R. I, 73 : File of correspondence from the Town Clerk's office relating to Broadgate House. In this file see Abstract of Title of Mr. and Mrs. Linday (1932) reciting deeds of various dates.

38. ibid.

39. Mellors [1916]. A small photograph of Stephen Armitage appears on page 50. The firm of Armitage Brothers dated from 1775 when a prominent Quaker, William Fox, opened a business as corn merchant, wholesale and retail grocer and seed merchant in High Street and Victoria Street, Nottingham. His son, Samuel Fox, a Quaker philanthropist, who, like all members of his firm, wore traditional Quaker dress, brought an Armitage into the business by marrying Miriam, daughter of John Armitage, who farmed land round Trent Bridge. The Armitages were active in Nottingham municipal affairs for many years, and one sat on the first Town Council to be elected after the Municipal Reform Act of 1835. Their High Street shop was demolished for road widening in 1901. See A. Gilbert, *Recollections of Old Nottingham* (1904) and *Victorian Nottingham* 9 (1972). J.J.Armitage lived at The Grange, Beeston [Allen 1907].

40. 'Notts Register of motor cars and motor cycles, 1903'. *Thoroton Society Record Series* xxi (1962) 65-79.

41. N.U.M.D., U.R. I 73

42. ibid.

43. ibid.

CHAPTER VII

LENTON HALL AND ITS ESTATE

Introduction

One of the original purchasers of Milward estate land from Messrs. Pares and Paget in 1798 was John Wright, who acquired a large tract of the northern side of the estate together with most of it on the Trent valley floor. Indeed, as reckoned by the Land Tax assessments for 1799 he bought rather more than half of the whole Milward estate. Buying and selling land was an important part of John Wright's business activity, and he subsequently 'enlarged the estate by various purchases of land both in this and the adjoining parish of Beeston'. Some of these transactions have been mentioned earlier (Chapter V) and others are noted below.

On his land within the present University campus Wright built the mansion called Lenton Hall, said by some to have been called at first Lenton House, and although no positive evidence for this has been found other than a badly placed name on the First Edition O.S. one-inch map it is true that the present Lenton House was known by several different names before the 1830s, none of them Lenton House. Lenton Hall now forms the western end and original nucleus of Hugh Stewart Hall, containing the Warden's quarters, the Senior Common Room and other accommodation. William Stretton of Nottingham and Lenton was commissioned to design and build the Hall, which seems to have been completed and occupied only in 1804 [1]. The area of its grounds and park in the mid-19th century, some 130 acres, was very similar to that occupied by the farmer Thomas Stevenson in 1798, but Lenton Hall park included land in the west earlier associated with the Beeston Lane farm and the Odd House (Lenton Abbey) farm, and excluded not only the land east of the Keighton Closes and south of Cut Through Lane, but also an area in the north-east that was sold off at an early stage to Thomas Wright Watson, a Nottingham hosier, who built the house called Lenton Firs upon it (Chapter IX). Part of Watson's land was later incorporated into Wollaton Park, as described in (Chapter XIII).

Antecedents of the Wright family at Nottingham

John Wright, alias Camplyon, of Stowmarket, Suffolk, who died in 1559, left landed property to be divided between four sons. Then three further John Wrights - son, grandson and great-grandson - each 'alias Camplyon', yeomen of Stowupland, Stowmarket, and buried respectively in 1592, 1641 and 1658, were followed by yet another John Wright (1614-1683) (Figure 46) the first member of the Wright family known in the Nottingham area, where the beginnings were unhappy. Inheriting money, probably from his grandfather in 1641, but no land, this Captain John Wright purchased land at Skegby. He was a Parliamentary officer in Colonel Whalley's Regiment of Horse, and later in Colonel Hutchinson's Regiment of Foot, of which he raised his own company at Nottingham in 1643. In July 1661 he was arraigned before the King's Bench but discharged for lack of evidence against him [Bailey 1853 907]. In 1663 he was arrested again, and imprisoned for eight years at Newark Castle without charge (other than his attachment to the Commonwealth) by a county Deputy Lieutenant under Charles II. He was 'a fierce and unrepentant Puritan', and on his release he settled at Nottingham, 'a congenial centre for Puritans' and probably took up residence in part of the old Thurland Hall [Bailey 1853, 1257]. He married a Miss Mosely in about 1659 and had four children, of whom the only one to leave issue was the eldest son, Thomas Wright (1660-1730). Thomas married Hannah Rotherham of Dronfield, and left seven children. He was the great grandfather of the John Wright who built Lenton Hall, and was the first Wright to appear on the roll of 'freemen' or burgesses of Nottingham, enrolled in 1687 as 'Thomas Wright, ironmonger'. His eldest son 'Samuel Wright, ironmonger' was admitted to the burgess roll in 1717, and died unmarried in 1753; but the youngest son, Ichabod (a 17th century Puritan name) born in 1700 and also an ironmonger, who was made burgess on his coming of age in 1721. He had married in 1720 Elizabeth,only daughter of John Wildbore of Nottingham. The later Wrights discussed below were all descendants of this first Ichabod.

Wrights' Bank

Ichabod Wright (1700-1777) established a banking business in about 1760 [2] with his two eldest sons, John (1723-1789) and Thomas (1724-1790), who survived him by little more than a decade. In 1760 Ichabod was described as an ironmonger of Long Row, and 'a gentleman and Christian extensively engaged in the Baltick Trade in Timber, Iron and Hemp ....and Lead' [Bailey 1853 iii 1256: Hunter 1961 35], at first with his brother Samuel and then with his eldest sons John and Thomas. In conditions of scarcity in 1756 he claimed to have brought up the river [Trent] 1,500 quarters of grain in the first half of the year, with nearly 700 sacks of flour, mostly delivered direct to the bakers. On the evidence of a threatening letter demanding a reduction in the price of corn, to which Ichabod responded in Cresswell's Nottingham Journal of 14-21 August 1756, it seems that Ichabod Wright and son then

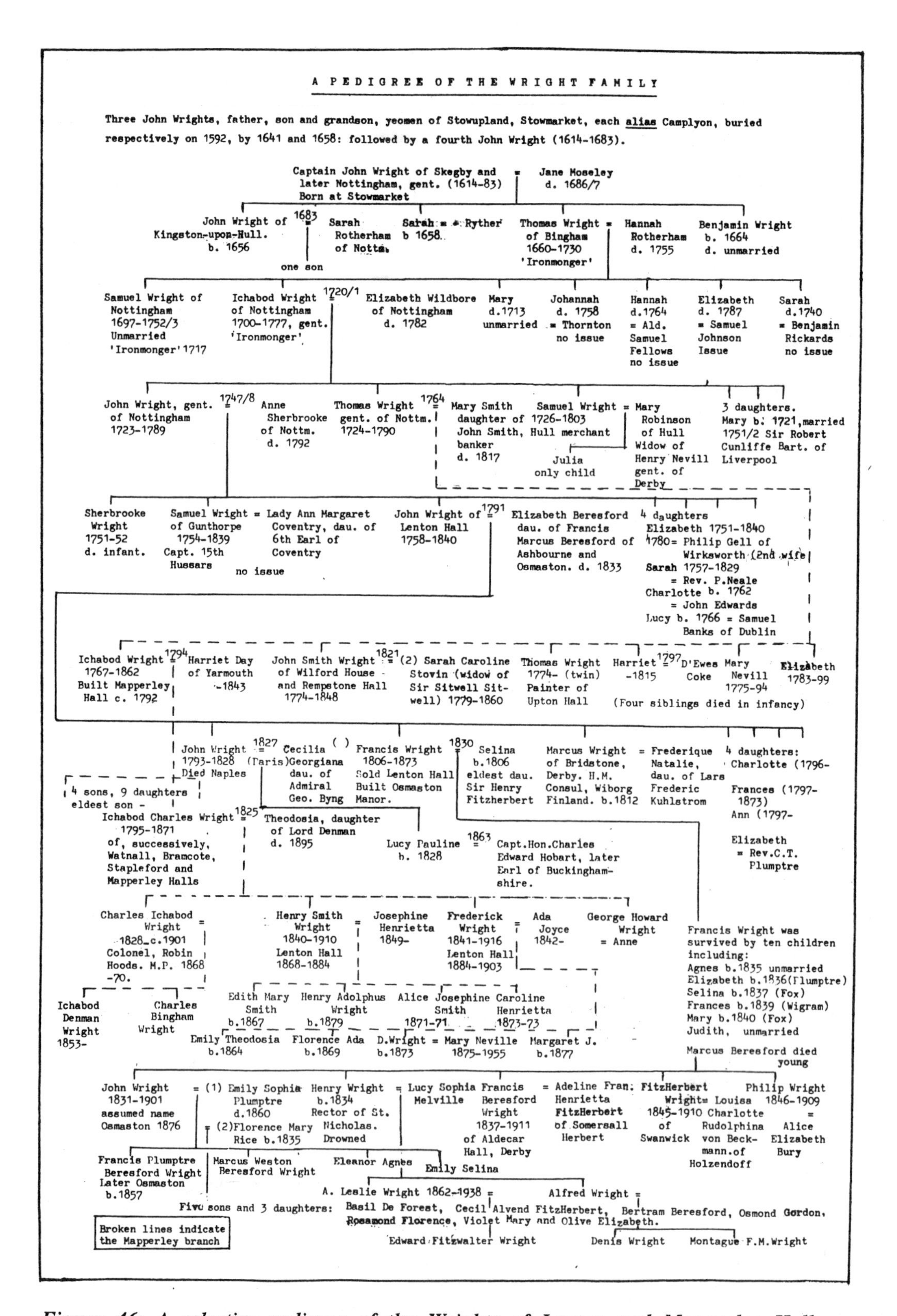

Figure 46: A selective pedigree of the Wrights of Lenton and Mapperley Halls

commanded the trade in corn and flour up the river Trent to Nottingham. Ichabod's third son, Samuel Wright (1726-1803) entered the burgess roll in 1750 described as 'merchant', and his connections with Hull point to his involvement in this continental trade. Ichabod's three daughters were Mary, who married Sir Robert Cunliffe in 1752, Elizabeth and Hannah (d.1823). His two eldest sons, John and Thomas, who helped to run the bank, were the founders of the two main branches of the Wright family which were directly involved in the history of Lenton Hall - the Lenton and Mapperley branches respectively. After Ichabod's death in 1777 the bank was run by John and Thomas, and then, from 1790, by their respective sons John (b. 1758) and Ichabod (b. 1762) who thereby became free to marry, had the resources to pursue more wide-ranging careers in commerce and industry on their own accounts, and build their mansions which eventually became the two chief men's Halls of residence of University College Lenton Hall in about 1800-04 and Mapperley Hall in about 1794 John Wright took full advantage of the opportunity: Ichabod did not. The eventual outcome was that John abandoned banking in 1830, leaving the bank entirely in the hands of members of the Mapperley Wrights.

Wrights' bank, like Smiths', played an important part in the 19th century development of the city and region of Nottingham - as well as in the enrichment of the Wright family. In its earlier years the bank business was subsidiary to the ironmonger's and showed some lack of enterprise. It was too cautious, for example, to finance Richard Arkwright's exploitation of his improvement of Hargreave's spinning jenny which made Jedediah Strutt's fortune. 'When Messrs. Wright, bankers of this town, withdrew their advances from Arkwright they recommended him to apply to Mr. Strutt' [Sutton 1852 35, 79], and the partnership between Arkwright the engineer, Strutt the industrialist and Need the financier flourished greatly until about 1783. But the success of the bank eventually 'placed the families of Wright of Mapperley and Lenton among the first class of untitled magnates of the land' [Bailey 1853].

The bank remained for 40 years in the premises on Long Row, the back part of which ran through to Parliament Street and contained warehouses used in the iron business, which continued actively until the bank moved to new premises at the top of Swine Green (called Pelham Street after about 1810). The Long Row premises were taken over by Alderman Swann, and occupied in the mid-19th century by Tompson and Son, drapers and mercers. Stretton recorded [3] that 'the house and premises now [1814] occupied by Ed. Swann Esq., and previously by John Wright Esq., who was then [before 1795] an Iron-Monger and a Banker (the Bank being on the same premises) and was in the latter end of the 17th century an Inn, the Sign of the Antelope'. Edward Swann was a grocer, Mayor of Nottingham in 1805 and 1812, uncle of Henry Kirke White the poet, and father of Charlotte Octavia, the formidable wife of Alfred Lowe of Highfield House. The site of the bank on Pelham Street was part of that occupied by the ancient mansion of the Gregory family in 1796 (see Chapter IV). Altered internally in 1881-93 the bank took its modern form in 1898, when conveyed to Capital and Counties Bank (earlier known as Nottingham Bank) which was absorbed into Lloyds Bank in 1918. The 1898 takeover was a very important event for the Mapperley Wrights - and for the history of the campus, as will be shown later in this chapter.

John Wright (1723-1789) married Anne, daughter of John Sherbrooke, a Nottingham merchant and manufacturer, and was the father of three sons and four daughters The eldest son, John Sherbrooke Wright, born in 1751, died in the following year. The two surviving sons were Samuel (1754-1839) and John (1758-1840). Samuel pursued a military career in the 15th Hussars. He was 'of Gunthorpe' and married Lady Ann Margaret Coventry, daughter of the 6th Earl of Coventry; and he leaves this story. Samuel probably had no need of a banking career, for by then the Wrights were very wealthy. Samuel's brother John was the banker and industrialist who built Lenton Hall.

Thomas Wright and the Mapperley branch

Thomas Wright, the first Ichabod's second son, in 1766 married Mary, the second daughter of John Smith, of the other great Nottingham banking family, which is discussed at greater length in Chapter XV. The connection between the two families is indicated in Figure 47. Eventually Wrights' Bank became part of Lloyds and Smiths' of the National Provincial, since 1962 the National Westminster. Thomas and Mary Wright had three sons and three daughters in addition to those who died as infants. The eldest son was Ichabod Wright (1767-1862) who built Mapperley Hall, married Hariett Maria Day of Norwich in 1794, and by her had three sons and ten daughters. In August 1790 Thomas bought Mrs. Newdigate's house, then occupied by a Captain Plumb, in Castle-gate and Hounds-gate (now called Newdigate House) with the paddock between Hounds-gate and Friar Lane, and is said to have rebuilt part of it [Robertson (Stretton) 1910]. This was the house, originally built in the mid-17th century, in which Marshal Tallard lived after his defeat by Marlborough at Blenheim in 1704, and where he is said to have introduced celery cultivation [Hammond 1926 32]. It was sold in 1817 after Mary's death. Thomas, however died in 1790. He had received the Mapperley estate in 1777 by deed of apportionment, and his son Ichabod inherited it from him, and built Mapperley Hall probably about the time of his marriage in 1794.

This second Ichabod Wright (see Appendix 22), who lived to the age of 96, was an active man of strong personality and powers of leadership, who was widely respected - even venerated in his later years. He joined the bank in 1782 and became a partner in 1794. Around his new Hall he enclosed Mapperley Park and planted many trees there. He and his family promoted, and were large donors to Carrington church and National Schools, and his 13 children all cooperated in furnishing the church. Ironically the church's first funeral was that of Ichabod's wife, Harriet. A keeper of horses - he owned at least one racehorse in 1795 [Sutton 1852, 221] - Ichabod became Captain Commandant of the Nottingham Town troop of Volunteer Yeomanry Cavalry that was enrolled in 1794 when public safety seemed to be in

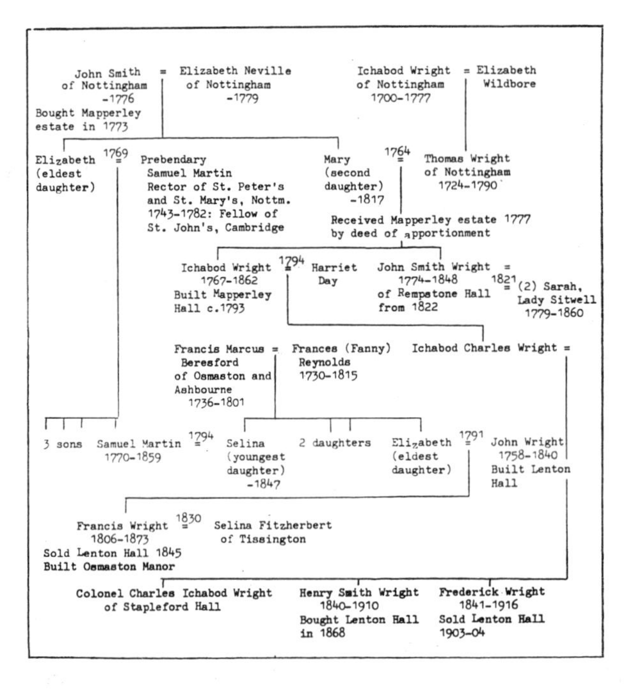

Figure 47: Interconnections between the Nottingham banking families of Wright and Smith

question. The 67 men of the Town Troop, after a 'grand field day' on 3 October 1794, were given 'a sumptuous evening entertainment at Thurland Hall by Ichabod Wright'! [Sutton 1852, 215]. In June 1808 Ichabod succeeded Colonel Elliott in command of the Nottingham Volunteers.

Mapperley Hall will be mentioned again several times, and eventually in connection with its establishment as the chief Hall of Residence for men of the University College in 1906, with Professor Henderson as Warden. Lenton Hall, built by Ichabod's first cousin, John, joined it as the second Hall of Residence in 1930. Ichabod Wright's eldest son, Ichabod Charles Wright (1795-1871) of Watnall Hall, who married a daughter of the first Lord Denman, was the father of Henry Smith Wright, M.P., who brought back Lenton Hall estate into the Wright family by purchasing it from Lord Middleton in 1868, and of Frederick Wright who followed his brother there. They are discussed further below. Ichabod Charles Wright was one of the brightest, and in later life one of the most eccentric members of the family. An outline of his career, and in particular an account of his scholarly publications, is given in Appendix 22.

The second son of Thomas and Mary Wright, and brother of the second Ichabod, was John Smith Wright (1774-1848) of Rempstone Hall, and earlier of Wilford House, the chief benefactor and the first President of the Nottingham Mechanics Institution. He was a senior partner in the bank. He married as his second wife in 1821 Sarah Caroline, widow of Sir Sitwell Sitwell. She founded the Midland Orphanage at Lenton, and died in 1860 aged 81, to be buried at Rempstone. Eventually it was Thomas Wright's descendants, including John Smith Wright, who remained in banking until the end of the 19th century, while John Wright's family's interests became concentrated on industry, especially in Derbyshire. It was these Lenton Wrights who formed 'a classic example of a family rising through several generations from minor gentry to great wealth from commerce, and then investment in land and industry' and by 1790 they were among the wealthiest families in Nottingham. By John Wright's generation they were one of the dozen families that dominated the Industrial Revolution in the East Midlands north of the Trent [Riden 1973 17], most of which remained prominent well into the present century.

John Wright (1758-1840) who built Lenton Hall

John Wright (Figure 48), son of John Wright, was 30 years old at his father's death in December 1789. and was closely involved, in partnership with his cousin Ichabod, in the operation of the bank, which was prospering. He also inherited land near Nottingham, and the family's Derbyshire estates at Ripley, Hartshay and Riddings, all close to the site of the later Butterley ironworks. He was then able to widen his business interests to include dealing in land and mineral exploitation, including iron manufacturing - perhaps a natural progression from the Long Row ironmongery with which he was still involved - and investing in canal shares and turnpike trusts. His major industrial interest came to be the Butterley company , but as a good banker he was always on the lookout for potentially profitable investments, on both his own account and the bank's.

John Wright and the Butterley Company

John Wright was one of the four partners of Outram and Company, the enterprise formed to establish an ironworks and exploit the coal reserves of the Butterley Hall estate in the early 1790s. The story of Butterley and John Wright's connection with it really begins with that of the Cromford canal, which extended the Erewash canal northwards to provide an outlet to the Trent for the coal owners of the upper Erewash valley. The first leading supporter of the northwards extension of the Erewash Canal (in May 1787) was Rev. D'Ewes Coke of Brookhill Hall, Pinxton, a landowner whose son married John Wright's neice Harriet in 1797, and a party of proprietors met in July 1787 to discuss it. In December 1788, after opposition from the Erewash Canal's committee had been ameliorated by a meeting at Matlock chaired

Figure 48: John Wright (1758-1840)

by Sir Richard Arkwright on 30 August 1788, Francis Beresford of Ashbourne was appointed solicitor to the group. In the party was Joseph Outram, a substantial Alfreton land agent, whose son Benjamin, probably the author of an earlier survey of the line of the proposed canal, acted as secretary. The meeting accepted William Jessop's report of a second survey, by E.G.Fletcher, and decided to promote a Bill. Pushed by 23-year-old Benjamin Outram the Cromford Canal was authorised in July 1789, and the proprietors' committee, including Beresford, on 4 November 1789 appointed William Jessop as principal engineer for the project, with the young Benjamin Outram, trained as a surveyor, as full-time 'superintendent of the making of the canal', under the eye of the busy Jessop. Thus three of the Butterley partners, Beresford, Outram and Jessop were brought together by 1789. It was Jessop who pointed out in his report that the Cromford Canal was to pass through a site with great iron-making potential - Butterley. Beresford, Outram and Jessop all took shares in the Cromford Canal company in 1789. They were joined three years later by John and Ichabod Wright, with 17 shares between them, and John Wright's involvement culminated in his becoming chairman in 1809.

The canal had a revolutionary effect on the upper Erewash valley, and in particular 'its promotion was the occasion of the establishment of a company that was to lead and to a large extent dominate the revolution' - Outram and Co., founded by 26-year old Benjamin Outram in 1790, funded by Francis Beresford as his original informal partner and joined in 1791 by John Wright and William Jessop. 'In accordance with the spirit of the age' [Mottram and Coote 1950] it intended to establish an ironworks and exploit the coal workings on the Butterley Hall estate, which had been bought by Beresford in that year from the Home family. The partnership deed executed on 10 December 1792 bound the four partners for 60 years in equal shares of £6,000. They described themselves as 'Traders together in getting and smelting Ironstone, casting and manufacturing Iron, getting and burning Limestone and getting Coal and Slack'. The company was renamed The Butterley Company in 1807 after Outram's death. Outram and Co. began trading by opening pits on the Butterley Hall estate and selling coal. In October 1793 the full opening of the Cromford Canal made expansion possible: but already, in 1791 and 1792 Beresford had bought land for a limestone quarry at Crich, and land for a wharf on the canal a mile from Crich, where limekilns were in commission by April 1793.

The four requisites for the development of Butterley brought together in 1791 were entrepreneurial ability and drive in the person of the remarkable Benjamin Outram; capital, provided by Beresford, a wealthy country attorney of Ashbourne, who made the initial purchase of the Butterley Hall estate of 200 acres in June 1790, and by the banker John Wright; improved communications, in the field of which Jessop and Outram were outstanding, and to a degree complementary; and technical improvements to the blast furnace and the steam engine. Outram, the initiator and man of ideas, was fully aware of the crucial importance of transport, especially to heavy industry. William Jessop, an able engineer and surveyor, was a man of great energy and practical versatility, with special expertise in canal construction and operation, already with a national reputation. Francis Beresford, prominent in connection with the Cromford canal, contributed mainly money and a beautiful daughter who married John Wright in 1791, an event which cannot have been unconnected with John's joining Outram and Co. only weeks after his marriage. Wright himself brought assured financial backing for the enterprise in the form of both liquid capital and overdraft facilities, and a traditional family knowledge of the iron industry, as well as conveniently situated land and minerals with which he was prepared to part on generous terms, doubtless with his own long-term interests in mind. Together the four founders who entered into a legal partnership in 1792, constituted 'a formidable combination of visionary and practical talent'. Further details of Outram, Beresford and Jessop are given in Appendix 23.

The early success was due to the skill and ability of Outram as manager, and to ready access to substantial funds - 'a powerful combination of entrepreneurial ability in need of finance and landed and commercial wealth looking for new forms of investment'. The first 15 years at Butterley were dominated by Outram; the next 10 by his memory [Riden 1973]: but after his death on a visit to London in May 1805 John Wright progressively increased his financial hold on the company which he had financed in its first 15 years - a vital factor in its success. Outram was the only active partner at Butterley itself, for Beresford, tied to his legal practice, played no direct part in running the business, Wright was busy at his bank and took little active part at first, while Jessop's role was mainly advisory. However, Wright's wealth put him in a dominant position financially, for Outram at his death had paid for less than half his quarter share, while Jessop paid in instalments financed by Wright.

John Wright, the 'solid capitalist' of the concern, bought out the Beresford share in 1806 for £ 10,000 from his brother-in-law John Beresford who had inherited it on his father's death in 1801. Outram's share, inherited by his widow in 1805 but only partially paid for, was the subject of Chancery litigation which led to the dissolution of the partnership in 1813-14, with Margaret Outram assigning two parts of her share to John Wright, and one part to William Jessop. Jessop died in November 1814, leaving his share of the company to his son William, who managed Butterley with Joseph Outram after Benjamin Outram's death in 1805, and was one of the most respected ironmasters in the country until his death in 1852. The elder William's second son, Josias (1781-1826) was involved with the company's Indian venture and was engineer to the first two railway companies in the East Midlands - the Mansfield and Pinxton (1817) and Cromford and High Peak (1825). William Jessop's eldest son, Major John Jessop, was a professional soldier who was badly wounded at Waterloo, and retired thereafter to Butterley Hall. He renounced his succession in the partnership in 1839. Thus Francis Wright, who succeeded to John Wright's estate in the following year, was very much the senior partner in the company, especially since John owned the Butterley Park estate on his own account, and had also purchased the Butterley Hall estate, earlier a partnership asset. The Butterley Company, however, remained a partnership between successive members of the same families until 1888 when it became a private limited company, dominated by Francis Wright's sons.

In 1815 the Butterley company was already making cannon, steam engines and ironwork (for example, the Vauxhall Bridge in 1814). From 1815 to 1830 the new partnership of John Wright and the second William Jessop was busy extending its properties at home and its markets abroad, for example in Calcutta (1825) and Spain. In the 1820s Butterley was a show works - the largest coal and iron company in the East Midlands and the largest single coal owner. It was upon these foundations that John Wright's son Francis, from 1830 to 1873 built up further the great integrated Butterley coal and iron industry of the Erewash valley, where the Butterley Works alone already employed 2,000 people in 1844, and by 1862 the company produced one fifth of Derbyshire iron and 7-800,000 tons of coal a year. Francis Wright remained the driving and directing force of the concern for 43 years, while his father, John, the backbone of the company for forty years, never played a part in its management.

The later Butterley shed iron smelting early in the 20th century and evolved into a large engineering concern, though retaining coal mining interests until nationalization in 1947. In 1968 the company was bought by the Hanson Trust, which developed the brick making and building materials side and sold on the engineering works, which have since changed hands several times, but are still in business.

John Wright's wife and family

John Wright's deep and increasing involvement at Butterley was almost certainly precipitated by his marriage. On 2 April 1791, little more than a year after his father's death in December 1789, John, then aged 33, married Elizabeth Beresford (1759-1833), the eldest daughter of Francis Beresford of Ashbourne by Fanny, only daughter and heiress of Benjamin Reynolds. Hoppner's portrait of Elizabeth is in the National Gallery. Two months after his marriage John Wright became a business partner of his father-in-law [Bailey 1853 1257]. This connection with one of the oldest families in the county firmly established John Wright in Derbyshire society, and laid the foundations for the growth of his family's Derbyshire property, which by his death had become very extensive. After their marriage John and Elizabeth lived in Willoughby House at the top of Low Pavement in Nottingham (not at his Long Row business premises), 'late the residence of Rothwell Willoughby Esq., sold to Mr. Ichabod Wright, merchant' (John's grandfather) in 1765 according to Thomas Bailey [1853 1277]. The house was 'later used as an academy by Messrs. Biddulph and Son' [4]. It was built about 1738 and survives.

John and Elizabeth Wright moved to their new house, Lenton Hall in about 1804. They had three sons and four daughters. Their eldest son, John, born in 1793 at Willoughby House, died in Naples in 1828. In 1827 he had married in Paris Cecilia Georgiana, daughter of Admiral the Hon. George Byng, and they had a daughter, Lucy Pauline, who eventually married the Earl of Buckinghamshire (Capt. the Hon. Charles Edward Isobart). After John came Charlotte (b.1796), Frances (b. 1797) and Ann (b. 1799), who remained unmarried and are mentioned again in connection with Lenton Firs. Francis (1806-1873) and Marcus (b. 1812) were born at Lenton Hall. Francis inherited John Wright's estates on his death, aged 81, on 21 April 1840. Marcus, described as of Budsgrove, Derby, became H.M. Consul at Wiborg, Finland, having married Friderique Natalie, daughter of Count Lars Frederic Kuhlstron, Councillor and Master of the Rolls for Finland.

John Wright as a dealer in land and landed estates

Besides his partnership with his cousin Ichabod at the bank, John Wright was 'largely engaged on his own account in carrying on the extensive ironworks at Butterley and in the purchase and sale of estates'. In this last role he not only bought property in Derbyshire , but also more than half the Milward estate in Lenton in 1798 and 1799, and soon afterwards other land in Lenton, including that upon which much of New Lenton was soon to be built, to his great profit. In 1818 he bought Langar Hall and Langar-cum-Barnstone parish from the Howe family [Bailey 1853 iv 299], and in particular from Sophia Charlotte (1762-1835) the eldest daughter of Admiral Lord Howe (1726-1799), who had married Penn Assheton Curzon, first Viscount Curzon of Penn. John Wright broke up the estate and dismantled the old Hall, which was vulnerable to fire (since many beams went through the chimneys) and built a smaller house on the same site, the present Langar Hall [Huskinson 1952 54-59]. Langar Hall will be mentioned again in Chapter X (Lenton Abbey) since Mrs. Annie Bayley bought it in 1899 and bequeathed it to her son Harold in 1904. As a banker John Wright had an eye for potentially profitable investments other than land, and in particular turnpike trusts, canal companies, and later railways, which paid regular dividends on investments. Indeed these, with the bank, supplied his income, for the Butterley enterprise paid no dividends until 1830 when he retired, profits being retained in the company, which in part explains its rapid expansion and success. John Wright remained a Nottingham and Lenton man, but his son Francis whose role at Butterley was much closer, and who was not connected with the bank at Nottingham, became a Derbyshire man.

The Land Tax assessments of the early 19th century reveal John Wright himself as occupier of part of the farmland he had purchased in Lenton in 1798-99, which he probably farmed through a bailiff. Nothing is known of his actual farming enterprises, but he appears to have been well enough known as a progressive agriculturalist to receive the dedication of a book on the new 'Scientific Agriculture' by W. Grisenthwaite, proprietor of a 'gents' boarding school at King's Place, Nottingham [Pigot 1831]. The book was first written as an outcome of attendance at one of Coke's agricultural meetings at Holkham, though it is not known whether John Wright was himself present. In the dedication of a second, enlarged version of the book in 1830 the author referred to John Wright's 'lack of ambition for public distinction', his zeal for the promotion of agriculture, and for legislative protection to encourage investment of capital in it, and his energy and skill in management, referring also to his long life of practical observation , and his retirement to 'the bosom of your truly Christian family' in the tranquility of 'the country'.

John Wright as a public figure

John Wright was early a well-known public figure in the town. He was High Sheriff of Nottinghamshire in 1796, when he was invited by a body of electors to stand for Parliament as a candidate in the Whig interest. He declined, but 'so far lent his countenance to the part as to nominate Dr. Crompton'. The John Wright who in 1788 occupied the chair when the Revolution of 1688 was celebrated in Nottingham 'with great eclat' by a public dinner in the Great Room, Thurland Hall, 'to which about 50 gentlemen from among those of the highest respectability in the town sat down' [Bailey 1853 128] may have been his father, who died in the following year. Thomas Bailey [1853 1258] suggested that it was a remarkable fact about the Wrights of both Lenton and Mapperley that although 'four or five generations appear in regular order of succession from father to son upon the burgess roll, not one of them has ever filled an office in the municipal body of the borough'. He thought that this was in part because throughout their first century at Nottingham, while heads of family were open to the temptation of coveting civic honours, the largely self-perpetuating governing body 'consisted mostly of Presbyterians, whilst the Wrights, down to the generation of which the venerable Mr. Wright of Mapperley House is the living representative, were steady and zealous Independents, a sect generally held in greater dislike by their non-conforming brethren of the former denomination than were even the Episcopalians themselves ... . Since that period the social position of the Wrights has been such as to have raised them above the acceptance of borough corporate offices had they even been tendered to them'. Mottram and Coote [1950] even suggested that it appeared as if Cromwellian disputes had survived as well as Cromwellian blood; but S.D.Chapman [1967 63] points out that Ichabod Wright, like Samuel Need, was a member of Castlegate Congregational church, and 'excluded by resolution of their own society from membership of the Corporation'.

Lack of municipal office did not prevent John Wright from engaging in social action. For example, on 4 March 1816 'a meeting of gentlemen was held at Thurland Hall, John Wright Esq., Lenton, in the chair, when it was resolved to commence the Nottingham Subscription Library'. This led to the purchase for £ 2,750 on 12 April 1820 of Bromley House, Market Place, Nottingham for the use of the Nottingham Subscription Library [Bailey 1853 IV 278 and 313]. John Wright also held parish office as churchwarden in 1809 and 1810, and the virtually compulsory office of Overseer of the Poor in 1808.

The character of John Wright

In character John Wright is an enigma, and he left little behind him by which his character can be truly judged. According to Riden [1973] the picture that emerges from a few surviving letters is of a prudent, conservative man, not a little bewildered in his later years by the enormous changes that had taken place during his lifetime. Yet some of his business activities appear as rashly speculative. For example, in the 1820s we find 'this normally shrewd and cautious man' the largest shareholder in the original difficult 31-mile Cromford and High Peak railway, finally authorized in May 1825 and opened in 1831 with the largest capital of any railway company. It incorporated nine inclined planes - mostly with Butterley beam engines. Indeed John Wright seems to have had a compulsive penchant for investment in communications. As late as 1829 he put £65 into a proposed but abortive Whaley Bridge to Manchester railway, and in 1832, two years after his retirement at the age of 72 he was attending Midland Counties Railway meetings and pledging substantial support (see Chapter XIII).

As early as the post-war depression early in the century John Wright was fearful of bankruptcy at both Butterley and the bank, and although recovery began in 1818 he seems to have remained pessimistic throughout his life. In the 1820s he took part in the controversy on banking reform and the Corn Laws. His pamphlets which, like his letters, were almost invariably pessimistic, included 'Remarks on the erroneous opinions which led to the new Corn Law: and also those of the Bullionists on the circulating medium, and pointing out the only protection to agriculture' (1823), and 'To the Right Hon. the Earl of Liverpool' (1826-27). Later he became obsessed with the prospect of bankruptcy, and it is doubtful whether he enjoyed his decade of retirement. Rarely did he strike a note of optimism, and the two preceding years had certainly been a time of stress. Only two months before his retirement he was writing to his agent Goodwin at Butterley about the 'awful and disturbing State of the Country': but he was then suffering from a failure of judgment on the Cromford and High Peak affair, and, worse, the death of his eldest son and heir John in January 1828 only 7 months after his marriage to Cecilia Georgiana Byng. In 1830, too, his cousin Ichabod found him selfish, and with an ungentlemanly, domineering manner in the disagreement that precipitated the withdrawal of John from the bank partnership.

Yet in 1830 this 'prudent, thoughtful man, with a trace of the ancestral puritanism still flowing in his blood' was an elder statesman figure in the economic life of the East Midlands, and his family's bank an important link in the regional economy, 'even though he does not at once attract attention in the way that Benjamin Outram or Sir Richard Arkwright does as one of the heroic figures of the local industrial revolution'.... 'Wherever one turns, whether to look at a list of shareholders in a canal or railway, or a list of turnpike trustees, or subscribers to a charity, or almost any kind of committee, the Wrights, and in particular John Wright, dominate the scene' [Riden 1973].

Lenton Hall: the house and grounds

During nearly 40 years residence John Wright's contribution to the character of the landscape of the present University campus was immense, involving no less than total transformation from farmland of the simplest kind to sophisticated residential parkland over a large part of its area. From soon after his death in 1840 until 1868, with the Lenton Hall estate owned by Lord Middleton and the Hall occupied by tenants, little change or development took place to alter the outcome of John Wright's creative work. The site of the Hall, on the ridgetop of the Leen-Tottle Brook interfluve, was chosen in part for the views it offered in most directions. Lawson Lowe [1871 24: 1876 136] described how the Hall occupied 'a considerable eminence....in a well wooded and beautifully undulated park some 120 acres in extent'. The undulations were mainly natural features, but the trees were planted mainly by John Wright. 'The mansion, from its commanding situation, overlooks Wollaton Park, and the woodland scenery of that beautiful demesne together with the great lake and the Hall form a landscape not easily surpassed. From another side Nottingham Castle and the town are seen to considerable advantage'.

'The gardens surrounding the mansion are extensive, and were very tastefully laid out and planted by the late John Wright' [Lowe 1871]. The plan of 1881 [5] (Figure 52) shows kitchen gardens to the north-east of the Hall, and ornamental grounds to the south-west, incorporating the ancient marl pit, trimmed and suitably planted, but leaving an open vista from the house across the Trent valley, now blocked by post-war shrubbery. The westward view across the 'downland' is also now obstructed by shrubbery and trees dating from early in the present century, when Lenton Hall Drive was extended past the Hall to give access to the new houses Lenton Mount and The Orchard. Parts of the ha ha wall round this part of the garden are still visible, including a section cut off in Lenton Mount (University Club) garden. The mature beech trees, and some sweet chestnuts along the inner side of the ha ha wall probably date back to John Wright's planting. Wright also planted copses in the park, and a cordon of trees alongside Derby Road as far west as Lenton Eaves, which was certainly begun before 1810 [6], the original 'natural' oak trees and hazel scrub (see Chapter XIII) being replaced by beech, chestnut and elm. A ring count on a beech tree near to Derby Hall uprooted by a gale gave a germination date of about 1800.

Lenton Hall itself received less general approbation than its grounds and park, perhaps partly because it was regarded as pretentious. Lowe [1871: 1876] described it as 'a large Pseudo-Gothic structure standing in a well timbered park', and 'a large square stone mansion in the Gothic style, ornamented with small embattled turrets'. A more recent description notes its 'simple Gothic design' with arched porch, turrets and battlements to a slated mansard roof, sash windows and central gabled feature to the garden [Notts.C.C, 1972]. Brand [1985] suggests that the building 'retains something of the style or taste of William Stretton' its architect, with its Gothic features and seven castellated bays, rather than attributing its characteristics to the taste of John Wright. Stretton was highly regarded as architect and builder in his time, and was responsible for many well-known Nottingham buildings (see Appendix 21).

The late Dr. William Neil [1980], former Warden of Hugh Stewart Hall, thought the style of the building 'an intriguing mixture of Georgian-Gothic. The basis is pure Georgian, as can be seen from the windows, the Senior Common Room and the Warden's drawing-room. On the other hand the battlements and turrets, which are original, suggest the Romantic Revival of the late eighteenth century, and possibly inspired the alterations of 1905′ (described below). 'The Warden's drawing-room is a perfect example of eighteenth century Georgian style, beautifully proportioned, with full-length windows and a deli-cately decorated ceiling. Unfortunately the original Adam fireplace was replaced at some date by Victorian marble, which, however, might well have been worse. The present Seminar Room, with its massive fireplace, and the adjoining kitchen combined to make the servants' hall. Domestic staff were lodged in what is now 'E' corridor, and the present Senior Common Room was the dining room of the mansion'. It is not known whether Dr. Neil was aware of the severe damage done to the interior of the house by a major fire in July 1845, described below.

Francis Wright at Lenton Hall (Figure 49)

In retrospect it is seen that the Butterley enterprise which John Wright came to dominate, and in which he invested heavily, was essentially, for him, a repository for capital and not a source of income. The rapid growth and consolidation of the company, especially through the post-war depression, owed much to the fact that no regular income was drawn from it by Wright, and regular dividends were first paid only from 1830, the year of his retirement. Francis Wright, aged 23, was given all his father's shares, worth about £110,000 and took over in June 1830. For him the priorities were different. Until his retirement John Wright remained active in the bank, but in that same year serious disagreement between John and Ichabod Wright led to the dissolution of the partnership at Wrights' Bank, so that the Butterley business took over from the bank as a chief source of income for the Lenton Wrights. It was probably this development rather than longstanding family connections that led inevitably to the sale of Lenton Hall in 1845 and the westward migration of the Lenton Wrights to Derbyshire.

In 1830 Butterley, skilfully managed by William Jessop junior, employed 1,500 and soon became the largest iron company in the East Midlands, and even larger than Barber-Walker

Figure 49: Francis Wright (1806-1873)

in the coal trade. With the advent of the young Francis Wright as a director the ruling minds at Butterley from 1830 onwards became even more adventurous and progressive. From their involvement in canal and road making (for example, the Derby to Alfreton turnpike in 1803) they turned to railways, the rapid growth of which presented pioneering opportunities for Butterley's heavy engineering - for example in bridge construction (Trent Junction 1839), viaducts (over the Derwent south of Derby), and later stations (St.Pancras 1869). Railway track increased from 2,000 to 5,000 miles in the six years 1843 to 1849. One of the first acts of Francis Wright as a Butterley partner was to subscribe in 1832 with his father £10,000 towards the cost of the Nottingham-Derby-Leicester railway connection (see Chapter XIII). As senior partner - effectively the proprietor - and director of the firm and titular head of the family, by the end of his reign of 43 years at Butterley he was 'the admired and unquestioned master of his own and of his vast industrial family'.

John Wright was buried in April 1840 in the family vault that he had erected in the south-west corner of the graveyard of the Priory church in 1823 [Lowe 1871 30] and where his wife Elizabeth was buried in 1833. Mural tablets on the north-east wall of Lenton parish church commemorate them, and their niece Annie, wife of Richard Perrin, who died at Lenton Hall in 1838. Orange's Nottingham Directory for 1840, presumably prepared in 1839, already named Francis Wright as the occupier of Lenton Hall. It is possible that John Wright moved to Lenton Firs in 1838 or 1839 (since he paid the rent there from Lady Day 1838 until Lady Day 1840) to live with his three unmarried daughters who became the official tenants of Lenton Firs at Michaelmas 1840 [7], while Francis had assumed the position of householder at Lenton Hall. John left only £18,000, having already distributed his wealth among his children.

Like his father, Francis Wright (Figure 49) married into an old Derbyshire landed family. In August 1830, within weeks of gaining his directorship at Butterley, he married Selina, the eldest daughter of Sir Henry Fitzherbert of Tissington, Derbyshire. It has been suggested that they went to live 'in the vicinity of The Park', but more likely that they took up residence immediately at Lenton Hall. They had eight children during the next ten years, seven of them in successive years. The Census Enumerators' Books of 1841 [8] give some idea of the life-style of the young Wright family in the early years of Victoria's reign. Francis and Selina, both aged 34, then had one son and five daughters at home - Agnes (6), Elizabeth (5), Selina (4), Francis (3), Frances (2) and Mary (1) - while their two older sons, John and Henry, who would have been 10 and 7 years old respectively, were not enumerated, and were probably away at school. The couple kept nine living-in servants, mostly young [9], while another, John Campion, probably a coachman, lived with his wife at a lodge. The lodge is thought to have been at the exit of Lenton Hall Drive to Derby Road, existing in 1823, and probably even before 1810, but rebuilt in about 1860. The 'proofs' associated with the litigation in 1823 between Lord Middleton and John Wright [10] described (p.36) a meeting of the Trustees of the Nottingham to Derby and the Lenton to Sawley turnpikes (who included John Wright) on 4 May 1810, at which Lord Middleton complained that 'a part of the south side of this road (Derby Road) from the cottage belonging to John Wright Esq. to the garden of the toll-gate' had been 'lately taken in and a quick fence planted next to the road....'. This cottage cannot have been other than a lodge at the entrance to Lenton Hall Drive. At the sale of 1867-68 discussed below its replacement was described as newly built. No farm bailiff was mentioned at the 1841 census, though the Sanderson map of 1835 shows buildings on the site of Lenton Hall Farm, and White's Directory for 1844 mentioned a bailiff called James Wilson at 'The Hall'.

Four additional children were born to Francis and Selina Wright after Lenton Hall was sold. They were Fitzherbert (b.1845), Marcus Beresford (who died an infant), Philip (b.1846) and Judith. The marriages of two of Francis Wright's daughters into the Fox family of Derby have a special interest. Charles (later Sir Charles) Fox, son of the first physician to Derby General Infirmary and founder of the local Mechanics Institute, broke away from his family's medical tradition to become an engineer, and senior partner of Fox and Henderson. He built Crystal Palace in ten months and was knighted for it. His eldest son, Charles Douglas Fox, later Sir Charles, married Mary, Francis Wright's fifth daughter, and seven years later Francis Fox, the second son, married her elder sister Selina. Selina died in 1900, a year after her youngest daughter, Lucy Adeline, married Ernest Beresford Fitzherbert Wright, who thus had Francis Wright as both uncle and father-in-law !

His Fitzherbert and Beresford connections eased the passage of the young Francis Wright into smart East Midlands society, but he may have been an uncomfortable companion, uninterested in wine, women (apart from his wife) and song, and 'horses were for drawing his carriage'. He was a serious, pious young man, a forerunner of Samuel Smiles in his devotion to hard work and self-help, with a social conscience that urged him to help those less fortunate than himself so long as they were God-fearing Protestants not given to drink, gambling or other forms of loose living and frivolity'. He was fortunate in his people at Butterley - William Jessop the younger, an active, able partner; Joseph Glynn, F.R.S., engineer; and George Goodwin as manager-agent. Francis took over at Butterley on the eve of a decade of railway mania in the 1840s, and a huge demand for rails, wheels and bridges. 'Ariel', one of the engines on the inaugural run by rail from Nottingham to Derby on 30 May 1839 was built by 'Jessop, Wright and Co. at Butterley works'. It reached Derby in 46 minutes and returned in an astonishing 30 minutes. With Butterley's affairs going well under the now experienced and highly capable William Jessop, Francis had time to concentrate on the well-being of his workers, with the model village of Ironville his first great achievement (1834-1860). Reports to the Home Office by H.S.Treachery [Parliamentary Papers between 1844 and 1859] praised the Erewash valley and Butterley in particular for the interest taken by the Masters in the well-being of the workpeople. 'Most of this came after 1830, and most of the leadership came from Butterley, especially from Francis Wright'; but it began before 1820 with John Wright and William Jessop. 'The Wrights had an enviable reputation in Nottingham in the early 19th century as philanthropists' [R.A.Church 1966: Riden 1973 36].

Francis Wright sold Lenton Hall with its park of 130 acres to Digby Willoughby, the 7th Lord Middleton, on Lady Day 1845 [11] but he retained his other property in Lenton, including the Dunkirk farms. He moved to Osmaston Manor near Ashbourne, where he built a large mansion. The move must have been prompted by family reasons as well as business convenience, for not only was Francis's wife Selina a Derbyshire woman but so was his mother, and it was through her that Francis inherited Osmaston. She was the eldest of four co-heiresses, daughters of Francis Beresford of Osmaston (for whom Francis Wright was named) by Frances, daughter of the Rev. Benjamin Reynolds. Francis Beresford died in 1801 leaving the Osmaston estate to be shared among three daughters, and John Wright bought out the shares of the other two. It was therefore only after the death of John Wright in 1840, Elizabeth having died in 1833, that Francis Wright would be in a position to build his new mansion at Osmaston. Incidentally, as a further example of the linkage of the Wright and Smith families it may be noted that the youngest of the four Beresford sisters, Selina, Francis Wright's aunt, in 1794 married Samuel Martin (1770-1859), rector of Warsop for nearly 60 years, the eldest of four sons of Prebendary Samuel Martin, rector of St. Mary's, Nottingham, who died in 1782 after being thrown from his horse. The Prebendary had married in 1769 Elizabeth, eldest daughter and co-heir of John Smith the Nottingham banker, whose second daughter Mary married Thomas Wright in 1764 and became the mother of Ichabod Wright of Mapperley Hall and John Smith Wright of Rempstone Hall.

During his five years as resident owner of Lenton Hall and its estate Francis Wright contrived to leave a considerable mark on Lenton parish, as well as serving as High Sheriff of Nottinghamshire in 1842 and as a county magistrate. He was churchwarden at the old Priory church from 1839 until 1844-45, when he left Lenton with his family. At the time the Rev.

George Brown, curate 1839, vicar 1840, was pressing the need for a larger church and a day school for the poor, to both of which appeals Francis Wright responded by presenting a site for each - perhaps appropriate gifts in view of the profit made by his father in buying and selling the land upon which the original New Lenton was built [Godfrey 1884 213: Bailey 1853 555].

Francis made an initial gift of £1,500 towards the cost of building the new Holy Trinity church, and his three sisters at Lenton Firs added £500. By March 1841, with £3,200 raised, the building contractors, Manning and Keeting of Rugby, could proceed to the design of H.I.Stevens of Derby, in the Early English style, using stone from Coxbench, Derbyshire. There were nearly 700 sittings on the ground floor and 340 for children in the west gallery (which was reduced in 1894). On 11 June 1841 Francis Wright and his sisters laid the foundation stone and treated the 60 workmen to dinner at the White Hart. The original estimates of cost soon proving unrealistic, Francis added £500 to his gift before the stone laying and a further £1,000 later, and his sisters provided a further £500, but this still left the church indebted. It was opened on 6 October 1842, but was later criticised because its tower was too small - the result of lack of sufficient funds - or over-ambitious planning.

The east window in the new church is inscribed along the bottom 'Erected by his sons, friends and tenants in memory of Francis Wright Esq., the Founder of this church. Born December 21st 1806: Died February 24th 1873'. Other memorial windows in Holy Trinity include those to Thomas Adams of Lenton Firs (see Chapter IX), to Albert Ball's mother, Loius (1913) and wife Harriett Mary (1931), and to Henry Kirk, a Nottingham lace manufacturer who until his death in April 1911 lived at The Oaks, Broadgate Beeston, now redeveloped for student residence (see Chapter XVI). The chief later benefactor of Holy Trinity, however, was William Goodacre Player of Lenton Hurst (see Chapter XII), who presented the present reredos in 1911 replacing a stone one of 1858, and replaced the 1847 organ in 1906, and provided the carved wooden screen separating the nave from the chancel in 1931.

The famous font of the 11th or 12th century, from the original priory church, carved from a single block of gritstone, was moved to Holy Trinity from the small church in Old Lenton, which closed, and was partly demolished to provide material for a Chapel of ease at Hyson Green. The chancel and vestry were eventually blocked off from the derelict nave, and services resumed there, until with development in Old Lenton and Dunkirk a new nave was built in 1884 and rededicated to St. Anthony.

The Rev. George Browne's call for a day school for the poor was met when Francis Wright presented the land upon which the National Schools were built for 130 boys and 120 girls in 1841, the first voluntary school in Lenton (now the Sikh temple on Church Street). The school building was opened by Francis Wright on 25 April 1842 and was extended in 1855. The original vicarage adjoining the church was replaced by one built on its tennis court. It is now called Unity House, with the ground floor providing parish rooms and with self-contained flats upstairs. A garage and petrol station now occupies its former vegetable garden.

Francis Wright after 1845 and Osmaston Manor

Francis Wright's sale of Lenton Hall took effect on Lady Day 1845 when the family had already moved, presumably to an existing house at Osmaston in which they lived until about mid-1849. The huge neo-Tudor Osmaston Manor, designed by H.I.Stevens of Derby (architect of Lenton Holy Trinity church) was begun in May 1846, and the Wrights were able to move in on 11 July 1849. The highly ornate, pseudo-Gothic mansion 333 feet long, had 49 bells on its bell board, and none of them serving the ten rooms provided for manservants and ten for maids. There was a 40-feet dining room, and a salon 73 feet long, extensive Italianate gardens and glasshouses on which Paxton is said to have advised.

The house had three especially impressive features in addition to the 80 feet long conservatory, a racquet court, the stables with 17 stalls full of white horses, the bakehouse, brewhouse, washhouse and other provisions for a quite large community. The special features were, first, the absence of chimneys on the house, smoke passing through cellars in a smoke tunnel, and beneath the kitchen garden to a 150-foot smoke tower which later failed, but was the only part of the original building to survive its demolition in 1966. Second, there was a railway system in the cellars with hydraulic lifts to distribute coal round the house: and thirdly a clock tower with a perforated parapet reading 'Work while it is day'. They were regarded at the time as manifestations of the emerging technological age rather than as ostentation by the nouveaux riches.

The house took 3 years and 2 months to build, and prayers for the builders were led once a week by Francis Wright ! When Francis, Selina and six sons and six daughters moved in they entertained to dinner 300 workers and tenants. Three years later there was a similar dinner for John's 21st birthday celebration, but the Wrights did not entertain at Osmaston's 'Christian barracks' (except for clergymen or missionaries). Francis was a long distance commuter from Osmaston to Butterley several times a week, and in the absence of a railway probably drove himself the 20 miles by carriage - he was a fine horseman and driver though he abhorred racing and hunting.

Tenants in new cottages found Francis a kindly landlord - providing they attended church regularly - but Ashbourne people held him in lower esteem. As chairman of the Ashbourne bench he closed several public houses, and when he bought the lordship of the manor he removed the cattle market to a site on the outskirts of the town, and even tried to ban the ancient football game through the streets - acts of 'arbitrary Puritanism'. He thought services in the parish church of St. Oswalds corrupting - bordering on the Anglo-Catholic - and 'displeasing to the Almighty, with whom he was on excellent terms'. He therefore built the rival St. John the Baptist 'Free Church of England' - free, it was said, to follow the form of worship laid down by Francis Wright - opened in 1871 but not licensed by the Bishop until 1883.

'Rabidly "antipapist" evangelicals' like Francis Wright regarded public schools set up by the Woodard Trust, with Anglo-Catholic leanings and comparatively low fees, as subversive, brainwashing the young. So Francis organized the founding of Trent College, whose religious guidance would have had an opposite bias, and he sold the idea to patrons such as the Duke of Devonshire, the Bishops of Leeds and Lincoln, Earls Howe, Manvers, Spencer, Lichfield and Harrowby and Sir Oswald Moseley. He found the site at Long Eaton and called the early meetings. The Duke of Devonshire laid the foundation stone in 1866, and Trent College opened in April 1868 with 53 boys and a house named after Francis Wright. It adopted his family motto, 'Ad Rem', usually translated as 'To the point', but by Wright as 'Whatever thy hand findeth to do, do it with thy might'. The school built a chapel to his memory in 1875, and his portrait (Figure 49) hangs in the school dining room. The Wright family maintained an interest in Trent College as long as the old Butterley company lasted, and up to 1947, when the mines were nationalized, six sons of Butterley employees (reduced to two after 1947) were admitted annually at the firm's expense.

Francis Wright was a great layer of foundation stones and opener of bazaars, usually connected with the church, though with his slight stammer he was easier talking with his miners than with his peers. It was said in retrospect that he was a man of modesty, humility and moral courage, devout and generous to the church, and becoming in his later years essentially liberal and reformist in outlook. He died after a short illness within days of the completion of one of the greatest of the Butterley works - St. Pancras station - on 24 February 1873. His funeral was attended by all the tenantry and 1,200 of the Butterley workforce. His estate was worth £1.4 million. The Derbyshire Advertiser's account of his spectacular funeral at Osmaston was reprinted in hard-back along with its report of the British Association's 1866 visit to Butterley. Admitting that 'Mr. Wright had not the gift of fluent and powerful speech' it excused his frequent changes of political allegiance between Tory and Liberal parties as an example of putting principle before party; made much of his 'modesty and humility' and of his benefactions, including the cost of 39 churches, some of them in the Vale of Belvoir where his mother's family originated; and used the word 'convictions' as a euphemism for 'bigotry'. But in particular the account emphasized his strong sense of duty, one of the more admirable qualities expected of a Victorian gentleman; and, indeed, 'although he was born in the reign of George III in 1806, Francis Wright was the epitome of the Victorian English gentleman. It is impossible to imagine him belonging to any other nation at any other time, or, for that matter, to any other social class.... His virtues and his defects of character - for he possessed none of the more tempting vices, and strongly opposed them - were those of the Victorian era writ large'.

John Osmaston and the Lenton Wrights after Francis

At his death on 24 February 1873 Francis Wright was survived by ten of his twelve children, five sons and five daughters. Each daughter got an income of £500 a year. The second son Henry was a clergyman (as one suspects his father would have liked to be), rector of St. Nicholas' church in Nottingham. The third and fourth sons, Francis Beresford Wright and Fitzherbert Wright each received two-fifths of the capital of the Butterley company, and there were shares for both the Rev. Henry and the youngest son, Philip as 'sleeping partners'. The industrial mantle fell upon Francis Beresford and Fitzherbert Wright who controlled the company, with the third William Jessop as junior partner until he retired in July 1882. Jessop died soon afterwards, having sold his one-fifth share to the Wrights, who now had total ownership. Subsequently the holdings were reorganized so that Francis Beresford and Fitzherbert each held 3/10 of the capital, leaving 2/5 for the representatives of the Rev. Henry, drowned boating on Coniston Water, and Philip, settled at Mellington Hall, Montgomery and High Sheriff of that county. The company was still run by the two senior partners. However, it was the Rev. Henry's son, Albert Leslie Wright (1862-1938), the so-called Great Man of Butterley, who dominated the business as its managing director from the beginning of the 20th century until his death in 1938. Meanwhile the banking business had long since passed entirely into the hands of the Mapperley branch of the Wright family.

To John Wright, his eldest son, Francis Wright left £125,000 and all his real estate, which included much of southern Lenton: but John either refused or was not offered control of Butterley or even a place in the firm. He rarely saw eye to eye with his father, and was never associated with the company, so this was probably by mutual consent. Although he lived at Osmaston Manor only intermittently, John changed his surname to Osmaston. He eventually moved to Kent, closed the house and put it up for sale, his mother moving to Yeldersley Hall nearby. He was also soon selling off his Lenton property, which began the development of Dunkirk, as shown below.

John Osmaston's withdrawal from involvement in the Butterley Company appears to have consigned him and his descendants to obscurity in the Derby and Nottingham areas. In 1883 he sold Osmaston Manor to Sir Andrew Barclay Walker, the donor of Liverpool's Walker Art Gallery. By 1908, when it was the seat of Sir Peter Carlow Walker (who had married Ethel Blanche Okeover) no Osmastons were mentioned in the Court Guide and County Blue Book [Deacon 1908]. Sir Andrew's grandson, Sir Ian Walker-Okeover, offered Osmaston Manor for sale after moving to Okeover Hall, Staffordshire, but as no buyer was found he had the Manor demolished in 1966, though retaining the estate. Aldecar Hall, occupied by Arthur Fitzherbert Wright until just before the second world war, suffered a similar fate, for although Monty (Montague) Wright wished to convert it into a training centre for mining engineers the N.C.B. was not interested; so it was pulled down in about 1962. The Derbyshire Blue Book in 1908 included a number of the former Lenton Wrights, generally prominent and wealthy through their association with the Butterley Company, and readily identified by their Christian names. The Board of the Company included, for example (in the years given) Ernest Beresford

Fitzherbert Wright J.P. of Yeldesley Hall, Derby (1911-30); F.E.Fitzherbert Wright, V.D., D.L., J.P., High Sheriff 1902, of The Hayes, Swanwick, Alfreton, third son of Francis Wright (1888-1910); Francis Beresford Wright, M.A., J.P. of Worton Court, Warwick, earlier of Aldecar Hall, Derby, second son of Francis Wright (1888-1911); and Henry Fitzherbert Wright, J.P., of West Hallam Hall (1902-44).

The connections of the Wrights with the University campus ended for a generation in 1845, for while Francis left Lenton Hall his three elder sisters, Charlotte (by then 49), Frances (48) and Ann (46) left Lenton Firs, and built a house called The Lodge adjoining the school and opposite to the vicarage and Holy Trinity church in Lenton, where for many years they lived 'lives of active benevolence and religious work'. In 1851 they provided the Infant School south-west of the church over the railway crossing (later a bridge). However, the sale of Lenton Hall and park left much farm property in southern Lenton in the hands of Francis Wright, and he retained it throughout his life. His eldest son, John Osmaston, having lived at Osmaston from the age of 15, was essentially a Derbyshire man, and he cut his family's ties with Lenton soon after his father's death in 1873 by selling off - 'recently' it was said in 1884 [Godfrey 1884] - 'the whole of his property in the parish of Lenton to various purchasers'. It was this sale that made possible the residential growth of Dunkirk, which began immediately.

The origins and growth of residential Dunkirk

Before pursuing further the history of Lenton Hall and its park after Francis Wright sold them in 1845, the outcome of the Lenton land sales by John Osmaston will be examined. Residential Dunkirk was developed immediately following the sales, and it is relevant to this study because the area was part of the priory demesne, and that the part of it west of Montpelier Road was included in the area allocated for long-term University use under the city's postwar development plan. However, since the University has as yet only nibbled at the designated area in Dunkirk in minor and marginal ways it seems appropriate to discuss its history at this point rather than in Chapter XVI, which summarises the acquisition and physical development of the campus as it now exists.

The story relates almost wholly to land bought by John Wright in 1798-99, and, indeed, the developments beginning in the early 1880s were bounded sharply on the west side by the former Keighton Closes owned by the Gregory estate, which showed little interest in developing its property. It was also confined to a single farm, Dunkirk Farm. Before the Osmaston sale the census Enumerators' Books from 1841 to 1881 show that the population of Dunkirk was limited to a handful of farmers and farm labourers. Subsequently the population grew steadily, not because of any new industry offering employment there, but mainly through the initiative of a 'property developer', Frank William Johnson in organizing the sale of freehold building plots to prospective private householders through a subscription scheme devised by him [12].

By John Wright's will dated 1 August 1835 (he died on 21 April 1840) his 'manor or lordship of Lenton priory' together with freehold lands in Lenton and Beeston (other than those bought from Charles Upton and Mrs. Mary Sills in 1803 that remained unsold) were bequeathed to Francis Wright for life, with the remainder in trust to Francis Martin and John Sherbrooke Gell for the use of his grandson, John Wright for life, and then to his sons according to seniority in tail male [13]. Ledgett Wong, of about 12 acres, was excluded by a codicil of 1838 when Marcus Martin became the second trustee on the death of J.S.Gell. On 23 June 1853 John Wright (later Osmaston), the grandson, married Miss Eleanor Plumptre at Eastwood, and on 9 March 1857 their eldest son, Francis Plumptre Beresford Wright, was born at Hulland House near Ashbourne, and he was baptised at Osmaston parish church in September 1876. It was some three years after Francis Wright's death and burial at Osmaston that his son John, by deed poll, assumed the surname Osmaston. On 25 June 1877 he mortgaged for £20,000 (with life assurance) all his farms, lands and hereditaments in Lenton and Beeston, and in 1878 the mortgage was increased to £35,000. Whether John Osmaston was in financial difficulties is not known. His son Francis was 21 on 9 March 1878, and an income of £500 a year, or more if he married, was provided for him up to the age of 25, possibly from Lenton farm rents.

Among the properties mortgaged was Dunkirk Farm, of 100 acres, tenanted by Thomas Wood from the mid-1840s. Wood's original home was in St. James Street, Nottingham, and it is probable that a bailiff managed the farm for him - probably William Mills from 1848 or earlier to 1861 or later, followed by William Cutts in 1871. Wood paid £294.14s. 2d. a year in rent. The mortgage on Wood's farm was revoked by indentures of June 1878 and May 1880. On 30 December 1882 about 44 acres south of the Tottle Brook were sold for £4,295.12s. 6d.. Earlier in the same year, on 24 March, an indenture between Henry and Marcus Lewis (1) [14] and Frank William Johnson(2), 'gentleman' of Dunkirk House (as he called Dunkirk farm-house) recorded agreement for a sale for £6,580 as beneficial owner of one divided moiety [15]. This related to the balance of the 100 acres of Wood's farm north of the Tottle Brook. Wood himself is believed to have died in 1880 [Wright 1879: Census 1881] and was followed briefly by Mrs. Mary Wood, who occupied the farmhouse and the southern half of the farm, some 44 acres sold in December 1882.

Frank William Johnson, who bought all this land, was the prime mover in the residential development of Dunkirk. His father, Joseph Birley Johnson, licensee of the News House inn on Leenside, died in August 1881, leaving his son money enough to buy Dunkirk Farm. F.W.Johnson had no intention of farming the land, but planned to develop it for housing. At that time only farm tracks served it, and an early move of Johnson was to seek building regulation approval in 1882 for a street, following an existing track, from his Dunkirk House near the railway to the junction between Abbey Lane and Dunkirk Road. He named it Montpelier Road. About the same time, on 27 July 1882 he formed the Dunkirk Freehold Land Society, the object of which was 'the purchase of an estate in Old Lenton, subdivision of it into allotments and roads 'as shown on the Constitution Deed', and division of such allotments among the members'. There were monthly meetings between 1882 and at least 1889 to collect contributions. A committee of nine was empowered to make roads, sewers, drains etc.. Allocation to members was made by a complicated auction system, with 'the premiums obtained for choice of plots' to be applied 'for the benefit of the Society'. The paid secretary of the Society was Arthur Birley Johnson of New Basford and the Treasurer was F.W.Johnson himself. Johnson's main gain, however, was probably obtained from building most of the houses east of Montpelier Road. The 108 allotments in the scheme, presumably laid out by Lawrence Bright, the surveyor of the Society, varied in size from 2390 sq. yards (value £298.15s.0d.) to about 450 sq. yards, but most were about 7-800 sq. yards (6 to 7 plots per acre). The committee was to approve all plans [16].

After Montpelier Road in 1882 there were plans for Cavendish Street, Gibbons Street (another existing track), Marlborough Street and Bunting Street in 1883, and others followed. Johnson was fond of using his family names. For example, Gibbons was the maiden name of his wife Millicent, and there were Millicent Villas (1895), a row of 8 houses on Montpelier Road; Claude Street after his son Claude; Birley Villas (1901) and Percy Villas (1902), both on Montpelier Road, after his sons Frank Birley Johnson and Frederick Percy Johnson; and Johnson Cottages (1903) on Claude Street. The first houses Johnson built were, in 1883, Dunkirk Villas, a row of 8 houses, and in 1886 five houses on Marlborough Street (the name plate for which has crumbled).

It will be noticed that all these houses were east of Montpelier Road. The roads planned west of Montpelier Road, both north and south of Beeston Road, were the work of the Osmaston Freehold Land Society, which probably began operations a little later than the Dunkirk society, and which appears to have purchased most or all of its land from F.W.Johnson.

It is not known whether the Osmaston trustees were involved. The Osmaston Freehold Land Society submitted plans for all the roads in that part of Dunkirk north of Beeston Road in 1886. Presumably it was this society that proposed the layout including Paul Street, Hartington Street and Roberts Street west of Montpelier Road sometime after 1904, an area that was never developed, possibly in part because of the first world war, but almost certainly because of drainage problems associated with the Tottle Brook. Figure 50 shows the progress made by the two land societies by the outbreak of the first world war. Much of the land intended for housing was then still shown as allotment gardens, a feature of private housing schemes in other parts of Nottingham such as Carlton. The western half of the Osmaston area north of Beeston Road was only sparsely built upon, and there were only two houses on Beeston Road west of Lace Street. By the late 1930s, however, this area was almost completely built over. By contrast, west of Montpelier Road only a few houses had been added, between Bunting Street and Dunkirk Road.

In fact F.W.Johnson had moved on. In the 1890s the directories described him as 'grazier and builder', but grazier presumably on the strength of letting land to butchers. In the 1900s he was called 'grazier, auctioneer and valuer' - but valuer mainly of public houses, a number of which he bought and sold himself. Again, in the 1890s he was building extensively in the Castle Boulevard area of Lenton. By the turn of the century he was wealthy, and in 1905 he moved to a palatial mansion that he bought in The Park, called Duke William Mount. In 1906 he let Dunkirk House and the remains of Dunkirk Farm to Thomas Aram, but he remained active in property development. For example, in about 1904 Johnson bought the Abbey Tavern in Friar Place, Lenton, and in 1912 he had Friar Place demolished and built there four shops called the Johnson Building together with the public house named after him.

A local opinion in the 1880s was that a new suburban railway station at Dunkirk on the Nottingham-Derby line was being seriously mooted, but it is difficult to decide whether this was a stimulus to building development at Dunkirk or a response to it. Certainly it was probably the rumour about the station that led Johnson to build the Dunkirk Hotel, and to make it so large [17]. A rival hotel was already being built on Osmaston land at the corner of Beeston Road and Abbey Lane, probably in response to the same rumours, but by the time that was finished the Dunkirk Hotel was already open. Consequently the Beeston Road house never obtained a licence, and stood empty for many years. Only in about 1920 was the building finally occupied, the ground floor for the manufacture of 'Castle's Consumption Cure', the first floor by the local Labour Party, and the top floor by Cyril Fordham's cane furniture factory [18] .

After F.W.Johnson's death in 1934 some property was sold, and the rest managed by trustees who included his son Frederick Percy Johnson, after whose death in 1952 all the remaining properties belonging to Johnson were sold. The University of Nottingham acquired a number of houses in Dunkirk, and some 7 acres of undeveloped land with drainage problems fronted by Montpelier Road where Roberts Street, Paul Street and Huntington Street had been proposed early in the century. This may have led to the inclusion of the land in the area earmarked for University use by the first post-war Nottingham Development Plan.

Lord Middleton' tenants at Lenton Hall, 1845-1868

Having bought Lenton Firs by 1814, at least partly to facilitate the diversion of the Nottingham to Derby turnpike road and allow part of the Lenton Firs land to be incorporated into Wollaton Park, and having bought Lenton Abbey house and land from the Green family in 1831, the Middletons were able to complete their cordon sanitaire - if that is how they viewed it - by the purchase of the Lenton Hall estate in 1845. This transaction gave them the entire frontage on Derby Road from the south between Sandy Lane (now part of Clifton Boulevard) and the Tottle Brook (now Woodside Road). The three estates, however, retained their separate identities with little adjustment [19] and were occupied by different tenants until they

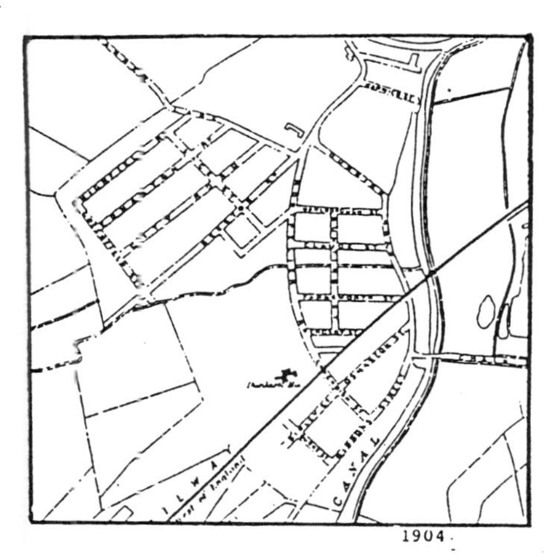

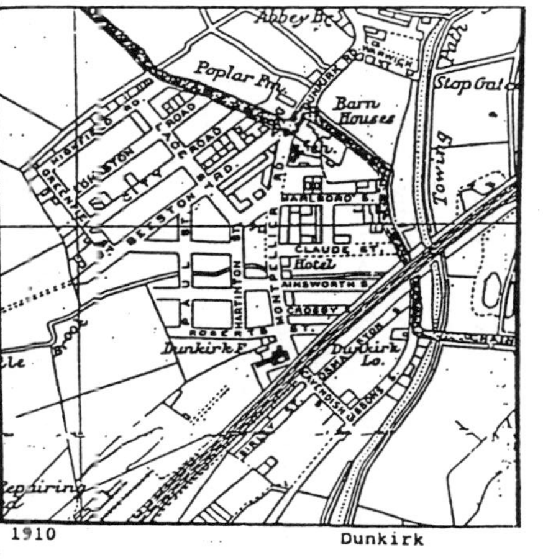

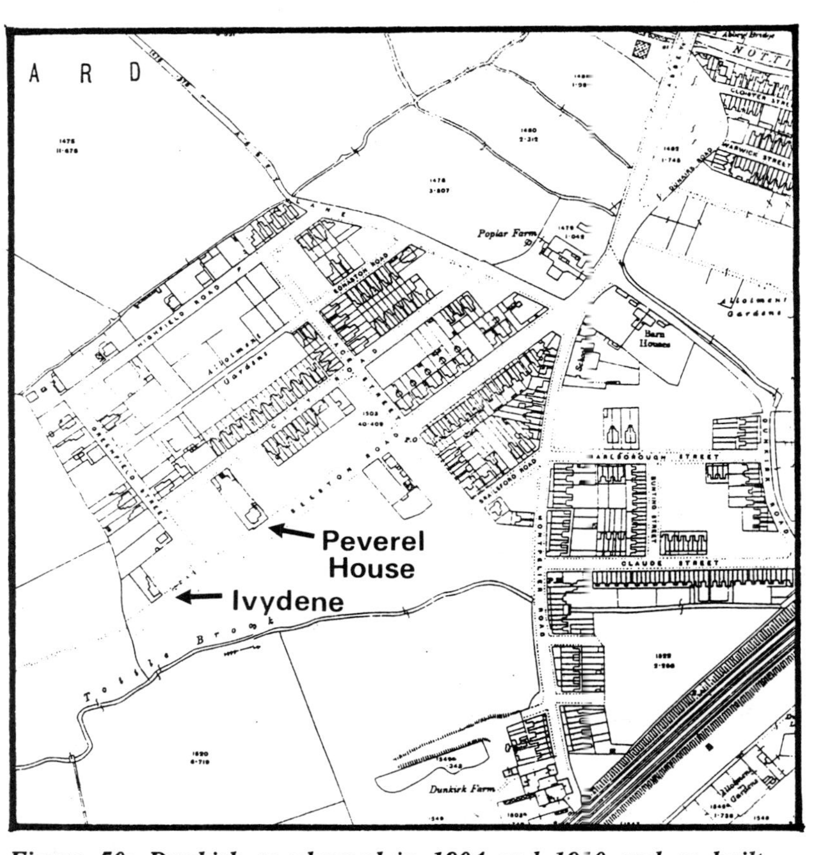

Figure 50: Dunkirk as planned in 1904 and 1910 and as built by 1913
Left: *two maps from the 'Lenton Listener' No. 42 (Oct-Nov) 1986, crediting NCLS.*
Right: *part of O.S. 25-inch map published 1915. The proposed streets west of Montpelier Road were not developed probably through poor drainage.*

were all resold in 1868-69. During its 23 years in Middleton ownership Lenton Hall and its park had four known tenants - Captain J.A.Legard, John Morley, Mrs. Louisa Wildman and Louis Baillon. The first two were each resident for about seven years, and the third and fourth for uncertain though shorter periods, Baillon known only on the authority of Lawson Lowe [1871].

Lord Middleton's Lady Day rental for 1845 contains information about the purchase of Lenton Hall estate, and the assignment of the house and land , including the transfer of 15 acres west of Beeston Lane (now occupied by sports pitches) to Isaac Fisher, the tenant of the Lenton Abbey estate. The first occupier of Lenton Hall and its estate, from 1845 to 1853, was Captain James Anlaby Legard, R.N., K.T.S. (1805-1869). Preparation of Lenton Hall for Captain Legard and his family was interrupted by a spectacular disaster which might easily have ended the history of the Hall, and which must influence the dating and interpretation of some of its interior features. An amusing account of the incident in the 'Nottingham Review' of 25 July 1845 is worth quoting [20].

'On Saturday night last a fire broke out at Lenton Hall near Nottingham which happily was discovered in time to prevent the entire destruction of the premises. Two months since, Francis Wright esq. removed from Lenton to Osmaston in Derbyshire, and having disposed of the Lenton property to Lord Middleton the house was untenanted and unfurnished and undergoing a thorough repair, and was expected to be ready in a few days time for Captain Layard (sic) MP for Carlon (sic) its future occupier.

'One of the servants, Thomas Fairfield, left in charge of the house, closed the window shutters, and an hour and a half afterwards did not notice any smoke or fire, and he and John Mather (a servant from Wollaton Hall) remained together during the evening. At half past ten Thomas Smith, a groom in the employ of Mr. Wright but living in Lenton, happening to look from his chamber window towards the Hall saw a great light and flames bursting from the windows. He instantly set out and in breathless haste gave the alarm. The fire by this time had burnt the shutters and caught the ceiling and was raging with great fury, threatening entire destruction.

'Fairfield actively set about putting out the fire, and Mather got a horse and rode off to Wollaton Hall, from whence two engines were instantly despatched accompanied by the whole of the servants. He then went into the village, called at the Public House where the Middleton Lodge of Oddfellows were assembled entertaining a party from the Dow Lodge, and the whole of the company, 85 in number, ran off and formed an excellent fire brigade. Messengers were sent to Superintendent Whitworth, [and] Inspector Parnham, policeman Fox, Cooper, Vaux and Whitehead were on the spot in less than an hour, as were also Chief Constable Harris with the Town Engine and several policemen under his command.

'Mr. William Hickling, landlord of the Rose and Crown, and Mr. James Hull of the Travellers Rest, with the company of their houses, all repaired to the fire, and a large crowd, including the whole of the Beeston Light Horse (a term given to the rabble of that village) quickly surrounded the house.

'A rigid inspection then took place under the direction and personal superintendence of Mr. Chowler, Steward to Lord Middleton. Walls, ceilings, rafters, shutters, beams and some floors gutted. Walls had been batted to keep them dry, which had no doubt contributed to the hasty manner of the fire'.

After this inauspicious beginning Captain Legard's tenancy of Lenton Hall lasted for eight years, during which he became a respected and popular figure in the neighbourhood. Born in 1805, and thus 40 years old when he came to Lenton, James Legard had two distinct but powerful links with the Willoughby family, and it may be supposed that either or both were involved in bringing him from Yorkshire to Lenton. The first connection was through his first wife, Charlotte Henrietta, described in 1848 as 'a deceased daughter of the said Henry Willoughby the elder by his late wife' [21], and thus a sister of the 8th Lord Middleton. However, James Legard remarried in 1845 [Mason 1969 93,100], and it is therefore unlikely that

Charlotte Henrietta ever herself lived at Lenton Hall, even allowing for the rapidity of remarriage in early Victorian times. It is equally unlikely that the purchase of the Lenton Hall estate by Lord Middleton had any direct connection with her. Her elder son, Algernon Willoughby Legard, was born in 1842, and her younger son, Cecil Henry Legard in 1843 or 1844. Despite this connection there is no indication that Captain Legard occupied the Lenton Hall estate without paying rent.

The second connection, perhaps even more significant - and indeed the first may well have arisen out of it - was Captain Legard's long and close relationship from his boyhood with Rear Admiral Sir Nesbit Josias Willoughby, the 'Hero of Mauritius' (1777-1849), born at Aspley Hall the fifth son of Robert Willoughby of Aspley and Cossall and his second wife Barbara, and thus a cousin of Lord Middleton [Mason 1969]. In his naval career James Legard is probably to be regarded as a protege of Sir Nesbit. Like Sir Nesbit he went to sea as a very young boy, and at the age of thirteen in about 1818 he was posted to HMS Tribune as a 'volunteer' [22], probably as Captain Willoughby's personal servant, though he came from a wealthy family. After recovering from yellow fever in Jamaica through careful nursing by an unnamed negro woman, and through a prolonged convalescence 'in the loving care of Admiral Sir Charles and Lady Rowley' [Mason 1969 100] he returned to England in his ship, the Tribune, at a time when many junior officers were being paid off; but though only a midshipman he was kept on, by reason of either his ability or his connections, and remained a serving naval officer until 1852, only shortly before he left Lenton Hall to return, in retirement, to his native Yorkshire.

During the 1830s James Legard's connection with Admiral Willoughby was maintained or resumed. He frequently visited Sir Nesbit at his London home in Montague Street, and probably helped him with his book 'Extracts from Holy Writ' published privately in 1839. He was certainly the admiral's amanuensis after he became blind in his surviving eye, dealing with his voluminous correspondence, some of which survives. Legard subsequently acted as Sir Nesbit's executor, and after his death in 1849 took charge of all his papers, filling his sea chest with those now known as the Willoughby Manuscripts, to be found in the Middleton collection housed in the University's Hallward Library a short stone's throw from the house in which Captain Legard was living at the time. The documents, still in the old sea chest, were found by Colonel Sir J.D.Legard of Welham Hall, Malton, Yorkshire, Captain Legard's son, when he moved house in 1892, and he sent them to Lord Middleton [23]. Lady Middleton [1905] wrote that Colonel Legard 'gave us the Admiral's old sea chest containing such old papers, letters, ships' logs etc. as Captain Legard had not felt it incumbent upon him to destroy'.

The household at Lenton Hall in 1851 [24] (Table 15) comprised James Legard, with his second wife Catherine, then aged 39, and like her husband born in Yorkshire, together with their young children James Digby aged 4 years (later to become Colonel Sir James Digby Legard, K.C.B.) and Allayne B. Legard aged 3 years, both born at Lenton. Also enumerated then were three older children born of Catherine's earlier marriage, Henry F. Beaumont (18), Mary C. Beaumont (16) and Richard T. Beaumont (13), all described as 'scholars at home' and all born at Scarborough. Not present at the census, and probably away at school, were the two sons of James and Charlotte Henrietta (nee Willoughby) named Algernon Willoughby Legard (1842-1923), later Sir Algernon Legard, and Cecil Henry Legard, for both of whom financial provision had been made by Digby, Lord Middleton in 1848 [25]. Sir Algernon Willoughby Legard, who lived to be 81, was Master of the Rufford Hunt in the 1880s and 'a member of a family always devoted to field sports'. Indeed, his very brief stay at Cambridge University is said to have been chiefly occupied in riding to hounds.

The Legards, evidently wealthy, in 1851 employed at Lenton Hall a resident domestic staff numbering 12, at least five of whom appear to have been brought from Yorkshire with the family. In addition to a groom and a stable boy, as in 1841, there was a dairymaid, Jane Lightfoot from Yorkshire, indicating that dairying was one of the farming operations in the park,

Table 15.
Household at Lenton Hall in 1851

Name	Age	Position in family: occupation	Place of birth
James A. LEGARD	46	Head, tenant. Retired Commander R.N. on half pay. County J.P.	Ganton, Yorks
Catherine LEGARD	39	Wife (second wife) [Legard's first wife, Charlotte Henrietta was daughter of Henry Lord Middleton]	Brompton, Yorks
James Digby LEGARD	4	Son	Lenton
Allayne B. LEGARD	3	Son	Lenton
Henry F. BEAUMONT	18	Stepson. Scholar at home.	Scarborough
Mary C. BEAUMONT	16	Stepdaughter. Scholar at home.	
Richard T. BEAUMONT	13	Stepson. Scholar at home. [These three were children of Catherine Legard by an earlier marriage. Two sons of James and Charlotte Henrietta Legard named Algernon Willoughby LEGARD and Cecil Henry LEGARD, beneficiaries of the (later) will of Henry, after the death of Digby, 7th Lord Middleton, were not in residence at Lenton Hall.]	
William CHURCHILL	31	Butler	Cheltenham
John WILSON	20	Footman	Barton, Notts.
John HALLAM	24	Groom	Leicester
James LANGSDALE	14	Stable boy	Wollaton
Mary COE	48	Housekeeper: widow	Westmorland
Jane PEACOCK	34	Lady's maid	Muston, Yorks.
Fanny COUPLAND	25	Nurse	Lincs.
Ann BENNETT	28	Laundry maid	Worksop
Ann EAST	24	Housemaid	Lincs.
Eliza GREGORY	27	Kitchen maid	Yorkshire
Eliza BOSTOCK	15	Nursemaid	Yorkshire
Jane LIGHTFOOT	22	Dairy maid	Yorkshire

At this date there is no mention of either Lenton Hall Lodge or of gardeners' cottages associated with Lenton Hall, although in 1861, when Lenton Hall was untenanted at the census, a coachman and his wife, Joseph and Ruth Whitehead, both aged 47 and born at Newstead were recorded in the Hall, and a gardener's cottage was occupied by John (39) and Mary Kidger (44) with their daughter aged 3 years, born at Lenton, and their boarder, George Harvey (43) an agricultural labourer. Lenton Hall Lodge was unoccupied. In 1868 the Lodge was 'newly built and forms a pretty object at the entrance of the park, abutting on the turnpike road'. It was probably built in 1861-62. At the 1841 census an earlier Lenton Hall Lodge was occupied by a male servant, John Campion aged 27 and his wife Caroline.

supervised by a farm bailiff at Lenton Hall Farm. Lascelles and Hagar's Commercial Dictionary of Nottingham for 1848 named John Clayton as the farming bailiff, but by the 1851 census John Hall, now a widower, had moved up from Lenton Abbey with his daughter and granddaughters.

In fact little is known of the details of life at Lenton Hall during the eight years of Legard's tenancy. Evidently James, a county magistrate, was very well regarded locally although he appears to have taken little part in Nottingham's public life and affairs, possibly because he spent much time in London and at sea. On 4 April 1853 a public dinner at the White Hart Inn was given by the parishioners of Lenton to 'Captain James Anlaby Legard, R.N., J.P., previous to his leaving the neighbourhood, as a mark of respect for the uniform kindness and courtesy shown by him to all parties during his residence in the parish' [Godfrey 1884 470]. James Legard seems to have been a man of attractive personality and presence. A crayon drawing of him in a family history written by his son, Colonel Sir J.D.Legard, to whom 'he was fond of telling stories about the great Willoughby who had made a sailor of him' (many of which were repeated by Sir James to his relatives the Middletons) shows him as a man of young middle age, remarkably handsome. 'It is not a very strong face, but the sketch would make anyone think "What a delightful fellow that must be !"' [Mason 1969 100].

In 1853 the Legards moved back to Yorkshire, to Kirkby Misterton, though James remained an acting magistrate for Nottinghamshire for a number of years after his removal [Wright 1858]. He died in 1869.

The second of Lord Middleton's tenants at Lenton Hall was John Morley of the firm J and S. Morley, silk and cotton doublers of Queens Road, Nottingham. Morley was at Lenton Hall by the beginning of 1854, since he was included in both Wright's and White's Directories for that year. He was still there in 1860 according to Drake's Directory, but had probably moved out by the spring of 1861, when the census recorded only a coachman and a gardener at Lenton Hall [26]. The coachman and his wife were both born at Newstead, suggesting that Lenton Hall was already being prepared for occupation by Mrs. Wildman, the next tenant - if she was not already installed. In 1862 Mrs. Wildman and her sister Miss Preisig were certainly in residence. During the six years of John Morley's tenancy the various Directories - Wright's, White's and Drake's for example - also named Thomas Bayley and J.G.Seyrig as occupiers of Lenton Hall, calling them both 'proprietors', although Thomas Bayley had not yet moved to Lenton Abbey and John Gotlobs Seyrig, an engineer, lived on Park Road, New Lenton. Since John Morley appears to have paid an unchanged rent of £440 a year for Lenton Hall [27] it is clear that the Hall and park were not let separately, and the probable, though unconfirmed explanation is that Morley sub-let parts of the park for grazing.

Louisa Wildman (c.1802-1877) said to be a daughter of F.Preisig of Appenzal, Switzerland, and widow of Thomas Wildman of Newstead Abbey, was the tenant of Lenton Hall estate for several years from 1861 , and was followed by Louis Baillon [Lowe 1871]. Little is known of 'Mrs. Colonel Wildman' herself, and her early life is the subject of speculation. But much is known about her husband, Colonel Thomas Wildman (1787-1859) D.L., J.P., and this should be outlined first.

Colonel Wildman was the eldest son of Thomas Wildman, M.P. (1740- 1795) the third son of a yeoman of the Bowland area of Lancashire who went to London, became a solicitor, and rose rapidly in wealth and social position, becoming a member of Lincolns Inn in 1773 and influential among lawyers, with houses in fashionable Bedford Square and at Bacton Hall, Suffolk. From a position of trust, through unscrupulous and fraudulent betrayal over a period of many years of the interests of the son of the vastly wealthy William Beckford (who died in 1770 leaving as his heir his nine-year old son William) Thomas Wildman senior and his two younger brothers dishonestly acquired great wealth including several large Jamaican estates at William Beckford's expense [Coupe 1991].

Thomas Wildman junior, only nine years old when his father died, inherited the major part of his wealth on reaching his majority in 1808, when he left Christ Church, Oxford without graduating and joined the 7th Hussars. He served with them in Spain in 1808 and 1809; was in the retreat to Corunna; and subsequently took part in all the actions of his regiment in the Peninsula in 1813 and 1814 . He was a veteran of Waterloo, and as aide-de-camp to Lord Uxbridge (the Marquis of Anglesey) he was with him when he was wounded and lost his leg. He also served as equerry to HRH the Duke of Sussex.

Colonel Wildman was wealthy enough to buy Newstead Abbey with its park and estate of nearly 5,000 acres from Lord Byron the poet, his friend and schoolfellow at Harrow from

1801 to 1805. He paid £94,500 in November 1817, shortly after his marriage in London to Louisa in 1816 [28] . Louisa thus spent virtually the whole of her 43 years of married life at Newstead. Thomas Wildman was one of the four 'chief mourners' at Lord Byron's funeral in 1824 [Sutton 1852 384-5]. After his purchase of Newstead he lost no time in becoming, for 40 years, an outstanding Nottingham personality.

Wildman spent large sums on restoring and improving Newstead Abbey in keeping with 'the Byron tradition', and, although his work there was criticised by some for 'earlying-up' it received approval from many for its integrity and taste. It is to Wildman and his architect John Shaw (1776-1832) that we owe the survival of the Abbey in its present form [29] . Lord Byron's attachment to Newstead was emotional, even sentimental, for he lived there very little. He moved to Newstead from Cambridge in 1808, aged 20, and passed over the residential part of the Abbey in the following year to his mother, who had been living at Burgage Manor, Southwell. Byron married in 1815 and left England in 1816, never to return alive. He died on 19 April 1824, and was buried at Hucknall on 16 July 1824 after his embalmed body had been put on view at The Black Moor's Head, Pelham Street, Nottingham. Wildman, on the other hand, 'had the good fortune to enjoy his outlay for 42 years until his death in 1859'. In 1861 the estate was bought from his executors by William Frederick Webb, an eminent traveller and 'sportsman' and a personal friend of both H.M.Stanley and David Livingstone, who wrote perhaps his most important book, 'The Zambesi and its tributaries' while staying at Newstead for some months in 1864-65. W.F.Webb's grandson, C.I.Fraser, sold Newstead in 1931 to Sir Julian Cahn, who presented it to the City of Nottingham on 16 July 1931 (see Chapter XII: Redcourt).

Colonel Wildman, whose portrait is reproduced by Coupe [1991 51] was soon widely admired and respected in the Nottingham area, despite the discreditable story of how his immediate forebears came by the means and property which provided £94,500 for the purchase of Newstead, and a further £100,000 for its rehabilitation. High Sheriff in 1821, a county magistrate, and Deputy Lieutenant for Nottinghamshire, he became a lion and leader of Nottingham society, and remained in the public eye until well after the middle of the century, as may be deduced from his activities as recorded in Sutton's 'Nottingham Date Book', especially pages 372 to 386. 'The Little Colonel' was a courteous man, popular as an after-dinner speaker and as chairman and speaker at public meetings, political or charitable. He was also prominent in local military affairs and in 1829 he replaced the Duke of Newcastle as Commandant of the Sherwood Rangers (Yeomanry) formed in 1819-20 [Fellows 1895 31-32], but later resigned for political reasons. He was called to the burning of Nottingham Castle in the Reform Bill riots of October 1831, but as a county magistrate and not as a military man.

In politics Wildman was a radical, supported by his close friend the Duke of Sussex, and was active in the Liberal cause. After nominating a 'Reform' candidate for the elections of 5 May 1831 he was the chief speaker at an 'immense' public meeting in Nottingham Market Place in May 1832 to protest against opposition to the reform of Parliament. On 13 September 1833 Wildman presided over a 'grand Masonic festival' at the Exchange Hall, supported on his right by H.R.H. the Duke of Sussex and Lord Rancliffe, and on his left by Lord Churchill and the Mayor, John Heard' [Sutton 1852 442]. One of his major social assets was his personal friendship with the Duke of Sussex (brother of King William IV) to whom he was equerry, and who often stayed at Newstead and was introduced to Nottingham life by his host. Wildman named Sussex tower which he built at Newstead after him.

Colonel Wildman was not himself connected with the University campus, but Louisa Wildman was also well-known in local society, and may be supposed to have enjoyed many of her husband's social connections which must have influenced her move to Lenton Hall after his death. The Wildmans enjoyed the prestige and influence that would make the Colonel's widow a tenant very acceptable to Lord Middleton [30] . There was a persistent rumour, now thought unlikely to be true, that Louisa and her sister Caroline Preisig were illegitimate daughters of the Duke of Sussex, possibly because of the combination of the following facts, taken in association with the Duke's long and close association with Thomas Wildman.

Louisa, born in 1802, was only 14 years old at the time of her marriage in 1816. She and her younger sister Caroline were both born in London. Family tradition has it that Thomas first met Louisa in Spain, presumably in 1813-14 when she would have been 11 or 12, and it is not known why Preisig should then have been in Spain. A visitor to Newstead in 1851, looking at a miniature of Louisa, was told by her 'That was painted of me at seventeen when I had been a wife two years'. A lady visitor to Newstead of about 1820 [Grant 1988 178] wrote '...Colonel Wildman was not settled there, it was undergoing repairs, having just been bought from Lord Byron. ... Colonel Wildman was a West Indian and very rich. He had made one of those queer marriages some queer men make - educated a child for his wife. She turned out neither pretty nor clever, but she satisfied him and was well-liked'. The marriage was childless. Caroline Preisig, who never married, went to live with Thomas and Louisa at Newstead, and half a century later with Louisa at Lenton Hall. She evidently outlived her sister, for the Nottingham Borough Records for 1880 record the presentation to the Castle Museum by her of the sword worn by Colonel Wildman when he was High Sheriff. The Borough Records for 6 July 1896 refer to gifts to the museum of local portraits, including those of the late Colonel Wildman of Newstead Abbey and of Mrs. Wildman.

Although Louis Baillon lived at Lenton Hall in the later 1860s according to Lawson Lowe [1871] - and as an immediate neighbour and contemporary he should have known - Baillon's status is not clear, whether guest, joint occupier or sole occupier, and the actual date of Louisa Wildman's departure is not known, though it was certainly not 1860, when according to Coupe [1991] 'she left Nottinghamshire and went south to Hove where she died in 1877'. Documentary evidence (see Table 17) shows her to have been tenant of the Lenton Hall estate at least as late as 1866, but she may have held a fixed term lease and let to Baillon after she had left. A very prosperous merchant, Baillon was the French vice-consul at Nottingham. He had followed William Cartledge in residence at Woodthorpe Hall, where he employed five servants including a coachman. Fry [1989] includes a photograph of Baillon, but little else is known about him. His residence at Lenton Hall must have been brief.

Lenton Hall park in the 1860s

Lord Middleton's estate in Lenton was surveyed in 1863, probably with a view to its valuation and sale. The resulting map [31] shows the character and use of the park during the tenancy of Louisa Wildman. It contained a consolidated 115½ acres, bounded by Cut Through Lane, Lenton Firs land, Derby Road, and the Lenton House estate. Except for Lenton Hall Field of about 3 acres - the old 1838 quarry floor on free-draining Lenton Sandstone with a high water table - which was cropped (as it was a century later), and several small copses and the gardens and orchard of the Hall, the whole area was described as parkland. The orchard, on stronger soils south of the Clifton fault along the boundary with Lenton House lands down to Beeston Lane, probably supplied the Hall. The orchard south-west of the Hall, in which the house called The Orchard was built in 1904, did not then exist. One unbroken tract of parkland of about 66 acres occupied the entire slope from Beeston Lane eastwards (now often called 'the downland') and across Lenton Hall Drive to beyond the site of Cripps Hall, and appears to have been divided from a further 17½ acres extending down to Cut Through Lane. It formed a striking contrast with Lenton Abbey, which was all arable farm land except for 'The Lawn' and paddocks immediately around the house, farmstead and garden. Lenton Firs, too, was different, with its smaller lawn, and beyond it grass fields. This is not to say that Lenton Hall park was agriculturally unproductive, for the presence of a farm house and buildings, and the employment of resident farm workers in 1851 and 1871 suggest that both cattle and sheep as well as horses grazed the parkland, while Lenton Hall Field produced fodder crops as it did until it was obliterated by dumping in 1959-60.

During the second half of the 18th century the establishment of farm holdings on the Milward estate had been associated with subdivision of the Abbey Fields, a process reversed by the 19th century development of Lenton Hall park. In 1823 Samuel Brownlow of Lenton, aged 77, recalling pre-turnpike days, said: 'The Abbey Fields were larger formerly than they are now, but have since been divided into less inclosures', and Thomas Stevenson, who farmed much of the land from 1775 until Lady Day 1799 remarked that 'since the defendant [John Wright] bought the land he has thrown the closes together into one' [32]. By 1863 the plantings of the early part of the century were coming to maturity. Little is known in detail about the landscaping of the park, except from its results, and the incorporation of the old marl quarry into the gardens, and the planting of a variety of tree species there would be of particular interest. Various exotic species were used in the gardens, but the beech was especially favoured, with some sweet chestnut (*Castanea sativa*) and these are seen in John Wright's plantings inside his ha ha wall, alongside Derby Road near Derby Hall, and in several copses in the park.

Of the tree formations that existed before the park was formed little now remains. The double row of elms bordering that part of the Sawley turnpike abandoned in about 1805, and prominent on the estate map of 1863, on 19th century Ordnance Survey maps, and on Sanderson's 2-inch to the mile map of 1835 (conventionally by a single line of tree symbols) existed in fragmentary form until recent times (Figure 90) but the last remnants succumbed to Dutch elm disease in the 1970s. The oak trees bordering Derby Road on both sides in the early 19th century, many well over 100 years old then, have also largely gone, though some still survived in 1863, among other trees planted by John Wright on the narrow strip taken in from the turnpike despite his undertaking in 1809 not to do so [33] (see Chapter XIII).

It is most likely that land sales were already in mind when the survey of 1863 was made. Wollaton Hall was no longer a favourite residence of the Middletons, and was leased in 1867 to Henry Akroyd; and the sale in 1867-69 of the Middleton property included in the present University campus had for some time been delayed only by legal impediments. Lenton Abbey and Lenton Firs, as will be shown later, were sold to wealthy sitting tenants, but the Lenton Hall estate was a more complicated matter, and Lord Middleton and his advisers were considering alternative plans for its disposal well before its sale. Among the Middleton papers is an undated bundle which includes a document suggesting that 50 acres should be cut off from Lenton Hall park to provide building plots, and since the plans attached to the sale particulars of 1867-68 were identical to the survey of 1863 it is probable that the sale and breakup of the estate was under consideration soon after 1860 at the latest [34].

The sales particulars of 1867-68 [35] related to the estates of Lenton Hall, Lenton Firs, Lenton Abbey and Beeston Fields. The sale was to be by auction by Messrs. Pott and Neale of Wheeler Gate, Nottingham and London on 5 June (presumed 1867) at the George Hotel, Nottingham, but Lenton Hall was not legally sold until 1869, the required disclaimer being dated 1 March 1869 [36]. The particulars for Lenton Hall included a lithograph of the Hall (Figure 51) viewed from a point opposite to the entrance to the Hallward Library (the favourite point for photographs of the Hall), showing the large conservatory north-east of the main house. The extensive ancillary buildings further north-east are not seen. They included a large coach and stable block approximately on the site of the present dining hall and kitchen of Hugh Stewart Hall, and are displayed on the 1:500 O.S.map of 1881 (Figure 52). The sale description commended a 'first class mansion', with 'bedrooms in great number', airy and pleasant; out-offices ample and convenient; stabling, carriage houses, farm buildings, compact and well arranged; walled kitchen garden, well stocked with choice fruit trees, etc.. There were vineries of most productive character, extensive conservatories, orchard houses and forcing

LENTON HALL, NEAR NOTTINGHAM.

SOUTH EAST VIEW

Figure 51: Lenton Hall in about 1868 viewed from the south
[From sale brochure of Middleton estate in Lenton.]

pits on approved principles; beautiful pleasure grounds and well planted plantations. Details of the sales of 1867-69 are given in Table 16.

The return of the Wrights to Lenton Hall

The purchaser of the Lenton Hall estate in 1869 was apparently Henry Smith Wright, (1839-1910) of the Mapperley branch of the Wright family, a partner in the family banking firm of I. and C.Wright, although it is questioned below whether the purchase was by Henry on his own account or for the bank. The transaction brought the Hall and the surrounding land back into Wright hands after a break of 24 years, at a cost of £23,000 [37]. The relationship of Henry to Francis Wright, who had sold the estate in 1845, through their common descent from Ichabod Wright (1700-1777), grandfather of John Wright who built the Hall, has been explained above (see Figure 47).

The scholarship of Henry's father, Ichabod Charles Wright (1795-1871) is discussed in Appendix 22. Henry Smith Wright, president of the Nottingham Literary Club in 1891, was himself a translater of classical writers, notably Virgil. He was Conservative M.P. for Nottingham South for nine years from 1886 - after he had left Lenton. He was first married to Mary, only daughter and heiress of William Cartledge of Woodthorpe Hall (who was succeeded there by Louis Baillon - see above) and they had an only daughter, Edith Mary. Mary died in 1866, and Henry married as his second wife his cousin Josephine Henrietta, daughter of the Rev. Adolphus Wright, rector of Ickham, Kent, and moved to Lenton Hall. There they had a son and two daughters who both died in infancy, Alice Josephine on 25 May 1871 and Caroline Henrietta on 24 February 1873, commemorated on a slab near the end of the chancel of Lenton church.

Figure 52: Lenton Hall in 1881: the house, garden and farm
[Reduced from O.S. 1:500 map, Nottingham sheet XLII5.2 (1881)] Note lines of open view from the Hall over the 'downland' and to Wollaton Park, and south-westwards over the Trent vale.

Table 16.
Some details of the sale of Lord Middleton's estate in Lenton in 1867-69

Property	Tenant in 1866	Lot	Area	Purchase price	Purchaser
Lenton Firs	Thomas Adams (a)	4	19a.1.15	£ 6,500 (1)	Thomas Adams
Lenton Abbey & tan yard	Thomas Bayley	2	68a.0.39	9,000 (1)	Thomas Bayley Bayley paid twice as much for land in Beeston
Lenton Hall	Louisa Wildman	1	115a.7.09	23,000 (2)	Henry Smith Wright
Lenton Fields land (b)	Henry Hadden	3	14a.2.17	2,000 (2)	J.H.Lee. Lee paid £ 2,100 of which Bayley kept £ 100.
Lenton Eaves		5		441 (1)	Benjamin Walker
Lenton tannery			1a.1.33	2,100	Thomas Bayley

(a) Held under lease for 14 years from 25 March 1862
(b) Lenton Fields, 'formerly arable, now [1869] pasture and meadow. Set limitation on building. Included 1r.18p. of woodland. Conveyance to Lee 21 October 1869 with Thomas Bayley involved. Indenture enrolled 9 March 1869.
(1) Sold under disclaimer of 1867.
(2) Sold under disclaimer of 1 March 1869.

Total area of Lenton parish in Wollaton Park 201a.0.34, valued at £377.16s. per annum.

Data mainly from UNMD, Mi 3 G10, G11 and G12.

The Census Enumerators' Books for 1871 [38] give details of Henry Smith Wright's household at Lenton Hall (Table 17). Henry, then 31, and his 22-year-old wife Josephine Henrietta, with Edith Mary (4) and Josephine Henrietta's children Henry Adolphus (1) and Alice Josephine (1 month) were attended by ten servants resident at the Hall, ranging from the housekeeper Sarah Brown, a 46-year old widow, and John Brown the butler, to Walter Tom Brown aged 11, 'page-boy'. There was also a nurse and a nursery maid. The nearby farm house was occupied by John Fowle the farm bailiff and his family, while two cottages were occupied by gardeners Isaac Smith with his wife and young daughter, and Alfred Mabbott with his daughter. The 'newly built' Lodge (until recently called the West Lodge and part of Wortley Hall) was the home of the coachman Henry Tyers and his wife and adult son [39].

Henry Smith Wright lived until 1910, when he was aged 71, but he was at Lenton Hall for only a few years, probably to 1878, when he 'sold' Lenton Hall and part of the surrounding park to his younger brother, Frederick Wright. Henry took the place of Thomas Adams of Lenton Firs as churchwarden in 1873 but retained the position only until 1875, although Kelly's Post Office Directory recorded him at Lenton Hall in 1876, as did Morris's Directory in 1877, and the conveyance of the Hall [Rotheras] is dated 12 November 1878. Fred Wright was a member of the family bank like Henry. He moved to Lenton Hall after living for many years at Radcliffe-on-Trent. In 1881 the census recorded him in residence at Lenton Hall with his wife, Ada Joyce, their daughters Emily Theodosia (17), Florence Ada (12) and Margaret J. (4), and an eight-year-old son [40] (Table 18). There were also George Wright, a younger brother of Frederick, a student of Theology at Trinity College, Cambridge though 35 years of age; Anne

Table 17.
Household at Lenton Hall in 1871

Name	Age	Position in family: occupation	Place of birth
Henry Smith WRIGHT	31	Head, owner: banker and landowner	Quorndon, Derbys
Josephine Henrietta WRIGHT	22	Wife	Ickham, Kent
Edith Mary Smith WRIGHT	4	Daughter	Woodthorpe,Nottm
Henry Adolphus WRIGHT	1	Son	Lenton Hall
Alice Josephine Smith WRIGHT	1 month	Daughter [died 25 May 1871]	Lenton Hall
John BROWN	41	Butler: married	Beeston, Notts.
Sarah BROWN	46	Wife. Housekeeper	Clifton, Notts.
Jane Emma GUY	26	Unmarried. Lady's maid	Woburn, Beds.
Agnes BOYCE	31	do. Nurse	Langham, Norfolk
Kezia Louisa MARTIN	25	do. Housemaid	Derby
Hannah WIDDOWSON	18	do. Kitchen maid	Derby
Mary FLETCHER	17	do. Nursery maid	Thurgarton, Notts
Walter Tom BROWN	11	Page. [Son of butler ?]	Clifton, Notts.
Thomas William RISE	17	Unmarried. Stable boy	Derby
Joseph SPURR	16	do. Garden boy	Sherwood, Nottm.
Cottage on Lenton Hall estate			
Isaac SMITH	36	Married. Gardener	Langar, Notts.
Jane SMITH	35	Wife	Woolsthorpe Lincs
Elizabeth Ann SMITH	5	Daughter	Woolsthorpe Lincs
Another cottage			
John FOWLE	51	Farm bailiff	Wollaton, Notts.
Ann FOWLE	54	Wife	Ranskill, Notts.
Susan FOWLE	27	Daughter. Lace folder	Sherwood, Nottm.
Henry FOWLE	21	Son unmarried. Railway porter	Sherwood, Nottm.
George CASS	4	Grandson	Nottingham
Another cottage			
Alfred MABBOTT	54	Widower. Gardener	Radcliffe on Trent
Martha MABBOTT	33	Daughter unmarried	Radcliffe on Trent
Lodge to Lenton Hall			
Henry TYERS	52	Coachman	Rempstone
Hannah TYERS	54	Wife	Whatton
Henry TYERS	25	Son unmarried. Bookkeeper	Leicester

Data from Enumerators' Books of the 1871 census.

Wright, Frederick's sister-in-law (possibly the wife of William Howard Wright) [41] ; and a neice, Frances Cropper. The full domestic staff comprised six women and four men as well as a governess from Aschaffenburg, Bavaria. In the 'farmhouses' near the Hall (one of them earlier called a cottage) lived John Fowle, shepherd (described as farm bailiff in 1871) with his wife and grandson, and assistant gardener Alfred Mabbott with his daughter Martha, a laundress, both remaining from the time of Henry Smith Wright. The gardener Nathan Pownall lived with his wife Elizabeth and two sons, one of them a 'Fine Art dealer's apprentice', in a gardener's cottage, and the coachman, William Price and his wife Jane, a dressmaker, occupied Lenton Hall Lodge at the end of the drive.

Table 18.
Household at Lenton Hall in 1881

Name	Age	Position in family: occupation	Place of birth
Frederick WRIGHT	40	Head. Banker and farmer of 100 acres, employing 3 men and boy	Quorndon,Derbys
Ada Joyce WRIGHT	39	Wife	West Leake Notts
Emily Theodosia WRIGHT	17	Daughter scholar	Radcliffe, Notts
Florence Ada WRIGHT	12	Daughter scholar	do.
D. WRIGHT	8	Son scholar	do.
Margaret J. WRIGHT	4	Daughter	do.
George H. WRIGHT	35	Brother of Fred. married. Undergraduate student of Theology at Trinity College, Cambridge	Bramcote, Notts
Anne F. WRIGHT	39	Sister-in-law of Fred. Married	Horbling, Lincs
Frances M. CROPPER	17	Neice of Fred. Scholar	Thornton Fields
Ann SHEPHERD	35	Cook unmarried	Kneeton, Notts
Jane LOVETT	43	Lady's maid do.	Kegworth, Leics.
Emma BUDD	32	Nurse do.	Arkent, Yorks.
Mary HOBBILL	21	Housemaid do.	Ockbrook,Derbys
Mary I. CROSS	18	Under-housemaid do.	Willington, do.
Betsy MORLEY	18	Kitchen maid do.	Thoroton, Notts
Robert EDWARDS	63	Butler married	Duffield, Derby
Frank COOPER	21	Footman unmarried	Hinckley, Leics
Frank WHITWORTH	18	Groom do.	Radcliffe
John PICK	17	Farm servant do.	Eaton, Leics.
Clara SCHUSSLER	44	Governess do.	Aschaffenburg
Farmhouse, Lenton Hall			
John FOWLE,	60	Shepherd married	Wollaton, Notts
Ann FOWLE	65	Wife	Ranskill, Notts
George CASS	13	Grandson scholar	Nottingham
Cottage, Lenton Hall			
Alfred MABBOTT	64	Widower Assistant gardener	Radcliffe Notts
Martha MABBOTT	42	Daughter Laundress unmarried	Radcliffe
Gardens, Lenton Hall (cottage)			
Nathan Hyde POWNALL	49	Gardener married	Disley, Chesh.
Elizabeth POWNALL	53	Wife	Shrewsbury
John POWNALL	16	Son: Stone mason's apprentice	Radcliffe
George POWNALL	14	Son: Fine Art dealer's apprentice	do.
Lenton Hall Lodge			
William PRICE	31	Coachman married	
Jane A. PRICE	35	Wife Dressmaker.	

Data from Census Enumerators' Books RG 11/3340 p. 2

Thus in 1881, the year of publication of the O.S. 1:500 map [42] which depicts the Hall and grounds in considerable detail (Figure 52) Lenton Hall housed the menage of a typical well-to-do Victorian middle class family numbering over 30 people. Fred Wright, J.P., then 40 years old, was described as a banker and farmer of 100 acres (presumably the park) employing as a farmer three men and a boy. These workers would be gardeners Nathan Pownall and Alfred Mabbott and the shepherd John Fowle (replaced in the 1890s by Richard Butler, called farm bailiff) together with 17-year-old John Pick, a 'farm servant' living in the Hall. But Lenton Hall park was obviously not a normal commercial farm. The park would be grazed by draught (including coach) horses and riding horses, and the sheep attended by John Fowle would function as 'lawnmowers', but there is now no indication of dairying or of field cropping although there may have been seasonal grazing by cattle, particularly on the land retained by Henry Smith Wright.

The interests of Fred Wright outside his business and family and Holy Trinity church are not well known. Although not sharing Henry's intellectual pursuits he succeeded him as Treasurer of the Mechanics Institution, and retained the office for many years after 1879 [Green 1887]. Perhaps both elections owed something to family tradition, for their father Ichabod Charles Wright was a vice-president in the 1840s and their brother Charles Ichabod Wright followed in 1874-78.

The breakup of the Lenton Hall estate, 1878-1905

The sale of the Dunkirk farms by John Osmaston has been discussed earlier in this chapter, and at about the same time the dismemberment of Lenton Hall park began. In 1878 Frederick Wright 'bought' from his brother Henry only part of the parkland surrounding Lenton Hall and its gardens (Figure 53). Although this included a corridor to Derby Road in the form of Lenton Hall Drive on the ridgetop, and another at the turnpike tollgate alongside the present Lenton Hurst, it is immediately apparent from Figure 53 that Henry Smith Wright was retaining

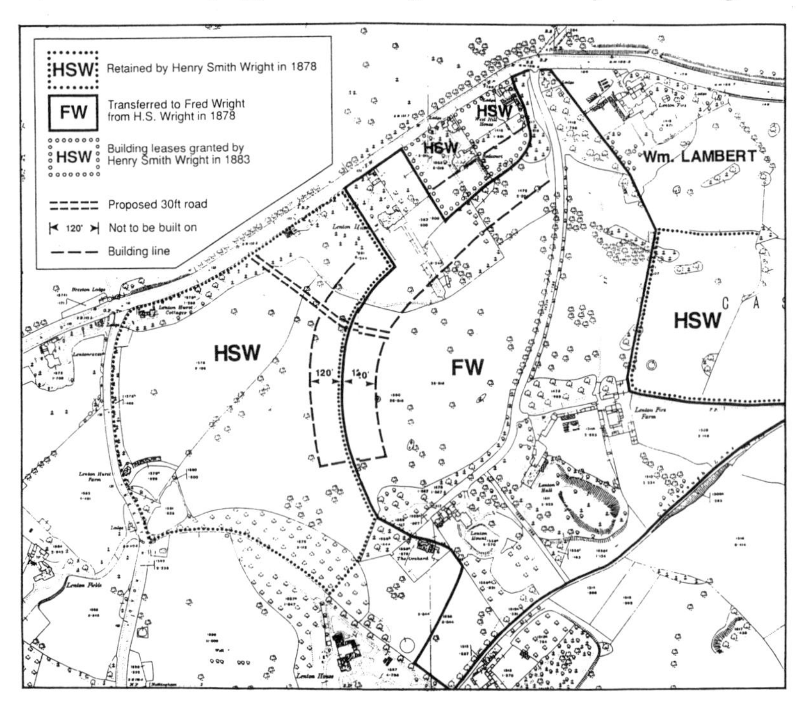

Figure 53: The partitioning of Lenton Hall park, 1878
[Courtesy of Messrs. Rotheras. Base map reduced from the 1915 O.S. 25-inch map]

in his name nearly all the public road frontage with the clear intention of selling or leasing building plots. A 30-feet wide road was also planned, with a sewer. On 12 November 1878 Henry covenanted in respect of the parts of the park retained in his name to observe a restriction on building nearer than 40 yards from the boundary between the two properties created (Figure 53) and it was probably this covenant that subsequently protected the park from extensive building development other than the two large houses alongside Derby Road - West Hill House and Redcourt. However, Henry Smith Wright retained possession until the turn of the century of the western part of the 'downland' and the Beeston Lane frontage, as well as of a tract of land running down to Cut Through Lane along the Lenton Firs boundary, and he evidently envisaged the potential of these other areas for building development. The conveyance of 1878 and the plan and restricting covenant are held by Messrs. Rotheras, the University's solicitors.

J.T.Godfrey [1884 202] commented that 'a portion of the park surrounding the mansion has been leased in detached lots, and is now being built over'. The lessor was, of course, Henry Smith Wright, who will almost certainly have had in mind the partitioning of the park and building on it even before his own purchase of the estate in 1869. In June 1866 Lord Middleton was advised that 'Mr.Moore thinks that Lenton Hall with 50 acres or so of land judiciously selected would sell well, and that the remainder of the estate with the adjg property could be sold in building plots without interfering at all with the value of Wollaton Park. A similar exchange would be necessary as in the case of the other estates mentioned above before this property could be disentailed and sold' [43] . A decade later Henry Smith Wright was putting these Middleton suggestions into effect.

Godfrey's reference to building alongside Derby Road in 1884 related to West Hill House (later called The Cedars , subsequently occupied by Paton College and now, as Paton House, by the University's Institute of Planning Studies) and to Redcourt (later occupied by the University's Institute of Education and now part of Lenton and Wortley Hall of Residence). The history of these two houses is discussed in Chapter XII. The boundaries of their large gardens, and the location of the buildings conform to the conditions agreed in 1878, and the paddocks behind them, still distinguishable, also reflect the arrangements outlined in Figure 53, though they were purchased freehold in 1903. Further west along Derby Road Lenton Eaves had been built already in 1875, but Lenton Hurst was not to appear until the close of the century.

Frederick Wright lived at Lenton Hall until 1903, when the whole estate was sold and he 'removed from Lenton', where he had done 'much useful work' [Mellors 1912 19]. Although it probably had a different cause, discussed below, his move probably marked his retirement from his business appointments, which included the joint local directorship (with Charles Bingham Wright) of the Capital and Counties Bank Limited of Carlton Street, the successor of Wrights Bank from 1898; Treasurer of Nottingham Savings Bank [Allen 1895]; and a directorship of the Employers' Indemnity Company Limited of St. Peter's Gate. His later home was 'The Forest', Nottingham [Deacon 1908 398] and he died on 4 September 1916, aged 76. A mural tablet to his memory in Lenton parish church, describing him as 'late of Lenton Hall', records that he was churchwarden of the parish for 26 years. The same tablet commemorates his wife, Ada Joyce, who died on 29 November 1920 aged 78, and a second tablet honours the memory of their daughter Hilda Dorothy Price, who died aged 32 after an operation on 21 November 1913 at Karachi. Meanwhile Henry Smith Wright, with an address at 4, Chelsea Embankment in 1900, made his home at Averley Towers, Farnham, Surrey, where he died in 1910. He had disposed of the remainder of his property in the former Lenton Hall park to William Goodacre Player and Thomas Shipstone. The various conveyances relating to this and other sales of land that followed were recited in what amounts to an abstract of title of W.G.Player when he was selling Lenton Hurst Farm and Lenton Hurst house to Sir Thomas Shipstone in January 1930.

On 6 September 1898 Frederick Wright sold to W.G.Player the plot upon which Lenton

Hurst was built, together with land behind the house which became the formal garden, and further land behind the garden of Redcourt. Lenton Hurst was first mentioned in Wright's Directory for 1900, having been built in 1898-99. Player also bought land from Henry Smith Wright in 1900, probably for a westward extension of the garden; but his largest purchase from H.S.Wright was that of 18 February 1903, when about 28 acres extending to Beeston Lane and to the top of the 'downland' were conveyed to form Lenton Hurst Farm. In July of the same year a further conveyance involved Albert Ball as well as both the Wright brothers, and related to land south-west of Lenton Hall, involving agreements concerning restrictions on the nature of future development. The deed of 1903 released W.G.Player from any legal commitment vis-a-vis the proposal of 1878 which had been incorporated in earlier deeds, to build a 30-foot wide road between Lenton Hurst and Lenton Hall.

Albert Ball (later Sir Albert, Mayor of Nottingham and father of the well-known airman V.C. of the first world war) was involved in the sale of Lenton Hall and parts of the park, probably as selling agent on behalf of Fred Wright. Alderman Ball (1883-1946) was always described as a 'land and estate agent', but he also had other business interests, for example as one of the three directors of W.Cooke and Company, bleachers, and chairman of Nottingham Grand Theatre and Estate Limited [Allen 1907]. At the time of the Lenton Hall sale he lived on Sherwood Road, Lenton, but later moved to 43 Lenton Road, The Park, with his business address at 9 Cheapside, Nottingham [Wright 1910: Kelly 1916], and in 1917 was at Sedgley House, The Park. Covenants made between various purchasers on 15 July 1903 indicate that this was the date of most of the Lenton Hall transactions although there were others in 1904 [44]. In addition to more garden land sold to W.G.Player, Ball sold land near to Lenton Hall to the builders of Lenton Mount (now the University Club), and The Orchard, W.S.Hemsley and A.T.Richards respectively. Members of the University will know that the surviving trees of a Lenton Hall orchard dating from about 1890, from which The Orchard derived its name, are still productive, and in autumn shed fruit, especially pears, on to the extended Lenton Hall Drive from both sides.

The enforced sale of Mapperley and Lenton Hall estates in 1903-04

The sale of Lenton estate land by Fred Wright has been detailed above; but it is by no means certain that this is a full and true representation of the course of events. In the first place it may be questioned why Frederick Wright, after living there for over 20 years, should decide to sell his palatial home and estate in 1903 with every sign of urgency, and apparently below its real value. The Lenton sales coincided in time with the sale of Mapperley Hall and the Mapperley Park estate, and though not parts of the same transaction they may have had a common cause. Both took place as a sequel to the absorption of the bank of I. and C.Wright into the Capital and Counties Bank in 1898. Although Ichabod Charles Wright, the eldest son of Ichabod Wright, remained at Mapperley Hall for some time after the death of his father, and is said to have granted the lease of the Hall and part of the land to Edward Manlove in 1869, the transfer of the same lease to William Lambert in 1877 was not made solely by his eldest son Charles Ichabod Wright, for his younger brothers, Henry Smith Wright, then of Lenton Hall, and Frederick Wright, then of Radcliffe-on-Trent were co-leasers. It is not known, in fact, whether Mapperley Hall was owned privately by the Wrights or by their joint business, Wrights' Bank, though Charles Bingham Wright was living there in 1900, his father, Colonel Charles Ichabod Wright having his home at Radcliffe Hall and Watcombe Park, Torquay, and Henry Smith Wright having moved to Surrey twenty years earlier. Equally, it seems possible that Lenton Hall was bank property, and not owned individually by Fred Wright.

The Mapperley auction of 20 March 1903 was forced upon the Wrights by a judgment of the High Court. In June 1898 Capital and Counties Bank paid £110,000 for Wrights' bank premises on Carlton Street and the goodwill, the takeover of the customers' accounts and for local directorships, and a further £97,747 for the bank's investment portfolio. Frederick Wright of Lenton Hall and Charles Bingham Wright of Mapperley Hall were appointed local directors. But at the end of October 1902 Capital and Counties brought an action against Colonel Charles Ichabod Wright, Frederick Wright, Charles Bingham Wright and John William Davey, 'retired bankers', and Nevill Wright and Francis John Carter, solicitor of Torquay, which was heard by Mr. Justice Joyce in the Chancery Division. The bank sought a declaration that it was entitled to a lien on money due under arrangements for the purchase of Wrights' Bank four years earlier from the four partners. They also asked for 'the realization and sale of the former bank's remaining unsold assets', and his lordship ordered a sale and realization without prejudice. In respect of two other actions the judge directed, on 10 November 1902, a sale by the court of certain securities given by Charles Ichabod and Charles Bingham Wright on the Mapperley and Basford estates the Mapperley Park estate as detailed in indentures of 8 February 1873 and 15 May 1900, the second of which designated Charles Ichabod Wright, N. Wright and F.J.Carter as trustees.

The sale of Mapperley Park estate by Morris and Place on 20 March 1903 created tremendous local interest, mainly because it included with Mapperley Hall some 130 acres with frontages on Mansfield Road, Woodborough Road and Lucknow Drive, prospectively very valuable building sites, the subsequent development of which has been described in some detail by K. Brand [1986-87]. The buyer, for what was regarded as the knock-down price of £74,000 was S.P.Derbyshire of Derbyshire Brothers, Chartered Accountants, acting for a syndicate. While evidence that the Lenton Hall estate of Fred Wright was subject to a similar order cannot be cited, it must be deduced that its sale, mainly in July 1903, but handled in a different way, was closely linked to the Mapperley sale of four months earlier because of the ramifications of the interconnected business and private interests of the Mapperley Wrights. The sale by Henry Smith Wright to W.G.Player of the land that became Lenton Hurst Farm on 18 February 1903, soon after the judgment and one month before the Mapperley auction, may well have been associated too. The sales had wide consequences. Thomas Shipstone probably bought Lenton Firs in 1903 because of the availability of Lenton Hall park land held by both Frederick and Henry Smith Wright: and the purchase of Lenton Firs led to the removal of William Lambert (earlier resident at Mapperley Hall) from Lenton Firs to Redcourt, where he spent the last two years of his life (see Chapter IX).

Soon after its sale at auction Mapperley Hall was purchased by the Corporation to be equipped and opened as a Hall of Residence for male students of the University College's School of Education founded in 1890 with 26-year-old Amos Henderson as its head. The versatile Henderson, much involved in student affairs, teacher of mathematics and geography, College Director of Music and Professor of Education from 1906 when the Hall opened, became the first Warden of Mapperley Hall [Tolley 1990]. Confirming the Hall's association with teacher training Henderson was succeeded as Warden by H.A.S.Wortley, also to become Professor of Education and then the last Principal of the University College, following Hugh Stewart. Further discussion of Mapperley Hall may be found in Appendix 22.

The sale of Lenton Hall park in 1903-04 led to the building of only two new houses. An agreement dated 15 November 1904, under which Alfred Thomas Richards of the Imperial Laundry, Radford Boulevard was allowed to take a pipe from the house he was building across land owned by W.G.Player to Cut Through Lane shows that The Orchard could not have been occupied before early 1905. The land in question was the eastern part of the site of the present Education building, and it had been sold to Player by Albert Ball earlier in the year. Lenton Hall Drive was extended beyond the Hall to serve Lenton Mount and The Orchard, and a grassy drive, now widened as Library Road, was made from it to Cut Through Lane, leaving the south-west corner of Lenton Hall garden within the boundary of Lenton Mount. The remains of the Hall's original ha-ha wall can still be seen there, separating the mature beech trees on the

Lenton Hall side of it from the newer plantings, mainly evergreens, on the Lenton Mount side. Land was also sold freehold to S.H.Sands of West Hill House (the house itself being built on land held as leasehold from Henry Smith Wright) to extend his garden. The most important land sale, however, was to Thomas Shipstone, who had just acquired the Lenton Firs estate, and who purchased not only the greater part of the land sold by Frederick Wright, which included Lenton Hall Farm (to become Lenton Firs Farm) but also the land running down to Cut Through Lane which had been retained by Henry Smith Wright in 1878. Shipstone later added to this, in 1930, the Lenton Hurst estate to consolidate in his ownership a large part of the northern half of the University campus.

The land transactions of 1903-04, though hedged about by various restrictive covenants legally controlling the type of permissible future development, were clearly designed to take maximum possible advantage of the development value of the Lenton Hall estate at that time. But bereft of its park and its farm, and left with only a seven-acre garden, the Hall itself, though attractive enough, had become a distinctly unattractive economic proposition for a private owner, being too large and too old, bearing in mind that there was no extensive landed estate to support its upkeep. Lenton Hall had no fewer than six different owners in the twenty years from 1904 to 1924.

The subsequent history of most of the 19th century park is pursued in later chapters in connection with the houses of its new owners, but perhaps it should be mentioned here that some of the persons said to be purchasers in 1903 were evidently mortgagees who had advanced part of the purchase price of the land or the houses associated with it [45]. They included Henry Wilkins Roberts of 38 Bridgford Road (of H.W.Roberts, merchants of Stanford Street); Edwin Marshall of 7 Gregory Street, Lenton, a timber merchant; George Mather of Park Ravine, The Park (partner in Bauman Ludewig and Co., merchants and shipping agents of Pilcher Gate); and William Lewin [46] - all businessmen likely to have capital to loan.

Owners of Lenton Hall after Frederick Wright

Lenton Hall with its garden was finally purchased on 28 November 1904 by George Cresswell Bond, M.I.C.E., a civil and mining engineer of Mann's Chambers, Park Street, Nottingham. Before buying Lenton Hall he was living at Aspley House, 236 Alfreton Road, and he later moved to 12 Regent Street, Nottingham. He was born in 1862, a son of Richard Banks Bond, and was a large property and minerals owner in Oxfordshire, Warwickshire and Northamptonshire, and a Freeman and Member of the Livery of the City of London. He may have been a seeker of grandeur - he was granted Arms giving Lenton Hall as his address [47] - but also seems to have been an astute businessman. In 1904 he paid only £4,000 for Lenton Hall and gardens, and on this sum had a mortgage debt of £3,500 when he sold it less than three years later, in 1907, for £8,000, having spent a considerable sum on the building. Bond had a loan of £2,500 from a J.T.Brewster, who died in 1905, and his executors were involved in the sale of the Hall in 1907.

In 1905 Bond made two particular alterations to Lenton Hall. A projecting french window was installed in the dining room (the present Senior Common Room, and earlier the Hall library) 'adding a Wren-like touch to the architectural mixture'. It was as if this side of the house was being promoted at the expense of the north-west-facing facade, now screened by shrubs and trees. Secondly, the entrance hall, now part of the Warden's quarters, was reconstructed, and with its pseudo-Gothic pillars and arches, its quaint stucco figures and oriental minstrel gallery it was 'more reminiscent of Horace Walpole and Strawberry Hill than the Edwardian era', and was seemingly 'a fascinating attempt to recreate a period piece'. Bond's initials, with the date, may be seen above the french window in the S.C.R. [Neil 1980].

When Edward Powell purchased Lenton Hall on 6 July 1907 he paid £4,500 to G.C.Bond and £2,500 and £1,000 to his mortgagees. Powell's family home was Plas-y-bryn near

Newtown, Montgomeryshire, but he was living on Broadgate, Beeston because he was the chairman and managing director of Humber Limited, the motor car and cycle manufacturers of Beeston and Coventry. Humber had large works at Beeston at the corner formed by Humber Road with the present Queens Road (then called New Lane and Hassock Lane respectively) [48] . In 1908, the very next year, the Humber Company, although it originated at Nottingham, began to move its work completely to Coventry, with serious effects on the prosperity of Beeston. The company had been formed in 1887 by Thomas Humber, a moulder (a 'mechanic' according to Mellors [1916]) who lived at 65 Northumberland Street, Nottingham, where, in a blacksmith's shop behind his house and with the help of his wife he began to make 'velocipedes' in 1868 at a rate of one a week. 'The Boneshaker' was his development of the French velocipede of 1867, and the 'spider wheel' was a Humber improvement. By 1891 [Kelly 1891; Wright 1891] Thomas Humber was living on Broadgate, Beeston, but it is not known whether he was succeeded in the same house by Powell. When the company left Beeston it was employing between 1,400 and 1,500 workers there, and its departure meant moving about 3,000 people, with 600 houses falling vacant. The Humber factory was bought by Mr. A.W.Black, M.P., and became a lace factory. Other cycle works south-west of Beeston station, later purchased and greatly enlarged by the British L.M.Ericsson Manufacturing Company making telephone apparatus (now Plessey) were built by Messrs. Humber and Goddard, with railway access nearby.

Edward Powell sold Lenton Hall on 30 June 1911 to Charles Alfred Hingston for £5,100, with the aid of a £3,000 mortgage from Frederick Wadsworth of Nottingham, paid off in 1918. Hingston, a member of the firm of Gifford, Fox and Company, brown net manufacturers of High Pavement, Nottingham, moved to Lenton Hall from Cliff House, Radcliffe-on-Trent [Wright 1907] in 1911 [Kelly 1912] and was still in occupation in 1920 [Wright 1920]. On 7 July 1919 he sold land to W.S.Hemsley, the builder of Lenton Mount, probably to extend Hemsley's garden at the expense of his own.

By a conveyance dated 12 March 1921 (not seen by the writer, but said to include a plan delineating the property) Hingston sold Lenton Hall and its garden to none other than Sir Jesse Boot for £9,000, and went to live at Barton Lodge, Ruddington [Kelly 1922]. This transaction took place a few months before Sir Jesse, during that same summer, decided to offer the valley-side part of the Highfield estate as the site for new University buildings instead of the Trent-side land he had offered a year earlier (see Chapter XVI). Therefore the purchase appears to have had no connection with the College project, but may have been associated with his plans for a model industrial village on the Highfield estate - possibly as his own residence alongside it, his son John having bought the nearby Lenton House a year or so earlier. But Lady Boot having declined to leave her house in The Park it is perhaps surprising that Sir Jesse did not then envisage a role for Lenton Hall in the projected College scheme. After three years, when the new College building was already taking shape, Sir Jesse sold Lenton Hall, by a conveyance of 30 June 1924 to Helen Barnsdale for £9,136, probably the price he had paid for it plus sale costs.

Helen Barnsdale was the eldest daughter of Sir Frank Bowden, the founder and head of the Raleigh cycle company. Her brother, Sir Harold Bowden, lived at Beeston Fields before moving to Bestwood Lodge, Arnold. Helen was the wife of Major John Davison Barnsdale, who in early 1924 lived at 25, Lenton Road, The Park. His mother, Mary Barnsdale, had occupied The Orchard throughout the first world war from 1913 probably to 1919 (see Chapter XII) so that he would undoubtedly be familiar with Lenton Hall. He was the third son (of the ten children) of Oswald and Mary Barnsdale, who lived at Arnold and then Mapperley Park. They were cigar makers in Nottingham, and also had an interest in Daybrook Laundry, started by Oswald's uncle. Oswald died in his forties. Jack and Helen Barnsdale whose sons Tony and Richard were recently living at Kingsley Green near Haslemere and near Farnham, Surrey respectively, lived at Lenton Hall from its purchase by Helen until 1930, but it is not known whether the Hall was occupied at all between 1921 and 1924 when owned by Sir Jesse Boot.

Hugh Stewart Hall

It seems appropriate to continue the story of Lenton Hall here rather than in Chapter XVI since the College did not, in fact, own it (through the Corporation as trustee) until 1935. The new University College opened in 1928, and the surviving small men's Hall of Residence at Mapperley, purchased by the City Council in 1903 for leasing to the College, then at Shakespeare Street, soon proved to be both too small and too distant from Highfields as the only men's Hall, although it had been convenient for Shakespeare Street. According to Wood [1953 103] the College, at the instigation of Principal Hugh Stewart, paid £10,000 for Lenton Hall in January 1930, and Lord Trent, in the year before his death, agreed to pay for alterations needed to provide accommodation 'for 40, or, if possible, 80 students'. There is an element of myth in this version of events. It was the imminent influx at very short notice of an additional 100 students announced in early 1930 by the Board of Education that precipitated the hurried 'purchase' of Lenton Hall, and although it was occupied by the College and greatly altered internally from 1930, Helen Barnsdale remained the legal owner until 1935. By an indenture dated 25 March 1935 Helen, 'wife of John Davison Barnsdale formerly of Lenton Road, The Park, then of Lenton Hall, but now of Frensham Beale Manor near Farnham, Surrey, Gentleman' sold Lenton Hall for an agreed price of £10,000 to the Corporation of Nottingham as trustees of University College, Nottingham ... in fee simple'. This indenture must have been prepared in 1930 at the latest, for Lenton Hall was described in it as a capital mansion house, with coach houses, laundry, stables, outbuildings, vinery, greenhouses, yards, gardens, gardeners' cottages and out offices. The area of the Hall and its grounds, including a moiety of the roads on the north-west and south-west sides was 7a.1.34½.

Lord Trent declined, on principle, to take responsibility for the purchase of Lenton Hall, but was willing to fund its conversion, and indeed its extension. As a result, since the College had no available capital, there was a hurried arrangement for purchase by payment of the insured value (£10,000) in six annual instalments, beginning with £1,000 in 1930, and ending with £1,000 by March 1935, with provision for re-entry and sale by Helen Barnsdale in case of default on payment of any instalment, but with possession on 15 April 1930. The proposal to buy Lenton Hall as 'an additional hostel' under this arrangement was made in February, and the decision to do so was taken on 8 March 1930 [49]. With remarkable generosity Lord Trent, on this flimsy basis, provided funds for conversion and equipment. He wrote on 28 April 1930 from Villa Springland, Cannes, to W.J.Board the Town Clerk, who was also Honorary Secretary of University College: 'It is my intention to bear the entire cost of the present alterations to Lenton Hall to make it suitable for the first 40 students, and then to ascertain what would be the amount involved to extend the accommodation for a further forty. If at all possible I shall be happy to finance this also, as I would like to go right on with the building whilst the workmen are on the spot, but I will inform you of my decision in due course...'. The letter continued: 'I am very anxious to see more hostels around the University, for I attach the greatest possible importance to these as having a great influence on the life of the students, apart from the training they receive at the College'.

Accommodation for the first 40 students was needed in September 1930. Mrs. Barnsdale did not vacate the house until 30 April, a fortnight later than agreed, so that Morley Horder, the architect, and Sir James Carmichael the contractor had little time. In addition to renovation there was a new residential block to be built to add to the converted accommodation in the old Lenton Hall, and it is clear that this could not have been completed by September 1930, especially since it must have involved substantial demolition, including that of the vinery and the single-storey building behind it [50]. But the Board of Education 'recognized' accommodation for 43 students at Lenton Hall on 15 December 1930, so it must have been ready for the Spring term, 1931 [51] .

Dr. William Neil outlined the alterations of 1930 in a commemorative pamphlet of 1980. The small kitchen annexe and back staircase were pulled down and a first addition of 15 study bedrooms on three floors was made (A4-8, B1-5, D1-5), which with the old Hall provided accommodation for 43 students. Two rooms of A-corridor were used as a kitchen and a scout's room. The rest of the 'scouts' slept in the cottage at the cycle sheds. The present Warden's drawing room was the students' dining room and the present S.C.R. was used as the J.C.R.(later to become the library).

Alterations made during the summer of 1932 increased the number of student places in Lenton Hall from the 43 of 1930-31 to 57 and then to 60, an expansion made possible, according to a letter from the Registrar dated 5 May 1933, by 'the conversion of the range of buildings previously used as coachhouses, garages and stables into a dining hall and kitchens, and the erection of a temporary common room in the grounds' [52] . Nine more study bedrooms, three on each floor were added (A1-3, B3-8, D6-8). The large rooms on C-corridor on the second floor of the old Hall were divided. For a short time the present S.C.R. became the dining room, and the Junior Common Room 'moved out to the stables'. Then a wooden hut was built in the stable yard to serve as a Common Room and the rest of the stable buildings were converted into an open-raftered kitchen and dining room, with staff rooms above, which together with the cottage in the grounds previously occupied by the engineer provided accommodation for all men servants. The removal of the kitchen gave six additional bedrooms and a rearrangement of the Warden's quarters added more, to provide 14 rooms on the ground floor. The temporary dining room became a library. The University College prospectus of 1932 contains a photograph of Lenton Hall with the first study-bedroom block (Figure 54).

After the death of Lord Trent in June 1931 further extension of Lenton Hall did not attract funding from his estate, but in the mid-1930s, a time of severe pressure on the College's finances, priority over all other developments was given to further extending the Hall. A letter of 19 March 1940 from the Registrar stated that Hugh Stewart Hall, as Lenton Hall had then become, cost the College a total of £89,000, 'but certain additions were carried out by Lord Trent and we have no knowledge of the actual cost' [53] . The large extensions of the mid-1930s were financed by a large loan of £67,000 from the Corporation, which added to the £10,000 original purchase price paid by instalments leaves £12,000 to account for. Allowing for the servicing of the loan, part of this must represent the cost of the work of 1932-33. It was possible to provide collateral for the large later extensions only in the form of the property itself, the deeds of which were in the Town Clerk's hands by 4 April 1935 after the final instalment of the purchase price had been paid. But almost a year earlier, on 28 April 1934, W.B.Starr and Hall, architects and surveyors of 12 Victoria Street, Nottingham, wrote to the Town Clerk that they would proceed with plans and estimates for the new buildings [54] .

The building operations of 1935-37, by Messrs. John Cawley Ltd., added the terrace blocks I to M, followed by the central F- block, entrance hall, reception room, dining hall with billiards and table tennis room below it, and kitchens, all completed by April 1936 when 100 students were in residence. By September 1936 N-block, and the south-east wing, with a new Junior Common Room (now the library) and scouts quarters above were finished, to complete an open-sided quadrangle extending into the former kitchen gardens. The enlargement brought the number of residential places up to 116, and the Hall was finally opened formally on 7 January 1938 by the Duke of Portland, President of the College, who named it Hugh Stewart Hall. By that time Professor H.A.S.Wortley, earlier a Warden of Mapperley Hall, was Principal of University College, but 'in view of the late Principal Stewart's espousal of the original purchase and his close interest in the successive enlargements, it was appropriate that the Hall should receive Hugh Stewart's name' [55] . The Hall's subsequent development within

Figure 54: Lenton Hall in 1932 and Hugh Stewart Hall in 1938
Above: *The extension north-east of the original Hall is that financed by Lord Trent (Jesse Boot) in 1931-32.*
Below: *The further extensions to the Hall were built in 1935-37, and formally opened in Spring 1938 by the Duke of Portland, who renamed the Hall in honour of Principal Hugh Stewart.*

the College and University is outlined in a booklet, 'Hugh Stewart Hall, 1930-1980' compiled for the celebration of the first fifty years as a Hall of Residence.

NOTES

1. Barley and Cullen [1975 38] gave the date of 1804, probably following Blackner [1815/1985 252 fn.]. There was certainly some delay in building, and Thomas Stevenson was allowed to stay on his farm for a year or more after its purchase by Wright - though this letting did not include the site of the Hall and its gardens.
2. Sutton [1852 50] gave the date of establishment as 1759. Thomas Bailey [1853 1256] favoured 1761. Others have given 1764.
3. See *The Stretton Manuscripts* by William Stretton of Lenton Priory, published privately by G.C.Robertson of Widmerpool in 1910 (p. 164). The documents were owned by J.T.Godfrey, and many are now in the Nottinghamshire Archives Office.
4. According to William Stretton [N.A.O., DDTS 6/4/4, Notebook No. 29, p.6] 'The house occupied by Mr. Lewis Alsop on the Low Pavement was built by Rothwell Willoughby Esq., minister of St. Peter's 1742-44, in 1738. He was a great naturalist and antiquary. After his death it was sold to John Wright Esquire, Banker, who on retiring to his House at Lenton sold it to Lewis Alsop, an eminent attorney'.
5. O.S. 1:500 map (Ten Foot Series) 1881. Copy in N.A.O..
6. N.U.M.D., Mi 1/16/1(a) (1823)
7. N.U.M.D., Mi R 31 (1838), Mi R 32 (1839 and 1840)
8. Census of 1841, Enumerators' Books, H.O. 107/858
9.

Female servants:	Elizabeth Robertson (20)	Anne Smith (15)
	Mary Facon (30)	Hannah Cope (20)
	Mary Capewell (14)	Mary Turton (14)
Male servants:	Francis Sadler (30)	Thomas Bingham (15)
	Frederick Beresford (20)	

10. N.U.M.D., Mi 1/16/1a, p. 36
11. N.U.M.D., Mi R 36, a Middleton estate rental for 1845, annotated: 'Purchased of F.Wright Esq. Lenton Hall and 130 acres of land...'. 'Lenton Hall and estate purchased from Lady Day 1845'.
12. A good account of F.W.Johnson and his part in the Dunkirk developments was published in *The Lenton Listener* 49 (Dec.-Jan. 1987-88). Lenton Local History Society.
13. N.A.O., DD 958/1 (1883): Abstract of title of Mr. F.W.Johnson.
14. The trustees for John Wright's will
15. N.A.O., DD 958/5
16. N.A.O., DD 958 (1882): Rules of the Dunkirk Freehold Land Society.
17. The present Dunkirk Hotel was built behind this original one.
18. *The Lenton Listener* 49 (Dec. - Jan.) 1987-88
19. Isaac Fisher, tenant of Lenton Abbey, was charged an additional rent of £18.15s. 0d. in the rent schedule at Michaelmas 1845 for 15 acres west of the northern end of Beeston Lane, much of it the former Abbey Field Close exchanged to John Wright in the Beeston Inclosure Award of 1808-09, thus restoring it to the farm of Lenton Abbey. [N.U.M.D. Mi R 38 (1845) Lady Day rental].
20. The writer is indebted to Mr. S. Zaleski for this reference.
21. N.U.M.D., Mi 3 G 60, Bundle 12 includes an indenture, Lord Middleton's of 18 May 1848. On page 11: 'On the death of Henry Willoughby the elder, or with his consent...but not before the death of Digby...raise for the portion of each of the two children of Charlotte Henrietta Legard, a deceased daughter of the said Henry Willoughby the elder by his late wife, viz. Algernon Willoughby Legard and Cecil Henry Legard, a sum...'.
22. N.U.M.D., Mi 2 F 70 (9 October 1818)
23. N.U.M.D., Mi 2 F 837 (1892). The Willoughby Manuscripts number almost 1,000, and form the Mi 2 F group of the Middleton papers. They give details of many members of the extensive Aspley Willoughby family in the first half of the 19th century.
24. Census of 1851, Enumerators' Books. For Lenton H.O. 107/2129, pp. 4-143, 178-181 and H.O. 107/2130, pp. 4-35; taken 5 April 1851.
25. N.U.M.D., Mi 3 G 60, Box 6, Bundle 12. The settlement of 1848 provided for not more than £6,000 to be raised for the portions of A.W. and C.H.Legard, but not before the death of Digby, who became the 7th Lord Middleton and died unmarried in 1856. In 1867 [N.U.M.D., Mi 3 G 22] interest 'less income tax' was being paid half-yearly into banks at York and Scarborough on these sums invested for the Legard brothers, but in April of that year 'The two sums of £6,000 to wch Messrs. C.H. and A.W.Legard became entitled under the sd. settlt. of 18 May 1848 were duly paid and discharged'.
26. Census of 1861, Enumerators' Books, H.O. 107/858-9 RG 9/2947

27. John Morley's rent is given in a Middleton estate rental for 1859 [N.U.M.D., Mi R 41].
28. Robertson (Stretton) [1908] 197. Carter [1866]. Nottingham Public Libraries Staff [1937]. Robert J. Smith [1979]. Byron had made an abortive sale to T. Claughton of the whole estate for £145,000 in 1813, but Claughton could not raise the money.
29. T.J.Pettigrew to the British Architectural Association, 1854. [See Bailey 1853 II 409]
30. Lawson Lowe called Mrs. Wildman's sister 'Clara'; and as her near neighbour it would be supposed that he knew her well.
31. N.U.M.D., Mi P 6 (1863) (map) and Mi 2 S 3 (1863) (schedule and key to the map, appearing as 'Reference to Plan No. 2') and indicating that the map was by Sturgess and covered all the property of Lord Middleton in Lenton at that date.
32. N.U.M.D., Mi 1/16/1a-1d, 1823 - in the summary of evidence.
33. ibid.
34. N.U.M.D., Mi 3 G 33. This bundle includes a document giving details of several estates of which Lord Middleton was tenant for life. Schedule 4 is Lenton Hall estate, 130a.1.20, annual value £440. In blue pencil in the margin is written: 'To be sold. 50 acres to be cut off for building land'. Also 'House 1,000, 55a. 13750 = 14750'.
35. N.U.M.D. Mi 4 E 137. The date should be 1867 and not 'about 1880' as given in the index.
36. N.U.M.D., Mi 3 G 10
37. ibid. - Schedule of deeds 1867 - sales. Particulars of estates sold: Lot 1, under disentailer of 1 March 1869, £22,342.18s.10d after deducting expenses of sale.
38 Census of 1871, Enumerators' Books. For Lenton, RG/3499, p. 4 to end and RG/3500, 4-32 and 52-63.
39. N.U.M.D., Mi 4 E E 137. The sales particulars of 1867 stated that 'The entrance lodge is newly built, and forms a pretty object at the entrance of the park, abutting on the turnpike road'.
40. Census of 1881, Enumerators' Books RG 9/3340 and 3341.
41. According to Wright's Directory of Nottingham the occupier of Lenton Hall in both 1881 and 1883 was William Howard Wright of the banking firm (the youngest brother of Henry and Fred. Wright was George Howard): but Kelly [1881] named Frederick Wright, as did the census.
42. O.S. 1:500 map (10.56 feet to the statute mile or 41.66 feet to the inch). For Lenton Hall see Sheet XLII.5.21. Notts. Archives Office holds maps of the area at this scale, dated 1881 and 1882.
43. N.U.M.D., Mi 3 G 11, 5 June 1866
44. N.U.M.D., UR I67: Town Clerk's correspondence. Many of the deeds are in the keeping of Messrs. Rotheras, the solicitors of the University.
45. A list of the names is to be found in a letter from the Town Clerk to Principal Wortley dated 9 February 1938. [N.U.M.D., UR I 67].
46. It is not known whether the William Lewin mentioned was of Gunthorpe Hall, Lowdham (of C. Martin and Co.) or was William Lewin, iron founder (of the firm of J. Redgate) living at Cedar Mount, 73 Cromwell Street.
47. N.A.O., DD 804
48. J.T.Godfrey (ed.) *Allen's Red Book, Almanac and Annual Register* (1907) 122.
49. N.U.M.D., UR 67 (1930-38)
50. Compare O.S. 1:500 map of 1881, the lithograph of about 1868 and photograph of c. 1932.
51. N.U.M.D., UR 467 (which includes the letter of 15 December 1930)
52. ibid.
53. N.U.M.D., UR 456
54. N.U.M.D., UR I 67 (1930-38). William Beedham Starr (c. 1865-1953) of Nottingham prepared the layout of the Edwardian part of the Mapperley Hall estate and designed many of its grander houses. He was the architect of the Apollo Works (Home Brewery Company) in the early 1920s, and of many interwar public houses in the Nottingham area.
55. For Hugh Stewart see, for example, E.Weekley (ed.) *Hugh Stewart, 1884-1934: some memorials of his friends and colleagues* with a foreword by the Duke of Portland. John Murray, London 1939, pp. xi, 83.

CHAPTER VIII

LENTON HOUSE AND LENTON FIELDS

Lenton House

Matthew Needham, who built Lenton House
The lands of Lenton House estate
Matthew Needham's family and their friends
High Pavement Chapel and the Unitarian influence
Financial problems 1830
The Reform Bill rioters 1831
Caroline Needham at Lenton House, 1840-50
Mrs. Anne Thorpe's lease, 1851-58
William Needham and his occupation of Lenton House, 1858-62
Chief Constable Captain Henry Holden's lease, 1862-65, and the sale to W.D.Paget
The Thorpes at Lenton House for half a century
Wentworth Ernest Claye in residence, 1914-19
John Campbell Boot' s purchase (1919) and sale (1946) and the research station
Gift of the site of the Jesse Boot Conference Centre to the University

Lenton Fields

Mrs. Catherine Turner and her boarding school for Unitarian girls
Purchase by Henry Hadden (c. 1859) and James Holwell Lee (1867)
***Occupiers** 1880-1946*
William Heape Walker (1880-88)
William Forster (1894-1900)
Joseph Spendlove (1900-07)
Richard Granger (1907-27)
Stephen C. Armitage (1927-46)
Purchase by the University

LENTON HOUSE

Lenton House and Lenton Fields, situated on opposite sides of Beeston Lane, are linked historically because they were built for the same owner, and were at times called by the same name - Lenton Fields House, or variants of it. Fields House, Lenton Fields and High Fields are names used by the Directories apparently interchangeably. For example, Dearden [1834 49] recorded that Matthew Needham was resident at Lenton Fields under the head 'Seats of the nobility, gentry and clergy', but on page 137 it was Highfields; and both refer to Lenton House, because Lenton Fields was not built in 1834. At one stage Lenton House was called Lenton Laurels. Since the two houses devolved independently after the middle of the 19th century their histories will be pursued separately, although cross reference will be inevitable.

Matthew Needham, who built Lenton House

Matthew Needham the younger 'of Wilford' (1768-1840) was the only surviving son of Matthew Needham, gentleman, of High Pavement, Nottingham, a 'surgeon and apothecary' - effectively the latter - and perhaps appropriately so in view of the recent history of Lenton House. Martha (née Messiter) the first wife of the elder Matthew Needham, had three children who all died in infancy. Sarah, Matthew senior's second wife, widowed before 1793, was the sole heiress of William Lee, gent., a hosier of Wilford [Godfrey 1884 202] and she had two daughters, Anne and Priscilla, and one son - the younger Matthew. William Lee bought from the Handleys (see Appendix 10) the large white house near the village school and across the Green from Wilford church . His daughter, Matthew Needham's mother, enlarged it considerably [Barker 1835 55] and it was later sold to Samuel Newham, then to W.S.Burnside, and by 1835 to R. Leeson.

Anne married Robert Phillips of Lancashire, and Priscilla, mentioned later, died unmarried. The younger Matthew, born in 1768 and at school at Quorn in Leicestershire in 1777 [1] was apprenticed to a Nottingham hosier from 1783 to 1790, when, at the age of 22, he was enrolled as a burgess (freeman) of Nottingham. Many apprentices in hosiery were sons of landed proprietors, and large premiums were common. The same was true of mercers (such as Joseph Lowe - see Chapter VI) and a high proportion of hosiers had family resources to mortgage for major industrial expansion. Matthew's maternal grandfather, William Lee, left most of his property to Matthew in 1792 on condition that he changed his name to Lee, and it is surprising in view of his later reputation for rectitude that he never did so. In the following year he was a 'master hosier' in partnership with James Nixon on High Pavement [Stalker 1793]. He was still a partner over 40 years later [Thomis 1968]. Thomis [1968 186] notes that in 1814 the Luddites destroyed, not particular types of frame but 'frames belonging to particular employers who were in disfavour with the men ... Needham and Nixon, two hosiers who had refused to pay their men a rise had their frames sought out and broken along with another, James Hooley, an intimate friend of theirs who had been associated with them in their stand against the Union'. In 1818 the firm was Needham, Nixon and Alcock [Sutton 1818 54].

Using his inherited property in a marriage settlement Matthew Needham married in 1795 Mary Manning, one of the daughters and co-heiresses of William Manning, a wealthy East India merchant and shipowner of Ormesby near Norwich. Matthew and Mary lived at Wilford, presumably in William Lee's former house, until Lenton House was built in 1800, a date engraved in slate on the house, and confirmed by M.C.M. [1910]. Land purchase dates would not have allowed an earlier completion of the building (see Chapter V). William Needham was born at Wilford in July 1799, and Ann at Lenton in March 1801.

In 1799, in two stages (see Chapter V) Matthew Needham bought a part of Miss Milward's estate lying west of the Lenton Hall estate, and in 1800 built Lenton House upon it. This original house - the western part of the present house - in two storeys, was extended on the east side in 1816 in three storeys - probably a nursery wing with its barred windows and servants' bedrooms above [Train undated, c.1973]. Details of the architectural features and alterations (about which Dr. Norman Summers was consulted) as well as the furnishings, are given in Keith Train's pamphlet. A single-storey range of buildings across the entrance courtyard, roofed with Welsh slate, has a dentil course near the eaves which suggests that it was contemporaneous with the 1816 extension. A coachhouse to the north dates only from 1890, built for W.B.Thorpe. A recent summary description of Lenton House is: 'Early to mid-19th century, two-storeyed stuccoed villa with pilasters and two-storeyed bow window and bay window. Eaves to hipped slated roof. Enclosed entrance court, much altered, especially doorway' [Notts. C.C. 1972 13]. Lawson Lowe [1871] described it as 'a large mansion of irregular form'.

The lands of the Lenton House estate

About 28 acres of land formed the Lenton House estate. This excludes the land of Lenton Fields, purchased from James Green of Lenton Abbey in 1808-09 (see Chapter V) and much later additions above Lenton House mentioned below. The deeds of sale have not been seen by the writer, but Train described the original purchase comprising a cottage and three closes called The Grass Close, the Lower Highfield or Barn Ground, and the Home Field or House Close, amounting in all to 27a.1.0 (amended to 27a.3.0 in a sale plan of 1865). These three fields, the second and third forming one close called Hill Field Close, or High Field Close of 16 acres [2], and the first 'a piece or parcel of the High Field Close next the Field' (Abbey Field) in 1684, made up the holding of Rose Parker in the later 17th century, held by her on a 21-year lease from Lady Day 1681 (see Chapter IV). She paid £16.10s.0d. for it [3].

As recounted in Chapter V (see Figure 30) the Lenton House estate land was part of a larger farm holding totalling about 68 acres in the late 18th century, held by Messrs. Hopkin and Hooton from 1782 onwards, and before that by Messrs. Hague and James [4]. It was sold by Miss Milward with the rest of her estate to Messrs. Pares and Paget on Old Lady Day 1798. Before 11 July (the date of the land tax assessment) they had re-sold it to the sitting tenants, Richard Hooton, yeoman, of Nottingham and William Hopkin the elder of Lenton. Both were innkeepers, Hooton being in 1799 landlord of The White Hart at Nottingham (not Lenton), and of The Bull, Fisher gate [Sutton 1852 241 3], and Hopkin the landlord of the Three Wheatsheaves on Derby Road in Lenton. Richard Hooton, 'maltster' of Fisher-gate, was described as 'gent' by the Nottingham Directory of 1815, and Sutton [1818] named him as one of six Junior Councilmen elected in 1798. By 1832, when he appears to have been living at Woodthorpe Hall, he was 'maltster and brickmaker'.

While nothing is known of the tactics involved in the land sales, it is apparent that John Wright, having decided where to build his new Hall, secured the westward vista from it by buying the Fourteen Acres and Fourteen Acres Meadow (now usually called 'the downland') from Hooton and Hopkin - part of their Beeston Lane farm. Matthew Needham may have been blocked by Wright's purchase, or the prospect of it, because he secured land taxed at only 18s.8d. a year by June 1799, and only a year later was he taxed an additional £2.16s.0d. for the rest of the Lenton House estate land, which was presumably not wanted by John Wright for his park. Matthew Needham paid £2,931.5s.0d. for his land in 1799.

Matthew Needham built his house in a commanding position near the top of a south-west facing slope, where the outcrop of the Plains skerry reduced the slope in a slight terrace feature. At the bottom of the slope, alongside Beeston Lane, was a cottage, and farm buildings

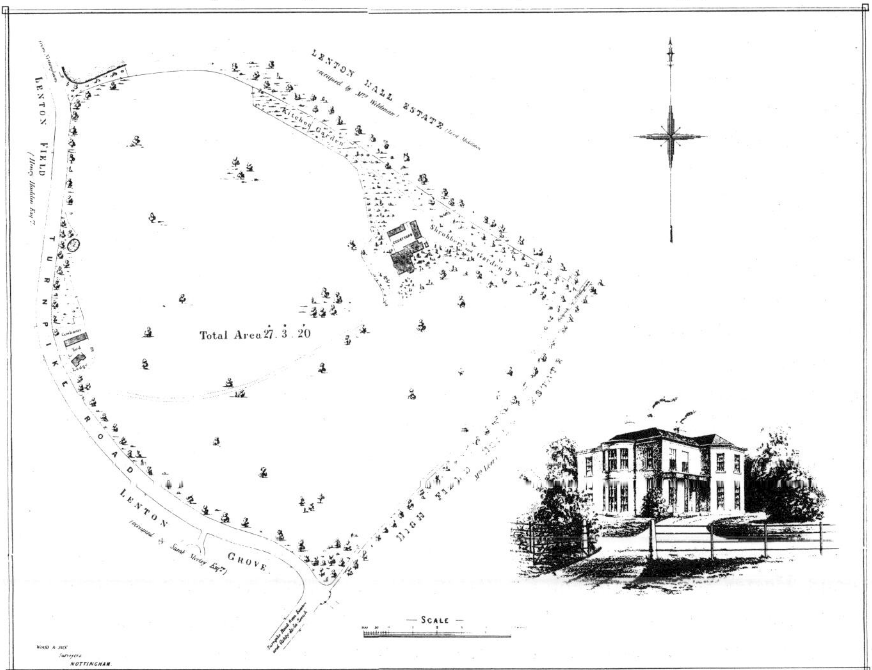

Figure 55: Lenton House and its estate in 1865
From the 1865 sale catalogue. [NAO DD 236/1]

associated with it. These were certainly present in 1831, and the original cottage occupied by the bailiff or sub-tenant of Hooton and Hopkins was on the same site, and probably was the same building, so that the Boots Company may have recently demolished what was probably the oldest building on the entire campus - though not the most distinguished. The cottage farmstead was occupied by William Gibbins in 1831, and one of his predecessors there was a coachman named Thomas Warren. The farm was marked on Sanderson's maps of 1834-35. The lodge and cottage now surviving on Beeston Lane at the ends of the two drives are of much more recent origin.

The soils of the estate are potentially much more productive than those of most of the campus, the stiff red 'marl' soils of the higher part, and the more varied soils of the lower parts being both cohesive and well drained. For most of the 19th century, however, except for the gardens near the house, the emphasis was on grass and small-scale dairying for the needs of the household, with scattered trees promoting the desirable park-like appearance. Only from the 1930s did the emphasis change to intensive arable usage in the artificial context of a horticultural research station, a condition that has now been reversed.

Matthew Needham's family and their friends

Lenton House remained in the ownership of the Needham family until 1865, though it was let to others from 1851 to 1857 and again from 1862. Matthew Needham himself lived there for forty years until his death on 1 August 1840. He and his wife Mary had nine children. The first three, born at Wilford before 1800, were Hester, who died at the age of six months; a second Hester, who was severely handicapped, and was dependent on nursing until her death in 1825; and William, born in 1799, who eventually inherited and later sold the estate. The six children born at Lenton House were as follows.

Anne (1801-1865) was a talented artist, and in 1835 married William Enfield (1801-1873), solicitor, eldest son of the Town Clerk of Nottingham, and himself Town Clerk from his father's death in 1845 until 1870. They lived at 18 Low Pavement, later called Enfield House.

Lucy, born 1803, was married in 1827 to Richard Martineau, son of John Martineau, a London brewer. Constance Martineau, her daughter, mentioned later as a pupil at the school at Lenton Fields, was the author of 'Memories of Lenton' (1910).

Caroline (1805-1850) was born and died unmarried at Lenton House.

John Manning (his mother's maiden name), born 1807, married Jane, daughter of John Fordham of Royston, Cambridge in 1831

Mary Priscilla, born 1809, married in 1838 Samuel Greg of Bollington, Cheshire.

Eleanor Sara (1813-1880) married in 1841 at High Pavement Chapel, Henry Enfield, brother of William Enfield, Anne's husband. Henry too was a solicitor, practising mainly in London. He became Chief Clerk in Chancery, and Secretary to the Commissioners in Lunacy, returning to Nottingham on retirement in 1864 to become a J.P., and to take an active part in public life. Both Sara and Henry were buried in Lenton Priory churchyard. They had two daughters, Mary and Ellen, and a son Henry (b. 1849) who gave up Law for Art, married Elise Schmitt of Dusseldorf, and lived for many years in Berlin.

Though inoculated (vaccination was not yet available) the first Hester died of small pox. The second Hester was intelligent but helpless. A housekeeper was kept to allow Mrs. Needham to spend more time with Hester and with her other children. Anne (Figure 56) was well known for her wide interests in charity, education and religion, as well as for her art. Pictures by her were published in 1854 in a folio volume 'Sketches in Nottinghamshire' [see Godfrey and Ward 1908 31,77]. Among her subjects were the Castle, Bridlesmith Gate,

Windmills on the Forest, Trent Bridge, and Wilford Church and Wilford ferry. The profits went to the Midland Institution for the Blind. 'Wilford Ferry Boat 1854' is reproduced in Victorian Nottingham [Iliffe and Baguley, 6, 46]. Anne was for many years a superintendent of the girls' part of the High Pavement Sunday School, working with Mrs. Turner (see below) [5]. She was the authoress of several hymns which were set to music by Henry Farmer of Lenton. Her husband William Enfield was a kindred spirit, described by the Dictionary of National Biography as 'a leader of all philanthropic efforts at Nottingham'. Anne's death on 16 July 1865 after a long and painful illness is commemorated in 'An address and extracts from a sermon delivered by Rev.F.W.Clayden on the decease of Mrs. Enfield', which was printed for private distribution. In the Arboretum a drinking fountain 'much resorted to by the children' was the gift of Anne and William Enfield in 1859.

Lucy's marriage to Richard Martineau was very beneficial to the Needhams, as will appear below. Their acquaintance began on the family's biennial visit to old Mr. Manning at Ormesby, Norwich, when the young people became friendly with the family of Thomas Martineau, and especially Caroline Needham with Harriett Martineau, a future authoress. The marriage of the youngest of Matthew Needham's daughters, Eleanor Sara, to a second Enfield brother is not surprising in the circumstances of the time, for the Enfields were close family friends, and 'when the family walked to chapel in Nottingham William, Henry and Maria Enfield sometimes walked part way back with us' [6].

From the beginning Matthew Needham was prominent and respected in Lenton. He was one of the larger subscribers to a fund to finance the Lenton Volunteers set up at a meeting on 11 August 1803 to discuss measures to meet the feared French invasion, and in September was described as Superintendent of Lenton parish and Treasurer of the fund. His offer to provide a horse for a guide, however, did not match the offers of equipment made by some of the large farmers, such as John Wright (2 waggons, 6 horses and 2 drivers), John Chamberlain

Figure 56: Anne Needham (Mrs. William Enfield) in 1859
Photo. S.Redgate, Bromley House. [NUMD Hi 3 P 79] Courtesy High Pavement Chapel trustees.

(the same), and William Wigley (1 waggon, 1 cart, 5 horses and 2 drivers); but it compared with those of Francis Evans (1 tilted cart, 1 horse) and James Green (1 cart, 2 horses and a driver) [Godfrey 1884 465].

High Pavement Chapel and the Unitarian connection

Matthew Needham's parents were Anglicans, and he was himself a churchwarden at Old Lenton in 1805 and 1806: but the Mannings, his wife's family, were prominent Nonconformists, and Matthew became a Unitarian of the congregation of High Pavement Chapel when it was converted to that sect. The original trust deed for the chapel was executed in 1691. It was built on land belonging to Sir Francis Willoughby of Cossall, and alongside his town house. In 1754 it was registered for the use of Protestant-Dissenters (Presbyterians) [Bailey 1853 1226] but made a new start in 1802. In that year the chapel was rebuilt to cater for the large numbers attracted by the lively intellectual stimulus offered by pastors George Walker, F.R.S., a prolific writer on a wide variety of subjects, and James Taylor, who arrived in 1802, and took the congregation over to the Unitarians, the most free-thinking of the Protestant bodies. 'The largest body of Dissenters in Nottingham before the Methodist movement added a new dimension to nonconformity, and certainly the most influential in the years before and during the Evangelical Revival was the congregation of Presbyterians who assembled at their Chapel on High Pavement' [Thomis 1968]. According to Train Matthew Needham's name occurs in the Vestry minutes from 1822 to 1837, but he had joined the Unitarians many years earlier. When the Needham children were old enough they walked with their parents to chapel in the city every Sunday morning, a return distance of some six miles. Matthew's widowed mother lived on in Nottingham to 1817 with her younger daughter 'Prisca', who lived for a further 30 years in the 'neat little house' on Castle-gate, near St. Nicholas' church, on the spot where the Women's Hospital stood earlier in this century [M.C.M. 1910]. It was a regular place of call on Sundays for the Needhams after chapel, and Aunt Prissy was a regular visitor at Lenton House.

The great importance of High Pavement Chapel (which now houses the Lace Museum) in the economic life and development of Nottingham in the late 18th and early 19th centuries has been emphasized by Malcolm Thomis [1968]. It was certainly of central importance in the intellectual and social life of the Needhams. The community included the Enfields, the Needhams' influential friends, and also the Lowes of Highfield House, whose children were baptized at 'The Presbyterian Meeting House' from the mid-18th century onwards. It included economic innovators and the leaders of the political life of Nottingham. In the Enfields they had a monopoly of the Town Clerk's office for 126 years. In the last quarter of the 18th century 12 of the 15 mayors had worshipped at High Pavement, and as late as 1833 local Tories claimed that four-fifths of the officers of the Corporation came from High Pavement [Thomis 1968 99].

It could be said that members of High Pavement Chapel dominated Nottingham Corporation from 1689 to 1832. The Rev. George Walker was not only an outstanding religious leader but also a powerful political influence. He was a friend and correspondent of Joseph Priestley, and a former pupil of Adam Smith at Glasgow. Under him, in the last quarter of the 18th century High Pavement Chapel 'became a centre of progressive political as well as religious thought. Walker became the voice of Radicalism in the East Midlands, ably supported by his friend Major John Cartwright, and carried many of his wealthy congregation with him' [Chapman 1967 188-89, 195]. At least nine cotton spinners, including Charles Morley, Thomas Oldknow, Henry Hollins and Harry Green were also Unitarians. Leading figures in other cotton-worsted centres in the Midlands were also Unitarians, and leaders in provincial society and of progressive political thought in the East Midlands. Philosophic Societies were started - for example by Dr. Erasmus Darwin at Derby in 1784.

The Unitarians were also closely involved in education, and this may well explain the existence of Lenton Fields, as will be shown later. James Taylor lived and kept a school at the bottom of Short Hill behind High Pavement, while his co-pastor and later successor, Benjamin Carpenter, ran a day school in a house on the south side of High Pavement, 'well patronized by some of the leading families of the town, such as the Lowes of Highfields'. The school at High Pavement Chapel was supported by prominent Nottingham industrialists, but they tended to send their own sons to the Standard Hill Academy, run by Unitarians, but providing a commercial rather than a technical education. The education of the Needham children is only sketchily known, though it is certain that they were not educated at the Charity school adjoining the chapel, where 40 boys and 24 girls were educated free, and partly provided with clothing. The Needham girls had governesses up to 1822, including a Miss Stone, who had a school in Lenton and was very unpopular, and a Miss Mitchell, a full-time resident governess to the younger children for a time [M.C.M. 1910].

The Rev. Henry Turner, son of Rev. William Turner of Newcastle-on-Tyne, who succeeded Dr. Hutton as co-pastor of High Pavement Chapel with Rev. James Taylor in 1817, used to go to Lenton House to give Latin lessons to John and Mary Priscilla Needham. The boys attended Mr. Taylor's boarding school, 'to which Unitarians sent their sons from distant parts of the Kingdom', and fellow pupils there included the Enfields. 'Some of them used to come out to Lenton sometimes to spend a chance holiday, among them Sam Greg' - the future husband of Mary Needham [M.C.M. 1910]. After Mr. Taylor's school at Short Hill broke up John Needham was sent to 'old Mr. Turner in Newcastle, and afterwards to Dr. Carpenter at Bristol'. After the death of Henry Turner in 1822 his young widow, Catherine, started a school at 11 Market Street, Nottingham, where it remained for about nine years before moving to Park Row as virtually a denominational girls' school for Unitarians. It was a very small school, to which Ellen and Mary Needham used to walk to have lessons with Isabella and Caroline Phillips, the only boarders, and a few others including Eliza Hunt (afterwards Lady Fellows), Maria Enfield (later Mrs. Withers Dowson) and Eliza Smith (later Mrs. Alfred Paget). The education provided by Mrs. Turner is discussed below in connection with Lenton Fields House, which was built for her by Matthew Needham, and to which she moved with her school in about 1837.

Matthew Needham's change of religious affiliation to Unitarianism may betoken a flexible and lively mind, with a liberal and generous outlook. The liberal attitudes of the Needham family were shown, for example, in their hospitality to refugees from the continent, and in particular their emotional friendship in 1824 with Italian refugees after the abortive Piedmontese revolution of 1820, which is described in some detail by M.C. Martineau [1910]. Because they shared liberal, nonconformist, progressive interests and attitudes, as well as worshipping together at High Pavement, it is not surprising that the Needhams and the Enfields enjoyed a close friendship that led to two marriages when the two eldest sons of Henry Enfield of Short Hill, Low Pavement, Treasurer of the Town and Town Clerk 1815 to 1845, William and Henry, married Anne and Ellen Sara Needham. Associated with the legal profession in Nottingham throughout the 19th century, and providing Town Clerks through most of it, all the Enfields were prominent in public life as well as prominent Unitarians.

Richard Enfield (1817-1904) of Bramcote Grange, Henry's fourth son, and partner with his brother as solicitors, is of particular interest in respect of the origins of Nottingham University. Regarded as ahead of his times in educational matters he was 'a moving spirit in the higher education first developed in the town by the work of the People's College and then in the Mechanics Hall evening classes, leading to the University Extension Lectures' (which were suggested by his wife, Mary P.H.Dowson, granddaughter of Rev. Pendlebury Dowson, a famous liberal divine) 'and to the building of University College'. A contemporary wrote that in 1871 he 'led the movement towards the University College' [Williams c.1883 38], and in a

University College Souvenir of 1913-14 a portrait of Richard Enfield has the caption 'One of the Founders of the College', bracketed with Rev. J.B.Paton as responsible for the University Extension arrangements. The cash offer that led the Town Council to erect the University College was made through him, and he was a member of the governing body of the College from its beginning. His educational, professional and charitable interests and offices ranged over a remarkably wide field [7] . The third of Henry Enfield's four sons, Edward (1811-1880) also had a distinguished career, and was prominent in charitable work in London. He became President of Manchester New College, London, and one of the Moneyers of the Mint. In 1867 he became Treasurer of University College Hospital, London, and a guiding spirit in its management. As a Unitarian dissenter he shared largely in non-sectarian efforts for the poor in East London.

This discussion of another, better-known family, associated with the Needhams by friendship, religion and outlook and by marriage, is intended to convey something of the atmosphere of intellectual stimulus, social activity and earnest philanthropy of the circle in which they moved, arising from a responsible recognition of their privileged and prosperous life-style and resting on a close-knit and stable family life. The dissenting Radicals were characteristically upper middle class, and paternalistic in their attitude to the working class. The Unitarian doctrine of justification by works alone was an important influence on the old dissenting families, and also on their friends and connections, leading to a strong emphasis on the value of humanitarian action. The welfare of workers was a moral as well as an economic concern: but their doctrinaire attachment to unpopular political views and to a free market economy made the Unitarians targets for angry resentment [Chapman 1967].

Financial problems in 1830

In the early 1830s the life of the Needham household was disturbed by two near disasters, one financial and the other accidental. Matthew's eldest son, William, became associated with iron founding and coal mining undertakings in Monmouthshire, and Matthew was induced to invest most of his capital in them in the 1820s. In 1830 they proved to be bad investments, and only help from the Martineaus and other Unitarian friends allowed the Needhams to stay on at Lenton House, where the 1830s were hard times after the gracious living of the 1820s.The consequences of the sudden financial difficulties for the whole household are described in Constance Martineau's book, pointing the changes from 1826 when 'our Lenton life was at the height of its prosperity', with regular London seasons for the older children while the governess, Miss Mitchell, stayed at home with the younger ones, to the more austere life-style that soon followed. Despite help - 'Richard [Martineau] has offered £100 a year' - 'all these servants will go as far as we can foresee'. There was severely bruised pride. The disaster was to be kept secret, and 'there are the concerts, and papa will offend Mr. Lowe and all the people by not subscribing. There is not a person we know who does not subscribe'. William's new fiancee from Bristol was induced by relatives to break off the engagement. Fortunately the engagement of John Needham to Jane, daughter of J.G.Fordham, a banker of Royston, went ahead, and his father-in-law 'helped set up John in the brewing business, and a brewery was built for him in Beeston, where John and Jane lived in the brewery house for five years until the business failed in 1836 [8] . White's Directory for 1832 included under Beeston 'John Manning Needham, brewer'. Matthew Needham's financial circumstances appear to have recovered fairly quickly since he was able to build Lenton Fields house for Catherine Turner and her school in the mid-1830s.

The Reform Bill rioters, 1831

October 1831 was a dangerous month for all the families in the isolated houses on the present campus, and more dangerous for the Needhams than for most. After news of the defeat of the Reform Bill in the Lords reached Nottingham on the evening of Saturday, 8 October, at the height of the Goose Fair, rioting began and was to last for several days. On Monday, 10 October, despite a public meeting in the market place, where 20,000 people were addressed by Colonel Wildman and others [Williams c. 1883] [9] and resolutions in support of the Bill were passed, Colwick Hall was sacked and Nottingham Castle set on fire and destroyed, lighting up the whole district between 8 pm. and 2 am..

The next morning the rioters went to Beeston, and around midday burned down the silk mill owned by William Lowe of Nottingham, a prominent anti-Reform Tory. On the way to Beeston some used Cut Through Lane, while others, using Derby Road, called at Lenton Firs, where they had an acrimonious exchange with the aged Dr. Storer in his garden, and took a quantity of his carrots [10]. On their return journey, after 'regaling themselves at the expense of the publicans' [Bailey 1853 378] they went to Lenton House where, in the absence of both Matthew and John a great deal of disorder was caused, graphically described in letters written to Lucy Needham at the time [11]. The intruders cleared the house of food, ale and wine, 'at the same time laying their hands upon any portable article, which they carried off, together with about £40 worth of plate' [Bailey 1853]. The rioters then visited Lenton Hall, where 'John Wright gave them what money he had about him'. Arriving at Beeston Lane end, on their way towards Wollaton Hall, the mob made a half-hearted attack on Wollaton Park gate 'by what is now the second lodge, but which was then only an ordinary five barred gate' [Williams c.1883 16]. Inside the park a small garrison of the Wollaton Yeomanry awaiting them under the command of Colonel Hancox charged the rioters, and took 16 or 17 of them prisoner, since 'the mob were assembling as it was supposed for the purpose of attacking his lordship's mansion' [12]. Several were tried at the Assizes in January 1832, five sentenced to hang and four to transportation for life for burning down Lowes' mill. After appeal two were reprieved and three hanged [13].

It is not known whether in normal times the families resident on the campus had close or distant social contacts or relationships with each other. However, they seem to have come together to cooperate in the face of this dangerous situation, though they were contemptuous of Lord Middleton, 'The Wrights have taken refuge at Beeston, poor things. The mob went there after here, but Mr. Wright met them and gave them money, and they went away'. 'Mr. Fisher [of Lenton Abbey] has called twice and we have made an agreement with him that whoever was attacked should ring their great bell ...' and the others would call out the Yeomanry. 'Seventeen men sit up at Mr. Wright's, one on top of the house'. There was great support for the Needhams from the Enfields, with visits, food supplies and other help; and they took away plate for safety. But 'as to Lord M. it is a perfect farce to hear how he takes care of his own precious, crazy self and nobody else' [14].

It would be inappropriate at this point to pass on without reminding the reader of Matthew Needham's weather record, one of the earliest in the district, which began in 1809 and ended only with his death (see Chapter I). It seems very possible that it was Matthew Needham's example that fired the interest of Alfred Lowe and his sons in meteorology, and contributed to the eventual scientific eminence of Edward Lowe [15]. It would have been of great interest to compare the temperature record for 1810-40 with that of the post-war decades kept by The Boots Company at almost the same spot, and to have calibrated the early 19th century record from the modern readings, but the former are lost and the latter were immediately destroyed when the research station closed some years ago.

Mrs. Mary Needham died, probably from cancer, at the age of 68 in August 1837, and her death was followed by that of 71-year-old Matthew in 1840 [16]. The Lenton burial register described them respectively as of High Fields and of Lenton Abbey Fields. Both were buried in Old Lenton churchyard in a vault inscribed 'M.N. 1822'.

Caroline Needham at Lenton House, 1840-1850

At Matthew Needham's death in 1840 only Ellen and Caroline remained unmarried, and by Matthew's will, written in 1838, these two daughters were to have the Lenton House estate until their marriages or deaths. Thereafter the estate was to pass to William, though not (by a codicil of 1839) if he was bankrupt or insolvent - perhaps an echo of Matthew's bitter experience of financial disaster associated with William's activities in business. The Misses Needham were at Lenton House according to Pigot's 1842 Directory: but in 1841 Ellen had married Henry Enfield, leaving Caroline alone at Lenton House, and dependent on Richard Martineau and other members of the family to augment a slender income in order to afford to remain there. The relatives helped by staying at Lenton for long periods in the summer.

Caroline never married. She had an emotional relationship in 1833-34 with a Polish refugee, one John Bartisch d'Elia, who paid particular attention to her on his frequent visits to the house - but borrowed money from other members of the family. Mrs. Catherine Turner's letter to Lucy Martineau in 1833, warning about his dubious antecedents, indicated that they were actually engaged. After some months he disappeared. Caroline 'of High Fields Old Lenton' died in March 1850 and was buried in the Needham vault in Old Lenton graveyard: and since William was solvent the estate went to him! Caroline was still named by Slater's Directory of Nottinghamshire at Lenton House in 1857, seven years after her death.

The Census Enumerators' Books of 1841, the year after Matthew Needham's death, mentioned a house called Lenton Field House, which was occupied by Catherine Turner and her school boarders [17]. The next house listed was Lenton Laurels House, a name encountered only in this single reference; but this was Lenton House. The census listed only three servants, Hannah Newton (25), Mary Brown (11) and Thomas Hewitt (20). The next entry, Lenton Laurels Lodge, was occupied by William Gibbin (46) an agricultural labourer, his wife Hannah and their children Hannah (20) a milliner and dressmaker, William (18) an agricultural labourer and Mary (17). Letters written to Lucy Needham after the Reform Bill riots of 1831 included a reference to advice given to Mrs. Needham by Gibbin when the house was being ransacked, and Gibbin lived at the farm belonging to Matthew; that is, the cottage with farm buildings alongside Beeston Lane (opposite to the entrance to Nightingale Hall), called The Lodge in the middle 19th century and now demolished [18] (Figures 55, 58).

Mrs. Anne Thorpe's lease, 1851-58

The census of 1851, taken in the year after Caroline Needham's death, recorded at Lenton House (under that name) 24-year-old Fanny M. Thorpe, 'landed proprietor's daughter', with a visitor, Eleanor Stewart and her infant son, together with five living-in servants and a coachman with his wife and four small children at the farmhouse on Beeston Lane. Fanny's mother, Mrs. Anne Thorpe, held a 7-year lease from William Needham from either 1850 or 1851, and was recorded by the Directories as the occupier of 'Field House' from 1853 to 1857. The Thorpe family of Coddington Hall, Newark, were in business as maltsters. Mrs. Thorpe appears to have brought her domestic staff to Lenton with her, since while Fanny Thorpe and Eleanor Stewart were born at Newark, Eleanor's son Arthur, and Harriett, youngest child of the coachman Benjamin Rooth were born at Coddington, the groom William Armstrong at Collingham, housemaid Mary Ann Poole at Gonerby and the cook, Elizabeth Cragg at Doddington. In 1858, at the end of Mrs. Thorpe's lease, William Needham himself moved into Lenton House.

William Needham and his occupation of Lenton House, 1858-62

Despite the financial difficulties arising from William Needham's partnership with George Kenrick and his sons in the ironworks at Varteg, Monmouthshire, about 1830 - referred to earlier as the cause of severe difficulties for the whole Needham family - William remained at Varteg, where Mary and Ellen Needham paid him a long visit in the spring of 1832. In November or December 1836 he married at Trinity Church, Euston Road, London, Camilla Ann Bosanquet of Dingstowe Court, Monmouthshire. She was an anomaly in the Needham family - a strict Anglican churchwoman and Tory, very different from the Needham women and their husbands. She never became close to them [M.C.M. 1910]. William and Camilla had two daughters, Mary Camilla Laetitia, who married Arthur Ogilvie, and Hester Georgiana, born respectively in 1841 and 1843. In 1840 'the business at the Varteg was about to be given up, leaving them [William and Camilla] without a home', and in May 1841, with Camilla recovering from a long illness, they moved to a new home near Cardiff, where William was employed as manager of an ironworks [19].

After a decade near Cardiff William and Camilla Needham moved again, this time leaving South Wales, but not taking up Lenton House, where Mrs. Anne Thorpe had just been granted a lease. The industrial management experience of William Needham in the iron trade enabled him to join the management of the Butterley Company in 1851-52 on the retirement of William Jessop the younger after 46 years in charge there, for 37 of them as 'junior partner' [Christian 1991 111]. Jessop was a 'working partner', and his shares passed to a third William Jessop, son of his brother John and too young to take over a major company: so Francis Wright took on William Needham as a 'salaried partner' for four years while the young Jessop was gaining experience - probably 1852-56. During this period William Needham and his family lived in Butterley Company property, first at Alfreton Grange, and then at Aldecar Hall after Francis Wright had bought it, probably in 1854 [Vice 1854]. A Commissioners' Report in 1853 referred to William Needham as the 'resident partner of these works': but although he was a hard and purposeful manager, as the Butterley records show [Riden 1973] he was never a partner. Over one-third of the Jessop shares in Butterley were held by George Jessop, who returned from India and soon took up residence at Aldecar Hall, probably in 1858 or 1859, when he sold his shares to Francis Wright. The Needhams, therefore, moved to Lenton House, where Mrs.Thorpe's lease expired. But they remained there for barely four years, for Camilla died in 1862, William found living at Lenton House too expensive, and the property was let again.

In 1861, at the census, William Needham was described as aged 62, a Justice of the Peace and a landed proprietor, living with his London-born wife Camilla and their daughters Mary Camilla (20) and Hester Georgiana (or Georgina) (18). There were two living-in servants, Anne Briggs (35) and Harriet Stevenson (32) and a butler, Thomas Herritt, born at Beeston, who occupied Lenton Fields Lodge [20] with his wife Hannah, a washerwoman, and their 8- and 12-year-old children. William Needham's somewhat unsettled business and domestic life should not obscure the fact that despite his difficulties he was a considerable and respected figure, 'Deputy Lieutenant for this county and Justice of the Peace for the counties of Nottingham, Derby and Monmouth' [Lawson Lowe 1871].

Captain Henry Holden's lease, 1862-65, and the sale to W.B.Paget

The tenant who followed William Needham at Lenton House in 1862 was Captain Henry Holden, son of Robert Holden of Nuthall Temple [Wright 1862]. Henry Holden was Chief Constable of Nottinghamshire for over 35 years, from 1856 to 1892. He was the youngest of five brothers of a Derbyshire family which bought Nuthall Temple [21]. When his tenancy at Lenton House expired in the summer of 1865 Captain Holden moved to Bramcote, where he lived at The Grove [White 1885] part of the Bramcote Hills estate before moving to Bramcote Hills itself in 1892, when the estate passed to him on the death of his sister, Mrs. Sherwin-Gregory (see Appendices 9 and 17) [22].

But already, on 24 May 1865, the 'capital family mansion' of Lenton House with 'extensive gardens and pleasure grounds and park-like lawn adjoining' had been sold by auction at the George Hotel to William Paget of St. Anne's Manor, Sutton Bonington, a member of a branch of the Ibstock Paget family for £5,800 [23]. The solicitor for the conveyance was William Enfield, William Needham's brother-in-law. Train [c.1973] gave an area of 27a.3r., 2 roods greater than that of 1799, because 'Matthew Needham had bought an additional piece of land in 1819 from John Wright of Lenton Hall', but the writer has not been able to trace this transaction.

The sale particulars described Lenton House, fairly, as 'one of the most delightful residences in the vicinity of Nottingham. It is situated on a pleasant elevation with south and west aspects, and the beautifully timbered lawn slopes down to the turnpike road.' The house contained a dining room, 24 by 17 feet, drawing room 30 by 18 feet, a library, housekeeper's room, and excellent kitchens, servants' hall and other offices. There were 13 bedrooms, 4 dressing rooms and 4 attics. Adjoining the house was a four-stall stable, a double coachhouse and other outbuildings, and near the entrance lodge a barn, stable, cowhouses etc.. The house was sold with about 27 acres and 3 roods of land forming the 'extensive gardens and pleasure grounds and park-like lawn adjoining', and included the farmstead on Beeston Lane described above (Figure 55).

William Needham needed money: but fortunately the purchaser did not pursue the vendor's suggestion that 'without interfering materially with the enjoyment of the Residence, several eligible sites for Villa Residences might be divided off from the Lawn'. It will be recalled that Lord Middleton's agents were at the same time thinking along the same lines in their proposed development of Lenton Hall park. Perhaps William Paget had too little time to begin housing development along Beeston Lane, for he died four months after his purchase, and the property was placed in trust for his eldest son, William Byerley Paget of Southfields, Loughborough.

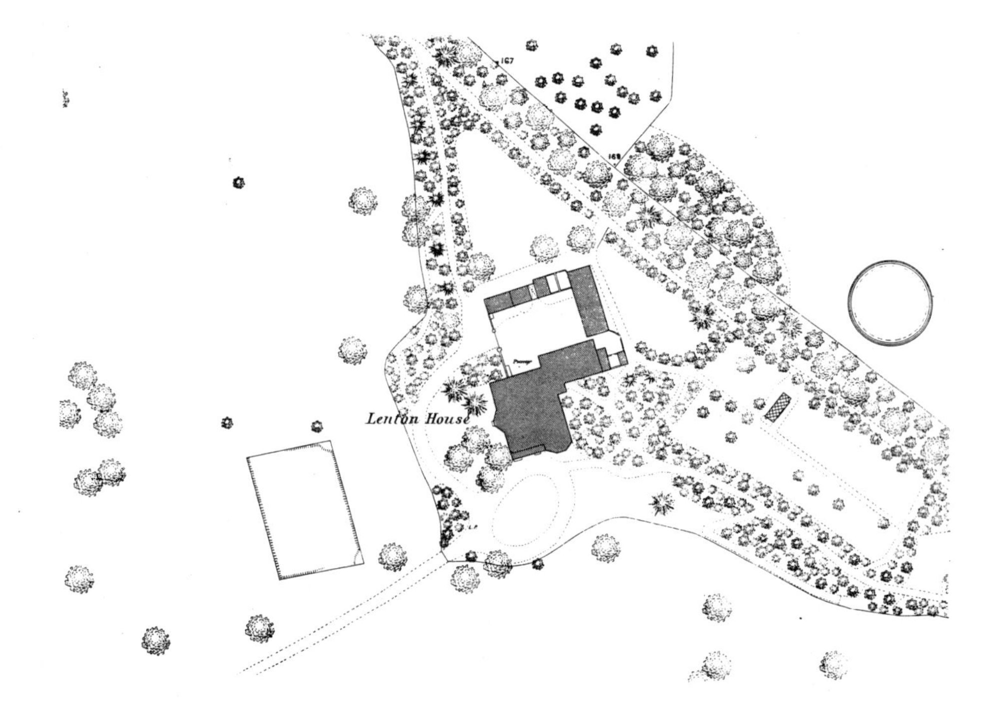

Figure 57: Lenton House and garden in 1881
[Reduced from O.S. 1:500 plan, Nottingham, Sheet XLI.8.24] Note the dewpond on land then in Lenton Hall Park.

The Thorpes at Lenton House

Mrs. Anne Thorpe's tenancy of Lenton House in 1851 to 1858 has been mentioned, and within a decade Thorpes were back there in the persons of John Thorpe of Nottingham, a corn merchant and maltster and his family, after the house had been unoccupied in 1866 [Wright 1866]. At the census of 1871 John Thorpe was 69 years old, and his wife Elizabeth was 73. Staying with them were their daughter, Sarah Burrows (38), wife of a lace manufacturer, her 8-month old daughter, Maude Elizabeth, and two other grandchildren, John E. Cropper (12) born in America, and Elizabeth Jane Cropper (10), with a governess, Eleanor Evans Brentnall (24). The father of the Cropper children was presumably Lionel Cuthbert Cropper, a nephew of W.B.Thorpe and one of his executors named in 1902, but dead before the sale of the estate in 1919. Four female servants completed the Thorpe household in 1871 - Elizabeth Westmorland (49), Sarah Wykes (35), Eliza Spowage (19) and Ann King (25), while Joseph Lee aged 55, the gardener, lived at 'Mr. Thorpe's Lodge, Beeston Lane' with his wife Hannah and gardener son Francis.

John Thorpe died in 1875, and was succeeded by his son William Blankeley Thorpe, also a corn factor and maltster, with premises at 56 Poplar Street and The Malthouse, Milk Street. In 1881 he arranged a new 5-year lease of the Lenton House estate with W.B.Paget, the owner, at a rent of £250 a year. At the end of the lease, on 21 June 1886, Thorpe bought the estate for £10,000 and subsequently extended the house. He seems to have lived on a more lavish scale than his predecessors at Lenton House, for at the census of 1881 [24] the five young Thorpe sisters then at home - Edith Mary (12) Suzy M. (10) the twins Ethel and Hilda (9) and Catherine (5) - were cared for by six female servants, including a nurse and a governess, as well as a coachman, while Joseph Lee the gardener and his wife remained at Lenton House Lodge [25]. William Thorpe lived at Lenton House until his death in July 1914, a few months after his wife Mary died [26]. The twin sisters were still at Lenton House in the early years of this century. One of them married Dr. William R. Smith, who lived on Middle Street, Beeston, and later at The Willows, Dovecote Lane, before retiring to Norfolk . [27] .

In view of the purchases of Lenton House and Highfield House in 1919-20 by John Boot and his father, Sir Jesse, it is interesting to note that W.B.Thorpe was not only a Nottingham maltster, but also a director of the Joint Stock Bank, and was a founder director of Boots Cash Chemists (Western) in 1897 together with H.D.Browne, a wealthy city stockbroker [Chapman 1974 122]. Jesse Boot banked with Nottingham Joint Stock Bank until it merged with London City and Midland Bank at the end of 1905. The Joint Stock Bank made vital advances of capital to Jesse Boot when he was building his Goose-gate shop, and for later ventures. The real founder and first chairman of the Joint Stock Bank was Thomas Adams of Lenton Firs (see Chapter IX). In 1901 W.B.Thorpe of Lenton House [Allen's Red Book 59] was a director of the three companies of Boots Cash Chemists, Eastern, Western and Lancashire. Perhaps Thorpe should be regarded as the unwitting originator of the sequence of transactions through which the future University of Nottingham came to occupy its present campus - but excluding, ironically, Thorpe's own Lenton House estate.

Wentworth Ernest Claye in residence 1914-1919

After the death of the Thorpes in 1914 their trustees seem to have let the Lenton House property for the war years, and W.E.Claye had moved there by 1916 from Bramcote Hills, where he lived from 1908 or earlier. He remained until the estate was sold in 1919 to John Boot. Arthur Mapley, gardener to W.B.Thorpe in 1914 was replaced by Francis George, 'head gardener to W.E.Claye', although meanwhile, in 1915, there was John Gilson, 'gardener to the Thorpe estate'. The Thorpes' coachman, Joseph Rule, lived at the Beeston Lane lodge, but the farmhouse there was in 1916 occupied by J.C.Chapman, 'farm bailiff to W.E.Claye', and Chapman stayed on after the sale of 1919 as 'dairyman' to John Boot [Wright 1916, Kelly

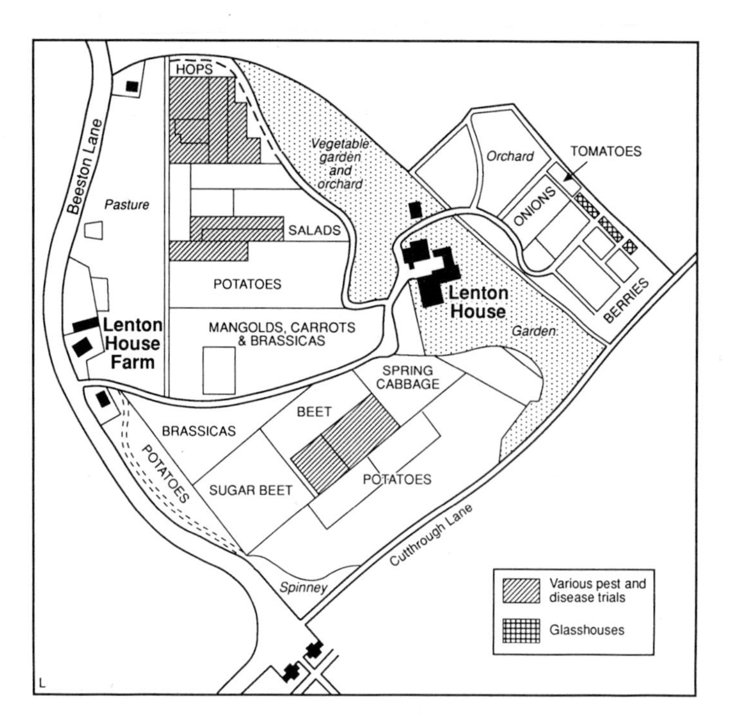

Figure 58: Lenton House estate developed as horticultural trial grounds 1946
[Redrawn from sale catalogue of 1946]

1916-1936].

John Campbell Boot's purchase (1919) and sale (1946)

The Lenton House estate was sold in December 1919 to John Campbell Boot (1889-1956) for £9,500. John Boot, the first Chancellor of the University, was educated at The Leys School and Jesus College Cambridge. In 1914 he married Margaret Joyce Pyman, daughter of a wealthy shipowner. He served in the first world war as a Captain in the Robin Hood Battalion, The Sherwood Foresters, and on his return bought Lenton House as a private residence [28]. Soon afterwards, in 1920, aged 31, he took over the chairmanship of Boots Pure Drug and associated companies, and some matters relating to his period as chairman are discussed in Chapter XII in connection with Lenton Mount. On his father's death in 1931 he succeeded as the second Lord Trent, a title that lapsed on his death without a male heir in March 1956.

John Boot employed a dairyman in the 1920s, but the land use of the estate was completely transformed in the late 1930s. In 1937 part of The Lawn, south-east of the house, was used in a horticultural research project - at first on mercury seed dressings - with Arthur W. Billett (later well known as a broadcaster) in charge. In 1939 the ploughed area was much expanded to promote the 'Grow More Food' campaign in collaboration with the Ministry of Food and the Ministry of Agriculture, with the broadcaster C.H.Middleton involved. By 1944 nearly the whole area of the estate outside the garden was in use for experimental purposes (Figure 58).

On 11 April 1946 Lord Trent sold the whole estate to Boots Pure Drug Company for £40,000, and in 1947 Lenton House became the Company's guest house. Laboratories and

Figure 59: Aerial view of part of the campus from the south in 1969
In addition to Boots' Experimental station the view takes in the Halls of the northern campus and most of the Central Area.

glasshouses were built, and the estate became Lenton Research Station, engaged in research and development of agricultural and horticultural chemicals in association with a fruit farm at Thurgarton and the Koree Research Station in Australia. Comparison of the maps of the estate from the sale catalogues of 1865 and 1946 (Figures 55 and 60) shows that about 4 acres had been added in the north-east, abutting on Cut Through Lane. This land was bought by John Boot from W.G.Player of Lenton Hurst for £3,516 in 1928 when Player was disposing of his land within the present campus, preparatory to moving from Lenton Hurst to Whatton Manor. It was ploughed up for wartime food cropping in October 1939 (See Figure 14). It contains the old dew pond, and the present Education building extends on to it, though the north-western part is retained in the Lenton House estate. In recent years the research station has been run down, and part of the land in the north-west, adjoining the University estate alongside Rutland Hall, and with a generous frontage on Beeston lane, has been presented to the University by Boots plc. as the site of the Jesse Boot Conference Centre, together with a large capital gift towards its building.

Until recently there were three cottages on the Lenton House estate alongside Beeston Lane. Lenton House Farm included with the cottage a farm yard and a barn and implement shed. It was demolished a few years ago when it was no longer needed to house machinery used in cultivating the closed Experimental Station land. It had existed since at least 1780, and was occupied by a succession of tenant farmers, farm bailiffs, dairymen and the like, (not always being run to serve the needs of Lenton House) including John Christopher Chapman (farm bailiff) in the 1930s and Thomas Sharman in 1956. At the northern end of the estate's frontage on Beeston Lane was The Cottage, built in the later 19th century, probably as accommodation for coachmen since from the 1920s it was occupied by Lord Trent's chauffeurs, for example James Stanley Rayner (1932), George Hume (1936) and Albert Parkes (1956). The Cottage has recently been completely renovated and now provides office accommodation for the Jesse Boot Conference Centre. Lenton House Lodge, on the south side

Figure 60: Portrait of Mrs. Catherine Turner c. 1836
Engraving by J. Gilbert. [N.U.M.D. Hi 3 P 52] Courtesy of High Pavement Trustees

of the entrance to the main drive to the house is much more recent, and does not appear on maps prior to the first world war. In 1932 its occupant was John Armstrong, a stud groom, and in 1956 George Reynolds.

LENTON FIELDS

In the Directories of the mid-19th century Lenton Fields House can be distinguished from Lenton House only by the names of the occupiers, and the first occupier of Lenton Fields was Mrs. Catherine Turner (Figure 60), for whom it is said the Matthew Needham built the house. There is good evidence to show that Lenton Fields was built in 1836. It was not shown on Sanderson's 2 inches to one mile map of 1835 (surveyed 1830-34), and Mrs. Turner's school was still at Park Row in that year [Pigot 1835], but she was living at Lenton Fields in July 1837, when she gave great help and comfort to the Needham family during Mrs. Needham's last illness. Constance Martineau wrote [M.C.M. 1910 51] in a reference to the death of Mary Needham 'The end came on the afternoon of that day [25 June 1837]. We were at Lenton at the time, and I remember I was to spend the day at Mrs. Turner's, who then lived at Lenton Field, a house my grandfather had built for her, about ten minutes walk from his own'. The house was included in the First Edition O.S. 1-inch map published on 1 July 1839 [29]. Although it is puzzling to find Matthew Needham building a house with school accommodation for a friend in the mid-1830s, when he was in considerable financial difficulty, it is less surprising if one can appreciate the high degree of sympathy, gratitude, admiration and affection in which Mrs. Turner was held by Matthew and his family. She visited Matthew frequently during his last period of ill health. One day William said to his father 'What a nice person Mrs. Turner is !' and Matthew responded 'I don't know such another. So much judgment, good sense and kindness - it is wonderful how she ingratiates herself with young and old, and how many seek her advice on all subjects. I don't think there is another such woman in the world'. [M.C.M. 1910 59].

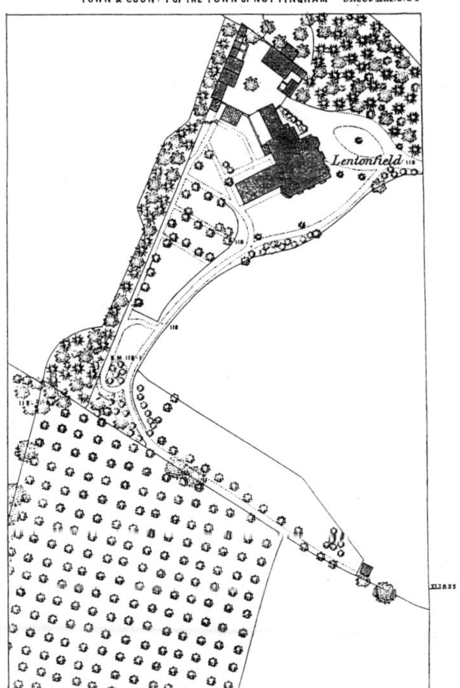

Figure 61: Lenton Fields house and garden in 1881
[From O.S. 1:500 plan: Nottingham Sheet XLI.8.24 (1881)] The name given then was Lentonfield.

Lenton Fields House has been described briefly as follows [Notts.C.C. 1972 3]. 'Early/ mid 19th century, 2-storeyed stuccoed villa, 3 windows. Channelled ground storey with arched windows. Cornice and blocking to slated roof. One storey bow window and added bay. Altered entrance at side. One storey rear wing with eaves to roof'. The single-storeyed wing on the west side of the house is clearly contemporaneous with the main structure, and evidently a schoolroom, though at present subdivided into study-bedrooms. The extension to the rear probably included dormitory accommodation. The list of architectural details hardly does justice to what is perhaps the most pleasing and well proportioned of the old houses on the campus, especially before its chimney stacks were removed some years ago. In time and style it stands alone on the campus, some 35 years later than the six original mansions and 25 years older than the Lenton Firs extension, and 40 years older than the oldest of the newer group of mansions, Lenton Eaves. It was built in the year that Victoria succeeded William IV.

Catherine Turner and her boarding school for Unitarian girls

The antecedents of Mrs. Catherine Turner (Figure 60) and her school are of some interest in connection with the origin and construction of Lenton Fields House. Catherine Rankin was a cousin of Rev. Dr. James Martineau, D.D., and she married Rev. Henry Turner in 1820 [30]. Henry Turner, whose father, Rev. William Turner had a school at Newcastle-upon-Tyne (to which John Needham was sent), founded the famous Literary Society there and was very well known throughout the Unitarian body, came to Nottingham from Bradford in February 1817. He had been educated at Glasgow University and York College, and he was a teacher like his father. 'He was warmly loved by the congregation, and especially by the young people in whom he took the greatest possible interest. A volume of his sermons was published after his death at their request'. He formed a Discussion or Mutual Improvement Society. He lived on Fletcher-gate at the corner of Byard Lane in a house that became the offices of Messrs. Johnstone, Williams and Walker, and took pupils there. He also gave Latin lessons to John and Mary Needham at Lenton House, and Mary (as Mrs. Greg) later wrote 'We all became much attached to Mr. Turner, and when he married Miss Catherine Rankin of Newcastle his congregation subscribed to furnish his house' [M.C.M. 1910]. Henry Turner's untimely death took place 'about two years after his marriage, after a very short illness' and was 'my first great sorrow'. Clearly his young widow received kindnesses from the Needhams at this time, and he was buried near to the Needhams' vault in Lenton Priory churchyard, commemorated by 'a plain square monument' with a Latin epitaph (Lawson Lowe 1871 [31]).

Henry Turner died aged 29 on 31 January or 1 February 1822, and Catherine soon afterwards started a small girls' school to support herself, initially perhaps at the house in Fletcher-gate, but before long in Market Street, where Henry had had an 'academy' in 1818, the year after his arrival at Nottingham [Glover 1818], and the boys' school became a girls' school. Keith Train [c.1973] wrote that in 1822 Catherine Turner 'started a girls' school in Park Row, Nottingham. Soon after Matthew Needham built a house for her, confusingly called Lenton Field or Lenton Field House, which she used as a school, and among her pupils were his younger daughters and later his grandchildren'. This needs considerable qualification. Mrs. Turner's school in 1822 was at 11 Market Street, and in 1828 and 1831 was described by Pigot's Directories as a Ladies' Boarding School. It moved to Park Row in 1831 or 1832 (White [1832] first gave the Park Row address in its list of 'academies') and it was still there in 1835 [Pigot 1835]. The house on Park Row, which had a sunken garden, was immediately opposite to the entrance to East Circus Street. Mary Needham was one of Mrs. Turner's first pupils (at Market Street), and with her younger sister Ellen (Eleanor) walked into Nottingham and back three times a week for lessons. Mary's eldest daughter was Mrs. Turner's hundredth and last pupil. Matthew's youngest daughter was 23 when Mrs. Turner moved to Lenton Fields, so that only his grandchildren could have been to school there - for example, Constance Martineau and Amy Greg.

The school was throughout very small, for Mrs. Turner 'never took a larger number than she could keep under her own influence, and a most valuable influence it was'. It was also very different from the typical 'dame's school' of the time in the standard of education offered, and 'it was widely known throughout Unitarian circles in England, and many of the best-known [Unitarian] families sent their daughters to Mrs. Turner for their education'. Ten girls were resident at Lenton Fields at the 1841 census. They were Maria Hansfield (15) and Elizabeth Hansfield (15), Mary Paget (15), Fanny White (15), Sarah Swaine (15), Susan Hatton (13) and Ann Hatton (14), Emma Henrick (12), Catherine Turner (11) and Constance Martineau(10). Constance wrote of 1840: 'I went to Mrs. Turner's every morning for lessons for 2, 3 or 4 hours according to the day of the week, and never, surely, did school life begin more happily' [M.C.M. 1910]. In 1841, when the school reopened (after Christmas) Constance went back to Lenton House to live with her aunts, now alone there after Matthew Needham's death, but had to become a boarder at Lenton Fields because of the illness of her aunt Camilla, and was recorded there by the Census Enumerator. In 1842, after the Christmas holidays 'I took up my abode at Lenton Field', and 'became more completely a Lenton Field girl'. Among the girls listed above Catherine (Kitty) Turner, a new pupil from Manchester, is not known to have been related to Mrs. Turner. Mary Paget may have been a daughter of Charles Paget of Ruddington Grange, although the two Paget girls at the school in 1851 were both born at Leicester, and presumably belonged to the Birstall branch of the Pagets. The ten girls in 1841 were looked after by two teachers and three domestic servants. Eliza Swanwick was the assistant teacher, and the domestic staff were Ruth Hunter (30), Charlotte Bell (20) and Elizabeth Brompton (15). Miss Swanwick, only recently arrived, was 'young, genial and sympathetic' and was soon very popular.

The 1851 census [31] shows that there were still ten pupils boarding at Mrs. Turner's school. They were Anna Taylor (15) and Bertha Taylor (13), both born at Diss, Norfolk [32], Alice Taylor (14) born at Ellichpore, Julia Keyman (14) of Nottingham, Lucy Taggart (14) London, Ann E. Paget and Harriett Paget (13), both Leicester, Clara White, born at Loughborough, Nina Radice (9) and Amy Greg (10) of Styal, Cheshire, Matthew Needham's granddaughter. Such names as Paget and Styal are familiar among the Unitarian textile manufacturing families [Chapman 1967 198] [33]. The Dublin-born teacher Eliza Swanwick, now 40, had been joined by a third teacher, Eliza Wilson (25) born in Glasgow. There were still three domestic servants in the house [34]. Three teachers to ten pupils is a staff-student ratio that testifies to the fact that Mrs. Turner provided an expensive education as well as a good one, and it was only for daughters of very well-to-do Unitarians.

The education provided at Lenton Fields was broadly based and ambitious. Botany studied in the field was enjoyed greatly. Some girls 'read with Miss Swanwick Buckland's Bridgwater Treatise, a geological work which first impressed upon me that we must not look to the Bible for scientific truth ... an astounding enlightenment to me' [M.C.M. 1910]. Books read and studied with Mrs. Turner included Burke on The Sublime and Beautiful, Alison on Taste, Paly's Moral Philosophy and Lingard's History of England. The pupils were taught to play piano, draw, dance, speak French; and also to think, and 'to have an earnest purpose in life'. Mrs. Turner always encouraged an intelligent interest in public affairs, and used to read the debates - for example that on Peel's 1844 Dissenters Chapel Act - as they appeared day by day. There were visiting teachers. Among them was Mr. Spencer of Derby, father of Herbert Spencer [35], who 'came once a week to give lessons on natural philosophy. The aim ... [was] to teach us to think, to find out things for ourselves, and explain in clear language the reason of them'. With more advanced pupils Spencer went on to astronomy, electricity and other sciences. This was very different from the regime of most private schools at that time.

Yet in some respects, perhaps, ideas outside school were less advanced. For example: 'It was about this time that we began the habit of going on fine mornings before breakfast to Tuttle Brook for a drink of fresh water. I think it was Aunt Anne who introduced the custom as an encouragement for getting up early. She wrote a poem about it' [M.C.M. 1910 69]. But Anne Needham, the artist, was not educated by Mrs. Turner, and had married Henry Enfield in 1835 and left Lenton House the year before Lenton Fields was built. Robert Mellors [1916 29] mentioned that the Tottle Brook 'was regarded in the olden times as having beneficent medical qualities'!

Constance Martineau wrote that Mrs. Turner 'kept school' for 28 or 29 years, but this was an underestimate. She was still at Lenton Fields in 1858 [Wright 1858], and since she opened her first school in 1822, and since 'my Aunt Mary's eldest daughter' Amy Greg (aged 10 in 1851) was said to be her hundredth and last pupil, she probably retired before she reached the age of 60, in 1858 or 1859, and subsequently lived on Park Terrace [White 1864 272]. She lived for a further 35 years, and died in 1894 at the age of 94, having survived her husband, after only two years of marriage, by more than 70 years [M.C.M. 1910]. After Mrs. Turner's retirement the school was carried on for a time by Miss Eliza Swanwick and Miss Marie Wirz, and then by Miss Wirz and Miss Buob, but perhaps in different premises because by the census of 1861 William Needham had sold Lenton Fields to Henry Hadden, a hosiery manufacturer aged 46, who was already in residence with his cook, Mary Drury (49) and a housemaid, Elizabeth Morrel (25).

In her retirement Catherine Turner remained very active on behalf of High Pavement Chapel, which was throughout at the centre of her life. She was a teacher at the Sunday School there for 50 years, and superintendent for 25 years. When at Lenton Fields she used to take her pupils over on Sundays to take a class in the school, chartering a 'fly' for those unable to walk both ways. When she retired from Sunday School work, aged 80, she was presented with an address, and in an obituary in the 'Inquirer' of 12 May 1894 Dr. Martineau paid tribute to her in these words: 'She was a gentle and gracious woman, and an old scholar speaking of very much earlier days than I can remember once said to me that when in the company of Mrs. Turner and Mrs. William Enfield (Anne Needham, her co-superintendent) he felt he was associating with "beings of a higher sphere". She kept her youthfulness and interest in life to the last'. In her will she left over £ 700 to Mr. Benjamin Dowson (husband of Amy Greg) to be used by him as he might think best for the benefit of High Pavement Chapel and its schools. Most was used, appropriately, to restore and improve the schoolrooms.

Purchases by Henry Hadden (c. 1859) and James Holwell Lee (1867)

Henry Hadden was a member of J. and H. Hadden and Co., hosiers and glove manufacturers with a factory on Stanford Street, Nottingham. This firm originally came to Nottingham from Aberdeen in 1787 to channel supplies of hosiery yarn from Scotland to the Midlands, where there was a scarcity [Chapman 1967 101]. Lenton Fields house was built on less than 5 acres bought by Matthew Needham from James Green after the major part of the Home Abbey Field (Abbey Field Close) had been allocated to John Wright in 1809, a small area by comparison with the land attached to the other old houses on the campus. The Middleton estate map of 1863 [36] shows that Hadden had lost no time in renting the Abbey Field Close (which had been restored to Lenton Abbey farm after Lord Middleton's purchase of the Lenton Hall estate in 1845) together with the remainder of the land west of Beeston Lane, by then in two closes with a combined area of 14a.2.17, which now forms the Beeston Lane playing fields. It included a strip of woodland which now separates Lenton Fields house from the sports grounds.

Henry Hadden owned Lenton Fields for less than a decade, and in 1867 he sold the 4½ acres and the house to James Holwell Lee, J.P., of the firm Lee and Gee, and went to live on the Ropewalk [Wright 1871]. The land was described as 'fenced off from, and formerly the south or south-east end of a close of James Green commonly called Home Abbey Field'. Lee next acquired from Thomas Bayley of Lenton Abbey the 14½ acres mentioned above, 'adjoining, and forming an irregular triangle at the angle formed by Beeston Lane with Derby turnpike'. This was a triangular transaction (see Chapter X below) being part of the sale of all Lord Middleton's Lenton estate [37]. Lee, owning Lenton Fields, already occupied these fields, and this transaction, by detaching the land from the Lenton Abbey estate, may well have preserved it from council house development in the 1920s. The conveyance from Lord Middleton to Lee placed restrictions on the type of building development to be permitted on the land, and Lenton Eaves was the only type allowed.

This land was now in two closes, of 5a.3.23 and 8a.1.16, with 1r.12p. of woodland. On the southern part of the smaller field Lee realigned the drive to Lenton Fields house from Beeston Lane, and immediately north of the entrance built a lodge for his gardener (see Figure 59) the site of which is today marked only by a few ornamental conifers surviving from the garden, behind a wall of Bulwell stone. The lodge, together with 871 sq. yards of land, was sold to the Corporation for road widening in 1927 by S.C.Armitage, then the owner, and the lodge was demolished [Rotheras] (Figure 62).

At the 1871 census [38] J.H.Lee, aged 52, the owner and occupier of Lenton Fields house, was described as a magistrate and landowner, and a cotton spinner and hosier employing about 100 people. Elizabeth Lee was his second wife, the ages of their children in 1871 - James P. (7), Lawrence B. (6), and Reginald (5) showing them to have been a generation apart from children of an earlier marriage. These were Ann Elizabeth (27), Charles Leslie (23), 'hosier', and William Thomas (20), 'cotton spinner', all living with their parents, and the sons apparently associated with their father's businesses. Three female servants lived in, and Robert Hamilton, aged 34, the gardener, lived with his wife Ann at 'Mr. Lee's Lodge, Beeston Lane', newly built on land bought only in October 1869.

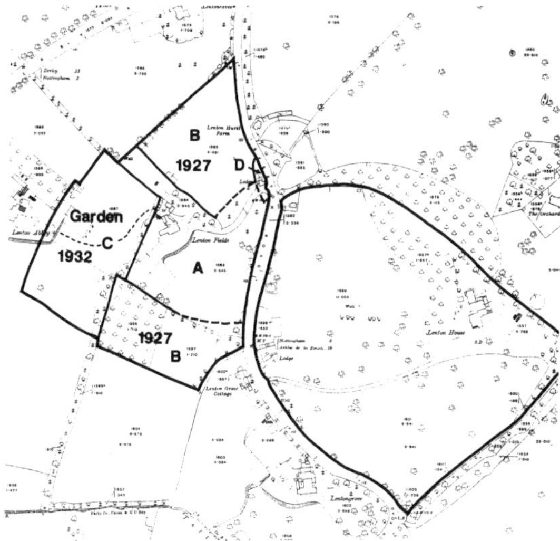

A	-	Lenton Fields as purchased by Richard Granger in 1907
B	-	Land purchased by Granger in 1917
A B and D	-	Estate purchased by Armitages in 1927
D	-	Sold to Corporation for road widening in 1928
C	-	Land bought by Armitages in 1932 - a remnant of the Lenton Abbey estate

Figure 62: Lenton House and Lenton Fields estates
[Base map reduced from O.S. 25-inch map of 1915] Stephen Cecil Armitage and Hilda Winifred Armitage in 1927 purchased Lenton Fields from the trustees of Richard Granger

Occupiers of Lenton Fields, 1880-1946

Figure 61 depicts Lenton Fields house and garden in 1881. James Lee was still living at Lenton Fields in 1876 [Kelly 1876] but was apparently about to leave. On 17 April 1875 he had sold the 8-acre field to Benjamin Walker junior, then of Beeston, for £3,349, and Walker built his house called Lenton Eaves in the north-east corner of it in that same year (see Chapter XII). Lee was succeeded at Lenton Fields by **William Heape Walker**, younger brother of Benjamin Walker junior, and also a member of the family firm of Benjamin Walker and Co., who had been living with his father in 1877 and 1879 at Lenton Priory in Old Lenton [Morris 1877]. Benjamin Walker senior must have died then, for in 1881 William Heape Walker, aged 30 and unmarried, was at Lenton Fields with his mother, Emma Walker, aged 66 [Wright 1881, Kelly 1881] [39]. Lee was at Newcastle Drive, The Park in 1881 according to the electoral register, in which he qualified in Lenton because he still owned Lenton Fields. In 1881 Benjamin Walker junior, aged 38, had succeeded his father of the same name as head of the lace manufacturing business at Spring Close. The Walker household at Lenton Fields in 1881 was served by Fanny Wickenton (27) a cook, Elizabeth Wright (25) a housemaid, and a coachman, Henry Harwood (25) who lived with his wife Ann at Lenton Field Lodge.

William Heape Walker was still at Lenton Fields in 1887 [White 1887] but in 1889 (James H. Lee) and in 1891 and 1895 (Mrs. Elizabeth Lee) the owner was named by Wrights' Directories, suggesting that there was no tenant (and that James Lee had died in about 1890). It is thought that W.H.Walker left in 1888. The next known tenant, William Griffith Forster of the Beeston Brewery Company, was at Lenton Fields in 1894 [White 1894] and 1897 [Wright 1897]: but Joseph Spendlove, an embroidery manufacturer at 19 Castle-gate, Nottingham, was named on Beeston Lane in 1894 [White 1894], 1895 [Kelly 1895] and 1897 [Wright 1897], and it is known that he was the owner and occupier of Lenton Fields in 1900 [Briscoe 1901]. It is certain that he followed Forster there, for a conveyance in the care of Rotheras refers to the 'Mansion or dwelling house called Lenton Fields with the outoffices, stables, gardens, pleasure grounds, lodge and croft comprising 6.632 acres ... formerly in the occupation of William Griffiths Forster, late of Joseph Spendlove and now or recently of the vendor' (Richard Granger). It appears that in the 1890s Spendlove lived for some years at Lenton Grove before he purchased Lenton Fields and displaced Forster. Lenton Grove was vacant in 1904 [Kelly], with Spendlove at Lenton Fields, and his coachman, Joseph Rule, occupying the lodge built by James H. Lee.

By the end of 1907 Richard Granger, a lace manufacturer, had bought and occupied Lenton Fields, and Spendlove was living in 1908 at The Willows, West End, Beeston [Kelly 1908]. Granger lived at Lenton Fields for about 20 years, and after his death his executors on 20 August 1927 sold the property to Stephen Cecil Armitage of Cavendish Crescent for £3,650. The attached land was 6.632 acres when Granger bought the property, and was said to extend to 6.451 acres when bought by Armitage [Rotheras]. In the same year, 1927, 4.149 acres, earlier part of the Home Abbey Field, were added. The 6.451 acres was the field lying now between Nightingale Hall and the drive from Beeston Lane to the Sports Centre, and the 4.149 acres lay north of the drive. Armitage immediately sold 871 yards for road widening as mentioned above. Land to the south, up to the boundary of Lenton Grove's grounds, some 3.423 acres, was conveyed separately from Granger's executors to Hilda Winifred Armitage, spinster of Beeston for £1,650, and on 17 September to S.C.Armitage. Later, in 1932, a further parcel of 4a.1.23, forming the easternmost part of the Lenton Abbey estate, was conveyed to Armitage for £2,000 [Rotheras]. Nightingale Hall is built on a former orchard which was conveyed to Richard Granger in 1917 as part of the 3.432 acres, and then to Miss Hilda Armitage and S.C.Armitage in 1927. By these accretions the property attached to Lenton Fields House was extended in area to 16.568 acres.

Stephen C. (later Sir Cecil) Armitage was a Nottingham solicitor with the firm Eking,

Morris and Armitage of Long Row in 1916, and not to be confused with Stephen Armitage of Broadgate House, Beeston. After some 20 years he sold Lenton Fields House and the whole 16½ acres of land to University College Nottingham on 2 May 1946 for £16,000. Nightingale Hall was built on it in 1947. For a short time Lenton Fields House provided flat accommodation for members of the teaching staff, including Mr. and Mrs. H.A.Moisley (Geography) and Mr. and Mrs. A.Aitken (Zoology), but it then became an annexe to Nightingale Hall, being opened with accommodation for 21 students after the summer vacation of 1950, at the same time as Lenton Eaves.

The conveyance of the Lenton Firs estate to the University of Nottingham on 24 March 1950 indicates that 'Lenton Hall Farm' was occupied by S.C.Armitage. This is taken to be an error for Lenton Hurst Farm, which had been rented by Armitage from Sir Thomas Shipstone, who had bought it from W.G.Player; and Armitage presumably farmed the Lenton Hurst land together with his own 16½ acres of Lenton Fields across Beeston Lane, from the Lenton Hurst farm buildings, where his bailiff would have lived (for example Joseph Tinsley in 1956). He continued to operate Lenton Hurst Farm for a time after Lenton Fields had been sold to the University (though he now lived at Hawksworth Manor, where he followed Sir Alexander Russell Birkin) ending with the building of the men's Halls and the demolition of the farm buildings to make way for Rutland and Sherwood Halls in 1963 (see Figure 126).

NOTES

1. Extract from a letter written by Matthew Needham senior in August 1777: 'Mr. F. was at Quorn last week, says our dear boy there is exceeding well' [M.C.M. 1910]. M.C.M. was Constance Martineau, who was the daughter of Richard Martineau and Lucy Needham, and was Matthew Needham's first grandchild. She quoted profusely from family letters, and from a manuscript called 'Recollections' written by her aunt, Mrs. Greg, nee Mary Priscilla Needham, about her childhood. M.C.M.'s book was heavily drawn upon by K.S.Train in his undated pamphlet on Lenton House published for the Boots Company, as it has been also for this account.
2. The connection with 1684 was made by Godfrey [1884] following the schedule of lands in N.U.M.D., Wadsworth 52, 'Copy of the parcels in the conveyance from Miss Milward to Messrs. Pares and Paget, 28 and 29 March 1798'. A copy of the appropriate part of the schedule of lands at the sale of 1684 is found in N.U.M.D., Wadsworth 50. The terrier of 1684 does not name a Hill Field Close, and neither do those of 1731 and 1743; and the correct name is probably High Field Close.
3. N.U.M.D., Wadsworth 50
4. N.A.O., Land tax assessments for Lenton. Most years from 1780 to 1832 are held.
5. A joint portrait of Catherine Turner and Anne Enfield in oils, dated c. 1860 is in the University's Manuscript Department Hi 3 P 81.
6. M.C.M. [1910]; Mrs. Greg's 'Recollections'. Maria Enfield (1806-84) married John Withers Dowson, attorney, of Norwich. Anna Enfield (1814-60) married in 1835 at Bramcote, Septimus Dowson, merchant of Geldeston, Norfolk.
7. Richard Enfield was closely associated with the Mechanics Institution, the General Hospital, the Midlands Institution for the Blind, the Coppice Lunatic Asylum, the Midland Orphanage, the Eye Infirmary, Bromley House Library and the School of Art. He was president of the British and Foreign Unitarian Society in 1885-86, was twice president of the Nottingham Incorporated Law Society, and was for 35 years Sunday School Teacher and superintendent at High Pavement school. His friend, Rev. Dr. J.B.Paton is discussed in connection with Paton House (originally West Hill House) in Chapter XII.
8. In 1832 John Manning Needham paid land tax of 2s. a year on his brewery property, on land belonging to his brother William. John himself had other land in Beeston taxed at 2s. 7d.. When the brewery failed John joined the Martineau brewery in Chiswell Street, London. John and Jane had three children, William Manning, Manning and Fanny, who married William Dalton Holt of Liverpool.
9. N.U.M.D., Mi F 12 : Letter of 1 December 1831.
10. Edward Harrison, Dr. Storer's gardener, testified at the trial of the arrested rioters that a dozen or fourteen men came into the garden at Lenton Firs, and told Dr. Storer that it was a revolution, and he had better get out of the way or he would be hurt. Storer forbade Harrison to give them carrots: they cursed him and said they would have what they liked. They came back in the afternoon. Another version [Barker 1835] was that the venerable Dr. Storer boldly came out to confront the rioters and induced them to depart.
11. N.A.O., Dowson Mss. 523/1-3. Among the comments was 'What a happiness that the Brewery is not finished!.' The Yeomanry coming from Wollaton scoured the field and arrested two.

12. N.U.M.D., Mi F 12 : Letter of 1 December 1831.
13. Iliffe and Baguley, Victorian Nottingham, 8, 38.
14. N.A.O., Dowson Mss. 523/1-3. Colonel Hancox had garrisoned the Hall with a body of colliers, with several pieces of cannon, and the Wollaton Yeomanry were stationed near the entrance.
15. K.C.Edwards (ed.) Nottingham and its Region (1966) Appendix I. Lawson Lowe [1871] wrote that Matthew 'rendered considerable service as a meteorologist at a time when the science of meteorology was little studied'.
16. M.C.M. [1910] gave a detailed description of the circumstances of the death of both Matthew and Mary Needham.
17. Census of 1841, Enumerators' Books H.O. 107/858
18. N.A.O., Dowson 523/1-3, quoted at length by M.C.M. [1910]. William Gibbin probably died soon afterwards since Mrs. Hannah Gibbin was living on Market Street, Beeston in 1844 [Glover 1844]. During Caroline Needham's last years at Lenton House the farmstead and farm land were let, since Lascelles and Hagar's Commercial Directory of Nottingham for 1848 lists among the farmers of Lenton William Snow of Lenton Field. Indeed, 'William Gibbin, cowkeeper' [Glover 1832] himself may have been a rent-paying tenant in Matthew Needham's time.
19. Earlier, in 1841 William and Camilla were staying at Lenton House, for Constance Martineau, who went to live there and attend the Lenton Fields school wrote that because of complications following Camilla's confinement 'I was sent to board at Mrs. Turner's ... as neither the aunts nor the maids had any time to attend to me'. [M.C.M. 1910].
20. This still referred to the farm house, because the lodge to Lenton Fields was not built until after 1869, and neither lodge at the two Beeston Lane entrances to Lenton House had yet been built.
21. The second brother was Colonel Robert Holden (1805-1872) of Nuthall Temple, which was inherited from his father who lived at Darley Abbey. The third brother was Rev. Alexander A. Holden, M.A., who owned Nuthall Temple in 1881.
22. Captain Holden (see Appendix 17) was still at Bramcote Hills in 1900 [Kelly 1900].
23. Lord Middleton was informed in a letter of 26 July from Joseph Moore, his agent, that 'Mr. Needham's property, Lenton House and land 28 acres, has been sold to Mr. Paget, Sutton Bonington for £ 5,800. I do not think it dear at that price'. N.U.M.D., Mi E 33/1 (1865).
24. Census of 1881, Enumerators' Books. For Lenton, RG 11/3340. 9 April 1881.
25, The resident domestic staff at Lenton House in 1881 was:
Mary Ann Gunn (17) kitchen maid: Eliza Thorpe (25) housemaid
Jane Stewart (17) nurse : Mary Shelton (38) lady's maid
William H. Gunn (23) coachman : Clarissa Elliott (53) governess
Elizabeth Westmorland (59) cook - also in 1871.
26. Wright [1913] named him, but in 1915 recorded John Gilson, Beeston Lane, 'gardener to the Thorpe estate', and W.B.Thorpe and his wife were dead.
27. Beeston Local History Society, 13, September 1974. Dr. Smith lived on Middle Street West in 1904. In 1908 Joseph Spendlove was living at The Willows, West End, Beeston after selling Lenton Fields (see below).
28. John Boot had other homes - 32 Smith Square, Westminster, and Glenborrodale Castle, Acharacle, Argyll. [Baylis 1935].
29. For the correct date of the quarter-sheet see Chapter XIII, fn. 41.
30. Whether Mrs. Turner could be said to be distantly related to the Needhams by marriage after Lucy Needham married Richard Martineau in 1827 is questionable. The Martineaus were descended from a Huguenot family who came to England on the revocation of the Edict of Nantes in 1685. James Martineau is said to have been so much affected by attending the funeral of his friend Rev. Henry Turner in 1822 that he gave up engineering for a religious life. He became Principal of Manchester New College in succession to Rev. James Taylor.
31. Census of 1851, Enumerators' Books: for Lenton H.O. 107/2129-2130. Taken 5 April 1851.
32. Mr. and Mrs. Lombe Taylor of Diss were Unitarians, visited by the Needhams when on holiday at Cromer in 1839 [M.C.M. 1910 54].
33. See Mary Rose, The Gregs of Quarry Bank Mill: the rise and decline of a family firm 1750-1914 (1986).
34. The domestic staff at Lenton Fields in 1851 were Anne Belfield (29) housemaid, Elizabeth Fougas (18) cook, and Maria Keeting (16) kitchen maid.
35. Herbert Spencer (1820-1903), born at Derby, lived for four years in the house that became the Spread Eagle Inn on Alfreton Road, Nottingham. After early struggles he became a prolific author of philosophical books.
36. N.U.M.D., Mi P 6 (maps) and Mi 2 S 3 (reference book to plans): by Sturgess, 1863. See Plan No. 2.
37. N.U.M.D., Mi 4 Da 4 (1869), Conveyance from Lord Middleton and others to J. Holwell Lee Esq., 21 October 1869: Thomas Bayley of Lenton Abbey of the second part. The fields were originally to be sold to Bayley for £2,000, which had not yet been paid, and Bayley agreed to the sale to Lee for £2,100, of which he retained £100.
38. Census of 1871, Enumerators' Books. For Lenton RG/3499-3500. In 1869 James Lee was still living in Sherwood according to Fry [1989 19]. In 1901 [Allen 1902] and 1903 W.H.Lee was one of three directors of Lamb and Lee Limited, hosiery manufacturers of Lamartine Street, Nottingham.
39. See also Census of 1881, Enumerators' Books. For Lenton RG 11/3340-3341.

CHAPTER IX

LENTON FIRS

Thomas and Elizabeth Watson: the Georgian house and its land
Lord Middleton's purchase, 1813
Lord Middleton's tenants, 1815-1867
Alexander Foxcroft (b. 1770) 1815-23: the diversion of Derby Road and splitting of Lenton Firs estate.
Dr. John Storer, F.R.S. (1747-1837): physician, innovator, organizer and speculator.
The Misses Wright, Charlotte, Frances and Ann, 1838-45
Thomas Adams (1807-1873) 1845-67 (and owner 1867-73): lace merchant.
The Victorian house and lodge (1861-62)
David Mitchell, gardener.
John Adams, 1873-76
Robert Arthur Hollins, 1878-81
Edward Cope, 1881-89
Alderman William Lambert (1823-1905): 1889-1903: Lace finisher, sportsman, and builder of the Theatre Royal.
Sir Thomas Shipstone (d.1940) brewer: bought Lenton Firs in 1903
Further purchases: Lenton Hall Farm 1905; Lenton Hurst Farm 1930
Lenton Firs grounds
Lenton Firs (formerly Lenton Hall) farm after 1940.
Lenton Firs as H.M.Forces convalescence hospital 1941 and as Hall of Residence for women, 1946-50
The University purchase 1950

The Georgian house and its builder

In 1798 John Wright bought the whole of the northern corner of the former priory demesne fronting the Nottingham-Derby turnpike road as far west as the present Lenton Eaves. After a year or two he re-sold a substantial area in the north to Thomas Wright Watson, a Nottingham hosiery manufacturer, who built the house called Lenton Firs on the highest part of his portion. (Figure 63). The house was much enlarged in the mid-19th century, and until recently (1987) was the nucleus of Wortley Hall of Residence, which has now been converted for use by the University Department of Architecture.

It must be admitted that the antecedents of Thomas Wright Watson are not entirely clear to the writer. Thomas Bailey [1853 96] described Thomas Watson as a 'merchant and manufacturer' and one of the two sheriffs of Nottingham in 1782. He also referred to the 'extensive firm of Watsons and Nelsons' which occupied the premises on Fletcher-gate 'where the extensive business of the Messrs. Morley is now [1853] carried on. This firm, 'like all the rest of the old manufacturing establishments in the town, perished before the new principles of trade and manufacture introduced by youthful competitors, to which they could not at once conform themselves'. In 1793 there was a firm of hosiers called J. and F. Watson and Co. Ltd., probably the same business as that referred to by Willoughby [1799] as 'Watson and Co., Hosiers, Fletcher-gate', the only reference to a Watson by that Directory, and presumably the firm with which Thomas Wright Watson was associated. It is believed that his father was also Thomas Watson, since he was probably the 'Mr. Watson junior' whose death was recorded in the diary of Prebendary Charles Wylde on 19 April 1802 [1] while his

Figure 63: Lenton Hall, Wollaton Hall and Lenton Firs in 1812
Although this well-known engraving is entitled in some versions 'Wollaton Hall from the river Trent', the viewpoint must be the bridge carrying the Dunkirk Road-Chain Lane over the Beeston Canal. The whole view is foreshortened. On the right is the Georgian Lenton Firs house. The trees in the middle distance line the Tottle Brook.

father may have been the partner in the firm Samuel and Thomas Watson, 'manufacturers of hose in general' [Bailey 1784 414] and the writer who had prefaced a pamphlet in the controversy surrounding the forced resignation of William Smith from the office of mayor in 1789 with 'a short, sensible and temperate address to the inhabitants of Nottingham [Bailey 1853 96].

Lawson Lowe, unusually for him, was incorrect in stating that Watson purchased his estate from Messrs. Pares and Paget, and also that Lenton Firs was built by T.W.Watson 'about the year 1792' - almost a decade too early. Watson was not among those named in the land tax list for Lenton approved on 27 June 1799, and his name was appended to the list of 1800 only at a late stage. By June 1802 he was replaced in the land tax schedule by his widow.

Thomas Watson's Lenton Firs estate, about 38 acres in all, was much larger than it became after 1822. It included the Lodge Field of 17a.2.10, the Six Acres Close west of the Lodge Field, on which the house was built, and parts of Sand Hill Field and Sandy Field, all relatively recent subdivisions of the old Abbey Field. Lodge Field, lying 'against Derby Road' (the old turnpike now lost within Wollaton Park and Wollaton Park housing estate) was sometimes known as the Summer House Field after the so-called Summer Houses, the twin lodges which until 1792 stood at the old entrance to Wollaton Park from the old main road, near to the present park entrance gate off Middleton Boulevard [2] . Lodge Field extended south-east from the turnpike immediately west of the Wollaton Park entrance, across the present road called Adams Hill and east of the drive called Wortley Close (Figure 21 and 89). The western boundary of the Lenton Firs estate ran from the place at which Lenton Hall Drive, now a pedestrian entrance to the University, met Derby Road, south-eastwards round the present woodland below the squash courts, and from a point below the drive to the Cripps Health Centre eastwards to the junction of Cut Through Lane with Sandy Lane near to the present tower block. A witness in a law suit of 1823, Thomas Roe, described how Watson felled some old oak trees that stood 'upon the bank between the [old] road and that field' (Lodge Field). Lenton Firs estate was essentially residential, and not agricultural, being composed largely of coarse, sandy land of the Nottingham Castle Formation, traditionally rabbit warren, but with a fringe of better soil on Lenton Sandstone.

According to a large square monument near the door of the old Priory church at Lenton, Thomas Watson died aged 44 on 20 April 1802. His daughter Mary, aged 5, died on 30 September 1801, and his son Henry, aged 17, on 8 May 1802 [Lawson Lowe 1871 31]. Elizabeth Watson, having lost her daughter, husband and son in seven months, perhaps from some contagious disease such as influenza or tuberculosis, lived on at Lenton Firs until her death in 1813. The Nottingham Journal of 15 May 1813 advertised the sale of Lenton Firs and its estate by auction, describing it as 'a very compact and desirable Freehold, Tythe-free Estate called Lenton Firs, comprising a well built modern Mansion House with offices of every description, an excellent garden, hot house, pleasure ground, and about 38 acres of good arable, meadow and pasture land ... situate ... on a delightful Eminence on the south side of the Turnpike Road leading from Nottingham to Derby, opposite to Wollaton Park (from whence it is abundantly stocked with game) and commands a beautiful view of Nottingham and Belvoir Castle, the Trent Vale, Clifton Grove and surrounding country. The house is fit for the reception of a large genteel family, and Possession may be had immediately after the sale'. The solicitors were Bolton and Payne of Nottingham.

Lord Middleton immediately bought the house and land from 'Watson's assignees' - the first of the three purchases by which he added the whole Lenton frontage on Derby Road opposite Wollaton Park to his estate. A reason for the later purchases was to be able to prevent threatened building development opposite to Wollaton Park at a time when Wollaton Hall was still a favoured residence of the Middletons. But the particular reason for this first purchase was that Lord Middleton wished to extend Wollaton Park eastwards to the Nottingham Canal across the former Beck Field, and to move the entrance to it from approximately its present position off Middleton Boulevard to the Derby Road crossing of the canal and the river Leen at Hillside, where the impressive Lenton Lodge entrance now stands in isolation. This intention was clearly in mind before Lenton Firs came on to the market, because in 1812 Lord Middleton was obtaining an abstract of title of the Gregory estate which had owned the southern part of the former Beck Field since its inclosure in 1768, and he probably purchased that part of Beck Field between the old turnpike and the present Adams Hill east of the intersection with Middleton/Clifton Boulevard in that year.

Lord Middleton 'agreed with the Trustees of the turnpike road to make a new road 20 yards wide and build a bridge, in consideration of having the old road conveyed to him, which have been done' [3]. This took place in 1822. The sharp diversion of Derby Road to its new line down Adams Hill (Figure 89) was inconvenient to the public road users because it introduced a gradient too steep to be comfortable for horse-drawn vehicles, a difficulty that was not encountered on the historic line of the road. The land between the old and new lines of Derby Road - some 16 acres of Lenton Firs land, mostly from the Lodge Field, and over 22 acres of Gregory estate land of the former Beck Field - was taken into Wollaton Park behind a new wall, and an embankment inside it which was planted with trees.

Lenton Firs was left with only about 19½ of its original 38 acres, and this required an adjustment of the rent value of the property, and eventually a correction of its land tax, which was reduced from £4.2s.0d. to £3.4s.0d. in 1828. Mid-19th century cadastral maps show a double line of trees from the old Wollaton Park entrance to the new one at Lenton Lodge, with an alignment that suggests that an avenue was planted in anticipation of a road diversion in 1812, before Lenton Firs came unexpectedly on to the market with the death of Mrs. Watson. Lenton

Firs house was originally situated well back from the turnpike road, and large-scale 19th century maps appear to indicate by a line of trees joining gaps in the roadside banks the original well-graded line of access, a drive running from the old main road southwards and then south-westwards to the Georgian part of the present house. The diversion of 1822 (discussed further in Chapter XIII) brought the turnpike road much nearer to the house, and resulted in the short, steep access drive that we see today.

Lord Middleton's tenants, 1815-1867

Between its purchase by Lord Middleton in 1813 and its sale in 1868 Lenton Firs was occupied by a succession of rent-paying tenants.

Alexander Foxcroft (b. 1770) 1815-1823

The first Middleton tenant was Alexander Foxcroft, who entered the Middleton estate rental in 1815, occupying Lenton Firs house and a field together with Dog Lane Close (later called Nutt's Close) and paying a half-yearly rent of £47 [4]. The Foxcroft family had been prominent in legal and public affairs in Nottingham in the 18th century, and five Foxcrofts were sheriffs between 1731 and 1762 [Bailey 1853 1168,1228,1239,1248]. John Foxcroft was named as attorney to the Commissioners in respect of Trowell bridge in April 1766 [Meaby 1947 107] and he was a Senior Councilman. He died in 1779 [Sutton 1852 59]. An earlier Alexander Foxcroft was a solicitor who was elected a Senior Councilman in 1762. He died in 1774. Alexander Foxcroft of Lenton Firs was aged 53 in 1823, and was described as Clerk to the Trustees of Derby Turnpike Road [5]. Earlier he was known as an attorney of James Street, Nottingham [Holden 1805 237]. It is probable, though not certain in view of his youth, that he was the person described as Attorney and Steward of the Mayor's and Sheriff's courts for the town of Nottingham in the 1790s [6], and was appointed by the Tories at the election of 1802 to organize the raising of signatures for a petition to Parliament for an annulment, and who denied charges of dishonesty in that exercise [Thomis 1968 88-91]. It must be said, however, that the conjunction between Foxcroft's profession, his appointment with the Turnpike Trust, his tenure of Lord Middleton's property (Lenton Firs) and Lord Middleton's anxiety to divert the turnpike road through Lenton Firs land is intriguing to say the least.

At Michaelmas 1818 Alexander Foxcroft was paying £205 a year in rent for Lenton Firs[7], but in the 1820 rental 'Notice' was written against his name in the Lady Day rent schedule, and 'Under discharge' in that of Michaelmas [8]. However, Foxcroft's rent continued until 1823[9], when he gave evidence for Lord Middleton in the trespass suit against John Wright relating to his alleged encroachment on the turnpike road [10] (see Chapter XIII). The rent was reduced to £ 42 a half year at Michaelmas 1821, presumably because Foxcroft was now denied the use of the 16 acres that were being incorporated into Wollaton Park, or was suffering inconvenience caused by the deterioration of access to Lenton Firs. In 1823 settling-up payments were being made by Foxcroft for rent, dilapidations and 'use of fixtures', and were being made to him for what appear to have been improvements made by him at Lenton Firs - 'For floors, stairs, shutters, bath stoves and chimney pieces £115.0s.0d. : Stove in the hall and manure left £12.0s. 0d.'. This was in the year after the diversion of the Nottingham-Derby turnpike down Adams Hill was successfully completed. Little is known of the Foxcroft household during their tenure of Lenton Firs, except that Lenton Priory church registers show that Herbert, an infant son of Alexander and Sarah Foxcroft, died on 6 October 1817 aged five months.

Dr. John Storer, F.R.S. (1747-1837) (Figure 64)

Lenton Firs is missing from the Middleton rentals for the years between 1824 and 1827 inclusive. A brief for litigation in 1823, which is discussed in some detail in Chapter XIII [11] reads

Figure 64: Dr. John Storer, FRS (1747-1837)
[From a portrait that once hung in Bromley House]

Figure 65: Thomas Adams (1807-1873)
[From a portrait that hung in the basement chapel of Adams' warehouse on Stoney Street in Nottingham Lace Market]

in part: "Mr. John Wright, Banker of Lenton, claimed all the land ... between the alteration of the wall opposite Dr. Storer's house and the bridge in Beeston Field'. Dr. John Storer, M.D., F.R.S., succeeded Alexander Foxcroft at Lenton Firs, but while Foxcroft is not heard of there after 1823 Storer did not appear in a Middleton estate rental until Old Michaelmas Day 1828 [12] and was not named in the land tax assessments for Lenton until 1830. He did figure in the Beeston land tax returns as early as the mid-1790s on account of land he had purchased there, probably on the advice of Francis Evans, later of Lenton Grove. It is not known, therefore, whether Dr. Storer moved into Lenton Firs in 1823 or 1828, or on some date between.

Dr. Storer paid rent of £91 a year for Lenton Firs in 1828. He wrote in 1832: 'I live in a very pleasant retirement at Lenton Firs, built by Mr. Watson, hosier, and sold after his death'. A pencilled note in the Old Lady Day rental for 1837 reads: 'Dr. Storer died 17 September 1837'[13] . He was 90 years old, and was buried in the village churchyard at Hawksworth, Nottinghamshire, where his only son, Rev. John Storer, M.A., J.P. (1782-1837) was rector from 1808. He, in turn, had three sons, Dr. Storer's only grandchildren. They were a second Rev. John Storer, M.A., J.P., born 1811, himself rector of Hawksworth 1837-1850, immediately following his father of the same name, and afterwards of Combe Court, Surrey; Dr. Charles Storer, M.D., of Lowdham Grange (1813-1891); and George Storer of Thoroton Hall, Thoroton (1815-1888), M.P. for South Nottinghamshire in 1874. Thoroton is within a mile or two of Hawksworth in the Vale of Belvoir.

John Storer was a physician of distinction, but very much more than a popular doctor, and he was a very well known and prominent public figure in Nottingham for many years. Born in July 1747 at Kinross, the son of Rev. John Storer, incumbent of Fossoway, Kinross, he attended Glasgow University on a Theology course, but emerged with a degree in Medicine. He came to Nottingham in 1781 after serving for ten years as an Army Medical Service surgeon with a Scottish regiment in the war of the Spanish succession in Holland, followed by a period at Grantham from 1777, shortly after his first marriage, to Mary, second daughter of James Douglas of Carlisle and widow of W.H. Middlemore of Somerby Hall, Lincolnshire. Storer quickly established himself at Thurland Hall as the leading physician in Nottingham, and from the beginning took a leading part in the successful establishment of the General Hospital.

The founding benefactor of the hospital was John Key of Fulford Hall near York, born at Leadenham, Lincolnshire in about 1688, married to Anne Usher, and resident at Nottingham where his sons John and Ellis were bankers. A distinguished forbear refounded and endowed Gonville Hall, Cambridge as Gonville and Caius College. John Keys died in January 1778 leaving £500 for a County hospital at Nottingham, providing £1,000 was raised by public subscription within five years [Jacob 1956 13]. A two acre site at Derry Mount was provided, half by the Duke of Newcastle and half by the Corporation. After meetings in August and October 1780 John Simpson's plan was approved, and the foundation stone was laid on 12 February 1781 by the mayor. The building was opened on 28 September 1782, followed by a procession to St. Mary's church, a public dinner at Thurland Hall, and a concert and ball at the Assembly Room. Later hospital buildings were designed by T.C.Hine in 1856 and 1877.

John Storer was the first and leading physician of the General Hospital, with Dr. John Davison and Dr. Snowdon White as colleagues, each on duty for a week. The four honorary surgeons, who included Thomas Wright and John Attenburrow the senior surgeon, a vigorous promoter of inoculation in the early years of the century, were subordinate to the physicians (who in earlier times were usually ecclesiastics). Thus Storer was effectively the leader of the medical staff. After 20 years of honorary service he retired in 1802 with the title of 'Consulting Physician Extraordinary for Life' to the Infirmary but remained at Thurland Hall on Carlton Street, Nottingham [14] to carry on his private medical practice for many more years, and was very active in the intellectual, social and political life of the city until in 1828 he retired completely to Lenton Firs, where he lived until his death in 1837. His first wife, Mary, died on 19 July 1803, and on 20 November 1805 he married Miss Lois Turner, daughter of Rev. Hammond Turner, rector (and lord of the manor) of Hawksworth, who was succeeded as rector there by Dr. Storer's son John three years later. Lois was John Storer's near contemporary, born in the year after him and died in the year before him, aged 88. John Storer's name is commemorated at the General Hospital today in the John Storer Clinic for patients with drugs/psychiatric problems.

An innovator and organizer outside the medical sphere, Dr. John Storer was prominent as early as 1784 in the movement to establish a Sunday School for the children of the poor [Sutton 1852 158]. He was a leading instigator of action to establish the Vaccination Institution, and the General Lunatic Asylum at Sneinton [15], the forerunner of Mapperley and Saxondale Hospitals. He was a founder, and the first President (1816-19) of the Nottingham Subscription Library, (still existing at Bromley House on Angel Row, founded in 1816 and by 1844 containing over 10,000 volumes - a notable centre of cultural activity [16]. His portrait looks on to the staircase there, and he is also commemorated in Storer Street off Carlton Road, almost opposite to where the Asylum once stood.

Storer was a corresponding member of the Literary and Philosophical Society of Derby, and for many years President of the local auxiliary of the Bible Society. He headed the list of those who signed a bill calling for a meeting at the Exchange Rooms in 1824 to consider founding a Mechanics Institute, perhaps the very first of a series of events that ultimately led to the foundation of Nottingham University, although the Mechanics Institution was not, in fact, established at St. James Street until December 1837, two months after Dr. Storer's death [Becket 1928] [17].

It is surprising, even startling, to find Dr. Storer engaging in a substantial joint business venture with Francis Evans that failed spectacularly - the establishment of a large brewery in Nottingham, intended to supply a large proportion of the needs of the district [18]. Evans, an attorney, had rooms in Thurland Hall like Storer. In 1792 Storer and Evans, with Alexander Green as a nominal partner [19] bought about two acres of land from John Stirland, a Nottingham watchmaker, at the high cost of nearly £2,500, and in early 1794 had completed a large brewery building said to have cost £15,000. Though conducted with 'a degree of spirit requisite for so large an undertaking' the business was suddenly closed down after only two years, the stock of porter sold off in 1797, and all the movables auctioned. The buildings were occupied as a barracks in 1799, and after the troops left most of the buildings were demolished and small tenements built with the materials and given the name Poplar Place. Blackner [1815:1985] described the project thus. 'The first wholesale brewhouse was opened in Goose-gate in 1792 by Mr. Thomas Simpson: and after about thirteen years pursuit in the concern he brought it to a close. The next wholesale brewhouse was erected on a most extensive scale where now stands Poplar-place, and was opened in 1794 under the firm of Henry Green and Co., but the concern by no means answered the expectations of the wealthy part of the firm: and it was shortly given up' [20].

The Misses Wright, Charlotte, Frances and Anne, 1838-1845

The new tenant of Lenton Firs in 1838, after Dr. Storer's death, was none other than John Wright of Lenton Hall, who had initially sold the land to Thomas Watson, and he paid a half-year rent of £80 in 1839, a substantial increase [21]. It is not known whether John Wright moved into Lenton Firs himself with his three unmarried daughters for whom the house was rented, but it seems unlikely, though Francis Wright and his family were well established at Lenton Hall in 1840, the year of John Wright's death, and Francis was regarded as the householder at Lenton Hall by the time Orange's Directory for 1840 was published [22]. By Michaelmas 1840 the Misses Wright were the tenants of Lenton Firs [23] and they remained there until 1845, the year in which their brother Francis sold Lenton Hall and moved to Derbyshire. Thomas Adams then took over the tenancy of Lenton Firs and the Wright sisters removed to Lenton village. Frances, Charlotte and Anne built their house called The Lodge on land owned by Francis on Church Street, opposite to the new Holy Trinity church, and lived there for many years, 'full of alms-deeds and good works' [Mellors 1912] which included the building of the infant school nearby in 1851. They were still at Lenton Lodge, New Lenton in 1877 [Morris 1877], aged 80, 81 and 78 respectively.

At the census of 1841 [24] Charlotte, Frances and Anne Wright, aged 45, 44 and 42, and each described as 'Independent', were recorded at Lenton Firs with Elizabeth Plumptre (45) and her presumed children Sophia and Charles, also described as independent, and probably friends, later to become relatives when John Wright (eldest son of Francis) and their nephew, married Eleanor Plumptre at Eastwood on 23 June 1853 (see Chapter VII). They would be well served domestically at Lenton Firs, for in 1841, in the restricted accommodation of the Georgian house, there were nine living-in servants in addition to others at Lenton Firs lodge, which was in the outbuilding block north of the house. The living-in staff in 1841 were:

Elisa Mitchells (37)	Mary Hensley (31)	Mary Bradley (30)
Marianne Brown (15)	Susan Greenleaf (26)	Sarah Gregory (22)
Sarah Vann (29)	Francis Vann (29)	William Ireland (20)

and at the lodge Robert Hodgson (38), Sarah Hodgson, his wife (38) and Sarah Brown (62).

The Misses Wright were still named at Lenton Firs in the Old Lady Day rental of 1844, to pay the £50 half-year's rent, but with the later annotation 'Now Adams Thomas', and in the Michaelmas rental Thomas Adams was charged [25]. In 1843 Adams was living at The Towers, Nether Street, Beeston [Glover 1844, 'taken 1843']. White [1844] gave the same address for

1844, when 'The Misses Wright of Lenton Firs are building a handsome stuccoed mansion nearly opposite the new church'; so Thomas Adams appears to have moved to Lenton Firs in late 1844 or early 1845.

Thomas Adams (1807-1873); tenant 1845-67 and owner 1867-73.

In many respects Thomas Adams (Figure 65) was the typical Victorian captain of industry, an innovative entrepreneur of modest beginnings, becoming successful in business and moving to a quiet country residence within easy reach of the city as his prosperity increased. In other respects he was unusual. Professor J.D.Chambers wrote: 'It is a relief to turn from these barbarities [child labour] to enlightened large employers such as Thomas Adams, who anticipated some of the better practices of today ...' [26]. Born at Worksop in 1807, the son of a maltster who died when he was a child, Thomas was apprenticed to a Newark draper for seven years before moving to London. After being tricked into going to France, where he was robbed, he eventually returned to London and worked in the warehouse of Bodens, a Derby based lace firm earlier in partnership with John Heathcoat. He came to Nottingham in 1830 and established a similar business on Stoney Street, able to buy lace from the 1200 or so makers of plain and decorated net in the town and surrounding villages, and distribute the fabric to wholesalers and retailers. The lace trade was booming, and his enterprise quickly developed into a firm with nine partners, which built a large new warehouse on Stoney Street in 1855 to the plans of Thomas Chambers Hine. Adams came to be regarded as 'the foremost lace merchant of Nottingham'.

In 1832 Adams had begun a long partnership with James Page, a fellow Anglican and Tory, and a small number of manufacturers to form Adams, Page and Company. The railway link with London soon gave impetus to the business, which eventually became Thomas Adams and Co., famous for its regard for the welfare and comfort of its workers and their families, and not neglecting their spiritual welfare. The new building of 1855 on Stoney Street, where about 400 were employed, contained a dining room, a washroom, a chapel - with a chaplain, the Rev. Edward Davies. Even in 1930 services were still held in the chapel on a regular basis [Ginever 1930] although it is unlikely that employees were still fined for non-attendance [Iliffe and Baguley 1974]. There was apparatus, by Alfred Penny, for circulating warm air through the building [27] . The Adams warehouse was generally regarded as the most architecturally impressive of all the warehouses in the Lace Market, and served as a model for others. In some respects it looks more like a country mansion than a warehouse, and at the time was criticised as too grand for its function, although Hine's vision was of 'a visible symbol of the community and its important trade' [28].

Mellors [1912] wrote of Thomas Adams: 'His character was developed by industry, frugality, fixity of purpose, sincerity, truthfulness, strong domestic affections, great liberality and above all the fear and love of God, carrying with it a deep sense of responsibility'. Whether employment of nine resident domestic servants can be regarded as frugal may be open to question, and Mellors added 'Of course he had his imperfections and faults ...[but] ... humility was one of his distinguishing features'. He was surely, however, a deeply religious man who carried his principles into his business life, and emerged as the leading evangelical layman of his day in Nottingham. In Mellors' words he was 'a man of unassuming manners, earnest piety and unbounded benevolence in the support of schools and churches' though himself a poor speaker. The articles of association when Adams and Page became Thomas Adams and Co. Ltd. in 1865 included among its objects those of establishing, managing and assisting churches, chapels, schools, libraries, banks etc. etc. for the benefit of persons employed by the company, their relatives and others, and to employ a chaplain of the Established Church to conduct services.

Adams was active on committees of the General Hospital, was a member of the Board of Guardians, and was a magistrate. Elected to Nottingham Corporation as early as 1836 as a Tory he was denied any opportunity of office as alderman or mayor by the Whig majority, but he was held in high regard by people from many walks of life, and it is said that 10,000 people attended his funeral. Adams Hill, on which he lived at Lenton Firs for nearly 30 years, was named in his honour. The second window on the south aisle of Lenton parish church is the Adams window, dedicated to his memory by his friends and neighbours. Another window to his memory is in St. Mary's church in Nottingham. In Lenton church there is also a tablet on the south wall which reads: 'Animo Fidique. To the memory of their beloved father, Thomas Adams of Lenton Firs, J.P. for the Borough and County of Nottingham: this tablet is erected by his grateful children. He was born 5th February 1807, fell asleep in Jesus May 16th 1873, and was buried in the Church cemetery'...'Also in memory of their beloved mother Lucy Adams, born August 28th 1807, died August 28th 1874'. St. Phillip's church on Pennyfoot Street was designed as a 'Thomas Adams memorial church' [29].

Thomas Adams married Lucy Cullen, daughter of a Nottingham businessman, at St. Mary's church in 1830, the year of his arrival at Nottingham. They had ten children, and in 1851[30] eight were at Lenton Firs, where the household included Thomas and his wife Lucy (43), daughters Catherine L. (19), Frances (18) and Ann (16), all born at Nottingham; Samuel (10) and John (8) born at Beeston; and Mary (6), Elizabeth (4) and Arthur (1) born at Lenton Firs. There was also Catherine Adams, Thomas's unmarried sister, and seven living-in servants, together with William Smith (called 'gardener' in 1861) and his wife Mary at 'Derby Road', that is, Lenton Firs Lodge north of the house. The Georgian house must have been extremely crowded, but it was not enlarged until a decade later.

The Census Enumerators' Books of 1861 [31] recorded three daughters - Catherine, Frances and Ann - still at home, together with 20-year-old Samuel and 18-year-old John, both described as lace merchants, presumably in the family business. There were now as many as nine servants packed into the house, as follows:

Luke Antcliffe - butler:	John Pride - footman:
Thomas Cross - groom :	Ann Cowlishaw (28) - cook:
Elizabeth Garner (45) housemaid:	Susan Cooke (23) - housemaid:
Emma Wardle (18) - kitchen maid:	Emma Bacon (18) - housemaid:
Elizabeth Richardson (33) - laundry maid.	

William Smith, gardener, and his wife Mary (54) were at the lodge. After a further decade, in 1871 [32], only Catherine Lucy, the eldest daughter, now 39, and Elizabeth (24) the youngest, remained at home, but in a much larger house and still served by as many servants -

Charles Naish (57) - butler:	Thomas Tatham (20) - footman:
Matthew Hopewell (23) - groom:	Martha Turner (42) - cook:
Elizabeth Aronn (33) - lady's maid:	Ann Palmer (18) - housemaid:
Rebecca Burrow (35) - housemaid:	Betsy Hill (16) - kitchen maid:
Elizabeth Richardson (43) - laundry maid.	

Only the laundry maid and William Smith the gardener, now 67, remained from 1861. Two other gardeners now lived in a new cottage at Lenton Firs, David Mitchell with his wife Rebecca and seven children aged from 17 to 1 year old, with Tom Raw, a 14-year-old gardener probably lodging with them. The cottage of the Mitchells was the present East Lodge, built as part of the improvements begun in 1861, and in the Middleton estate survey of 1863 called the Far Lodge.

The Victorian house and lodge

When Lenton Firs house is viewed from the west today two quite different styles are immediately apparent, indicating two distinct phases of building (Figure 66). It is clearly seen that there are two houses fused together, and that the present rear portion, best seen from the

Figure 66: Lenton Firs house from the west, showing the fusion of the Georgian and Victorian buildings dating from 1800 and 1861
The large glasshouses, partly ranged along the wall left (with a surviving heating pipe) were built between 1863 and 1873, when Adams died.

north-west side, is much older than the south-east facing facade. The contrast in styles is heightened by the contrast between the light grey stucco and slated roof of the Georgian house and the bright red brick and the tiled roof of the taller Victorian addition. Lenton Firs was 'modernized' or partially rebuilt and greatly extended in 1861-62 to take its present form, and the improvements began in 1861 with the building of the East Lodge. The cost of £840 involved an unusual arrangement, by which the materials were supplied by Lord Middleton and the labour by Thomas Adams [33]. The extension and improvements were followed by the grant of a 14-year lease to Adams at the unchanged rent of £160 a year from 26 March 1862 [34]. The lease stipulated that the three closes of pasture land must not be ploughed, broken up or converted into tillage; nor must the gardens and grounds be altered, or the premises sub-let without approval, and this was endorsed by Thomas Adams' signature.

The greatly enlarged mansion, the new access drive on the east side and the new Far Lodge (more recently called East Lodge) at its exit on to Adams Hill, called for appropriate reorganization of the gardens and employment of more gardening staff. The O.S. 1:500 plan of 1881 (Figure 68) shows the enlarged Lenton Firs house and gardens, and the extensive glasshouses are a prominent feature, as they were at other large houses on the campus. Only some backing walls and the marks of old hot water heating systems remain to be seen today. The glasshouses dated mainly, though not entirely, from the time of Thomas Adams's extensions and reorganization in the early 1860s. Those who operated them were men of high skills and training - the expert horticulturists of the heyday of Victorian gardening. It was such men, of whom sadly little is known beyond their names, who were the real creators of the landscape content that gives the University campus its special character rather than their employers, the estate owners or tenants.

David Mitchell, gardener (Figure 67)

Thanks to the researches of his great granddaughter, Mrs. Iris Keeble, we do know something of David Mitchell, 'gardener', who moved into the new Far Lodge at Lenton Firs with his family in 1862 when aged 36. He was characteristic of the type. Born at North Grimston, part of Lord Middleton's estate of Birdsall Hall, Yorkshire, which became the favourite and principal home of the Middletons, he began his working life as a gardener's lad at Birdsall Hall. In due course he moved to Chatsworth, where he trained as a landscape gardener and horticultural engineer under Sir Robert Paxton. Mitchell looked after the plants sent from Chatsworth to the Great Exhibition of 1851. In the following year he married Rebecca Hobbs, born at Wells, Somerset, but then living near Derby, where her father was employed in the paper industry, and from where her whole family emigrated to North America about the time that she married [35]. After a brief period near Derby David and Rebecca Mitchell moved to Nottingham in 1854 or 1855 to live at Sherwood, where they remained until after the census of 1861. Sherwood was just being developed, with many large houses, all with glasshouses, offering employment opportunities for a horticultural engineer. After living briefly on Butchers Lane (now Wollaton Road) Beeston, they moved into the new Far Lodge at Lenton Firs, probably in late 1862, and an extension of the glasshouses there followed.

David Mitchell was a man of parts, and was held in high respect by the Adams family. He was widely read and owned many botanical books. He was artistic, a violin player and a competent painter and draughtsman, excelling in water colour landscape painting. Four of the Mitchells' ten children were born at Lenton Firs Far Lodge, and one died there in 1866. Their tenth child was born in 1874 after they had left Lenton Firs following the death of Thomas Adams in 1873 and of Mrs. Adams soon afterwards. They remained in Lenton, living first at 22 Church Street and later on Lenton Boulevard, and David was much sought after by residents of the new houses in The Park, Nottingham because of his reputation for fine peach and grape production. He died in 1900, and his gravestone (commemorating also his wife Rebecca who died in 1916) is in Lenton churchyard, with that of his eldest son, Francis, also a gardener, who was educated at Thomas Adams's expense.

Figure 67: David Mitchell, gardener, and his wife Rebecca [Courtesy Mrs. I.M. Keeble]

Purchase of Lenton Firs by Thomas Adams

Within six years of the 1862 lease the whole estate of Lord Middleton south of Derby Road was advertised for sale, a total area of 462 acres including Beeston Fields Farm west of the Tottle Brook [36]. The property included 'All that capital messuage or mansion house ... called Lenton Firs, with the gardens, pleasure grounds, coachhouses, stabling and outbuildings ...' and three closes of pasture land called Far Lodge Close (8a.0.12), Abbey Field Nook (2a.3.22). and Lawn (3a.3.35) . The house and gardens covered 4a.1.26.. In less formal terms Lenton Firs was described as 'a handsome residence, parts of which were recently built, containing large dining and drawing rooms and other ground floor sitting rooms, a cellar and kitchens and other offices, large entrance hall and ample accommodation in bedrooms and dressing rooms. The kitchen garden, pleasure grounds and shrubberies are most complete, and the situation is unparalleled for beauty. The approach is from the turnpike road with a newly erected entrance lodge abutting on the same. The stabling and carriage house and other outbuildings are convenient and abundant'. 'This lot is held under a lease by the present tenant, Thomas Adams for ... 14 years, nearly nine of which are unexpired'. Thomas Adams himself bought the house and land for £6,500 (£6,316 after deductions) under a disentailer of 1 March 1867 .

In his later years Adams developed a new business interest - the Nottingham Joint Stock Bank established on his initiative in 1865. He was its first chairman, and established close connections with Birmingham banks. Six directors were in the lace trade and the other three were Birmingham bankers. The enterprise was highly successful, though its character changed with time. By 1905 it operated 28 branches. Of the four directors in the late 19th century one was S.H.Sands, the chairman, who built West Hill House (now Paton House) next to Lenton Firs in 1884, and another was W.B.Thorpe of Lenton House, a director of Boots Pure Drug Company. This bank was the source of most of Jesse Boot's finance in his rapid development. In 1905 it was absorbed in the London City and Midland Bank Limited which in 1918 became the London Joint Stock Bank, and finally part of the Midland Bank in 1923, with its head office still at its original premises on Victoria Street, Nottingham.

Thomas Adams had planned for his sons Samuel and John to succeed him in his business, and of the 11,200 shares issued by Thomas Adams and Company Thomas himself held 6,650 and Samuel and John shared 2,350. But both sons died young, Samuel in 1870, three years before his father died on 16 May 1873. Thomas left estate valued at £90,000. The memorials to him in both Lenton church and St. Mary's, Nottingham reflect the importance of his business in the Lace Market near St. Mary's, and the high regard in which he was held in the village of Lenton. His widow remained at Lenton Firs for a year until her death, when the property passed to her surviving second son, John Adams. He was there in 1876 [Kelly 1876] when Lenton Firs was named as his residence [Lowe 1876], but he was not mentioned by Morris's Directory of 1877, and it is thought that he had died. However, Lenton Firs apparently remained in the ownership of a member of the family until 1903, for in that year its sale to Thomas Shipstone was negotiated with a Mr. Adams according to Shipstone's daughter's autobiography written in her old age [Snell 1969]. Although the business passed out of the control of the Adams family it maintained its momentum for two further generations, to peak soon after the turn of the century, when it employed over 2,000, with 1,400 workers, mainly women, at Stoney Street making up ladies' wear for world-wide markets.

Although Kelly's Directory of 1881 recorded Edward Cope living at Lenton Firs, Wright's Directory for the same year showed Robert Arthur Hollins in residence, suggesting that one was replaced by the other. In 1877 a Mr. Edward Cope lived at 17 Arboretum Street, while Robert Arthur Hollins was on Cavendish Road South, The Park. In 1879 Robert Arthur Hollins was named at Lenton Firs [Wright 1879] and he seems to have occupied the house from 1878 until late 1880 or early 1881. William Hollins and Company, which had been established at Spring Close, Lenton from 1856 onwards, sold their Lenton mill and moved machinery to Radford in 1882 (see Chapter XIV) and this brief tenancy of Lenton Firs may have been connected with the move. Robert Arthur Hollins is not to be confused with Richard Arthur Hollins, assistant manager to William Hollins himself, and in the 1870s running the firm's Pleasley works [37] .

The full development of Lenton Firs is shown in Figure 68. The Census Enumerators' Books of 1881 show that by mid-1881 Edward William Cope, J.P., aged 40, of Cope and Ward, lace manufacturers, was living alone at Lenton Firs, attended by five house servants - William Clements (36) butler, Elizabeth Giles (44) cook, Eliza Brentnall (25) housemaid, Mary A.

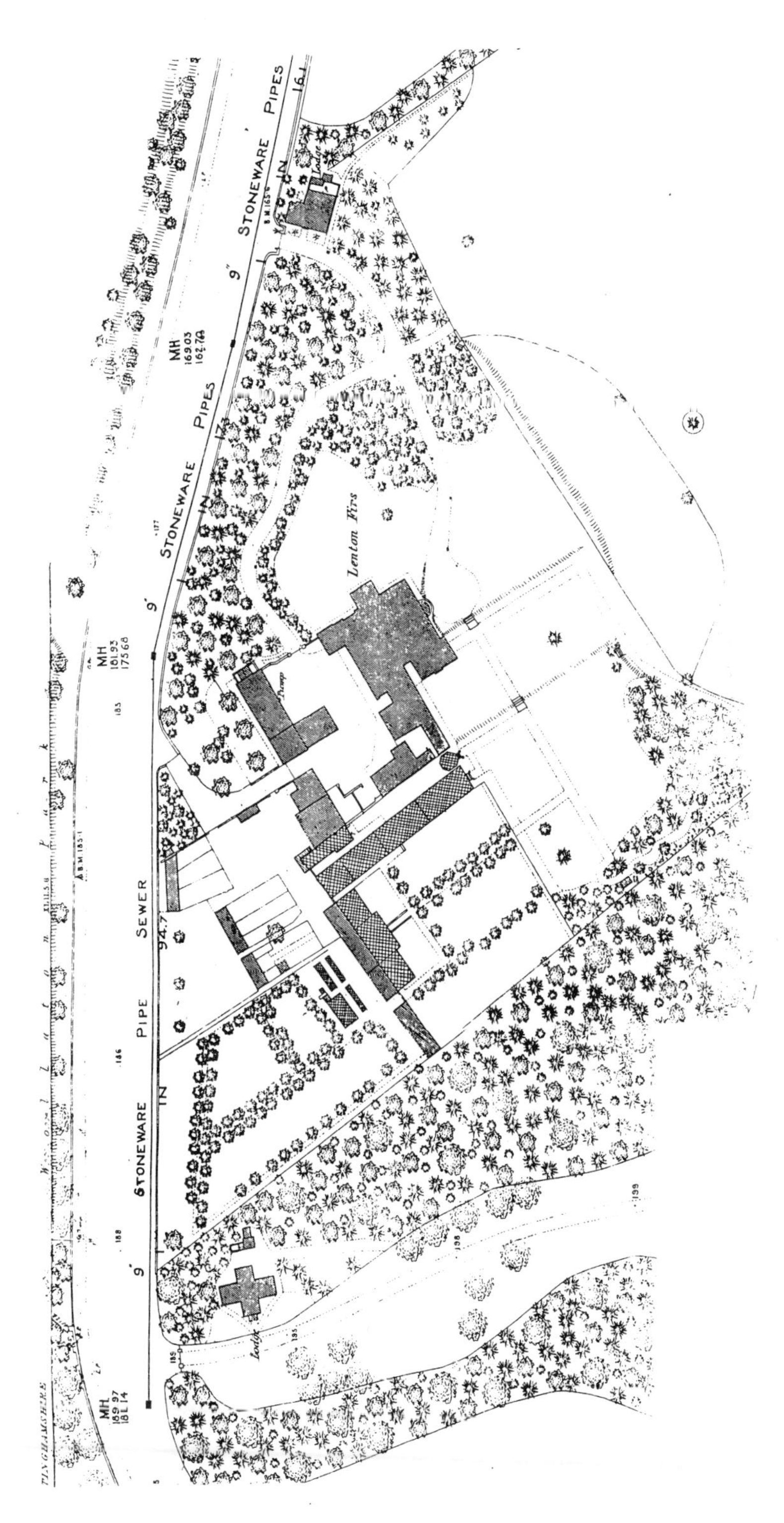

Figure 68: Lenton Firs and its garden in 1881
The lodge, drive and woodland in the west (left) were in the Lenton Hall estate. Note the extensive glasshouses and the pig or poultry pens. The Wortley cedar tree was not then, apparently, fully grown.

Cresswell (19) kitchen maid and Henry Smith (21) groom. Coachman Oswell Shepherd (28) was at Lenton Firs Lodge with his wife Florence and two young children, Ada and William Edward: John Dixon (37) gardener occupied Lenton Firs gardener's lodge No. 1 with Eliza his wife and six children under the age of 13: and William Smith (20) under-gardener was at Lodge No. 2. Edward Cope was still at Lenton Firs in 1887, and probably remained until William Lambert moved in to take his place, probably in 1889 [Wright 1887 1889]. Little is known of Edward Cope, or of his connections, if any, with Edward Cope, 'railway contractor' of Church Hill Close, Old Lenton in 1848, and 'road contractor' living on Gregory Street, Lenton in the 1850s and 1860s, but he was evidently the same person as the Mr. E.Cope, J.P. who was living at Chilwell Hall in 1891 [Brown 1891 254].

Alderman William Lambert (1823-1905) : 1889-1903 (Figure 69)

William Lambert is a very well-known character - another powerful and energetic personality who retired from a very active business and public life to the calm of the Lenton parkland. In 1889 he had lived for ten years at Mapperley Hall, a mansion that has had repeated links with the University campus, including its use for 33 years (1906-1939) as a hostel for men students of the University College [38]. William Lambert lived at Clarendon House, 19 Clarendon Street in the 1870s before moving to Mapperley Hall by 1879 [Wright 1871 1879 1881], and his brother John Lambert lived at Ellesmere House, 17 Clarendon Street throughout the 1870s. When William leased or rented and moved to Lenton Firs in 1889 he again became a near neighbour of his brother John, who had built and occupied Redcourt in 1884 (Chapter XII). By the turn of the century John Lambert junior, son of William Lambert, occupied Ellesmere House, his uncle John's earlier home [Wright 1895 1905: Kelly 1904] and in 1903 William moved from Lenton Firs into Redcourt.

Born in 1823 and educated at Nottingham High School, William Lambert was in partnership with his brother John as bleachers, dyers and lace dressers, and their business was very lucrative. Their large and imposing premises on Lower Talbot Street remain a prominent feature of the Nottingham skyline, a listed building of five storeys with towers, but long deserted and the object of wrangling between would-be developers, conservationists, public bodies and planners. It has recently undergone major rebuilding and repair after severe gale damage in early 1989 [39]. Like Thomas Adams the Lambert brothers were regarded in their time as model employers, 'men of sterling character and rare compassion, strong churchmen and members of St. Matthew's church, Talbot Street'. The large, airy rooms of their Talbot Street works contained 230 employees, mainly women and girls aged 13 and upwards since the Lamberts refused to employ children under 13 years of age. William Lambert was connected in business not only with bleaching and dyeing, the leading industry of the Leen valley, but also with banking as a director of the Nottingham and Notts. Banking Company: and he was chairman of the Nottingham Real Estate Investment Company and of the Colwick Park Racecourse company.

Outside business William Lambert was a magistrate, councillor, sheriff of Nottingham in 1859 and mayor in 1874 and 1885, being elected alderman in 1875. For many years he was a member of the Corporation's Public Works and Recreation Grounds Committee, and its chairman between 1898 and 1901 when Bulwell Forest, Lenton Victoria Park, Vernon Park and other open spaces, including Lenton and Radford recreation grounds, were secured for public use. The first pile of the Victoria Embankment was driven by Alderman Lambert in May 1898, and the completed work was opened by him in July 1901.

The Lambert brothers together are perhaps more celebrated as the builders of Nottingham's Theatre Royal, now splendidly restored. It was originally designed to seat 2,000, by C.J.Phipps of London and Bath, and was constructed in a mere six months in 1865, at a cost of £15,000, as 'a temple of drama'. The brothers decided that the only way to provide a worthy theatre for Nottingham was to build one, and hope that their fellow townsmen would help to make it a place of culture, and in March 1866 they issued a prospectus inviting applications for shares. The theatre was opened on 25 September 1865 and was very successful. Robin Beynon [1978] has written that 'John and William Lambert ... saw their creation in a rather didactic light. The opening night address by the manager, Walter Montgomery, included such clauses as "We hope rather to add to the number of those who seek a healthful pleasure in intellectual recreation...and...with a well conducted theatre and with a company of ladies and gentlemen, what is to prevent drama from fulfilling its greatest mission, namely a teacher of the highest morality, nay, even the gentle handmaiden of religion"'!

William Lambert hunted for over 40 years. He was an original member of the Robin Hood Rifles, and as Captain Lambert (he later became Major) in 1865 - a year of successes for him - he was the winner of the Duke of St. Albans' cup for rifle shooting. He was a genuine representative of the genre Victorian entrepreneur, public figure and sportsman - and a suitable one to see out the 19th century history of this northern corner of the campus. He died aged 82 in 1905, having moved along from Lenton Firs, which he rented or leased to Redcourt, built by his brother John, when Thomas Shipstone bought Lenton Firs in 1903 [40] .

Sir Thomas Shipstone, brewer, 1903-1940 (Figure 70)

Sir Thomas Shipstone, Kt., J.P., chairman and managing director of the brewing firm Shipstone and Sons of Basford from 1922 to 1940, was born in 1851, the third of four sons of James and Eliza Shipstone. James (d. 1897) in 1852 started a small brewery on Mansfield Road from which it moved to Basford as the business grew. Thomas was taken into the business in 1883, soon after his eldest brother James. He lived at Lenton Firs for nearly 40 years, from his purchase of it in 1903 until his death on 17 October 1940. He moved there from Edwalton Manor which he had bought in about 1890 and which was a property similar to Lenton Firs, with its glasshouses and small fields. He brought several of his employees with him, including Sharp, a coachman-groom, 'Cherry-nose' Faulkes, the head gardener, who always wore a

Figure 69: Alderman William Lambert (1823-1905)

Figure 70: Sir Thomas Shipstone (1851-1940)

bowler hat, and probably the poultryman Cooper and his wife. Thomas Shipstone was knighted in 1922. His wife, Eliza was a daughter of John Loverseed, a prosperous Nottingham builder.

Despite a sketchy education Thomas Shipstone, short in stature, dapper in appearance, and, to his family, generous, emotional and affectionate, though reserved and independent, was a keen and assertive business man. During his period at Lenton Firs he extended his ownership over most of the north-western side of the present University campus, the small estate of Lenton Firs being augmented by his purchases from some 19 acres to almost 100 acres. Indeed, it is possible that his original purchase was made in the knowledge that other, adjoining land was about to come on to the market. As the Lenton Hall estate was breaking up Shipstone was able to buy Lenton Hall Farm (renamed Lenton Firs Farm) with its land on the high ground from Fred Wright, and the land below Lenton Hall running down to Cut Through Lane from Henry Smith Wright. Arthur Footit was his farm bailiff, living in the farmhouse adjoining Lenton Hall gardens from before 1912 [Kelly 1912] to about 1923 [Wright 1923 Kelly 1923]. On 1 January 1930 Sir Thomas bought Lenton Hurst Farm with about 26 acres from W.G.Player for £11,000 together with Lenton Hurst house (Rotheras) (see Chapter XII).

Some insight into the nature of life at Lenton Firs in the time of Sir Thomas Shipstone can be gleaned from the autobiography of his daughter Annie [Snell 1969], though Mrs. Snell's dates and chronology are often uncertain. Mrs. Snell had two sisters who became Mrs. Mabel Frances Ratcliffe, and the much younger Mrs. Helena Kathleen Mackness (Nellie). The internal arrangements and furnishing of the house, as well as its pictures, can also be visualized from the catalogue for the sale of contents by Messrs. Place and Kirk on 24-28 February 1941. The house itself was not drastically altered when it became a Hall of Residence. Much of the modern stained window glass, said to be indicative of Thomas Shipstone's taste, was preserved; the library remained a library; and the drawing room opposite across the large pillared entrance hall, furnished for Mrs. Shipstone, became the Junior Common Room. From the dining room, which was enlarged by taking in the billiard room (still identifiable by its stained window glass) the aviary was visible across the lawn, its denizens including an old white cockatoo which was eventually sent to the aviary at Nottingham Arboretum. The aviary at Lenton Firs was shown, but not named on the O.S. 2½-inch map and the O.S. 6-inch Provisional edition map revised to 1938, but was not on the Second edition O.S. 6-inch map revised to 1899. White fantail pigeons were kept in the 1930s over the stables under the small ornamental clock tower, and both pigeons and chimes will be remembered by former residents at Hugh Stewart Hall who used the nearby 'bus stop at the top of Adams Hill.

Figure 71 depicts the facade of the house and a vista in the garden of Lenton Firs in about 1930. Two large kitchen gardens supplied the house, and are now occupied partly by single-storey buildings, mainly former study-bedrooms converted into studios for students of the School of Architecture, and partly by a large lawn. Several large glasshouses produced oranges, nectarines, peaches and grapes as well as more mundane crops. Social life at Lenton Firs was overshadowed before 1920 by the fact that Mrs. Shipstone suffered from a degenerative spinal illness from which she died in 1919. Special footpaths were made, wide enough to take her bath chair. The broad York stone path running south-west from the front of the house to the woodland, and a disintegrating statue survive, but a summer house alongside it was destroyed by fire in about 1960. A second, once delightful and beautifully built summer house in the secondary sycamore thicket on the sandstone knoll south of the house, also probably provided for Mrs. Shipstone's use before the sycamores took over (but greatly appreciated later by users from Wortley Hall Close) stood sadly vandalized, derelict, and neglected for many years, and a recent valiant partial renovation which saved it from final destruction has not restored its charm (Figure 72).

At Lenton Firs the same head gardener who had served the Shipstones at Edwalton Manor House, Edwin Faulkes, supervised the gardens until the death of Sir Thomas in 1940,

Figure 71: Lenton Firs house and a view of the garden in about 1930
[From Snell 1969]

Figure 72: Derelict summer house in the grounds of Lenton Firs, built before the first world war
[January 1988]

living in East Lodge. He was given scant justice by Mrs. Snell, who wrote that Faulkes 'helped in the gardens', especially with the lawns, and 'looked after the pony Tiny who pulled the lawnmower'. The coachman, Eli Sharp, lived in the small lodge attached to the stable block according to Mrs. Snell but he was not mentioned in the Directories after 1922, when a coach was no longer used, and he was succeeded by the chauffeur Edwin Thomas Matthews. Lenton Hall Lodge was acquired by Shipstone with Lenton Hall Farm, and was called Lenton Firs Lodge after 1920, when Samuel Hall, who had been chauffeur to Mrs. Shipstone occupied it. It has been known as West Lodge in more recent years. The lodge attached to the stable block with the clock tower was built for Shipstone, and was thus not shown on the O.S. Second edition 6-inch map revised to 1899. Both East and West Lodges were eventually converted by the University into study-bedroom units as parts of Wortley Hall.

Lenton Firs Farm after 1940

In Sir Thomas Shipstone's time Lenton Firs Farm, the former Lenton Hall Farm (Figure 73), continued to function in much the same way as in the 19th century, though effectively bounded on the west side by Lenton Hall Drive. It was a grassland farm, stocked with beef cattle, many of the Highland breed, usually bought on visits to Scotland, and often with the help of the expertise of Mr. Machin of Papplewick [Snell 1969]. It was also grazed by horses during the earlier period when Sir Thomas was keenly interested in breeding, breaking in and showing pedigree horses. The farm supplied Lenton Firs house with eggs and poultry, and after the mid-1920s, when Fred Waring was farm bailiff, the occupier of the farm was called 'poultry-man to Sir Thomas Shipstone'. The 'poultrymen' included William Thomas Cooper in the later 1920s and John Herbert Clarke in the mid-1930s [Kelly 1928, 1936: Snell 1969].

Figure 73: Lenton Firs Farm and beef cattle seen from the site of the Social Sciences building in about 1930
[From Snell 1969]

In 1940, shortly before his death, Sir Thomas Shipstone sought a tenant farmer to replace Mr. Blatherwick, who then ran Lenton Firs Farm for him. William Barsby took the tenancy, to operate the farm on a commercial basis despite its mainly sandy soils of limited fertility [41]. From a small beginning Barsby built up a pedigree Friesian dairy herd, with poultry and pigs as secondary enterprises, and he grew fodder crops, particularly mangolds, on Lenton Hall Close, the former sandy quarry floor of 1838 now deeply buried beneath the Social Science car park and the slope of imported marl below it, and also on the sandy land on which Cripps Hall now stands. With the modernization of the farm, from the connection of an electricity supply to the installation of modern milking machines, the dairy herd grew to about 50 cows by the time that William Barsby's tenancy was ended in 1955, and the University's large-scale development and building began on the farm. Bill Barsby died at East Leake on 18 February 1986, aged 76.

Lenton Hurst Farm was acquired by Sir Thomas Shipstone in 1930, and little is known of the nature of the operation of this small holding before that time, when Thomas Skerrit was farm bailiff for W.G.Player of Lenton Hurst. After 1930 the farm was let to S.C.Armitage (later Sir Cecil Armitage) who had then recently bought Lenton Fields, and who was still the occupier in 1950 when the University purchased it, some four years after Lenton Fields had been bought from Armitage by the University College [42]. In Armitage's tenure the farm specialized on the breeding of pigs, and the row of pig pens along the eastern side of Beeston Lane and along the north-west side of the fence marking the line of the old Sawley turnpike in front of Derby Hall are prominent features of the contemporary O.S. 6-inch maps (see Figure 116). There was no sign of such structures on Armitage's land across Beeston Lane. He evidently remained as the University's tenant after he had removed to Hawksworth Manor until the whole farmstead was demolished to make way for the building of Rutland and Sherwood Halls (Figure 126) and pigs were still rooting in the field in front of Derby Hall until late 1962.

Lenton Firs as wartime convalescent hospital and Hall of Residence

After Sir Thomas Shipstone's death in 1940, and following the sale of its contents in 1941, Lenton Firs was quickly converted as a convalescent hospital for members of H.M.Forces, with Dr. W.Blandy as the medical officer, and was formally opened by the young Duchess of Portland. The patients in 'hospital blue' clothing were familiar figures in the park during the next few years. This use was not inappropriate, since Sir Thomas was another resident of the future campus (with Sir Louis Pearson of Lenton Grove and Mr. W.G.Player of Lenton Hurst) to have been a generous benefactor of the General Hospital [Hogarth c.1949], of which he was President in 1927 and 1928. Among his gifts to the hospital was a second new operating theatre in 1932, following closely on that given by Sir Louis Pearson in 1931, a ward named after him, and another new theatre in 1938 [Jacob 1951). Lenton Firs, however, did not pass into the hospital's ownership like Lenton Grove, but the house was rented from 1946 by the University College for use as a small Hall of Residence for women under the joint Wardenship of Professor Arthur Radford and his wife. It remained so for five years until it was developed as a men's Hall, and named Wortley Hall in honour of the last Principal of the University College.

In 1950 the University was able to purchase both the Lenton Firs estate and the Lenton Hurst estate from Shipstone's executors, a total area of over 95 acres, and it was this transaction which allowed the University to start to implement its grand development plan. The sale indenture dated 24 March 1950 between the executors, Sir Charles John Pain of Low Pavement, Annie Eliza Snell of Edwalton Lodge (Sir Thomas's daughter, mentioned earlier) and Lt.Commander George John Mackness, R.N. retired of Arlington Drive (his son-in-law) and the University in the persons of Alderman Sir Francis Hill and Mr. Hedley Pickbourne, recorded an agreed price of £22,000 for the 85.48 acres extending from Clifton Boulevard to Beeston Lane. In view of the provisions of the newly published development plan of the city the University had no serious competitor. The document, a photocopy of which is held in the Bursar's Department of the University, contains a schedule of some 19 conveyances incorporating covenants on parts of the joint estate dating from 1898 to 1937, of which 13 were of 1903-04 and involved Albert Ball as a party in the disposal of the Lenton Hall estate (see Chapter VII).

The further topographic history of the Lenton Firs and Lenton Hurst estates is touched upon in Chapter XVI below.

NOTES

1. Prebendary Charles Wylde's diary (typescript copy), N.U.Hallward Library, Local Studies section: Not 1 D25 WYL.
2. N.U.M.D., Mi 1/16/1a. The 'Summer Houses' were described by witnesses in the law suit of 1823, Middleton v. Wright (see Ch. XIII)
3. N.U.M.D., Mi 1/16/1a : Brief for the plaintiff, p. 5 et seq.
4. N.U.M.D., Mi R 7: Rental for Lady Day 1815. 'Recd Mr. Foxcroft's rent for the Firs, £ 47.0s.0d. 8 April.'
5. N.U.M.D., Mi 1/16/1a (1823) p. 35.
6. N.A.O., *Directory Extracts, Nottingham and Newark, 1791-98*, 50.
7. N.U.M.D., Mi R 11 : Middleton estate rental for Michaelmas 1818 and Lady Day 1819.
8. N.U.M.D., Mi R 13. 'Notice' was also written against the names of John Burton, Richard Chamberlain, John Hopkin and John Wilkinson, probably because land occupied by them was about to be incorporated into Wollaton Park.
9. N.U.M.D., Mi R 16 : Middleton estate rental for 1823.
10. N.U.M.D., Mi 1/16/1a (1823) and Mi R 14 : Middleton estate rental for 1821.
11. N.U.M.D., Mi 1/16/1d : 'The Brief'.
12. N.U.M.D., Mi R 21 : Rental, Old Michaelmas Day 1828. Includes the entry : 'Storer M.D. Doctr. £ 45.10.0d.'. Lenton Firs is missing from the rentals for the years between 1824 and 1827 (N.U.M.D., Mi R 17-20).

13. N.U.M.D., Mi R 30 : Old Lady Day rental for 1837.

14. Thurland Hall, dating from the 1430s, was the residence of Thomas Thurland, 'a great merchant of the staple'. It came to the Holles family by purchase, was substantially rebuilt by the Earl of Clare in 1626, and was the largest house in 17th century Nottingham, taxed on 47 hearths in 1674. It later belonged to the Duke of Newcastle [Blackner 1815/1985 67]. John Storer immediately took up residence there when he arrived in Nottingham in 1781. Thurland Hall was demolished in 1830-31.

15. *'The articles of Union ...for ...a General Lunatic Asylum near Nottingham'.* S. and J. Ridge, Newark, 21 March 1811. Resolutions - John Storer M.D., Vice-President, in the chair. (The President, the Duke of Newcastle, was a prestige figure only.) 25 April 1810 - Agreement between J.P.s and subscribers and benefactors for an asylum at Sneinton, which was opened on 12 February 1812.

16. I. Inkster [1978]. The mathematician James Green (of Green's Mill, Sneinton) joined in 1823.

17. Becket [1928 11] wrote: 'A plan to form a Mechanics Institute took shape, but was abandoned in favour of a less ambitious scheme to found a library for mechanics and apprentices, which materialized owing to the efforts of Dr. John Storer, F.C.S. ... Henry Enfield, Town Clerk 1815-44, and Thomas Wakefield' - the Artisans' Library.

18. For further details of Dr. Storer's achievements see Mss. Collection, Saxondale Hospital, and his obituary in the Nottingham Journal of 13 October 1837.

19. William Stretton, *The Stretton Manuscripts* ed. G.C.Robertson (1910) discussed (pp. 220-21) the supply of beer and porter to Nottingham and District in the 18th century, and provided details of the venture of Storer and Evans.

20. Henry Green is mentioned again in Chapter XIV as a businessman with a variety of interests.

21. N.U.M.D., Mi R 31 : Middleton estate rental 1838. A pencilled note against the Lady Day rents reads: 'Dr. Storer dead - now Jno. Wright Esq.'.

22. James Orange, *Nottingham Annual register ... and Directory for 1840* p. 89 : 'Lenton Hall - F. Wright: Lenton Firs - J. Wright Esq.'

23. N.U.M.D., Mi R 32 : Middleton estate rental 1840.

24. Census of 1841, Enumerators' Books. For Lenton, H.O. 107/858.

25. N.U.M.D., Mi R 34 (1845)

26. Prof. J.D.Chambers, 'A century of change', in *The People of Nottingham*, a souvenir of the Exhibition, Albert Hall Institute, 25-29 September 1951, p. 5.

27. For a description of the building's facilities, including Alfred Penny's apparatus for circulating warm air, and the basement chapel and its daily services, see D. Lowe and J. Richards, *The Lace Heritage: a guide to Nottingham Lace* (1984) Ch. 2 - 'Thomas Adams and his empire' pp. 5-14.

28. Nottingham Journal 1855. See *Nottingham's Heritage - a view of conservation in the city* (1985) p.9 (Nottingham City Planning Dept.) for a good print of the building. See also M.W.Barley and R. Cullen, *Nottingham Now* (1975) Nottingham Civic Society: photo. p. 28, No. 69.

29. St. Phillip's church, Pennyfoot Street, demolished in 1963, was designed by R.C.Sutton and consecrated as a memorial in 1879.

30. Census of 1851, Enumerators' Books. For Lenton, H.O. 107/2129

31. Census of 1861, Enumerators' Books. For Lenton, 2447 and 2450

32. Census of 1871, Enumerators' Books. For Lenton, RG 9/3499 and 3500

33. Mr. K. Brand believes on stylistic grounds that the architect for East Lodge - and therefore for the new house - was T. C. Hine, who had designed Adams's warehouse on Stoney Street, completed in 1855.

34. N.U.M.D., Mi Da 8/11, 26 March 1862 : Counterpart lease of Lenton Firs with 19a.2.00 of land for 14 years, rent £ 160, by Lord Middleton to Thomas Adams.

35. Personal correspondence with Mrs.I.Keeble. See also Iris Keeble, 'We have a cowboy in our family tree', *Notts. Family History Society* 6, 7 (April 1990) 20-24.

36. N.U.M.D., Mi 4 E 137. The date suggested on the document is about 1880, but the correct date in 1868 or thereabouts, and the plans included are the same as those of the 1863 survey. All the property was to be sold by auction by Messrs. Potts and Neale on 5 June (year not given, but probably 1868) at the George Hotel.

37. See Chapter XIV and Pigott [1949 87]. William Hollins and Co., formerly of Vyella House, Nottingham, Somercotes and Hucknall are still in business as shirt manufacturers at Hucknall.

38. The Mapperley Hall estate was sold in the early years of the century for development. Since the Board of Education had been stressing from 1903 the need for a hostel for students at Shakespeare Street whose homes were outside Nottingham, and offered increased grants for such students, the Corporation bought Mapperley Hall and rented it to the University College Council. It opened for students in 1906.

39. See *Nottingham's Heritage* (1985) p. 12, which suggests that Lambert's factory is strongly reminiscent of Wollaton Hall. See also Andrew Hamilton in N.C.S.N. 67 (April 1985) 9-11.

40. *Nottinghamshire at the opening of the Twentieth Century* (1901) has a brief biographical note on William Lambert, with a photograph (p. 188). Many photographs of the Lambert family are included in Iliffe and Baguley's *Victorian Nottingham* 16 (1976). William's son John, an enthusiastic pioneer photographer, produced some well-known photographs of the city, including some from the vantage point of the tower of Lamberts' factory.

41. *The Lenton Listener* issue for May-June 1985 includes, under the title 'The Farmer's Tale', an account of the life and work of Bill and Gladys Barsby at Lenton Firs Farm.

42. The indenture of sale to the University in 1950 wrongly refers to the property as 'Lenton Hall Farm'.

CHAPTER X

THE LENTON ABBEY ESTATE

Introduction

The schedule of the Milward estate lands conveyed to Messrs. Pares and Paget on Old Lady Day 1798 [1] described the farm holding later called Lenton Abbey as a 'messuage, tenement or farmhouse and several closes or grounds inclosed ... lying in Lenton and Radford' in the occupation of the representatives of the late John Clayton, deceased, and 'now or lately called by the names' given in the following list.

Far Fan Broom Close	9a.0.12
Near Fan Broom Close	10a.0.22
Middle Broom Close with the stackyard and lane adjoining	12a.2.00
Near Broom Close or Home Close with the yard, garden and site of buildings	6a.2.33
The Four Acres or Broom Close	4a.1.00
The Long Meadow or Broom Meadow	8a.1.04
The Eight Acres or Broom Close	8a.0.22
The Home Abbey Field	11a.1.09
The Second Abbey Field	12a.1.18
The Hind and Far Abbey Fields	17a.2.12
Total	100a.1.12

The seven closes incorporating the name Broom aggregated about 59 acres, and are thought to represent the Great Broom Close of the 16th-17th century. The Home Abbey Field and Second Abbey Field brought the area up to 83a.3.00. Clayton had also occupied the adjoining close called the Hind and Far Abbey Field - part of the Far Abbey Field in 1684 [2] - which brought his land holding to just above 100 acres (Figures 21 and 30). This farm, which came into being as a distinct and separate holding between 1730 and 1745, formed the basis of the Lenton Abbey estate of the 19th and early 20th centuries.

John Clayton had died only a few weeks earlier, for the Nottingham Journal of 9, 16, and 23 December 1797 advertised the forthcoming sale by auction at the Black Moor's Head, Nottingham on 27 December 1797 of some property of Miss Milward in four lots, three of which were closes near to Lenton village, but the other 'a complete farm' of 'upwards of 100 acres of rich land in a ring fence, with a farmhouse etc., divided into 11 closes in the occupation of Mr. John Clayton of Nottingham'. The description is of a consolidated tract of land, probably the first independent farm holding on the estate since the Dissolution. The farm adjoined 'the turnpike-road from Nottingham to Derby, and also the Branch out of that road towards Sawley', bounded west by the Tottle Brook, and south-west by land owned by Francis Evans and not in the Milward estate [3] .

The Odd House Farm as it may be called (see below) was probably chosen for auction in December 1797 because it was an independent unit, and estimated to be worth enough to redeem Miss Milward's 50-year old mortgage of £3,000, now called in by James Graham, without the need to sell the whole estate, because transfer arrangements were completed in an indenture dated 8 December 1797, the day before the farm was advertised for auction [4]. It is uncertain whether the auction was successful because actual possession following the sale was to be on the following Old Lady Day, by which time the purchases at auction 'will be required to be completed'. Pares and Paget, in fact, purchased the entire Milward estate with the exception of Trent Wong on Old Lady Day 1798 [5] and James Graham joined Miss Milward in the conveyance, as described in Chapter V. The Odd House farm, somewhat reduced in area, was re-sold by Pares and Paget one week later, on 4/5 April 1798 to James Green of Wollaton, and the balance of the 100 acres was sold to John Wright and Francis Evans [6] .

The area purchased by James Green was 72a.3.10, including the 23a.2.27 of the Home and Second Abbey Fields, while Francis Evans and John Wright had 9a.3.30 and 17a.2.12 respectively of Clayton's former holding. This partition of the farm in 1798 had an influence on the boundary of the University campus on the west side 150 years later. The Hind and Far Abbey Fields lying alongside Derby Road immediately west of the old (pre-1805) part of Beeston Lane, were bought by John Wright to form the western extremity of Lenton Hall park, enabling him to move this part of the Sawley turnpike westwards soon afterwards, as related in Chapter XIII below. The area between Derby Road and the old and new lines of Beeston Lane was later called The Three-cornered Close [7] . Within a few years, as a result of the Beeston inclosure award of 1808-09 (see Chapter V) Wright was able to extend his land still further west to the western boundary of the present sports ground in front of the University Sports Centre, thus reducing further the area of Lenton Abbey farm in Lenton.

Francis Evans bought land contiguous with his own property on which he was to build Lenton Grove. The land apportioned to Evans - the Eight Acres and part of Broom Meadow - was already agreed at the time of the sale, showing that James Green had earlier made arrangements to buy the farm, and may possibly have done so at the time of the auction. Evans reimbursed Green for his share of the purchase price of £4,780 in respect of his 10 acres, and the sale to Green and Evans was effected in a single indenture. Green was to have 'All that the north-west end or part of the Long Meadow or Broom Meadow as the same is fenced and divided from the south-east end thereof, conveyed or intended to be conveyed to Mr. Francis Evans, and which said several closes or grounds inclosed, including the remainder of the said

Long Meadow and a close called Eight Acres or Broom Close conveyed or intended ... by the said Thos. Pares and Thos. Paget to the sd. Francis Evans were in and about the year 1684 in five closes....'. This brought Green's area to 72a.3.10.

The earlier history of the Lenton Abbey estate

J.T.Godfrey [1884 209] stated, incorrectly, that the Lenton Abbey area, 'a portion of the priory demesne lying near the western extremity of Lenton parish ... appears to have been sold off at an earlier period' (than 1798), adding, however, the partial truth that 'this part has been known for at least two centuries as the Abbey Fields'. Perhaps Godfrey knew of the alienation of the Lenton Grove land, earlier also called Broom Close (see Chapter XI) and had been misled by it. The farm has been shown in earlier chapters to have formed the westernmost part of a 200 acre tract called the Abbey Fields covering virtually the whole of the northern part of the University campus west of the present ring road, used in medieval times as open arable land, but since the Dissolution chiefly as 'dry pasture land', and in the later 16th and the 17th centuries as sheep walk. However, on account of the character of the soils of this western part of the Abbey Fields, arising from the geological conditions - fairly cohesive but well drained and comparatively fertile - this was the first part of the Abbey Fields to be enclosed. Arable cultivation appears to have been re-established, though as part of a mixed farming system, in the last years of the 17th or early years of the 18th century. For the same reason Lenton Abbey Farm in the 1860s was largely arable land when the rest of the former Abbey Fields was parkland. It would not be surprising, therefore, if a farmstead was built there in the early 18th century.

In 1684 the Abbey Fields, 'all those fields, pieces or parcels of Pasture ground', were occupied by Messrs. John Scattergood and Alcock, who paid £41 a year for them under a lease running from 1682 to 1695. They contained an estimated 200 acres [8]. In 1731, although the Abbey Fields of 200 acres were still recorded, there were also on the estate two unlocated messuages or tenements with the gardens belonging [9]. In 1743 two distinct farms were described (and no 'Abbey Fields') and one of these was the undoubted forerunner of Lenton Abbey - a messuage or tenement held with two Broom Closes and Broom Meadow, occupied for a yearly rent of £24.10s. by Hugh Standley [10]. The second farm in 1743 was that worked from Abbey House at the eastern end of the estate (see Chapter VII).

'There was an old house here, which has been conjectured to have been originally the grange or farmstead of the monastery' wrote Godfrey [1884]: but no evidence has been found to support the latter speculation. A grange of the priory in that location would be difficult to understand, though a barn or crewyard might be more likely, and it is thought that the farmstead occupied by Hugh Standley in 1743 was probably the first building on the site. A house on the site of Lenton Abbey was shown on the map of Nottinghamshire by John Chapman, printed for W.Faden in 1785 but surveyed in 1774. It was named 'Odd House', the meaning of which is not known, but might be 'strange' (if, for example, it was a barn conversion), or 'old'; or it may have had a meaning now lost. Chapman's map shows another 'Odd House' on the site of the present Sherwin Arms inn at Bramcote.

The farmhouse mentioned in the 1798 sale terrier, and depicted on Chapman's map in 1774, was the house that Hugh Standley occupied in 1743, and this is the first known mention of Lenton Abbey as a distinct, independent, functioning farm unit, which had come into being probably after 1731. A decade after 1743 a Mr. Wilkinson was the occupier, for his son, William, a progressive and prosperous farmer in Lenton in the 1820s, and probably the originator of the famous Lenton Shorthorn herd discussed later, (Chapter XV) was born there in 1759 [11]. Details of the tenancy of Lenton Abbey farm in the 18th century come from the highly informative evidence of a number of witnesses in the case of a prosecution for trespass in 1823, further details of which are given in Chapter XIII. William Wilkinson said in 1823 that he was born in the house then occupied by Mr. Ray, but this must be incorrect, since the farm house at Lenton Abbey was built by James Green. Wilkinson returned to the farm in 1774 aged 15, and lived and worked there for nine years (to 1783) and 'had that farm in his hands'. Thomas Roe, a year younger than William Wilkinson, was a labourer there, who came to Lenton in 1776 and lived and worked on the farm 'now Green's' (in 1823) for several years, probably from 1776 to 1783 for Wilkinson. After 1783 Roe (or Rowe) occupied Milward estate land earlier held by Widow Welsh (Figure 29) and probably then lived in Lenton village. On the evidence of the land tax assessments John Clayton of Nottingham replaced William Wilkinson at the Odd House farm in 1790 [12]. Clayton was named as a Nottingham victualler in the Universal British Directory of 1793.

James Green's building of the house and farmstead of Lenton Abbey

Lenton Abbey house, which has been described as an 'early Victorian villa', was built in 1798-1800, at least 35 years before Victoria's accession, though it has subsequently been altered and extended. Its name, Lenton Abbey, is a pure invention by James Green, and highly misleading. The old part of the house is said to have very thick walls in parts, so Green's mansion is presumed to incorporate parts of the fabric of the old farm house occupied by the 18th century tenants. Green built also a house for the farmer or bailiff who worked the land. This information comes from an Abstract of Title produced for the sale of the estate by Lord Middleton in 1867 [13], which refers to an indenture of 11 March 1815 (a form of marriage settlement between James Green and his second wife, Elizabeth Horst of Blackheath) in which Green was 'seized of a capital messuage or mansion house and hereditaments' which he agreed to place in trust. A marginal annotation by C. Butler dated 1830 (when Lord Middleton was about to buy the estate) reads: 'The capital messuage or mansion house is, I presume, a new erection in the lands conveyed by the indenture of 4/5 April 1798. A farm house was conveyed by these deeds, which I presume is the farm house mentioned in the particulars of sale'. It was not: it was the Odd House. An undated rejoinder by W.G.B. states: 'The capital messuage ... is for the most part a new erection - the old farm is retained ... the offices of the present mansion. The farm house now standing is a small house for the bailiff, and was built by Mr. Green'. This must be the house occupied by Mr. Ray in 1823. It is now called The Cottage, and architecturally forms an integral part of the range of former farm buildings, now converted into dwellings, round the former farmyard at its northern corner.

The Odd House farm as it had been held by John Clayton before the sale of 1798 was diminished by assignment of land at the sale to John Wright and Francis Evans, and the farm in Lenton parish lost further land through the Enclosure award for Beeston in 1808-09 [14]. John Wright, who owned land in Beeston, was awarded an allotment in the 'several closes, pieces or parcels of ground called Beeston Field Closes in Beeston', lying alongside the Tottle Brook opposite to James Green's Broom Meadow. Then this allotment of 10a.3.28 was surrendered to Green in exchange for 10 acres of Green's Home Abbey Field of 11a.1.09 adjoining Wright's Hind and Far Abbey Field near Beeston Lane, and called Abbey Field Close on the Beeston enclosure map. At the same time Matthew Needham of Lenton House purchased from James Green the remainder of the Home Abbey Field together with the south-eastern part of the Second Abbey Field of 12a.1.18 - the land upon which he later built Lenton Fields house. 'This exchange was made and possession taken, but no conveyance executed. Mr. Wright will convey the legal estate in these fields and an abstract of his title is preparing': but no conveyances were necessary under the Enclosure Act. Thus already in May 1808 James Green's land tax in Lenton decreased by £1.14s.11d. from £8.12s.2d. to £6.17s.3d., while that of John Wright increased by £1.5s.4½d., and the balance of 10s. 4½d (sic) was due from Matthew Needham.

An undated plan of the Lenton Abbey estate [15] which incorporates these changes, but includes the name of Francis Evans, who died in 1815, is probably to be dated 1815 or a little earlier, and may have been associated with James Green's marriage settlement of 1815 referred to above. It may be noted that a similar map attached to the sale papers of 1830 discussed below may well have been surveyed earlier, and from its content probably in about 1809 (Figure 74). An indenture of 24 December 1816, certified on behalf of James and Elizabeth Green with the trustees of the 1815 settlement, the 'sale' to Matthew Needham of Lenton House and his heirs etc. in trust, 'all such and so many and such parts of the messuage, closes, lands and other hereditaments comprised in the 1500 year term' except 'the pieces or parcels of land sold and conveyed by James Green to the said John Wright, William Jamson, Jonas Bettison and William Manning, and also except a certain piece or parcel of land belonging to the said Jno Wright situate in Beeston ... and all the estate etc. ... to hold the same unto Matthew Needham ...'. According to its label this assignment related to 54 acres, and continued: 'As to Lot 2. Abstract of assignment of term of 1500 years'. The contemporary map of the estate lists in its schedule about 59 acres in Lenton parish, corrected from 57 acres.

Soon afterwards, on 26/27 May 1817, James Green the elder put the estate in trust for his three children, Susanna and James, both also of Lenton, and Henry Gilson Green, gent. of Newark, aged 18. These deeds list an area of 62a.3.9, including Home Abbey Field and Second Abbey Field. The brothers were to pay one-third of the rent to Susanna for her undivided third part. On 25 September of the same year Susanna Green married William Batley of Blackheath, and on 12/13 February 1819 the Green brothers released to Benjamin Elisha Batley, an oil merchant of the Barbican, their two undivided third parts, to hold subject to a life interest in the house and garden and an annuity of £200 or £300 [16]. The reason for the alternative annuities was that if Elizabeth, James Green's second wife and presumptive widow, were to decline to live in the mansion after the death of James her annuity would be increased from £200 to £300. In the event she did decline to live at Lenton Abbey. In May 1825 [17] the property of the brothers Green - or their expectations - was mortgaged for £2,500 to a Thomas Herrington subject to the life interest of their stepmother Elizabeth Green under their father's will. Matthew Needham of Lenton House was again involved as trustee, as in 1815.

Little is known about James Green during the 30 years between his purchase of the Lenton Abbey estate in 1798 and his death in 1829, and nothing is known of his first wife, Sarah, who died aged 60 in 1811 and was buried at Lenton. Before 1798 James was very much in the public eye as the superintending engineer (under the broad direction of William Jessop) for the construction during the 1790s of the Nottingham Canal and of the Nottinghamshire section of the Grantham Canal (described in Chapter XIII below). His task was onerous, and he faced many serious difficulties that were not of his making, stemming from the very nature of the enterprise and the fact that his employer was a committee of people with often divergent views and interests. He was publicly blamed, unfairly, for the high cost of the project which over-ran its budget in a time of inflation, and it is not known that he ever worked as an engineer again, but he appears to have farmed his estate and he certainly took some part in local life, for example, as churchwarden at Lenton in 1808 (with John Wilkinson) and in 1809 (with John Wright). In 1803 he was involved with the local anti-invasion plans and offered transport in the form of two horses, a cart and a driver, and he was Overseer of the Poor for Lenton in the same year [Godfrey 1884 467 and 337).

James Green's sub-tenants, 1798-1829

The land tax assessments indicate that Green farmed his land through a resident farm bailiff down to 1813, but redemption of the tax deprives us of later detail, and he ceased to be responsible for the tax himself by 1818, when his name was replaced by those of T.Ray, T.Hall and J. Cheetham. Ray is known to have been living at Lenton Abbey in 1822-23 [18], probably in the farmhouse, and later evidence shows that he leased the agricultural estate during the

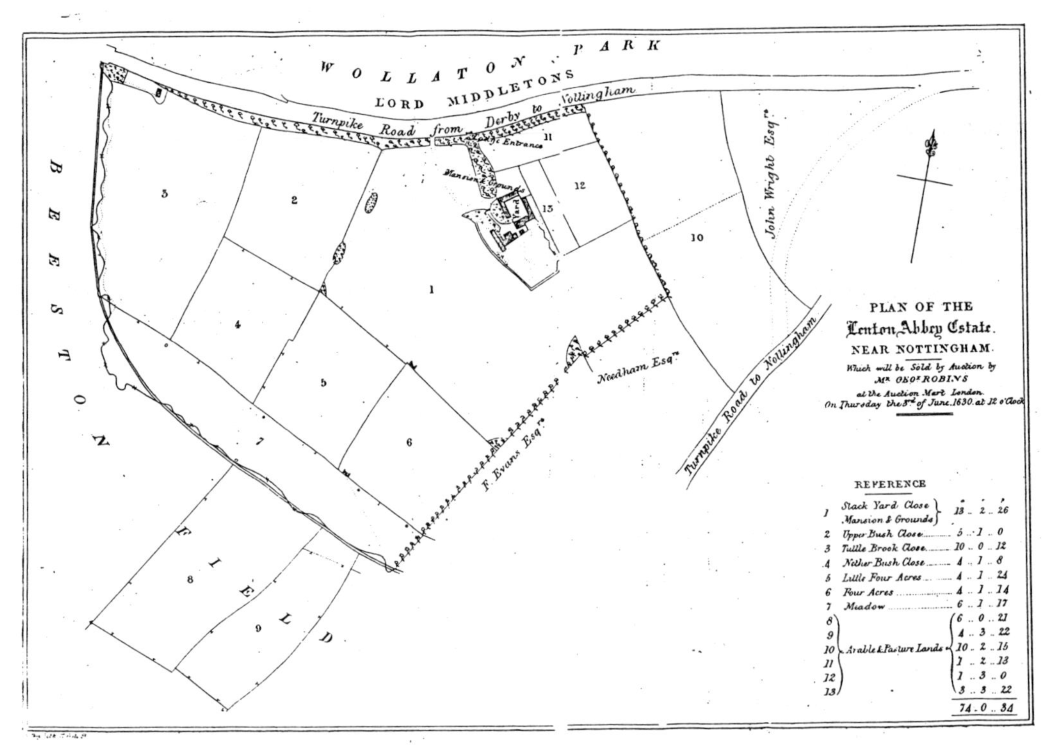

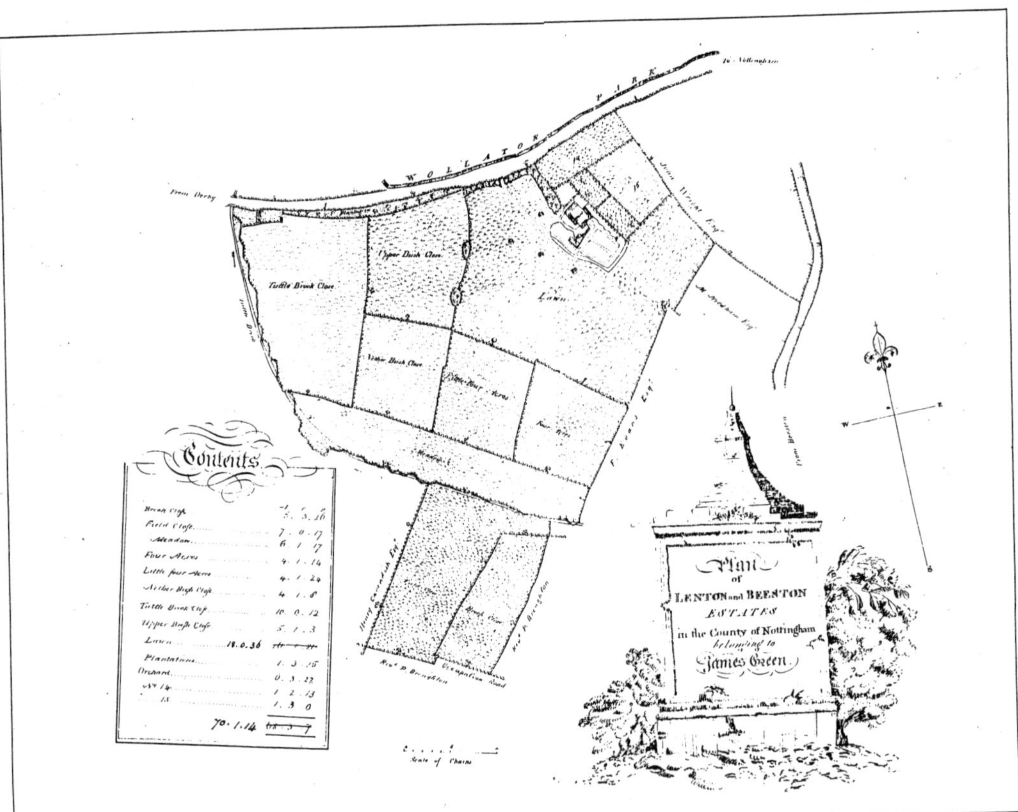

Figure 74: Maps of the Lenton Abbey estate of James Green in about 1809 [NAO DD 669/1 (1830): NAO BE 2 S (c. 1809)] For discussion of dates see text

1820s, and perhaps from 1818 , sub-letting some land to others - probably the two fields in Beeston parish. In 1830 'the property was demised a few years ago to Mr. Ray at a low rent of £300 a year' and 'in one short year it falls again into possession'. Whether Ray's lease included the mansion throughout is not known, but in 1830 (after Green's death) Ray 'has sub-let the residence and gardens to S. Fisher Esq., the respectable occupant'. It seems possible that in his later years James Green may have been unable to manage his own affairs, especially after - perhaps even before - his dubious second marriage, and the legal transactions after 1815 certainly suggest that his affairs were being conducted by others

Purchase by Lord Middleton - sale particulars of 1830

After James Green's death in early 1829, when he would have been about 80 years old, there was a great hurry to realize his assets and implement his will - to sell the estate urgently in order to redeem the mortgage, share the proceeds of the sale among the heirs, and secure the annuity for the widow, Elizabeth. Having been put up for auction on 9 August 1829 without a sale being made, a second auction was arranged for 3 June 1830, to be conducted by Mr. George Robins at the Auction Mart, London [19] . The sale was to be 'in one lot and peremptorily', for the house and '74 acres of rich land'. The sale description of the estate, with the house and garden, included 'a small farmhouse' which was 'judiciously placed at the end of the plantations' and probably refers to the cottage near the Tottle Brook bridge which today immediately overlooks the Lenton Abbey traffic island. 'All the buildings essential to a Pleasure Farm are entirely shut out from view'.

The sale particulars of 1830, like those for Lenton House and Highfield House estates many years later, made much of the potential value of the estate for profitable residential development, and in language which shows that in imagination and panache, not to mention pomposity, the estate agent of today would have little to teach his predecessor of 1830. Some of the prose is worth repeating for its own sake. 'Although not renowned for its similarity to an Abbey (to which character it does not aspire), [it] is justly famed in Nottingham and its vicinity for its quiet, gentlemanly outward form and excellent accommodation. It were impossible after passing THE SPLENDID CHATEAU OF LORD MIDDLETON and his immense and far-famed domain, not to turn aside and repose on Lenton, its unpretending friendly neighbour, and then enquire "who has the good fortune to possess and the good taste to have completed this domicile of comfort ?". It is seated in grounds laid out in excellent order, the American plants are well selected, and feather to the ground, and the flowering shrubs in little myriads pour forth their sweet perfumes in every direction. THE LODGE ENTRANCE and communication thence through the grounds of this Paradise in miniature are demonstrative proof of the superior tact that must have presided over the whole arrangement'.

The potential value of Lenton Abbey as a dairy farm was obvious. 'But it is confidently believed the time is not far distant when this little territory will put on an entirely new character. The wealthy merchants of Nottingham must of necessity recreate occasionally after their daily avocations, and it may be asked with great confidence "where can they gratify this laudable propensity so well as at Lenton ?" for though not three short miles from the bustle and confusion [of Nottingham] it is as quiet and retired (and the writer is almost inclined to add as interesting as if it were the most admired scenery of North Wales) ....Mr. Robins expects that this domain will soon be ornamented by first-rate villas, and each of them, from their proximity to the town, may be designated the "rus in urbe"....'. An additional virtue of the location was that the Wollaton Park estate across Derby Road 'cannot be built upon'. Ironically it was Lord Middleton himself who bought the estate, though whether at auction or subsequently is not known, the indentures being dated 8/9 March 1831, and with 60 acres and not 74, the land across the Tottle Brook in Beeston parish not being included. Following Lenton Firs (1813) this was the second stage, to be followed by Lenton Hall in 1845, in the Middleton acquisition of the entire Derby Road frontage of the campus west of Clifton Boulevard.

Lenton Abbey house in 1830 had four 'best bedchambers' with a dressing room, and two principal spare bedrooms as well as three attic chambers. There was a drawing room (20 by 17 feet), a dining parlour (22 by 18 feet) and a library or breakfast room. A kitchen, larder, scullery, dairy, butler's room and storeroom with men's sleeping room over, extensive cellaring 'of good temperature and very dry'; and ample detached offices, including a brewhouse with a laundry over it completed the domestic accommodation. There were two coachhouses, ample stabling (connected with a 'snug little paddock') a farmyard with barn, stabling etc., and other buildings including the small farmhouse.

Susanna Batley and her brothers on 8/9 March 1831 'contracted with Henry, Lord Middleton for the absolute sale to him of the mansion house, land and hereditaments in fee simple, free of land tax' for £11,970 [20]. The transaction was subject to redemption of a mortgage of £2,500, originally to Thomas Herrington, now to Maria, wife of John Marshall, deceased executor of Herrington. Susanna was to receive one-third of the sale price of the estate, with her brothers sharing the rest after paying off the mortgage, all subject to the life interest of Elizabeth Green (£300 a year). The property sold extended to 60a.0.08. Its plan was said in Lord Middleton's abstract of title in 1867 to be 'in the margin of the first skin of the now abstracting indenture' (which has not been located) and the estate was in the occupation of I. Fisher Esq. and Mr. Ray or their undertenants.

Lord Middleton's tenants at Lenton Abbey

Captain Isaac Fisher and his wife Ann, 1829/30-1859

The successor of James Green at Lenton Abbey house was Isaac Fisher, already in residence at Lenton Abbey in 1830, when the sale particulars indicated that he rented the house from Mr. Ray, who then held a lease of the whole estate. Fisher may have moved in only after James Green's death, however, since Pigot's Directory for 1828-29 recorded a Captain Fisher living at Stapleford, while the 1831 edition mentioned him at Lenton Abbey. Fisher took over the whole estate on the expiry of Ray's lease, and the Old Michaelmas rental for 1831 confirms that he was the first of Lord Middleton's tenants of the Lenton Abbey estate, paying a half-yearly rent of £150, which had been established earlier to cover Elizabeth Green's pension under her husband's will [21]. Whether Ray left the farmhouse is not known, but Fisher remained, paying the same rent, until his death in 1845. In that particular half-year he paid an additional half-year rent of £18.15s.0d. at Michaelmas for 15 acres of land (now mainly a sports ground adjoining the Indoor Sports Centre) which had been part of Lenton Hall park, newly purchased by Lord Middleton in 1845 [22]. This restored to Lenton Abbey the 10 acres transferred from it to John Wright in 1808-09, and added a triangular area in the angle of Derby Road and the new part of Beeston Lane, on part of which Lenton Eaves was later built. Ann Fisher, Isaac's widow, remained at Lenton Abbey until about 1859 [Wright 1858 294] when the property was leased to Thomas Bayley [23]. The Fishers had occupied the mansion for 30 years.

The Census Enumerators' Books of 1841 and 1851 provide further details of the occupancy of Lenton Abbey mansion and its ancillary cottages towards the middle of the 19th century. In 1841 [24] Isaac Fisher, who was a prosperous lace manufacturer then aged 57, lived in the mansion with his wife Ann (55), two manservants (George Holt (25) and George Gilsthorpe (30)), and four maidservants (Mary Thompson (30), Sarah Gilbery (25), Helen Cowley (20) and Harriett Wood (35)). Lenton Abbey Lodge was occupied by two other servants, William Bayley (25) and his wife Louisa (27). Lenton Abbey farmhouse (known as The Cottage at the present day) where Mr. Ray had lived, was then the home of John Hall (50), agricultural labourer, his wife Hannah (55) and daughter Ann (14), together with Hannah Bostock (26), her three young daughters, and Sarah Wright (25). John Hall's description as agricultural labourer indicates that he probably acted as farm bailiff for Isaac Fisher.

At the 1851 census [25] the widowed Ann Fisher, now aged 70 and described as 'fund holder', was still at Lenton Abbey, living with her niece Sarah Wood (42); but all other members of the household had changed. The six living-in servants were all of local origin, as follows: William Harrison (24) butler, born at Ruddington; Robert Rushton (29) coachman, Elston; Mary Drury (39) cook, Linby; Fanny Langsdale (35) housemaid, Bramcote; Mary Borrowcliff (17) kitchen maid, Wollaton; and Sarah Townsend (50) laundress, from Oxton. The gardener, Robert Stafford from Doveridge, with his wife Elizabeth (43) and six children, the four youngest born at Lenton, occupied Lenton Abbey Lodge, while at the farmhouse was Benjamin Cope (45) from Mapperley (Derbyshire), 'agricultural labourer', his wife Mary (45), born at Kegworth, and their two sons and a son-in-law, all called agricultural labourers, as well as a younger son at school. John Hall, who lived in the farmhouse in 1841, had moved up the hill to become farm bailiff at Lenton Hall Farm. The local origins of the domestic and farm staff contrast with the diverse and more distant origins of the staffs at Lenton Hall and Lenton House.

Thomas Bayley and his forbears (Figure 75)

Thomas Bayley (1813-1874) (Figure 76) proprietor of the large and growing 'fellmongery' business engaged in tanning and dressing leather at works alongside the river Leen and Nottingham Canal on Leengate, Old Lenton, leased Lenton Abbey from Lord Middleton in 1859-60. However, he could not buy either Lenton Abbey or the site of his tannery until legal restrictions on their sale were removed in 1868-69. By his will Henry, 6th Lord Middleton, in 1848 devised his property in Lenton to the use of his successor Digby, the 7th Lord Middleton, for life, and to his sons in tail male. Special disclaimers after exchanges were required before the property could be sold [26] .

The Bayley leather business had been established by Thomas Bayley's great-uncle Isaac Bayley (1756-1836), who before 1790 had come to settle in Nottingham before moving to Lenton. He was joined in the business in 1793 by his brother Thomas Bayley (1750/1-1835) who had previously had a school in Chester. Isaac and Thomas were the fourth and third sons respectively of another Thomas Bayley of Sandbach, Cheshire (1706/7-1761) and Mary Venables of Macclesfield. A Bayley pedigree begins with yet another Thomas Bayley or Bealie (died 1587) of Sandbach [Phillimore 1910 I 269-70] (Figure 75).

Isaac Bayley took over the site on which the tannery was established in 1795, as the Nottingham canal alongside it was opened for traffic. It was the only land in Lenton then owned by Lord Middleton (outside his Wollaton Park) and the Middleton estate rentals from 1788 to 1794 inclusive show that it was occupied by a Mrs. Wood at an annual rent of £2.2s.0d. [27] . In 1795, when Mrs. Wood was three years in arrears with her rent, Isaac Bayley became the occupier at the same rent [28] , and the same entry was repeated annually to 1809 [29] . In 1813-14 [30] Isaac Bayley was still the only Lenton name in the Middleton rental, but now paying £30 a year. The increase was presumably on account of development of the site, and extension of the tannery in 1809, when the rent was increased to £25 [31] . In 1809 the premises were described as 'House, skin house, skin pits, garden and croft, and two gardens lately purchased of Mr. Edge'.

Isaac Bayley featured in the Middleton rentals until 1837, when his name was replaced by those of Thomas Bayley and John Shaw [32] . Isaac married Elizabeth Copley of Hoby, Leicestershire (1765-1843) in 1795, the same year as his first occupation of the Leen-gate site, and he is presumed to have lived on the site. The house he built later in New Lenton, Holly Cottage, appears by its photograph [Phillimore 1910 277] to be in a style much later than 1795. It was in Middleton Place [White 1832] or Lenton Sands [Dearden 1834]. Isaac's children were not associated with the leather business. His son, also Isaac, died abroad, and his daughter Ann married Lorenzo Christie, a lace manufacturer who lived on Middleton Place, New

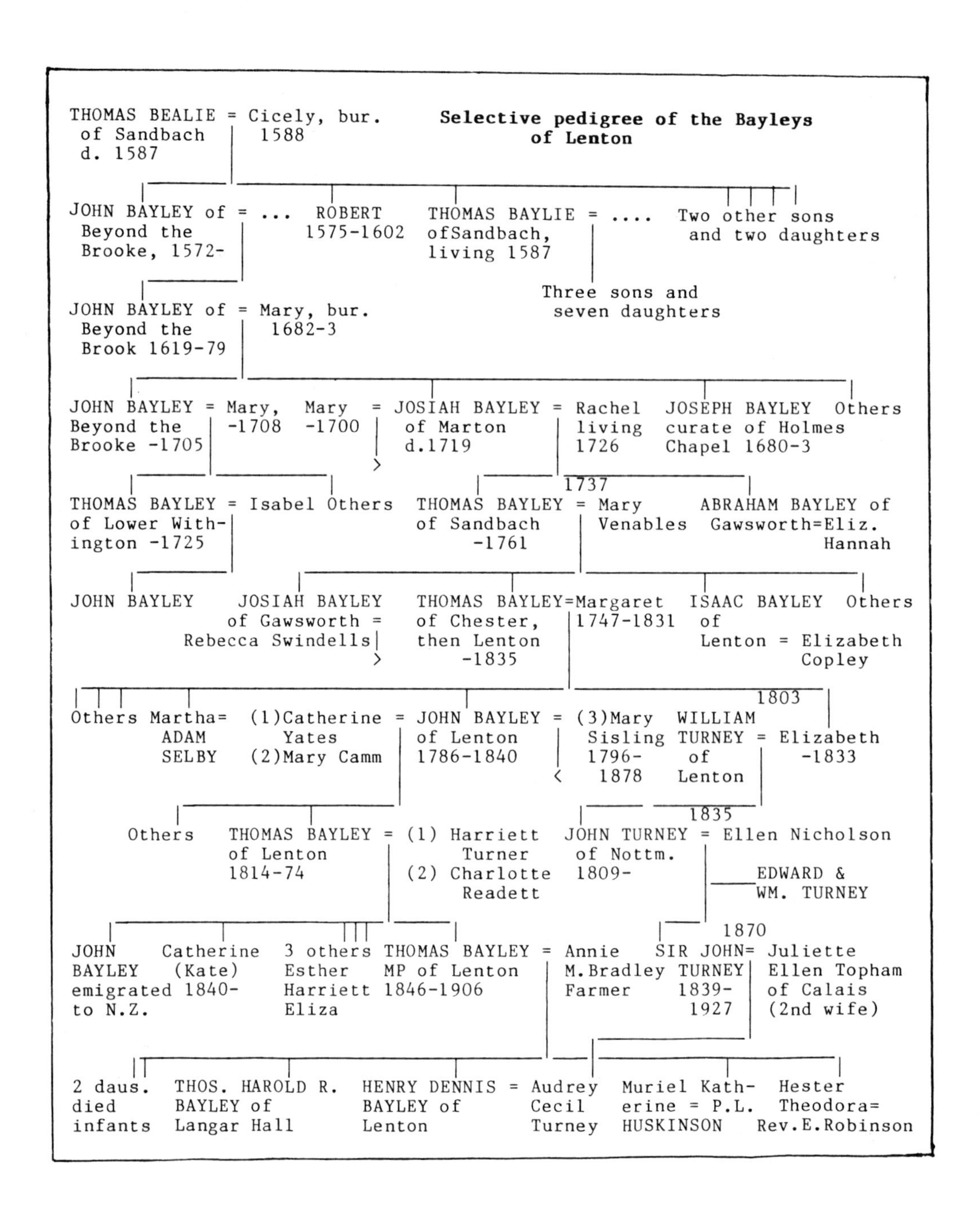

Figure 75: Selective pedigree of the Bayleys of Lenton

Lenton [Glover 1832]. Their son, Richard Copley Christie, M.A., (died 1901) was Chancellor of the Diocese of Manchester from 1872 to 1893.

The forty-year business partnership of Isaac Bayley and his brother Thomas ended in 1835 when Thomas died, aged 84, and was buried in Lenton Priory churchyard. Isaac died in the following year. Thomas was a strict Scotch Baptist, and conducted services at his home and at Park Street Chapel in Nottingham. He and his wife Margaret (1748-1831) had four sons and two daughters. Martha (1781-1879) born at Chester, married Adam Selby and had a son, Isaac (died 1879), a schoolmaster at Carrington. Elizabeth, also born at Chester, married in 1803 William Turney, and had seven sons, one of them the father of Sir John Turney Kt., head of the firm of Turney Brothers, also important leather producers, whose daughter Audrey Cecil married her cousin, Henry Dennis Bayley of Lenton Abbey, grandson of Thomas Bayley the elder, and mentioned again later. The large Turney leather works near Trent Bridge survived into the years after the second world war. Whether it had direct business connections historically with the Bayley enterprise is not known, though the family connection is clear enough. Of the four sons of Thomas Bayley only the youngest, John, survived him - and he by only five years - and he appears not to have succeeded to control of the business on Leen-gate despite the statement by Mellors [1912 20] that he 'carried on the leather business'. It was John's son Thomas who leased Lenton Abbey in 1860.

The Thomas Bayley who died in 1835 was described as a fine preacher, 'full of pithy sentences and proverbial sayings. He dressed in the old-fashioned way, with knee breeches and brass buttons' [Mellors 1912 20]. His son John was also a religious man, a preacher, and pastor of a Scotch Baptist church in Nottingham. He was married three times. His first wife was Catherine Yates of Longton, Staffordshire, who died in 1818 aged 30, having had four children of whom two survived childhood. Their daughter Catherine (1818-1884) married Michael Shaw of Lenton, a leather dresser [33] and their son Thomas took over the leather business in 1836 after the death of the two aged brothers Isaac and Thomas, his great-uncle

Figure 76: Thomas Bayley senior (1814-1874) and junior (1846-1906)

and grandfather respectively. John Bayley married his second wife, Mary Camm (died 1825) in 1821: there were no children. In 1826 John married a third wife, Mary Sisling of Bottesford (1796-1878) and had four further children, all born at Lenton. Mary (1832-1898) married Samuel Charles Hardy in 1862, without issue: and there were Annie (1834-1851), John (b. 1835) and Elizabeth (1836-1885) who married Alfred Saxton, a Nottingham lace manufacturer, and died in Birmingham.

Thomas Bayley (Figure 76) - 'the elder' in the context of Lenton Abbey - took over the business in 1836 at the age of 22, in partnership with John Shaw, a member of a Lenton farming family [34] . They paid the rent jointly from 1837, and under the partnership the leather works on Leen-gate expanded quickly. By 1859, when he leased Lenton Abbey, Thomas had opened other tanneries at Giltbrook and Newark, and founded the Digby Colliery Company of which he was the principal proprietor. As early as May 1841 Lord Middleton furnished materials for an extension to the tannery 'up to £150', and the rent was increased to £150 a year from Lady Day 1842 [35] . Soon after his move from Parkside, Nottingham to Lenton Abbey Thomas Bayley was described by the census enumerator of 1861 as 'leather dresser and farmer of 347 acres' - land which included Beeston Fields Farm adjoining Lenton Abbey across the Tottle Brook, and probably also part of Lenton Hall park. His businesses then employed 252 men, 52 boys and 25 women, but eventually he employed over 2,000 workers, and the leather works at Lenton accounted for 450-500 of them.

Thomas married his first wife, Harriett Turner, at St. Mary's church Nottingham in 1837, the year in which he took over the business. Harriett died aged 30 on 10 August 1846, having had six children, of which three died young - Esther (1838-52), Harriett (1842-46) and Eliza (1844-45). The others were Catherine (Kate), born in 1840, who lived at Lenton Abbey until her death in 1920 - a well-known local personality (Figure 79); Thomas Bayley (the younger) (1846-1906) (Figure 76) who inherited the business and the estate; and John Bayley, said to have done useful work in the promotion of temperance education and social improve-

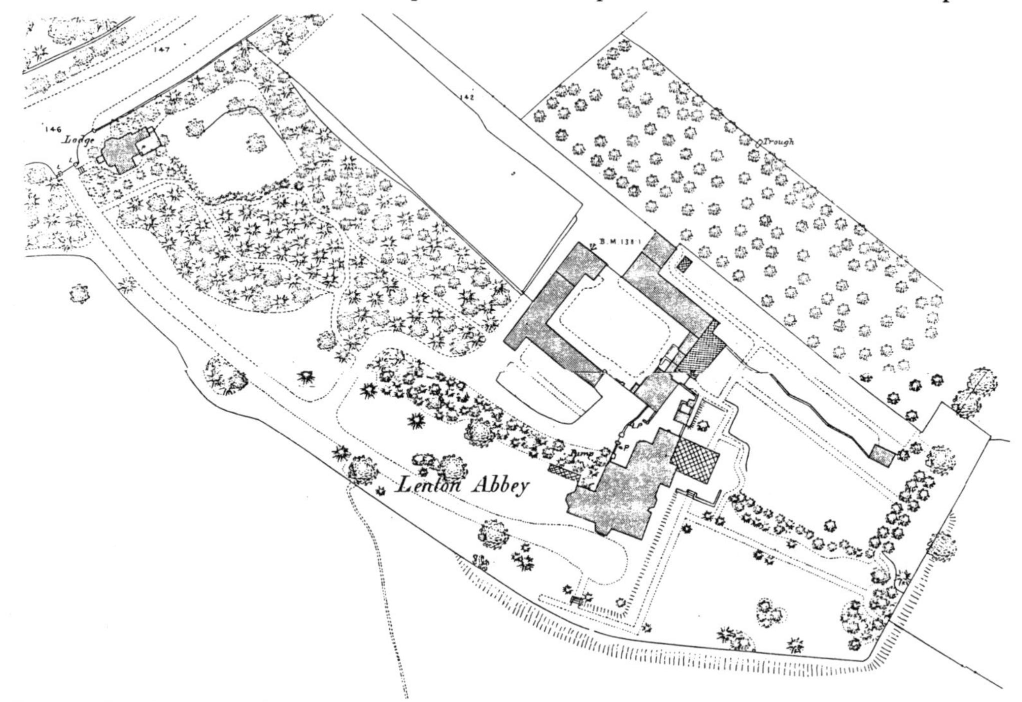

Figure 77: Lenton Abbey house and grounds in 1882
[Reduced from O.S. 1:500 Nottingham sheet XLI.8.24]

ment in Lenton and Nottingham before emigrating to New Zealand. Thomas Bayley the elder's second wife, Charlotte Readett (1834-1892) of Beaumond Cross, Newark (Figure 79) had no children.

In 1861 [36] Thomas Bayley the elder was still only 48 years old, and a man of great energy and very pronounced religious and political views. With his second wife Charlotte, daughter Catherine (Kate) (20) and son Thomas (14), children of his first marriage, he was served in the house by a footman and three female house servants. Ephraim Pendleton (50), agricultural labourer, was at the farmhouse with his wife Sara Matilda and two young daughters, while John Sibson the gardener, aged 37, his wife Sarah and three young children lived at the Lenton Abbey Lodge into which they had recently moved from West Bridgford.

A strong Baptist like his father John, and grandfather Thomas, and himself a preacher of note, Thomas Bayley the elder spent his Sundays preaching in Nottingham and the surrounding district. He was interested in social reform, and during the 'cotton famine' visited Lancashire with his industrial neighbour Benjamin Walker, whose lace factory on Commercial Street, Spring Close, almost adjoined Bayley's leather works on Leen-gate. In Lancashire in December 1862 they observed the working of retail cooperation, which had been introduced at Rochdale in 1844. On their return they called a meeting of their workpeople in Lenton, and on 28 March 1863 formed a committee to establish and manage the Lenton Industrial and Provident Society. With Bayley as chairman for eight years, and Walker as secretary and later president, they brought their combined business capacities to bear in the enterprise. This society was the direct forerunner of the Lenton and Nottingham Cooperative Society, which later dropped Lenton from its name, and is now the Greater Nottingham Cooperative Society.

Benjamin Walker and Thomas Bayley knew each other if only because both lived in the Sion Hill-Parkside locality before moving to Old Lenton. They were enlightened employers, took a keen interest in the welfare of their employees, and 'may be regarded as the Robert Owens of the Nottingham district' [Leeman 1944 4]. Leeman's book makes clear the close connection of the initiative of Bayley and Walker with the Lenton Temperance Society, and the meetings in its Reading Room (provided by Bayley) between August 1858 and May 1863. Benjamin Walker of Parkside was chairman of the Temperance Society, and others involved were John Bayley, Miss Kate Bayley and Miss Walker. Both Thomas Bayley and Benjamin Walker were champions of Nonconformity and opposed to the monopoly of the Church School in Lenton. Both opened reading rooms at Lenton, Bayley's adjoining his works on Leen-gate and Walker's at the back of the New Inn. Among his other activities Bayley was the prime mover in building Circus Street Hall as a Baptist chapel, and for the cost, which was unsubscribed, he took from the Trustees promissory notes, publicly burning a £100 note at each succeeding annual anniversary. He was lay rector of Beeston, and in business was an original director of the Nottingham Joint Stock Bank.

The wills of the owners of landed estates were often designed, through the operation of a succession of designated heirs, to impede their break-up, and special legal disentailers were required before land could be sold off. This was the case with the Middleton estate in Lenton. It became possible to put on the market several parts of the Middleton estates in 1867-68, and they included Lenton Abbey mansion and farm, and Bayley's tanyard [37]. Thomas Bayley was able to buy the Lenton Abbey estate in 1868, eight years after leasing it, under a disentailer of 1867 [38]. He paid £8,508.2s.5d. for it [39]. The sale was originally intended to include the Lenton Field closes bordering Beeston Lane, but once more these were detached from Lenton Abbey and sold as part of a triangular transaction to J.H.Lee [40].

At the same time as his Lenton Abbey transaction Thomas Bayley made a larger purchase - of 11 Lots in Beeston - chiefly Beeston Fields House and Farm, for which he paid Lord Middleton a total of £19,650 [41]. Subsequently Benjamin Walker junior bought land from J. Holwell Lee upon which he later built Lenton Eaves.

The favourable conditions for agriculture on the Lenton Abbey estate as compared with much of the rest of the former Abbey Fields has been mentioned in connection with the early development of an independent farm there in the early 18th century, and the distinction was still apparent in the later 19th century. A map of Lord Middleton's Lenton estates in 1863 [42] shows that while the Lenton Hall estate was almost all described as park, Lenton Abbey was quite highly cultivated - a true agricultural holding, which is reflected in the shading employed on the contemporary O.S. six-inch map. The gardens and orchard were divided from The Lawns, an area of grassland which served as a miniature park, by a ha ha wall, and the grassland of The Lawns was continued north of the house in two small paddocks. Otherwise the whole area from Beeston Lane to the Tottle Brook, with the exception of the alluvial meadow land along the brook itself, was described as arable land, reflecting the relatively fertile soils developed on the lower formations of the Mercia Mudstone rocks and river terrace gravels.

At the sale of 1868 Lenton Abbey house was described as a commodious residence. 'The house is in good condition, beautifully situated in park-like grounds well sheltered from the north by a belt of fine trees. There is an entrance gate lodge, recently built, abutting on the turnpike road: good stabling, carriage house, farm buildings, most productive gardens and well planned pleasure grounds' [43]. Lawson Lowe [1871] described 'a large well-built mansion, surrounded by extensive grounds, considerably altered and improved by the present proprietor, Mr. Thomas Bayley'.

The successors of Thomas Bayley the elder at Lenton Abbey

Thomas Bayley the elder died in 1874, only six years after he actually purchased Lenton Abbey estate. He was sixty. The two of his children who were most prominent in public life, and interesting personalities in their different ways, were Thomas Bayley the younger (1846-1906) and Catherine (Kate) Bayley, the spinster daughter who remained in residence at Lenton Abbey until her death in 1920. Thomas, who had lived at Lenton Abbey from the age of 14, remained there until 1874, the year of his father's death and of his own marriage. At the 1871 census the 24-year-old Thomas was described as a leather manufacturer, while his father was simply 'landowner', suggesting that the younger Thomas was already shouldering the responsibilities of running the multiple family business, then called T., J., and T.Bayley [Wright 1871].

In 1874 Thomas married Annie, daughter of Henry Farmer of Flora Cottage, Birch Lane (now Sherwin Road) Old Lenton, not far from the Leen-gate leather factory. Henry Farmer (d.1891) was very well known as a musical composer, conductor, teacher and publisher of music, and for over 40 years organist at High Pavement Chapel. He was also founder of the firm of his name trading in musical instruments and acting as a city ticket agency until swept away by the recent redevelopment of the Theatre Royal area. His father, proprietor of a music hall, and his nephew and neice were all musicians. Henry conducted the Nottingham Sacred Harmonic Society (founded by Alfred Lowe of Highfield House) for 14 years, was a skilled violinist, and composed many pieces designed for easy playing. It is not known whether Annie was a musician; but in 1873 Thomas Bayley was a director of the Albert Hall (or Temperance Hall) while Annie's father was closely involved with the musical concert arrangements at the Hall. Thomas built Peverel House in The Park, Nottingham, and occupied it until his death. Thus in 1877 Morris's Directory and Gazetteer of Nottingham recorded two Mrs. Thomas Bayleys, one, Charlotte, widow of Thomas the elder at Lenton Abbey, and another, Annie, at Peverel House, Cavendish Street.

The career of Thomas Bayley junior is summarized in a note accompanying his portrait in 'Contemporary Biographies' [Briscoe 1901]. Born in 1846 at Lenton he was educated at Amersham and privately. He was elected M.P. for Chesterfield in 1892, and remained a member until 1905, the year before his death, sitting on several Royal Commissions during his

Parliamentary service. He was for many years a member of Nottingham Town Council and was Sheriff of Nottingham in 1881: was a Justice of the Peace for the county: and as a member of Nottinghamshire County Council from its formation was one of the first county aldermen. Like his father he was a promoter of non-sectarian education, and chairman of the governors of the non-sectarian school, for which memorial stones were laid in 1873 by Mr. A.J.Mundella and Mr. Benjamin Walker (the younger) of Lenton Eaves (see Chapter XII). He was chairman of both Digby Colliery Company and Manners Colliery Company, a director if the Daimler Motor Company, and of A. and J.Shaw Ltd., leather manufacturers of Grantham [44] .

Thomas and Annie Bayley had six children. Two daughters died in infancy, and two others, Muriel Katherine (b.1880) and Hester Theodora (b. 1887) married, respectively, Percy Lambe Huskinson of Epperstone, a civil engineer, in 1899 at Westminster, and Rev. Edward Robinson, vicar of Car Colston, at Langar church in 1908. Their two sons were Thomas Harold Readett Bayley, born at Peverel House in 1876, and Henry Dennis Bayley, born in 1878. Thomas Bayley was said to have three residences in 1901 [Briscoe 1901), including Lenton Abbey, where he did not live, and Ringwood Hall, Chesterfield, in his Parliamentary constituency; but they did not include the Hall at Langar, where both Thomas (in 1906) and Annie (in 1904, aged 54) were buried in the churchyard [45] . Phillimore [1910] stated that it was Mrs. Bayley who purchased the Langar Hall estate in 1899, and that she died at Langar Hall on 23 August 1904. Thomas died at Peverel House. It is not known whether any estrangement in the family was involved, but Langar Hall was bequeathed by his mother to the elder son, Harold Bayley, educated at Uppingham and described in 1910 as a 'musical composer and colliery owner, unmarried and living at Langar Hall'. A list of Thoroton Society members in 1917 had him at North Lodge, The Park, and in 1935 T.H.R.Bayley was a priest of the Nottingham diocese, living at 8 Upper College Street, Nottingham [Baylis 1935]. It was H.Dennis Bayley, the younger son of Thomas and Annie Bayley, who appears to have inherited Lenton Abbey, and lived there. He is discussed further below.

Figure 78: The two sons of Thomas Bayley junior, Dennis and Harold
Colonel Sir Dennis Bayley, KBE, DL, moved to Hunmanby Hall, East Yorkshire: Rev. T. Harold R. Bayley lived in The Park, Nottingham, and later on Upper College Street

Charlotte and Kate Bayley (Figure 79)

It is thought that Thomas Bayley the elder willed a life interest in Lenton Abbey to his widow Charlotte and his unmarried daughter Kate, both of whom remained there to the end of their lives. Although the census of 1881 recorded only Catherine Bayley in residence she was described as 'daughter', and Directory entries as late as 1891 show that Kate's widowed stepmother, Charlotte (Figure 79) was still at Lenton Abbey. Charlotte died in 1892, and thereafter Miss Kate Bayley was the head of the household, and so remained, aged about 80, twenty-five years later, in 1920 [Wright 1920]. She died in 1921. She was remembered as a lively and forthright character into her old age. She was politically active in the cause of the Liberal Party, and in 1910 was President of the Chesterfield Women's Liberal Association (in the Division where her brother had been M.P. from 1892 to 1905), and President of the Nottingham Castle Ward Women's Liberal Association [Phillimore 1910].

The chief public work of Kate Bayley, however, was in the local social field, and she is best known for founding and substantially maintaining Beeston Orphanage, and for founding

Mrs. Thomas Bayley
neé Charlotte Readett

Miss Kate Bayley

Mrs. Thomas Bayley
neé Annie M.B. Farmer

Mrs. Dennis Bayley
neé Audrey Cecil Turney

Figure 79: Some women of the Bayley family
[From Phillimore 1910]

the Nottingham Day Nursery, one of the first creches in the country. The orphanage foundation was probably a fulfilment of the wishes of her father, for the Records of the Borough of Nottingham for 1875 note [46] that under the will of 'the late Thomas Bayley, fellmonger' he offered £2,000 towards an asylum for orphans, on condition that another £10,000 was subscribed within five years of his death: but the money was not raised. Mellors [1916 31] confirmed that Miss Bayley founded the Beeston Orphanage 'in accordance with a wish expressed in the will of her father, Mr. Thomas Bayley', and with the cooperation of friends, including Lady Turney who built one of the cottages. Sir John Turney was Kate Bayley's second cousin, and Lady Turney Sir John's second wife, married in 1870.

Henry Dennis Bayley

Dennis Bayley (Figure 78) born 1878 the second son of Thomas and Annie Bayley, and educated at Uppingham like his brother, and by tutors, was described as a colliery owner and leather manufacturer, and he was certainly at Lenton Abbey with his wife in 1910. It was he who carried forward into his generation the family interest in the leather business and its association with Lenton Abbey. He had been married at St. Margaret's, Westminster on 22 September 1903 to his distant cousin Audrey Cecil Turney (Figure 79) the fourth daughter of Alderman Sir John Turney of Gedling. Their daughters Catherine Turney Bayley (b. 1904) and Barbara Bayley (b. 1907) and their son Thomas Dennis Readett Bayley (b. 1906) were all born at Lenton Abbey. It is not known whether Kate Bayley lived at the house as a separate household, but Dennis Bayley and his family lived there for some 20 years until Kate's death, and there is evidence that he was regarded as the householder. For example, a new lodge 'for H. Dennis Bayley' was built in 1914 at the Derby Road end of the entrance drive, to plans by Wheeler and Waite [47] .

During the forty years from 1874 to 1923 Lenton Abbey house remained little changed except that at some date between 1881 and 1901 (on map evidence) it was somewhat enlarged by building out a two-story bay on the south-east side (Figure 80). Little is known of the use of the farm land in these years, when the estate was probably farmed independently of the house. The agricultural labourer (or bailiff) Ephraim Pendleton of 1861 was replaced in 1871 by a coachman, Thomas Harston (24) with his wife and infant son living in 'Lodge, Bramcote Road' according to the census, while the gardener John Sibson remained at the 'Lodge to Mr. Bayley's'. This was called Lenton Abbey Lodge in 1881, when coachman J.Hayes occupied the 'Farmhouse'. No farm workers lived in the mansion, where the resident staff in 1881 numbered only two - Annie Upton, a cook, and Elizabeth Attenborough a housemaid - serving only Charlotte and Kate Bayley. The Directories lack entries for Lenton Abbey's ancillary buildings before 1915, when Tom Staniland was named as chauffeur to H.D.Bayley, and Richard Wortley as his gardener. In 1916 Tom Staniland was 'agent', Robert Ward chauffeur and Ernest Clark gardener to H.D.Bayley; and in 1922 Edward Dudley was agent and William Kemp gardener [Kelly 1916, 1922]. Captain Dennis Bayley's 'agent' presumably managed his affairs during his absence on war service.

W.F.M.Weston Webb, purchaser of Lenton Abbey in 1923, vendor in 1925

Colonel Sir Dennis Bayley KBE DL was already living at Hunmanby Hall, East Yorkshire by 1920, and Harold Bayley in The Park, though earlier at Langar Hall, his mother's home. Kate Bayley died in 1921 and by a conveyance dated 23 April 1923 the house and land were sold in fee simple to Wilson Fulford Marriott Weston Webb. The vendors were the four surviving sons and daughters of Thomas and Annie Bayley - Thomas Harold Readett Bayley, Sir Henry Dennis Readett Bayley, Muriel Kathrine Huskinson and Hester Theodora Robinson [48] . Sir Dennis owned Burton Joyce Hall, now demolished [Charlton 1978], but it is not known whether he ever lived there.

Figure 80: Lenton Abbey house from the South in about 1908
[From Phillimore 1910] Note the two-storey bay built out on the south-east side of the house, probably in the 1890s. The former entrance drive is now a garden, and access to the house is through the former farm yard.

Weston-Webb, born in 1851 and already 71 years old when he bought Lenton Abbey, was a yarn merchant, who with great enterprise built up wide foreign contacts and developed the substantial Nottingham firm of Holland and Webb Limited, with branches in Chemnitz, New York and many other places, world-wide [49]. His life was one of movement, not only around the world in pursuit of his business interests, but also from house to house, many of which he altered to meet his own taste and needs. He came to Nottingham in 1874, married Emily Maxwell in 1876, worked in partnership with Charles Holland until he died in 1882 (and was buried at Beeston), and then was given a partnership by Samuel Hollins, owner of an old merino-spinning concern at Bolton. Samuel Hollins and Company failed to adapt to changes in demand and was killed by competition, mainly from William Hollins and Company of Pleasley. Holland and Webb became a limited company in 1901, with Weston Webb as chairman. He had bought Gedling Manor, with 900 acres reaching to Burton Joyce, from Lord Carnarvon in 1899, and moved there from Winkfield Park, but left in 1902 on account of the supposed ill effect of the low-lying situation on his wife's health. After buying a house on The Ropewalk, Nottingham in late 1905, he immediately sold it, and moved to Peverel House in The Park, which became vacant on the death of Thomas Bayley the younger. He bought Peverel House in 1908, though the family spent much time at Seacroft, Skegness, where he had a bungalow. But having decided to retire in 1912 he sold Peverel House and bought Toddington Manor, adjoining Woburn Abbey, Bedfordshire.

A serious accident to his son John in 1922 was blamed for the onset of an illness from which Weston-Webb's wife died at Scarborough, and lonely and restless he moved to a hotel at Nottingham to resume his business interests. 'Eventually I rented Lenton Abbey....Once more I decided to buy, and once more my friend Mr. Bromley was called in to put my house in order. All my seven children were away except my little girl. My life was utterly miserable...'. However, in 1923 Weston-Webb married a Miss Hodges who he had met at Mentone. 'We proposed to live at Lenton Abbey, but on the advice of doctors I went to the south of France'. The couple both had many friends there, and they built a spectacular house at La Tour de Baonssit. 'With my usual luck I was able to dispose of Lenton Abbey to the Corporation of Nottingham, and at this present time [1928-29] this property is gradually being built over'. Kelly's 1925 Directory reported Weston-Webb at Lenton Abbey, together with the Hon. Geoffrey Hope Morley and a gardener, James Pogson. Morley may have been a temporary tenant. The Corporation bought the estate on 21 December 1925.

Lenton Abbey housing estate and later owners of the mansion.

Lenton Abbey council housing estate, more of it on the former Beeston Fields farm west and south of the Tottle Brook than on former Lenton Abbey estate land, was very quickly laid out, with provision on the Lenton Abbey side for a recreation ground and church. On 25 March 1926 most of the remaining part of the Lenton Abbey property, not required by the Corporation for council housing, was sold to solicitor Douglas McCraith for £6,500 [50]. For this modest outlay McCraith obtained Lenton Abbey house with two lodges, a cottage and other buildings, and some 13a.1.21 of land - prime building land in a very desirable location. On the western half of this land the Charles Avenue private housing estate was soon developed, leaving a 3-acre field in the east on which the major part of the University Indoor Sports Centre was later built.

Douglas McCraith, M.A., J.P. (b. 1878) son of Sir J.W.McCraith, was educated at Harrow and Trinity College, Cambridge, and became a member of the firm of Maples and McCraith. Later, as Sir Douglas McCraith, he was described as a notary public, and Clerk to the Commissioners of Income Tax [Kelly 1936] [51]. Before acquiring Lenton Abbey he had lived at 19, Cavendish Crescent North, and then at Ashley House, Park Drive, The Park, Nottingham. He was also of Normanton Grange, Normanton-on-the-Wolds (Plumtree) [Kelly 1916 1925, 1928, 1936]. In 1932 or thereabouts McCraith sold the remnants of Lenton Abbey, except for a lodge, to T.D.C.Taft, and Lenton Abbey Lodge separately to Mrs. E.S.Fisher, whose daughter, Mrs. M.E.Watson, sold it to the University of Nottingham on 18 September 1969 for £6,350 [52]. Lenton Abbey was not mentioned in Kelly's 1936 Directory, when McCraith was listed at Plumtree, and conversion of the house and buildings by Mr. Taft may well have begun.

Taft set in train alterations which converted Lenton Abbey house and its various outbuildings, mainly disposed round a former farm or stable yard into flats for renting commercially. When the property came on to the market again in late 1975 or early 1976, some forty years on, it had been altered to provide a spacious house, occupied by Taft himself, together with six flats in the main building and three other dwellings developed from the stabling and opening on to the cobbled courtyard. There was also the Cottage, part of the courtyard complex, which was the original small farmhouse built by James Green for his bailiff. The area of the buildings and grounds was 1.59 acres. The purchaser in 1976 was the University of Nottingham, which acquired Lenton Abbey as an investment property, uninfluenced, it may be hoped, by the historical misrepresentations of the sale brochure [53].

The rapid sale and development of the Lenton Abbey estate was taking place during exactly those years in which the new University College buildings were being constructed and the original campus laid out on the opposite side of the present campus. It is interesting, though fanciful, to speculate as to whether this integral part of the geographical unit now largely occupied by the University would have been purchased, or otherwise earmarked for eventual use by the University envisaged by Sir Jesse Boot, had the scale of the post-war growth of the University been foreseen.

Finally, before leaving Lenton Abbey, the topographic history of which was dominated by the Bayley family whose members occupied it from 1860 to 1923, it may be noted that Bayleys' leather dressing works on Leen-gate, Lenton, which contributed increasingly to employment provision for Spring Close in the second half of the 19th century (see Chapter XIV) eventually closed down in the early 1960s, having been in operation for over 170 years. Unfortunately, as so often happens when old businesses close, it appears that all the company's documentary records were destroyed at the same time. Although most of the old buildings on Leen-gate were demolished the chief buildings of the leather works were spared, and were occupied by the Bell Fruit Company, which remained until the mid-1980s. Since then some of the buildings facing the Queen's Medical Centre across the reconstructed former canal bridge have been converted for residential use.

NOTES

1. N.U.M.D., Wadsworth 52: 'Copy of the parcels in the conveyance from Miss Milward to Messrs. Pares and Paget dated 28 and 29 March 1798'. The list was printed, with a few omissions, in Godfrey [1884] 196-198. A schedule of that part of the Milward estate supposed to form Lenton Abbey Farm, and the content and dates of relevant indentures, are copied in N.U.M.D., Mi 3 E 4: '1684-1867 Abstract of title of Henry Lord Middleton and Hon. Digby W.B.Willoughby to a freehold estate called Lenton Abbey' with notes and opinion by C. Butler. The document contains some errors and uncertainties in identification of land.
2. N.U.M.D., Wadsworth 50 and 52. N.U.M.D., Mi 3 E 4
3. It will be shown in Chapter XI that Francis Evans built Lenton Grove on land that he had owned for some years before the sale of the Milward estate, and the tenurial devolution of this and is traced. It extended from Beeston Lane (alongside the present Florence Boot Hall) north-west to the Eight Acres Close, which Evans bought in 1798.
4. N.U.M.D.,Mi3E4.
5. N.U.M.D., Mi 3 E 4, 28/29 March 1798 : Indentures of lease and release by (1) James Graham of Lincolns Inn (2) Elizabeth Milward, spinster of Marylebone (3) Thomas Pares the younger of Leicester and Thomas Paget of Scraptoft.
6. N.U.M.D., Mi 3 E 4 (Abstract of title) recites: 4 and 5 April 1798, by indentures of lease and release tripartite between (1) Pares and Paget (2) James Green of Wollaton, gent. (3) Francis Evans of Nottingham, gent.. In consideration of £4,780 paid to Pares and Paget by James Green, Pares and Paget grant and sell to James Green and Francis Evans, in their actual possession, the property listed. The Hind and Far Abbey Fields were, of course, missing from the list.
7. N.U.M.D., Mi 1/16/1a (1823) p. 39 : 'The old guidepost used to stand at the corner of the close called the Three Cornered Close between Derby Road and the Beeston branch'.
8. N.U.M.D., Wadsworth 50, 25/26 January 1684 (copy).
9. N.U.M.D., Wadsworth 51 : Copy parcels in the deed of 1731.
10. N.U.M.D., Wadsworth 21 : Copy of the premises at Lenton mentioned in the deed of sale of 5 and 6 August 1743.
11. N.U.M.D., Mi 1/16/1a to d (1823).
12. In 1780 Wilkinson's land tax was said to be £10.16s.8d., while Mr. Hall was to pay £5.7s.8d. for Trent Wong: but in 1782 the sums were interchanged, and Wilkinson's successor, John Clayton, paid £5.7s.8d.. It is surprising that Clayton's 100 acres at the Odd House should be assessed at only half the tax demanded for less than 100 acres of meadow land subject to seasonal flooding. In 1800 the tax on Trent Wong remained unaltered, but James Green paid £8.12s.2d. for a much smaller Lenton Abbey than Clayton's. This discrepancy is unresolved.
13. N.U.M.D., Mi 3 E 4
14. N.A.O., Copy of the plan attached to the Award made in 1809. Copied by E.A.Bush, Surveyor, Beeston. The Award, in typescript is attached.
15. N.A.O., BE 2 S : Plan of Lenton and Beeston estates in the County of Nottingham belonging to James Green. Scale in chains. Undated (c. 1815).
16. N.U.M.D., Mi 3 E 4, p. 37: 12/13 February 1819 : Indenture of lease and release between (1) James Green the younger and Henry G. Green (2) William Batley of Barbican and Susanna his wife, and (3) B.E.Batley.
17. N.U.M.D., Mi 3 E 4
18. N.U.M.D., Mi 1/16/1 (1822-23) .
19. N.A.O., DD 669/1 : Lenton Abbey sale particulars (1830)
20. N.U.M.D., Mi 3 E 4
21. N.U.M.D., Mi R 24 : Lord Middleton's estate rental for 1831
22. N.U.M.D., Mi R 38 : Rental for 1845
23. Drake's Directory for 1860 showed that Thomas Bayley, tanner, was at Lenton Abbey. He had paid the Michaelmas rent, or part of it - £80.10s.0d. for 1859. See N.U.M.D., Mi R 41.
24. Census of 1841, Enumerators' Books: H.O. 107/858

25. Census of 1851, Enumerators' Books: H.O. 107/2129
26. N.U.M.D., Mi 3 G 33: 'Schedule of several estates of which Lord Middleton is now tenant for life'.
27. N.U.M.D., Mi R 1
28. N.U.M.D., Mi R 2
29. N.U.M.D., Mi R 3 and Mi R 4
30. N.U.M.D., Mi R 5
31. N.U.M.D., Mi S 3: A valuation of the estate of Henry, Lord Middleton, by Jonathan Teal, p.31.
32. See N.U.M.D., Mi R 6 (Lady Day 1814) to Mi R 26 (Michaelmas 1833) - rentals recording a rent of £30 a year which then increased to £40 a year until 1839 (N.U.M.D., Mi R 27 to 29). But at Lady Day 1837 the entry against Isaac Bayley, £20 a half year, was - 'Dead' (N.U.M.D., Mi R 30).
33. It is not known whether Michael Shaw was a member of one of the branches of the Shaws of Lenton, but he was probably a younger son of John and Elizabeth Shaw, the parents of John Shaw (1805-1864) who was Thomas Bayley's partner in the leather business.
34. John Shaw (1805-1864) was a son of John and Elizabeth Shaw, grandson of John (1746-1808) and Elizabeth Shaw, great grandson of William and Anne Shaw (married 1743) and great, great grandson of William and Elizabeth Shaw who took over the farm of The Hall, the largest house and largest farm in the Gregory estate in Lenton, earlier occupied by John Garland, father and son.
35. N.U.M.D., Mi R 33 and 34 (1842). The 1844 rental explained the increase in rent - for fellmonger's premises £20 a half year and for new building material £5. (N.U.M.D., Mi R 36)
36. Census of 1861, Enumerators' Books: for Lenton 2447 and 2550.
37. N.U.M.D., Mi 4 E 137 and Mi 3 G 10 : Schedule of sales 1867: Schedule of Middleton estates furnished by Mr. Chouler (Lord Middleton's long-serving Steward). The 1866 tenancies included in Lenton 'Thomas Bayley, House, land and tanyard, 68a.0.39'. In a '7th schedule' the industrial premises were separately described - 'Thomas Bayley, a freehold house and outbuildings: land adjoining used as a tanyard, 1a.1.33.'.
38. N.U.M.D., Mi 3 G 10 : Particulars of estates sold. These included as Lot No. 2, Lenton Abbey - under the will of Henry, 6th Lord, and disentailer of 1867 - £8,508.2s.5d.. Lot No. 5 was the later Lenton Eaves land, £433.6s.9d. under the same disentailer. Lenton tan yard was 'in exchange with the settlement trustees' - £2,018.5s.9d..
39. N.U.M.D., Mi 3 G 12 (a volume) : Statement of sales of settled estates of Henry, Lord Middleton in 1867 and 1868: No. 2 - Lenton estate. The schedule included Lot No. 2, purchased by T. Bayley: purchase money £9,000, deduction £491.17s.7d. - £8,508.2s.5d.. Also Lenton tannery purchased by Thos. Bayley: purchase money £2,100, deduction £81.14s.6d. - £2,018.5s.6d.. In the same schedule were sales to J.H.Lee and B. Walker.
40. N.U.M.D., Mi 4 D 4 : Conveyance from Henry, Lord Middleton et al. to J.Holwell Lee Esq., 21 October 1869, with Thomas Bayley of Lenton Abbey of the second part. In March 1869 Lord Middleton agreed to sell this land to Thomas Bayley as the then occupier for £2,000. This was not paid immediately, and Bayley agreed to sell the land to Lee for £2,100. Lee accepted limitations on building development.
41. The details are substantially repeated in N.U.M.D., Mi 3 G 33.
42. N.U.M.D., Mi P 6 (map) and Mi 2 S 3 (reference book).
43. N.U.M.D., Mi 4 E 137
44. It is not known whether this leather business had any direct connection with the partnership between Thomas Bayley's father and John Shaw. Shaw was still a partner in 1856 [Fyfe 1856] and probably until 1860 or later. He died, aged 69, in October 1864 and was buried in the new Lenton churchyard, where his wife Margaret (d. 1869) was also interred [Lowe 1871 33].
45. Both Thomas and Annie Mary Bradley Bayley are commemorated by a brass tablet in Lenton parish church. There were other connections between Langar and the University campus. William Peverel, founding Lenton Priory, gave it two parts of the tithe and church of Langar. John Wright of Lenton Hall bought the estate and his son Francis 'took down the mansion, divided the park into meadows and felled the timber' [Lowe 1876 80-81]. Phillimore [1910] provides details of the history of Langar Hall, with pictures of it dated 1676, 1792 and 1910.
46. Records of the Borough of Nottingham 244, 2 August 1875 (note).
47. Deeds and documents relating to Lenton Abbey Lodge are held by Messrs. Rotheras, and include an abstract of title to it.
48. The conveyance to W.F.M W Webb is recited in an abstract of title to Lenton Abbey, held by Messrs. Rotheras.
49. Most of the details about Weston-Webb, and the quotations below come from his book *The autobiography of a British yarn merchant* (1929).
50. The Lenton Abbey housing estate built for the Corporation in 1924-29 comprised 880 houses built by F. Perks and Son Limited of Long Eaton. It is shown nearing completion in an aerial photograph of 1929 in Oxley and Richmond [1989 20].
51. McCraith was a member of the City Council 1905-1930, Alderman 1920-1930, and chairman of the Watch Committee. He was chairman of Notts. County Cricket Club in the 1930s. He was appointed Chief Regional Information Officer by the Ministry of Information after the outbreak of war in 1939.

52. The Lodge was inherited by Mrs. Margaret Ellen Watson under the will of her father, Samuel Fisher in 1951. See abstract of title held by Messrs. Rotheras.

53. A copy of the sale brochure is in the University library (Special Collections) as pamphlet Not 4 PD 64 ABB. The statement by the agents, Harlow, Shelton and Co., that Lenton Abbey house was originally 'a nobleman's or Gentleman's Sporting or Country Residence' and was built on the site of Lenton Priory could hardly be more false.

CHAPTER XI

LENTON GROVE AND ITS ESTATE

Introduction

Lenton Grove house was built in about 1800 for Francis Evans and now, with added accommodation, houses the University Music School. The house was described in 1972 [Notts.C.C. 1972] as 'an early/mid 19th century plain stuccoed villa of two storeys, five windows: bracketed eaves to hipped slated roof: simple entrance: irregular, altered rear'. Its simple Georgian style in fact reflects its turn of the century date. The same source draws attention to the gateway on Beeston Lane, given the same date - a pair of modest stone piers with incised gothic decoration and ball filials, and plain wrought iron gates 'of interest only in conjunction with the house'. Lawson Lowe [1871 21] described Lenton Grove's 'sheltered situation with a pleasant southern aspect near the boundary of the parish. The house (as its name indicates) is almost entirely surrounded by a grove of trees in which is an extensive rookery'. Its original name of Lenton Shrubbery suggests that the trees were planted by Francis Evans at the beginning of the 19th century. The plan of the house on the 1881 O.S. 1:500 map (Figure 81) shows what appears to be a conservatory or cloister running the whole length of the south-facing facade, a feature reminiscent of its near neighbour Dagfa House on Salthouse Lane, Beeston. Entries for 1842 in the diary (1838-42) of Miss Elizabeth Nutt Harwood of Beeston (mentioned in Lenton Local History Society's Newsletter of February 1992 - just 150 years later) include mention of 'a visit to Lenton to see Mrs. Markham's new conservatory', which effectively dates this feature to 1841-42. The architect of Lenton Grove is not known.

It was supposed by Godfrey [1884 203] following Lowe [1871 26] that Lenton Grove was one of the original houses built on the former priory demesne on the break-up of the Milward estate in 1798; but this was not the case [1]. Its small park certainly included some land in the north-west - the Eight Acre field (6.98 acres) and part of Broom Meadow (0.34 acres) - that was purchased by Evans in 1798 from Paget and Pares by arrangement with James Green who bought the Lenton Abbey land (see Chapter X above); but this area, upon which Ancaster Hall now stands, was not the site of the house and garden of Francis Evans. The advertisement of 1797 for the sale of the Lenton Abbey farm held earlier by John Clayton [2] described the

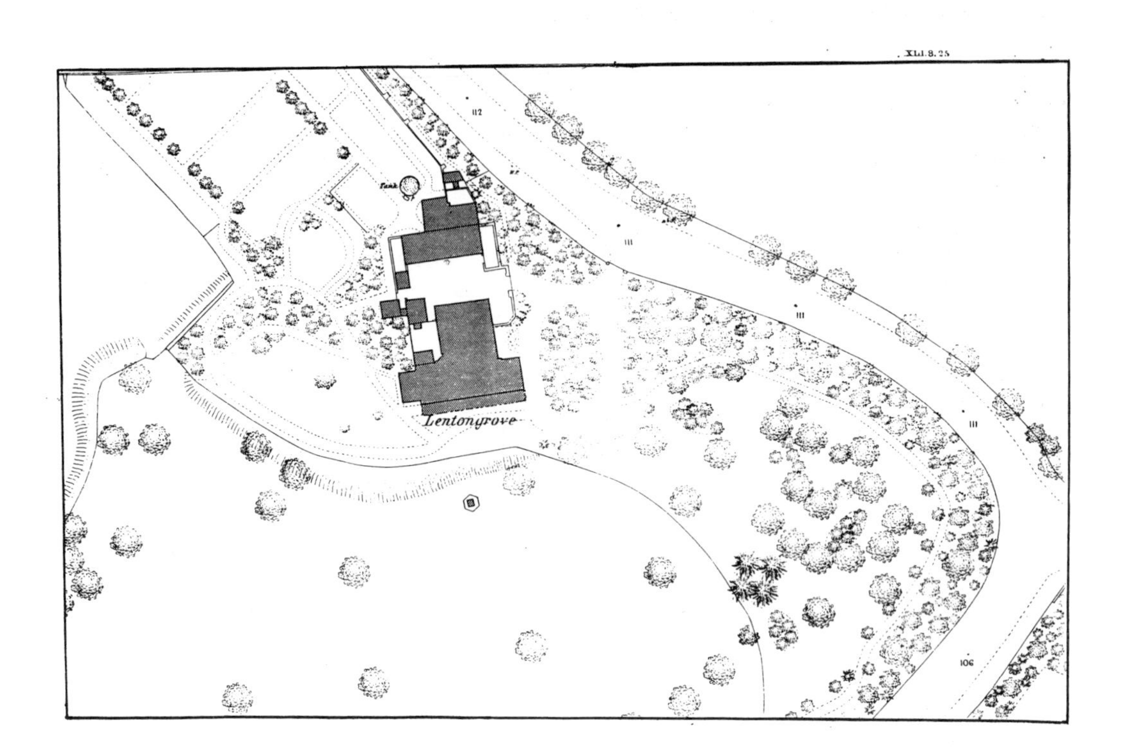

Figure 81: Lenton Grove in 1881
[Reduced from O.S. 1:500 map, Nottingham, Sheet XLI 8.25]

farm as having 'upwards of 100 acres' within a ring fence, and adjoining the turnpike road from Nottingham to Derby and also the Branch out of that road towards Sawley'. Unless the diversion of Beeston Lane a few years later is taken into account this description could mean that the whole of the Lenton Grove land was included within the farm, but close examination of the 1798 schedule of Milward estate lands indicates that this cannot be so. The major part of the Lenton Grove land in Lenton had no tenurial connection with Lenton Abbey farm. It is not known conclusively whether it was originally part of the priory demesne, but for both geographical and historical reasons it almost certainly was, as will be shown below.

Francis Evans and his forbears

Francis Evans was a well-known Nottingham attorney, a partner in the firm of Evans and Middlemore, Attorneys and Masters Extraordinary in Chancery [3], and at one time was 'Steward to John Plumptre Esq.' - whose daughter he married in 1783 [4]. He held the office of Prothonotary of the Court of the Honour of Peverel, and in the 1780s was 'of Nottingham, gent.' [5]. His father, Robert Evans (1709-1779) was also an attorney-at-law, and had chambers at Thurland Hall in Nottingham, where Dr. John Storer, a friend and business associate of Francis Evans (see Chapter IX) lived from 1781. Robert Evans married as his second wife Dorothy (1721-1797), daughter and sole heiress of Rev. Henry Francis, whose wife, also Dorothy, was co-heiress of John Hacker (1667-1735) of Trowell, the last male heir of an old Nottinghamshire family that included the regicide Colonel Francis Hacker [6]. A mural tablet in Trowell church commemorates two Evans children who died in 1760 and 1768, and also 'Robert Evans, died July 10, 1779 aged 70 years', and 'Dorothy Evans, died August 14 1797 aged 76 years'. Stretton recorded these inscriptions and added 'Note: this family went to reside at Lenton, where their son Francis was buried in 1816': but it is unlikely that this refers to Robert Evans and his wife [7]. Francis Evans took the oaths as Under-sheriff in 1777 and 1781; his father Robert did so in 1753.

Tenurial history of the Far Broom Close, 16th to 19th century

The tenurial history of the Lenton Grove land in Lenton down to the end of the 18th century can be clarified by study of earlier rentals or surveys of the former priory demesne and from other sources. In a 'rental' of the former priory estate in about 1554 a Richard More was the tenant of land called the Hill Close, which was unique in that it was 'neither parcel of my Lady Stannop nor Alex' (that is, Alexander Wright) but was 'in lease before recit'. It was meadow, but the rent was not given [8]. Both the tenant and the field name are significant, as will be shown below. The 'surveys' of fields and closes of the former priory demesne in the early 17th century [9] include one of Brome Close, described in several parcels with a total area of over 51 acres, but it is not clear whether this included Broom Pasture or Close where Lenton Grove was built, and which was later distinguished as Far Broom Close. A document dated 3 October 17 Elizabeth recording an inquisition into the boundaries of the manor of Lenton [10] included the following description of a section of the western boundary of the manor. '...From Terry's Close [11] by the exterior hedge of a certain close called the Rounds and then following the Hedge towards [word omitted] called Tuttleberry Gate and from thence by the Hedge of a certain close within the aforesaid manor of Lenton called Broom Close towards [Derby] Gate and thence by the Hedge of a certain field belonging to Francis Willoughby...' Tuttleberry Gate is identified as Beeston Lane here.

In the terrier made when the estate of the priory demesne was sold in 1684 [12] we find 'A piece or parcel of pasture ground, part of a close called The Broom Close, containing by estimation 12 acres', occupied by John Moore (or his assigns) - a forbear, possibly the grandfather, of the John Moore of 1780, who appears in the land tax schedules for both Beeston and Lenton [13]. Moore's Beeston holding was taxed at 14s.10½d. a quarter year in 1780, and remained unchanged to the end of the century, though by 1792 or earlier Mrs. Elizabeth Moore, John's widow was the owner and Henry Attenborough the occupier. John Moore also had land in Lenton for which he was taxed in 1780 at 12s.4d. a quarter (£ 2.9s.4d. a year) and he occupied it himself. From 1783 H.A.Attenborough was recorded as the occupier of this land at the same tax. In 1786 William Hodges and Attenborough appear to have been trustees, and William Hodges was devisee, presumably under John Moore's will, while Attenborough was the occupier.

In 1791 the Hodges-Attenborough land tax assessment for Lenton was reduced to 4s.10d. a quarter (19s.4d. a year), and in the same year Francis Evans appeared for the first time as a landowner in Lenton, taxed at 7s.6d. a quarter (£1.10s.0d. a year) - exactly the amount by which the Hodges-Attenborough tax was reduced. Clearly Francis Evans had purchased part of Elizabeth Moore's estate in Lenton, and there is no doubt that this purchase was of the Lenton Grove land. Not only did Evans continue to pay the same tax on this land after 1798, but the fact that John Hodges owned the Hill Closes (including the site of Florence Boot Hall) at the time of the Beeston inclosure (1809), divided from Lenton Grove only by the Sawley turnpike (Beeston Lane), is circumstantial confirmation of the identification. Further, the land beyond, now University playing fields, was named Moore's Hassock (in Beeston parish). Comparison of areas and taxes suggests that Evans' purchase was of the order of 10 to 12 acres, and this, added to the 7.32 acres of Milward estate land purchased from Pares and Paget in 1798 would represent the whole of his land in Lenton. The 7.3 acres was taxed at £1.8s.3d.

a year in 1798 [14], adjusted to £1.8s.8d. from 1799 onwards.

The century gap between the John Moore of 1684 and the John Moore of 1780 is bridged by the terriers of 1731 [15] and 1743 [16]. In 1731 the deed distinguishing Dame Sarah Winford's jointure lands from Thomas Cookes-Winford's estate recorded no occupiers' names, but Broom pasture was there, with an area of 12 acres. In 1743 Jno. Moore was paying an annual rent of £12.10s.0d. for the Far Broom Close and the Rounds Close [17]. This seems to be proof that the Lenton Grove land was until 1743 at least a part of the estate of the priory demesne, but was subsequently - if not actually in 1743 - alienated by sale in the same way as the Sixty Acres was in 1698. But no documentary proof has been found for the transaction.

Francis Evans' speculations

There is no evidence that Lenton Grove house was built before about 1800, but equally no proof that it was not, and it is of interest to question why a city attorney should wish to buy a few acres of rural farm land at the western extremity of Lenton parish in the spring of 1791. The date is significant. In April 1791 Francis Evans also bought one of the Combs closes in Beeston, lying alongside the west bank of the Tottle Brook in the angle between the Nottingham to Derby turnpike and the southern end of the present Wollaton Vale [18]. Dr. John Storer, Evans' friend and neighbour at Thurland Hall bought another Comb close at the same time [19]. Francis Evans was in fact a speculator, as his expensive and failed venture into large-scale brewing in 1792, also with John Storer, (and with someone else's money) showed (see Chapter IX); and these land purchases were probably purely speculative. They were based on Francis Evans' expectations for the proposed Nottingham Canal.

In his dual role of Clerk to the company building the Cromford Canal, which received Parliamentary approval in 1789, and Secretary to the committee planning the Nottingham Canal, to divert Cromford Canal traffic from the Erewash Canal to the Trent at Nottingham (he was nominated in November 1790) Evans was obviously privy to William Jessop's survey of his preferred route for the Nottingham Canal made in the winter of 1790-91. Jessop's proposed line ran from west of Wollaton village down the Tottle Brook valley (alongside the present Wollaton Vale and Woodside Road) to gain the Trent vale by Florence Boot Hall. Had it been chosen there is little doubt that the Tottle Brook valley, and perhaps University Park, would have been industrialized in the same way as was the Leen valley when the canal was built through it above Lenton. The Lenton Grove estate in Lenton parish was in 1791 potentially a prime industrial site, and it was the only land on the east bank of the Tottle Brook not in either the Milward or the Middleton estate, and thus unavailable for purchase. Similarly the Combs closes were the lowest lands on the west bank of the brook above its discharge on to the Trent vale not in the common open field of Beeston, and thus similarly unavailable. The intervention of Lord Middleton, who insisted that the Nottingham Canal must serve his own coal mines, and threatened to withdraw financial support unless it did, led to Jessop's withdrawal, ostensibly through ill-health, in June 1791. James Green's revised route in the autumn of 1791 (see Chapter XIII) must have been a severe blow to Francis Evans' speculative hopes.

Evans made the best of his ill-fortune, not only by building his mansion at Lenton Grove, but by initiating and promoting vigorously moves to inclose the parish of Beeston, where in 1792 he owned land occupied by John Pearson of Chilwell that paid 8s.8½d. a quarter (£1.14s.8d. a year) in land tax. In addition to his small Combs close he owned two old enclosures, the Glead Wongs, which lay between the end of the present Dovecote Lane and the Nottingham Rugby Club ground. On account of this modest holding Evans benefited very greatly in the inclosure award of 1809 by receiving as allotments, through exchanges, the tract of land alongside Lenton Grove across the Tottle Brook through which Woodside Road now runs from the southern boundary of the Lenton Abbey housing estate as far as the present University Boulevard, and up to Salthouse Lane, as well as an extensive strip of land alongside the Beeston

Canal [20]. It is perhaps not surprising to find Francis Evans in the forefront of pressure for inclosure from the 'proprietors'. It was he who signed the 'Notice to Proprietors' dated as early as 24 December 1796 giving information about the proposed inclosure of Beeston that was published in the Nottingham Journal of 7 January 1797, only months after the Nottingham Canal was completed, and only months before plans to sell the Milward estate were revealed.

Lenton Grove 1815-1904

In October 1807 Francis Evans was described as 'late of Nottingham and now of Lenton Shrubbery, gent.' [21], and even in 1815 when he died he was of 'Lenton Shrubbery' [Sutton 1815 121] although his house was already known by the more mellifluous name of Lenton Grove in 1810 [Laird 1810]. His widow, Dorothy Evans 'gentlewoman' continued to occupy Lenton Grove for a further 25 years, and was named there by Dearden [1834 37] and by Orange [1840]. However, in 1841 only domestic servants were enumerated at the census [22], which suggests that Dorothy Evans died about this time whether the domestic staff were hers or employed by a succeeding tenant. It is possible that Mrs. Markham was already in residence, though absent on the census date, and had already ordered her new conservatory.

Francis Evans left no son, and the property ultimately devolved to his eldest daughter and co-heiress Miss Anne Elizabeth Evans, though at first it was in trust, with the land tax paid by Francis Evans' executors. It is unlikely that Miss Evans lived at Lenton Grove after her mother's death, though she remained the owner until her own death at an unknown date, probably about 1881 [23]. Godfrey [1884 203] described the property as 'vested in [her] representatives' and the only part of the priory demesne 'still in possession of the descendants of the gentlemen who bought the various portions when the manor of the priory demesne was divided in the latter part of the 18th century' - a somewhat misleading statement as was shown above. Lawson Lowe [1871] overlooked Dorothy Evans' continued occupation of Lenton Grove until at least 1840 in writing that Francis Evans died in 1815, and 'Lenton Grove has since then been occupied by tenants, and is now the property of Miss Evans'.

During the 1840s Mrs. Frances Markham lived at Lenton Grove. Lowe [1871] wrote that Lenton Grove 'was for some time the residence of Mrs. Frances Egerton Markham, widow of the Venerable Robert Markham, Archdeacon of York, and grandmother of 'the present Henry Robert Clifton Esq., of Clifton Hall, who changed his surname of Markham for that of Clifton upon succeeding to the estates of that ancient family'. Frances Markham was the sister of the 8th Clifton baronet who died in 1852, and thus aunt to the 9th baronet, the last of the male line of the ancient Clifton family, Sir Robert Juckes-Clifton (1826-1869) [24].

Mrs. Markham's tenancy was long before her brother died, and some 25 years before her grandson inherited the Clifton estates, for at the 1851 census Mrs. Harriet Kingston and her family occupied Lenton Grove [25]. Mrs. Kingston, then aged 63, was a lady of independent means described by the census enumerator as a 'fund holder'. She was presumably widowed, and with her at Lenton Grove were two unmarried daughters, Louisa (27) and Laura (24). Two granddaughters were there, both born at Nottingham - Eleanor E. Orlebar (10) and Mary L. Orlebar (8) - and a grandson, Vere B. Orlebar (4) born at Birmingham. There were five living-in servants - the usual number at Lenton Grove - and they included a French lady's maid, Eliza Sudant (24) born at Calais, and a young governess, 16-year-old Edith Emily Bott, which suggests that the children were permanent residents. At the Lodge, standing opposite to the drive to Lenton House from Beeston Lane, the residents of 1841, Anthony Smithers and his grandson, and Hannah Hudstone, a servant, had been replaced by Thomas Belfield (51) described as a groundkeeper/farm bailiff with his wife Catherine and nephew Thomas Clark (17) a lace maker [26].

Mrs. Kingston's stay at Lenton Grove, like Mrs. Markham's, was fairly brief, for although she was still named there by White's Directory for 1854, Samuel Morley had replaced her by the 1858 edition. Between these dates there was an even briefer tenancy, that of William Morley of the firm J. and S. Morley. According to Lawson Lowe [1871] 'Lenton Grove was occupied by William Morley Esq., since whose death it has been the residence of his son, Samuel Morley Esq.'. John Morley of the same firm occupied Lenton Hall in 1854 and 1858. The Samuel Morley of Lenton Grove is not to be confused with the more famous Samuel Morley, head of the firm I. and R. Morley, who had a home in London, and later served as M.P. for Nottingham. In 1861 [27] Samuel Morley of Lenton Grove, born at Nottingham, was aged 42, unmarried and described as a landowner. His unmarried sisters Ann (40) and Eliza (32), both described as 'Independent', with incomes from property investments, lived with Samuel at Lenton Grove, with five living-in servants and a coachman at the Lodge [28] .

The census of 1871 [29] still recorded Samuel Morley as the householder at Lenton Grove. He was then aged 53 and still unmarried, living with his unmarried sister Ann, his neice Susanna Morley aged 21, and another of his sisters, Sarah (46) with her husband John Wells Leavers (53), a cotton merchant. George and Zillah Savory and three of their children remained at the coachman's lodge on Beeston Lane, and the living-in servants were Maria Brandon (55), Emma Barton (32), Eliza Beet (30), Margaret Ann Stewart (16) and Henry Langsdale.

Samuel Morley appears to have given up the tenancy of Lenton Grove shortly after 1871 [30] and in about 1874 the occupier was Francis George Rawson, a solicitor, Clerk to the Justices of Nottingham in 1865 at the age of 31, and a partner in the firm of Freeth, Rawson and Cartwright (later Freeth, Cartwright and Sketchley) of Low Pavement [31] . In 1881 Francis Rawson, then aged 47, his wife Sarah Ann (48) and their daughters Catherine Emily (17) and Frances A.E. (20) made up the family, and as usual there were five living-in servants, now all female [32] . These five, with their birthplaces, were: Catherine R. Smith (45) of Nottingham, Harriett Farmer (38) of Holt, Worcestershire, Fanny Hawksworth (24) of Markham, Notts., Ellen L. Williams (23) of Huntingdon and Louise Curyon (14) from Norfolk. A coachman, Henry Peberdy (36) and his wife Virtue lived at Lenton Grove Lodge.

It is not known how long after 1884, when they were named by Godfrey, the Rawsons remained at Lenton Grove, which may have been unoccupied for a time in the 1880s. There are some puzzling deeds relating to land on the Beeston side of the Tottle Brook in 1884-87, but Lenton Grove remained in the hands of 'The trustees of the late Miss Evans' until at least 1901[33]. The Directories failed to mention Lenton Grove again until 1897, and even then no tenant was named [Wright 1897]. In 1904 the house was definitely unoccupied [Kelly 1904], but it is shown in Chapter VIII that Richard Spendlove lived there from 1895 or earlier until about 1899.

Sir Louis Pearson at Lenton Grove, 1905-1943 (Figure 82)

The next known resident at Lenton Grove was Louis Frederick Pearson, later Sir Louis Pearson, C.B.E., J.P. (1863-1943), head of the Beeston Foundry Company which he founded jointly with his brother Henry John Pearson of Beeston and Bramcote (1850-1913). Louis moved from The Grove, Devonshire Avenue, Beeston to Lenton Grove in 1904-05, but seems to have purchased the property only in 1926 [34] . He was born at Chilwell House, the son of John Royston Pearson, and was educated privately. He married Gertrude Potter in 1889, and their son Henry Thomas Royston Pearson was born in 1896. Sir Louis' elder brother Henry, who lived on Broadgate, Beeston, was chairman of the foundry firm, called Foster and Pearson in 1897 [Wright 1897] but in 1901 called Beeston Foundry Company, with Louis a director and D.H.Pearson Secretary [Allen 1901 57]. Henry, a keen ornithologist and a specialist on Arctic and northern Russian birds, died while on an expedition at Luxor, Egypt in 1913, and Louis succeeded him as chairman of the firm.

Henry had been the chief benefactor of the Beeston recreation grounds for which Sir Louis, more closely associated with Beeston than with Lenton, presented the bandstand and

Figure 82: Sir Louis Pearson (1863-1943)
He lived at Lenton Grove from 1905 until his death in 1943. [From F.H. Jacob 1951]

the 'children's shed' in 1908. He will be remembered publicly, however, chiefly as a generous benefactor of Nottingham General Hospital [Hogarth c.1949] which owes much to members of the Pearson family, including Lt.Col. N.G.Pearson of Bramcote, Sir Louis' nephew, Chairman of the Nottingham No. 1 Hospital Management Committee from 1948. Sir Louis was president of the General Hospital in 1924-25, and for ten important years, between 1932 and 1942, he was chairman of the General Hospital Monthly Board following the resignation of William Goodacre Player of Lenton Hurst. He was the donor of the Pearson Theatre, an up-to-date operating theatre opened by Lord Moynihan in 1931, and among his many other large gifts was the Pearson Hall, a room for the use of nurses. He raised £12,000 towards Pearson House the nurses' home begun in 1939, £1,000 towards extending The Cedars, and £5,000 towards the Rope Walk wing, and he endowed two beds. He also built a covered way leading from the Board room to the Nurses' Home in memory of his daughter Gladys, who was a V.A.D. nurse during the first world war.

Sir Louis retired from the chairmanship of the hospital in 1942 on account of ill health, in the year before his death on 5 November 1943. He had bequeathed Lenton Grove to Nottingham General Hospital, and by a conveyance of 23 April 1945 an executor, W.N.Parr, conveyed the house and immediate grounds, together with the two Lenton Grove cottages to the Trustees. In the following year Nottingham Corporation bought about 22 acres of land from Pearson's trustees, including over 14 acres in Beeston, extending to Salthouse Lane (which had been allotted to Francis Evans in 1809 by the Beeston Inclosure Commissioners) and through which the southern end of Woodside Road was built. The Corporation also bought further land bordering Lenton Abbey housing estate, on which Ancaster Hall is built [35]. Lenton Grove house was used as a rheumatism clinic for some time, up to 1950 [Kelly 1950], but was then unoccupied even after it was purchased by the University from Sheffield Regional Hospital Board in 1952.

Lenton Grove Cottage on Beeston Lane near the northern end of the estate, originally the ground keeper's dwelling, was occupied by Sir Louis' chauffeur Arthur Reid in 1932 and 1941, and the New Cottage alongside it by his gardener, James William Pacey. William H. Pratt lived at Lenton Grove Cottage in 1950 and 1956, and the New Cottage was occupied by William Brown in 1950, and by G. Palmer, the Vice-Chancellor's chauffeur in 1956.

The purchase of 22.75 acres of Lenton Grove and Lenton Mount land by the University was described in the University's Annual Report (Report of the Council) of 1952. The 1953 Report stated that the Music School would occupy Lenton Grove, although after its unoccupied years 'apart from repairs and the provision of heating necessary to prevent further deterioration nothing has yet been done beyond the consideration of plans'. The Corporation's purchase of land in 1946 was to provide for the completion of Woodside Road, begun with the building of Lenton Abbey housing estate in the 1920s and planned as part of the city's outer ring road. This road having been completed the University was able to acquire the land on either side of it, that between the road and the Tottle Brook as a green buffer overlooked by the women's Halls, and an area of 7.398 acres between Woodside Road and Salthouse Lane (obtained in exchange for a piece of land west of Nightingale Hall assigned to the Corporation) upon which student flats now stand and are being added to [36]. The former Lenton Grove estate now contains residential provision in Halls and flats for about a thousand of the University's students.

In conclusion it may be mentioned that the flooding of Beeston Lane at the University's West Entrance, above the Tottle Brook's already culverted section from Beeston Lane to University Park at the paddling pool, became more frequent and serious during the 1950s in consequence of the accelerated run-off in the upper part of the brook's catchment area through extensive housing development and the associated culverting there. At a financially difficult time the University was compelled to culvert the brook below Willoughby and Ancaster Halls, and complained bitterly about the great expense of the work in its Annual Report for 1958-59.

NOTES

1. N.U.M.D., Wadsworth 52. 'Copy of the parcels in the conveyance from Miss Milward to Messrs. Pares and Paget dated 28 and 29 March 1798'. No item which might refer to the land on which Lenton Grove was built can be identified in this schedule,.
2. 'Nottingham Journal', 9th, 16th and 23rd December 1797.
3. Universal British Directory, 1793
4. Prebendary Charles Wylde's diary (typed transcript in University of Nottingham Library, Special Collections) records that Mr. Plumptre of Mansfield died 5 February 1782, and on 7 April 1783 Mr. F. Evans and Miss Plumptre married.
5. Bailey's Nottingham Directory 1783 287 and 1784 410. A marginal note on an abstract of title of Henry, Lord Middleton in 1867 (N.U.M.D., Mi 3 E 4) states that 'Mr. Evans who was the well known and respectable attorney and banker in Nottingham has been many years dead....and as his death is so well known in the neighbourhood a certificate of his burial will not be considered necessary.... Mr. Evans was buried at Lenton 11 October 1815'.
6. Briscoe 1881 130-138 - Major Lawson Lowe: 'Some account of the Hacker family of West Bridgford'. Lowe's pedigree included Col. Francis Hacker, the Parliamentary officer to whom the warrant for the execution of King Charles I was addressed, and who commanded the troops involved and was himself executed after the Restoration. The pedigree ends with Francis Evans.
7. Robertson (Stretton) 1910. Prebendary Wylde's diary gave the date of the death of 'Mr. Frank Evans' as 5 October 1815, and confirmed the date of the death of 'old Mrs. Evans'.
8. P.R.O., Rentals and Surveys, Portfolio 24, No. 12, 'Lenton Monastery - Rental (Eliz ?)'. Undated, 15 mss.
9. N.U.M.D., Mi 1/38/41 undated.
10. Quoted by J.T.Godfrey (1884 28-31). The original document was from the Office of the King's Remembrancer in the Exchequer, 'Inquisitio tangens divisiones manerii de Lenton per metas et Bundas a manerio de Wilford'. Mich. Eliz. ro. 381 (Mon. Ang. v. 110)
11. The 'Terry's Close' of Godfrey's transcript is almost certainly a misreading of Jervys or Jervis Close, which was located near the Lenton boundary with Beeston by the Horse Doles.
12. N.U.M.D., Wadsworth 50. This document is a copy of a list of the premises sold by Sir William Hicks and his wife to Thomas Winford.
13. Land tax assessments for Lenton and Beeston made annually from 1780 to 1832 inclusive, normally in May or June, are held at the Nottingham Archives Office. Unfortunately they are now committed to microfiche and in the writer's experience are very difficult to use. The relationship between Moore and Hodges is clarified by the Beeston inclosure apportionment.

14. Land tax assessment for Lenton of June 1798, distinguishes the land bought by Francis Evans on or shortly after Old Lady Day 1798 from that bought by him earlier.
15. N.U.M.D., Wadsworth 23a (1731)
16. N.U.M.D., Wadsworth 21 (1743)
17. The Rounds closes on the Trent valley floor lay along the boundary with Beeston between Beeston Hassocks and the Beeston canal. Edward Attenborough, renting a Rounds close for £ 4 a year was the next entry in the schedule.
18. N.U.M.D., Mi 2/53/35 5 April 1791. Robert Singlehurst to John Storer and Francis Evans, both of Nottingham. 3a.2.01, late in the tenure of Robert Lacey. Also Combs Close, 1 acre: lease for 1 year.
19. N.U.M.D., Mi 2/53/36 6 April 1791. Release of a close in Beeston, Mr. Singlehurst to John Storer M.D. and trustee. Comb Close, 1 acre, abutting Far Field on the south side. Consideration £300.
20. Evans was awarded 26a.3.26 'for lands and rights of Common and two ancient inclosures .... called Gleadwonge', transferred by exchange to John Fellows. He received, after exchanges, 30a,3.26 of Tuttle Brook Field, neatly contiguous with virtually the whole of the Lenton Grove land in Lenton, increasing the area of a compact Lenton Grove estate to about 50 acres. The further award of meadow land on both sides of the Beeston Canal suggests that Evans was still interested in possible industrial development along the local canals. A copy of the inclosure award map for Beeston is held in Nottingham Archives Office. The formal reference is 46 Geo. III, c52 (Private) 1806 Award 11 November 1809.
21. N.U.M.D., Mi 2/53/37 October 1807
22. Census of 1841, Enumerators' Books, H.O. 107/858 for Lenton. At the house were Hannah Campey (40), Phoebe Brown (30), Hannah Chilton (27), Hugh Silverwood (24), Mark Learman (25): and at the Lodge Anthony Smithers (60), Anthony Smithers (7) and Hannah Hudstone (40).
23. Among the owners of land in Beeston referred to by Kelly's Directory for 1881 were 'The trustees of the late Miss Evans'.
24. The spendthrift Sir Robert, MP for Nottingham in 1861, 1865 and 1868 (though unseated for bribery in 1865) died of typhoid fever in 1869, and his cousin Henry Markham succeeded to the estates but not to the baronetcy. The estates afterwards passed to the descendants of Marianne, sister of Sir Robert and wife of Sir Hervey Bruce, whose great grandson, Lt.Col. Peter Thomas Clifton, sold Clifton to Nottingham Corporation in 1952 [Train 1969,1973, 13-14].
25. Census of 1851, Enumerators' Books, H.O. 107/2129-2130. 5 April 1851.
26. The living-in servants in April 1851 were: Edith Emily Bott (16) governess, Eliza Sudant (24) lady's maid, Anne Suter (34) cook, Elizabeth Dolman (22) housemaid, and John Cheeseman (34) butler.
27. Census of 1861, Enumerators' Books H.O. RG9/2447 and 2450.
28. The servants in 1861 were: Fanny Allsop (30) housemaid, Elizabeth Fletcher (21) housemaid, Elizabeth Dunmore (20) cook, Suzanna Bradley (13) kitchen girl, John Morley (19) groom. The coachman, George Savory (36) with his wife Zillah and their son and five daughters, all under 12 years old, lived at the Lodge.
29. Census of 1871, Enumerators' Books RG 3499 and 3500
30. Wright 1866 and 1871 gave James Morley as the tenant of Lenton Grove, but in 1865 he lived on Derby Road, New Lenton [White 1865] and Samuel Morley was still the householder at Lenton Grove at the 1871 census.
31. As early as 1858 Wright's Directory referred to George Rawson, Clerk to the Magistrates, of Low Pavement - then only 24 years old. He is not to be confused with George Rawson of The Hall, Bestwood Park. F.G.Rawson was a native of Leicester though his wife and two daughters were born at Nottingham.
32. Census of 1881, Enumerators' Books RG9/3340 and 3341.
33. See the sale map of the Highfield estate, 1901: N.U.M.D., Accession 23.
34. The conveyance, dated 4 May 1926, is with Messrs. Rotheras. Sir Louis Pearson may have leased Lenton Grove before this date.
35. The 22.055 acres of land was conveyed to Nottingham Corporation by Mr. Parr on 22 August 1946 for the sum of £13,014. Codicils to Pearson's will of 1938 had added P.F.Granger (1939) and W.N.Parr (1940) to his executors. The north-western part of the Lenton Grove land had been occupied by 'the late Dr. A.G.Taylor'.
36. University of Nottingham Annual Report 1958-59: Report of the University Council.

CHAPTER XII

THE LATE VICTORIAN AND EARLY EDWARDIAN HOUSES

Introduction - building on the disintegrating Lenton Hall estate.
Lenton Eaves (1875)
Benjamin Walker junior built it and lived there 1875-95
Benjamin Walker senior and Benjamin Walker and Co.
Later residents: John Piggin 1896-1903
Walter Carrington Fowler 1903-11
John Morris 1911-47
Purchase by the University (1948) and subsequent changes of use.
West Hill House (1884) (= The Cedars = Paton House)
Samuel Herrick Sands built it and lived there 1884-1905
Herbert J. Snook and Mrs. Snook 1905-48
Paton Congregational College 1948-68
Purchase by the University (1968) and later use
Redcourt (1884)
John Lambert built it and lived there 1884-c.1890
Thurlow Astley c.1891-94
Charles Robert Hemingway 1895-1903
William Lambert 1903-05
John Thomas Linsley 1905-c.1941
Sir Julian Cahn 1941-42
Purchase by the University 1945-46 and occupation by the Institute of Education
Lenton Hurst (1898-99)
John Player, founder of the tobacco company
William Goodacre Player built the house and lived there 1899-1930
Lenton Hurst house and its site
Lenton Hurst gardens and cottages
Lenton Hurst Farm
Sale of Lenton Hurst and subsequent uses
Lease of the house (1945) and purchase of the estate (1950) by the University
W.G.Player as public benefactor
Lenton Mount and The Orchard (1904-05)
Lenton Mount
William Sydney Hemsley built it and lived there 1905-25
Captain John Eric Greenwood 1926-53
Greenwood and Boots
Lenton Mount gardens
Purchase by the University 1953
The Orchard
Alfred Thomas Richards built it and lived there 1905-13
Mrs. Mary Barnsdale 1913-c.1919
H.B.S.Toone c.1919-1940s
Purchase by the University 1950 and subsequent uses.
Postscript - Lenton Close (1934)
Henry B. Fletcher, builder of the house, and Mrs. Fletcher.
Purchase by the University 1959 to be part of Cripps Hall.

Introduction

The first signs of an imminent break-up of the old order of the six original estates on the campus were apparent almost 20 years before it actually began, in the discussions involving Lord Middleton and his advisers in about 1863 about possible building development on the Lenton Hall estate, and the similar ideas being advanced by William Needham before he sold the Lenton House estate in 1865. The latter came to nothing, but the former was followed by the Middleton sale of 1868-69. Henry Smith Wright, purchaser of the Lenton Hall estate, began its fragmentation in 1878 by selling only part of it to his brother Fred with the Hall, and making plans for the development of the rest, as outlined in Chapter VII. Although it is not clear from available records whether Benjamin Walker purchased the site of Lenton Eaves in the 1868-69 sale or later, he bought further land and built the first of the Victorian houses in 1875.

Between 1875 and 1905 six houses had been added to the six original mansions (Figure 83). Lenton Fields (see Chapter VIII) was anomalous in status and intermediate in date. In 1884 J.T.Godfrey wrote that parts of the park surrounding Lenton Hall had been leased, and were being built upon. He was referring to West Hill House and Redcourt, built beside Derby Road immediately west of the exit of Lenton Hall Drive. West Hill House was later called The Cedars, and subsequently was occupied by Paton Congregational College, and renamed Paton House. It is now occupied by the University's Institute of Planning Studies. Redcourt, later occupied by the newly founded Institute of Education, is now part of Lenton and Wortley Hall.

Lenton Eaves, near the former junction of Beeston Lane with Derby Road opposite to the Beeston Lodge entrance to Wollaton Park, eventually an annexe of Florence Boot, Nightingale and Willoughby Halls in turn, and now the premises of the University Non-Academic Staff Club, was already ten years old when the Directories first recorded West Hill House and Redcourt in 1885. Lenton Hurst was built some 15 years later, completed in 1899, when its owner, W.G.Player had purchased only a small area of land from Frederick Wright of Lenton Hall, and it was mentioned first in Wright's Directory for 1900. The history of these four Victorian houses alongside Derby Road will be outlined in order of their seniority, followed by the two houses immediately south-west of Lenton (now Hugh Stewart) Hall, built in the first decade of the present century - Lenton Mount and The Orchard.

LENTON EAVES (1875)

Lenton Eaves, the earliest of the Victorian houses on the campus, was built for Benjamin Walker junior, of the lace-making firm of Benjamin Walker and Company, earlier known as Elsey and Walker, which had its factory on Commercial Street, Spring Close, and is discussed in Chapter XIV below. The land for Lenton Eaves and its garden was sold by Lord Middleton in 1869 (see Chapter X) probably to J.H.Lee of Lenton Fields, since Benjamin Walker was not mentioned in the deed of conveyance of the two fields in the angle of Derby Road and Beeston Lane, from Henry, Lord Middleton to J. Holwell Lee on 21 October 1869 [1]. However, an undated summary of the proceeds of the sale of Lord Middleton's estates in Lenton and Beeston, in a bundle of papers in the Middleton collection, lists Lenton Eaves as Lot 5, sold to B. Walker for £433.6s.9d. [2]. Although other papers in the bundle appear to date from 1877 Walker had already built Lenton Eaves by 1875 [3] and he was certainly living there by 1876 [Kelly 1876]. In 1875, also, Walker bought 8a.1.16 from Lee for £3,310. It appears that Benjamin Walker may have negotiated the purchase of the site of the house and garden sometime between 1869 and 1875, with Lee, Lord Middleton and Thomas Bayley of Lenton Abbey all involved, before the financial aspects of the sale of the Lenton Abbey estate to Bayley had been completely implemented. The indenture of 1869 imposed building restrictions which determined the type of development to be allowed - as on the Lenton Hall estate - and for this reason it may be said that the survival of the parkland along the Derby Road frontage of the University campus followed from Lord Middleton's care for the quality of environment

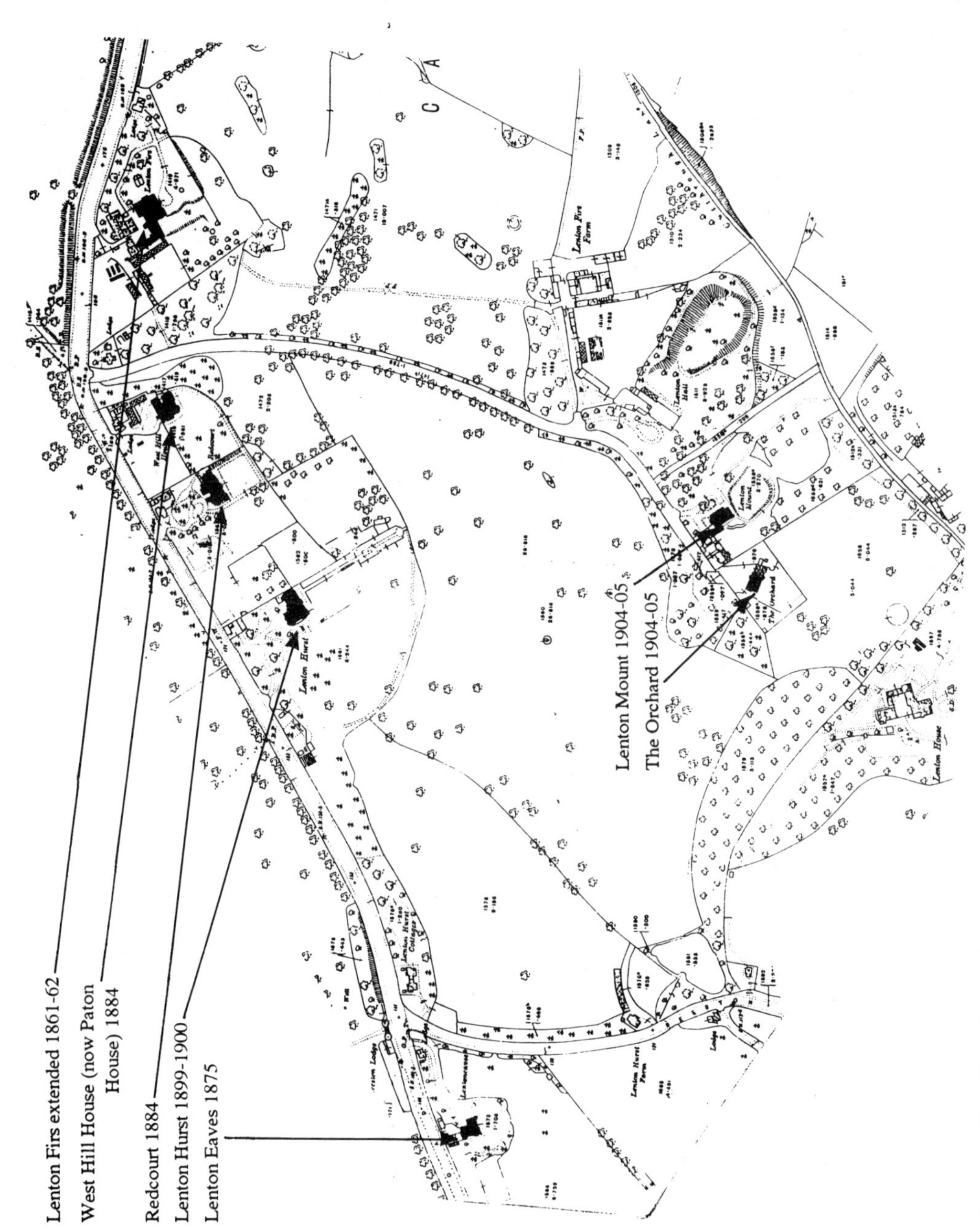

Figure 83: The Late Victorian and Early Edwardian houses
[Base map reduced from O.S. 25 inch map of 1915]

in the vicinity of his own park across the road. The coachman's cottage that now stands adjacent to the path giving access to Derby Road from Beeston Lane was built at the same time as the house.

Benjamin Walker senior and junior, and Benjamin Walker and Co.

Benjamin Walker junior of Lenton Eaves, born 16 March 1843, was 38 years old in 1881, and mention of the name in the Directories before the mid-1860s usually refer to his better-known father. We encounter Benjamin Walker senior in 1842 as a metal dealer on Derby Road [Pigot 1842], and in 1844 as an iron, steel and metal dealer and roller on Sion Hill (Derby Road) [Glover 1844]. Benjamin Walker 'gentleman' lived at Hazard's Yard, Long Row. In 1848 he was still described as a metal dealer on Derby Road, but also as a lace manufacturer at Spring Close [Lascelles and Hagar 1848], and by 1850, with a house on Derby Road, he was simply a lace manufacturer in Lenton, and had apparently given up his metal trading interests [Slater 1850]. In 1862, and probably earlier, he lived at Lenton House, Lenton Terrace, Parkside (or Sion Hill) [Wright 1862], on the north side of Derby Road between the former Sand Field and Canning Circus, which was probably the site of his metal trading premises [Drake 1860]. At Parkside, Lenton Terrace had five houses, one occupied by Benjamin Walker, and William Walker, another leading lace manufacturer, lived in one of the five houses of Wellington Terrace.

In about 1869 [4] Benjamin Walker senior moved to the house called The Priory, Old Lenton, built by William Stretton for himself early in the century (see Appendix 21), succeeding there John Bayley (elder brother of Thomas Bayley the elder of Lenton Abbey) who emigrated to New Zealand. It was this Benjamin Walker who was closely associated with his contemporary Thomas Bayley the elder in the educational and social work in Lenton described in Chapter X. He is said to have died in 1883, after 20 years' connection with Lenton Cooperative Society, established by Walker and Bayley in 1863. Their collaboration evidently owed more to the neighbouring sites of their factories at Spring Close and Leen-gate respectively than to the proximity to Lenton Abbey of Lenton Eaves, built a decade later by Walker's son.

The family of Benjamin Walker junior of Lenton Eaves in 1881 [5] comprised his wife Clara Louise (37), born in America, two sons, Ben Marvell Walker (8) and William Stanley Walker (5), and a daughter, Louisa D. Walker, aged one year. Ben Marvell appears to have been born in 1873, but it is not known where his parents were then living [6]. The household at Lenton Eaves also included a governess, Ada A. Britten (23), Emily Amanda Wynn (31) a nurse, Sarah Collishe (26) a cook, and Angela Beighton (20), a housemaid. A coachman, Mark Willshaw, and his wife Hannah (34) occupied Lenton Eaves Lodge, adjacent to the road junction.

Benjamin's younger brother, William Heape Walker, also a member of the Spring Close lace business, was living with his parents at The Priory in 1879 [Wright 1879], but by 1881 was renting Lenton Fields, where his mother, Emma, was also enumerated at the census, only a stone's throw from her eldest son at Lenton Eaves. This suggests that Benjamin Walker senior had died before mid-1881. William was aged 30 and unmarried in 1881, and he rented Lenton Fields from W.H.Lee until at least 1894 according to various Directories. Benjamin Walker was still at Lenton Eaves in that year [White 1894, Wright 1895], but although he was still named in 1901 as a director of Benjamin Walker and Co., and was replaced in that position by F.J.Bradley only in 1903 [Allen 1901 1903] by 1896 he was succeeded at Lenton Eaves by John Piggin [Wright 1895]. Presumably William left Lenton Fields at about the same time.

John Piggin soon gave way to Walter Carrington Fowler, variously described as managing director, colliery proprietor and mining and civil engineer, who occupied Lenton Eaves from 1903 until 1911 [Wright 1902 et seq.]. The next occupier of the house, John Morris, a laundry proprietor, lived there for 30 years, and was still recorded in Kelly's Directory for

1941. A succession of gardeners occupied Lenton Eaves Lodge, including Walter Jamson from 1912 to 1920, and Richard Emmons and Lee Jones in the 1920s.

The University owned Lenton Eaves, together with Lenton Fields and its land by 1948, when it received its charter, and in 1950 Lenton Eaves was attached to Florence Boot Hall as an annexe with accommodation for 20 students. Although not included in the University Calendar until 1951-52 it was described as a Hall of Residence by Kelly's Directory in 1950, by which time it had been rejected as a home for Paton Congregational College, which bought The Cedars (Paton House) instead (see below). William H. Scott then occupied the lodge. In 1959, when Florence Boot Hall acquired The Oaks, The Pines and Broadwood in nearby Beeston as annexes, Lenton Eaves was transferred to Nightingale Hall. Within a few years it was transferred again, this time to Willoughby Hall, which opened in 1964. One reason for these changes was that Lenton Eaves, as an annexe, was never liked by students, who thought it to be dull, with its high Victorian ceilings, and unacceptably noisy from Derby Road traffic, as well as offering inadequate privacy through multiple room-sharing; so in the 1970s it became a clubhouse for the University's non-academic staff. An excellent bowling green was laid alongside it to replace that lost when the Hallward Library was built. The club's original clubhouse was brought from the Science precinct and reassembled alongside the house to add to its facilities. In 1984 a sympathetic addition was made to the front of the house, and this now masks the lower part of the original facade, and in the opinion of many positively enhances the aesthetic quality of what was a rather ordinary, large, mid-Victorian red-brick villa.

WEST HILL HOUSE (= THE CEDARS = PATON HOUSE) (1884)

After Lenton Eaves a decade passed before the next building development - West Hill House and Redcourt. Both were built on long building leases granted by Henry Smith Wright. West Hill House was built in 1884 for Samuel Herrick Sands, J.P., described as a 'machine holder' [White 1885-86] the term commonly used to describe lace and hosiery manufacturers in the early days of factory development, when several firms might share buildings and their power installations. Sands lived in the house for 20 years, until 1905, with Harold Sands, 'engineer and millwright', presumed to have been his son. Samuel was living at Eastbourne in 1908, though still listed among the Nottinghamshire justices [Deacon 1908 381], and Harold, described as F.S.A., was in 1917 living at Charing near Ashford, Kent.

In business Alderman Samuel Sands was a director of the National Telephone Company and of the Nottingham Patent Brick Company, chairman of Nottingham Joint Stock Bank on Victoria Street (one of the other four directors being W.B.Thorpe of Lenton House), and chairman of Nottingham Suburban Railway Company [7]. The Suburban Railway was a 3½ mile double track line from Trent Lane junction (near the Great Northern Railway station in Nottingham) to Daybrook, completed in 1889 [Anderson 1973 116-118]. The company was independent until absorbed by the L.N.E.R. in 1923. It had three stations, and served 40,000 people and two large brickyards, but difficult terrain and a level change of 200 feet made it expensive to both build and operate. Although it was virtually killed by the introduction of the cheaper electric trams running direct to the city centre in 1901, and its intermediate stations were closed in 1916, it did not close completely until 1951.

It is not known whether Samuel Sands was a descendant of James Sands, 'grocer' in 1793 [8]. He was active in public affairs as well as in business. Mayor of Nottingham in 1891, he was also honorary secretary of the Subscription Library at Bromley House, founded under the leadership of Dr. John Storer, and one of its 21 trustees.

When West Hill House was taken over by Herbert D.Snook, J.P., in 1905 its name was changed to The Cedars [Wright 1905], which was probably not unrelated to the fact that the family home of the Snooks in Sherwood (to which James Snook moved from Hawthorn Cottage in the 1870s) was also called The Cedars. H.D.Snook was a director of the family firm,

J.Snook and Company, wholesale clothiers and warehousemen of Hounds-gate, which in 1902 had four directors, James Snook, and F.W., J.B., and H.D. Snook. A photograph of the Snooks Building on Hounds-gate can be found in a recent book on conservation in Nottingham [9]. A city magistrate like his predecessor at the house, Herbert Snook remained at The Cedars for some 40 years. The names of some of his early chauffeurs, who occupied the lodge by the entrance gate from Derby Road are known - Beecroft Brown in 1906, Arthur Stennet in 1912, J. Sutton in 1913 and Sidney H.Taylor in 1915.

Paton Congregational College 1948-68

The later history of West Hill House is of interest in providing an example of the piecemeal acquisition of the campus by the University, but more especially through the circumstances by which it came to be called Paton House, its present name. These include the 20-year academic relationship between the University and the Paton Congregational College to which Mrs. Snook sold the leasehold house and garden in 1948, and a much earlier connection. Paton College was named for the Rev. John Brown Paton, M.A., Hon. D.D. (Glasgow), (1836-1911), the founding principal of the Congregational Institute established at Nottingham in 1866. The Institute or College on Forest Road, Nottingham, opened in 1868 in 'a handsome brick building in the Gothic style', was a college for training young men for the Independent or Congregational ministry [10]. J.B.Paton lived for 43 years in the house forming the west wing of the Institute. An account of his career was given by Robert Mellors [1924] and a definitive biography was written by his son John Lewis Paton, High Master of Manchester Grammar School. Mellors suggested that Paton was appointed because of his 'boundless energy, joined with spiritual power, a love of knowledge, his delight in imparting it, and the experience gained in training lay preachers at Sheffield'. Paton was not, of course, personally associated with The Cedars, but his memory should be honoured in the University as one of its real founders. F.S.Williams wrote a century ago 'The Rev. J.B.Paton ... with James Stuart of Trinity College, Cambridge, devised the University Extension Lectures out of which the University College eventually grew [Williams c.1883 38]; and Dr. E.M.Becket [1928 23] of the Department of Education, who wrote a history of University College, remarked that 'a warm comradeship' grew up between Paton and Richard Enfield, counterparts in character, and they were joint movers in promoting the Cambridge Extension Lecture programmes.

This early connection was revived and extended when Paton College moved to The Cedars [Turner and Wallace 1968] [11]. In 1946 the College decided to sell (for £20,000) its Tollerton Hall and estate which had been requisitioned during the war, and search for a new home. Principal Wortley of University College suggested that it might establish itself in a temporary building on the campus in order to allow its desired association with University College to develop. Later Lenton Eaves was suggested, since the University College decided to buy its land but did not require the house; but Lenton Eaves was thought to be 'inadequate though not impossible'. A large house with grounds in Mapperley Park was considered, together with other properties. Eventually, in April 1948, before it was earmarked for University use by the city's development plan The Cedars came on to the market. Part of the five acres of grounds was freehold, but the house and other buildings were held in leasehold dating from the transaction of the 1880s though with a possibility of purchase.

Although the house was deemed suitable, and the gardener's lodge, garage and storage space desirable, it was known that the University College (whose charter was imminent) wanted to acquire it to add to Redcourt. It was therefore thought politic for Paton College to withdraw its approach to the vendor, though prepared to offer £8,000 for the leasehold and £4,000 for the freehold land behind, with a ceiling of £14,000. The Acting Principal of University College, Professor Robert Peers, and the Registrar, Mr. Hedley Pickbourne, had indicated informally that the University College was determined to buy The Cedars 'whatever the price' because it constituted an integral part of the general scheme for the campus when University status was achieved. Paton College, it was thought, might be allowed to rent it for a limited period in view of the contribution it might make to an infant Department of Theology. However, by July 1948 the University College had to withdraw from negotiations because the Treasury would not advance the necessary funds, and with a district valuer's price of £8,500 it wished Paton College to revive its negotiations. Planning approval was obtained, and the purchase made by Paton College. Under pressure from the vendors Mrs. Snook's gardener, Mr. Richardson, was allowed to stay on until he retired in May 1956.

For Paton College the eventual outcome was not entirely satisfactory, for the Nottingham City Development Plan included the whole of The Cedars property in the area designated for the University campus. The College opposed this in 1954, though still cooperating with the University - for example, in improving the entrance (later closed) to Lenton Hall Drive later in the same year. Eventually, in 1968 Paton College moved to Manchester to merge with the Congregational 'Northern College' there, the removal being completed by mid-September so that the Department of Architecture and Civic Planning could move in before the end of November. The 105th annual report of Paton College in 1968 expressed pleasure at the promise by the University to retain the name Paton House for the building to commemorate not only 20 years of valued association, but also the role of J.B.Paton as a moving spirit, with Richard Enfield and Canon Morse, in arranging the Cambridge University Extension Lectures from which the University College directly sprang. 'What was for the University an unfortunate financial stringency in 1948 was our gain'. Although the sale of the buildings and grounds was put in the hands of John E. Mitchell and Sons, the town plan, restricting the use of the property to 'educational institutions other than schools' ensured that the only purchaser in the market was the University, which paid an agreed price of £34,000 with the concurrence of the District Valuer. Mrs. Sullivan, living at the lodge with her husband, moved to work at the University Club at Lenton Mount.

It must be hoped that the unit building that obscures the south facade of the house, and which is visually offensive particularly because of its siting, can be removed soon, when Paton House, like its neighbour and contemporary, Redcourt, should merit a place among 'Buildings of Special Interest' [12] .

REDCOURT (1884)

Redcourt, lying immediately west of West Hill (Paton) House, was built at the same time, in 1884, and also on land leased by Henry Smith Wright after he had left Lenton Hall. This handsome house has been described as early mid-19th century [13] which is grossly inaccurate, as are most dates suggested by this source. It has two main storeys; seven windows plus five to return; and is said to be of simple Gothic design, with 'arched porch, turrets and battlements to a slated mansard roof'. There are sash windows, a central gabled feature to the garden, and 'large extensions to the east' of unknown date but of identical style. Indeed it is questionable whether the 'extension' is to be regarded as later than the main body of the house.

The house was built for John Lambert, partner with his brother William in the firm of W., J. and T. Lambert, bleachers, dyers and lace dressers, whose factory on Talbot Street, Nottingham was discussed in Chapter XI in connection with William Lambert's tenancy of Lenton Firs. Partners in business, and in building the Theatre Royal in 1865, the brothers were neighbours on Clarendon Street in the 1870s, with John occupying Ellesmere House and William at Clarendon House, and they were the two councillors representing Byron Ward. But in 1879 William Lambert moved to Mapperley Hall and in 1884-85 John moved to the new Redcourt.

Like West Hill House, Redcourt, with John Lambert in residence, was first mentioned in Wright's Directory for 1885. John did not, in fact, long survive there, for although he was present in 1889 when William moved from Mapperley Hall to Lenton Firs, he was not mentioned in 1891 by Wright, and is not found in any later Directory. It is assumed that he had died. He was succeeded at Redcourt by Thurlow Astley [White 1894], whose tenure was also brief, since by 1895 at the latest he had been succeeded in turn by Charles Robert Hemingway [Wright 1895]. Hemingway was a member of the firm of Logan and Hemingway, railway contractors. He remained at Redcourt until 1903, when it appears that William Lambert moved into it from Lenton Firs (after the latter was sold to Sir Thomas Shipstone) and died there in 1905 [Kelly 1904,1905]. Redcourt was presumably still owned by one or more members of the Lambert family, if not by William himself. Shipstone was in residence at Lenton Firs in 1905, but apparently still at Edwalton Manor in 1904 [Kelly 1904].

Astley and Hemingway were tenants at Redcourt, but John Thomas Linsley purchased the property, probably in 1903, and remained there for 36 years. According to Jack Hill, the son of one of Linsley's chauffeurs, he was a Hull brewer who preferred to live near Nottingham. A memorial tablet on the south wall of Lenton parish church reads: 'In affectionate remembrance of Alice Stickley Linsley, the dearly beloved wife of John Thomas Linsley of Redcourt, Lenton, Notts., who departed this life March 25th 1920, aged 56 years'. The altar service books were also inscribed in memory of Mrs. Linsley, 'for 14 years a constant worshipper in this church'. Redcourt, like West Hill House, had its chauffeur's lodge (originally coachman's lodge) alongside the entrance gate from Derby Road, and the service rooms of the house were also on this north side, with the main rooms looking south and south-west over the gardens to Lenton Hall park. For many years Walter Herbert was the Linsleys' chauffeur, and certainly occupied the lodge in 1908 and in 1920.

It is understood that Sir Julien Cahn occupied Redcourt for a time during the second world war, but his occupancy must have been very brief, since J.T.Linsley was still named there in 1941 [Kelly 1941] and Sir Julien died in 1943. The chief residence of the Cahn family was Stanford Hall near Loughborough, which was bought by Sir Julien from the Radcliffe family in 1928 and sold in 1944, after his death, to the Cooperative Union, with the family moving to Bournemouth. But Cahn's business interests in a retail furnishing company centred on Nottingham, and he was well known nationally for his fine cricket ground at West Bridgford (now public land) where he arranged matches between 'Sir Julien Cahn's XI' and touring Test teams (he was president of Notts. County Cricket Club in 1938). Evidently Redcourt was intended to be his town house in the difficult war years. His generous donations to local charities, and his gift to the City of Nottingham of Newstead Abbey and its grounds (bought from C.I.Fraser, grandson of W.F.Webb in 1931) were recognized by a knighthood in 1929 and a baronetcy in 1934.

Redcourt was conveyed to University College Nottingham by Lady Phyllis Cahn in January 1946. It is now part of Lenton and Wortley Hall, and contains the Warden's residence and some other accommodation. It was bought with three acres of land, and was adapted for use by the newly formed Institute of Education, directed by Professor Michael Lewis, a former lecturer in the Department of Education who became Vice-Principal of Goldsmiths College London during the College's wartime stay at Nottingham, and returned to live at Redcourt with his wife, Hilda Lewis, the novelist. The Institute removed to the present Education building when that was vacated by the Departments of the Faculty of Law and Social Science, and the new Lenton Hall was rising alongside Redcourt.

LENTON HURST (1898-99)

Lenton Hurst was built in 1898-99 for William Goodacre Player (1866-1959), a director of John Player and Company, the tobacco manufacturers (Figure 84). Plans having been submitted to the City Council for the erection of Lenton Hurst, P.F.Heathcote (1985) gave the date of building as 1896-97, which was when Arthur Marshall the architect designed altera-

Figure 84: William Goodacre Player (1866-1959) of Lenton Hurst
[The later portrait from Jacob 1951]

tions and additions to John Dane Player's residence at 'Fernleigh', Woodborough Road, Alexandra Park (now the Nottingham Hospice); but the indenture for purchase of the site of Lenton Hurst is dated 1898 [Rotheras] and W.G.Player was first recorded in residence at Lenton Hurst in 1900 [Kelly 1900]. He was the younger of the two sons of John Player, the founder of the firm, who were together mainly responsible for the development of the business after the untimely death of their father at the early age of 45.

J.D.Chambers [1951] named John Player, with Jesse Boot and Frank Bowden, the founder of Raleigh Industries, as the three newcomers whose success, through a similar combination of industry and imagination, staved off depression in Nottingham due to the competition of the United States and Germany in the city's staple industries towards the end of the 19th and in the early 20th century. He was born at Saffron Walden on 11 July 1839, the third son of John D. Player, a local solicitor and a principal founder and minister of the sect of Particular Baptists in the town, who died in 1850, leaving his family in straightened circumstances. The Player family is believed to have been at Deptford in the early 17th century, but a century later Stephen Player moved to the Saffron Walden area. His son, also Stephen, married three times, and his third wife, Elizabeth Dane Cambridge, was the mother of Joseph Player (1764-1837) who had three sons and five daughters. The youngest son, John Dane Player (1800-1850) had six children, and his third son was the John Player who moved to Nottingham in 1859, looking for work, which he obtained first with a draper. By 1861, aged 22, he was in business on Beastmarket Hill in the centre of Nottingham, adjacent to the then cattle market, as agent for Prentice and Company's agricultural manures and seeds, but selling loose tobacco as a sideline. In 1863 he married the widow of Thomas Whiteley of Stapleford, nee Anne Goodacre, who had one son, Arthur, and they lived over the shop at No. 5

Beastmarket Hill. The sons of John and Anne Player, John Dane and William Goodacre were born on 24 November 1864 and 23 January 1866 respectively.

In 1868 John Player entered the tobacco trade seriously, and was soon selling packed tobacco under his own name. By 1874 he had opened a second shop, in Market Street, and then moved his family from Beastmarket Hill to No. 7, Belgrave Square, off Goldsmith Street. In 1877 he bought 45 Broad Street from his original competitors, William Wright and Sons, whose business was founded 54 years earlier, and whose Broad Street factory, employing 150, produced enough tobacco to supply the Nottingham district. By the following year he had moved his home to a modern house called Walden House at the top of All Saints Street. He reorganized the packing department at Broad Street to draw attention to his own brands, and introduced the Nottingham Castle trademark. Having moved house once more, to 6 Park Valley, The Park in 1881, he had bought a large site in Radford off Alfreton Road, and had three factory blocks built, designed by Charles Sutton , two of which he let to lace manufacturers, which may suggest that he lacked confidence in the lasting appeal of cigarettes [14] . After building the Castle factory north of Outgang Lane (Hartley Road) in 1883-84, and transferring there the Broadmarsh employees, John Player died, on 9 December 1884, at the age of 45, when William Goodacre and John Dane Player were aged 18 and 19 respectively. His career had followed a course similar to that of Jesse Boot, except that Player moved earlier into manufacturing, while Boot built up a very large retail business before entering upon manufacturing himself.

John Player's executors, who included his widow, carried on the Company until the young Player brothers took control in 1893, both still in their twenties. Even by 1887 they were marketing their 'Navy Cut' cigarettes. They took over a business poised for further expansion, and they succeeded brilliantly. They became a limited company in 1895, and by 1900 had taken over the two lace factories at Radford, and employed about 1,000 workers.

In 1901 the American Tobacco Company, headed by J.B.Duke, was ready, with a new mass production cigarette machine, to invade the British market, having acquired Ogdens of Liverpool; so thirteen leading tobacco manufacturers, including John Player and Sons, combined to meet this challenge by forming the Imperial Tobacco Company, of which the Player brothers became directors. By the outbreak of war in 1914 the workforce at Radford was 2,500, and by 1926, when the Player brothers retired, it had doubled to about 5,000. Lenton Hurst was built by W.G.Player at the peak of his fortune and powers, and he moved with his wife Mabel from Forest Road at about the turn of the century. Although he lived for a further 60 years, 30 of them at Lenton Hurst, and died in 1959 aged 93, he retired from business in 1926, before the building of the largest Nottingham factories.

Other factories were built between 1895 and the retirement of the Player brothers, including one at Dublin, but the 6-storeyed Players No. 2 on Radford Boulevard, with a floor area of 220,000 square feet, and producing only cigarettes, was not built until 1931-32, designed by Imperial Tobacco's own architects and built by William Woodsend. This building, demolished in 1986, was regarded by Pevsner as Players' most stylish, as well as most expensive factory. Players No. 3 was built behind it in 1938-39, and the year after came the bonded warehouse on Ilkeston Road. After the second world war production and employment continued to grow, reaching a maximum of 11,000 in the late 1950s, when Players were producing 13 brands of pipe tobacco and 11 of cigarettes. The Head Office opposite to the Radford factories, completed in 1967, was designed by McMorran and Whitby, who were responsible for several buildings on the University campus - Cripps Hall, Lenton Hall and the Education building (see Chapter XVI). Two years later, on a 45 acre site on Lenton Industrial Estate, the £14 million Horizon factory designed by Arup Associates, the most advanced in the world was begun, and it opened in November 1972. This was followed by the closure of No. 1 Factory in 1974 and No. 2 in 1976, and by 1983 the whole Radford complex was surplus to requirements. Part of No. 1 became a car park, and Nos. 2 and 3 were demolished in 1986, when Players became part of the Hanson Trust which acquired Imperial Tobacco. By this time there were only 2,700 workers, and by 1990 only 1,990. The site of Nos. 2 and 3 is now the 'Castle Retail Park', with Texas Homecare and Aldi supermarket, and the head office building has been acquired by the Nat-West Bank, so the Radford connection has gone completely, and only the Horizon Factory is left.

Lenton Hurst house and its site

The imposing Lenton Hurst house was designed by architect Arthur Marshall, and built by Thomas Fish and Son. The solidly, indeed lavishly built red brick and slated mansion originally comprised four morning, dining and drawing rooms, a large billiards room, and 9 bedrooms, together with stabling and a coachhouse alongside Derby Road. The architect's abilities were proved by his earlier work, including a large house on the Park estate, which incorporated 'a number of characteristic Marshall-type features such as fancy gables and ornamentation' [Heathcote 1985] [15] , and was built for Marshall's friend Samuel Bourne. He is best known, however, for such buildings as the Russell Chambers (King Street/Long Row) completed in 1896, Bagthorpe Infirmary and workhouse (now the City Hospital), an assignment for which Watson Fothergill and others competed and which took six years to build and was opened in 1903; and Hawtonville Hospital, Newark (1905) and several workhouses.

The site of Lenton Hurst is of historical interest, the house being situated immediately east of the junction with Derby Road of the old Sawley turnpike (Beeston Lane) before its diversion in about 1805, and Lenton Hurst garages probably occupy what was the garden of the turnpike tollhouse before the turnpike gate was abolished and the keeper's cottage removed in 1870. The former gateway to Lenton Hurst, still represented by a recessing of the fence to Derby Road, with some of its surviving stonework, was almost exactly the point of junction of the two turnpikes. On a map of Derby Road in 1823 [16] (see Chapter XIII) a similar indentation is seen immediately west of the tollgate, and an 'old guide post' stood there until the early years of the 19th century, on the south side of the road junction. From this point a depression can be seen crossing the lower part of Lenton Hurst lawn towards Derby Hall, marking the line of the old Sawley turnpike before 1805. On the Wollaton side of Derby Road opposite to Lenton Hurst a stone marked on the map of 1823 stood where the parish boundary between Wollaton and Lenton met Derby Road on that side, and identification of this boundary point on the modern map confirms the exact location of the tollgate and the old road junction on the south side of Derby Road. A drive or track which in the early 19th century ran from Lenton Hall towards the tollgate cannot now be traced at the Derby Road end, but the retention of a corridor to Derby Road by the rump of the Lenton Hall estate at the sale of 1878 may be significant [17] . It was the land on which Lenton Hurst was built.

Player's land on the campus was purchased in three stages, by separate transactions. The land on which the house was built, together with the formal garden behind it, and an adjoining similar rectangular plot on the north-east side, which together formed the corridor purchased by Frederick Wright from his brother, was bought by Player in 1898. In 1903 there were two further conveyances, the first, dated 18 February 1903, being of 27a.3.23 from Henry Smith Wright, then of Averley Tower, Farnham, Surrey, for £9,065.9s.4d. [Rotheras]. This was the land on the west side of the Lenton Hall estate that had been retained by H.S.Wright when he sold the hall and the remainder of the central part of the park to Frederick Wright in 1878. On 15 July 1903 W.G.Player bought additional land, this time from Frederick Wright (with Albert Ball). This was the remaining upper part of the 'downland' west of Lenton Hall Drive and Cut Through Lane apart from the area upon which Lenton Mount and The Orchard were about to be built. The greater part of the purchases of 1903 became Lenton Hurst Farm, although some land was added to the gardens of Lenton Hurst house.

Lenton Hurst gardens and cottages

The gardens of Lenton Hurst, augmented by land purchased in 1903 extended south-westwards to the present main entrance to Derby Hall, and south-eastwards across the present Beeston Lane into the site of Lincoln Hall and its car park. There was a kitchen garden on the north-east side of the house. The pleasure garden was planned with care, and is said to have been created in about 1905 by Gertrude Jekyll (1843-1932), the essence of whose style lay in a 'sophisticated, though apparently artless re-use of cottage garden motifs', arranging species in carefully graded associations of colour, shape and texture. In this case there was a combination of formality in the rose garden with informality in the rock gardens and in the lawn running down to the old turnpike. It is questionable, however, whether Miss Jekyll was responsible for one of the most individual design features of the gardens - the attractive layout of alleys through shrubberies converging on a lawn which formed a charming open-air theatre for the Wortley Hall play in later times [18]. This feature was largely destroyed in the construction of the University road (Beeston Lane) where it passes Lincoln Hall, and only short remnants of a few alleys remain. The feature was not shown on the O.S. 6-inch map of 1913, which shows, however, a layout quite different from that of the O.S. 6-inch Second Edition map of 1901.

Lenton Hurst cottages were built in about 1906, the more easterly one being occupied in 1907 and 1920 and 1928 by W.G.Player's long-serving chauffeur William Marriot, and the westerly one by his gardener, Joseph Slack in 1907 and Frederick Roberts in 1920 and 1928. The cottages were therefore not shown on the O.S. map of 1901, when Player had not yet bought the land on which they stand.

Lenton Hurst Farm

W.G.Player built Lenton Hurst farmstead soon after 1903 on a site between the present Rutland Hall and Beeston Lane, very near to the road, which has now been moved slightly westwards to accommodate Sherwood Hall. The farm buildings extended eastwards from the cottage as a south-facing crescent overlooking the pool (see Chapter I) which has been filled in to form Rutland Hall car park. The pond may have served for watering stock over a long period in view of the absence of any natural source of surface water in the vicinity. Although the former farmstead formed a building group of considerable merit and interest it was demolished in 1963 (Figure 126) to make way for what is now mainly a plot of grassland in front of Rutland Hall. Thomas Skerritt was the farm bailiff for W.G.Player at Lenton Hurst Farm in 1907, and he remained there until at least 1928, and probably until 1930 when the farm was sold to Sir Thomas Shipstone.

Player, and his farm bailiff, gardener and chauffeur were all mentioned in Kelly's Directory for 1928, but were absent from that of 1932. On 31 December 1928 Player sold 4½ acres of land between Lenton House and The Orchard for £3,516 to John C. Boot (later the second Lord Trent) of Lenton House, and it was added to the Lenton House estate. Much of this land (which includes the 'dew-pond') was eventually sold to the University to provide part of the site of the present Education building. On 1 January 1930, one year later, Player sold to Sir Thomas Shipstone of Lenton Firs 'the cottage with farm buildings' called Lenton Hurst Farm, together with about 26 of the 27a.3.23 of his original purchase of 1903 [Rotheras]. The map for this sale shows Sir Thomas as already owning all the land along the north-east boundary, together with Lenton Hurst house and its gardens.

It is not, perhaps, surprising to find that the tenant of Lenton Hurst house in 1932, and until the death of Sir Thomas Shipstone in 1940 was Frederick M. Ratcliffe, the manager of Shipstones' brewery. Ratcliffe may have stayed longer, because it was only in 1945 that Lenton Hurst house was rented by the University College for the use of residential courses for members of H.M.Forces organized by the Department of Adult Education, then at Shakespeare Street. There were also courses for others, for example for German teachers, although the demand decreased in later years. In 1950 the University was able to purchase the whole of the Lenton Firs estate, including Lenton Hurst house and farm, and for a time the house became a detached part of Wortley Hall, until Lenton Hall was built alongside and absorbed it [19] . Lenton Hurst Farm was let by Sir Thomas Shipstone during the 1930s and 1940s to S.C.Armitage, (later Sir Cecil Armitage) who had bought Lenton Fields in 1927, and it was developed as a pig farm. Pig pens are shown on the O.S. 6-inch maps of the time on the land south of Sherwood and Derby Halls, and pigs were still on this land until 1962 when Derby Hall was completed.

After retiring in 1926, and selling his house and land in Lenton at the beginning of 1930, W.G.Player removed to Whatton Manor where he lived until his death, aged 93 in June 1959, (and where his daughter, Miss Player, lived until her death in 1987). He was very rich (leaving £1,606,739 at his death) and throughout his life was a generous benefactor to churches and hospitals, with a particular interest in Nottingham General Hospital, to which he gave over £180,000, used especially for provision of buildings. He was a member of the 'Monthly Board', the hospital's governing body, from 1906, and its chairman between 1926 and 1932; and according to R.G.Hogarth, a surgeon associated with the hospital for over 50 years, he was an excellent chairman, 'conscientious, painstaking and an inspiration to all who served with him' [Hogarth 1949]. He was also President from 1915 to 1918, when the hospital's facilities were under pressure in wartime conditions. His gifts began then, in April 1915, with half the cost of temporary buildings (to which he later added a balcony for 20 more beds) followed by half the cost of a further temporary building in 1917, and in October 1915 he financed the reorganization of the X-ray Department and provided its equipment [Jacob 1951]. In November 1919 he was chairman of a new Extension Subcommittee, and from 1924 chairman of its successor. The Rope Walk Wing opened in April 1927 was largely his gift (£50,000) with the other major contributions from his neighbours on the campus, Sir Louis Pearson of Lenton Grove and Sir Thomas Shipstone of Lenton Firs, and in 1929 he presented the new children's ward named for his wife Mabel Player. At the opening in October 1932 of the new Player Wing towards which he gave a crucial £25,000, tributes were paid to his 'generous spirit, kindliness, encouragement and forbearance'. 'He has probably given more money to the hospital than any other benefactor we have known'. Other monuments to his generosity may be seen in the 'Castle Ward', and the 'Jubilee Wing' added to the Mabel Player Ward, as well as the Memorial Nurses' Home. His brother, John Dane Player, was also a generous benefactor of the General, Children's and Women's hospitals.

With W.G.Player's resignation from the chairmanship of the Monthly Board on 16 March 1932, his task of almost daily supervision of the affairs of the Hospital passed to Sir Louis Pearson of Lenton Grove, but he continued to serve on committees, and as late as 1943 Castle Ward was added above the Player Wing at his expense.

William Goodacre Player was 'a man of very retiring disposition, never wanting to place himself in the limelight, nor to draw any personal glory from what was achieved'. Before the first world war he bought an estate at Ednaston near Brailsford, Derbyshire, and commissioned Sir Edward Lutyens to design a house there, completed in 1912-14 according to Pevsner, and 'perhaps the most perfect country house that Lutyens designed'. But Mabel refused to accept it as their principal home, and although Ednaston Manor remained in the family, and William frequently fished in the trout stream there, the Players continued to live at Lenton Hurst. William and Mabel clearly retained a warm affection for Lenton, and long after they moved away they still took a close and benevolent interest in the parish, and supported it financially. For example, William was largely responsible through his gift of funds for making possible the provision of the two new churches that opened in 1938, one at each end of the campus along Derby Road - St. Mary's Wollaton Park and St. Barnabas, Lenton Abbey [20] -

following an appeal launched in the early 1930s by the Rev. R.Skipper. Player bought the site of St. Mary's Wollaton Park and paid for the entire building together with a church hall and curate's house, which were built in 1937.

LENTON MOUNT and THE ORCHARD (1904-05)

Both Lenton Mount and The Orchard were built in 1904-05 on land sold off through Albert Ball after Frederick Wright was forced to dispose of Lenton Hall and the remains of its estate. They are the newest of the original private houses on the campus with the exception of H.B.Fletcher's house, called Lenton Close, on Lenton Hall Drive, now part of Cripps Hall (and, of course, the houses of the Lenton Abbey housing estates, municipal and private). Neither house was mentioned in Kelly's Directory for 1904, or in Wright's for 1905, but both figured in Kelly's Directory for 1908. The Orchard was in the early stages of building on 15 November 1904, when A.T.Richards concluded an agreement with W.G.Player of Lenton Hurst for a water pipe to be carried from Cut Through Lane across Player's land now occupied by the Education building [Rotheras]. The house of Lenton Mount, with alterations and additions, is now the University Club, and the University (Hallward) Library has been built in its garden. The Orchard is occupied by University teaching accommodation after being used to house successively the Departments of Law and Politics.

LENTON MOUNT

Lenton Mount house, now extended, has been is use as the University's Staff Club for the past 40 years. It was built for William Sydney Hemsley, managing director of Hemsley and Co., Limited, and he remained there until 1920 or later [Wright 1920]. Before the first world war his coachman, Frederick Nurse, lived in the cottage alongside the house and the coachhouse-stable which was later converted into garages. Frederick Mitchell was the owner in 1925 [Kelly 1925] and probably several years earlier. It was Mitchell who on 31 March 1920 bought from T.S.Pearson-Gregory some 48 acres of land, part of that called the Alexander Wright Closes in the 16th century and including The Keightons, and Bacon, Quarrel, Ley and Great and Little Mare Closes [21]. This land was purchased by Sir Jesse Boot very soon afterwards, for it became the eastern end of University Park and of the campus of University College after 1932, and of the public playing fields across University Boulevard.

Mitchell was succeeded at Lenton Mount by Captain John Eric Greenwood, J.P., LL.B., M.A., A.C.A., (Figure 85) who moved there from The Park estate in 1926, and who remained there until he retired to Dorset and the University took over the house and garden in 1953. Greenwood was a man of many talents, whose career holds especial interest because of his important role in the history of the Boots Company, especially during the 1920s - a fascinating story recounted in his autobiography, published posthumously [Greenwood 1977, Part I, 3-76]. The book illuminates the public school-Oxbridge-Club culture operating in business between the wars, and provides insights into the characters, great achievements - and foibles - of Jesse and Florence Boot (Lord and Lady Trent) and their son John, the second Lord Trent and first Chancellor of the University of Nottingham.

Greenwood's family were well-known City stockbrokers (Greenwood and Co.). His grandfather was co-founder in 1858 of Deloitte and Company, one of the world's largest firms of chartered accountants, and after taking the Law Tripos at King's College, Cambridge John Greenwood was articled to a leading London firm of accountants before taking a wartime commission. He served in the Grenadier Guards with distinction and was mentioned in Dispatches. After the war, when Sir Jesse Boot was having worries about increasing production costs, his younger daughter Marjorie drew his attention to her friend Tommy Greenwood's brother John, whose qualifications and connections impressed Sir Jesse. John Greenwood was in fact already well known nationally as captain of Cambridge University

Figure 85: John Greenwood and his rock garden at Lenton Mount
[From J.E. Greenwood 1977]

Rugby Club (1912) and a member of the England XV that won the triple crown in 1912-13, and again Cambridge captain in 1919 and about to become captain of England (through 1920). Chapman [1974] has suggested that he was seen by Jesse Boot as a 'counterweight to his son John', who was allowed no executive function in the firm before his marriage, even though he had matured during five years' wartime service in France with the Sherwood Foresters. Greenwood, with no business experience, was brought to Nottingham in February 1920 as a director of the chief Boots subsidiary company (Boots Cash Chemists Eastern) with a large salary, and was appointed in December as 'expense controller'. He married Doris Mary Radford in 1921. He remained financial director of Boots, and an executive director of the company throughout the rest of his working life although Sir Jesse retired from active business only a few months after appointing him.

As a director of the Eastern Company John Greenwood had access to unpublished accounts that contained some surprising features, including large undisclosed reserves and an alarming overdraft [Chapman 1974] and he was instrumental in greatly increasing the company's profits in the early 1920s. He was also closely involved in the sale of Boots Pure Drug Company in 1920 to the United Drug Company of America (which provided Sir Jesse with the funds that enabled him to endow the University College with its new campus and the Trent Building) and, with John Boot, in the reorganization of the direction of the Company that followed (see Chapter XVI). From 1933, however, after Sir Jesse's death, Greenwood's influence declined.

John Boot led a consortium of British financiers which bought back the company from the United Drug Company (which had fallen on hard times during the American depression) and Boot became chairman and managing director. Although Greenwood was given a seat on the board his authority, and that of his associates connected with the American era waned. Despite his estrangement from John Boot, however, he remained a director for a further 20 years. When Lord Trent suffered his first serious illness in 1951, and the question of succession arose, Greenwood and J.P.Savage, a lifelong Boots employee who had been Greenwood's assistant, were appointed joint vice-chairmen: but Savage was virtually nominated as chairman by Lord Trent one evening in 1953 at Lenton House [Chapman 1974). At this juncture Greenwood retired, his position and his responsibility for shops, retail staff and overseas trade being taken over by Willoughby Norman, son of Sir Henry Norman, M.P., who married Barbara, Lord Trent's eldest daughter, and in due course became chairman of Boots.

John Greenwood's career outside business is described in his pleasant and well illustrated book 'A Cap for Boots' (a title that he seems unlikely to have chosen himself) published two years after his death in 1975 on his 84th birthday. He was twice President of the Rugby Football Union, in 1935-36 and 1936-37, a most unusual honour. He was sought after as a member of such public inquisitional bodies as the Civil Service Tribunal (1936-1949); the Catering Wages Commission; Courts of Inquiry into the Omnibus Dispute (1946) and the Road Haulage Dispute (1947) as well as the Royal Commission on the Taxation of Profits and Income (1951). He also served locally as chairman of the Nottinghamshire War Bonds Committee. His social and sporting life, and involvement in public affairs was as remarkably full and varied as his business activities.

Lenton Mount gardens

Although John Greenwood wrote that he did not become really interested in gardening until his retirement to Dorset, the five-acre garden of Lenton Mount was a celebrated one. It includes a spinney on the north-east side of the house that is dominated by tall beech trees contemporary with those near the present entrance to Hugh Stewart Hall and surrounding its gardens and tennis courts. The beeches at Lenton Mount stand on and behind a steep bank which represents degraded remains of the original ha ha wall round Lenton Hall gardens, cut off when the Lenton Mount plot was sold for building in 1903-04. The evergreen trees in front of the bank are clearly much younger, and less than 90 years old.

Greenwood and his wife Doris were keen tournament tennis players in the 1920s, and Lenton Mount garden included hard and grass tennis courts of high quality. During the second world war Mr. Dan Maskell, stationed at Loughborough in charge of a physical rehabilitation unit, was a frequent visitor, with other players of high class (such as Ernest Wittman, the Polish Davis Cup player, and Herman David, later chairman of the All England Club) to use these courts. There was also a notable rock garden at Lenton Mount, now partly occupied by the extended dining room of the University Club. A photograph of part of it (Figure 85) looking towards the croquet lawn, appears in Greenwood's book. The garden was, indeed, delightful, and the writer recalls in particular a magnificent standard specimen of Wisteria sinensis of some antiquity approximately in the position of the present Hallward Library dustbins. It probably received suitably lavish attention, for Greenwood employed three gardeners, and a chauffeur who mowed the lawns. He was particularly interested in his tennis lawn, was a member of the Sports Turf Research Institute at Bingley, and took advice and help from Boots Horticultural Research laboratories under Arthur Billett across his garden fence. He wrote: 'Lord Trent and I were neighbours at Lenton, with a field between his house, Lenton House, and my house, Lenton Mount. He gave his half to Boots to establish a research lab, greenhouses etc., and one of our employees, A.W.Billett was put in charge'. When Billett retired he became nationally known as the co-presenter, with Mr. Percy Thrower, of the BBC2 programme 'Gardeners' World' [Greenwood 1977 202]. Arthur Billett still took part in BBC television gardening programmes until his recent death.

Today 'Jenny' Greenwood's tennis courts and much of his garden are occupied by the Hallward Library, though most of the levelled croquet lawn survives between the Library and the University Club. The winding footpath leading from the Club to Library Road marks the original boundary between the ornamental grounds of Lenton Hall and open parkland, and leads across the road to a better-preserved portion of the ha ha wall, though lacking its original dyke, round the garden of Hugh Stewart Hall to the Social Science building. A bowling green constructed for use by University staff in the 1950s is now beneath and alongside the south-east corner of the Hallward Library building.

THE ORCHARD

The Orchard was built for Alfred Thomas Richards, the managing director of the Imperial Laundry, Radford Boulevard. It was situated in an orchard of Lenton Hall which had probably been in existence only since about 1890 on cartographic evidence, and the surviving fruit trees, mainly pear trees, still bear fruit profusely, and scatter it between The Orchard and Lenton Mount on the road and paths.

Richards was succeeded at The Orchard in 1913 by Mrs. Mary E.A.Barnsdale, the mother of John Barnsdale, who occupied Lenton Hall with his wife Helen (nee Bowden) in the 1920s [Wright 1913-14]. Before 1920, however, Harold B. Smith Toone, another 'director' lived at The Orchard, and doubtless owned it, for he remained there until at least 1941 [Kelly 1941]. Toone was associated with the firm of B.Toone and Co., of Gambles Factory, Newdigate Street, Nottingham, Jacquard Card Punchers [Wright 1920]. The business was later called A.S.Toone and Sons. jacquard card manufacturers and plywood manufacturers of Dulwich Road, Radford. The firm was mentioned in Kelly's Directory for 1950, the year in which the University bought The Orchard: Toone was not, and had retired or died.

Toone's predecessor at The Orchard, Mrs. Mary Elizabeth Alice Barnsdale, living in 1904 at Lucknow Drive, Nottingham, was said to be a cigar manufacturer, a director of Robinson and Barnsdale Limited [Kelly 1904]. She was the widow of Oswald Barnsdale, who died in his 40s, and presumably was in business with her second son, Sandford Oswald

Barnsdale, tobacco broker of Long Row, who lived on Dagmar Grove, Alexandra Park. In 1907 Mrs. Barnsdale was one of three directors of Daybrook Laundry Company [Allen 1907 111], but no family or other connection is known with A.T.Richards of the Imperial Laundry, her predecessor at The Orchard, and her laundry interest arose from the marriage of one of her sisters to John Robinson of Daybrook Laundry [22]. In 1925 Mrs. Barnsdale lived at 43 Tavistock Drive.

POSTSCRIPT : LENTON CLOSE (1934)

The last 'residual' house on the campus acquired by the University (other than Lenton Abbey) and the newest, is Lenton Close. Built very much in the contemporary modern style of the 1930s it was delightfully situated on Lenton Hall Drive opposite to the present Cripps Hall, and was designed to take full advantage of its environment and aspect, with a curving facade facing south-south-west, and an open outlook across the 'downland' beyond its large, sunny garden, with lawns running down to the fine spreading 'park' beech tree which still, fortunately, survives. The garden has been mostly lost, absorbed into the park.

The house was built for Henry Bowmer Fletcher, who was able to buy land on Lenton Hall Drive immediately beyond the grounds of The Cedars (Paton House) from Sir Thomas Shipstone in 1933 (covenant dated 30 November). Fletcher was a member of the Nottingham firm of surveyors, estate agents and auctioneers, Turner, Fletcher and Essex. He died in the 1950s, but Mrs. Fletcher remained at Lenton Close until it was taken over by the University to become an annexe of Cripps Hall when it opened in 1959. The hard tennis court of the Fletchers has remained a valued amenity for members of the University, including Cripps Hall, for the past 30 years.

NOTES

1. N.U.M.D., Mi 4 Da 4 (1869)
2. N.U.M.D., Mi 3 G 33 (undated)
3. A tablet with the date July 1875 left of the front door records the date of completion and occupation of Lenton Eaves.
4. Morris' Directory for 1869 named John Bayley as the occupier of The Priory, but recorded The Priory as the home of Benjamin Walker.
5. Census of 1881, Enumerators' Books. For Lenton RG 9/3340-3341
6. The Mr. Walker at Spring Villas, Beeston about 1870 [Morris 1869 Wright 1871] was John Benjamin Walker, who headed another lace firm, J.B.Walker and Co., of High Pavement, Nottingham and Sandiacre, and who later lived on Cavendish Crescent North in The Park, Nottingham. Benjamin Walker junior recorded at West End, Beeston in 1879 could not have been the Benjamin who by then had been living at Lenton Eaves for four years.
7. P. Howard Anderson, *Forgotten Railways: the East Midlands* (1973) 117-118 (with map and photograph).
8. The Universal British Directory, Nottingham and Newark, 1793.
9. Nottingham City Planning Department, *Nottingham's Heritage - a view of conservation in the city* (May 1985) p. 30.
10. *Visitors' Guide Book to Nottingham* Printed and published by G.H.Shepherd, Angel Row, Nottingham.
11. A.R.Turner and Ian H. Wallace, 'Materials for the history of Paton College, Nottingham' (undated typescript). Much of the detail in the following paragraphs comes from this pamphlet.
12. Notts. County Council, *Buildings of special architectural interest* (1972).
13. ibid.
14. K. Brand, 'Richard Charles Sutton'. *N.C.S.N.*,69 (Jan. 1986) 4-6
15. The house, called 'The Brightlands', built in 1885, had a large hall, 3 reception rooms and 11 bedrooms, and thus was comparable in size to Lenton Hurst.
16. N.U.M.D., Mi 1/16/1c (1823)
17. This track is clearly shown on Sanderson's map of 1834, and it can be discerned on the O.S. First edition 1-inch to 1 mile map of 1838. It does not appear on the larger scale estate plan of 1863, which shows the toll gate and toll house (N.U.M.D., Mi P 6).

18. Mr. Fred Weiss produced the Wortley Hall play each summer for many years until his death, and the lawn at Lenton Hurst, as well as other parts of the garden, were used to stage it when Lenton Hurst was an annexe of Wortley Hall.
19. Miss Jeremiah, later Mrs. Fred Weiss, supervised the domestic arrangements at Lenton Hurst both during its time as a centre for residential courses and later, as Domestic Bursar at Wortley Hall.
20. A photograph taken at the dedication of St. Mary's, Wollaton Park, including W.G.Player, can be found in 'The Lenton Times' No. 1, (October 1988) 14-16 .(Lenton Local History Society)
21. L.A.O., 4 PG 108
22. I am indebted to Mrs. Clair Harlow of Woodthorpe, Mrs. Barnsdale's great grand-daughter, for interesting details of the Barnsdale family which have not been pursued in this account.

CHAPTER XIII

COMMUNICATIONS ON AND AROUND THE CAMPUS: ROADS, CANALS, AND RAILWAYS

Introduction

Until the rate of economic and social change accelerated two hundred years ago roads formed a very stable element in the pattern of landscape in both town and countryside. Subsequently advances in technology and great geographical changes in the character of the University district, as elsewhere, have led to great changes in both through routes and local communications by road, water and rail, in which some ancient routes have maintained or increased their importance while others have ceased to function, and some entirely new ones have appeared. In this chapter the history of roads and tracks on and around the University campus is described, and the place of canals and railways briefly discussed. In order to place each into its regional setting and historical context the reader may refer to Chapter XIX, 'Communications' in the British Association's publication 'Nottingham and its Region' [Edwards ed. 1966 315-339].

The turnpike roads

The chief through roads associated with the campus area in the 18th century were those from Nottingham to Derby and to Birmingham, both of which were turnpiked in 1758 (Figure 86). The latter diverged from the former near the present Lenton Hurst, where a toll gate was established. There is good reason to suppose that the Nottingham to Birmingham road - the Sawley turnpike - became important only with the increase in wheeled traffic, and probably little before the end of the 17th century, but the Nottingham to Derby road is much older, and dates from before the Conquest. An inquiry in 1569 recorded the Nottingham-Derby road as one of the four 'comon high ways' through the lordship of Lenton [1], but the Nottingham-Birmingham road was not among them. The Derby road formed part of the ancient boundary of Lenton parish or lordship and of the demesne of Lenton Priory, established in the early 12th century, and undoubtedly formed a property and administrative boundary still earlier. The way from Birmingham to Nottingham crossing the river Trent at Sawley ferry, and following the valleyside gravel terraces through Chilwell and Beeston to the point where these end near Florence Boot Hall, faced there a steep climb up Cut Through Lane which could not be negotiated by wheeled traffic, and therefore diverged along the Tottle Brook valleyside to take advantage of the gentler gradient of Beeston Lane and join the Derby-Nottingham road near Lenton Hurst. The ancient track called Cut Through Lane, leading directly to Nottingham Castle is discussed below.

The 'king's highway' running south-westwards out of Nottingham was called Derbigate as early as 1301, Derbistrete in 1352 [Cameron 1976] and in 1335 was described as 'regiam viam quae ducit versus Lenton' [2]. From the top of Sion Hill (Canning Circus) it headed for the Leen ford at Hillside, forming the boundary between Lenton's Alwell and Sand Fields down to Lenton Sands. Its line was determined largely by considerations of physical geography, in connecting the lowest hard-bank fording points of the river Leen at Hillside and the river Erewash at Sandiacre by the most gently graded and dry-ground but reasonably direct route. By circling north-westwards and then south-westwards from Hillside through what is now Wollaton Park housing estate it negotiated the steep west side of the Leen valley, and from the Tottle Brook at Lenton Abbey used the gently graded east-west valley leading to the 'gap' between Bramcote village and Bramcote Hills, running mainly over rocks of the Sherwood Sandstone group. It was diverted between Hillside and the top of Adams Hill in 1822 for reasons discussed below.

As wheeled traffic increased, the maintenance of main roads by local statutory parish labour, which had been the system since 1555, became impracticable, and although the principle remained, from about 1760 onwards parishes could apply to Quarter Sessions for the imposition of a highway rate in addition, usually 6d. in the pound. From 1663 the turnpike (toll road) system was superimposed, with the local gentry as trustees, which allowed more effective maintenance of the busier roads. The situation was especially serious when coal was a major item of trade because its carriage was especially damaging to unmetalled roads. For example, at Lenton Sands traffic cut a deep narrow 'hollow way' in the soft Lenton Sandstone, and in 1740 colliers had to be sent by Lord Middleton from his Wollaton pits to improve it [Blackner 1816 (1985) 57].

In 1773 restrictions were imposed by statute as to the maximum number of horses to be used to draw waggons and carts on highways other than turnpike roads [13 G 3 c78]. With wheels 9 inches wide waggons could use six horses, and carts five horses. Vehicles on wheels or rollers 16 inches wide and thus less damaging to the road surface, might be drawn by any number of horses 'or other cattle' (two oxen being equivalent to one horse). Licences could vary this because of the bad state of the roads. On turnpikes narrower wheels paid higher rates.

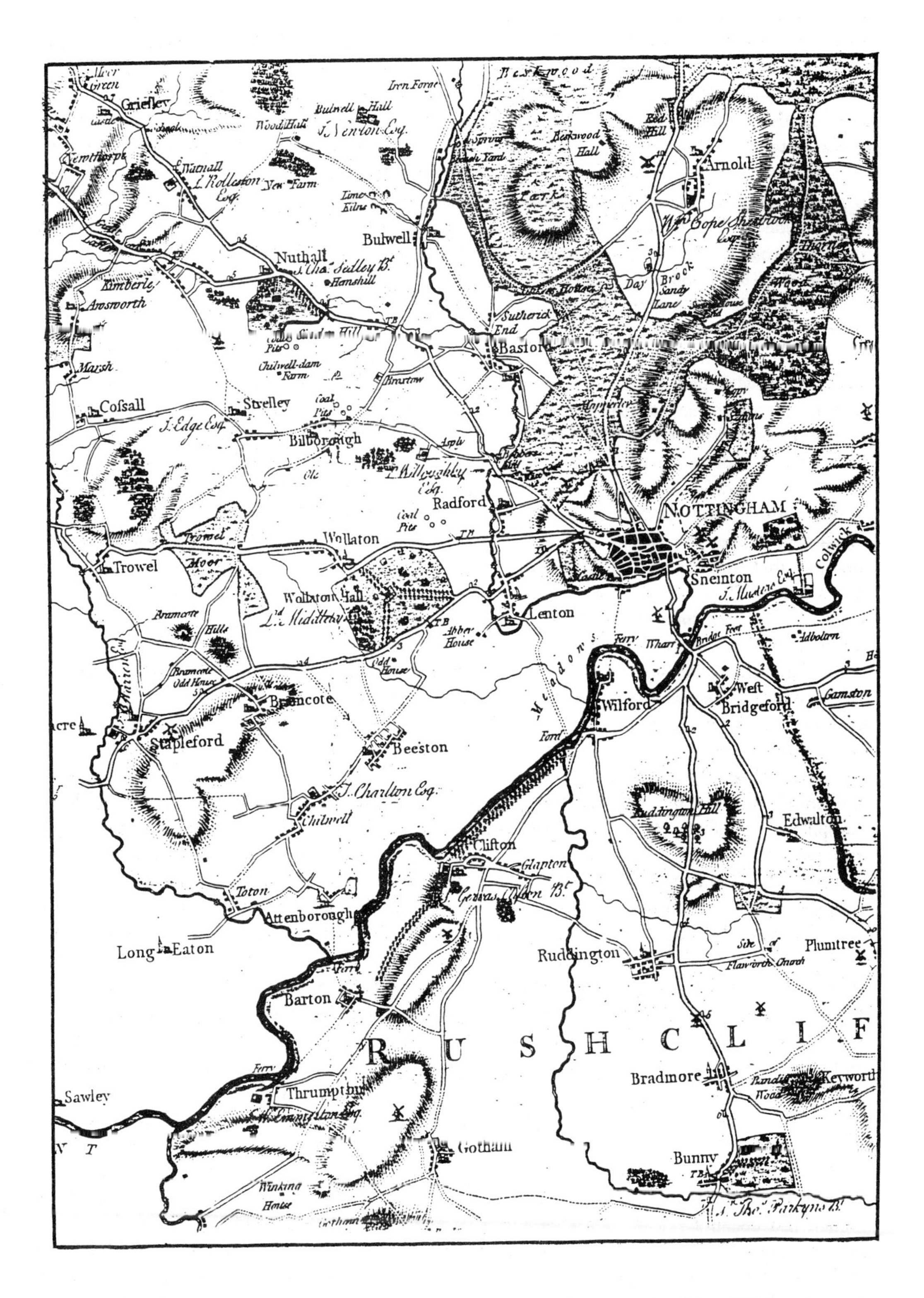

Figure 86: Part of Chapman's map of Nottinghamshire surveyed in 1774 (reduced) [NAO N 27 L] Courtesy N.A.O.

More horses were allowed on steep hills, and local Quarter Sessions orders included one of 5 October 1767 for Nottingham to Trowell (James Foxcroft, Clerk to the Trustees) and another of 13 January 1772 for Nottingham-Derby/Lenton-Sawley Ferry (James Foxcroft). On 25 November 1775 William Hopkins of Lenton was convicted for using narrow-wheeled waggons on the turnpike road [Meaby 1947 101]. Even in 1799 the amending Turnpike Act increased the annual composition of the parish of Lenton to £5 because the previous 10-shilling charges 'are by no means equal to the injury the inhabitants of such towns do to the said road in passing thereon' and it required that the inhabitants' vehicles had 'wheels not less than 6 inches wide'. The maintenance problem remained extremely serious until the MacAdam method of road surfacing was devised [3], and MacAdam and Telford were at the height of their fame in the 1820s and early 1830s.

Before it was turnpiked by the Act of 1758 [4] which was subsequently amended and extended by further Acts, the Derby Road past the campus was narrow, pot-holed and rutted, and overhung by trees. According to the House of Commons Journal of 5 March 1759 the Lenton to Sawley part of the main route from Nottingham to Birmingham and The West was in many places so narrow that two carriages could not pass each other. The preamble to the 1758 Act noted that the roads 'from the Guide Post [by Lenton Hurst] near certain lands called The Abbey Lands in the parish of Lenton, through Beeston, Chilwell, Toton, Long Eaton and Sawley ... to Sawley Ferry are in a ruinous condition and in several parts very narrow and incommodious, and dangerous to passengers, and the said Roads cannot be effectively amended and kept in repair by the ordinary Course provided by Law'. The Lenton to Sawley road met that from Sawley to Tamworth, turnpiked in the same year, at Sawley Ferry, but an Act of May 1779 provided for a bridge to be built over the river Trent 'at or near Sawley ferry', and the ferry was superseded by the Harrington Bridge built under an Act of 1787-88 [28 Geo.III, c80].

The turnpike trustees were empowered to erect 'such gates or turnpikes in or cross any part or parts of the respective roads and also such Toll Houses near the same as they ... shall think proper'. A toll bar was set up and a toll house built at the junction of the two turnpikes near the present Lenton Hurst, and they remained for 112 years. This bar, and that on Derby Road just above Chapel Bar, and another a hundred yards down the hill from Barrack Lane (opened only in 1854) were immediately demolished in November 1870 when the last Derby Road Turnpike Act expired. By this time the medium and long distance travel by road which brought most of their income to the turnpikes had declined so much through competition from the railways after about 1840 that the turnpike trusts were in serious financial difficulty, and local turnpike Acts were allowed to expire without renewal. By 1851 many trusts were insolvent.

By the 1758 Act the surveyors of the trustees of the Sawley and Derby turnpikes might 'dig, gather and take away any gravel, furze, heath, sand, stone or other materials for repairing the said roads out of any river or brook, or out of any waste grounds ... without paying ... and where sufficient materials are not to be there had they may be taken from private grounds ...' and payment made. It is thought that the pond now filled in to form Rutland Hall car park was probably in origin a quarry for road-building material used either by the Sawley turnpike trust or by John Wright when he diverted Beeston Lane in about 1805.

The amending Act of 1799 noted that the Trustees had made great progress in repairing and widening both the Derby road and that 'from the guide post in the parish of Lenton to Sawley Ferry', but had borrowed much money which could not be repaid until the road had been further improved, and traffic and income further increased. Despite the still poor condition of the roads regular fast coach services were operating past and through the present campus in the 1790s. For example, in 1793 a Birmingham coach left the Black Moor's Head, Nottingham , every day at 7 a.m., and a coach to Derby ran every Wednesday and Saturday afternoon from the Spread Eagle Inn [5]. In 1797 the Nottingham to Birmingham 'accommodation post coach' ran from the Black Moor's Head Inn through Castle Donington, Ashby, and Tamworth to Birmingham in ten hours, claiming that this route was six miles shorter than any other, by using Sawley Bridge rather than Trent Bridge. It left at 8 a.m. every Tuesday, Thursday and Saturday. The inside fares were 8s. to Ashby and 18s. to Birmingham, and outside fares 5s. to Ashby and 10s. to Birmingham. In 1798 the old Nottingham to Birmingham coach ran from Mr. Gray's and from Mrs. Lart's (The Bell Inn) at 8 a.m. every weekday, to the Swan Hotel and the Castle Inn, Birmingham - 'a light, four-wheeled carriage with good horses and plated harness to go post'; inside fare 12s., outside 6s. By 1831 there was a four-horse coach from Nottingham to Birmingham via Beeston Lane called the Birmingham Dart, which called daily at Beeston at 8.30 a.m., and on the reverse journey at 3.30 p.m.. We should visualize the horses of these scheduled service coaches of nearly 200 years ago galloping across Lenton Hurst lawn below the toll gate, through the site of Derby Hall's east entrance and Edale House, and on between Sherwood and Rutland Halls to the sharp corner where the narrow, tree-lined Beeston Lane joined Cut Through Lane; and then emerging beyond the Tottle Brook valley on to the unfenced road now called Broadgate, crossing the open common arable field of Beeston called Tuttle Brook Field.

In the 1820s and 1830s, just before the arrival of the railway, long distance passenger and mail traffic by horse-drawn coaches reached a peak of importance, although the canals now carried most heavy goods, produce and materials at their much slower pace. Regular scheduled coach services connected all the chief centres of population on a daily basis, usually with inns providing stabling and associated facilities as their points of departure and arrival. In 1825 [Glover 1825 29] and 1832 [White 1832 29] for example, the Royal mail coach called the Birmingham Dart, mentioned above, with the royal arms on its door panels, the upper parts black and the lower parts a deep crimson, ran daily down Beeston Lane from Nottingham to the Castle Inn, Birmingham. It left the White Lion Hotel (later called The Lion's Head) in Clumber Street every weekday morning at 8.00, and travelled at an average speed of 10 m.p.h. including stops, exchanging horses in 10-mile stages. It was backed up by the Birmingham Dart light post coach running daily from the Lion Inn at 10 a.m. [Dearden 1834 14]. From the Black Boy Hotel the Hark Forward coach left daily at 6.45 a.m. for Birmingham, Warwick and Coventry. Several coaches ran daily along Derby Road to Derby, taking two hours - the Derby Royal Sovereign at 6.45 a.m. and the Derby Times at 11 a.m. from the Lion Hotel; the Derby, Burton and Lichfield Champion at 6.30 a.m., and the Derby Tally-Ho at 3 p.m. from the Black Boy; and the Derby Royal Defiance at 3.30 p.m. from the Maypole Inn, Long Row. Other Nottingham to Derby coach services were called The Favourite, the Union and the Lord Nelson. Yet in 1853 only one coach service from Nottingham was listed - that to Sheffield from the Maypole Inn - and none plied along Derby Road and Beeston Lane. The railway had taken over all except local traffic, the turnpike trusts withered away through a drastically reduced income, and the toll bars did not long survive.

Derby Road in about 1820 and the roadside gardens

A vivid and detailed picture of Derby Road in the later 18th and early 19th century is provided by the evidence of elderly witnesses in the litigation of 1823 between Lord Middleton and John Wright of Lenton Hall [6], and illustrated by a map attributed to Lord Middleton's employee Chouler (Figure 87). Wright was being sued for trespass after a series of provocative actions by him, ostensibly to establish his ownership of a narrow strip of land between Derby Road and Wollaton Park wall now occupied by the footpath there. Wright was probably provoked by Middleton's purchase of Lenton Firs in 1815 and his high-handed diversion of Derby Road down Adams Hill in 1822; and personal dislike, jealousy and vindictiveness are more likely reasons for his actions than avarice or assertion of legal rights. Lord Middleton won the case.

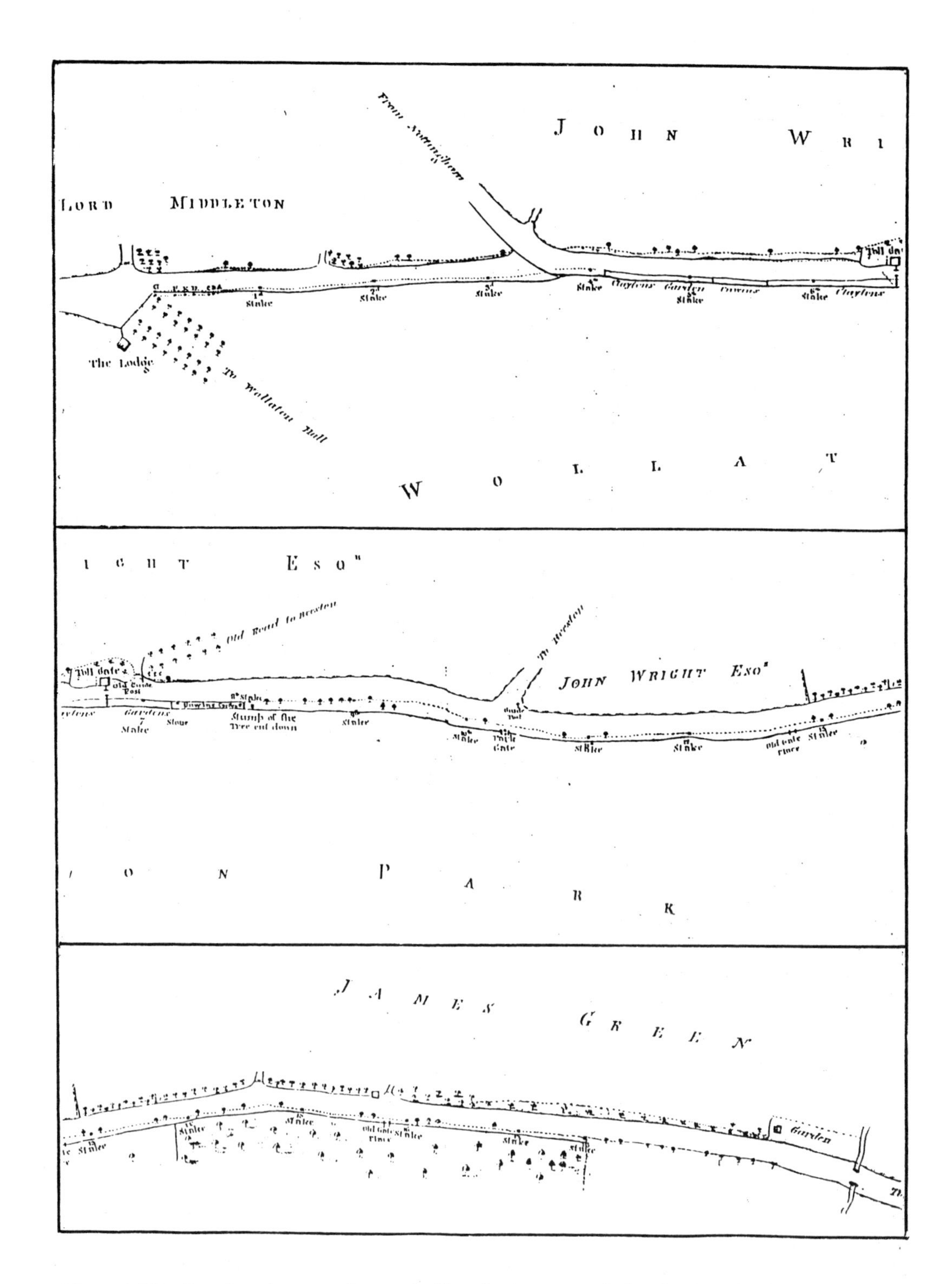

Figure 87: Overlapping sections of Chouler's map of Derby Road, Lenton, bordering the University campus, 1822-23

(Reduced) [From NUMD Mi 1/16/1c (1823)] Note the original entrance drive to Lenton Firs; the lodge that replaced the 'Summer houses' opposite Sandy Lane (gated); former entrances to Wollaton Park; roadside gardens and layout of the toll bar.

The Wollaton Park wall was built after the purchase of the Sixty Acres in 1698 and before the memory of the oldest witnesses of 1823 - in the 1720s according to Iliffe and Baguley [1983 37]. The Abbey Fields on the south side of the road were enclosed by quickset hedgerows and wooden rail fences. Joseph Kirkland (70) said: 'There was always a quick [hawthorn] fence to the whole of the Abbey estate between that and the turnpike road'. Richard Chamberlain (61) a Lenton farmer whose father had rented 'Abbey land' confirmed this, and had heard his father say that he first planted quick there and had some difficulty in raising it, 'there being so many rabbits that cropped it' - not surprising since this was formerly the priory's rabbit warren. The lease of 1753 from Dame Elizabeth Cookes-Winford to Mr. Williamson, which was taken over by Mr. Chamberlain senior in 1760, incorporated a covenant that the tenant would 'plant quick sets in the hedgerows of the ring fence belonging to the closes called the Abbey Fields where the same were wanting, and stoops and double rails of good oak timber, and make necessary banks and ditches'.

The carriageway of Derby Road was much narrower than that of today, and even after it was widened to 15 yards under the Turnpike Act (the maximum the trustees could claim) there was land between the road and the fences on both sides. The narrow strip of 'treebord' or 'screed' on the Wollaton side was the subject of the litigation of 1823, to which we owe a detailed map of the road provided for Lord Middleton's brief, and probably surveyed and drawn by Charles Chouler the younger of Wollaton, under-steward to Lord Middleton. The screed was described by many of the witnesses of 1823, and William Hopkin, innkeeper (of the 'Three Wheatsheaves') stated categorically that the fences between the Abbey land and the turnpike 'have been brought forward by Mr. Watson [who died in 1801], Mr. Wright and Mr. Green' (of Lenton Firs, Lenton Hall and Lenton Abbey respectively). John Sleight of Wollaton, aged 78, and park keeper to Lord Middleton for 54 years, gave evidence that on the north side of the road the screed was being encroached upon by the surveyor of the turnpike more every year - presumably through pressure on the other side of the road - so 'about ten years ago [about 1812] a man called William Peet, a carpenter of Lord Middleton's, put down a number of posts as land marks at the edge of the screed and between it and the footway' (see Figure 87).

John Wright claimed that the screed between the park wall and the road was his, and although his case was weak he had tried to establish his right by allegedly removing from it four trees, four loads of underwood, four loads of branches, four loads of wood, and 40 loads of 'soil, earth and stones'. For the same reason he destroyed the fences of the narrow gardens that occupied most of the screed on the Wollaton side of the road from the top of Adams Hill opposite to Lenton Hall Drive down to the Beeston Lane entrance to Wollaton Park. These gardens, shown on Chouler's map (Figure 87) were made and worked by the men associated with the road - the 'surveyor' who was responsible for road repairs and maintenance, and the tollgate keeper at the tollhouse near to Lenton Hurst. Their gardens were in a sense analogous to the later 'railway allotments' alongside railway tracks near to railway stations.

Wright also encroached on the road from the south side by fencing off the screed there, especially in 1809, and planting trees on it, despite having undertaken not to do so. Alexander Foxcroft, Clerk to the Trustees of Derby turnpike road (see Chapter IX) presented evidence that at a meeting of the trustees of the two turnpike roads at the Black Moor's Head Inn on 4 May 1810, at which John Wright was present, Lord Middleton complained that various persons had been allowed to enclose parts of the side of the road opposite to his park wall. 'A part of the south side of this road from the cottage belonging to John Wright Esq. to the garden of the Tollgate having been lately taken in and a quick fence planted next to the road, Mr. Wright being present assures the Trustees that the part so taken in shall not hereafter be planted'. The cottage mentioned was probably an early lodge at the entrance to Lenton Hall drive, though none was shown on early maps or mentioned in census books before the existing lodge (called West Lodge in recent times) was built in 1861-62 to replace it. Some of the trees planted on this strip east of the tollgate must still survive, for John Wright appears to have got away with his encroachment without penalty. This leads to the intriguing possibility that the University, in its resistance to the conversion of Derby Road past the campus into a dual carriageway, in fact had no moral right to ownership of a strip of land along the whole north-western margin of the campus. James Green of Lenton Abbey had also fenced an encroachment on 'a screed of land opposite the wood [that is, Thompson's Wood] which was wider than that enclosed by Wright, and averaged 25 feet wide. It is clearly shown on Chouler's map. But Green made no claim to the screed along the park wall. The General Turnpike Act of 13 George III cap 78 prescribed penalties for inclosing 'waste' land within 30 feet of the centre of a turnpike road: but it was repealed by 4 George IV cap 126, 'the late General Act', passed in July 1822.

The tone of the local witnesses from whose evidence Lord Middleton's brief was made up in 1823 suggests that they resented the encroachments by John Wright, and his claim of ownership. Resentment may have been real in some cases, because the screed alongside Derby Road had been used not only for the digging of sand by the public, but also for grazing their animals. William Wilkinson, who was born at the Odd House (Lenton Abbey) and later returned to work the farm, described how his father, living nearby, rented the herbage of the lane from the toll bar down to the Tottle, on both sides of the road. This part of the Derby turnpike was then called Pomfret Lane. The parish of Lenton received the rent and applied it to 'parish purposes'. When the Steward of Miss Milward's Abbey estate, a Mr. Wild, heard of this he told Wilkinson not to pay, since the land and herbage belonged to the Abbey estate, and the people of Lenton had no right to them. No rent was paid thereafter. The owner of the Gregory estate, in his turn, instructed all his tenants to turn their cattle on to the lane, and the Abbey estate Steward took no action to prevent them from doing so. These events took place in the early 1780s. One witness in 1823, John Hopkin, a Gregory estate tenant, turned his sheep every summer from 1790 to 1802 on to 'Derby turnpike called Pomfret Lane' to pasture by the road sides which, except for the turnpike gardens, were quite open. Other people too grazed their asses and cattle there, and John Hopkin's father William, who rented Abbey land, also turned his horses there, where John had tended them many times [7]. Richard Chamberlain remembered Lenton people, including his father, turning their horses into the road beyond the toll gate 'to eat the cropping there, by Mr. Gregory's direction'.

John Hopkin's description of the screed as 'open' does not imply that it was all grassy. Samuel Brownlow of Lenton, aged 77 in 1823, remembered the road before 1759, and saw the building of the tollhouse. 'The road was narrower than now [1823] with nut trees and bushes on both sides'. He had 'gone a nutting' there as a boy, and confirmed that the road along the Abbey land was called Pomfret Lane, a name that properly applied only to that part of it west of the tollgate. At that time it appears that Beeston Lane was more used by traffic than Pomfret Lane. Many oak trees were growing on the screed alongside the Wollaton Park wall, and on the south side of the road in front of the fence bounding the Abbey Fields were bushes, hazel trees, briars and gorse, which John Wright later cut when enclosing the land in his fields. He planted trees in a strip varying from two yards to six or seven yards wide over a length of several hundred yards opposite the gardens - that is, from Lenton Hall Drive to beyond Lenton Hurst. A dozen years later he took away several oak trees, and rooted up the fences of the gardens along the park wall and carried away soil on the pretext that the road was too narrow - by reason, others claimed, of his own encroachment on the opposite side of the road.

In April 1813 John Martin, Lord Middleton's steward, had a row of stout stakes put along the roadside edge of the screed to allow the turnpike gate keeper and the road surveyor to fence off and cultivate their narrow strip gardens east of the tollgate. Originally all the screed on the park side, generally four yards wide (but wider before the road was turnpiked) was covered with oak trees, hazels, thorn bushes and briars. South-west of the tollgate there were 30 or 40 oaks, with spaces where others had stood, nearly in a row, generally 100, but some probably

200 years old, and probably originally hedgerow trees surviving from the 17th century boundary of the Sixty Acres. Other oak trees east of the tollgate where the gardens were made, and as far as the old entrance lodge to Wollaton Park had been cut down, and the secondary growth of brushwood cleared by the tollgate keeper and William Unwin, the surveyor, to make their gardens.

In the 18th century Derby Road, Lenton, was notorious as a favourite resort of highwaymen. Even as late as the early 1790s there were several robberies on the highway near to the Wollaton Park entrance lodge, which was then uninhabited, by footpads hiding in the bushes on the screed, and according to Joseph Kirkland's evidence the whole screed from the entrance lodge to the tollgate was cleared by order of Lord Middleton. But highway robbery continued, for in March 1802 Fernando Davis, a Sawley blacksmith, was hung and Henry Palmer eventually pardoned for robbing John Cockayne on the Derby Road in Lenton [Sutton 1852 253]. The surveyors of the road twice lopped the branches of trees on the screed which overhung the road with Lord Middleton's permission, first in about 1783, when the undergrowth was also cut, and again in about 1795-97 when bushes were grubbed up. The old entrance to Wollaton Park (very near to the present one) was replaced and widened in about 1791, and the park wall rebuilt over 50 yards some ten feet nearer to the turnpike road. A lodge built by William Stretton replaced the earlier pair of 'summer houses' at the entrance in 1792. These 'acts of ownership' were described by John Sleight, the former Wollaton Park keeper, Joseph Watson, a Retford bricklayer, and Thomas Stevenson of Abbey House, who farmed the Abbey land opposite. John Sleight and James Tatlow described how, west of the tollgate, Lord Middleton's employees had cut and carried to his woodyard between a dozen and a score of oak trees 'of an inferior sort' which were growing on the screed, while others had been lopped in 1794-95. Further west bushes were cut, and trees that hung over the road towards the corner of the park by the Tottle Brook were cut in about 1780 by order of Thomas Sampson, then the road surveyor, with Lord Middleton's permission, Sampson taking the timber and his labourer the brushwood.

The roadside gardens took advantage of the clearance of part of the screed. John Handley, one of Lord Middleton's gardeners living at Lenton, gave evidence in 1823 that 'about 21 years ago [that is, in about 1802] Lord Middleton gave him leave to make a garden to grow potatoes on the screed' about 100 yards above the entrance lodge, that is, on land taken into the park after the diversion of the turn-pike down Adams Hill, and therefore not shown on Chouler's map. He had the garden, fenced with thorns, for about three years, when Unwin, the surveyor, took part of it to make a footpath, and Handley gave up the rest. There was no footpath when he took the land, which he held rent-free. Later other gardens were formed alongside the park wall from opposite to the present Paton House to well beyond Lenton Hurst, partly by William Unwin the road surveyor, but more especially by the tollgate keeper, who was Thomas Widdowson for a period before 1820, Stephen Orrell in 1820-22 and Thomas Clayton from 1823 onwards. Unwin paid 1s. a year, and successive tollgate keepers 2s. 6d. a year to Lord Middleton, though it appears that the rents were charged retrospectively to establish 'exercise of ownership', since the Derby Road gardens first appeared in Lord Middleton's rentals only at Michaelmas 1820, called 'Lenton Acknowledgements' [8] .

It is not known exactly how long the individual roadside gardens survived. Although Thomas Clayton remained at the toll house into the 1850s the final entry recording the gardens in the rentals was in 1832 :- 'Deduct T. Clayton's garden, now in the Park - 1s.3d.' and in 1833 the gardens were missing from the rentals and did not reappear [9] .

Before the roadside gardens were made a 'serpentine' path wound among the bushes along the park wall, and those on horseback tended to use that side of the road 'to look over the wall to see the deer and game'. At various times, certainly after 1783, soil had been taken away from the screed to be spread on Lord Middleton's fields in Wollaton mixed with manure, and this was specifically described in 1808-09 for the section between Derby Gate (the new entrance to the park opposite to the end of the new northern section of Beeston Lane) and Green's house (Lenton Abbey). One of the objects was to lower the path alongside the wall to prevent people from climbing over it. Again, soil and sand was removed from the screed along the wall in a haphazard way by the general public was well as by Lord Middleton's employees. Sand had been dug for centuries for a variety of uses - in road mending, for spreading on floors, and as an abrasive cleaner. 'The people of Lenton used to fetch sand from both sides of the road between the entrance lodge and the tollgate until Lord Middleton stopped it', though his gamekeeper Isaac Wibberley still fetched sand from the park wall side of the turnpike to fill up holes made by the deer. The custom of digging sand at the roadside ceased about 1820 when Lord Middleton 'ordered the holes to be levelled and no more opened'.

The 'serpentine path' was replaced by a 'good raised footpath two yards broad made at the edge of the screed next to the road over the whole length of the gardens'. It was constructed by William Unwin, the surveyor of the road, who made some of the gardens. Unwin succeeded as surveyor John Barker of Beeston, who put up the guidepost for the new Beeston Lane in about 1804, and who had himself succeeded Thomas Sampson in his job in January 1784. Lord Middleton would have argued that this path formed by the turnpike surveyor was of dubious legality. The garden rents were paid to him, and the screed was in Wollaton parish, as shown by the periodic traditional beating of the bounds of Lenton [10], and the trustees of the turnpike had no power to extend the road on to it.

John Wright tried to justify his claim to ownership of the screed by arguing that the Abbey Fields were 'open field', though this was palpably untrue in any legal sense. Aged witnesses all agreed that there was always, at least since the road was turnpiked, an 'ancient fence' round the Near and Far Abbey fields to the road, and in the fence oak trees apparently over 100 years old. The Sawley branch was similarly fenced, with hedgerow trees [Chapman 1785]. Thomas Stevenson, who took over most of the Abbey land in question, testified that the 'old fence' ran all the way from the summer houses or entrance lodge 'quite through to Tuttlebrook' during his tenure, from 1775 until Lady Day 1799. In his last year he also had the field that he called the 'Three-cornered Close' between Derby Road (Pomfret Lane) and the Sawley turnpike - the land on which Derby Hall and Sherwood Hall now stand, and at the corner of which 'the old guide post' then stood [11], but he never claimed the screed 'on which several oaks grew'. Thomas Roe, a Lenton labourer who came to the parish in 1776, remembered Mr. Watson, who owned Lodge Field (and who built Lenton Firs) cutting down some old oak trees that stood upon the bank between the road and that field in 1800, and 'there was a few dwarf oaks upon the screed in question opposite to the Lodge Field which are now cut down'.

The diversion of Derby Road in 1822 (Figure 89)

The diversion of Derby Road from Lenton Hall Drive directly down Adams Hill to the Leen crossing at Hillside was mentioned in Chapter IX above. The map of the road associated with the litigation of 1823 was drawn immediately after the diversion. 'Lord Middleton was last year [that is, in 1822] desirous to enlarge his park, and he agreed with the trustees of the turnpike road to make a new road 20 yards wide, and build a bridge, in consideration of having the old road conveyed to him which have been done' [12]. The new shorter, but much steeper section of the road was built entirely for Lord Middleton's convenience as well as at his expense; but it was a change greatly to the inconvenience of the ordinary road user for a century because of the steepness of the upper part of Adams Hill facing horse-drawn vehicles - a difficulty that was not encountered on the better-graded though longer ancient line of the road, part of which Middleton thereafter enjoyed as an extension to his park drive. The disadvantage of the steepness of the new road was to be set against the provision of a wider carriageway and a good bridge over the Leen. According to Godfrey the new bridge replaced a ford and

Figure 88: Derby Road crossing of the Tottle Brook at Lenton Abbey in about 1925
Attribution unknown. View eastwards across one of the Comb closes and the brook to (left) the present Wollaton Vale, the site of The Priory Inn and Thompson's Wood, and (right) the Lenton Abbey estate. The present Woodside Road extends right from between the bridge and the cottage

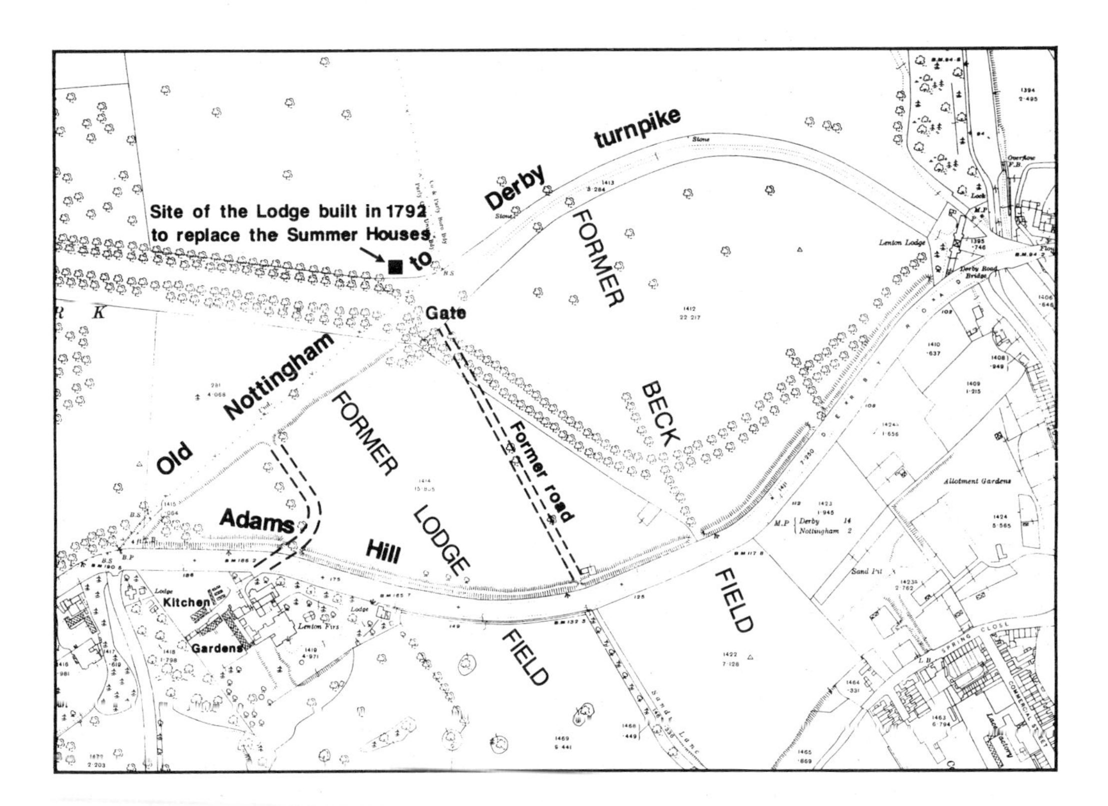

Figure 89: Old and new (Adams Hill) lines of Derby Road, diverted 1822
Reduced extract from O.S. 25-inch map of 1915 (revised to 1913) with added notes showing earlier features. The old turnpike was lost in building the Wollaton Park estate in the 1920s, and the present Wollaton Hall Drive follows a different line. Also see the Lenton Firs entrance drive through its own land before enclosure in Wollaton Park in 1822 (now built upon).

a small footbridge across the Leen, although according to Bailey [1853 IV 2 (p. 1277)] 'the bridge over the Leen near to Wollaton Park gates [was] erected at the expense of the Commissioners of the Nottingham and Derby turnpike' in 1766, and a bridge had been carrying coaches over the Nottingham canal for at least 25 years in 1822.

The exact point at which the new section of road diverged from the old road was obviously determined by the facts of land ownership, since it coincided with the place where the old road met the Lenton Firs estate boundary. That Lord Middleton had in mind an extension of Wollaton Park to the Nottingham canal and Hillside before he was able to buy Lenton Firs at the auction of May 1813 after Mrs. Watson's death, is suggested by the fact that in 1812 Coldham and Enfield, solicitors, provided an abstract of title of George de Ligne Gregory to his estate in Lenton and Radford for Messrs. Foxcroft, Hopkinson and Parsons, solicitors for Lord Middleton [13], who bought the former Beck Field land between the old Derby Road and Adams Hill below the present ring road, which the Gregory estate had owned since the inclosure of 1768. Nineteenth century maps of the area show a double line of trees dipping south-east and then north-east from the old entrance to the park to the new one, and these may represent a proposed new line of Derby Road before Lenton Firs became available for purchase. At the end of Lenton Hall Drive the encroachment on the turnpike road by John Wright was said to have made the transition from the old 15-yards wide road to the new 20-yards wide road too abrupt, and compelled Lord Middleton to rebuild part of the park wall west of the actual junction in order to give the new line of road a suitably smooth bend.

The new section of road was 'macadamized', a method of road surfacing then newly invented, and the sixth Lord Middleton was evidently delighted with it, not only because it opened the way for the building of the imposing new entrance to his park, Lenton Lodge, but because he was oblivious to the disadvantages of its line to everybody but himself. In a letter to his cousin and heir Digby Willoughby dated 24 March 1822 he wrote: '...Our Road is become very popular, everybody well pleased except Mr. Wright' [perhaps one of the few persons in the vicinity able to stand up against the powerful Middleton] 'and he has been obliged to draw in his Horns, which he wished to set full against me. It will be very handsome and a great improvement for the public and this place [:] the only regret I have heard is that the people will lose the pleasure of looking up the Avenue. I think it will be complete in another two months, and fit for the public ... Whether or no we shall get the wall finished this year I know not. But we shall set them on in three divisions beginning at each end and in the middle with separate gangs of men, and beginning in April, 7 months ought to complete it, and when they have completed it I will give them a Dinner in character in the Brick Yard' [14].

The Sawley turnpike (Beeston Lane) and its diversion in 1804-05

In an inquisition dated 3 October, 17 Elizabeth [15], made to record the course of the boundary of the manor of Lenton, part of the description ran: '....by the Exterior Hedge of a certain Close called the Rounds and then following the Hedge towards [words omitted] Tuttleberry Gate and from thence by the Hedge of a certain Close within the aforesaid Manor of Lenton called Broom Close towards ....[Derby] Gate...'. Tuttleberry Gate was evidently the lower end of the modern Beeston Lane between the Tottle Brook (now culverted) at the present west entrance to the campus and the sharp bend northwards at the Beeston end of Cut Through Lane. However, it is not known whether in Elizabethan times Tuttleberry Gate continued along Cut Through Lane or along Beeston Lane. The former, the direct riding route to the centre of Nottingham and the Castle, would have been an impossible way for wheeled traffic, and the latter was certainly a cart and coach road in the early 18th century, long before it was turnpiked. It seems likely that a lane or bridle road giving field access northwards in the 16th century was extended north-eastwards along the shallow dry valley to Derby Road at Lenton Hurst, providing a smoothly graded vehicular route towards Nottingham as the need arose during the second half of the 17th century.

The northern end of Beeston Lane (called Beeston Road before that name was usurped by a new road in Dunkirk in the 1880s) was diverted in 1804 or 1805 by John Wright, newly resident at Lenton Hall, who had purchased land hitherto farmed from the Odd House (Lenton Abbey) as part of his original land purchase in 1798. One of his objects would be to push public access to the periphery of his estate, then being planted and landscaped. A second object would be to extend the westward vista from Lenton Hall windows and gardens which is now sadly obstructed by shrubberies and conifers planted in about 1905, presumably in the interest of privacy when Lenton Hall Drive was extended to Lenton Mount and The Orchard.

The original line of the northern end of Beeston Lane is indicated by a double row of roadside trees, already shown on the map of 1823. Later O.S. 6-inch maps and other plans show this avenue, with a fence along the western line of trees, extending from the lower end of Lenton Hurst lawn, through the present Edale House of Derby Hall to its junction with the newer line of Beeston Lane near to Rutland Hall car park (Figure 90). The line of the road across Lenton Hurst lawn is now seen in a very well-marked depression. The tree lines, gradually reduced through the 19th century, were still recognisable on the 6-inch O.S. map (Provisional Edition) revised to 1938, and a group of elm trees, badly undermined by rabbits and by the pigs of Lenton Hurst Farm still survived at the opening of Derby Hall in 1963 (Figure 90). The elms, mainly wych elms, succumbed to Dutch elm disease, and only a solitary oak tree now remains as a possible representative of the avenue. Godfrey [1884] described how 'the Sawley branch ... ran along by the row of old elms in the park belonging to Lenton Hall, joining the present road near the small pond at the corner of the park', now filled in as Rutland Hall car park. He was incorrect, however, in stating that 'near the entrance lodge to Lenton Hall' the old Derby Road 'crossed the line of the present road'. This is disproved by the position of the old toll house near to Lenton Hurst.

It should be noted that a second diversion of this northern section of Beeston Lane was made in 1963, when the entrance to it from Derby Road was closed after a public enquiry. The entirely new campus road from Lenton Hall Drive past Lincoln and Derby Halls (also now called Beeston Lane) crosses the end of the former road towards the garden of Lenton Eaves, and then turns south to rejoin the old line by Rutland Hall car park . This diversion was made to increase the area available as the site of Sherwood Hall. The first few yards of the earlier Beeston Lane are now enclosed as part of the garden of one of the Lenton Hurst cottages, and only the footpath on its west side (there was no path on the east side) now survives in use there. A few of the conifers formerly lining the lane beyond also still survive. The remainder of Beeston Lane, apart from widening at the corner opposite to Cut Through Lane in 1923, when the new College entrance was being constructed (see Figure 91), and near the drive to the Sports Centre in 1927 (see Chapter VIII) and a general widening along its east side, probably resembles in general appearance the 'beautiful umbrageous road' described by Richard Allen in about 1870.

Lenton toll-gate

The Lenton toll-gate of 1759 incorporated a cottage with a small garden behind it. It remained in use for 110 years until its demolition in 1870. Its layout, as shown in Chouler's map of 1823 (Figure 87) suggests that the garden may have been formed from the end of the original line of Beeston Lane when the toll-gate was established, the road turning sharply as it joined Derby Road west of the toll-gate so that all traffic passed through the single bar. By 1823 Beeston Lane had been diverted for 20 years, and the gate shown near to the old guidepost was both a field gate and the entrance to a secondary drive to the north side of Lenton Hall, shown by pecked lines on Sanderson's map of 1835

Since it did not figure in the directories the chief sources of information about the keepers

Figure 90: Parts of the old Sawley turnpike, diverted in c. 1805
Above: *Looking up the line of the old turnpike south of Derby Hall in April 1963.*
Below: *The turnpike crossing Lenton Hurst lawn towards the toll bar and cottage. 1987]*

Figure 91: A narrow Beeston Lane at its junction with Cut Through Lane (right), 8 March 1923
The trees shown left have since been lost by road widening. [Photo. by Nottingham City Engineer's Department: NUMD Acc. 423]

of the toll-gate in the 19th century are the statements of witnesses in the trespass case of 1823, the Middleton estate rentals of the time, and the Census Enumerators' Books of 1841 to 1861. From the brief of 1823 we learn that Thomas Widdowson operated the toll-gate and lived at the cottage there from before 1813 until 1819, when he was succeeded by Stephen Orrill for three years, and he by Thomas Clayton, who remained until after 1851. It was these toll-gate keepers, with only a small cottage garden, who were able, from the nature of their employment, to make and cultivate the roadside allotments described above. Thomas and Hannah Clayton's three children, Ann, Thomas and Joseph, were born at the toll-gate cottage in 1825, 1826 and 1832, and grew up there. In 1851 Ann (29) a dressmaker, and Joseph, a labourer, were still living there, together with Hannah's 78-year-old mother, Ann Hallam, and 3-year-old Elizabeth Clayton, whose parentage is not made clear. William England was the toll collector in 1861, and lived in the cottage with his wife Esther, aged 49, and their sons William, a cutler, and Thomas a 'gentleman's servant', and their 13-year-old daughter Mary. England may well have remained until the toll-gate and cottage were demolished in 1870.

The gate and cottage were still shown on Sturgess's map of Lord Middleton's Wollaton estates in 1863, from which it appears that the actual toll house was located on the present pavement where Lenton Hurst coachhouse-garage was later built. The entrance to the old Sawley turnpike from Derby Road to the south appears to have become the entrance to Lenton Hurst drive in about 1900, and can still be identified by an inflection in the campus boundary fence.

Entrances to Wollaton Park from Derby Road, and the 'Beeston Tower'

In 1773 and earlier the entrance gateway to Wollaton Park on Derby Road (Pomfret

Lane) was opposite to the drive to the Odd House (Lenton Abbey farm) although a steep bank there today indicates a considerable subsequent lowering of the level of the road for grading purposes [16]. The significance of this location probably lies in the fact that it was an old right of way before the park wall was built in about 1720, and a public footpath continued the line south of Derby Road past the Odd House and across Brook Close to the end of Salthouse Lane and thence to the Sawley turnpike (Broadgate) and Beeston village. This path was also shown on much later maps into the present century.

Chapman's map published in 1785 but surveyed in 1774 shows a straight double row of trees defining an avenue from Wollaton Hall to the eastern corner of Wollaton Park lake, and continuing through what is now Thompson's Wood to Derby Road opposite to the unfenced drive to the Odd House (Figure 86). Woodland, though extending north over much of the distance to Wollaton village along the western margin of the park, was shown by Chapman only well to the west of the tree-lined avenue reaching Derby Road, and the present beech wood east of it must date only from the late 18th century at the earliest. The present avenue of lime trees extending up to the Hall is not 'the great walk between Wollaton House and the lake' which was 'set with acorns between Michaelmas and Christmas' in 1660, if only because it intersects the boundary of Lenton parish notionally indicating the boundary of the Sixty Acres purchased from John Sherwin only in 1698 [17]. Indeed the present avenue of lime trees dates from no earlier than the middle of the 19th century, for there is no indication of it on Sanderson's map of 1835 or on the O.S. 1st edition 1-inch map of 1839. The avenue shown by Chapman must have been felled, right to Derby Road.

In or before 1803 this entrance to Wollaton Park was closed and bricked up, and a new one opened about 200 yards nearer to the toll-gate, probably at the margin of new beech woodland. But it was in use for only a few years because a new circumstance had arisen - the diversion of Beeston Lane - and in 1805 Lord Middleton had his bricklayer, Watkinson, move the entrance to its present position, directly opposite to the new junction of Beeston Lane with Derby Road [18]. A drive from this new entrance could strike straight across Wollaton Park, now the golf course, in a fairly direct line to the east side of Wollaton Hall. This new entrance was called Derby Gate, but it was not served by a lodge for 30 years. None existed when the Reform Bill rioters attacked the gate on 11 October 1831 after burning down Lowes' Beeston silk mill on the day after the destruction of Nottingham Castle (see Chapter VIII). It was near to this gate and just within the park that a troop of yeomanry cavalry put the rioters to flight, captured 16 of them, and handed them over to the 15th Hussars at Nottingham barracks. However, 'Lodge' was marked on Sanderson's map of 1835, which was surveyed in 1832-35, and it was called Beeston Lodge on the O.S. 1-inch map of 1839. In 1853 W.H.Wylie wrote : 'The lodge at the south side of the park, standing on the Beeston road (sic) is commonly known as Beeston Tower, and Allen [c.1870] described it as 'a massive stone castellet', recalling the time before 1831 when 'an ordinary five-barred gate did duty there'.

Godfrey [1884] stated that the 'castellated' Beeston Tower was built by the seventh Lord Middleton (that is, by Digby, who held the title from 1835 to 1856): but being marked on Sanderson's map of 1835 it must have been built in 1834 or earlier, and by the 6th Lord. It was thus built a decade later than Lenton Lodge at the new main entrance to Wollaton Park at Hillside, which was designed by Jeffrey Wyattville for the sixth Lord Middleton in 1822-23, and it clearly had a different designer [19]. The Beeston Tower was, indeed, a poor relation of Lenton Lodge, which was very much the prestige 'front gate' of the estate, said to have cost £25-30,000 to build - an enormous sum at that time - and with architectural features reminiscent of Wollaton Hall itself. The lodge that it replaced, at the former gate on the old road, near to the present park entrance from Middleton Boulevard, and shown on the 1823 map, was described by Laird [1810 167] thus: 'This gate is a handsome elevation of stone, with a neat lodge and light iron railing ...'. It was built by Stretton to replace the 'summer houses' which did duty as lodges until 1791.

Beeston Tower or Lodge did not gain mention in directories until the present century, though Lenton Lodge was regularly recorded. An early occupier - possibly the first - was John Matthews, who lived there rent-free in 1838, 1844 and 1845 [20]. He was 70 years old at the 1841 census, living with 22-year-old Charlotte Matthews, a servant, presumably his daughter or granddaughter. He was still there, aged 81, at the 1851 census, with Mary A. Matthews, aged 40. John Matthews was Ilkeston born, and was described as a porter. He was succeeded by John Langsdale and his wife Elizabeth. Langsdale was described by the census enumerator as an agricultural labourer in 1861, a gardener in 1871, and in 1881, when 77 years old and without his wife, simply as 'lodge porter'. Kelly [1912] recorded Amos Ashford as 'caretaker', followed in 1913 by William Hartshorn, who remained at Beeston Lodge for some twenty years until, in 1925, when Wollaton Hall and Park were sold to Nottingham Corporation, his rent-free tenancy of the lodge, with 27 perches of land, was 'determinable with engagement as lodge keeper' [21]. Beeston Tower was a gatehouse, and its function disappeared when the estate was sold. It was let from time to time, but has been unoccupied since about 1960. More recently rubbish was removed and the interior of the lodge cleaned up in collaboration with the Notts. Building Preservation Trust, and 'further work awaits a decision as to the future use of this interesting structure' [N.C.T.N. 75 (1988) 26]. The drive running from the lodge towards Wollaton Hall across a post-war plantation and the golf course is only a faint depression now, and difficult to trace.

Today Derby Road carries very heavy traffic, both local and distance traffic, and links the outer ring road (with Middleton Boulevard and Clifton Boulevard) and the outer by-pass along Woodside Road and Wollaton Vale, all dual carriageway motor roads. Despite the geographical changes brought about by such events as housing development on part of the north side of Derby Road after the sale of 1925, the expanded traffic arrangements at the University's North entrance and the development of the Queen's Medical Centre, as well as the enormous residential developments in western Nottingham, Derby Road itself is still confined between Wollaton Park wall and the fences by which John Wright and James Green enclosed their probably illegal encroachments on the turnpike road. Despite repeated suggestions that a dual carriageway road should be constructed, Derby Road bordering the campus still has only a single carriageway with effectively single-lane traffic.

Other roads and tracks

Cut Through Lane and Spring Close

Cut Through Lane was formerly the shortest, most direct and almost straight route for travellers on foot or horseback between the villages of Beeston and Lenton - or between Sawley Ferry and Nottingham Castle. The centres of both villages - and Keighton between them in the distant past - lay on the south-east side of it. It was part of the track linking a string of villages along the north-west margin of the Trent vale, typically sited on patches of valley-side gravel terrace. However, between Beeston and Lenton the gravel terrace at the margin of the vale is absent, and the valleyside route had to climb the valley slope.

Cut Through Lane was part of a 'dry' route, running parallel to a second line of movement on the valley floor about 500 metres away, and here represented by the line of the present Queens Road, Beeston and Hassock Lane, the only remaining part of which is the short section alongside the University tennis courts to the sports pavilion. Formerly this could be traced much further north-east, parallel to University Boulevard, leading to a raised track just north of Dunkirk Farm. The function of Cut Through Lane differed from that of Derby Road, which was a through route between towns, while Cut Through Lane was part of a chain of parish tracks. It is difficult to accept the hypothesis of Holland Walker that it was part of a long-distance drovers' route [22] if only because it was too narrow to allow control of a moving herd, and there is no evidence for or likelihood of such traffic along it. Another suggestion, that Cut Through Lane was 'part of an ancient road from Lincoln to Oxford' seems to be equally fanciful. However, it did continue via Leen-gate and Birch Lane (later Sherwin Road) Lenton, and by Lenton Road through The Park direct to the city centre, passing north of the Castle to Hounds-gate or Friar Lane, shown for example on Badder and Peat's map of 1740, and on Sanderson's of 1835 as an unfenced road. Dearden's map of 1844 labels it 'Footway from Beeston, Lenton etc.'.

Godfrey [1884] wrote that 'just at the bend of the road [Beeston Lane] it is joined by the foot-road known as Cut-Throat Lane' (Figure 91). It is perhaps more logical historically to think of Beeston Lane as diverging from the valley-side line continued by Cut Through. As suggested earlier, Beeston Lane turns sharply northwards not because of the narrowness of Cut Through but because the direct line presented a steep slope across the Highfield fault up to the vicinity of Highfield House which would daunt all horse-drawn wheeled traffic. Beyond this, despite the 'cut-through' or cutting near the top of Bath Hill near Lenton Hall, the track sloped even more steeply in crossing the scarp of the Clifton Fault [23]. The turnpike road circumvented this barrier by following the gentler slope up to the present Lenton Hurst and joining the Derby turnpike there. Cut Through Lane therefore remained in the 18th century what it had always been - at best a packhorse or riding track that was too narrow to be called a bridle road.

Until the University campus was developed after the second world war Cut Through Lane remained virtually unchanged, and the mansions near to it all had alternative access by drives from Beeston Lane (Lenton House and Highfield House) or Derby Road (Lenton Hall), although the families often used Cut Through Lane when riding or on foot. The gradient near the top was further reduced in the later 19th century, and east of the Clifton fault line the track was widened in 1838 when the quarries were in use. Crossing the Cut Through Lane from the Education/Pharmacy gardens (now occupied by 'the cowsheds') to Hugh Stewart Hall involved steps down to the lane level on both sides. Very little of the original lane now survives, the only part preserving anything like its pre-war form being the footpath from Beeston Lane to the entrance to Highfield House, but even here the lower stone courses of the original fence on the south-east side of the path can be seen only in places at the lower end. This section survives because the parallel drive to Highfield House has been adopted as part of the cross-campus road rather than Cut Through Lane itself.

Eastwards from Highfield House, Cut Through Lane followed the footpath on the south-east side of the campus road, and ran closely alongside the former Engineering buildings; then past the temporary buildings, over the brow of the hill, and through the cutting, now widened to carry a road (Figure 92). The original lane was on the Botany garden side, so that its line crosses the new road called Keighton Hill some yards from its north-western end. It then ran past the south-east side of the isolated sandstone rock exposure along the line of the present access road to the district heating station, and passed on through the sites of the Science Library and the tower block to join up with Spring Close across Sandy Lane-Abbey Lane, now Clifton Boulevard. Before its industrial development (see Chapter XIV) Spring Close was similar to Cut Through - called a footway in the Inclosure Award of 1768 - leading to a narrow bridge over the Leen and later a canal bridge. The wider part of Cut Through Lane north-east of the Clifton fault line was for a very short time in the 1950s widened into a fine road - the main spine of the campus road system - but this was soon superseded by a new road layout required by plans for the development of the Science area (see Chapter XVI).

Ordnance Survey maps showed an irregularity in the south-east fence of Cut Through Lane at the apex of the former Little Brome Close near to the present Science Library, marking the point at which the lane was once joined by a footpath. This path is shown on maps of the

Figure 92: Cut Through Lane between the Social Sciences building and the Botany Garden, c. 1905 and in 1986

earlier 19th century running south on a meandering course across Keighton Close; past the site of the medieval tile kilns; between Bacon Close and Quarrel Close; and crossing the Tottle Brook between the Ley Close and Mares Close to reach the line of Hassocks Lane. Since the closes named all belonged to the 'Alexander Wright group', and the path did not cross any land belonging to the main demesne estate, it was evidently the way of access from Lenton village via Spring Close to the various fields that were let to different Lenton farmers by the Gregory estate. But since these fields were those of Keighton village lands in medieval times it might also be interpreted as a medieval track.

At the north-west corner of the Keightons, Cut Through Lane was joined, just west of the top of the present Portland Hill, by the sunken track of ancient origins that was described in Chapter II. It is conceivable that this track may have linked up with the footpath described in the last paragraph, and it seems possible that it remained in occasional use long after the disappearance of Keighton village, with which it has been associated.

The antiquity of Cut Through Lane itself is clear. It formed an important land boundary in the Middle Ages, when it separated the open fields of the priory demesne to the north-west from the closes of Keighton, while its extension eastwards, Spring Close, ran between the common arable Beck Field of Lenton to the north and the Abbey Closes, originally the dairy farm of the priory, to the south. As a road, however, it was doomed to remain undeveloped because of the steep slopes, for which skerry bands in the Mercia Mudstones were mainly responsible (see Chapter I). The inclosure award of 1768 [Godfrey 1884 319] confirmed its status as a public footway rather than a road, in the words: 'From the town of Lenton westward over the allotment of John Webb in Bull Close, to a footbridge over the river Leen, and from thence over the allotment of the said George de Ligne Gregory, No. 11, to a place in the said Lordship of Lenton called Abbey Field, where a footway has usually heretofore been from Lenton to Beeston'. A narrow, hump-backed bridge was later built over the Nottingham canal, linking Spring Close to Leen-gate.

Sandy Lane, Abbey Lane and the ring road

In an inquisition of 1569 [24] Bartholomew Hill, a Lenton husbandman, swore on oath that 'these ways hereafter namyd be the comon high ways through the lordship of Lenton -

one highway leading from Nottingham towards Derbie
one other way from Nottingham to Wollaton
one other heighway from Nottingham to Strelley
one other heigh waye from Nottingham to Mannsfield in Sherwoodde'.

A north-south road down the Leen valley through Radford and Lenton was not mentioned, but this was probably not because one did not exist, but because it was controlled by Lenton Priory until the Dissolution, and was not 'the King's highway'. Indeed, successive priors - Hobson, Annsley and Heath - had insisted that 'there was not highway over the River of Trent through the Lordship of Lenton', and it was said that 'the Queen's tenants sustain yearly by high ways used over Trent hurt damages to the value of £20'. John Toll, a Radford carrier, testified that 'there is another waie now used which goythe through the meadows over Trent, which way has been stopped by the late prior of Lenton and chained so that none could pass that way without licence of the prior, which way so used ... is yerely great damages to ye tenants ...'. Others confirmed this 'toll road'. John Taylor, a Lenton cooper, said he 'hath known there hath been a chain on the way by the cross next to the Abbey gate and one other chain over the river of Leen'. Much of the traffic at that time appears to have been Wollaton coal purchased by people living south of the Trent. Nicholas Gorsson, a Nottingham goldsmith, said 'that he hath known Mr. Andrewes of Gotham, gent., and other gent. crave licence of the prior to carry their coals some tyme that way'.

Most of the coal traffic to the Wilford ford followed a route southward from the Wollaton pits on the west side of the Leen valley. The road on the east bank, through Radford and Lenton villages (which led to the Prior of Lenton's retreat at Aspley Hall in the 15th and 16th centuries [Barley 1987]) was not a through route except in the sense that there existed a network of parish tracks. West of the Leen the coal traffic to the country south of the Trent seems to have followed mainly (though not entirely) an ancient lane that in the 13th and 14th centuries ran south from the 'lost village' of Sutton Passeys to the lost village of Keighton. This follows partly from the fact that the shallow surface diggings of the coal pits were in coal seams that crop out in the west of Wollaton parish, and that the destination of the packhorses, with their pannier baskets of coal, was in the first place the shallow ford across the Trent at Wilford. The route ran approximately along the periphery of the original New Park of Wollaton and of the Beck Field, and at the position of the present Dunkirk flyover and traffic island offered alternatives - either through Lenton via Abbey Street and then Wilford Road (hence the chain near the priory gate) or via Dunkirk Road and the significantly named Chain Lane, to join the line of Trent Lane and approach the ford over the common pasture and meadow of The Holmes. The present ring road follows approximately this line, with Middleton Boulevard and Clifton Boulevard leading both local and through traffic to Clifton Bridge, the modern equivalent of Wilford ford. The road through Old Radford, Faraday Road, Radmarsh Road, Gregory Street and Lenton Lane is now by contrast, a relative backwater. There were probably other coal routes, crossing Wollaton Park, as discussed below.

Middleton Boulevard was constructed in 1926-27 in conjunction with the development of the residential Wollaton Park estate, but as part of the projected Nottingham outer ring road. Abbey Boulevard (later called Clifton Boulevard) followed in 1937-38 as the next stage of the ring road, also a dual carriageway as far as the Dunkirk traffic island, and formed the eastern boundary of the post-war University campus until the Medical School and Teaching Hospital were built east of it. The next stage of ring road development, the extension of Clifton Boulevard to the new Clifton Bridge, was a post-war scheme, like most of Clifton itself. A large industrial estate has subsequently developed on either side of it on low ground, substantially raised in level by dumping, partly of fly ash from the now demolished Wilford power station on the east side, and of miscellaneous waste on the west side, the whole area of the former Holmes having been purchased by Nottingham Corporation from the Gregory-Harlaxton estate.

Clifton Boulevard replaced and engulfed the lane called Sandy Lane in the north for at least 150 years (Figure 93) and Abbey Lane in the south. The former, from Cut Through Lane up to Derby Road, has been complicated recently by connections made to the Q.M.C. and the main University campus, and by the new underpass. Before 1822 it extended on from its present intersection with Derby Road as far as the old Derby turnpike at the old Wollaton Park gate off Middleton Boulevard. Its name was descriptive of its course over the soft Lenton Sandstone, and its antiquity is confirmed by its status as the boundary between the Beck Field of Lenton manor and the Abbey Fields of the priory demesne. Old roads often coincide with property boundaries, and although it is usually not obvious which was cause and which effect this is one reason for their persistence as landscape elements. Sandy Lane became Abbey Lane south of the intersection with Cut Through Lane, and ran through former priory demesne land to its junction with Dunkirk Road. In land surveys and terriers of the 16th and early 17th century Abbey Lane was called Brome Lane - a name that may have applied also to Sandy Lane since that has a similar connotation. Like Sandy Lane, Abbey Lane was very narrow and unimportant before the 1880s, when it was widened and metalled as far north as Highfield Road to serve the residential area being developed by the Osmaston Freehold Land Society (see Chapter VII).

The extension of Wollaton Park and the construction of the park wall across Sandy Lane in 1822-23 effectively prevented any further use of the lane as a public road; but in fact it was already virtually moribund. Chouler's map of 1823 (Figure 87) gives no indication of any

Figure 93: Sandy Lane being graded for the construction of Abbey (later Clifton) Boulevard, 1936-37
Soft Lenton Sandstone overlooks the valley floor and Dunkirk. Note in distance, left to right, Wilford power station, the Dunkirk Hotel and the soap factory. [Photo. by courtesy City Engineer'sDepartment and NCLS]

extension north of the old Derby turnpike, and Sandy Lane was closed by a gate. The reason is clear. The opening of the Nottingham canal on a parallel line nearby had effectively robbed it of coal traffic over 20 years earlier. At about the same time, on 3 October 1796, after a special Sessions held at the Admiral Rodney (Wollaton) on 16 September 1796, Justices the Hon. Henry Sedley and Thomas Charlton ordered the diversion of a footway that ran across Wollaton Park from its north side on the Ilkeston turnpike to the [old] Derby turnpike at the lodge gates (off the present Middleton Boulevard), to a new line further east, outside the park wall [Meaby 1947 96-97]. Sanderson's maps of the mid-1830s show Sandy Lane as no more than a cart track, gated at both ends, running along a field boundary, but unfenced on the Lenton Firs side, and with a small diversion round a copse planted directly on its line, and later removed when a row of trees was planted along it. It remained a right of way, but no more than a footpath down to the 1930s.

The medieval origins of this north-south road as a track linking the extinct villages of Sutton Passeys and Keighton has been mentioned earlier. On 24 June 1301, for example, Roger, son of William de Lenton, granted to Hugh de Wollaton of Nottingham half an acre of arable land in the fields of Lenton and Radford (here Beck Field) 'lying in the Longebothem between the road which was called Cakethemgate on the east and the land of Henry de Wolaton on the west, and abutting upon the King's highway which is called Derbygate towards the south' [25] . We can locate this selion approximately, and Cakethemgate must surely be identified as 'Keightongate', phonetically if not etymologically. It was 'the lane towards Keighton' (from Sutton Passeys). Alan Cameron [1976] in a study of Sutton Passeys writes of the lane immediately at the east end of the village, known in the 14th century as Cross Lane[26], that it was 'cognate with the lane at the end of the village which leads to the south ... the lane towards Lenton', and 'the lane towards Keighton' [Cameron 1976 50]. Southwards this probably became Cakethemgate, which either extended into Sandy Lane or linked up with it. The extinction of both Sutton Passeys and Keighton villages in the second half of the 15th century (see Cameron 1976 57, and Chapter II above) must have greatly reduced the use of this route, which revived with the growth of coal traffic until that was usurped by the Nottingham Canal in the 1790s.

Old tracks on and near the campus

Several old tracks not so far mentioned, and of which only vestiges now remain in the landscape, functioned permanently or temporarily in past times as parts of the pattern of local routes for carts, riders, pack animals or pedestrians.

1. A fragment of a Wollaton coal road.

On the sandstone spur extending south-east from the Cripps Health Centre and the adjoining coniferous plantation there is a long, straight, narrow depression or shallow trench along the ridge slightly below its crest on the south-west side running towards the old quarry face overlooking the Physics-Mathematics car park (Figure 94). This depression ends abruptly where ground was cut away in grading the diverted Cut Through Lane. When this road was under construction in 1959 the depression could be seen in section, and was revealed as a former track, partially metalled with rough stones, including skerry and pebbles, and containing many small fragments of coal. Originally the track must have continued beyond the quarry face over the 'gorse covered hillock of considerable size' that was removed by quarrying in 1838 [Lawson Lowe 1871], descending to the intersection of Cut Through Lane/Spring Close with Sandy Lane/Abbey Lane. Because of its location it is highly unlikely that it was simply a farm track, but very probable that it formed part of a route along which coal was carted or carried from the Wollaton pits across what is now Wollaton Park to Wilford ford and beyond, joining

Figure 94: Part of an old track below Cripps Health Centre, probably part of a coal road from the pits at Wollaton to the ford at Wilford.
Viewed from south of the Cripps Student Health Centre. 1991

the route described above at its intersection with Cut Through Lane. It would have passed very close to the Keighton kilns, in which coal was used for several centuries.

Although William de Morteyn of Wollaton owned a coal mine at Cossall in 1283, and his son leased it in 1316, Wollaton's mines in the early shallow-mining phase of operation are thought to have been developed first in the second half of the 15th century [Smith 1989], and when the Willoughby family moved to Wollaton from Willoughby-on-the-Wolds around 1470 coal was already contributing to their income. The pits were all situated on the outcrop of Coal Measures in the Old Park of Wollaton, between Wollaton manor house and village and Bilborough. Five small bell pits and a 'levell pitte' were working in 1493, according to the will of Sir Henry Willoughby, and 8 to 10 pits were operating by 1526. The output in 1502 was about 5,000 tons a year, and averaged 6-10,000 tons from 1526 to 1547. There was a significant though irregular output through the 16th century, with a peak of about 15,000 tons a year by the 1580s. Thirty-five colliers lived at Wollaton in 1573, and the Wollaton colliery was a large undertaking using the most advanced technology of the time with the introduction of Cornish pumping methods in the early 1570s. The pits were drained by a sough first built by Sir Henry Willoughby in about 1480, refurbished in the early 16th century and rebuilt in the 1550s at great expense. The sough crossed Lenton manor (though not the priory demesne) and from Wollaton passed through Beck Field, Nether Thakholme Meadow, across Derby Road and through Alwell Field to discharge into the river Leen near Hell More (marked on the Sherwood Forest map of 1609). Before the Dissolution the prior of Lenton was paid an annual rent of 8 rooks, later increased to 12 rucks of coal a year or 24s. for the easement.

Much Wollaton coal was delivered and sold to local domestic users. Transport was a major element in the price of coal in the 15th and 16th centuries, and to carry it five miles from the pits raised the price by over 60 per cent, so that early mines usually served only the domestic market in their immediate locality. Wollaton pits, however, were near enough to river transport on the Trent to be able to serve economically an extensive market down-river to Newark and beyond, the coal being shipped mainly from 'the Nottingham Bridges', at or near Trent Bridge. However it was also sold in the parishes south of the Trent, and much crossed the river at Wilford. Coal was carried from the Old Park north of Wollaton village along several routes, the line chosen being determined by the best combination of directness and easy grading. The exact route or routes to the Nottingham bridges is not known, but one may have followed approximately the line of the sough. It is said that Coalpit Lane (see Dearden's map) leading down to Hockley, was opened up in about 1590 to make an easy gradient for handling the coal traffic from Wollaton pits, the route from Wollaton being probably through Radford - New Radford - Canning Circus - Back Side (Wollaton Street) - Coal Pit Lane and through to Beller Gate, Hollowstone and the Leen bridge, either embarking on the east side of the bridge or by the bridge itself via Bridge Foot, linking Fisher Gate with Narrow Marsh.

Some carts from the pits passed through Lenton village, along Wilford Road and the Holmes road to Wilford ford, near the present Clifton Bridge, and then to Trent Bridge south-east of the river. However, coal carried by horse or donkey pannier for the country districts south of the Trent, crossing at Wilford ford, could follow a more direct line, maintaining height across what is now Wollaton Park before dropping into the Trent vale at Lenton. The old track seen in Figure 94 must have been part of one or more such lines, probably crossing Derby Road a little west of the top of Adams Hill and continuing along Abbey Lane, Chain Lane and a precursor of Trent Lane to the ford. The popularity of the Wilford ford in 1593 led the Bellman of Nottingham, anxious to exact tolls in the town, to forbid (unsuccessfully) its use by coal carts [Smith 1989 10].

By the 1590s the Wollaton pits were fighting a losing battle against water. In the early 17th century, when the most accessible coal at Wollaton was worked out and the 130 feet deep pits struggled constantly against flooding, Humphrey Beaumont of Coleorton, Leicestershire took over the local industry by agreement with Sir Percival Willoughby and the Edge family. He made the Strelley pits economically viable by building a railed wagonway from them to Wollaton Lane - the first in England [Smith 1960] - and closed the Wollaton pits to ensure the competitiveness of those at Strelley. The former never recovered, and although Bartholomew Pearson a Beeston yeoman (who as a servant of Sir Percival had taken part in an ill-fated attempt to establish a colony in Newfoundland) leased them from Sir Percival in a succession of leases (with others), for example in 1618, 1627, 1632-33-34, he ran them down, and the workings were abandoned by 1644.

The use of the track on the campus for transporting Wollaton coal can therefore be dated to the period of about 160 years from about 1470 to 1630. As discussed in earlier chapters, from the Dissolution of 1538 onwards the Willoughbys leased from the Crown lessees the northern tract of the campus, the Abbey Fields, together with the Sixty Acres (in the present Wollaton Park) at least in part to ensure passage for coal from their pits to the lanes through the commons of The Greens and The Holmes leading to Wilford ford, and Sir Percival Willoughby in 1621 actually sub-let the Abbey Fields and the Warren for five years to Bartholomew Pearson 1621 when he was working the pits. Sir Percival's lease of former priory demesne lands from Sir William Hicks was, significantly, not renewed in 1630 (see Chapter IV) when the coal traffic across the campus had virtually ceased - a more convincing reason for Sir Percival's surrender of the lease than his persistent failure to pay his rents.

2. Lenton Hall to Lenton tollgate.

Sanderson's map of 1835 showed a track curving gently north-westwards from the northern end of Lenton Hall to join Derby Road immediately south-west of the Lenton toll gate. Although Chouler's 1822 map did not show the track it included a gate which must have served it, in such a position that it must date from after the diversion of Beeston Lane in 1804-05. The track may have been simply a drive from Lenton Hall with gentle gradients and avoiding passage through the toll gate for vehicles heading for Derbyshire where important business and family interests of the Wrights were located. However, it could be seen as in origin a medieval track along which marl was carted or dragged from the marl pit in Lenton Hall gardens to the arable Sixty Acres field north of Derby Road.

3. Hassocks Lane.

The short section of drive that runs alongside the tennis courts on the University sports ground is a remnant of the former Hassocks Lane, part of a valley floor route that paralleled Cut Through Lane, and avoided its steep gradients, though it would be subject to seasonal flooding. However the two routes were not alternatives because they led in different directions. An ancient road called Coventry Lane is said to have crossed the Trent at Attenborough [Godfrey 1884 13] (though there is no sign of the crossing place on Figure 95) with a branch turning eastwards near the river bank to pass below Chilwell and Beeston, and join up with the present Queens Road, and just beyond its junction with Humber Road pass forward along Hassocks Lane to the University sports ground. Before inclosure the road certainly existed from the junction with Dovecote Lane by Middle Pasture Road, later Queens Road, Beeston, and the short Albert Road, running into Hassocks Lane. Maps dating from before the 1920s show the line continuing past Hassocks Farm (near the present University sports pavilion) along tree-lined hedgerows over the meadows formerly called Doddesholme, and through the former Mares Closes; between West Tamworth and South Tamworth and linking up with an embanked track across East Tamworth immediately north of the former Dunkirk Farm. This may have led on via Chain Lane to the Church ford at Wilford. It is tempting to speculate that this track may have served medieval Morton, which was centred - if indeed it had a territorial centre - around Dunkirk Lodge and Dunkirk Farm. On the Beeston inclosure map of 1809

Hassocks Lane extended as far north-east as the public tennis courts near the middle of University Boulevard, giving access from Beeston to all the closes ranged along both sides of it, formed from Beeston Hassocks common pasture. Like Queens Road, therefore, Hassocks Lane was an enclosure road, and perhaps little of it coincided exactly with the line of the earlier track through the common grazing land.

4. The meandering footpath southwards from Cut Through Lane through the Keightons has been discussed above, and another footpath extending south in continuation of a track from Wollaton Hall to the old park gate as far as Broadgate, Beeston has also been mentioned. This path running south past Lenton Abbey, crossed the Tottle Brook to reach the end of Salthouse Lane. The right of way survived into the 1920s when Lenton Abbey housing estate was developed, but the southern end of the avenue in Wollaton Park was lost when the park gate moved, and is now indistinguishable within Thompson's Wood. The footpath to Salthouse Lane was partly maintained after the building operations by the preservation of pedestrian access from Woodside Road to Salthouse Lane. Almost parallel to it, but entirely within the open Tuttle Brook Field, was an unfenced road shown on Chapman's map surveyed in 1774, which extended the line of a footpath from Wollaton village alongside but outside the park wall from the point where Derby Road crossed the Tottle Brook to Beeston High Road (Sawley turnpike) approximately opposite to the present Regent Street, Beeston. This route disappeared in the Beeston inclosure of 1809.

5. One former footpath in the University district changed beyond recognition in the 1920s. It linked Lenton and Beeston directly through the lower part of the former Highfield estate. It might be thought that its replacement is the busy dual carriageway road of University Boulevard; but equally it could be claimed that the road is a new feature replacing Hassocks Lane , and that the footpath's true successor is the walk now winding through University Park on the south-east side of the lake. Neither interpretation is wholly acceptable. Beeston Road, Dunkirk represents the footpath at its eastern end, upgraded when Dunkirk was undergoing residential development in the 1880s. The widening and extension of Beeston Road in the 1920s under Sir Jesse Boot's scheme (discussed in detail in Chapter XVI) involved building University Boulevard on a line diverging from the former footpath, which ran alongside the screen of trees dividing it from the 'pleasure grounds' or miniature park with its 'fishpond' created by Alfred Lowe. Its line is now separated from the Boulevard by lawns and gardens, and its successor within the park, following the south-east shore of University Park lake, has a quite different function. At the Beeston end the original footpath crossed another at the southern apex of University Park. This led northwards along the east bank of the Tottle Brook (now culverted) to Beeston Lane at the University's west entrance, and southwards along the present drive into the University sports grounds to meet Hassocks Lane. The path from Dunkirk, crossing the Tottle Brook by a footbridge, continued south-westwards alongside Pasture Dike and via Fletcher Road and The City reached Middle Street and the old centre of Beeston village.

A note on canals and the river Trent

Where possible roads and tracks before the parish inclosures made use of common lands, which sometimes acquired or retained common status because they carried public roads. On a broader scale, however, good and reliable fords over major rivers such as the Trent were important factors in establishing the form of the through road networks down to the 18th century, and for that reason bridges have frequently been built at former major fords - for example, Trent Bridge, Sawley Bridge and recently Clifton Bridge. The north-south roads down both sides of the Leen valley converged at the northern apex of The Holmes. That from Radford, following Gregory Street and Wilford Road, crossing the Leen by the old bridge marked on Smythe's map of 1632 (later replaced by Clayton's Bridge) was joined by the road discussed above - Abbey Lane joining Dunkirk Road leading to Chain Lane [27]. The combined route crossed the common pasture and meadow to Wilford ford approximately along the direct line of Trent Lane, itself an inclosure road of 1768.

The ford at Wilford shoals was one of the best and most reliable along the Trent, for physiographic reasons related to its location below the knick point now represented by Beeston weir. The ford extended over several hundred yards, had a firm, gravelly bed, and at its shallowest point a summer depth of less than 20 inches; for example, 14½ inches in 1782, 20 inches in 1786 - the shallowest crossing along the whole course of the river through Nottinghamshire [28]. William Jessop, a famous canal engineer as well as Engineer to the Trent Navigation Company [Evans 1939 15] in his report on the river of 1786 (see Figure 95) was concerned primarily with navigation conditions, but he would have been well aware of the fact that the fords most favourable to road traffic were those least favourable for boat traffic. One of the major conclusions of his report was that some 'cuts' were needed for boats to circumvent the most difficult parts of the river, and especially three major fords. He stated that it was not an exaggeration to say that 'at the three Shoals of Holme, Nottingham Bridge and Wilford there must be kept, for the purpose of assisting the others upstream , six horses extraordinary: and that those horses, with their drivers, should earn 3s. a day or £ 280 per annum ...'. For technical reasons at that time regular dredging at the shoals was not feasible, and it would have had serious consequences by stopping road traffic completely. A dozen years later Nottingham Bridge and Wilford shoals had both been by-passed - by the Nottingham Canal and the Beeston Cut respectively. The 'cuts' represented a compromise between the conflicting interests of road and river traffic; but the Nottingham Canal had a different origin.

In 1796, the year before the first steps were taken towards the breakup of the Milward estate, Lenton's potentialities for industrial and commercial development were greatly enhanced by the completion and opening of the Nottingham Canal and the Beeston Cut. The short section of the Nottingham Canal between Hillside and the Abbey Street bridge, which now carries the river Leen water, is the only actual physical association of a canal with the campus, forming as it does the eastern boundary of the site of the Queen's Medical Centre. In respect of the history of the campus it is of interest not only because of the industrial and associated housing developments that it stimulated on the tract of land that was later to become the site of the University Hospital and Medical School - a late addition to the campus - but also because two men who were intimately involved in its planning and construction bought land and built mansions on the opposite (west) side of the campus in 1798. They were Francis Evans of Lenton Grove and James Green of Lenton Abbey.

The involvement of Francis Evans with the Nottingham Canal has been discussed at some length in Chapter XI, but little was said in Chapter X about James Green's contribution, which should now be considered. The 14½-mile Cromford Canal, which received Parliamentary approval in 1789 [29 G 3, c 74] was designed to provide access to the river Trent near Long Eaton for the products of industries along the river Derwent as far upstream as Arkwright's Mills at Cromford, via the earlier (1777-79) Erewash Canal from Langley Mill to Sawley [29]. Nottingham interests, especially local coal owners including Lord Middleton, alarmed by the proposed connection, in September 1790 called a public meeting for 5 November to discuss a 'navigable Cut from the Cromford Canal above Langley Bridge to pass through Trowell (or in whatsoever other Direction may upon a Survey be thought most eligible) and by the Side of the Town of Nottingham to the River Trent below the Bridge, near Sneinton Meadow' [30]. Mr. William Jessop was 'applied to' to act as Engineer for the intended Nottingham Canal. The Beeston Cut, under consideration at least as early as 1782 by the Trent Navigation Company to avoid the Wilford shoals, was also proposed [31]. A committee was appointed and a fortnight later resolved to appoint Mr. Francis Evans as Clerk and Mr. Jessop to 'explore the tract of

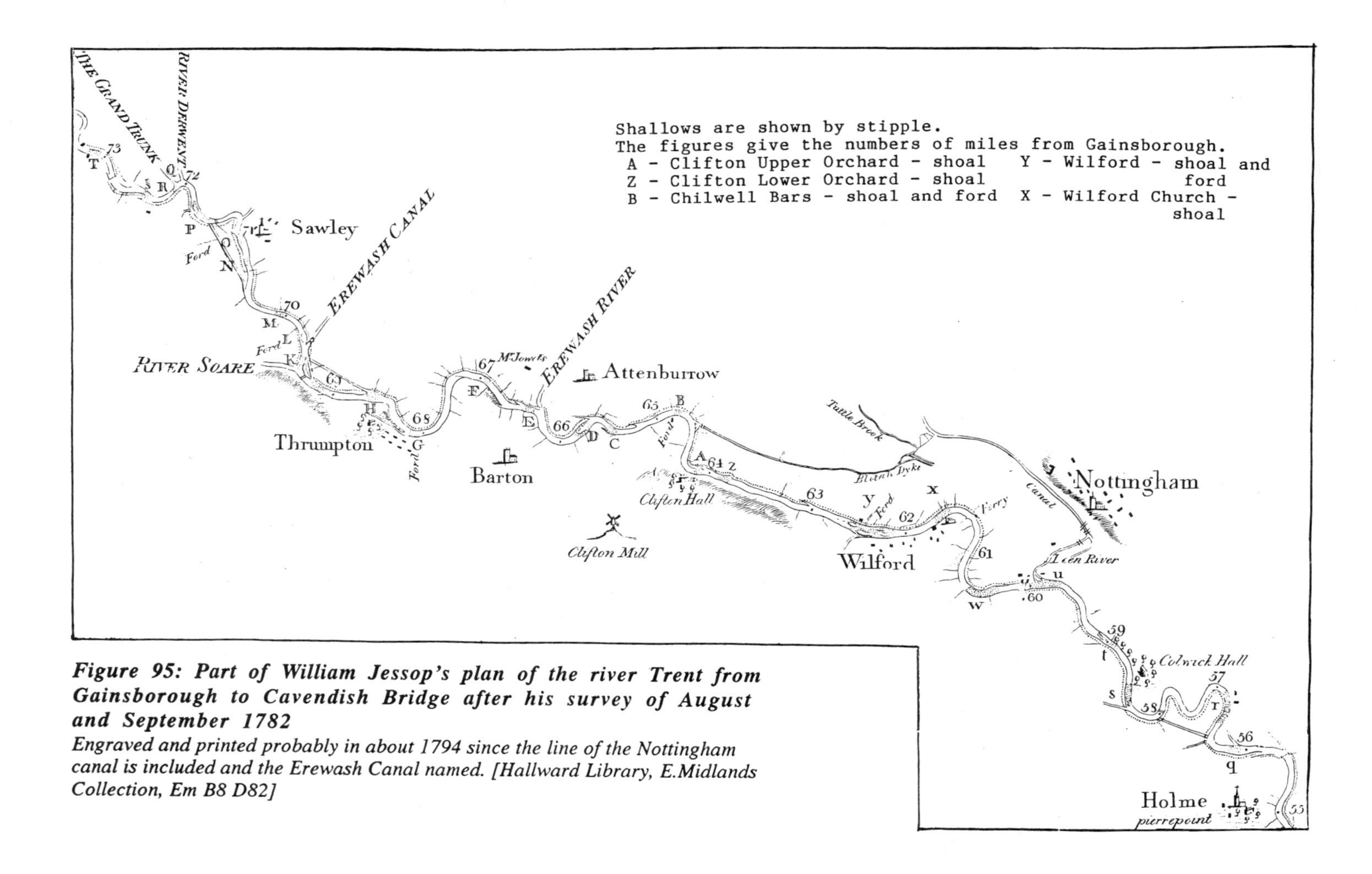

Figure 95: Part of William Jessop's plan of the river Trent from Gainsborough to Cavendish Bridge after his survey of August and September 1782

Engraved and printed probably in about 1794 since the line of the Nottingham canal is included and the Erewash Canal named. [Hallward Library, E.Midlands Collection, Em B8 D82]

Country for the purpose of making a navigable canal from the Cromford Canal to the Town of Nottingham and thence to the River Trent near the Trent Bridge, and also for the making of a collateral Cut from the Trent through Beeston Meadow to unite with the proposed canal at or near Lenton', and to make a survey and estimate, with special reference to the supply of water and probable extent of coal transport.

Evidently Lord Middleton was already pressing for his own route past his Wollaton pits and down the Leen valley to Lenton, for on 2 December 1790 'Mr. Jessop, having taken a general view of the country' [and clearly preferring the line down the Tottle Brook valley] 'gave his opinion that the Line recommended by Lord Middleton would on account of the extent of Deep Cutting and Tunnel be in point of expence almost unpracticable'. Lord Middleton persisted. On 15 June 1791 Jessop asked to be excused from his assignment, ostensibly through illness and pressure of other commitments, which was certainly formidable. He recommended James Green of Wollaton to make the detailed survey, but agreed that he could give general advice, and had given 'personal instructions to proceed in the Surveys' to Green.

In early August 1791 Parliamentary approval of powers to proceed were applied for, and on 29 September 1791 Jessop's report was considered. His recommended line was estimated to cost £52,211, plus £7,000 for reservoirs and £4,288 for the Beeston Cut. But a meeting at Nottingham Guildhall in late October heard that Jessop had reported that Lord Middleton would not assent to the canal unless a line on the east side of Wollaton Park was to be adopted instead of that proposed on the west side, at an additional expense of about £2,500 - a wildly optimistic figure in view of the fact that 14 locks would be required instead of two - and Green was later vilified on account of this unattainable budget, which was not of his making. In January 1792 the Bill was drafted to conform with Lord Middleton's proposal, and the Trent Navigation Company would not accept proposals for the Beeston Cut. Jessop's revised cost estimates totalled £49,920, including £45,185 for the Nottingham Canal and £4,735 for the Beeston Cut, sums more closely related to the original £50,000 limit of cost imposed than to reality. In early February the Beeston Cut was removed from the Bill, while Jessop and others met Lord Middleton again to discuss his objections.

The first General Assembly of the canal company at the White Hart Inn, Nottingham on 26 June 1792, when Jessop was to submit plans, specifications and estimates, formally appointed Francis Evans to be Clerk, with Benjamin Outram of Butterley Hall as Engineer, and James Green to 'superintend the making of the canal under the direction of Mr. Jessop'. Green was to attend to 'purchase of materials and the proper execution of the works, at £ 300 per annum out of which he is to find a clerk'. He was also to mark out an amended line of the canal at Wollaton (Figure 96). Advertisements in East Midlands newspapers in July show that Green lost no time in recruiting workmen and inviting tenders for supplies, and work on building the canal actually began on 30 July 1792.

Green's responsibilities were onerous, for he undertook to make contracts, appoint staff and workers, purchase materials, treat with land owners and deal with the innumeerable details of planning and construction. He continued to receive his salary until March 1795, beyond which he agreed to attend to final details of the work without payment. The canal opened for boats from the Trent to the newly formed town wharves at Nottingham on 30 July 1793, but the more difficult summit section with its many locks was not navigable until the end of July 1795. On 8 October 1794 Jessop was informed of the dissatisfaction of the Committee and the Proprietors with 'the erroneous construction of many works on the canal and the very large expenditure incurred'. This was certainly due in part to the adoption of Lord Middleton's line across the watershed to the Leen valley against Jessop's better judgment, but at this juncture was probably directed against Green, because a year earlier, on 22 October 1793 'objections were raised to Mr. Green having undertaken the construction of part of the Grantham canal' without the previous consent of the Committee, who 'expect that he shall

Figure 96: James Green's 1791 survey of the amended proposed line of the Nottingham Canal
Reduced copy of an original map deposited at the Local Studies Library, Nottingham [Courtesy NCLS]

continue to pay as much attention as usual to the making of the Nottingham Canal'.

James Green's heavy involvement in the construction of the Grantham Canal, authorized in 1793 [33 G 3 c 94] was very similar to, and under much the same auspices as that in the Nottingham Canal project. A plan for the Grantham Canal proposed by William Jessop was laid before the promoting committee on 29 October 1791, and at the first Annual General Meeting on 1 July 1793 James Green was formally appointed to be responsible for marking out the line of that part of the canal in Nottinghamshire from Cropwell Butler to the river Trent, together with a branch to Bingham that was never built, and he was called 'superintendent' of the building of this part of the Grantham Canal. All 33 miles of this canal were opened in 1797 after Green's final report in February 1797, about a year after the Nottingham Canal opened. In 1798 John Simpson appears to have replaced Green as superintendent, and so far as is known this ended Green's active career as a canal builder. In 1797-98 he would have been about 50 years old, since his first wife, Sarah, died in 1811 aged 60 [32]. In early 1798 he bought the land that became the Lenton Abbey estate and built his house there. The land transaction involved him in arrangements with Francis Evans, his Nottingham Canal colleague who already owned nearby land, and it is perhaps not too fanciful to suppose that James Green was led to Lenton Abbey through his acquaintance with Evans.

The Nottingham Canal, $14^3/_4$ miles long, and costing in the end £80,000, was completed in April 1796, and the Beeston Cut was necessarily opened at the same time. The Cut was authorized by an Amending Act for the improvement of the Trent navigation passed in 1794, and its construction began almost at once. It was envisaged quite independently, before the Nottingham Canal was first mooted, as a by-pass round the Wilford shoals for Trent river traffic by William Jessop in 1782. Jessop's map to illustrate his survey was published, updated, only in about 1794 [33] (Figure 95). It showed the line of the 'Intended Nottingham Canal' and an uncanalized Blotah Dyke: but Green's survey map of 1791 [34] showed an intended canalized Blotah Dyke as 'The Side Branch' from the river Trent above Beeston weir towards Lenton (Figure 96). South of Chain Lane Blotah Dyke followed the eastern boundary of the former priory demesne, and the Beeston Cut followed Blotah Dyke.

The proposals being made for the Beeston Cut (then usually called 'Beeston Meadow Cut') were not acceptable to the Trent Navigation Company in early 1792, and were removed from the Nottingham Canal Bill. The Cut was built later by the Trent Navigation Company itself, and Green was probably not involved since negotiations in early 1774 in respect of its connection to the Nottingham Canal were handled by Jessop. River traffic avoiding the Wilford shoals, boats that included those from the Erewash Canal, and some from the Cromford Canal, joined traffic on the Nottingham Canal at the Chain Bridge, Lenton, to travel through Nottingham to the river Trent below Trent Bridge. Some passed across the river to join the Grantham Canal. The introduction of this integrated system in the last three years of the 18th century was a great stimulus to industrial development in the area, and particularly in Lenton.

Occasional setbacks through human or natural agency included, for example, 'wilful breaches' of the canal banks in 1795 in the section alongside the present Queens Medical Centre, and floodwater passing from the river Trent through the Beeston Cut which caused serious damage to the Nottingham Canal in 1797 [35] . But traffic burgeoned, the barges carrying a wide variety of materials and goods. By 1808 tonnage income from the Butterley Company alone reached £1,000 a year. From the late 1830s, however, the advantages of rail transport exerted increasing pressure on canal trade. Although a petition prepared against the Midland Counties Railway Bill in February-March 1836 helped to persuade the Railways Committee of the House of Commons to order, on 13 April 1836, that the planned Midland Counties Railway branch into Nottingham be abandoned, the Derby to Nottingham line was opened in 1839.

Significantly the tonnage on the Nottingham Canal reached its maximum in 1840, and by 1852 it had halved, through progressive and rapid erosion by railway competition. The Nottingham Canal Company after long negotiations was taken over by the Ambergate, Nottingham and Boston and Eastern Junction Railway Company, which became part of the Great Northern Railway Company in 1861. The surviving canal traffic was mainly local movement of coal, gravel, roadstone and manure. By 1928 the Nottingham Canal was in disuse, the motor lorry having joined the railway in competition, and in 1937 it was finally abandoned except for the section from Meadow Lane lock in Nottingham to Lenton, connecting with the Beeston Cut, which was transferred back to the ownership of the Trent Navigation Company. Silting and flooding of the Nottingham Canal became such a nuisance that Nottingham Corporation purchased 3½ miles of it within the city boundary in 1952, proposing to make a green walk along its course, with pools for fishing and 'cascades in place of the locks'. Infilling and culverting began in 1955, but the plan was abandoned when the Raleigh Company bought the canal land adjoining its factory for development, thereby breaking the line of the canal and blocking any possible through walk. However, the 8-mile section from Balloon Woods to Langley Mill survives in fragmentary form. The Beeston Cut and the section of the Nottingham Canal linking it to the river Trent - the 'Wilford Shoals Bypass' - continued in use, but mainly by pleasure craft. The British Waterways Board neglected the towpath until in 1975 Nottingham Civic Society suggested that the Council should restore it as a public walk, an 'urban trail', now completed. Part of the canal itself has been given a new lease of useful life as a leisure amenity with the construction of the marina at Castle Meadow[36].

Railways

Although no railway line runs through the campus there are two historically important lines nearby, the Nottingham and Derby line through Dunkirk, skirting the playing fields, and the Nottingham and Mansfield line using the Leen valley. The former takes advantage of the low line formerly called The Rounds, and discussed in earlier chapters, and the extensive Beeston sidings, which closed in 1965, were developed here, mainly in Lenton parish. Its building in 1837-39 had an important if indirect effect on the physical landscape of the campus through the use of two quarries in the construction of the Dunkirk railway embankment in 1838. However, there was never a nearby station on this line, although an intended station at Dunkirk was rumoured more than once. The Nottingham-Mansfield line (1848) up the east side of the Leen valley had a particular connection with the campus only because of its influence on the industrial development of Spring Close in the second half of the 19th century, as will be shown in the next chapter. It passed between Old and New Lenton, with Lenton station conveniently located immediately north of its crossing of Derby Road, and Radford station in a similar position where it crossed Ilkeston Road. The Radford and Trowell branch (1875) taking off eastwards just north of Radford station paralleled the Nottingham Canal, and must have usurped some of its traffic.

The first known 'railway' in the Nottingham area - and perhaps in the country - was the short waggonway laid by Humphrey Beaumont to serve the Strelley coal pits in about 1604, and mentioned above. From the middle of the 18th century many other such rail tracks for horse-drawn trucks, usually making use of gravity, were used for short hauls of heavy materials, notably coal and mineral ores, from mines and quarries to the newly built canals in the valleys. The earliest railways in the modern sense, such as the Cromford and High Peak (1830-31) and the Leicester and Swannington (1832-33) still used inclines powered by stationary engines. The first true railroad in the East Midlands, the Nottingham to Derby section of the Midland Counties Railway, opened in 1839 though first planned in 1832, was similarly a response primarily to the needs of mineral transport, especially of coal. Although it stimulated the growth of Dunkirk later in the century, partly through unrealized expectations, the line was too far from the campus to affect it directly, except through the circumstances of its construction.

The Midland Counties Railway was conceived at a meeting of coal owners on 16 August 1832 at The Sun Inn, Eastwood [37] where a wall plaque commemorates a later meeting in November 1833 at which the decision to proceed was taken. Parliamentary notices for the building of the railway were deposited, but an Act was obtained only in 1836, after a stormy passage strenuously opposed by rival interests. The original subscribers to the project were Messrs. Barber and Walker (£10,000), John Wright (£5,000), E.M.Mundy (£5,000) and four others together subscribing £7,000 [38]. It would not be surprising, therefore, to find John Wright and his son and heir Francis (by now also a partner in the Butterley Company and leading forward its development) providing construction material for the three-mile long railway embankment running through Dunkirk from their nearby park. The two quarries from which the material was obtained have been described in Chapter I.

Work on the Nottingham to Derby line began in May 1837, directed by Charles B. Vignoles. At the beginning of 1838 1,000 men were busy, and by June 1838 some 4,000 men and 385 horses were engaged on this line and that from Derby to Leicester. In December 1838 4,035 men and 457 horses were employed, as well as a stationary engine and two locomotives[39]. From 4 June to 29 December 1838 1,462,430 cubic yards of 'earthwork' was executed at a cost of £197,781, and a substantial part of the operation must have been the transport of sandstone across the open fields down to the railway embankment at Dunkirk from the two quarries on the campus. It may be presumed that the greater part of the work was done in the summer and autumn of 1838, and the scale and intensity of the operation can be imagined. A view of the completed embankment is shown in an engraving published about four years later[40] (see Figure 97). The line was ready for use by the spring of 1839, and the inaugural train ran on 30 May 1839. A rail link from Nottingham to Leicester was effected by the opening of the line from Trent Junction to Leicester on 5 May 1840, and the Leicester to Rugby (Midland Counties) line opened 1 July 1840 gave a circuitous link to London.

The Midland Counties Railway Companion, printed in 1840 only a few months after the line opened, included the following passage [Allen 1840 9]. 'A little further on the towers of the lodge for Wollaton Hall may be distinctly seen: and, situate on the summit of a high hill, is the mansion of John Wright Esq., [that is, Lenton Hall]. In front of the house a large portion of the hill has been cut away, and the soil removed to form the embankment for the Railway for several miles, Mr. Wright having disposed of it to the Railway Company for that purpose. The neat country residence of Alfred Lowe Esq. of Highfields may also be seen.' In 1840 the scars of quarrying must have been very prominent, and although soon masked by vegetation except on near-vertical faces the marks of quarrying in the former Abbey Field were still visible on aerial photographs taken before the Science site was developed on the campus north-west of Cut Through Lane. Lawson Lowe of Highfield House wrote in 1871: 'On the eastern side of the mansion [Lenton Hall] towards the village of Old Lenton, there was a picturesque, gorse-covered sandy hillock of considerable size which was entirely removed about thirty-three years ago, and the soil used in the formation of the Midland Railway between Nottingham and Derby'. A continuation of the old coal track discussed above will have been removed with it.

The Lenton quarry tramway of 1838 (Figure 97)

Nothing now remains to show how the material from the 1838 quarries was transported down to the railway, but the route is known because of the accidental timing of the original publication of the southern two quarter sheets of the O.S. First edition one inch to one mile map in 1839 [41]. A track is shown running from near the junction of Cut Through Lane with Sandy Lane-Abbey Lane (Clifton Boulevard), alongside and a little west of Abbey Lane to the northern apex of the Dunkirk housing estate (not then in existence) and on past the site of the later Dunkirk Hotel to reach the railway near the former Dunkirk Farm house. The track was not shown on Sanderson's map of 1835, and it is missing from all later maps other than reprints of the original O.S. 1-inch map, suggesting that it was a temporary feature serving only the quarry in Abbey Field and, via Cut Through Lane, that in Lenton Hall Close. It was probably in use for less than a year.

Although its nature is not clear from the map, the track was almost certainly a tramway for horse-drawn trucks, being depicted by full, thin parallel lines, whereas an unfenced road would have been shown by pecked lines. It declined in altitude steadily and continuously from about 91 feet O.D. at Cut Through Lane to 85.5 feet at the northern apex of the housing estate, and crossed Beeston Road (then a footpath) at about 84 feet O.D., reaching the line of Montpelier Road at about 82 feet O.D.. There was a gentle downgrade over the whole length of the track to the railway embankment, just over half a mile, at about 1 in 270.

It is relevant to recall that Benjamin Outram and William Jessop the canal engineer, two of John Wright's three original partners in the Butterley Company in the 1790s (then called Outram and Company) were railway pioneers. Outram devised special trucks running on wooden rails, keeping the trucks on the track by bolting to the rails metal plates with flanges - the term 'platelayer' still survives. A good example of a flanged track with a truck is shown in a photograph of unknown date captioned 'The Little Eaton-Denby Railway (c. 1790)' reproduced in Edwards [1966 40]. Jessop transferred the flanges from the rails to the wagon wheels, and the pair adopted as the gauge for their 'railways' the traditional width between the wheels of the Derbyshire waggon or 'corve' of 4 feet 8½ inches, still the standard gauge of British railways. The trucks ran down carefully graded inclines under gravity when full, and the empty trucks were hauled back to the workings by horses - a method 'convenient for transporting heavy stuff a short distance'. Everything points to the fact that the Lenton quarry

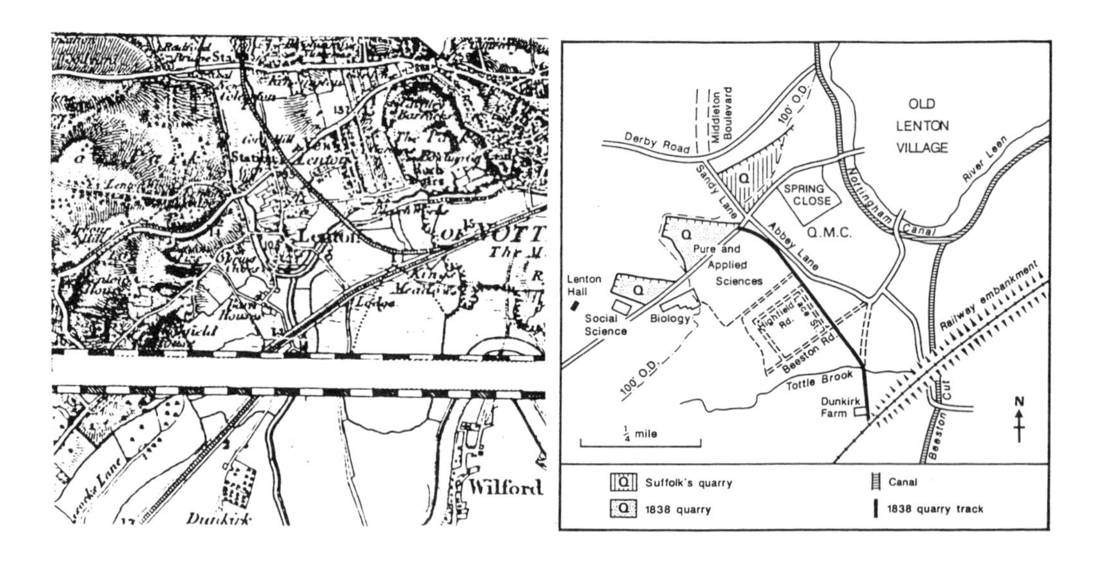

Figure 97: The 1838 quarry tramway from Lenton Hall park to the Dunkirk railway embankment

Above: *A print of 1842 showing the Dunkirk embankment. In middle distance left is Alwell Field extending from Lenton village to the Park estate, Nottingham.*

Below: Left *- Part of the O.S. First edition 1-inch map with later railways added but the tramway not removed.*

Right *- The line of the 1838 tramway through Dunkirk.*

tramway operated in 1838 according to this system.

NOTES

1. N.U.M.D., Mi 1/38/9. 'Expositions of witnesses taken at Lenton ... the 27 July 11 Elizabeth ... on behalf of the sovereign ...'. Endorsed 'About a way inclosed by Southworth. How bounded etc.'.
2. Records of the Borough of Nottingham, I 371 and 122.
3. J.L.MacAdam (1756-1835), appointed General Surveyor of Roads in 1827, devised the technique of constructing roads from angular, broken rock fragments in about 1820. Adams Hill was one of the first lengths of road in the area to use the system, in 1822 (see below).
4. The original Act was followed by further Acts in 20 Geo. III (1779), 39 Geo. III (1798), 59 Geo. III (1818) and 8 Geo. IV (1827). The Lenton to Sawley Turnpike Act was dated 1759 - N.A.O., cA 3/3/9.
5. The Universal British Directory of Trade, Commerce and Manufacture, Notts. and Newark (1793)
6. N.U.M.D., Mi 1/16/1 a-d. Notts. Lent Assizes 1823. Case in trespass, King's Bench. Lord Middleton pltiff. John Wright defendant. (1a - Brief: 1c - Map of Derby Road) The case did not come to trial for want of time, 'but the Judge referred it to be tried by Mr. Amos, and he decided from evidence that the land and trees were belonging to Wollaton Park'.
7. N.U.M.D., Mi 1/16/1 (1823). Evidence of John Hopkin and Richard Chamberlain.
8. N.U.M.D., Mi R 13, 23 November 1820. 'Lenton Acknowledgements'

   Stephen Orrill 5s. 0d. 2 years: for a garden by the park wall.
   William Unwin 6s. 0d. 6 years: for a garden by the park wall.

   N.U.M.D., Mi R 16, 1823 - 'Acknowledgements'

   Clayton 2s. 6d.
   William Unwin 2s. 0d.

   Lord Middleton's steward, John Nickleson Martin of Wollaton 'will prove receipt of rent for 6 years from gardens in occupation of William Unwin, one dug quite up to the park wall for 30 yards or more and at least 4 yards wide; in some places 15 inches deep and in all 12 inches at least, and the soil taken away'.
9. N.U.M.D., Mi R 16 (1823) : Mi R 19 (1826) : Mi R 21 (1828):
   Mi R 25 (1832) : Mi R 26 (1833). Stephen Clayton replaced William Unwin as road surveyor in 1826, when he already had other gardens. But the garden for which Clayton paid an annual rent of 1s. 3d. was said to be 'now in the park' in 1832. This suggests that Unwin and then Clayton had been allowed to cultivate Handley's potato garden for several years after the diversion of Derby Road.
10. John Sleight, former park keeper, described perambulations of Wollaton and Lenton boundaries, when he walked on the south side of the screed and Lenton people walked on the turnpike road. N.U.M.D., Mi 1/16/1, 'Proofs'. Richard Chamberlain perambulated the Wollaton parish bounds in 1799 and 1800, crossing the park wall near the toll gate with the aid of a ladder provided by Sleight, and went up the turnpike road and down to the entrance lodge, 'leaving the screed as in Wollaton'.
11. N.U.M.D., Mi 1/16/1. The traditional name of this field was Hind and Far Abbey Field, but it was not exactly the same since the line of Beeston Lane had been changed between his tenancy and his statement.
12. ibid. p. 5. See also N.U.M.D., Mi 1/18/1-2 'Indenture of 12 October 1822 (Deed enrolled 2 January 1823).
13. N.U.M.D., Mi 1/39/4 (1812)
14. N.U.M.D., Mi F 14/13 (1822)
15. Transcription in Godfrey 1884 27-31. Mon. Ang. v, 110.
16. N.U.M.D., Mi 1/16/1. p. 33; Evidence of William Wilkinson, who was born at the Odd House and later worked the farm as tenant.
17. N.U.M.D., Mi F 12: remarks of Rev. Killar. Much work on the development of the new Wollaton Park was taking place in the 1650s and 1660s, although the Sixty Acres (90 acres in area) forming the frontage to Derby Road between the Tottle Brook and Lenton Hurst was not owned by the Willoughbys until 1698.
18. N.U.M.D., Mi 1/16/1. Evidence of William Wilkinson.
19. N.C.S.N., 62, 14 gives 1823 as the date of Lenton Lodge. Sanderson's maps of 1834 and 1835 name only 'Park Gate' at the site of Lenton Lodge.
20. N.U.M.D., Mi R 31 (1838 rental) and Mi R 36 (1844 and 1845 rentals)
21. N.U.M.D., Mi 3 E 456. Indenture of 15 May 1925, under heading '7th Schedule - Tenancies'.
22. Lenton Local History Group, Broadsheet July 1975.
23. The gradient of Cut Through Lane was reduced artificially at its crossing of the Clifton fault line scarp at least once during the 19th century, producing a sharp cutting seen in Figure 92, which gave the lane its usual name. The lane was greatly widened in about 1950 between the Social Sciences building and the 'Botany Garden'.
24. N.U.M.D., Mi 1/39/9 (1569). 'About a way inclosed by Southworth'. 'Expositions of witnesses taken at Lenton ... the 27 July , 11 Elizabeth ... on behalf of the sovereign....'.

25. *Records of the Borough of Nottingham*, i, 371 (4236) 1301
26. The name appears to derive from a cross at the east end of the village in the 14th century, and not because the lane connected two village streets.
27. Dunkirk Road made use of a northward extension of the elongated common called The Greens, which is indicated in Figures 17 and 21 (Chapter III) although its exact boundaries are not known.
28. N.U.M.D., Rt N 3a (printed). 'A state of the depths of water upon the shallows in the river Trent between Cavendish Bridge and Gainsbro', as taken by W.Jessop, Engineer, in the months of August and September 1782, and also those taken by J. Smith, surveyor, on the 17th and 18th of July 1786: who was appointed by a Committee at Nottingham on the 9th of June last to survey the same'. Printed by George Burbage, Nottingham, 1786.
    N.U.M.D., Rt N 3b 'Report of William Jessop, Engineer, on a survey of the river Trent in the months of August and September 1782, relative to a scheme for improving its navigation'.
29. The Cromford Canal was opened in 1794. The engineers were William Jessop and Benjamin Outram, the two (of the four) founders of the Butterley Company who had technological expertise.
30. These data, and much in the following paragraphs, come from the Minutes and correspondence of the Nottingham Canal Company, which are transcribed with other material (but without historical commentary) in a bound typescript by the late Guy Hemingway, 'East Midland Canals'. A copy can be found in the Special Collections section of the Hallward Library, ref. Em G 24 HEM.
31. N.U.M.D., Rt N 3b (1782). Amending Act, 34 George III (1794): 'An Act to alter and amend an Act of the 23rd year of his present Majesty [1782] for improving the Navigation of the river Trent and for making and maintaining a navigable canal from the said river in the parish of Beeston to join the Nottingham Canal in the parish of Lenton ... and also certain Cuts on the side of the said River'.
32. W.P.W.Phillimore, Nottingham Parish Registers: Burials, Lenton (1904). Sarah, wife of James Green of Lenton Abbey, buried at Lenton, 23 November 1811, aged 60 years.
33. N.U.M.D., Plan, Em B8 D82. This plan, published in about 1794, is that drawn to illustrate Jessop's survey of the river Trent in 1782, delayed through problems of engraving.
34. 'A Plan showing the lines and the relative Situations of the intended Nottingham Canal and of the Erewash Canal and also the commencement of the Cromford Canal, of the Soar Navigation and of the intended Grantham Canal, surveyed in 1791 by James Green'. An original is held in the Local Studies Library, Nottingham.
35. Hemingway, op. cit., p. 197: '16 Feb. 1795: Breaches in the canal bank at Lenton were reported. 'From Mr. Chamberlain's land to the leather mill lock, part of the east bank has been washed into the canal'. On the west side between the leather mill lock and the footbridge to Beeston the bank had been 'wilfully cut' and breached, causing flooding. ibid. p. 210, 4 Dec. 1797.
36. Useful details, especially of 20th century changes and personal reminiscences of the canals in Lenton can be found in articles in the *Lenton Listener* No. 12 (May-June 1981) and the *Lenton Times,* No. 2 (May 1989), both published by Lenton Local History Society.
37. See, for example, R. Iliffe and W. Baguley, 'Old Nottingham Transport, a study in pictures'. *Victorian Nottingham* III, 3 (197.) and M. Higginson, *The Midland Counties Railway 1839-1989*: a Pictorial Survey(1989) Midland Railway Trust, p. 3.
38. *Nottingham Guardian* 8 January 1923
39. *Dearden's Miscellany* 1 (1839) 190. 'Collections'.
40. Frontispiece to John Curtis, *A topographical history of Nottingham and Nottinghamshire from actual survey* (1843-44). The engraving is entitled simply 'Nottingham'. The same engraving, slightly curtailed and entitled 'A train entering Nottingham through the Meadows' is printed in *Victorian Nottingham* (197.) and there dated 1839.
41. The quarter sheet that includes this feature will have been corrected on the 2 inches to 1 mile survey sheet up to 1838, before its engraving and publication on 1 July 1838. On the republished full sheet by David and Charles as their Sheet 35 (Sheet 71 in the Old Series of O.S. 1-inch maps) the date 8 February 1836 appears below the two quarter-sheets, but the bottom margins of the later northern pair of quarter-sheets, with their date of 1 July 1839 have been omitted in putting the full sheet together, and the earlier date printed below the full sheet of David and Charles is therefore misleading in respect of the date of the quarries and the track from them to Dunkirk. The David and Charles facsimile 1-inch map was produced from electrotype printings of the 1860s, with updated railway information: but the quarry track was not removed from the map. It is not known whether any traces then remained on the ground.

CHAPTER XIV

SPRING CLOSE, HILLSIDE AND THE QUEEN'S MEDICAL CENTRE

Introduction

The University campus was extended eastwards across Clifton Boulevard to the river Leen and the Nottingham Canal in the later 1960s to provide the site of the University Hospital and Medical School, the 'Queen's Medical Centre', mainly on former priory demesne land but partly on the former Beck Field. This extension was unexpected, for it contravened the city's Development Plan which twenty years earlier had zoned the land for industrial uses. It had been thought earlier that if a Medical School were to be established its natural site would be the Lenton House estate of the Boots Company: but this remained unavailable, and in the event there is little doubt that the site eventually chosen is a better one for its purpose in every way. The area's recent history is very different from that of the parkland across the boulevard; an area of small industries, old working-class housing, quarrying, allotments and semi-derelict land, overlooked by villas and gardens along the south-east side of Derby Road. Hillside, in the north-east corner, was a part of it, but is treated separately because its 19th and 20th century history was independent of that of Spring Close.

Tenurial history of Spring Close

Historically, the land between the river Leen (NE) and Clifton Boulevard (SW), and between Derby Road (NW) and Abbey Street (SE) was divided into two distinct units, probably from before the Norman Conquest, along the major physiographic boundary represented by the edge of the Trent flood plain, along which ran the ancient track from Lenton to Beeston via Cut Through Lane. The one-third of the area on the higher ground north-west of the Spring Close lane was the south-eastern end of Beck Field, one of the open, common arable fields of the medieval township of Lenton, with free-draining soils formed on Lenton Sandstone rocks. The remainder, on low, alluvial ground, was level, less well drained, and traditionally enclosed in grass fields that formed part of the dairy farm of Lenton Priory, within its demesne. The tenurial history of the two parts was therefore quite different. In 1938, when the writer first knew Spring Close (and in particular 'The Travellers Rest', the public house nearest to Hugh Stewart Hall and most frequented by its students) much of the area south of Spring Close road was still open land although part had become scrubby, and its drainage neglected. It was dominated by the closely built-up industrial hamlet, also called Spring Close, with factories and over 100 houses, now totally swept away.

Robert Mellors [1912] remarked that 'Spring Close tells of the presence of running water in a remarkable geological formation of contorted interglacial alluvium of the Trent'. In fact Spring Close was the name of a small field on the south side of the lane which included one (Snoton Spring) of a line of several springs emerging at the foot of the sandstone and gravel valleyside slope. A little further west was another, Romiley Spring, shown on a sketch made in 1846 (Figure 98).

The full tenurial history of Spring Close is not completely established. It may be thought to have been one of the Abbey Closes shown in Richard Smythe's map of 1632 [1] and owned by the priory until the Dissolution; but it was never named or identified in terriers and rentals of the former priory demesne. Instead it appeared in Gregory estate rentals in the 17th and 18th centuries, so it could not have been part of the Beck Field which was enclosed only in 1768. Smythe's map is too crude to show whether there was land of a third category between Beck Field and the former demesne. However, there is some evidence that there was an irregular

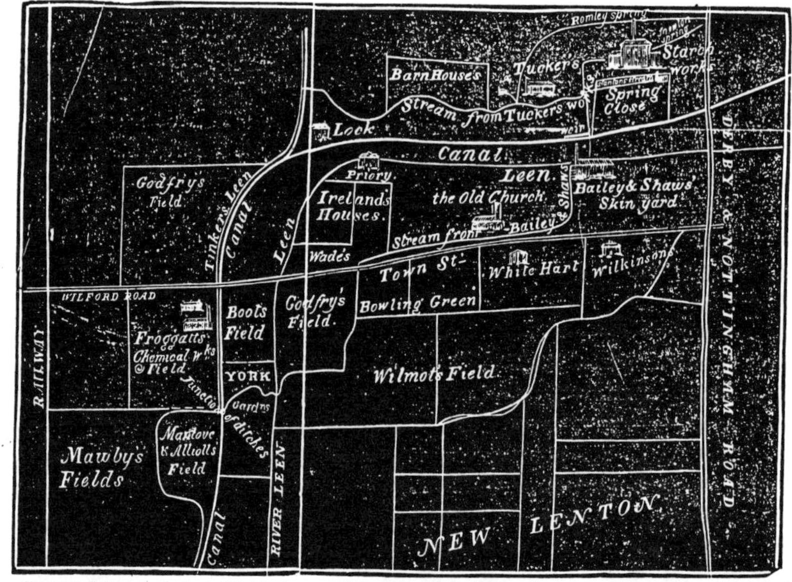

The reader will observe, upon looking carefully at the above engraved plan, that two springs exist in the north west corner, at the foot of the .... which divides the hamlet of Lenton from the Derby turnpike road; the stream from one of these springs passes through Mr. Tuckers' works, and is used by him in his process of manufacturing starch, and is joined by the other a little more to the south-east: the united streams then move gradually along until they fall into Tinkers' Leen, after passing under the canal, just above the lock; the amalgamated rivulets then pass through Mr. Froggatt's grounds, and at the bottom of his field are joined by another drain, which originates very near the same source as Mr. Tucker's stream, but arrives by a different route. This second principal stream, it will be observed, runs through Messrs. Bailey and Shaw's skin-yard, and is used by them in their business processes, and passing through the town street of Old Lenton, runs between Mr. Godfrey's field and Bowling-green into the York Gardens, when it also passes under the canal by a culvert, and forms a junction with the Tinkers' Leen and stream from Mr. Tucker's starch works, as before described. The whole then, in one continuous current, after passing around Messrs. Manlove and Alliott's field, runs along the side of the canal, through the Queen's Meadow, the Nottingham Meadow, and the Eastcroft, to the Trent. It will be necessary for the reader to make himself acquainted with these particulars, fully, to understand the details which follow.

Figure 98: Diagrammatic map of part of Old Lenton in 1846
[From the Nottingham Guardian, 25 September 1846.]

strip of 'waste' there, immediately below the low but steep cliff marking the edge of the valley floor, through which passed the ancient 'road' from Lenton to Beeston, continued along Cut Through Lane. In 1637 a petition by Marmaduke Marshall from Yorkshire to king Charles I, requesting the grant to him in fee farm of 'certain common or waste lands ... in Lenton and Radford' [Godfrey 1884 316-7] [2] included in its schedule the following:

'And one pcell of ground called Snowdenhole conteyning.. 3 acres
And one other pcell of ground conteyning .... 1½ acres
And one other pcell of ground conteyning .... 2 acres
And one pcell of ground called the Gorse conteyning.... 3 acres
And one other pcell of ground (lying ut supra) there
called the Becksyde, conteyning by estimation .... 3 acres'

This was evidently waste near Beck Field, and including the site of Snowdon or Snoton Spring. The petition was refused. George Gregory had recently bought the Crown manor of Lenton, and although no record of it is known this land was at least partly incorporated in the Gregory estate by 1651, when Christopher Stocks, a Lenton farmer, rented a 2-acre Snoton Close for £2.10s.0d. [3]. The area was given as 1½ acres in 1664 [4]. In 1725 [5] and in 1738 [6] Henry Brown, a smallholder, and in 1768 [7] his son Henry, rented a close called Hopyard, given an area of 3 acres in 1725 and 1738, and in 1768 2a.3.32, paying rent of £2.5s.0d.. This was the smaller western half of Spring Close. The larger eastern half, which may have been one or more of the other parcels mentioned in 1637, was rented by Arthur Beardsley for £4 in 1725, and called Spring Close. John Clarke was the tenant in 1738 and Stephen Weston , whose 52-acre farm in 1768 included 24 acres of the former Beck Field, paid £3 rent for his 3a.3.30.

In 1817-23 the eastern close - Spring Close proper - was not in the Gregory estate [8] and it had probably been surrendered in exchange to Rebecca Garland and George Brentnall following the inclosure allotments of 1768 [9]. The subsequent devolution of its ownership was extremely complex, involving six undivided parts in common (not joint) ownership, bankruptcy, mortgages of different undivided parts and sales, as may be seen from an abstract of title prepared for the purchase in 1802 by Samuel Goodacre a Sawley miller from Charles Upton and Mary Sills of property that included Lenton mill and three closes, one of which was Spring Close [10]. This transaction was of some significance, because had Spring Close remained in a major estate it would have been less likely to undergo piecemeal sale and industrial development in the late 1820s at a time when the lace industry was being established at a spectacular rate in parishes like Lenton just beyond the boundaries of Nottingham.

The Nottingham Canal and early industrial development, 1790-1830

Bleach yards

Industrial enterprises were being established alongside the newly built Nottingham Canal and the river Leen in the 1790s. They included tanning and leather works and bleaching works at Old Lenton, and soon afterwards a malting at Hillside. The leather industry prospered (see Chapter X) and expanded through the 19th century, and the malting survived until about 1900, but some other enterprises were shorter-lived. Part of the Seven Acres Close adjoining Spring Close was leased from the Milward estate in 1796 by Messrs. Killingley and Green, a textile firm planning expansion. Alderman Harry Green [11] had borrowed £800 in 1788, and they built Broadmarsh spinning mill in 1790-92 [Chapman 1967 84 and 140] but their bank loan greatly increased in 1795-96, and the Strettons built a bleach yard for the firm on Seven Acre Close in 1797. However, Green became bankrupt in August 1797, and in 1798, with Killingley now the sole tenant, the land was sold immediately after Lady Day to a Mr. Lock, though Killingley may have still occupied it as a bleach yard for a time. Lock died in 1809, and in 1818 James Nutt replaced Killingley as tenant, and bought the property in 1820. J.W.Killingley, 'gent.' was living at Lenton Terrace, New Radford in 1818 [Sutton 1818], evidently retired, and it is not known how long the bleach yard remained in operation, though it was marked and named on T.J.Ellis's map of 1824-25. A second small bleach works at Snoton Spring in the early 19th century ended in about 1835. It is discussed further below.

Early lace making and the lace boom

The establishment and growth of lace making at Spring Close is a longer and more successful story. The explosive growth of the industry and its associated residential areas outside the boundaries of Nottingham was brought about because the lack of space for expansion within the town, with its unenclosed common fields, directed an irresistible industrial pressure on to nearby villages, where suitable land commanded prices that were very attractive, especially to smaller land owners. 'Many of the [stocking] frames in Nottinghamshire and the adjoining counties were destroyed by the Luddites betwixt the years 1812 and 1816, and some of them were perhaps never replaced owing to their owners embarking in the lace trade, in which there are now employed in England upwards of 4,500 bobbin net machines belonging to above 1,380 owners, of whom nearly 1,000 work in their own machines, and enter both into the class of journeymen and masters. ... More than half of these machines are in Nottingham, Mansfield and the surrounding villages, and the remainder are mostly in Leicestershire [White 1832 197].

This boom in the lace trade was concentrated especially in the years 1823-25. On the introduction of the bobbin net machine invented by John Heathcote of Long Whatton near Loughborough in 1809 the multitude of lace machines other than the warp machine disappeared [Wylie 1853 300]. In 1823 Heathcote's 14-year patent expired, and 'such was the opinion of the profitable nature of the manufacture of lace that on the expiration of the patent people came from all parts of the kingdom to Nottingham to become lace manufacturers. There set in at that time an epidemic known as the twist fever, and farmers, butchers, bankers, publicans and bakers rushed into the trade, expecting to make rapid fortunes' (extract from a speech by Alderman Ward) [Williams c.1883]. 'All Nottingham went mad', with everybody wanting to make bobbin or twist net, and for more than two years ruinous speculation prevailed. The bubble burst in 1825, but 'hundreds of mechanics poured in' [Glover 1844] [12] and the sharp vicissitudes of the trade over the succeeding decades did nothing to check the rapid growth of the industry.

Spring Close 'village' originated in the growth of domestic-scale lace making in the 1820s and 1830s, although because of its outlying situation its beginnings were slightly delayed, and it was not involved in the boom of 1823-25. No building was shown on Wood's map of 1818-23, and in 1825 Glover's Nottingham Directory made no mention of the locality. The Poor Rate book for 1825 included Hillside by name, but not Spring Close [Godfrey 1884 47]. However, according to Pigot's Directory for 1828-29 the lace manufacturers of Lenton included Thomas and Samuel Shepherd (tattings), and both are known to have been at Spring Close in 1832 [White 1832] and were probably there in 1828 or earlier, while William Stanton is known to have established his workshop there in 1830 [13]. Lace making therefore first made its appearance at Spring Close in 1826-27.

In 1832 the bobbin net machines in Nottinghamshire 'are nearly all worked by hand, the broad machine having generally two men each, who work in four hour shifts' [White 1832]. Thus the physical expression of the early growth of lace making was in the form of dwelling houses, perhaps with workshops incorporated, and not of large industrial premises. Even after the introduction of new machines in 1833 had depreciated the value of the old hand machines, tending to 'sink the small owners into journeymen', the organization of production remained at the workshop stage, though after further improvements between 1839 and 1843 it was noted that 'since the panic of 1825-26 one-third of the machinery in the trade has passed out of the hands of the original owners' [Glover 1844].

A three-fold increase in Lenton's population in 30 years, from 893 in 1801 to 3,077 in 1831, took place mainly after 1821, an addition of 1,837 persons raising the parish population from 1,240 to 3,077 in a single decade: and of the 631 houses in the parish in 1831, 400 dated from after 1821 [White 1832]. Most of the new development was in three localities. First, the 'new village' of Middleton Place, the nucleus of New Lenton, was built on land enclosed from open field in 1768, allotted to Rebecca Garland and George Brentnall. Some 16 acres of this allotment, 'forming the site of New Lenton' was purchased by John Wright of Lenton Hall in 1804 'for £100 an acre and successfully sold for building purposes at £1,000 an acre, and so gave rise to this large and populous feature of the place' [Fyfe 1856 152]. This was a similar transaction to that identified as the beginnings of New Sneinton, when in March 1824 'two closes situated on each side of the Beck which divides Sneinton from Nottingham were knocked down in building lots at from 11s. 6d. to 24s. 6d. per square yard [Wylie 1853 363-64]. Second, Ison (Hyson) Green, another 'new village', was developed on land lying in the detached part of Lenton north of the Wollaton Road and enclosed in the second Lenton Inclosure, of 1799 [Godfrey 1884 328-333]. Third, Spring Close was 'another modern village, but of a much smaller population'. It was also much smaller in area and more outlying, but a genuine example of the contemporary form of industrial and residential development stimulated by the rapid growth of the lace industry.

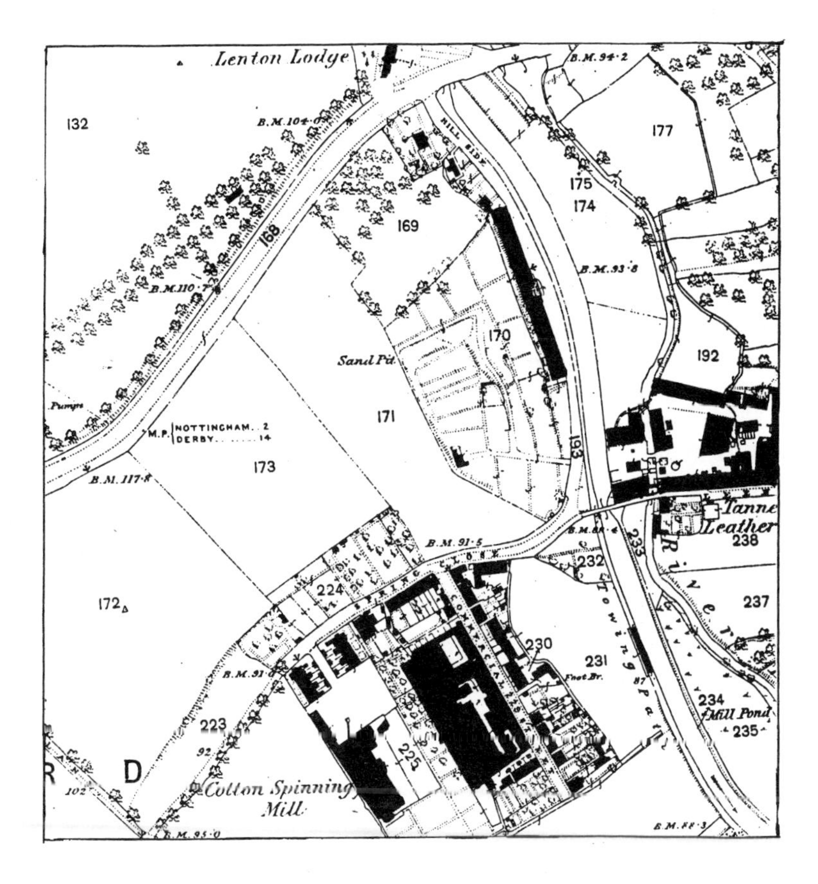

Figure 99: Spring Close and Hillside in 1881
Note sand extraction behind the malting at Hillside, and the undeveloped cotton mill with the spring of the former Tuckers' bleach works discharging into it from the north. [Reduced from OS 25-inch map of 1881]

The inhabitants of Spring Close named in White's Directory for 1832 - not necessarily a full list - were:

John Daws	Bleacher
George Ball	Bobbin net maker and hosier
Samuel Shepherd	Bobbin net maker
Thomas Shepherd	do.
George Stanton	do.
William Stanton	do.
Joseph Swain	do.
Thomas Towle	Shoemaker and Peacock beer house.

The Shepherds and the Stantons, at least on their first arrival, were probably the two-man teams required by the broad machine for its double working. Two years later Dearden [1834 134-37] named five of these six lace makers (excepting Joseph Swain) among the 25 lace makers listed in Lenton parish; and James Jackson of Spring Close, boot and shoe maker and 'retail brewer' had replaced Thomas Towle [14] . But directories are not always exhaustive, and Pigot in 1835 included George Ball of Old Lenton and William Stanton among the bobbin net makers but omitted the Shepherds, who certainly remained in business at Spring Close for very many years, and outlasted all the others named.

Growth of the village

The hamlet of Spring Close first became established along the south side of the lane called Spring Close which had been realigned by the Inclosure Award of 1768 to run along the margin of the former Beck Field, thus: 'From the town of Lenton westward, over the allotment of John Webb in Bull Close to a footbridge over the river Leen, and from thence over the allotment of the said George de Ligne Gregory, No. 11 to a place in the Lordship of Lenton called Abbey Field....'. Webb's allotment was the Bull Close and Leen Crofts, which became the site of Bayleys leather works, and allotment No. 11 was the southern part of Beck Field. Buildings soon spread south into the original Spring Close field, forming the northern end of what became Commercial Street, and eventually houses and factories occupied the whole of the original close, closely packed. The early footway soon became a cul-de-sac road leading east to Leen-gate by the canal bridge, and north to Derby Road by a lane alongside the canal past the Hillside malting, discussed later. Throughout the 19th century Spring Close looked east and north-eastwards, and not westwards to the meagre Sandy Lane. Sanderson's map of 1835, surveyed 1830-34, shows clearly the existence of the northern end of Commercial Street, and a building at its junction with Spring Close on the site of the Travellers Rest inn, probably the house of James Jackson, 'retail brewer, Spring Close' named by Dearden [1834 137]. There was also building west of Commercial Street (not yet named) in the position of Mitre Terrace and Walker's Yard.

By 1841 [15] 25 families lived at Spring Close, although there is no indication in the Census Enumerators' Books of how many were on Commercial Street. The heads of 18 of these families were lace makers; but few women were shown to be working in the industry. Although working the lace machines was then still men's work, it should be noted too that many wives had very young children, and there were few older children or unmarried people in the hamlet. The population of 127 in 25 houses included 23 married couples, one widow and one widower. Seventeen of the married men were aged 35 or less. There were five lodgers. About half the inhabitants were children aged 13 or less, and the average family size was over five. All except five of the householders were Nottingham born, a situation that was to change. Apart from a lodger with the (later) landlord of the Travellers Rest by far the oldest man at Spring Close was 57-year-old George Ball, confirmed by the census as a framework knitter, together with his son Thomas and 51-year-old William Tutin who also lived with him. William Stanton (absent at the 1841 enumeration) was prosperous enough to employ a resident servant. Richard Tucker, something of an anomaly, a starch maker living at Snoton Spring - not strictly part of Spring Close at that time - employed two people.

Tucker's starch factory

It is convenient to outline the history of the Tucker family and their starch making works at this point, before proceeding with further discussion of the development of Spring Close. Richard Grant Tucker, mentioned earlier as a small scale starch manufacturer in 1841, came to Lenton in 1835, aged about 48, from Middlesex, bringing his expertise in starch manufacture. He was a native of Tiverton, Devon, and since his eldest son was Richard Anstey Tucker, and a visitor in 1861 at census time was Abraham Anstey, aged 30, a medical student born in Devon, it is probable that his wife Clara was born Clara Anstey Tucker's daughter Sarah was born at Bromley in 1834, and his youngest son, Henry, at Lenton in 1837, and the year of his arrival at Lenton is confirmed by several local people interviewed in 1846 [16]. He established a starch factory at Snoton Spring, where a small bleach works relying on the same water supply had been located for many years. The position of the bleach works was shown as a building on Sanderson's map of 1835, surveyed in 1834 and earlier.

According to a local resident, Elizabeth Holland of the Barn Houses, speaking in 1846, an early occupier of the bleach works soon after 1813 was William Pearson, (though nothing was shown on the Gregory estate map of 1818-23) who was followed by John Hopkin, and finally by another, probably John Daws, who was named as a bleacher at Spring Close in 1832 [White 1832]. The works relied on the water supplied by Snoton Spring, one of a line of several springs emerging at the foot of the Lenton Sandstone slope of the valleyside. John Daws and son were listed as bleachers at Span Meadow, Lenton in 1831 along with Thomas Browne Milnes of the Lenton Works on Park Street Lenton, which probably used water from a spring on the eastern valley-side of the river Leen.

According to William Stanton [17] whose small lace factory or workshop adjoined Richard Tucker's premises, Snoton spring was in a garden, still occupied by William Pearson, labourer, in 1846, about 15 yards north of Tucker's garden; and its very clean, pure water was piped into Tucker's works, and left them 'at the bottom of Mr. Tucker's croft' in a very polluted state. The polluted stream turned east to join a pure stream which Stanton pumped from his 19 feet deep well, and at this point water from the 'weir dyke' - presumably overflow from the Nottingham canal - entered from the east. The combined stream flowed south-east sluggishly past the north-east side of the Barn Houses and beneath the Beeston Cut into the Tinker's Leen and thence alongside the canal towards the Trent. In its course through Lenton deposits of rotting material from the starch factory clogged the drains and gave rise to a grossly offensive stench. The problem had become increasingly severe since about 1840, and was thought to be associated with severe fevers causing deaths that affected Lenton more than any other part of the Nottingham area in the summer of 1846, and which led to a public inquiry. This would not be surprising, since many people used water directly from the dykes for cooking purposes. Equally or even more offensive and dangerous was the animal waste from the leather works of Bayley and Shaw which polluted the drains flowing through the village of Lenton along Leengate and Town Street (Gregory Street) and left deposits there. In the course of the inquiry in 1846 Richard Tucker had the effrontery, in his capacity as one of the Guardians of the Radford Union, to prosecute those through whose lands ran the drains polluted by his effluent for 'having a foul ditch running through their lands'. He was not the most popular incomer at Lenton, and at the County Hall proceedings 'very warm altercations' took place.

After about 20 years, in 1856, Richard Tucker's premises, consisting of a mill, a warehouse, boiler house, kiln and the private house where he lived, were leased to the firm of William Hollins, cotton spinners, which was expanding as the factory system became established, and was branching out from its base at Pleasley Vale [18]. Tucker was 69 in 1856. He died on 16 May 1867, aged 80 [19]. It is surprising to find him at the 1861 census still living at Noton (or Snoton) Spring with his unmarried eldest son, Richard Anstey Tucker, then aged 36, and his daughters Mary, Sarah and Hannah, employing two domestic servants. Evidently William Hollins needed the factory premises but not the house. Even more surprising is to find him apparently still active in the business as late as 1865 [White 1864, 1865] as a 'soap, British Gum and starch boiler'. But this cannot have been at Noton Spring. His second son, John, with his wife Clara Mary and two servants, were by 1861 living at Birch House, Sherwin Street, which until his death in 1854 had been the home of George Bradley, a lace thread maker [20], and John was called a starch manufacturer. In fact he was in partnership as Gill and Tucker, starchmakers in Sandiacre, and his father Richard was probably involved in the same business.

In 1873 William Hollins bought the freehold of the whole premises they leased at Snoton Spring, together with the engines and gearing to drive their machinery, representing an investment of about £5,000, with potential for expansion on the site, and they built a large cotton spinning mill there, occupying much of the western half of Spring Close. But in 1882 their Lenton mill was closed altogether, the workers and machinery transferred to Radford, and the premises sold to Benjamin Walker whose lace factory immediately adjoined them on the eastern half of Spring Close. By 1881 John Tucker had been able, at the age of 54, to retire from the starch making business [21] and was living at Birch House with some pretensions to grandeur describing himself to the census enumerator as 'gentleman', both his wife and his sister Hannah as 'lady', and one of their three servants, John Henry Horton aged 18 as 'page or footman'.

Continuing development through the mid-19th century

Comparison with the census data for 1851 confirms that the chief housing development at Spring Close during the 1840s had been along Commercial Street, and indeed house building was confined to this eastern half of the original Spring Close until after 1860. In 1851 there were 45 families, nearly twice as many as ten years earlier, and of this number 31 lived on Commercial Street. The heads of 32 families, or 71 per cent, as well as many members of these and other families, were engaged in making lace. Many of the sons of the earlier lace makers were in the same trade, while wives and daughters were most commonly described as lace menders. Wylie [1853 320] wrote; 'The husbands, fathers and brothers work the net machines; the wives, daughters and sisters...[in] embroidery or running the lace. The men work partly in factories but mostly in small houses; the women work partly in warehouses and partly in their own dwellings'.

Elsey and Walker's lace factory

The factory system was taking over at Spring Close, and by 1851 most of the male workers in lace were employed either in the workshops of the surviving small businesses such as that of Thomas Shepherd, who now employed 11 men on Commercial Street like his brother Samuel, and George Stanton, also now of Commercial Street, who employed 8 men; or in a larger enterprise established on Commercial Street in 1847-48 - the factory of Joseph Elsey and Benjamin Walker, 'bobbin net and lace makers' [Lascelles and Hagar 1848 170-80]. The 1851 census books described Joseph Elsey's employment as 'Lace manufacturing firm of two, employing 123 men, women and boys'. Small proprietors were described as 'lace maker' or 'machine holder'. The 123 employees of Elsey and Walker in 1851 heavily outnumbered the people employed in lace making and living at Spring Close, so the factory can be seen as attracting further house building nearby.

In the firm of Elsey and Walker, Joseph Elsey was probably the 'technical partner', while Benjamin Walker provided most of the capital. Elsey, aged 41 in 1851, arrived in Lenton only in the late 1840s via Nottingham and Basford according to the birthplaces of his children. Slater's Directory for 1850 described Benjamin Walker as a lace manufacturer, although he was new to the business, but did not mention Elsey. Joseph Elsey lived modestly on Commercial Street as did his brother John Elsey, one year his senior, and manager of the new factory. Joseph Elsey was missing from Kelly's Post Office Directory of 1855, and a review of local directories suggests that either he left the firm in 1854-55 or was bought out by Walker, though C.N.Wright's Directory for 1858 and for 1862 recorded Joseph Elsey, lace manufacturer, of Priory Villa, Old Lenton. Elsey appears to have been an innovator in manufacturing techniques, particularly in collaboration with John Livesey [22].

In the early 1840s Benjamin Walker senior, the dominant partner in Elsey and Walker, was an iron and steel and metals dealer and roller, with a warehouse and rolling mill on Derby Road, probably on Sion Hill between Derby and Alfreton Roads [23] Described as a gentleman he lived at Hazard's Yard, Long Row in 1844. Only in 1848 was he also described as a lace manufacturer at Spring Close [24], and by 1850 he appears to have given up the metal trade and was living on Derby Road. In 1866 his home was at Parkside (Sion Hill) [Wright 1866]. By the 1860s Elsey and Walker had become Benjamin Walker and Co., and had other Walkers in the business, including Joseph Benjamin Walker (Benjamin's nephew) from 1855, and Benjamin Walker junior his son, who built Lenton Eaves. Benjamin Walker senior, with a lace factory at New Lenton as well as that at Spring Close, moved to The Priory (built by William Stretton on the site of Lenton Priory when he was approaching retirement. He was still at The Priory in 1879, but died in 1883. It should be noted that it is not easy to clarify the various branches of the Walker family, and the firm of Walker and Co. on Hounds-gate was led by another Benjamin Walker, and should not be confused with the Spring Close firm.

By 1851 the growth of the village of Spring Close had reached a point at which the beginnings of service provision were appearing, in the form of several cow keepers - John Smith, George Ball senior (erstwhile framework knitter) and Henry Ball, all on Commercial Street; a shopkeeper, Matthew Hadden (or, more correctly, his wife Ann, since Matthew was also a lace maker) who had taken over the business of Frederick Holmes, named as a shopkeeper in 1848 [Lascelles and Hagar 1848]; and, in Joseph Hull, a 37-year-old master plumber and retail beer seller, the local publican, living at No. 11 Spring Close and providing accommodation for several lodgers as well as for a male and a female servant employed by him. Hull was at Spring Close by 1840 as a plumber, but in 1851 and 1853 he was described only as a beer seller, and in 1854 [Wright 1854] his house, on the corner of Commercial Street and Spring Close, an appropriately central point, was for the first time called the 'Travellers Rest'. Hull took over the function of Thomas Towle the shoemaker, who had started The Peacock by 1832 (presumably after the Beer House Act of 1830) and his successor by 1834, James Jackson, 'boot and shoe maker and retail brewer'. Joseph Hull was still described as a beer retailer 'of Beeston Road' (as Spring Close was then called) in 1855, but also as a plumber and glazier of Commercial Street.

The lodgers at the house of Joseph Hull, 11 Spring Close, in 1851 were a parchment maker with his wife and children, and four unmarried men who were leather dressers originating in different parts of the country. Another parchment maker together with three fellmongers were living on Commercial Street. All these were doubtless employed in the second large enterprise in the vicinity - the tan yards and leather dressing works of Shaw and Bayley on Leen-gate, immediately across the canal bridge, which was growing rapidly and drawing in workers from a distance. There was a leather mill of Charles Smith, 'skinner' on Canal side in 1841, but Shaw and Bayley were larger and growing quickly, so that by 1853 they could be described as 'the most extensive fellmongers in England [Wylie 1853 290] [25] and became increasingly important as employers of Spring Close people. In the 1851 census books women said to be employed as cotton winders or bobbin winders worked in the lace industry, for cotton spinning had not yet arrived at Spring Close.

The increase in houses and population

By 1851 Snowton Terrace had been built on the south side of the Spring Close road above Elsey and Walker's growing lace factory, and it is possible to trace most of the occupants through to 1881 despite the fact that the same houses were numbered differently in Snowton Terrace and Spring Close, and the order of entry in the Enumerators' Books appears to be inconsistent. In 1851 one of the eleven houses of Snowton Terrace was unoccupied at the census, but the occupiers of most of the rest were lace makers. No. 1 Snowton Terrace (= 13 Spring Close) on the corner of Commercial Street opposite to the Travellers Rest was tenanted by Matthew Hadden, aged 40, already mentioned as a lace maker who was also a shopkeeper. This house, suitably positioned, was still a food shop more than a century later, when occupied in the 1950s by William Hopkinson, a grocer like Matthew Hadden. The succession of tenants of this and other shops is shown in Appendix 24. Samuel Mason, aged 28, at No. 2 Snowton Terrace, was in 1851 a 'pattern leader' in the lace industry, and his 22-year-old brother Edward and Edward's wife Ann, who lived in the same house, were both lace designers - an artistically creative young household. Lascelles and Hagar [1848] specially named Edward Mason, designer and draughtsman in the lace industry, and if the 1851 census is to be believed Edward Mason was only 19 years old in 1848. Most of the tenants were young, and on the evidence of the ages and birthplaces of their children had been in Lenton for only a few years, so it is reasonable to link the building of Snowton terrace directly with that of the adjoining factory of Elsey and Walker, and likely that the houses were built by the firm.

Diversification of employment

The decade 1851-61 saw a continued rapid growth of both employment and population at Spring Close (Table 19). The Shepherds, Samuel and George, remained in business as workshop lace makers, and Elsey and Walker - Benjamin Walker only after 1854 - expanded vigorously. The population of Spring Close increased from 242 to 398 (+ 64.5 per cent): the total number in work rose from 97 to 166 (+ 71.1 per cent): and total lace workers increased from 60 to 113 (+ 88.3 per cent), some of whom were the adolescent children of existing lace workers there. However, although the number of heads of households employed in lace increased from 32 to 46, this represented a percentage decrease from 71 to 60.5, because an increased proportion of men were taking employment a Bayleys' leather works and in other, minor employment categories. Among these was cotton spinning, in which three men, all from Mansfield were employed, undoubtedly in connection with the leasing in 1856 by William Hollins and Company of Tuckers' starch factory to establish their spinning mill until their purpose built factory could be erected, at the same time as the silk spinning mill, the Sherwood Mill just off the Nottingham Road at Mansfield, was given up.

For the time being housing developments were still confined to the eastern part of Spring Close where Ebury Terrace was built south of the lace factory, and there was some further infilling of house sites on Commercial Street. Joseph Hull remained at the Travellers Rest until 1861, though with nine children and a daughter-in-law together with a servant and a plumbing apprentice all living at the inn no room was now available for lodgers. Shopkeepers, with their retail trading usually a secondary employment, came and went. For example, Matthew Hadden was named in 1854 but not in 1855; John Hudson was a retailer on Commercial Street in 1855 but not in 1858, when William Whitehouse was mentioned for the only time [White 1853: Wright 1854 1858: Kelly 1855]. In 1861 George Selby, grocer and Lois Shepherd (22) with Rebecca Deney her lodger, also grocers, were named at the census [26]. Further details of retail trading at Spring Close are given in Appendix 24.

Table 19 shows that the population of Spring Close remained virtually unchanged in the

Table 19.
Spring Close: population and employment in the mid-19th century

Year	Workers Total	Men	Women	Total in lace	%	Men in lace	%	Women in lace	%	Total in leather	%
1841	32	29	3	19	59.4	19	65.5	-	-	1	3.0
1851	97	65	32	60	61.9	41	63.1	19	59.4	9	9.0
1861	166	111	45	113	62.0	75	67.6	28	62.2	17	10.2
1871	210	131	79	117	55.7	64	48.9	53	67.0	35	16.7
1881	221	134	87	102	46.2	49	35.7	53	60.9	33	14.9

Year	Population	Families number	% increase per decade	Average size	Families relying on Lace Number	Lace %	Leather Number	Leather %
1841	127	25		5.08	18	72	-	-
1851	242	45	+ 80	5.38	32	71	2	4.4
1861	398	76	+ 69	5.24	46	60.5	12	15.8
1871	400	82	+ 7.9	4.88	41	50	13	15.9
1881	454	93	+ 13.4	4.88	32	34	19	20.4

decade 1861-71, a feature associated with a marked decline in average family size from 5.24 to 4.88 as the children of the earlier residents grew up and left home. But employment continued to grow, the number of workers resident there increasing from 166 to 210 (+ 26.5 per cent) although the lace industry had reached its peak and women workers were increasingly prominent in it. As male employment in lace declined at Spring Close, by 11 over the decade, women employed in lace increased by 25, almost doubling their number. More men found employment in the nearby leather works, the total from Spring Close doubling from 17 to 35. The leather business progressed steadily between 1850 and 1880, and became a Limited Liability Company, Thomas Bayley and Co., Ltd. in 1875. In 1861 the census indicated that Thomas Bayley employed 252 men, 52 boys and 25 women, and his work force nearly doubled by 1881, though only a proportion of these would be at the Leen-gate works. In about 1880, when additional buildings were erected covering more than two acres Thomas Bayley was said to employ 450 to 500 people. By 1877 [Morris 1877] Benjamin Walkers , with a second factory at Russell Street, New Lenton specialized in lace curtains, but later made also silk and cotton laces, fichus, nets etc. [White 1885] .

The lease of Tuckers' starch factory by William Hollins in 1856 and its eventual purchase in 1873, promised a major industrial development in the western half of Spring Close, called Snoton Close. The manager of Hollins' cotton mill, John Rylance lived on Commercial Street, but the 1871 census books very surprisingly recorded no other employee living at Spring Close. The move by Hollins was intended to expand their productive capacity, and they engaged in spinning 'merino' (merino wool mixed with cotton) and cashmere as well as cotton at Lenton. The company built Spring Terrace and Elm Tree Terrace adjoining the factory in the 1870s to house employees: yet at the 1881 census only No. 6 Spring Terrace was occupied by a cotton spinner, and only two men and five women from Spring Close were employed at this quite large factory. Evidently the decision to close the Lenton mill was already being implemented, and in 1882 the mill closed so that machinery and workforce could be concentrated at the sister mill in Radford - the so-called Old Silk Mill, which became the Coloured Mill, producing coloured yarns [Pigott 1949 78]. It occasions no surprise that the Hollins mill at Lenton was sold to Benjamin Walker, whose lace factory adjoined it.

In the 1860s Richard Arthur Hollins was in charge of the operations at Lenton and Radford. He was assistant manager to his uncle William Hollins, the leader of the firm and the force behind its expansion. In 1870 Henry Ernest Hollins, Richard's brother, became a second assistant manager in place of William Bryerley Paget, and took Richard's place in looking after the Lenton and Radford operations, while Richard ran Pleasley, both responsible to their uncle William. It appears that Robert Arthur Hollins moved to Lenton Firs from Cavendish Road South in The Park in 1878, and left in early 1881, just before the Lenton spinning mill closed down [Morris 1877, Wright 1879, 1881] but it is not known whether the two events were connected or where Robert Arthur Hollins fitted into the Hollins pedigree.

After 1860 the small fancy net making firms of Samuel, Thomas and William Shepherd survived for a time, and by 1864 Frederick and Henry Shepherd were also named as lace makers and machine holders [White 1864]. By 1871 Thomas Shepherd was aged 78, and William, a 'silk lace maker',employed only one man and a boy. Henry was not mentioned in 1871 [Wright 1871] and Samuel was missing in 1876 [Kelly 1876]. In 1881 Thomas, William and Frederick Shepherd were still in business [Wright 1881] but in 1885 none remained [White 1885]. Only Benjamin Walker and Company, much the largest lace firm, with 350 employees at the census of 9 April 1881 [27] was able through its size to respond effectively to changing demand, and one such change was the increasing importance of lace curtains, the machinery for which was suitable only for use in factories. In 1846 John Livesey of Lenton had produced an invention relating to vertical patterning which with other improvements suggested by Livesey 'were carried out by Elsey and Walker and other firms'. They were useful mainly in lace curtain production, which became Walkers' specialty, and they concentrated on making lace curtains until 1910 or 1911, when they closed. Other lines of production were probably taken over by John Benjamin Walker who set up business at Sandiacre in 1889 with all the plant and many of the employees moving from Spring Close [Berry 1989].

By the mid-1880s Benjamin Walker and Co. was in its heyday, and completely dominated Spring Close, though the leather industry across the canal bridge was also still growing. With more houses available between 1871 and 1881 population growth was resumed at Spring Close, and the number of people in work increased further, especially in the case of women. Families increased in number from 76 in 1861 to 93 in 1881 - not far short of the 101 households at Spring Close in 1956 [Kelly 1956]. But families relying on lace manufacturing, as indicated by the employment of heads of families, declined from 46 (60.6 per cent) in 1861 to 41 (50 per cent) in 1871 and to 32 (34 per cent in 1881; that is, from two-thirds in the later 1850s to only one-third in 1881. In the same period the families relying on employment in the leather industry increased to 19 (20.4 per cent).

The detailed large-scale map of 1881 (Figure 100) [28] does not quite mark the culmination of the development of Spring Close, in either housing or industry. There were still vacant house sites to fill on Commercial Street, and a further row was added to Ebury Terrace. A large new industry arrived, with additional industrial building on the western side of Spring Close. William Saxby and Company, dyers and bleachers, who took over the vacant Hollins factory in the mid-1880s [White 1885] remained until near the end of the century. Saxby and Wade, lace dressers and finishers (assumed to have been the same firm) left in the late 1890s [Wright 1897, Kelly 1900], and from 1903 the thriving firm of rope and twine manufacturers, William Coates and Sons took over the cotton mill premises and extended them, providing a boost in employment[29].

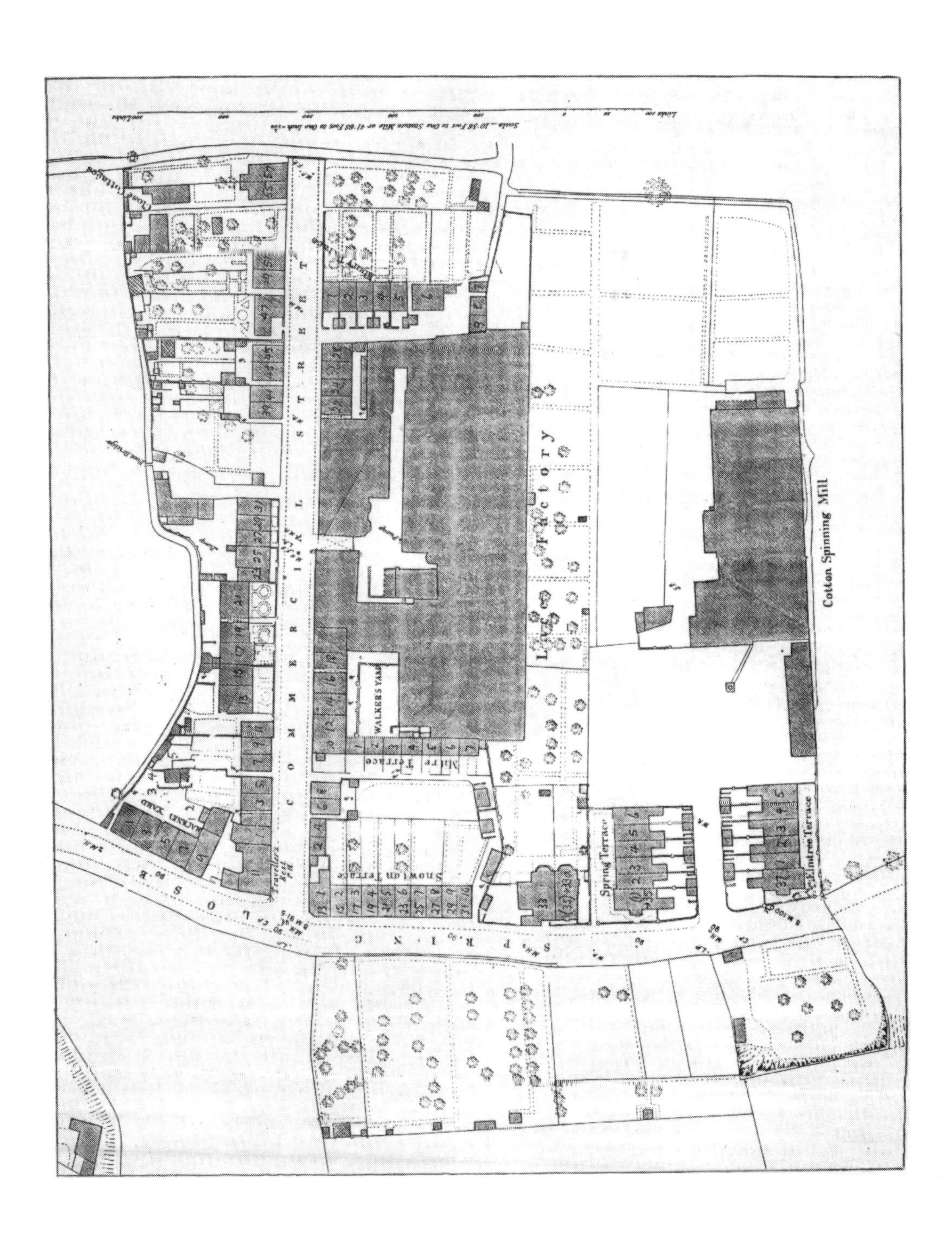

Figure 100: Large-scale map of the 'village' of Spring Close
House numbers have been added. [Reduced from OS 1:500 map of 1881]

William Coates' rope factory

William Coates began to make ropes on Dryden Street, Nottingham as early as 1840, later adding other sites, including by 1871 Bunkers Hill and St. Annes Well Road [Wright 1871] to become the leading firm of rope and twine makers in Nottingham, and producing in addition a wide range of associated products. From William Coates' death in 1894 his son Herbert controlled the business until he died, aged 88, in 1949. Acting upon the need to install new steam-driven machinery the firm concentrated all its ropewalk business in a great new covered ropewalk 100 yards long by 60 yards wide, opened at the old Hollins works at Spring Close in 1903. Employment soon grew to about 200, but the offices remained on Milton Street, Nottingham. After the first world war the firm developed a substantial sporting goods side, producing particularly tennis and badminton rackets and sports nets of various kinds. By a conveyance of 7 January 1920 Herbert Coates purchased from T.S.Pearson-Gregory 8½ acres of land fronting Spring Close and Abbey Lane, then occupied by William Henry Woodhouse, and comprising the fields numbered 65 and 67 on the Gregory estate map of 1818-24 [30], providing space for further post-war diversification.

Car hoods and horse-drawn delivery vans led on to a Coates motorised light delivery van introduced in 1927 - but unsuccessfully. Indeed the search for new products signified weakness rather than strength, and economic problems that led the firm into liquidation in 1935. Most of the Lenton works was sold off to the building and joinery firm of Simms, Son and Cooke, but a small part of the works was retained and later reopened, with about 20 workers concentrating on the production of tarpaulins, sacks and bags, but only to be sold to Simms, Son and Cooke after Herbert Coates' death in 1949. A new managing director, Marshall Wilkinson, took the firm to Montpelier Road, Dunkirk, and under Stewart Coates, Herbert's son, production from 1961 concentrated on various small cord and rope items, and special orders for awnings, covers and the like (including one from the writer for a garden hammock cover, satisfactorily executed !). The great William Coates and Sons of Spring Close reverted to a small family business at No. 10, Montpelier Road.

Replacements for lace manufacturing

Meanwhile, on the eastern side of Spring Close the closure of the Walker Company's lace curtain making business in 1910 freed factory space on Commercial Street which was taken up by other, smaller firms. In 1912 Robert Mellors wrote that 'the making of lace in Lenton has materially diminished, and other trades have taken its place', though A. and F.H.Parkes restored lace curtain making at the Albert Works until about 1922. New firms at Spring Close included Uttley and Bennett, mercerizers and dyers (1910-15); the Standard Machine Company, making machinery for hosiery, ties and insulating electric wires (1910-14); the High Speed Braiding Machine Company (1913-14); and Lenton Blouse Company (1913-14). These dates show that the outbreak of war ended some of these enterprises; but new firms took their places, such as George T. Barnabie, producing knitted underwear fabric (1914 or 1915-22) and Frank W. Smith, embroidery manufacturers (1912-25) [31].

In the post-war period Barnabie was succeeded by C.F.Sudbury, a hosiery firm (1922-32); Frank W. Smith by A and C Embroidery Company (1928-41) and Albert Carter Embroidery (1950-56-); Standard Lace Dressers (1936) by Cellular Clothing Company, lace finishers (1941-) and Textile Finishing Company, lace bleachers (1950-56-). In 1956 there were also Oscroft and Stokes, mechanical engineers at the Albert Works (1950-56-); F.I.E.Diesel Engineers (1956-); Clearmould Plastics (1950-56-) and the Danish Bacon Company warehouse(1950-56-). Simms, Son and Cooke has been mentioned earlier as an employer at Spring Close, where in the post-war period both the abandoned quarry floor in the north-west and open land useless for agricultural purposes to the south-east had become available for industry. The total textile emphasis of earlier years had been replaced by a heterogeneous collection of largely unrelated small industries. The jobs of the inhabitants of Spring Close had become equally diversified, and relatively few were in Spring Close.

Retail provision and its location

As Spring Close emerged from the lace boom period to become a more stable and balanced community and social unit, its services improved, and from the middle of the 19th century onwards day-to-day shopping needs were well catered for. There were the usual dressmakers, washerwomen (or laundresses), the cow keepers or dairymen, the coal dealer, market gardener and stonemason, and the cordwainer or bootmaker and repairer, supplemented by several retail shops. The licenced victualler - the Travellers Rest - was long-established in its location, and in place of casually distributed ephemeral shops at the houses of workpeople there was an increased tendency after the mid-century for certain particular houses to become established as shop premises, though the nature of the shop might change with the tenant.

The chief shop sites at Spring Close came to be Nos. 9 and 13 Spring Close, and Nos. 10, 15 and 25 Commercial Street. The periods during which these operated, and the nature of their business were as follows [32] :

9 Spring Close: 1864 to about 1924.
Briefly a butcher: then provisions and earthenware: thereafter probably a general shop.

13 Spring Close: 1858 to 1956 and later.
Mainly grocery, though James Beresford in the early 1870s was a fishmonger and greengrocer, and his successor in the 1880s, John Shaw, was a 'skinner and grocer', which means that he worked at Bayleys' and his wife ran the shop.

10 Commercial Street: 1864 to 1936 or later.
At first general groceries - George Selby kept the shop from about 1860 to about the end of the century; briefly fried fish around 1904-05; then greengrocery until the second world war, when it finished.

15 Commercial Street: 1860s to 1940s.
At first varied, with periods as grocer, small ware dealer and joiner and cabinet maker; but later chiefly haberdashery and millinery.

25 Commercial Street: 1890s to 1956 or later.
General shop.

A list of shopkeepers is given in Appendix 24. Business was also conducted from other houses for shorter periods. For example, Gregory Yarnall, and later his widow, carried on a retail business at 22 Commercial Street as a haberdasher and 'wardrobe dealer' from 1900 until the mid-1920s; and 37a Commercial Street was a shop from about 1912 into the first world war period, kept successively by Samuel Widdowson, J.C.Norris and Miss Alice Cocking. Market gardening was associated especially with No. 37 Spring Close in the 19th century, carried on by Thomas Nettleship, for example: and then, until the first world war, this house was a dairy. It may be added that only one school is known from Spring Close, and this was run for only a few years around 1890 by Mrs. Ellen Podmore at 33a Spring Close, at the western end of Snowton Terrace [33] . The distribution of the premises described above is seen in Figure 101.

Quarrying

One further industrial enterprise - the quarrying of sand - should be mentioned again (having already been discussed in a geological context) because it formed a very prominent

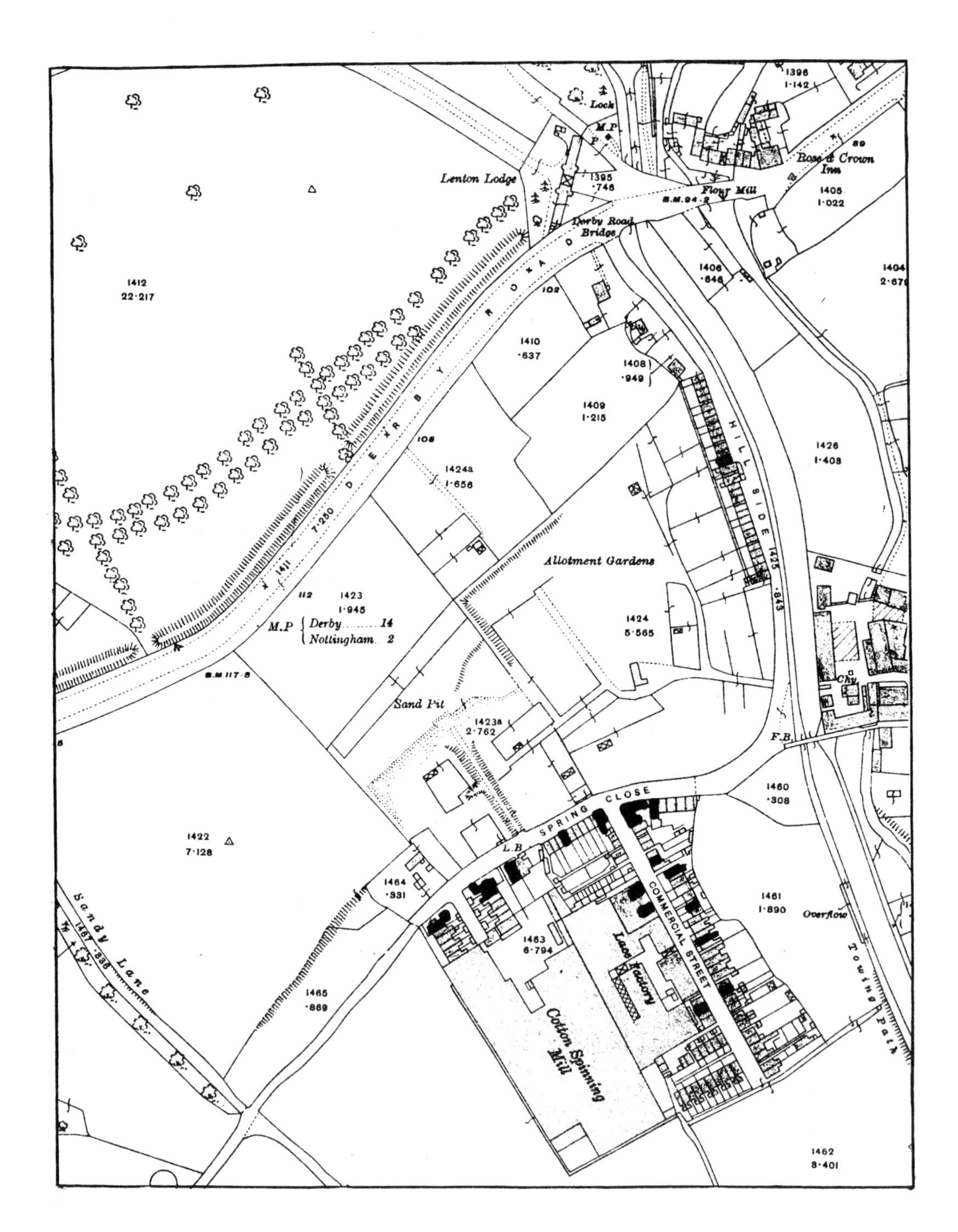

Figure 101: Spring Close and Hillside showing locations of retail shops
The retail shops operated during various periods - see Appendix 24. Note - since 1881 the Hillside malting had been converted into a row of small cottages, and further houses built at Spring Close. [Base map from O.S. 25-inch map of 1915]

feature of the general environment of Spring Close. The fine, red, soft sandstone called Lenton Sandstone is the country rock north of Spring Close, and the low cliff where it met the superficial deposits of the valley floor approximately along the line of the Spring Close road was the natural southern boundary of Beck Field. It formed well drained and reasonably fertile land, very easy to cultivate, and therefore popular as allotment gardens for the past century. Unauthorized removal of the easily dug material was widespread in the past, and for much of the 19th century both the Lenton Sandstone and its overlying glacial sand and gravel were worked commercially, latterly chiefly as moulding sand for the local iron industry.

Substantial working of gravel and sand began at the eastern end of the outcrop, nearest to the canal, and progressed westwards, although a quarry face in the close north of Elmtree Terrace was shown on the large-scale map of 1881 [34] and sand was dug at various points from time to time [35] .In the later 19th and early 20th century a sand pit located due north of the Travellers Rest inn had its exit to the canal bank. It appears from hachuring on maps of 1881 and later that this succeeded a working further east and north-east behind Hillside [36] , and by 1913 this eastern section was given over to allotment gardens, while there was sand quarrying opposite to the Spring Close factories, opening to Spring Close itself [37] . The western section of the sandstone slope, allotment gardens in the 1920s, was later, in its turn, quarried for moulding sand, and the quarry face had retreated halfway or more towards the gardens of the houses built alongside Derby Road by 1938 [38] . This area was worked out during the 1940s by the firm of Thomas F. Suffolk, called 'moulding sand merchants', which had begun operations by 1916, and in the 1950s and 1960s the floor of the worked-out quarry was occupied by several industrial premises (Figure 104). It must be questioned, however, whether either the quarrying or the industries that moved in behind it ever offered much employment for residents of Spring Close.

At the 1881 census 93 families lived at Spring Close: in 1956, 75 years later, 101 households were included in Kelly's Directory. If the eight newer houses in Spring Close Gardens and on the north side of Spring Close road are deducted this reduces to 93: but this is coincidental, for in the intervening years Mitre Terrace, with seven houses was lost, nine houses were added at Ebury Terrace, and there were gains by infilling and losses by abandonment on Commercial Street. Furthermore, the population will have declined because of a reduced family size; but it had been sustained at a rather constant level over some 80 or 90 years, during which obsolete local industries were replaced by more modern ones. But perhaps the chief reason for the retention of population in the old housing of Spring Close in recent times of increased individual mobility of workers had been simply the existence of the houses themselves in a relatively prosperous and still growing city region.

Comprehensive redevelopment for industry

Much of the old housing of Spring Close, some dating back to the 1830s, and, as a whole, run down and part of a drab and depressing local environment when stripped of nostalgia, was below the physical standard looked for in the post-war period. That it remained almost fully occupied might be attributed to the housing shortage and to the inertia of social cohesion. The Nottingham Development Plan dated 1952 allocated the residential areas of Spring Close and Commercial Street for industrial use, and expected the change of use to be completed in 6 to 20 years, that is, by 1958 to 1972. In the late 1950s and early 1960s 'comprehensive redevelopment' was fashionable, and by 1963 virtually all the older houses had been demolished, and only those built after 1870 remained [39] . The whole eastern part of the south side of Spring Close road as far as the western end of Snowton Terrace had gone, with the single exception of the Travellers Rest, together with all the houses on both sides of Commercial Street and those of its Yards - Hackney's and Walker's - and its Terraces, Mitre and Ebury. There was left only Spring Terrace and Elmtree Terrace, associated with the Hollins era, and the much newer houses on the north side of Spring Close road and in Spring Close Gardens, dating from the inter-war period.

It is sometimes said that the Spring Close area was cleared 'to make way for the Medical School and Hospital', but in respect of houses and population this is patently untrue, since the houses had virtually all gone, with their families rehoused, long before the question of building a Medical School and University Hospital had arisen. The Annual Reports of the University of Nottingham [40] record that the announcement of approval in principle for the establishment of a Medical School at Nottingham was made in Parliament on 27 July 1964, and the problem of finding a suitable site was addressed only later. A Public Enquiry on the acquisition of the site that was favoured took place more than three years later, in September and October 1967, with a favourable decision announced in March 1968: and an appeal and its delays meant that work could not begin on building before October 1969 - though in the event the construction of Phase I of the Teaching Hospital and Medical School began only in May 1971, seven years after the first approval. By this time all the houses at Spring Close had gone [41], though the row at Hillside remained. Because of its urban setting the open land south of Spring Close could not be farmed and was used for a variety of purposes, including a timber yard (Simms Son and Cooke), a petrol station on Clifton Boulevard, a large children's playground and several small, badly-built new houses on Abbey Street. The main clearance work for the Queen's Medical Centre therefore involved industrial buildings and sites, some of them by now long established, and it was from the firms using these that the chief objections to the siting of the Q.M.C. came. The objectors had a good case in view of the planning history, but they did not include earlier residents of Spring Close, most of them having left more than a decade earlier.

Hillside and its malting

Although only a hundred yards from the houses of Spring Close, the row of about thirty cottages alongside the canal bank between Spring Close and Derby Road was quite distinct in origin and in character, and for this reason is now described separately from Spring Close, though it is also now part of the Q.M.C. site. The malting from which the cottages were formed was also not mentioned among the early industrial developments for much the same reason.

The malting at Hillside, or 'Canalside', had ready access by the Nottingham Canal to Wollaton and Erewash valley coal, and via the Grantham Canal to Lincolnshire cereals, as well as to Nottingham and its breweries by road and to Newark by the Trent. The date of its establishment is not known, but it was certainly in existence in 1823, and may have been considerably earlier. For much of the 19th century it was owned by Samuel Hole of Caunton, whose family firm is better known for its brewing and malting interests at Newark, but it is not known whether the malting was actually built by them. Hole first appeared in partnership with a local man, John Harrison of New Sneinton, who may have started the Hillside business. Hole also owned a malting at Leenside [Dearden 1834 134] in partnership with Harrison, who was named as a maltster in Glover's Directory for 1825. Pigott [1828-29 652] included a maltster list with Samuel Hole of Lenton, and in 1832, when the Election Poll Book included Samuel Hole of Caunton as a freehold property owner in Lenton, White's Directory named two maltsters in Lenton - Hall and Harrison (probably a printer's error for Hole and Harrison) and James Pidcock of Middleton Place. Unfortunately the early directories of Nottingham - for example, those published by The Review Office in 1815, by Sutton in 1818 and by Glover in 1825 did not include details of Old Lenton, and thus any malting there would not figure in their lists of maltsters.

There is some evidence that if the malting was founded before 1818 it was not by Samuel Hole. Caunton manor and estate were bought from George Martin by Samuel Hole 'of Manchester, merchant' and John Hole of Newark, mercer and draper, in October 1819, with the aid of a mortgage from James Bradley of Caunton, which was reconveyed in 1823 [42] , though a Samuel Hole, farmer, of Caunton was mentioned in 1810. Samuel Hole of the Hillside malting was born in 1778, and was the father of James Hole, his successor as maltster, and of Samuel Reynolds Hole, Dean of Rochester (1819-1904) writer and famous rose grower. The balance of probabilities is that Samuel Hole came to the Hillside malting in the mid-1820s, and that it had been started by John Harrison, perhaps a decade earlier.

The Hillside malting was a large structure parallel to the canal, and shown by published large-scale maps to have been about 140 yards long. This estimate is confirmed by plans for its conversion to houses in 1902, discussed later (Figure 102) which show it to have been about 30 feet deep, giving a total ground area of about 12,600 square feet, or, excluding several cottages, over 10,000 square feet for the 'malt rooms' [43] . It is surprising, therefore, that J.T.Godfrey in his 1884 book on the history of Lenton, should fail to mention its existence, both in his itinerary for a walk round the parish and in his chapter on 'Manufactures' (pages 355-361), unless it was for a personal reason similar to that responsible for his omission to mention Benjamin Walker's lace factory which was largely responsible for the growth of Spring Close and Commercial Street, and was one of the largest employers of Lenton people. The malting was shown on the map of Gregory Gregory's estate in Lenton and Radford surveyed in 1818-23 almost exactly as it appears on large-scale O.S. maps later in the century. George Sanderson's map surveyed in 1830-34 faithfully represents the long, narrow building, but the 1st edition O.S. 1-inch map of 1838 is inaccurate as well as too small in scale to give a true indication of the buildings at Hillside. Chapman's 1-inch map of Nottinghamshire, printed 1785 but surveyed 1774, though much too early to include either canal or malting, does indicate building that would be at the northern end of Hillside and may represent one or more of the old cottages discussed below.

Samuel Hole continued to be recorded as of Hillside ('sometimes called Canal side') malting almost until his death in 1868 [Pigott 1842, Glover 1844, Lascelles and Hagar 1848, Slater 1850, White 1853, Drake 1865]; but in Wright [1866] and Morris [1869] it was James Hole, with William Daybell his foreman. James Hole remained proprietor of the Hillside malting, with Daybell as foreman, and later called manager, until the 1880s. He also carried on the Leenside malting, with W. Beecroft as manager.

The main business of the firm of S. and J. Hole was at Northgate, Newark, and with the progressive decline in the importance of canal transport as the century progressed the Hillside malting must have become increasingly marginal in location, and economically anomalous for a brewing enterprise based at Newark. In 1884 or 1885 the Hillside malting was sold to J. Pidcock and Co., with W. Pidcock the proprietor and Nathaniel Samuel Rawlings as foreman in 1887 [Kelly]. The firm of J. Pidcock and Company, already in New Lenton in 1842 [Pigott] had offices in Dean Street, Nottingham and malt rooms in Barker Gate and several other locations in Nottingham and Radford. By 1895, however, the Hillside malting had been sold again, this time to the brewers and maltsters William Henry Hutchinson and Son of the Prince of Wales Brewery, Percy Street, Basford, with offices at 20 Upper Parliament Street, Nottingham. James Hole of the Castle Brewery, Newark, retained the Leenside malting in 1900 according to Wright's Directory. The disadvantages of the location of the Hillside malting in the railway age, for an enterprise relying on the collection and assembling of bulky materials, especially barley, could not be gainsaid, and the malting ceased to operate in 1901 or 1902.

The early Hillside cottages

The Gregory estate map of about 1820 depicts three buildings between the northern end of the malting and Derby Road. What is not clear from published maps, but is apparent from the 1902 plans for conversion of the malting is that there were two dwellings (probably originally one, but extended and divided) attached to the southern end of the malting, and perhaps an integral part of the building, and two further dwellings, sometimes used as one, in the centre of it. But it is known from the Census Enumerators' Books for 1841 to 1881 inclusive that there were about 8 dwellings at Hillside in that period.

The most northerly building at Hillside is now known as Lyndale House, 363 Derby Road. In 1820 Derby Road did not pass that way, for its diversion down Adams Hill dates only from 1822, and Lyndale House faced the Nottingham canal and was part of Hillside. A recent article in 'The Lenton Listener' [No. 20, 1982] described this much-altered house as originally forming two tiny, closely adjacent, single-storey cottages (although if this interpretation is correct they were joined together before 1841). There is some suggestion that these two tiny cottages were represented by a single building symbol on Chapman's map surveyed in 1774, prior to the building of the canal and the other Hillside houses. If the four (originally probably three) cottages forming part of the malting building were all present in 1841, then the eight dwellings described in the 1841 census books must suggest that one, or, more probably, both of the two buildings between Lyndale House and the malting were subdivided into two dwellings. Sanderson's map of 1830-34 appears to show four buildings north of the malting, and it is possible that Lyndale House was, indeed, originally two cottages, or there was another cottage north of the malting then, of which nothing is known; but this is unlikely.

None of the eight Hillside dwellings were occupied by lace workers in 1841 [44] , for the rapidly growing urban village of Spring Close-Commercial Street was still very small and the factory system as yet undeveloped, so that special workshop facilities were required in the houses of lace makers, and the Hillside cottages were not built for that purpose. The processes of malting demand frequent attention from maltsters, and the incorporation of cottages within the malting building is understandable. No head of household at Hillside was employed in either lace or leather manufacture (at Bayley's tannery opposite across the canal bridge) throughout the period 1841 to 1881, although many younger members of the Hillside families did become lace workers, especially as Benjamin Walker's lace factory came into operation. Among the householders at Hillside the leading jobs were those of agricultural labourer (including gardener) and maltster. The former category was predominant among all Hillside workers at first, but disappeared in the 1860s as lace took over. The remaining categories of employment for the Hillside cottages were various, but malting was always represented, and there were at least three malting workers living at Hillside at each census between 1841 and 1881 except for 1861.

Further details of the earlier Hillside cottages and the families and individuals who lived in them are given in Appendix 25. In particular it is shown that the two buildings between the malting and Lyndale House were two pairs of semi-detached thatched cottages, probably belonging to two families in the mid-19th century, but usually occupied together by four households. The more northerly cottage was associated with the Pearsons and that near the northern end of the malting with the Kirkhams. Both cottages are seen on a photograph reproduced in the Lenton Times [No. 2 1989] though the more northerly is only partially visible. Although continuity is not certain their occupancy can be deduced (see Appendix 25).

Conversion of the malting into the Hillside Terrace

Until the census books for 1891 and 1901 become available there is little information about any changes in the Hillside cottages in the later 19th century. Fred Hilton in 1986 [Lenton Listener No. 39] described how 'between our terrace and Derby Road were two large houses, then two small cottages and finally Lyndale House', but it is not clear whether this implies that the southern cottages were larger than northerly ones or whether new buildings had appeared - which were certainly not shown on the O.S. 50-inch map of 1915 (revised to 1913). To the south, however, there were great changes, for in 1902-03 the malting was converted into cottages, increasing the number of dwellings on that site from three or four to 30. The 1902 conversion plan submitted by W. Savage, shows that the tiny cottages in the row were about 22 feet deep, compared with the malting's original 30 feet, and only about 11½ feet wide fronting the road, their floor areas, on two storeys, totalling only 500 square feet (Figure 102).

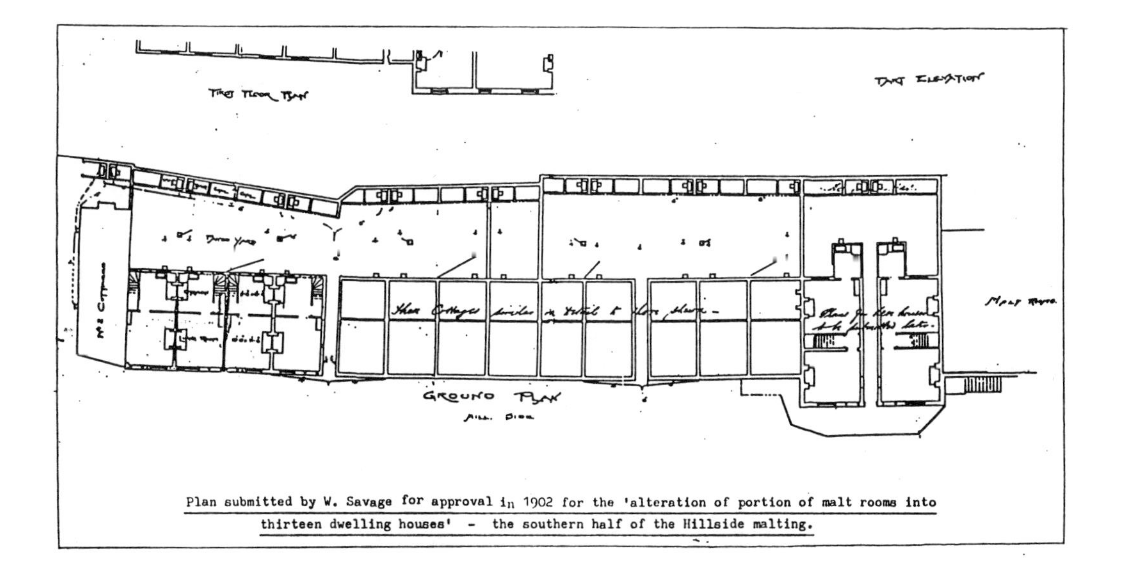

Figure 102: Plans for conversion of the Hillside malting to terraced houses in 1901-02
[Courtesy S. Zaleski and NCLS]

The total ground area of the 26 new cottages was less than three-quarters of the area of the malting rooms that they replaced.

After the building of the terrace the Hillside dwellings were numbered from north to south, the terrace itself being given even numbers from 18 to 72 inclusive, (as if a row with matching odd numbers was expected on the canal towpath) with the two surviving central cottages of the former malting numbered 44 and 46. But the house attached to the southern end of the former malting was un-numbered. Although shown as two dwellings in 1902 it was formed into one, as shown on the O.S. 1:2,500 map of 1915, and was occupied by Thomas Suffolk, who operated the moulding sand quarry behind. He remained there, according to the directories, from 1916 or earlier until at least 1941. Land south of this house contained premises occupied by Duckworth Brothers, coal dealers in the 1920s and early 1930s, and Kelly's Directories of 1928 and 1932 gave these the number 74 Hillside.

The numbering of Hillside is shown on the O.S. 1:1,250 maps of 1963. Evidently provision was made for eight numbered dwellings north of the Terrace, probably excluding Lyndale House, now with a gate to Derby Road although its front door and porch faced the canal, and numbered 363 Derby Road. It is not known which numbers were given to the old cottages there, but it is thought that the cottage near the northern end of the Terrace was No. 16, and the second old building 2/4, comprising two dwellings. Five 'new' houses built in about 1923 by W.J.Norris acquired the even numbers 6 to 14. According to Mr. Hilton 'the two small cottages were demolished to make way for them', which may be misleading because the five new detached houses (which remain today - see Figure 103) were built above the steep valley-side slope, and the lower strip of land on which the early cottages stood between the foot of

Figure 103: Aerial view of Spring Close and Hillside from the west, 1964
[Photo. by Messrs. Tempest, July 1964. Courtesy Mr. Beric Tempest]

the cliff and the canal formed their gardens and garage sites. The Hillside residents named in the directories from 1928 all lived in the new houses, and by then the old cottages were unoccupied or already demolished. Unfortunately their last occupiers are not known, although

Figure 104: Aerial view of the site of the Queen's Medical Centre from the north, 1964
Commercial Street has been completely demolished and few houses were left along Spring Close by this date. At top left the junction of the Beeston and Nottingham canals is seen; and concentric within the bend of Nottingham canal the former line of the river Leen and within its bend the site of Lenton Priory.

Mr. Hilton referred to a Billy Broughton, who lived with his grandmother in what was the last thatched building in Lenton.

Appendix 25 lists the householders of Hillside in 1936, 1941, 1950, and 1956, and in addition those in the new detached houses in 1928 and 1932. The lists are interesting because they show the wide variety of occupations followed by the residents of Hillside Terrace and reveal the considerable changes in tenancy between 1941 and 1950, doubtless associated with the upheavals brought by war, as compared with the relative stability in the years preceding and following. However, few names are known of the residents of the Terrace in its earlier years, but the 'village shopkeeper' or its equivalent is an exception. The only shop at Hillside was always at the same house, No. 42, near the middle of the Terrace, an example of the persistence remarked upon earlier (Figure 101). It was a grocery and sweets and tobacco shop throughout the existence of the terrace. In 1905 it was occupied by Mrs. Elizabeth Miller; in 1907 by Samuel Hogg; from 1910 or earlier until 1921 by Isaac Stevens; and then, briefly, by Henry Stevens. Then came Mrs. Anne Lowe until May 1926 [45] followed by Mrs. Elsie Nolan (in 1928) and Mrs. E. Husband (1932); and by 1936 it was Mrs. Laura Miller, who was still there in 1956.

The Hillside row suffered the same fate as Spring Close and Commercial Street and their Yards and Terraces, but in the case of Hillside the site has not even been built upon. On the University campus to the west many features of the earlier landscape have been incorporated into the modern one - houses, roads, gardens, trees: but here everything has been totally swept away, leaving nothing other than the road northwards from the bridge to Leen Gate and the abandoned quarry faces as reminders of everything that went before - the ultimate historical desert of 'comprehensive redevelopment'.

NOTES

1. N.A.O., RD 31. 'A Mappe of ye Lordshippe of Lenton and Radford taken the tenthe day of Julye anno 1632 by me Richard Smythe surveyor'. There is a scale of perches. Much of the map is heavily covered by opaque green paint, which renders its annotation virtually illegible in photocopy.
2. State Papers 1637 Vol. 369, No. 82
3. L.A.O., 2 PG 3/1/9 (1651). L.A.O. 1 PG 3/3/3/1.
4. L.A.O., 1 PG 3/3/1/1 (1664)
5. L.A.O., 2 PG 3/1/10 (1725)
6. L.A.O., 1 PG 3/3/5/2 (1738) : N.U.M.D., Mi 1/39/4 (1812) copy
7. L.A.O., 2 PG 3/1/11 (1768)
8. N.A.O., RD 4 L. 'Map of the estate of Gregory Gregory Esq. in the Lordships of Lenton and Radford in the county of Nottingham'. Surveyed by H.M.Wood in the years 1818 to 1823.
9. N.U.M.D., Mi 4 Da 2/10 20 February 1794 (copy)
10. N.U.M.D., Mi 4 Da 2/13. Of the three closes included two were occupied by Elias Roberts: the Spring Close was not. John Wright of Lenton Hall bought most of the other Upton-Sills property.
11. See S.D.Chapman [1967 84, 140]. Henry Green, a member of the High Pavement Chapel, was Mayor of Nottingham in 1793 [Stalker 1793]. The firm of Killingley, Green and Son were 'Manufacturers of hose in general' [Bailey 1783].
12. Glover [1844 125 et seq.] provides a good account of the replacement of the hosiery trade, which employed fewer hands in Lenton in 1831 than in 1811, and a review of the early development of the lace industry, with speculation on bobbin net machines in 1823-25, failures in 1825-26, gains in 1827, losses in 1828 (with working time restrictions), a rally in 1829, renewed depression in 1831-32 and despair in 1833-34.
13. 'Nottingham Guardian', 25 September 1846
14. In 1850, according to Slater's Directory, Thomas Towle, bootmaker, was in Kyte Street, New Lenton. The Beer House Act of 1830 allowed almost any householder to sell beer, and by 1832 there were at least four beerhouses in Lenton, of which The Peacock was one. It may have been no more than a back room of Towle's cottage.
15. Census of 1841, taken 8 June, Enumerators' Books. For Spring Close H.O. 107/858, pp. 34-37.
16. 'Nottingham Guardian' 25 September 1846
17. ibid.
18. F.A.Wells, *Hollins and Viyella: a study in business history* 1968, 78
19. Lenton Priory church registers N.A.O.
20. In the 1841 Census Enumerators' Books George Bradley (65) described as a lacemaker was living at Birch House with his wife Mary (65) and Caroline, aged 8, presumably his granddaughter. They had three servants. In 1848 [Lascelles and Hagar] he was called a 'lace thread manufacturer' with premises at Park Street, Nottingham. He was still at Birch House in 1853 [White 1853], by then aged 77, and in 1856 Fyfe [1856 113] called him 'the late Mr. Bradley': so he died in about 1855. The Tucker works at Snoton Spring was leased to Hollins in 1856, and John Tucker may have moved to Birch House then. He was certainly there by 1861.
21. Census of 1881, Enumerators' Books RG 11/3340
22. Godfrey [1884 357-58] recounted at length the achievements of John Livesey, especially in devising new methods of lace production, particularly for curtains, with 'the consecutive assistance of Elsey, Sisling and Cope' from 1846 onwards.
23. Benjamin Walker was described in 1842 as 'metal dealer' [Pigot] and in 1844 as 'dealer in metal, Derby Road' [Glover], and 'iron, steel and metal dealer and roller, Derby Road' [White].
24. Lascelles and Hagar 1848 - 'Benjamin Walker, Iron, steel and metal warehouse and rolling mill, Derby Road, and lace manufacturer, Spring Close, Lenton'.
25. Fyfe [1856 153-157] gave a detailed description of the working of 'the great fellmongers yard of Messrs. Bayley and Shaw, so well known in the American export trade'. Mellors [1912] noted that Isaac Bayley began the leather business at Lenton before 1790, and the Thomas Bayley of 1851 was the grandson of Isaac's brother Thomas, and co-founder with Benjamin Walker senior of the Lenton Cooperative Society. He bought and lived at Lenton Abbey - see Chapter X.
26. Census of 1861, Enumerators' Books RG 9/2447
27. Census of 1881, Enumerators' Books RG 11/3340 9 April 1881.

28. O.S. 1:500 map (10.56 feet to 1 mile, or 41.66 feet to 1 inch) of the Town and County of the Town of Nottingham, Castle Ward, sheets XLII.5.12, XLII.5.13 and adjoining sheets. Copies in N.A.O..
29. Much of the following detail concerning William Coates and Sons in Lenton is derived from an article in the *Lenton Listener* 24 (May-June 1983). The drawing of the Spring Close works in that article contains more than a little artist's licence, in that the houses of Spring Terrace and Elm Tree Terrace, which should have occupied the foreground (they were there from the mid-19th century until about 1960) have been spirited away to leave a broad roadway that never existed.
30. L.A.O., 4 PG (conveyance). See Wood's map (fn. 7 above).
31. The details in this paragraph are drawn mainly from the Directories of Kelly and Wright.
32. The data given are derived mainly from the Directories of White, Slater, Vice, Kelly, Wright and Morris for various years.
33. Wright's Directories of 1889 and 1891 included Mrs. Podmore's school: those of 1887 and 1894 did not.
34. O.S. 1:500 map (see fn. 28 above)
35. J. Shipman's geological map of 1884 shows 'Gravel Pit' in this location. His comment [Godfrey 1884 447] on a section drawn in 1879 that the red sand rock's highly contorted surface 'could be seen better about sixteen years ago. and before so much of it was cut away' suggests active quarrying here between 1868 and 1884. There was a working face here in the 1860s.
36. O.S. map, 6 inches to 1 mile, 2nd edition 1901 (revised to 1899)
37. See, for example, O.S. map 25 inches to 1 mile, 1915 (revised to 1913)
38. The O.S. 6 inches to 1 mile Provisional Edition map, claiming to be revised to 1938, shows only allotment gardens at the western end of the slope above Spring Close: but quarrying was already in progress when Clifton Boulevard was under construction in 1937, and the face had retreated substantially by 1938 when the writer visited the quarry as a student with Prof. H.H.Swinnerton.
39. O.S. map 1:1,250 or 50.688 inches to 1 mile, revised to December 1963.
40. Reports of the Council to the Court, printed in the Annual Reports of the University of Nottingham for 1963-64 to 1970-71.
41. O.S. map, 1:10,000, Sheet SK 5439 SE (1970-71)
42. N.A.O., Hole Papers
43. I am indebted to Mr. Stephen Zaleski for providing these details.
44. Census of 1841, Enumerators' Books. H.O. 107/858 p. 35. As mentioned earlier the Poor Rate Book for 1825 included Hillside, showing that the cottages were in existence then - an argument for an early date for the malting.
45. The *Lenton Times* No. 1 (1988) includes a note by Mrs. Anne Lowe, who had many customers from Spring Close - and one from Lenton Firs, Sir Thomas Shipstone, who walked to her shop to buy a cigar each morning, and was taken thence to his Basford office by his chauffeur, Matthews.

CHAPTER XV

TRENT WONG AND GROVE FARM

Introduction

Grove Farm, now used as University playing fields, is an extensive tract of meadow land alongside the river Trent at some distance from the University's main campus, though still within the parish of Lenton (Figure 105). It has been mentioned earlier as a detached part of the demesne land of the former priory, and it maintained its identity within probably unchanged boundaries from medieval into modern times. On 1 January 1960 a conveyance to the University from Mrs. Nellie Burnett, widow, with her son Colin as trustee, reunited in ownership these flood meadows with the University campus.

Trent Wong - priory demesne meadow.

A valuation of 1387 refers to 80 acres of meadow in demesne (in addition to six carucates of land), each acre valued at 2s. 6d. a year beyond the outgoings, which would total £10 a year[1]. In May 1538, on the Dissolution of the priory, a rental of Lenton and Radford distinguished its demesne land from lands of other categories of tenure, and the demesne schedule concludes with the meadow called Trent Wong, held with the rest of the demesne by Michael Stanhope at an annual rent of £8 for the Wong [2]. Stanhope's secondary lease of demesne lands, granted by the Crown soon afterwards, included 'a medow called Trent Wonge conteynyng by estimacon lvi acres lett among ye tennantts there' and valued at £8 [3]. This does not necessarily mean that it was no longer used in association with the farming of the rest of the priory demesne lands, but that it was divided among a number of tenants of the priory. Soon afterwards it was opened to wider uses, becoming subject to seasonal commoning. In 1545 it was involved in the 'award' of commons to the husbandmen and cottagers of Lenton by Henry Willoughby and Sir Hugh Willoughby [4], 'by the consent and agreement of the said husbands and cottagers thereof'.

The commoning system was operated by the 'burleymen', who were two husbandmen and one cottager 'who shall be elected by the homage of the township'. Under the agreement 'every husbandman for every oxgang of land shall have thre[e] be[a]sts pastures free, and every husband at his pleasure to take one of another['s] catell into his number for his pasture, but not to be taken of any strange or forigne'. In consideration of this the husbandmen 'as they been accustomed afore times shall carye and load at all times necessarye stone gravell and tymber for the reparation of the bryggs, causys and high wayes and car[ry]ing free'. Cottagers were to have for every cottage 120 beast pastures - interpreted as a total of 120 'gates' shared among them - 'paying for every beast 4d by year, the one half to be paid at Mayday at the puttyng in of the catell and the other half to be payd at Michelmas'. The money collected by the 'byrleymen' was used to pay 'the Kyngs rents and also Lords rents due and accustomed'; and the balance was to be 'bestowed to the common wealth of the towne as to the maintenance of the hyways, bryggs, causes [causeways] and scouryng of dychys by the cauling to of other too [two ?] honest men to the sayd burleymen wych shalbe elected by the township to se[e] the bestowyng of ye same'. Labourers were paid from this money for repairing 'hyways causeys bryggs and dychys'.

While this document provides for cattle to be put on common land on 1 May, at the beginning of the grass flush, the date was in practice delayed on hay meadows until Lammas (1 August), and the burleymen's accounts for Lenton in 1622 [5] show that this was the case at Trent Wong. A cessment (fol.1) on 13 May 1622 for the burleymen to pay for 'all those beast pastures that are wanting for the fraughtinge of the pasture that are put downe betweene Lammas and Michaelmas into pasture or medowes by the Jurye ...' at the rate of every beast 5d. and every horse, mare and ox 2d., provided £4.11s. 2d. for 219 beasts owned by 63 persons. The receipts for 1622 (fol. 2) are set out in six columns - Gates: Free gates: Taking gates: Lammas stage: Trent Wonge: and Ditche Silver: and 63 persons were accounted for. All 63 were charged under Trent Wong at between ½d. and 6d., and the total receipts for this only were £1.13s.0½d. for totals of 88 gates, 93 free gates, 127 taking gates. A second levy was made on 15 June 1622 (fol. 3) at a rate of 2d. a beast 'to be collected by Nicholas Stampe and Henrye Gardam, burlimen for Lenton'. A third cessment was made on 1 December 1622 (fol. 4-5) after the rate of 2d. a beast, 1d. a horse, and 4d a score of sheep. Disbursements by the burlimen (fol. 8) [6] in 1622 as well as payments (fol. 7) for 'those beasts pastures that are not fraughted after the rate of 12d. a beast' included payments to a swineherd; heathard, for tailing the pasture, mending the Cockbridge and the Leene bridge; and for work on roads and damming the river (presumably the Leen) [7]. All this as it applied to Trent Wong related to the aftermath, because it was let in sections as hay meadow by the holder of the Crown lease of the priory demesne [8].

The area of Trent Wong given in various rentals and terriers from the 16th century onwards was usually about 100 acres, though at other times about 50 acres. For example, in about 1539 the estimated area was 96 acres, and the rental of about 1554 gave the same area, though an undated survey, probably of the early 17th century recorded only 50a.12.14p. [9]. An undated document, earlier than 1604, estimated four score and sixteen - that is 96 acres again [10]. In connection with this variation it is interesting to find that the area of Trent Wong in the 19th century, between Beeston parish, the river Trent and the Lenton common pasture and meadow enclosed in 1769 was in two parts - 30 to 40 acres of closes in the north and 56 acres of open land, crossed by several footpaths in the south, suggesting that these two parts of Trent Wong were managed differently, and perhaps from an early date. The two parts are well distinguished on the O.S. 6-inch maps, especially the First Edition (Figure 105).

By the time of the rental of about 1554 [11] the secondary lease of the executed Sir Michael Stanhope had been granted to Alexander Wright, and it included Trent Wong, which still contributed £8 to the total rent of £22. 6s.0d. and was described as a meadow. Its value to the leaseholder was very considerable, for in the early 17th century 'Trent Wonge being enclosed, wch is not as yet walled, is valued to be worthe ye sum of £48' [12]. The Crown lease of 1601 to Thomas Cooper, Philip Hanmer and Thomas Hanmer [13] of the 'Alexander Wright closes' does not appear to have included Trent Wong with them, and its renewal in 1628 [14] (though

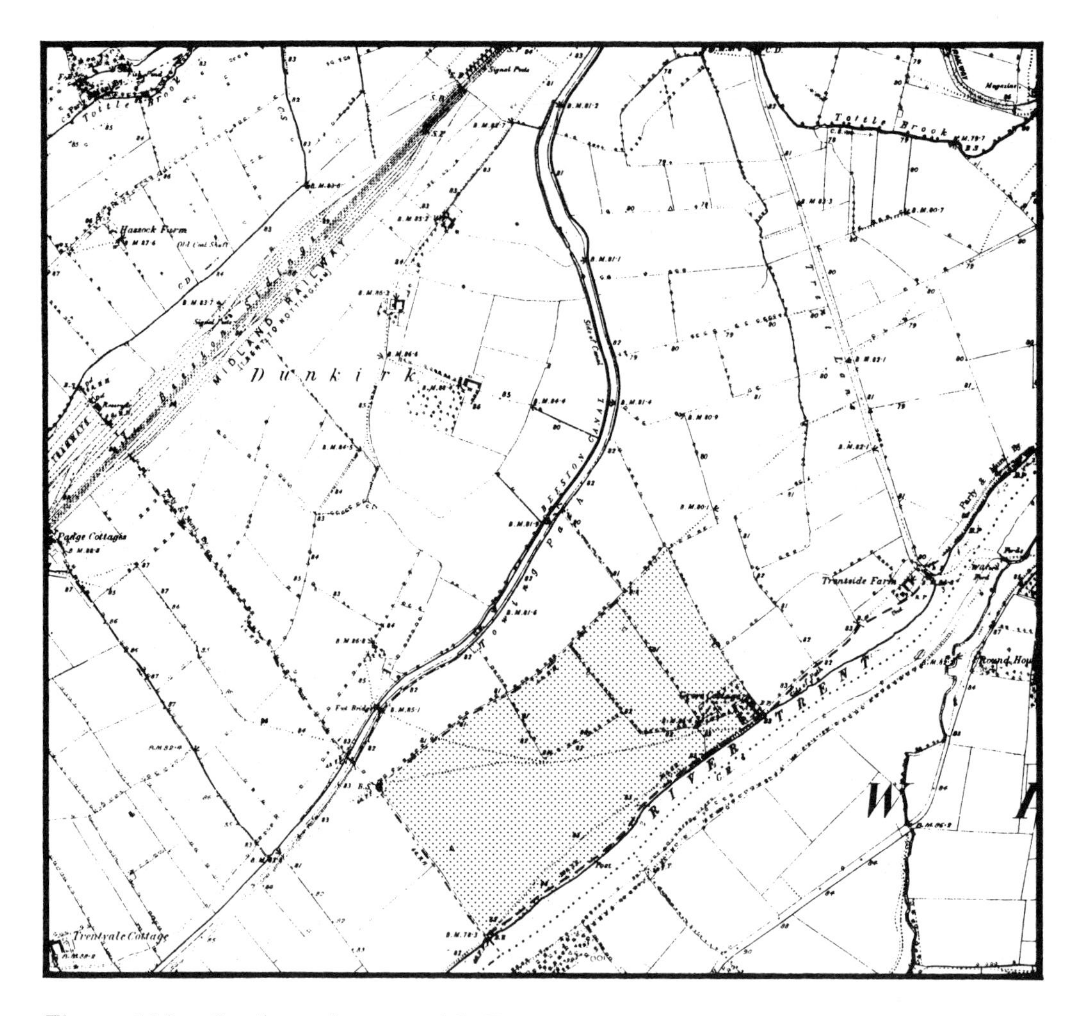

Figure 105: Southern Lenton, with Trent Wong and The Holmes
[From O.S. 6-inch map of 1883] Trent Wong is indicated by stippling. Note the proximity of Wilford ford.

reading is hampered by the decay of the manuscript) also appears to omit it. Although Trent Wong was not among the lands leased by Sir Michael Hicks to Sir Percival Willoughby from 1609 to 1630 [15] it was leased by Hicks to Robert Nixe for at least much of the period and was included with the main priory estate when it was sold by Sir William Hicks to Thomas Winford in 1684. It was then described as a piece or parcel of pasture land, about 100 acres in area, and occupied by Mr. Garland [16]. This John Garland, who lived at the Hall in Lenton village, farmed at that time the largest holding in the Gregory estate in Lenton.

Because of its distance from Lenton village, where the Lenton farmsteads were all located, and its proximity to the Wilford ford, Trent Wong was later more conveniently used by graziers living in Wilford, across the river. In 1731 and in 1743 it was rented by Benjamin Deverall, a Wilford grazier, for £61 a year, and was described as 'that piece of meadow or pasture ground called Trent Wong, containing by estimation 100 acres' [17]. Later tenants included a Mr.Hall, who in 1780 is said to have paid £5.7s.8d. a year in land tax for it [18] but in 1784 paid £10.16s.8d.. Hall was followed in turn by Abel Smith from 1787, Robert Smith from 1796 and Samuel Smith in 1797, and Samuel bought Trent Wong at the sale of the following year [19]. It is obviously significant that Samuel Stretton of Nottingham (see Appendix 21) with the Loughborough architect William Henderson (wrongly called Anderson in the Stretton manuscripts) 'finished building a new house for Samuel Smith at Wilford in 1781'. Henderson was also the architect for Stanford Hall, built 1771-74 . Pevsner dismissed Wilford House as 'a red brick box with some Adamish trim on the entrance'.

These Smiths were members of the banking family, and can be identified in the simplified pedigree (Figure 106). They were descendants of Thomas Smith (1631-1699), son of a Cropwell Butler landowner also called Thomas Smith (1593-1642), who is said to have founded the first private bank outside London soon after 1658 [20] based on a combination of a business as a mercer and revenue remittance. This was over 30 years before the Bank of England was founded in 1694. A stained glass window in the south transept of St. Mary's church, Nottingham commemorates Thomas Smith as the 'Father of English banking'. He bought the old Bank House on Peck Lane, which became his home, mercery and bank, with vaults in the cellars.

Smiths' Bank was eventually merged into the Union of London and Smiths Bank Limited in 1902, and after seven generations of Smiths this became in 1918 the National Provincial Bank, which in 1969 became the National Westminster. Its Nottingham branch was on South Parade [21] still known as the Smith branch. Samuel and Abel Smith, sons of the founder, were signing notes in the 1730s and 1740s, but the bank had been expanded by their eldest brother Thomas, who left it to Abel when he went to London soon after 1710. Abel Smith (1687-1757) was of East Stoke near Newark. Of his three sons George, created baronet, originated the Bromley family; John, from whom the Pauncefotes were descended, became a London merchant with the East India Company and was a director of the South Sea Company in 1775; while Abel, of Bulcote near Burton Joyce, carried on the Nottingham bank, established Smith and Payne's Bank in London, and opened branches at Hull and Lincoln. Abel was a Member of Parliament for three constituencies in the 1770s and 1780s. His town house was on South Parade, Nottingham, where his son Abel died in 1779. Abel senior is said to have died 'at his seat at Wilford' in 1788, though it was for his fourth son, Samuel, that a new house, Wilford House, was built in 1781 [22]. Robert Smith (1752-1838), Abel's third son, of the London bank, was created Lord Carrington in 1796, the year he is said to have rented Trent Wong, Abel senior having had it in 1787 [23]. Lord Carrington retired from the bank. He was Pitt's chief financial adviser, his agent in the money market, and an intimate friend. Two other sons of Abel Smith II, George of Selsdon, Surrey and John of Dale Park, Sussex and Bleadon Hall were Members of Parliament, and so were Abel junior, Robert and Samuel.

With Wilford House located very close to the major ford across the Trent which served the road crossing the Holmes to Lenton (Trent Lane) it is reasonably supposed that Samuel Smith, later of Woodhall Park, Hertfordshire, but then of Wilford House, bought Trent Wong direct from Miss Milward in 1798 because of its proximity to the house and not as a bank investment. It was the only part of the Milward estate not to pass through the hands of Messrs. Pares and Paget, having been 'sold, conveyed or assigned to the use of Samuel Smith ... ' [24] who remained the owner for many years, and probably until his death in 1834. Wilford House and Trent Wong passed to his youngest son, Henry, and both remained in the Smiths' ownership until 1920, although Wilford House was occupied by John T.Forman in 1892 after the death of Henry Abel Smith, and T. Bailey Forman, the Nottingham newspaper publisher lived there from 1922 until his death in 1938.

Samuel Smith redeemed his land tax on Trent Wong in 1803, so no values are available from that source, but the occupiers down to 1832 are known. Before 1810 these were Messrs. Breedon, Williamson and Facon jointly, followed by Edward Facon alone (1811-21), John Wilkinson and Robert Gregory (1822-23) and then John Wilkinson until at least 1832. Wilkinson was an important cattle breeder who is discussed further below. His farmstead 'adjoins the

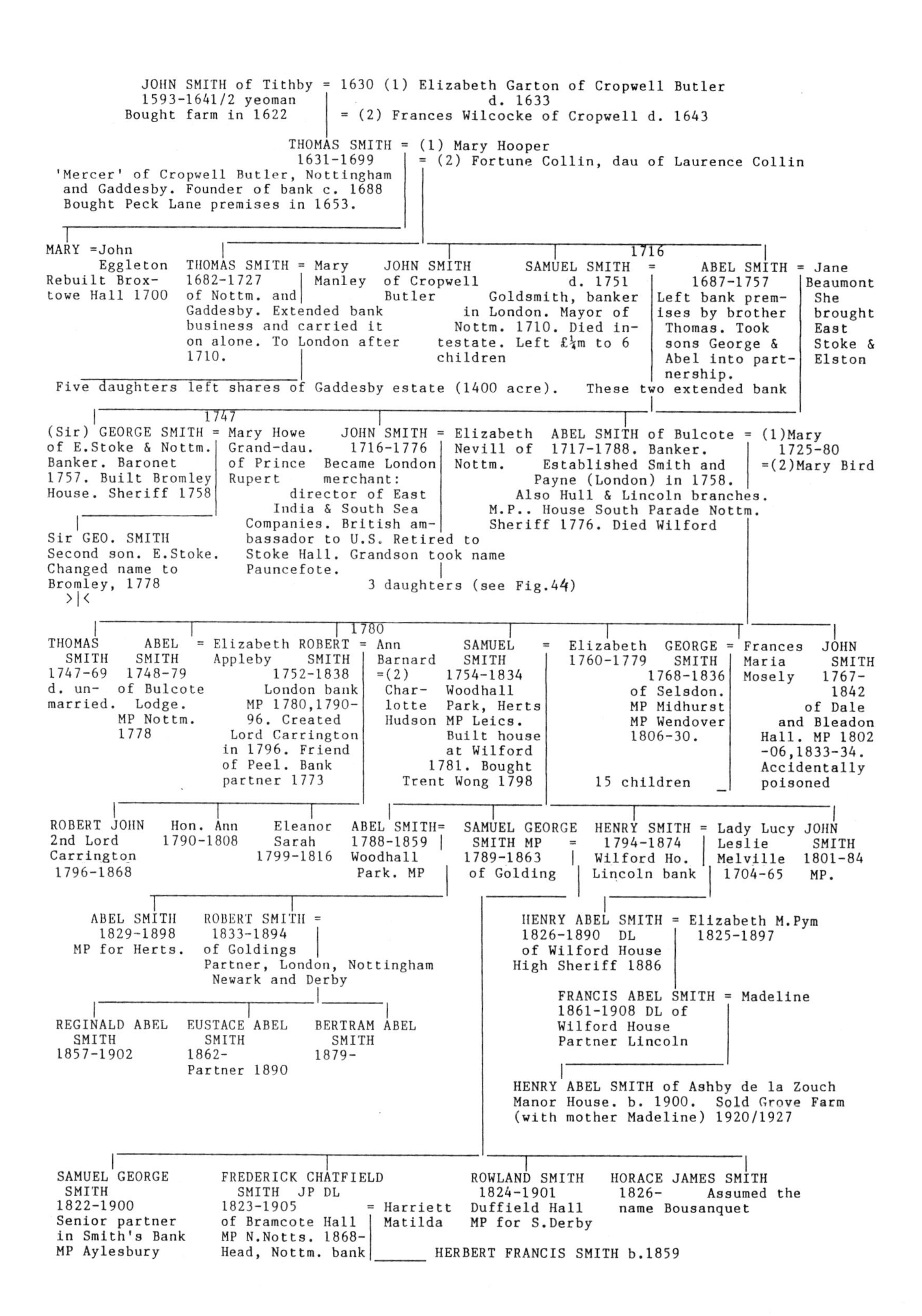

Figure 106: Selective pedigree of the banking family Smith

railway station above the intersection of Gregory Street, Lenton with the Derby Road'. Fyfe [1856 153] described 'the principal stock of this very superior herd of pure Shorthorns' which had been 'very carefully bred by Mr. Wilkinson himself for upwards of forty years' after his father had himself improved the breed. Many animals were sold off in 1854. Choice specimens had been introduced from other celebrated breeders' stock, and 'Mr. Wilkinson still keeps up a herd'. His father, William, was originally of the Odd House (Lenton Abbey) - see Chapter X.

Grove Cottage, Grove Farm and its tenants (Table 20)

The use of Trent Wong by John Wilkinson must have ended soon after 1832, with its establishment as an independent farm holding, with a farmstead, including a house called Grove Cottage built upon it. This may date from as early as 1834, the year of Samuel Smith's death, since buildings are shown on Sanderson's map of 1835 and the OS 1-inch First Edition map of 1836-38. Although these might represent only farm buildings, a house was certainly present in 1848, when Grove Cottage was named, and was occupied by Charles Shelton, aged 80, 'farmer and bone merchant' [Lascelles and Hagar 1848 26]. In the census books Grove Cottage was not named until 1881, but Charles Shelton's dwelling was one of three cottages at 'Trentside' in both 1841 and 1851. Shelton was aged about 70 in 1841. He appears to have employed a bailiff to manage the farm, living in a cottage on it with his family. Shelton kept two living-in servants, Matilda Whiteman (aged 45) and Mary Whiteman (20), probably mother and daughter, and probably relatives of Shelton since in 1851 Charles Shelton, aged 83, was living at Grove Cottage with his wife, his nephew John Whiteman, aged 27, and a maidservant.

Later occupiers of Grove Cottage are named in Table 20. At the 1881 census William Robinson Annibal (also spelt in other contexts Annibel, Annabel, Annabal, and Hannibal) aged 42 was there. He must have been at Grove Cottage since about 1870, when aged 21, on the evidence of the birthplaces and ages of his young children. In 1871 he was said to occupy 'Trent Cottages: Farm House'; but since he farmed 92-93 acres this must refer to Grove Cottage and Trent Wong. Trentside Farm, with 30-32 acres, was occupied by George Brewill, 'master butcher' in 1861 as well as in 1871 and 1881, so it is clear that John Harrison, farmer, must have occupied Grove Cottage at the 1861 census. W.R.Annibal kept servants, and was relatively prosperous as the tenant of this quite large holding. William Robinson Hannibal, 'Farmer, Dunkirk' (Kelly 1876) was probably the son of James Robinson Annibal, a lace manufacturer of Stoney Street, Nottingham, with a house on Mapperley Road [Wright 1858] who in later life appears to have lived at Caunton Manor [Brown 1891].

A third Trentside dwelling mentioned in the census Enumerators' Books as occupied by agricultural labourers or 'farming bailiffs' was a cottage on Grove Farm, also called Grove Cottage by Lascelles and Hagar's Commercial Directory of 1848. Thomas Charles was the occupier in 1841 and 1851, William Mills in 1861 and William Fuller in 1871. The tenants of the Trentside properties in the mid-19th century are shown in Table 20.

Henry Smith (1794-1874) 'of Wilford House', the third son of Samuel Smith, was confirmed as the owner of Trent Wong in 1845 by his inclusion in Curtis's History among the property owners of Lenton parish [Curtis 1843 44]. As a banker he was associated particularly with the Lincoln bank. He married Lady Lucy Leslie Melville (1794-1865), the eldest daughter of Alexander, the 8th Earl of Leven and Melville. Cornelius Brown, in about 1889, in an article on Wilford in the 'Nottinghamshire Guardian', describing a memorial plate to Henry, Lucy and three of their children, paid effusive tribute to 'these most estimable members of an eminent and honoured family', seeing Mr. Smith as 'the true pattern of an English gentleman, [who] won the love of all who knew him.' Lady Lucy Smith, 'widely known for her deep-toned piety and Christian zeal, after a life nobly spent in promoting religious and philanthropic movements in many parts of England, left a name which will long be cherished with reverence, affection

Table 20
Residents and tenants alongside the Trent in Lenton, 1810-1881

Trent Wong

1810	Messrs. Breedon, Williamson and Facon
1811-21	Edward Facon
1822-23	John Wilkinson and Robert J. Gregory
1824-32	John Wilkinson

'Grove Cottage' built by 1834

	Grove Farm	Grove Farm Cottage	Trentside Cottage
1841	Charles Shelton (c.70) Farmer Wife Elizabeth (c.65) 2 female servants	Thomas Charles (c.40) Agricultural Labr. 2 sons: 2 daughters	Sarah Lamb (c.70) Cottager Son Thomas Lamb (c.45) Agric. Labr
1848	Charles Shelton Farmer and bone merchant	Thomas Charles Farming bailiff	Thomas Lamb Farmer
1851	Charles Shelton (83) Retired grocer Wife Elizabeth (79) 1 female servant	Thomas Charles (55) Wife Elizabeth (60) Patrick Drigdarig (Irish labourer) 1 female servant	Sarah Lamb (82) widow, cowkeeper. Thomas Lamb (58) Labourer, single Jane Elvidge (nee Lamb) servant
1861	John Harrison Farmer Wife Elizabeth (38) 1 infant daughter 1 female servant	William Mills Labourer Wife Elizabeth (52) 1 daughter	George Brewill (47) Master butcher (in 1862 called farmer 2nd wife Sarah(27) 1 daughter, 3 sons
1871	W.R.Annibal (32) Farmer, 93 acres 1 man, 1 boy, 2 serv- ants. Wife Louisa 2 infant sons	William Fuller (45) Farm labourer Wife Elizabeth (55) 2 daughters	George Brewill (56) Farmer, 30 acres Wife Sarah (36) 3 adult children, 2 others. Father-in-law John Willoughby (82). 1 female servant
1881	W.R.Annibal (42) Farmer, 92 acres 1 man, 2 boys, 2 male farm servants Wife Louisa (34) 4 young sons		George Brewill (67) Farmer, 30 acres Wife Sarah (48) 1 daughter 1 man, 1 female servant

and esteem'.

Henry's son, Henry Abel Smith, D.L. (1826-1890) succeeded him both at the Lincoln bank and at Wilford House. He married Elizabeth M. Pym (1825-1877), daughter of Francis Pym. Grove Farm remained in the ownership of this branch of the Smith family throughout the 19th century, with Francis Abel Smith (1861-1908) of Wilford House following his father Henry Abel Smith. Francis was admitted as partner in the bank at Lincoln after his father in 1890. He probably left Wilford House on the death of his father, or earlier, since John T.Forman occupied it from 1892 to 1922, followed by T.Bailey Forman, after whose death in 1938 Wilford House was unoccupied until it was requisitioned for use in turn by the Military Police, the R.A.S.C., and Royal Ordnance Factory apprentices. After the war it was converted into eight flats for staff of the Nottingham Evening Post. Later, after being refurbished and extended by the owners, Forman Hardy Holdings Limited, it was tenanted by Messrs. Gleeds, the quantity surveyors who were largely concerned in the post-war building on the University campus.

Sales of Grove Farm

After the death of Francis Abel Smith on 20 March 1908 his widow, Madeline, did not remarry. Grove Farm was occupied in 1919 by John P. Woolley, and was sold to him by Madeline Abel-Smith in 1920, before her son Henry, born in 1900, came of age. At that time, in the immediate post-war period, over half of the 122 acres of the farm (including land across the parish boundary in Beeston) was classed as arable land, undoubtedly a brief legacy from its wartime use.

In 1925 Woolley's mortgage was transferred from Madeline Abel-Smith to her son Henry of the Manor House, Ashby-de-la-Zouch, and on 25 April 1927 Grove Farm was conveyed by J.P.Woolley and Henry Abel-Smith as mortgagee to H.R.H. the Prince of Wales for £8,500 [25]. The purchase was welcomed by the Journal of the Royal Agricultural Society especially because, having been successful as a Shorthorn owner the Prince was coming into possession of one of the historic sources of the dominant type of modern Shorthorn [MacDonald 1927]. John Wilkinson of Lenton, who had himself occupied Trent Wong (see above) formed the strain from which Amos Cruickshank 'at a critical juncture' fixed the 'Cruickshank Shorthorn' after visiting Wilkinson at Lenton in about 1852. At Grove Farm the cattle, 'including Lenton Lavenders and Lancasters that have been moved from Cornwall to the banks of the Trent have in a sense returned to the home of their ancestors' and 'will shortly be suitably accommodated in the way of buildings'. The Prince of Wales spent a large sum on the farm during the six years that he owned it, dividing the farmhouse into two, building two cottages, and modernizing the farm buildings. A small photograph of 'The Prince's Farm' can be found in L. Richmond's (undated) 'Rambles round Nottingham', p. 87.

It has been understood that the Prince of Wales bought Peveril House on Beeston Road, Dunkirk (see Figure 50) as accommodation for his farm manager, though this has been challenged recently. The substantial house was built between 1900 and 1905 [26] and in 1905 was owned by Alderman Houston, a baker [Wright 1905]. His garden reached back to City Road where his bakery was situated, together with a stable. The bakery is said to have remained in use during the Prince's occupancy, although Peveril House was occupied after the first world war by Frank Bird [Wright 1920: Kelly 1922]. Peveril House still survives, a little incongruously among the inter-war houses built along the whole length of Beeston Road west of Lace Street in the late 1920s and early 1930s.

The Prince of Wales sold Grove Farm by a conveyance of 3 October 1933 to George Reuben Shelton, a farmer formerly of Ruddington, for only £5,500, (excepting a narrow strip fronting the river, which was sold to Trent Navigation). It is not known whether G.R.Shelton was a member of the same family as Charles Shelton, who had occupied Grove Cottage a hundred years earlier. The price paid seems surprisingly small, even taking account of the depression in farming in the early 1930s. Shelton farmed the land for 13 years, but became increasingly worried about the occasional flooding (a positive quality when Trent Wong was all meadow land), and he sold Grove Farm, somewhat hastily in the opinion of his agents [27], in September 1946 to John William Burnett and his wife Nellie, formerly of Home Farm, Chaddesdon.

John Burnett died in February 1949, but his widow and son continued to farm the holding for a further decade. They spent very little on the upkeep of the buildings and other maintenance, and the property became run-down. Eventually Colin Burnett (as trustee) and his mother sold the farm in fee simple to the University of Nottingham for £26,000 on 1 January 1960. Its area was just over 120 acres, with a moiety of the adjacent river bed. It may be remarked that J.P.Woolley, and then, by deed poll of 25 March 1927 the Prince of Wales, had the right to take gravel by dredging from the river bed - the so-called Wilford Shoals - and on 21 August 1954 there was an agreement between the Burnetts and Hoveringham Gravel Company for extracting gravel on Grove Farm itself. Fortunately the plan was refused on 2 October 1956, and this planning decision may well have helped to precipitate the sale of Grove Farm to the University.

Physical character and flood works

The modern Grove Farm, with an area given as 121.304 acres in 1914, but in 1956 123.38 acres, calculated by compounding field areas given on Ordnance Survey maps, included about 29 acres in Beeston parish, so that the Trent Wong portion in Lenton was about 94 acres - very close to the 18th century figure. About 55 acres of this, the southern half, was undivided grassland on 19th century maps and on the revised O.S. 6-inch map of 1914. Less than 10 acres was classified as arable land, and this bordered the Beeston Horse Doles. By 1956, when about 63 of the 94 acres in Lenton could be classified as arable land, the largest field was less than 20 acres.

Though originally meadow, Grove Farm as a whole lies slightly higher than some of the adjoining land, and its gravelly soil drains well, which is why well over half could be called arable land in 1920. Geological maps [28] indicate that the whole of the surface of Trent Wong is alluvium; but this probably means that the area, except the house and farm buildings, was below the high flood level of the river Trent, and carries no implication about the lithological nature of the deposits and the freedom of the surface drainage. Floodplain deposits are normally coarser and thus better draining near the banks of the main river than elsewhere. The buildings of Grove Farm were not subject to flooding; but as part of comprehensive flood control measures on a regional scale a flood bank was constructed in the mid-1950s, making the whole farm with the exception of a few acres into washlands.

Because of the assumption of this status, and in view of the combination of level surface and normally good surface drainage ensured by the gravel subsoil, Grove Farm was eminently suitable for use as sports grounds: and there were buildings that could be converted for use as changing rooms. In view of the acute shortage of playing field space available to the rapidly expanding University the purchase of the farm, with quick access from the University main campus by good roads, was a most opportune and sensible investment. After a small exchange of land with Nottingham Corporation in October 1962 and May 1964 [29] the University Surveyor drew up plans to begin playing field development of 40 acres in 1965, the remaining land being farmed by the University School of Agriculture. A further 33 acres were developed in 1967, and more subsequently, with farm buildings converted in 1975 to provide changing rooms, stores and staff accommodation. But after 20 years the grounds are still not over-popular with the students who use them. It may be hoped that the University will eventually consider ways to ameliorate the winter bleakness of this flat and exposed tract of land by a programme of planting with tree species able to thrive under the special conditions of soil and drainage that prevail.

NOTES

1. J.T.Godfrey [1884 151-153]. Transcription of Add. Mss. 6164 f.502
2. N.U.M.D., Mi 1/38/31, May 1538 See copy of extract from the document reproduced on the back cover of this book.
3. N.U.M.D., Mi 1/38/2. The grant was by Henry VIII and was dated '11 day of May in the 2nd year of our reynge': but it mentioned Nicholas Heath, the last prior of Lenton, and the date given is thought to be an error for 1539. The lease was for 21 years.
4. N.U.M.D., Mi 1/38/3, 1 March 36 Hy VIII (1545).
5. L.A.O., 2 PG 13/5 (1622) - bundle. The receipts for 1622 are set out in fol. 6a.
6. The accounts for 1622 in the same bundle are in a very fragile and decayed condition. Fol. 6 gives rents received for 'the townes land and the common peeces with other receiptes generall by us', the burliman.
7. ibid. fol. 7. The inhabitants of the lordship of Lenton and Radford had to maintain five bridges, and were 'burdened in charges yearly toward the repairs of the said bridges to the value of £3.6s.8d. N.U.M.D., Mi 1/38/9 (1569).
8. For example: 'Rec. of Michael Freeman the 10th October for 6 acres of meadowe in Trent Wonge at 10s. the acre. 60s.'. - Misplaced item in the buildings accounts book at Wollaton, 28 Elizabeth (1586) - N.U.M.D., Mi A 60/5. For 80 acres at equivalent rent the total would be £ 40. This item shows that Sir Francis Willoughby leased Trent Wong during Lady Ann Stanhope's lifetime long after his lease of 1556 expired.
9. N.U.M.D., Mi 1/38/40(i): Mi 1/38/2 (1539) : and Mi 1/38/33 (c.1554)
10. N.U.M.D., Mi 1/38/40(i) : Names of ... parcels ... granted to Mr. Harrington ...' (undated).
11. N.U.M.D., Mi 1/38/33 (undated). This is a copy of part of P.R.O., Rentals and Surveys, Portfolio 24, No. 12, 'Lenton Monastery - Rental (Eliz, ?)' undated, 15 mss. The lease included the Keighton closes. Letters Patent granted in 1 Ph. and Mary.
12. N.U.M.D., Mi F 10/5 - said to be a rental of about 1636 although internal evidence suggests a date some 30 years earlier. See also N.U.M.D., Mi 1/38/35 - 'A rental of the grounds at Lenton Abbey: How the demesnes are lett by the quarter and by the year' (undated). (Nb. Lenton Abbey here means Lenton Priory)
13. L.A.O., 1 PG 2/8/Bundle 1: 1 - Inspeximus of Letters Patent: notes the lease of 24 July 43 Elizabeth (1601) to Thomas Cooper, Philip Hanmer and Thomas Hanmer, gents.
14. ibid. The original lease to Humfrey Hanmer by Elizabeth for 21 years was dated 25 Elizabeth (1583) and the lease for three lives to Winifred Hanmer, widow, and her sons Philip and Thomas appears to have been granted in 30 Elizabeth (1588). See L.A.O., 2 PG 1/7/2/5.
15. N.U.M.D., Mi 1/38/37 (i) to (xxx) (1609-1630)
16. N.U.M.D., Mi 3 E 4 - Abstract of title of Henry, Lord Middleton and Hon. Digby W.B.Willoughby to a freehold estate called Lenton Abbey, 1684-1867. Indentures of lease and release dated 27-28 January 1684. Note that the properties involved were in a different group, and additional to those copied in N.U.M.D., Wadsworth 50 and dated 25 and 26 January 1684.
17. N.U.M.D., Wadsworth 51 (1731) and Wadsworth 21 (1743). Benjamin Deverall (1696-1763) a member of a well-known Wilford family, married in 1732/3 Dorothy Constable (1708-1751), probably of the Constable family of Beeston. W.P.W.Phillimore and G. Fellows, Nottinghamshire Parish Registers: Marriages, VI (1904) 81.
18. N.A.O., Land Tax assessments, Lenton. The earliest extant assessment is dated 1780.
19. N.U.M.D., Mi 3 E 4 (28-29 March 1798). By deed poll of 29 March 1798 - the exception from the sale to Pares and Paget of certain hereditaments 'sold and conveyed or assigned to the use of Samuel Smith, his heirs and assigns ...'.
20. Among books on the history of the Smith family and their bank the following are useful sources (see Bibliography): Leighton-Boyce (1958), Easton (1903) including portraits, Bailey (1853), Jacks (1881), Firth (1916), Train (1969, 1973), Smith (1861), North (c.1910), Copinger (1907), Iliffe and Baguley (1983).
21. Iliffe and Baguley (1983) publish (p.12) a photograph of the bank taken in 1878.
22. G.C.Robertson (ed.) The Stretton manuscripts (1910) 227.
23. N.A.O., Land Tax assessments for Lenton
24. N.U.M.D., Mi 3 E 4
25. Deeds with Messrs. Rotheras, the University's solicitors.
26. On the north side of Beeston Road, west of Lace Street, only 'Ivydene' near the University entrance gate was present in 1899 (O.S. 6-inch map, 1901): Peveril House was present by 1905 [Wright 1905]: and a third house on the corner of Greenfield Street and Beeston Road had appeared by 1913 (O.S. 6-inch map, 1919).
27. This is suggested in a memo of Messrs. Walker, Walton and Hanson dated 13 September 1955, which is attached to the deeds in the care of Messrs. Rotheras.

28. See the geological map of Nottingham published by Arthur Brown, Borough Engineer, as amended from published Geological Survey maps by James Shipman and 'approved by W. Talbot Aveline'.

29. The legal documents which detail these exchanges are in the care of Messrs. Rotheras. A transfer of 6.09 acres to the Corporation was arranged in connection with the construction of flood control works, and the University received 2.7 acres plus £1,250.

CHAPTER XVI

THE ACADEMIC CAMPUS: LAND ACQUISITION AND PHYSICAL DEVELOPMENT

Introduction

Some of the events leading up to the establishment of University College on Shakespeare Street have been mentioned in Chapters VI, VIII and XII, in discussion of Highfield House, Lenton House and Paton House. The pioneering Cambridge University Extension Lectures at the Mechanics Institution, suggested in 1873, arranged on a visit to Cambridge by

Richard Enfield and Rev. J.B.Paton, and beginning in the winter of 1874, led to a gift from a friend of Enfield to provide permanent buildings for them. This was followed by a final scheme for a College in April 1876, a building start in July 1877 - with a rates levy in support - and an opening ceremony four years later. The City Council's plan of 1913 to raise the College to University status was extinguished by the first world war, but soon afterwards Sir Jesse Boot, having endowed a chair of Chemistry, provided the nucleus of a building fund for a University on a new site that he offered alongside the river Trent above Trent Bridge. Before building could begin Sir Jesse, in 1921, offered instead the Highfields site - a crucially important decision which has allowed the University of Nottingham to acquire and develop its fine, extensive campus over the past 40 years, on land which had been protected from earlier deleterious development by the historical circumstances which have been discussed at length in earlier chapters. Equally important, in practical terms, was Sir Jesse's further munificence in implementing his vision by paying for the new College buildings.

The University College campus, 1920-1948

Sir Jesse Boot, first Baron Trent, the founding benefactor: his antecedents and career

Sir Jesse Boot's gift of the original Highfields campus and its buildings, which culminated in the removal of the University College from Shakespeare Street to Highfields, initiated another revolution in the occupance and land use of a large part of the former Lenton Priory demesne - a change even more profound than that which followed the sale of 1798. The gift owed something to the fact that Jesse Boot was an East Midlander as well as a Nottingham man. His forbears can be traced to Richard Boote (died 1528) at Diseworth, Leicestershire in the 16th century, and his family lived in various Nottinghamshire villages, particularly Willoughby-on-the-Wolds for over 150 years [1]. Jesse was a grandson of an agricultural labourer of Radcliffe-on-Trent, and was born on 2 June 1850 at 71 Woolpack Lane, Hockley, in Nottingham, the only son of John Boot. John was himself an agricultural labourer at first, but later, after a breakdown in health in 1849, he set up as a herbalist at 6 Goose-gate, also in Hockley. John's first wife, nee Elizabeth Mills, who he married at Holme Pierrepont church in 1838, had died of tuberculosis in 1848, and their daughter, aged four, also died. John turned to revivalist religion and to his mother's interest in herbs and herbal medicine, and he became an intensely religious man, and a Wesleyan Methodist local preacher as well as a local leader in promoting 'medical botany'. Jesse Boot's mother, John Boot's second wife, Mary, the daughter of Benjamin Wills of Nottingham, was 34 when John Boot died in 1860 aged 44. Jesse was then ten and his sister Jane only eight months old.

Mary Boot, calling herself a medical botanist like her husband, kept going the small herbalist's shop on Goose-gate for some years while Jesse received an education, first at the school of Edward Todd Field in Hounds-gate, but from July 1861, when he was eleven, at the Agnes Mellors Free Grammar School (later called Nottingham High School) to which he had been elected by the Charitable Trustees of Nottingham. His secondary education was brief. Leaving school in August 1863 aged 13, Jesse immediately took charge of the family shop on Goose-gate in which he had helped his mother since his father's death. He studied pharmacy in his spare time but never, himself, became a pharmacist. In 1871, aged 21, he became a partner with his mother, selling simple herbal remedies and household materials such as soap, soda and candles. Wright's 1871 Directory recorded 'Boot and son, Herbalists, 38 Goose Gate' (that is, Mary and Jesse).

Jesse recognized as early as 1874 that herbalism was failing, and he entered the proprietary medicine business. He opened his first 'chemist's' shop at 18 Goose Gate, and though lacking capital he made headway by following the principle of large turnover and small profits for cash payment. With the untiring energy that was one of his most prominent traits he rapidly expanded his business. He bought numbers 16 and 18 Goose Gate in 1877, and redesigned them internally to produce his first big shop in 1883, when his business became a limited liability company and he became a 'Chemist and Druggist' [2].

After a serious breakdown in health in 1886 Jesse Boot took a recuperative holiday in Jersey, where he met Florence Rowe, 23-year-old daughter of a Jersey bookseller, and soon married her. In his courtship and marriage action followed intent with such speed that the bride's mother is said to have refused to attend the ceremony [3]. His quickness to make decisions was a characteristic that was later to be of great value to the University College. Florence Boot, with her experience of books and stationery, artists' materials, gifts and fancy goods in her father's shop in St. Helier, was largely responsible for the development of these lines at the new Goose Gate shop, which set a pattern for the large Boots department stores later, and perhaps even for the substantial printing business of Boots.

Jesse and Florence lived over the shop at 20 Goose Gate until 1892, when they moved to Carlyle House, Burns Street. Jesse continued to open additional shops until he had built up the largest retail chemists undertaking in the world. He had 60 shops by 1896. In 1892 the company began to manufacture its own drugs and other products, modern factories were built in Nottingham at the Island Street complex, originally a cotton factory, and the wholesale business grew rapidly with the retail. The whole organization became very complex, and in 1907 Boots Cash Chemists alone consisted of five distinct companies, with Jesse Boot chairman of all of them [Allen 1907]. By 1901 his home was 'Gardenhurst', South Road, The Park [Potter Briscoe 1901 173].

About the turn of the century Jesse Boot suffered a further breakdown in health, and rheumatoid arthritis subsequently confined him to a wheelchair and eventually made him a physically helpless cripple, though without impairing his intellectual energy and drive. He travelled in a specially constructed motorcar, and conducted much major business from his bed. Both before his illness and subsequently he owed much to the judgment and business acumen of his wife, Florence. The business continued to thrive, and in the war of 1914-18 supplied troops with such products as tablets for sterilizing water, and with effective box respirators against poison gas, of which 8 millions were made in a special factory together with the chemicals for a further 12 millions assembled elsewhere. Jesse Boot's labours increased, but at the same time his attention turned more and more to philanthropic activities, in recognition of which he was knighted in 1909 and became a baronet in 1916. In that year there were 600 Boots retail shops, and by June 1920, at his 70th birthday, Boots had 14,500 employees. Sir Jesse then retired from active chairmanship - but not from philanthropy.

The first University College benefaction

On 25 October 1920 Sir Jesse Boot received the Freedom of the City of Nottingham, one event in what was for him a most eventful year, and one of great importance in the history of the University campus. Sir Jesse was 70, and nearly nine months of illness in later 1919 and into 1920 had depressed him; and it was this rather than his age that led him - without the expected consultation with others - to sell his Pure Drug Company in 1920. The United Drug Company of America, led by Louis K. Liggett, is said to have paid £2½ million. According to Chapman [1974 145-6] it was agreed by the family after discussion with John Greenwood (see Chapter XII) that such a high price would be asked that the purchase would not proceed: but the price was accepted, and the unexpectedly large sum received by Sir Jesse may explain in part the size of his benefactions. He had just bought the Highfield estate. An indenture dated 19 November 1919 was followed by others dated 22 and 23 November and 23 December 1920, as recited in the void conveyance of 1 November 1923 [4]. The dates indicate that Sir Jesse was moving to purchase the Highfield estate before he sold his business; but after the sale he made

Figure 107: Jesse and Florence Boot and family at 'Plaisaunce' in about 1908
[Courtesy The Boots Company plc]

a series of large gifts in his native city, for which he felt a deep regard. He gave £50,000 towards the purchase of Woodthorpe Park 'in gratitude for a happy life'. In addition to large donations to Nottingham General Hospital (£50,000 to endow The Cedars, plus a further sum for improvements) and £10,000 to the Congregational College for a chair of Sociology, he formed the 'Sir Jesse Boot Social Trust Fund Ltd. for charitable purposes' with an endowment of £50,000. He contributed £8,000 towards rebuilding the Albert Hall, Nottingham, paid for an organ and provided three years salary for an organist. He helped the Club for discharged soldiers and sailors. But most significantly in the present context he offered funds for a site of 30 acres and a building on the Nottingham bank of the river Trent opposite to his house Plaisaunce to found an East Midlands University at a cost to him of some £250,000 [5].

The development and final extinction of the idea of an East Midlands University has been outlined by Wood [1953]. Sir Jesse had read a press report of an address by Alderman Edmund Huntsman (1865-1939) to a Leicester meeting in the summer of 1920 on the subject of the proposed East Midlands University. Huntsman (Figure 108) was a Nottingham solicitor who had handled much of Boots' business during the first decade of the century; who had once been Director of the infant Law Department at Shakespeare Street; and who was now a member of the Council of the University College. The report fired the interest of Sir Jesse, who telephoned Huntsman from 'St. Helier', and invited him there to discuss the idea [6]. A cheque for £50,000 for an endowment fund was sent to Huntsman the following day, and during the next twelve months a further £120,000 was promised for new buildings on the Trent-side site where the City War Memorial now stands - for which, incidentally, Sir Jesse paid. Alderman Huntsman became, effectively, Sir Jesse Boot's lieutenant in Nottingham in respect of his University College interests, not only during the 1920s but also, after Boot's death, through the 1930s.

Figure 108: Alderman Edmund Huntsman,
Mayor of Nottingham and Chairman of University College Council [Photo. by Millis]

The Highfields project

In 1920 Sir Jesse had plans to develop that part of the Highfields estate that now forms part of the University campus as a new factory community on the pattern of Bournville, or Port Sunlight, adjoining Lenton House and its estate which had been bought in December 1919 by his son, John Boot. He planned to site a new factory in the valley, with access to the railway and perhaps the canal. John Boot's purchase of Lenton House was made within a few weeks of Sir Jesse's move to buy the Highfields estate, and it is fair to assume a connection. Then, on 12 March 1921 Sir Jesse bought Lenton Hall. The physical attributes of the two contrasting parts of the Highfields estate were admirably suited to the factory and factory community plan, but Sir Jesse soon found that the United Drug Company had no intention of adopting his scheme for a model village, and his vision of another Bournville became translated into one of a great public park. Further, he found that his wife Florence, who enjoyed the social connections she had in The Park estate, was unwilling to move to Lenton [7]. At the same time there is evidence that in 1921 Sir Jesse was having doubts about the Trent-side site for a University, particularly in respect of noise disturbance, and it is said that in 1921 'Sir Jesse Boot had offered to buy the (Wollaton) Hall and grounds from the 9th Lord Middleton, as he was considering it as a possible site for Nottingham University College'; but 'the offer was refused' [8].

The problem was neatly resolved, according to Huntsman, by a chance remark made one day in the summer of 1921 by a companion of Sir Jesse, sitting with him in a car parked on the grass at the top of the slope overlooking the small lake (or fish pond) and enjoying the view across the Trent vale, to the effect that this would be a good site for a University. With characteristic speed of reaction to new ideas and their translation into action , Sir Jesse saw Huntsman the same afternoon, and within a few days had decided to offer much of the Highfield estate for the proposed East Midlands University instead of the riverside site [Wood 1953 82-83]. It was quickly decided to finance the construction of a park, winter gardens and campanile on the Trent embankment site, and to incorporate the proposed University with surrounding grounds as part of the grand scheme for the development of the Highfields estate for recreational and educational purposes. The area allocated for the University, some 35 acres, was not very different from that originally earmarked on Trent-side, but the potentialities were, and the change of plan made possible the great expansion of the spacious University of Nottingham that came 40 years later.

In fact work on the Highfields project had already begun in 1921. Before the end of 1920 Sir Jesse had engaged W.H.Radford, a Nottingham engineer, to plan a £200,000 scheme for a new boulevard - University Boulevard - to follow approximately the existing footpath from the end of Beeston Road, Dunkirk to Beeston village along the south side of the Tottle Brook, but raised above maximum river flood level. No direct road connection had existed hitherto between Beeston and Lenton other than Beeston Lane-Derby Road-Gregory Street (or Hillside), since Cut Through Lane was not useable by wheeled traffic. Although Boot may have had in mind his proposed new factories at Beeston and their connections with his existing works in Nottingham, just such a road had been under discussion for at least 40 years (see Chapter VI) and was already envisaged in the Nottingham Corporation Omnibus Act, while in the event the site actually chosen for the new Beeston factories was beyond the railway, and outside the Highfield estate [9]. The boulevard was to be flanked on one side by playing fields and on the other by a pleasure park and a fifteen-acre ornamental lake for boating, formed by extending in both directions along the foot of the Highfields valleyside slope the 'fishpond' formed by Alfred Lowe in about 1830. The pond had been formed by damming the Tottle Brook, and was fed by a channel reminiscent of a mill race leading water extracted from the brook near its crossing of Beeston Lane at the present west entrance to the campus - an arrangement that operated for nearly a century. Excavation for the new lake would provide the material to raise the level of the new boulevard, and the lake would fill by seepage, since excavation would reach three or four feet below the natural water table. This whole layout on the valley floor was now to be overlooked by the buildings of the College on the valleyside above. The University College project grew to occupy a major part of the remainder of Jesse Boot's life. Through it 'this man of plain, straightforward character found a welcome opportunity to use his wealth in what he regarded as a crowning service to his community'.

The Highfields scheme went ahead with great speed. It was carried through by a company established for the purpose - The Sir Jesse Boot Property and Investment Company Limited - described by the compilers of directories as 'builders'. The London architect Morley Horder, who did much design work for Boots shops, was recruited for the Highfield project. He was a great-grandson of Richard Morley, a Mayor of Nottingham in 1841 [Townroe 1928], and a member of the Sneinton Manor family, proprietors of the large Nottingham hosiery firm. A plan of development as envisaged by him at an early stage is attached to a void conveyance dated 1 November 1923 (Figure 109), and is seen to differ considerably in detail from the eventual outcome although the main outlines were not altered. An important element of the plan was the lido (now under redevelopment as an Arts centre), the largest inland swimming pool in Britain, measuring 330 feet by 75 feet and holding over $^{3}/_{4}$ million gallons. Water for the pool, when required was drawn from the lake and pumped in through a permanent pipe; and when the pool was emptied it was pumped into the nearby Tottle Brook. In summer the water was changed in this way each week when the lido was closed. At that time only water for drinking and for showers and toilet facilities was drawn from the mains. The buildings of the lido were designed with great care by Morley Horder, paying special attention to the problem of conferring some visual interest to a collection of 252 'dressing boxes', fitted with doors and other woodwork of untreated teak. The lido was the first part of the Highfields scheme to be made available for public use, and was formally opened in August 1924 by Hon. John Burns[10].

The excavation of the lake, supervised by W.H.Radford, was not simply a matter of enlarging the earlier Fishpond. The new lake, fed by seepage, was by-passed by the Tottle Brook. The formal layout of the terrace and gardens forming the central entrance to the public park from the central 'circus' of University Boulevard actually required infilling of part of the original pond as well as diversion of the Tottle Brook . Excavation below the water table was an essential feature of the scheme, to supply both water to the new lake and gravel to build the boulevard (Figures 110 to 113). Some 350,000 tons of material, including 240,000 tons of gravel were extracted.Some gravel was used in making concrete for the underpinning of the Trent Building, and the rest was carried in small trucks on a narrow-gauge railway from

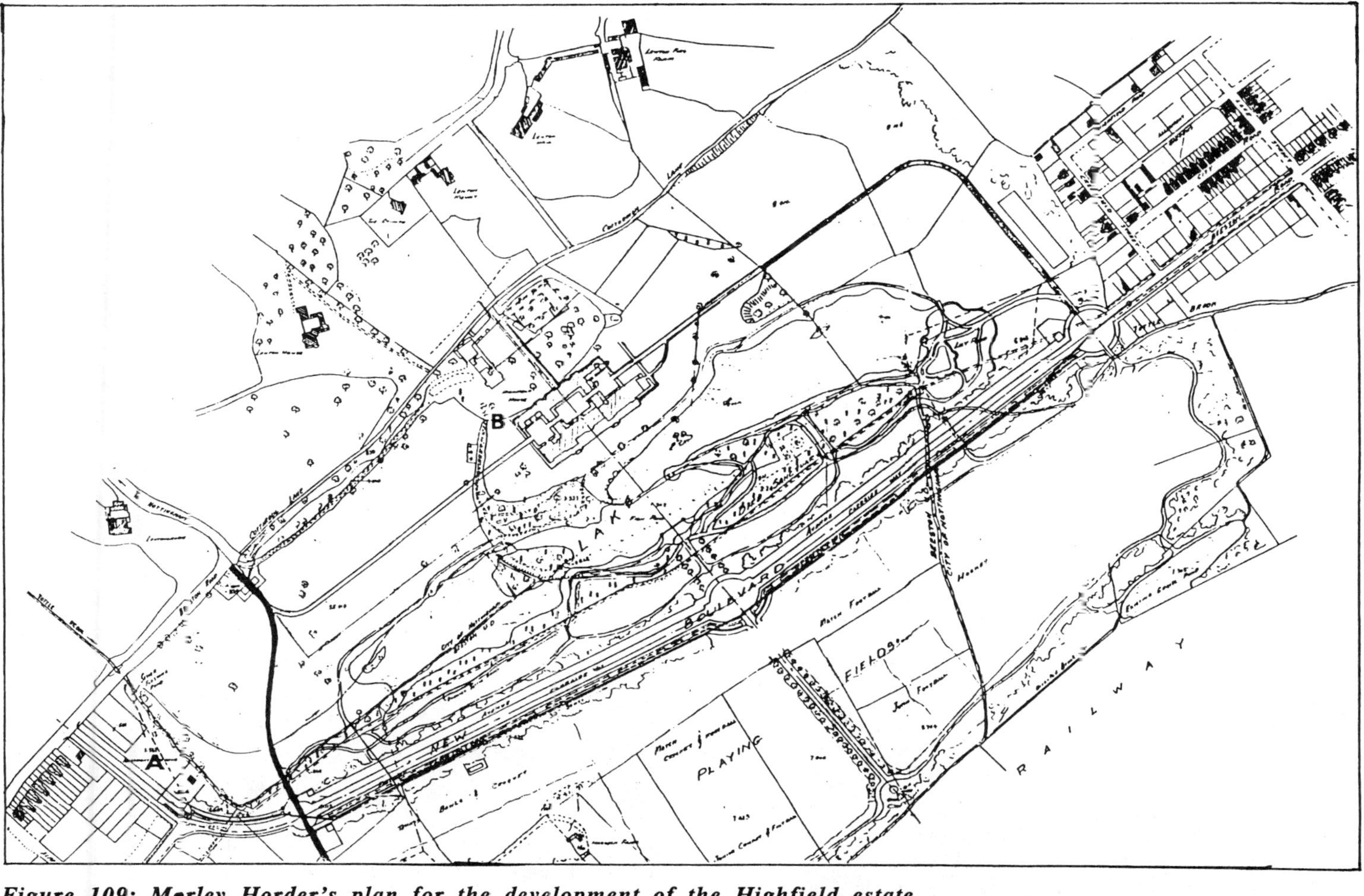

Figure 109: Morley Horder's plan for the development of the Highfield estate, 1922-23

Map attached to void conveyance of 1 November 1923. [Courtesy of the Bursar, University of Nottingham]

Figure 110: University Park lake under construction below the western end of the Trent Building in September 1924
This was part of the early 'fishpond'. Note containing walls of Bulwell stone. [UNMD Accession 423 No. 14]

Figure 111: University Park lake: excavation of the eastern reach
Note depth of the gravel deposit being removed. In distance, right, are two trains of trucks awaiting loading with gravel by mechanical digger. [UNMD, Accession 423 No.11 (undated)]

the bed of the lake to raise the new boulevard above the level of Trent valley floods, a real hazard at that time (Figures 112 and 113). Quantities of surface peat beneath shallow temporary pools were redistributed in the park to form a basis for planting the azaleas and rhododendrons which still present such a feast of colour in early summer. By April 1922 a substantial part of the embankment to carry University Boulevard was in being (Figure 113), the Beeston end having been constructed first. The eastern end of the lake was finally flooded in the winter of 1925-26.

Between 1922 and 1926 all the outlying works on lake, boulevard, lido, playing fields and pavilion, with the exception of the Lake Pavilion, progressed to completion, and the progress of the work can be followed through a series of dated photographs held in the University Department of Manuscripts [11] and in the Central Library, Angel Row. Playing fields and dressing rooms that had been acquired at Lady Bay near Trent Bridge in early 1920, very conveniently situated for the College on Trent-side then proposed, were exchanged for the present University playing fields on University Boulevard [12], and a new pavilion was built near to Hassocks Farm, which was demolished. The Lady Bay grounds remain as Boots athletic grounds today. The new facilities at Highfields were available for use by students in session 1924-25, long before the College moved from Shakespeare Street, and the pavilion, mainly paid for by Sir Jesse, but with a contribution from the Students' Union was opened in 1925.

The Lake Pavilion, originally intended mainly as a restaurant and ballroom - and always called the Tea Pavilion in the late 1920s - was equipped as a gymnasium after the College opened, and this remained its chief function until the University's Indoor Sports Centre was completed, although it was pressed into service during the period of the University's expansion as an examination hall, and later, for a time, as a University refectory providing lunches. It remains in Corporation ownership, though still used for some informal functions associated

Figure 112: University Park, eastern end, 2 February 1924
Note the narrow-gauge track for trucks carrying gravel from the lake excavation (right) to form the embankment for University Boulevard (left). The Tottle Brook can be seen. [NUMD, Accession 423 No.8]

Figure 113: The Dunkirk end of the University Boulevard embankment under construction
Note top right, trucks carrying material from the lake excavation for dumping, and left the Tottle Brook after crossing from University Park. [NUMD, Accession 423, No.7]

with the University. Early photographs of the interior of the Lake Pavilion can be found in B.S.Townroe's pamphlet of July 1928, and the College prospectus for 1937, for example, has a good photograph of the interior fitted as a gymnasium.

The public were given full use of the University Park in 1926. The deeds were formally transferred to the City Council in 1923, but transfer of the control of management was delayed until 1932, after Sir Jesse's death, and until that year the park staff, even including the catering staff at the Lake Pavilion, were employed by the Sir Jesse Boot Property and Investment Company. Sir Jesse had thoughtfully left a gift of £30,000 specifically to help in the upkeep of the park, and no doubt to help to establish high standards. He had also bought 'Ivydene' (see Figure 50) near to the entrance to the park at the end of Beeston Road, Dunkirk, for the use of the park superintendent.

The College buildings

Parallel with these public amenity developments the planning and construction of the new College buildings were proceeding in their own park (Figures 114 and 115). John and Sam Cawley, who had managed Boots' building department joined the Highfields team, and the foundation stone of the main College building (now the Trent Building) was laid on 14 June 1922 by Lord Haldane of Cloan: whereupon a further donation of £100,000 was received towards the building costs - always assumed to have come from Sir Jesse Boot. In the succeeding years, as he became completely disabled, Sir Jesse, having retired from business and handed over the chairmanship of his companies to his son John Campbell Boot, retired to Jersey from which his wife had come, but he continued to direct operations at Highfields in great detail, mainly through his chief agent in Nottingham, Alderman Huntsman, who had first inspired his interest

Figure 114: The Middle Circus, University Boulevard, in September 1924
In distance, left, Highfield House: right University College building (now called Trent Building) started. [NUMD, Accession 423, No. 3]

Figure 115: University College (Trent Building) under construction 9 November 1926
Great Hall and Lower Hall (now the Senate Chamber) not yet started, for reasons explained in the text. The lake is full. [NUMD, Accession 423, No. 22]

in the University project. Huntsman was *persona grata* with Sir Jesse, being leader of the Liberal group on the City Council, and so sharing his political sentiments; having worked for him in the past; and being, from 1921, chairman of the College Council. Though not at heart a politician Sir Jesse was for many years President of the Nottingham Liberal Association, was a generous subscriber to the Liberal Party, and numbered Asquith among his friends.

As mentioned in the Introduction to this volume the Trent Building has massive stabilizing foundations to counter any tendency to slippage as a consequence of geological conditions. Originaly it was intended that the building should be of Millstone Grit, but quite late it was found that insufficient seasoned stone was available in the early 1920s, mainly owing to curtailment of quarrying during the first world war, aggravated by rising costs in subsequent years. The lodges at the Beeston entrance to the campus and the terrace walling overlooking the lake are of Darley stone from the Matlock district, but the Trent Building itself is built of Portland stone. To some, including the writer, this appears to have been a fortunate mischance.

The new buildings at Highfields provoked a mixed public reaction. A mischievous D.H.Lawrence voiced the opinion of a minority in seeing the main building (the Trent Building) in Portland stone as an aesthetic 'iced cake', celebrating the business affluence of Sir Jesse Boot and little else. Lawrence's verse 'Nottingham's New University' was written in autumn 1925, though published in 1928: but the Trent Building reached second floor level only in 1926, and the tower was built in 1927, so his words can hardly rank as architectural criticism [13] . Frank Granger, the Vice-Principal [1928 26 et seq.] on the other hand was effusive in his eulogies on behalf of those who took a more favourable view. He suggested that the main front of the College building, over 400 feet long excluding the kitchens at the eastern end, owed its 'fine architectural effect' as viewed from University Boulevard to many causes. It faces south and 'meets the light'. It 'appears rising tall on a high slope amidst and against a spreading group of trees....The water of the lake contributes beautifully as a foreground like the lakes at Welbeck': and 'the terraces, not only in reality but in appearance, hold up the huge structure pressing down the Keuper clay which here comes lower down than in the eastern part of the city'. 'The uniformity of the windows is broken by the projecting centre tetrastyle and by the pilastered library and great hall at the two ends'. The tower, 'a later addition to the scheme....would have been more obviously led up to had there been eight, or even six columns in the centre of the front to extend the pediment', but without the tower 'the whole building would seem to sink towards the ground'. Other critics thought the tower too slender, and rising too abruptly from the mass beneath [Wood 1953 97] [14] . Granger described as 'brilliant and monumental' the way in which the architecture 'combined' with the landscape in the scheme - an aesthetic quality expressed in Partridge's painting 'Trent tower' of 1964 used as the front cover of this book.

The entrance gates (removed when the Beeston Lane entrance road was widened in more recent times) 'at once announce to the newcomer the sobriety of the general style' which the amateur could recognize as 'Palladian' by 'the columns or palisters taken up through more than one storey, as in front of the library' [Granger 1928]. Not surprisingly clipped holly hedges were used to point the Palladian style round the Trent Building and the entrance gate and lodges on Beeston Lane. The basic late Renaissance style, with the classical influence dominating the design, and decoraton largely eschewed in favour of the effects of mass, was thought to be characteristic of Morley Horder, an architect, according to Professor A.C.Wood, of 'purpose-ful and highly individual artistic talent', who found at Nottingham a task 'admirably suited to the reticence and discipline of his genius'. His unostentatious style, 'quiet, reserved, yet clearly distinguished by a sensitive, highly cultivated feeling for poise and taste', his artistry 'tinged with intellectualism and academicism' produced a 'sturdy' building of clear-cut if austere charm, catching the discipline and reticence of its classical forbears wedded to modern institutional requirements: a building of 'plain dignity' and 'assured yet comely strength' [Wood 1953 97].

This judgment of his art explains, according to Wood, why so much of Horder's work was academic, and 'it was no accident or chance that made him responsible for various new buildings at Cambridge and Oxford' [15]. Inside the new building the corridor walls 'are lined with a skirting of black Belgian marble' which 'furnishes the four monolith columns of the loggia' where the walls 'are covered with Hopton Wood marble of a yellowish-grey; elsewhere with a similar Belgian material'.

It is easy, over sixty years on, to smile at Professor Granger's effulgent description of the gifted architect and his new College building, standing alone on its fine site, unencumbered by a variety of other, later buildings. But few critics over the years can have been sillier than the writer of a report of a visit to Nottingham of the Thirties Society in 1986 [16] which ran:

> 'From Trentside the party went on to the University, Lord Trent's monumental seat of learning. Indeed his shop architect Morley Horder was brought in to design the Trent Building, begun in 1922 in the classical style that was believed to confer academic respectability on New Universities. (They did a similar thing at Leeds, and although it took thirty years it won the approval of a taxi driver who didn't like modern architecture but appreciated older forms. "T'University" he told me "that's classical: built by the Ancient Greeks"). Nottingham University, as it would become, was equally reassuring, even if the motifs in the Great Hall were more obviously Egyptian. Next door we saw the Portland Building, another 'interwar' survivor that didn't arrive till 1957, a late work of Cecil Howitt....'

If anyone was Sir Jesse's 'shop architect' it would have been Albert Nelson Bromley, whose commission involved designing shops in the manner of local vernacular tradition or using historic buildings as shops, while Horder's role was interior detailing reflecting local history.

While construction at Highfields proceeded apace in the mid-1920s the idea and ideal that had originally aroused the interest and generosity of Sir Jesse Boot, and a flood of interest and enthusiasm in many others - though large and corporate sponsors were disappointingly few - ran into the sand, mainly because of the withdrawal of cooperation from Leicester in the promotion of an East Midlands University in favour of a local Leicester campaign to promote Vaughan College. By February 1927, when the new gates at the west entrance to the new campus were already installed and carrying the motif of an East Midlands University, Alderman Huntsman had to admit that the regional idea could proceed no further, and it was dropped in favour of a University of Nottingham. The reasons for the abandonment of the East Midlands University idea were set out by Wood [1953 84-90]. Its effect was to deprive the Nottingham University project of much needed financial support from major sponsors.

The student residence problem

The main College building (Trent Building) had reached second floor level by mid-1926 (Figure 115) , and the tower was completed in 1927. By January 1928 Sir Jesse had agreed to pay for the immediate construction of the Great Hall, which it had been intended to add later, but as yet no provision had been made for student residence. Somewhat hurriedly, in 1928-29, Florence Boot Hall for 80 women students was built at the western end of the campus on the level fragment of the Beeston gravel terrace, formerly part of the Hill Closes overlooking the Tottle Brook (now culverted) and beyond it, in Beeston parish, surviving wartime allotment gardens. The land was given by Sir Jesse in 1926, and the building was paid for by Lady Florence Boot. A hard tennis court was included.

The new College buildings were opened in 1928 when the Arts and Science Departments of University College moved out from the city. The need to provide new residential accommodation was acute, especially because the four existing small student residences which served the College at Shakespeare Street were too far away from Highfields. They were:

Hollygirt, 44 Elm Avenue, Nottingham; for women (now an independent school):
Cavendish House, Burlington Road, Sherwood; for women in the Teachers Training Department:
Waverley House, 13 Waverley Street: for men:
Mapperley Hall, 53 Lucknow Avenue, Mapperley Park: for men in the Teachers Training Department.

Yet provision of accommodation to replace them was made very belatedly, and the circumstances of the acquisition and conversion of Lenton Hall (later called Hugh Stewart Hall) have been discussed in Chapter VII. This might suggest that until a late stage the new 'University' was still being viewed as a local institution with few students from homes outside the Nottingham area. But this would be a false conclusion, and the University College Council was well aware of the need for new residential provision, as was Sir Jesse Boot.

From January 1926 until at least July 1928, on the initiative of Principal Heaton, there were negotiations with the Central Board of Finance at Church House, Westminster, about the possibility of establishing a Church hostel in the presumptive University of Nottingham. A sub-committee of the Board chaired by Lord Grey arranged to meet and lunch with College representatives at the Guildhall, Nottingham in May 1926, but the meeting was cancelled at short notice in consequence of 'the Emergency which has arisen' - the General Strike. The church authorities were thinking of a hostel as 'the embryo of a Church of England College in the University of Nottingham' while the College side, including Alderman Huntsman and Sir Jesse Boot would insist on its being open to all denominations, and any Theological Faculty interdenominational. Two years later Professor Granger convened a meeting on 18 July 1928 to consider again the same proposal - for a church hostel, perhaps associated with St. Mary's church, and the appointment of a Warden. Nothing came of it.

It had been assumed, or at least confidently hoped that provision for residence would be made by sponsors other than Sir Jesse Boot, including some whose benefactions were diverted to Leicester. Certainly Sir Jesse himself had hoped that residences would be provided by other benefactors combined with public subscription. He wrote in a letter to Edmund Huntsman [17] 'As you know my first plan was to erect the University building only, leaving the Great Hall and the Hostel to be built in the future; but later, when I saw the plans coming out so well, I changed my mind....' and decided that '...as we had a trained body of workmen on the spot under such a skilled and enthusiastic manager as Mr. Cawley, we ought to take the opportunity of getting the Great Hall built as well'. This was written after Sir Jesse had visited Nottingham from his home in Jersey in the summer of 1927 after a two-year absence. He had originally promised to make up any shortfall of funds from the public for the Great Hall. 'Now....I have resolved to bear the whole expense of building the Great Hall myself'. Lady Florence was equally pleased, and 'will bear the whole cost of the Women's Hostel herself'. Sir Jesse added that one reason for his decision was to simplify appeals, so that the Endowment Fund (so vital to the prospect of achieving full University status) would be the sole public appeal.

Major building and engineering works such as those of the Highfields scheme must have repercussions in their neighbourhood outside the projects themselves. In this instance the construction of University Boulevard, a major new road that was certain to affect the pattern of traffic in Beeston and Lenton at a time when the nature and volume of road traffic was rapidly changing, was quickly followed by the widening of Beeston Road, Dunkirk by the City Council in 1924, and construction of the new section of Queens Road, Beeston and of Abbey Bridge, Lenton - and eventually the Nottingham outer ring road scheme with Woodside Road and its extension to the 'Balloon Houses', west of Wollaton. The total expenditure of over £ 1 million on the Highfields scheme included over £90,000 to cover the cost of acquiring and demolishing

35 old houses on Castle Boulevard which stood in the way of the new Abbey Bridge, built to link University Boulevard with Castle Boulevard and the inner ring road, and of providing 48 new dwellings to replace them. These replacements were the Penn Avenue Flats, Lenton, three 3-storey blocks, each containing 16 maisonettes with 3 or 4 bedrooms, designed for Sir Jesse Boot by Arthur Eaton and Son of Derby, and approved in February and March 1926. The new road, with Abbey Bridge, agreed in July 1924, required the purchase of about 16 acres of land from T.S.Pearson-Gregory (for £8,000). In the event few of the displaced families could afford to take up the new accommodation [18] .

In all the new buildings at Highfields, excluding the land, are said to have cost Sir Jesse Boot £438,000. His bounty extended to providing a new building for Engineering opened in 1930, re-equipping the Science departments and providing a dance floor in the Lower Hall (now the Senate Chamber) and altering and equipping an extended Lenton Hall and lending Broadgate House rent-free for five years as an annexe to the new Florence Boot Hall (see Chapter V). Sadly he was unable, through his illness, to witness the formal opening by King George V and Queen Mary in the Great Hall on Tuesday, 10 July 1928, but he was nearby and was able to talk with them. A few months later, in 1929, he was awarded a peerage as Baron Trent. He died at Millbrook, Jersey on 13 June 1931, and was buried at St. Brelades, having lived to see part of the Highfield estate converted by his munificence into the first stage of an ultimately much bigger University of Nottingham, on a campus much more extensive than he could have imagined. He remained, in his last three years, very active in promoting the well-being of the University College, and, as some would put it, interfering in the social development of the institution. One likes to think that in his last years the former Sir Jesse will have enjoyed his skirmishes concerning the governance of the new community of staff and students - albeit at a distance and through Alderman Huntsman - with another strong character in the person of Hugh Stewart, the independently-minded Principal appointed to succeed the retiring Principal Heaton in the summer of 1929.

F.S.Granger, quoted extensively above, also wrote one of three appreciative obituaries of the first Lord Trent collected as a supplement to an issue of the student magazine 'Gong'. Alderman Huntsman wrote, as chairman of the College Council, 'Lord Trent as I knew him' (reprinted from the Nottingham Journal of 15 June 1931); Principal Hugh Stewart's contribution was headed 'Benefactor and Friend'; and Professor Granger's was simply 'Lord Trent' (from The Times of 16 June 1931). Among his remarks Granger wrote of a meeting at Cannes in 1925 when Sir Jesse questioned him about building progress, and characteristically 'declared his purpose that the terrace overlooking the lake before the College should be used for tea by the staff and their friends like another and better known terrace at Westminster'. It was - by both staff and students, although it is now sad to reflect how changes in the geometry and geography of the University brought about by growth and progress have frustrated some of the simple and kindly plans of Lord Trent, among them this one. What was then 'before the College' is now behind it, and seldom visited by anyone for any purpose. Granger pointed out that Sir Jesse had Liberal sympathies although he was 'unpolitical', and 'his friendship with John Burns had an important effect upon the College landscape. Burns was proud of Battersea, and in an unguarded moment boasted of the size of the lake in Battersea Park. Sir Jesse ascertained the precise acreage and gave instructions that the lake at Nottingham should be "one size larger". His humour played around his schemes and those who should enjoy them'. 'A casual remark at a dinner party, with the mention of Mr. Morley Horder as "a poet in brick" led to the happy appointment which crowns the hill overlooking the lake with the dignity of Roman architecture'.

In an appreciation from within his own company H.J.Davis [1931] summed up the qualities of Jesse Boot as an outstanding personality who 'coloured everything with a glow of genius' through his background of pain. He possessed to an abnormal degree the quality of perseverance, and this led to a great capacity for organization and 'a readiness to see and to seize an opportunity, with a keen business sense and courage'. Jesse Boot, Lord Trent, was succeeded in his title by his son John Campbell Boot (1889-1956). The second Baron Trent (discussed above in Chapter VIII on Lenton House and Chapter XII on Lenton Mount) was to become the first Chancellor of the University in 1948, when it received its Charter.

The hiatus of the 1930s

The laying out of the original college campus at Highfields by Sir Jesse Boot and his architect, Morley Horder, the adaptation of Lenton Hall, with its seven acres, and of Broadgate House, Beeston as an annexe to Florence Boot Hall, and the forming of the sports grounds south of University Boulevard were all completed by 1930. The Arts and Science Departments of University College moved into their new accommodation on the campus in 1928, Electrical Engineering in 1932 and Civil and Mechanical Engineering in 1934, making use of upgraded contractors' office buildings behind the Trent Building. The Department of Mining and Fuels, and that of Dyeing remained at Shakespeare Street. As early as 1932 the original College campus of 35 acres was enlarged by a further 20 acres to incorporate part of the Keighton Closes to the east, through which the east drive already ran, and to presage, perhaps, later and greater acquisitions.

The 1930s, however, saw no further significant physical expansion or development of the College other than the further extensions to Lenton Hall, which were given priority. In fact student numbers declined from 695 in 1932 to 571 in 1937. The constraint on growth was essentially financial, arising in large measure from the failure to attract a sufficient number of large benefactors to join Sir Jesse Boot, partly due to the defection and competition of Leicester, compounded by general economic depression.

Financial and constitutional problems were closely linked, for while the College owed its establishment to the support, including financial support of the municipality, its progress towards independence and towards University status was severely hampered by its jealously maintained subjection to the Corporation. This was impossible to break internally, and only generous national funding introduced after the second world war finally freed the College to progress to the grant of its Charter as a University in 1948.

In 1903 a Charter of Incorporation had been granted to the University College, and a Court of Governors established which was dominated by representatives of the city. The property of the College was controlled by the city authorities as trustees, and although municipal financial support was vital to the maintenance of the College the lack of independence and freedom effectively stifled any further institutional progress, even on the new Highfield campus after 1928. Full University status, and with it enhanced academic standing and distinction awaited a change in the form of government, and an important step towards this was the Supplemental Charter and new statutes to provide a governing body widely representative of the East Midland area that was signed by King George VI in March 1938. The formal opening of the extensions to Lenton Hall, giving single study accommodation for 120 men, and its naming as Hugh Stewart Hall by the Duke of Portland in the same month, was a further earnest of a more expansive, extra-regional view of its functions by the College.

The 1940s: pre-planning and land purchase

The 1940s was a decade of transition from Collegiate to University status. The first half was preoccupied with the difficulties of the day-to-day operation of the College in wartime; of adjustment to heavy losses of both staff and students, especially men, to war service; and, not least, the problems of assimilating for the duration of the war two Colleges evacuated from London - Goldsmiths College, almost as large as the University College itself, and the Institute of Education. But the future was not entirely out of mind, and there were some who recognized that the state of social and educational flux and change to be expected after the war, with the prospect of a large injection of public funds into education, held out a promise of success for a renewed drive for University status. The vision of an end to the stand-still of the 1930s and the beginnings of a great expansion and extension in the 1950s proved to be well founded. The end of the war quickly brought back many returning ex-service men and women to swell student numbers and more than replace the student bodies of Goldsmiths College and the Institute of Education on their return to London. This influx, together with a new approach to University education in the country, introduced irresistible pressure for physical expansion. This was linked to progress in governance, and in June 1947 a petition to the Privy Council that led to the grant of a Royal Charter on 9 July 1948. This, in turn, was to trigger a tremendous expansion, already anticipated in some respects, and gave immediacy to planning for physical growth.

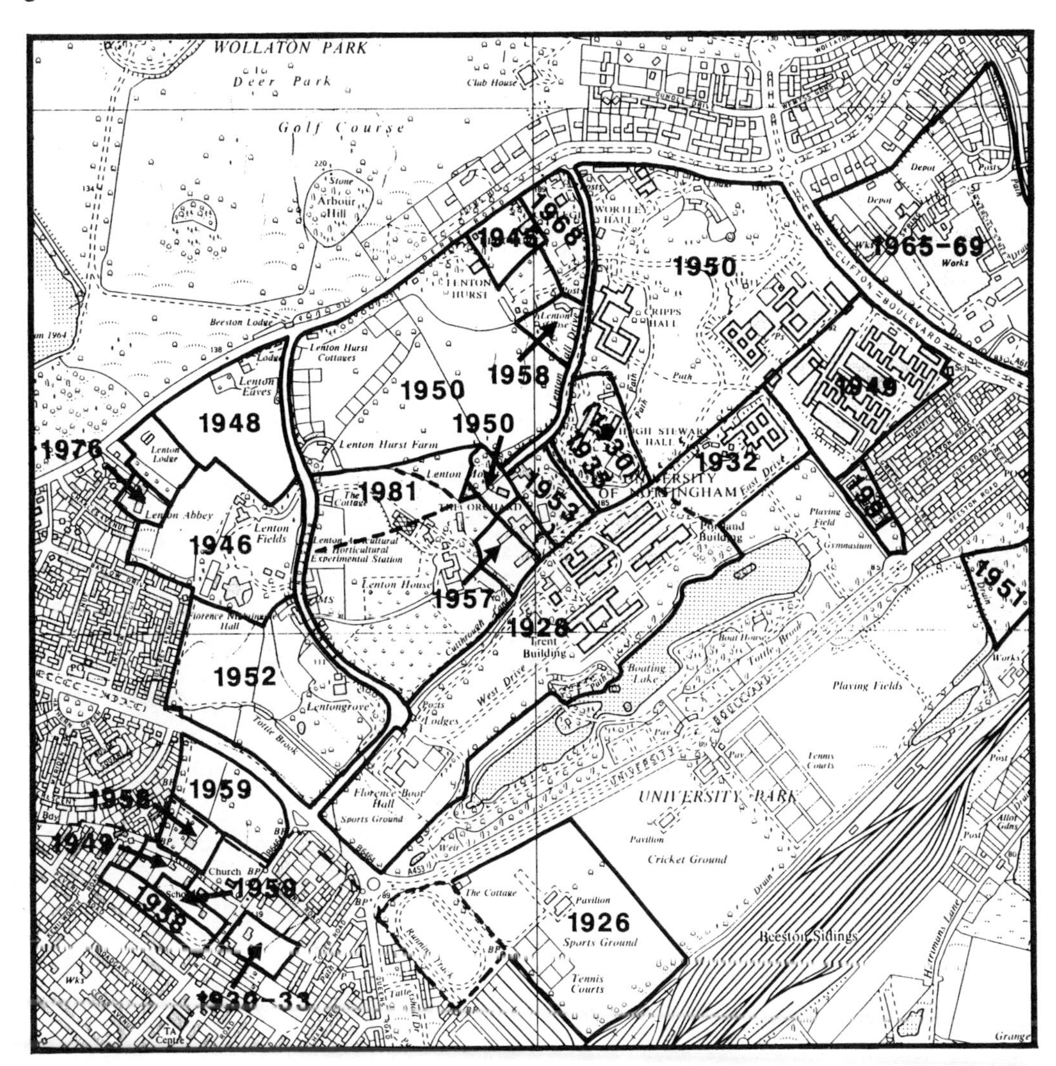

Figure 116: Dates of acquisition of land by the University
Base map shows progress made by about 1960 in the Science precinct, but residential provision only in its early stages. Note the pig pens of Lenton Hurst Farm where Rutland, Sherwood and Derby Halls are now built. [Base map from O.S. 1:10,000 map of c. 1960 reproduced by permission of the controller of H.M. Stationery Office, Crown Copyright.]

Wood [1953] commented that simultaneously with the building of three semi-permanent blocks ('The Cowsheds') in 1945, 'a start was made to secure for the College a hold on the cluster of fine old houses, once the homes of the most prosperous bankers and merchants of Nottingham, which lay between Highfields and the main Derby Road'. These substantially built houses, 'relics of an easier social epoch, establishments with extensive grounds....were obviously doomed to early "development" unless they were acquired to safeguard the present amenities and future expansion of the University'. The lustrum 1945-50 can be regarded as the University's pre-planning phase, during which its territorial requirements were established and most of the necessary property acquired. The city's development plan, as agreed by its Planning Committee in 1949 and published in 1952, allocated an area of 382 acres to the University's ultimate use - largely the northern part of the old Lenton Priory demesne - and by the end of 1950 234 acres had already been acquired (Figure 116).

The University campus 1948-1990

The largely 'empty' undeveloped campus of 1949-50 as it appeared from the air is seen in Figure 117. To the 88 acres of 1944 (including Hugh Stewart Hall and Broadgate House) were added Redcourt with three acres in 1945-46, the Lenton Fields estate of 19-20 acres with its house in later 1946, Lenton Eaves with 11 acres in 1948, and the Clifton Boulevard estate of government buildings, and The Woodlands in Beeston, together 17 acres in 1949. In addition the houses Lenton Hurst and Lenton Firs, both parts of the Lenton Firs estate, were rented by the College. These acquisitions were mainly opportunistic, not part of a well-defined plan; and being peripheral the houses included were of only limited usefulness in meeting the immediate pressures on teaching accommodation. Redcourt was adapted as accommodation for the newly established Institute of Education; Lenton Hurst was used as a residential college for short courses in further education, mainly for H.M.Forces personnel; Lenton Firs, with some added temporary buildings became a small Hall of Residence for women; and Lenton Fields

Figure 117: Aerial view of the campus in 1949

house temporarily provided flats for staff. The Lenton Fields and Lenton Eaves land was intended to provide sites for residences, as shown on early development plans, but in the event only one Hall, Nightingale Hall, was built, on Lenton Fields land, the earliest of the post-war, purpose-built Halls. It was only with the actual purchase from Sir Thomas Shipstone's trustee executors in 1950 of the Lenton Firs estate of 95 acres that a unitary campus became possible, and the pre-planning phase could be succeeded by serious, confident, planned physical development of the infant University. Even then there were lacunae such as Lenton Mount, Lenton Close, and the estates of Lenton House and Lenton Grove remaining within the University's estate.

Except for the unavoidable incorporation of buildings with sites pre-empted before 1950, notably Hugh Stewart Hall, in the future central area of the campus, and the Biology building on the margin of the future Science precinct, the new University was developed under a carefully conceived master plan. The constituent former estates discussed in earlier chapters were completely 'rehashed'. The two most important groups of planning principles governing the process related to the functional geometry of a University in respect of its academic, social and administrative interactions, and to the existing physical conditions such as steepness of slope, ground stability, access, and such relict landscape features worthy of preservation as groupings of mature trees and old buildings; and the reconciliation of all these to provide an efficient and pleasing environment for all the University's members. So, while many individual elements of the past survive in the present landscape of the campus and contribute to its interest and beauty, virtually nothing remains of its former pattern of estate organization and land ownership.

Development plans, 1948-1958, and building on the 'old campus'

Even before the Lenton Firs purchase hopeful plans for systematic development were being made with determination and optimism, led by the newly appointed Vice-Chancellor, Bertrand Hallward. The University Council, anxious to plan and site buildings in such a way as to maintain and enhance the natural beauty of the parkland, appointed Sir Percy Thomas consultant architect, and a model was made of his scheme of proposed development in 1949. His proposals were regarded as a very long-term plan, much of which was unlikely to be implemented for many years on account of the problem of attracting funding, as well as of acquisition of the required land. But with the sites of 'Lenton Fields Hall' (Nightingale Hall) and the 'Social Building' (Portland Building) already agreed, and with a new Biology building to be sited in accordance with Sir Percy's proposals (and completed in 1954-55) the broad allocation of areas to central functions, science and residence was in effect determined, and Sir Percy's 1949 scheme has been the starting point for all later planning.

The congestion brought about by the explosive post-war increase in student numbers was eased only marginally by the acquisition of a few old houses. The early post-war new building, severely constrained for financial reasons before the University's charter was granted, was confined to the original Highfields campus and (from 1946) the Lenton Fields estate. The most generally useful project was the first - the construction of the so-called 'temporary buildings', familiarly known as 'the cowsheds', mainly on the high ground east of the old Engineering buildings earlier used as the gardens of the Education and Pharmacy Departments, but also between Engineering and the main College building (Trent Building) called the 'Copse Blocks', seven lines in all . Three lines were built in 1945 and the remainder in 1948, with an addition in 1952. Initially they housed the Departments of Geography and Zoology, and substantial parts of Botany, Chemistry and Pharmacy, all from the Trent Building, together with an annexe of the University library, the museum, and additional staff rooms and lecture rooms, the Department of Mining and Fuels and an extension for Electrical Engineering. These versatile and adaptable buildings have since been used to house a variety of other academic Departments or parts of them, overflowing from the Trent Building and usually moving on later to occupy purpose-built permanent buildings elsewhere on the campus, thereby playing an indispensable role in the process of physical expansion of the University. Non-academic uses have become more prominent as academic pressures on accommodation have decreased, and the buildings now house the offices of the Directorate of Works (which includes the former Buildings and Surveyor's Departments), miscellaneous administrative units such as Graduate liaison and various student facilities including the Union shop, banks and the like, though some academic facilities for the Adult Education and American Studies Departments remain there.

Other early post-war developments on the original campus included an extension wing to the old Engineering buildings for Civil and Mechanical Engineering in 1949-52, and two major new buildings that were planned immediately after the grant of the Charter - the Biological Sciences building and the 'Union' building (later called the Portland Building), both with south-facing facades on to the East Drive, but very different in style. By 1948 the University Council recognized that it would 'be necessary to move science departments from the main building in order to provide more room both for the Library and for teaching and administration. The first Departments to move will be Botany and Zoology, for which a large permanent building is now being planned'. At the same time and for the same reason it was planned to move out all catering and Students' Union functions to a new Union or Social building.

The Biology building planned in 1948-49 by David du R.Aberdeen, (Figure 118) was to be an exciting modern architectural concept which was agreed in design and layout, and which, had it been built, might well have had an important influence on the architectural style of much of the University. Unfortunately it did not survive beyond the model stage because of a sudden financial cut-back by the government in October 1949. A totally different, workmanlike, not unpleasant but visually less exciting building designed in the University's Buildings Department at lower cost replaced it, and a start on building was made in January 1951, with a completion date of October 1952; but the work proceeded so slowly that the building was finished and occupied only in 1954.

Figure 118: David du R. Aberdeen's model of proposed new building for Botany and Zoology, 1949

The Portland Building's gestation was even more prolonged, even discounting the long preliminary discussions and arguments between the Union of Students, which wanted its own exclusive premises, and the University Council, which determined on a general amenities building to include art galleries, browsing library, bookshop, buttery, and a large, well equipped lecture room for public lectures, debates and the like, in addition to public and private dining rooms, kitchens, staff and student common rooms, large concourse lounges and a large ballroom, with, as a late addition, a crypt chapel - a project likely to attract public funding. The Students' Union was, however, much involved in the detailed planning. The architect was T. Cecil Howitt, D.S.O., born at Hucknall, Housing Architect of the City of Nottingham 1920-29 (when great areas west of the city, including the Lenton Abbey and Wollaton Park estates were developed), and architect of the Nottingham Council House. Howitt's plans, prepared by 1948, were initially approved in 1949, though a building start was not made until March 1953. Despite problems with water - presumably flowing from skerry bands in the Carlton Formation rocks (see Chapter I) - the building was completed for occupation in the summer vacation of 1956, and was formally opened on 26 October 1956 by Lord Kilmuir, though parts were still unfinished. Nicholaus Pevsner formally opened the Fine Art Department and galleries in the building in February 1957. Both the Portland Building and the Trent Building, which are connected by an underground tunnel, were named in 1953 in honour of the Duke of Portland and Lord Trent, respectively the second and first Chancellors of the University.

Developments on the extended campus from 1950

Adaptations of earlier buildings on the original campus, notably the Trent Building, to cater for new uses are indicated later. All the developments on the early campus from 1950 onwards were, of course, closely related to those proceeding elsewhere on the new, wider campus. The utilization of each of the estates added to the campus isoutlined below. Each was developed in a coordinated way as part of the progressive overall construction of the University to the plans of the consultant landscape architects and the architects of the individual buildings; and it is important to recognize that the principle of separation of residential from teaching and research areas, and the advantages of grouping Departments with related interests, usually in the same Faculty (comparable with the geographical concentrations found in industry) resulted in a particular type of development for each precinct rather than for each estate.

Lenton Fields estate, the first major purchase, was intended for residence, but only one Hall was built there, while the Lenton Eaves estate land, affected by mining subsidence, was ruled out for new building, and is now used for sports, with the indoor sports centre adjoining it on one side and the Non-Academic Staff Club in Lenton Eaves house on the other. Lenton Hurst Farm, part of the Lenton Firs estate, developed in 1961-65, and Lenton Grove estate, developed 1962-66, just a year behind, were both planned exclusively for residence. Four men's Halls and part of another were sited on the former, in a peripheral belt linking with three other men's Halls (now reduced to two with the lamentable closure of Wortley Hall) to the east. Three women's Halls and a 'close' of staff houses were placed on the latter to the south, between Florence Boot and Nightingale Halls, to form a block of five women's Halls and two closes. Thus an arc of 12 Halls partly encircled the 'green' area of the steeply sloping 'downland' and the Lenton House estate.

The Clifton Boulevard site was developed exclusively for teaching and research buildings, almost all for Departments of the Applied Science (now called Engineering) Faculty. The buildings of the Pure Science Faculty were sited on adjoining land of the former Lenton Firs Farm - the level floor of the 1838 quarry - to form the northern half of the Science complex, now very closely built up. This was developed mainly in 1958-65, but beginning modestly in 1955 and with several post-1965 additions. The Science Library at the western end and the tower block to the east both stand across the former line of Cut Through Lane, and link the two halves.

Before the recent addition of the MRI Centre, Cripps Hall with the Cripps Student Health Centre, and the (second) Social Sciences building adjoining the central area were the only other major new buildings on the Lenton Firs estate (outside Lenton Hurst Farm), which contributes much of the open space of the campus - the parkland responsible for much of its visual attraction and the road system. The eccentric siting of the MRI building raises fears that the erosion of the parkland has begun, and with it an abandonment of the principles that have safeguarded the main physical attraction of the campus. The Medical School and University Hospital with their associated residential and other buildings fill the area between Clifton Boulevard and the river Leen, which, though mainly part of the former priory demesne was not part of any of the private residential estates, and which was independently planned long after the development plans of the main campus had been implemented (see Chapter XIV).

Establishment of the infrastructure

The placement of individual new buildings and groups of buildings had to be planned in the context of a predetermined pattern of roads, drainage and water supply systems, district heating ducts, electricity and gas mains and other elements of infrastructure which could themselves be planned only after the general disposition of areas allotted to Arts, Administration, Pure and Applied Science and residence had been decided in the development plans of 1945, 1955 and 1958. Once the Lenton Firs, Clifton Boulevard and Lenton Grove estates had been acquired, and the broad layout of the campus recommended by consultant and landscape architects agreed - the location of Faculty areas, residential areas and open space - the road system could be planned, taking into consideration such factors as convenience and economy of internal movement, external road connections and entry points, incorporation of existing roads and provision of unobtrusive parking areas. It was at this stage, around 1950, that the type of use to be made of the earlier estates and their buildings was irrevocably determined, though many detailed changes in both building sites and roads were to be made as development proceeded during the 1950s and early 1960s.

By 1954, with the relative space needs of the Faculties clearer, G.A.Jellicoe was invited to up-date Sir Percy Thomas's landscape development plan of 1949 in collaboration with its author. Jellicoe's plan of 1955 (Figure 119) highlighted two major features: first, the general disposition of approved areas of development, already foreshadowed by the erection of the Biology building, Nightingale Hall and the Portland Building, and second, the progressive adaptation of the Trent Building as the main University Library. Thereafter planning became more detailed and specific - and more urgent, with the University facing a rapid doubling of student numbers to 4,000 by 1966. A series of major new buildings was begun in 1957. In 1958 the central area of the University was planned in detail by Donald McMorran, the architect of the Social Sciences and Education building (now Education alone) in that area, and of Cripps Hall and later Lenton Hall (now Lenton and Wortley Hall) (Figures 120 and 121). At the same time Basil Spence was performing the same task for the Science area, and was himself responsible for the Chemistry, Physics-Mathematics and main Engineering buildings.

Construction of the Science area went forward broadly as planned, though punctuated by sometimes heated debate and argument in the reconciliation of practical academic requirements of Departments with the aesthetic and architectural concepts of Sir Basil Spence and his colleagues. McMorran's vision of the central area, however, never materialized. The central area was seen as extending northwards from the Trent Building, as the main library, and the Portland Building, with union amenities and social and cultural provisions, to beyond Cut Through Lane, which was to be severed, with new buildings to cater for the faculties of Arts, Law and Social Science, and Education, together with a new Great Hall and Chapel, Senate House, administrative offices and a University Club. A combined Great Hall and

Figure 119: Model of Jellicoe's landscape plan of 1955
Above: *General view from the south.*
Below: *The proposed plan of the Central Area. The plan envisaged the eventual acquisition of Boots' Lenton House estate.*

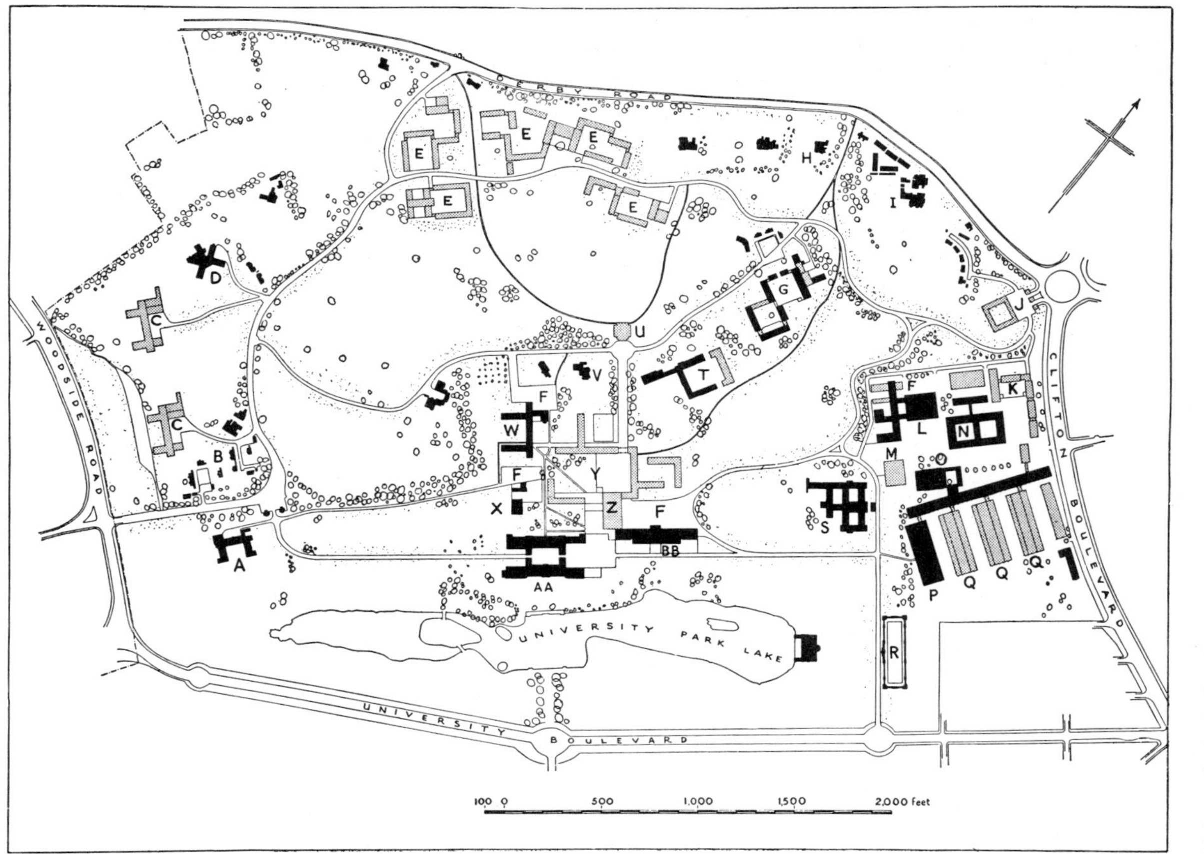

Figure 120: The development plan of 1958 - by Jellicoe and McMorran

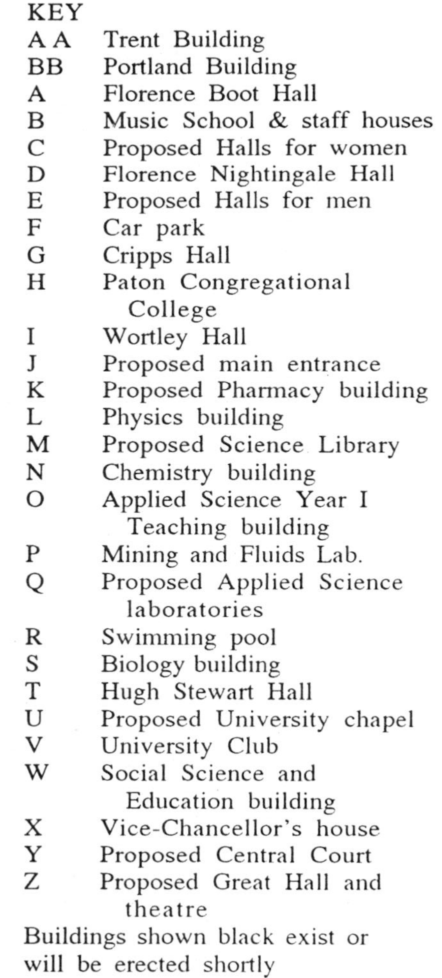

KEY

AA	Trent Building
BB	Portland Building
A	Florence Boot Hall
B	Music School & staff houses
C	Proposed Halls for women
D	Florence Nightingale Hall
E	Proposed Halls for men
F	Car park
G	Cripps Hall
H	Paton Congregational College
I	Wortley Hall
J	Proposed main entrance
K	Proposed Pharmacy building
L	Physics building
M	Proposed Science Library
N	Chemistry building
O	Applied Science Year I Teaching building
P	Mining and Fluids Lab.
Q	Proposed Applied Science laboratories
R	Swimming pool
S	Biology building
T	Hugh Stewart Hall
U	Proposed University chapel
V	University Club
W	Social Science and Education building
X	Vice-Chancellor's house
Y	Proposed Central Court
Z	Proposed Great Hall and theatre

Buildings shown black exist or will be erected shortly

Figure 121: Model of the 1958 development plan
Above: *General view from the south.*
Below: *The Central Area from the south-east.*

theatre was to form a unifying link between the Trent and Portland Buildings. The remaining buildings required when Law outgrew its quarters, and the growth of the main library required the expulsion of all Departments of the Arts Faculty and of the University administration from the Trent Building, were to surround a proposed central court lying approximately where the former Engineering buildings now stand, extending over the land between them and the present Hallward Library.

Although the McMorran plan was never implemented the Social Science and Education building (now Education only) was completed, partly on land from the Lenton House estate, but the whole plan was soon to be rendered obsolete by the decision of 1961-62 to build a completely new main University library. The Education building had been commissioned in 1957, and was, in a sense, caught up in the planning turmoil around 1958-60. It might have been built elsewhere at any other time. It was formally opened on 10 November 1961 by Mr.R.A.Butler. It was built mainly on a large, newly constructed car park - indicative of the confusion of the time - but it extended on to Boots' Lenton House land, two acres being exchanged for land adjoining the 'downland' (and now returned to University ownership). Glasshouses were moved and a row of specimen trees removed, though the University's arguments about the need to preserve Staff Club amenities (the Lenton Mount gardens) now ring hollow in view of the siting of the new University library there a few years later.

Once the land had been acquired the broadscale post-war planning of the campus owed very little to the earlier subdivision into its component estates, but was based on a variety of criteria, as mentioned above, including physiography and geology. It will be seen that with few exceptions the areas chosen for each precinct or group of large buildings were reasonably level or easily levelled, and with suitably stable foundation strata, while more steeply sloping land upon which building would have been more difficult and expensive, was left as open space, with cut and fill moderating the gradients of the internal roads crossing these areas.

The main internal road system was finally determined, and its construction begun in 1959, along lines substantially - even fundamentally - different from those laid down in the Jellicoe proposals. Considerable changes of plan were made at a late stage, for example in the area of the new men's Halls to reconcile the plans of the individual architects who had been commissioned to design the Halls; in the Science area, to conform to the advanced plans for that precinct; and subsequently in the central area as a consequence of a reconsideration of the library problem and the eventual use to be made of the Trent Building. The very first major new road construction proved to be premature. The upgraded old line of Cut Through Lane from the hill top through the centre of the area designated for Science buildings, serving the new main vehicular access to the campus from Clifton Boulevard, was doomed by Spence's plans for the precinct as well as by expectations of an explosive growth of traffic on the ring road almost before it was opened (Figure 122). Its replacement, diverging from the old line near to the present Social Sciences building to a new North entrance at the Derby Road - Clifton Boulevard (ring road) intersection, and a branch within the campus from the North entrance to the Science site, were opened by June 1960.

A branch westward from the new Cut Through Lane parallel to Derby Road was built up the valley between Cripps and Wortley Halls, and extended west beyond Lenton Hall Drive to serve the new men's Halls about to be built below. After the completion of Lincoln and Derby Halls, opened respectively in October 1962 and January 1963, this road was connected to Beeston Lane, which was cut off from Derby Road after public inquiries and closed as a public highway in September 1963, being effectively replaced in the local road network by the newly-completed Woodside Road. Beeston Lane was diverted to the west to extend the site of Sherwood Hall, which was about to be built. The Derby Road entrance to Lenton Hall Drive was closed to vehicular traffic to become a pedestrian entrance only. In 1967-68 the road named Keighton Hill was built to connect the old East Drive with Cut Through Lane and the

Figure 122: The site of the Science precinct from the west in May 1957
Above: *View north-eastwards from the site of the later Social Sciences building. In foreground the ploughed floor of the 1838 quarry below Lenton Firs Farm. At right the newly improved Cut Through Lane.*
Below: *View east-north-eastwards from the same place, overlapping. Note Lenton Sandstone mound, left centre, which now lies on the opposite side of the diverted Cut Through Lane.*

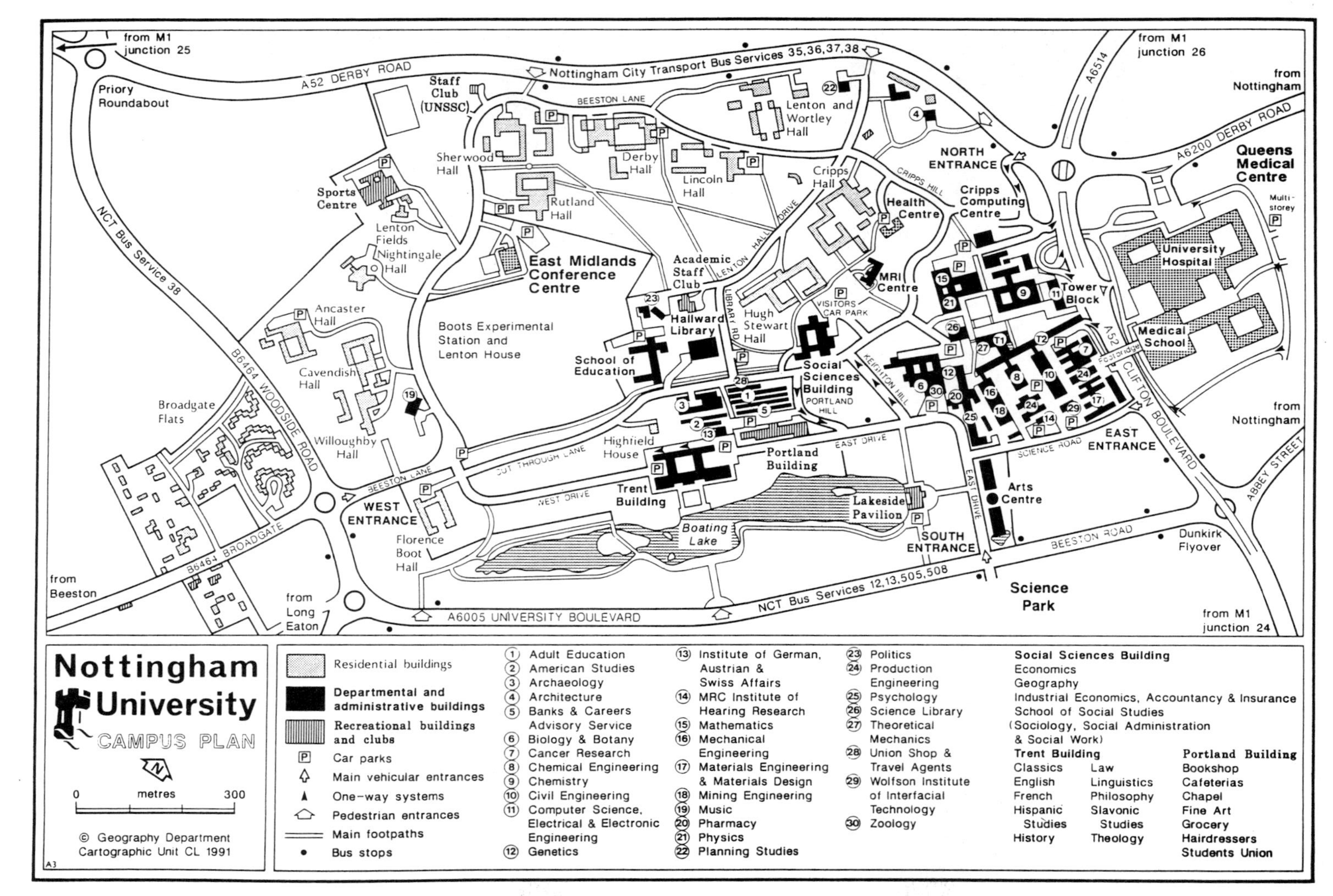

Figure 123: The campus precincts, clearly distinguishable from the shading of the buildings

Central area: Science precinct: Q.M.C.: Residential precinct: Northern outlier.

northern campus, and an entirely new element appeared when the Queen's Medical Centre required connection with the main campus across the busy Clifton Boulevard, which was effected by a vehicular subway and a pedestrian bridge.

From 1960 onwards, with road access and services in place or imminent, progress in the various University precincts was constrained chiefly by U.G.C. approval for the successive projects, and their inclusion in its funding programme. Stories of hurried sorties to London by Vice-Chancellor Hallward and/or the Bursar, Andrew Hendry, and of architects' plans lying in drawers awaiting any funds becoming unexpectedly available through failure to take them up elsewhere, suggest interesting, indeed exciting incidents in the history of the University, though only marginally relevant to this history.

Development of the precincts

It is now proposed to view the development of the campus as part of its continuing topographic history by presenting an outline of the developments on the different constituent estates, among them the Highfield estate that formed the original academic campus, and where, after the construction of the Biology and Portland buildings developments were to a degree determined in response to those occurring elsewhere on the campus.

The western campus - residential

The western margin of the main campus, bounded west by Lenton Abbey housing estate and east by Lenton House estate, extends from the University playing fields in the south to Derby Road in the north (Figures 124 and 125). Apart from the Music School and the residence-oriented indoor Sports Centre and playing fields, it is wholly residential in character. It is made up of the former Lenton Grove, Lenton Fields and Lenton Eaves estates, with additions from the Highfields and Lenton Abbey estates, and, recently, in the form of the Jesse Boot Conference Centre, from the Lenton House estate.

The Lenton Fields estate, with its house and 20 acres, was the first substantial post-war purchase by the University College in 1946, and it now includes Nightingale Hall, the first new postwar Hall, with Nightingale Close of four staff houses, the Sports Centre and considerable open space. The Hall, originally called Florence Nightingale Hall, was planned for 126 women students in 1947 by Cecil Howitt, designer of the Portland Building, for a 1948 start and 1950 completion. The Nightingale family had been closely associated with the University College when living at Lea Hurst in Derbyshire. The Hall opened partially in January 1951 with 60 women, mostly transferred from Lenton Firs Hall when that was being converted into a men's Hall (Wortley Hall), and was fully occupied by 144 women (including those in Lenton Fields house) in October 1951. It remains substantially unaltered. Lenton Fields House was divided into flats for academic staff from 1947 to 1950, before becoming a dormitory annexe for 21 Florence Nightingale Hall students in 1951. Nightingale Close of staff houses was completed and occupied in 1953.

The second major building on Lenton Fields land is the Physical Education and Indoor Sports Centre. Negotiations with the city authorities in 1960 for a joint project of sports halls and an Olympic standard swimming pool based on the lido site at the eastern end of the campus ended in rejection by the city in 1961 - an outcome that undoubtedly would have incensed Sir Jesse Boot. Coventry now has the pool planned for this scheme - the country's premier swimming venue. Predictably the lido soon became derelict, and in recent years has seemed to be in danger of being taken over by a private developer. At the time of writing an 'Arts Centre' is being built on the site by the University to replace the art galleries expelled from the Portland Building to make way for a business school. The outcome for the University of the city's rejection of the 1960 proposal was the present Sports Centre at Lenton Fields, which is based on an ingenious adaptation and extension of a redundant aircraft hangar, the actual building

Figure 124: Aerial view of the University campus in 1972
Under construction - Willoughby Hall extension and the Medical School.

Figure 125: Aerial view of the originally women's Halls along the western side of the campus, viewed from the south.
South to north - Florence Boot, Willoughby, Cavendish, Ancaster and Nightingale Halls and Lenton Fields. Florence Boot Close, the Music School and Nightingale Close are included. For original men's Halls see Figure 59.

being designed by F.S.Eales to incorporate the steel framework already purchased (Figure 125). When in 1964 the city again declined to participate the project was crucially supported by the Cripps family trust. The work of construction finally got under way in spring 1969 and was completed in the spring of 1970 at a cost of about £166,000 to the U.G.C., the Cripps Foundation and the University's Endowment Fund in almost equal parts. Squash courts were added in spring 1977, supplementing those built in 1961 near to Cripps Hall. The Centre was formally opened on 28 April 1970 by Dr. Roger Bannister, together with Cripps Hall extensions and the Cripps Student Health Centre, all made possible by the munificence of Sir Cyril and Mr. Humphrey Cripps. The final choice of the site for the Sports Centre owed something to its central position among the residential Halls, the proximity of ducts of the district heating scheme, and adjoining open land sterilized, at least temporarily, by subsidence.

Lenton Eaves, with 11 acres, was purchased by the University in 1948 at a time when it had no use for it, and the house was offered to Paton Congregational College, which declined the offer. Eventually, in 1951 it became one of Florence Boot Hall's dormitory annexes, housing 15 students. It was transferred to Nightingale Hall in 1958, and, after being hawked around various other Halls by the Warden - unsuccessfully - to Willoughby Hall. In 1975, exactly 100 years after it was built, and thoroughly disliked by generations of students because of its shared rooms and the traffic noise from Derby Road, it was adapted for use by the University's Non-academic Staff Club, whose earlier, wooden clubhouse was moved from the Applied Science area and re-erected alongside - a final happy outcome. The 15 students then resident at Lenton Eaves were moved to houses that the University had bought in Dunkirk. There is a recently built, and remarkably sympathetic extension to the front of Lenton Eaves house. The bowling green adjoining the house replaces that which was lost when the new Hallward Library was built at Lenton Mount. The rest of the land of Lenton Eaves has become playing fields, especially for Hall sports, but with an area of all-weather surface provided with floodlighting and used in association with the Sports Centre nearby. Initial levelling of seven acres begun in autumn 1956 was halted by mining subsidence caused by the final operations of Wollaton Colliery, and was completed only in 1958-59 after a period for land settlement, which was relatively short on account of the shallowness of the coal workings. Whether residential building was ruled out on account of the subsidence risk at that stage is not clear, but it should be noted that a strip of Lenton Eaves land was cut off by the westward shift of Beeston Lane to become part of the site of Sherwood Hall.

The 20 acres of the Lenton Grove estate east of the Tottle Brook, purchased with Lenton Grove house from the Sheffield Regional Hospital Board in 1952, was developed for women's residence. The house, after several unoccupied years, was in some disrepair, and there were no immediate plans for it; but after extension, and with purpose-built studio accommodation added in 1954-55, it was opened in 1955 as the Music School, to which study rooms were added in 1956. The outbuildings alongside Beeston Lane, originally mainly for farming operations, were taken over by University maintenance staff in 1955.

Several staff houses, called Florence Boot Close, built in 1958-59, were the first residential development. In 1961 plans were produced for three new women's Halls on Lenton Grove land, though the earlier Jellicoe plan envisaged only two. They were slightly later than the corresponding group of men's Halls on Lenton Hurst Farm. Willoughby Hall was designed by Richard Turley and W.H.Williamson of Newcastle, who had earlier been awarded the contract for a second Hall planned for Lenton Fields land (which was never built) after a competition in 1950. It was begun in May 1962, though as a somewhat shrunken version of the original plan, and was occupied in January 1964. It was extended in 1972-73. Cavendish and Ancastor Halls, which soon followed, designed by the same architects, are mirror images of each other. Cavendish was started in November 1964 and occupied in January 1966: Ancaster, started at the end of 1964, opened in October 1966. These three Halls were planned as an architectural unit, with special attention given to their visual harmony when viewed from the new Woodside Road across 13 acres of grassland fronting them between the new road and Tottle Brook, land surplus to the Corporation's road-building requirements and bought by the University in 1957 to 'preserve the amenities of Florence Nightingale Hall and the Department of Music'. Although the extensions of both Willoughby and Ancaster Halls have encroached upon it substantially, this tract of the former Lenton Grove estate in Beeston parish remains open land, serving the same purpose for the later Lenton Grove group of Halls, as well as for the more recent Broadgate flats development south-west of Woodside Road. Already over 1,000 students - and rising - live on the former Lenton Grove estate

The northern campus - residential

The University's men's Halls (the three most westerly, Rutland, Sherwood and Derby now mixed Halls like Willoughby and Ancaster of the Lenton Grove group) continue the residential belt of the western side of the campus eastwards along its northern margin and then south to Hugh Stewart Hall in an arc that partially surrounds the 'downland' (Figures 124 and 126). Except for Hugh Stewart Hall and Lenton-and-Wortley Hall, and both of these partially, all are on land formerly in the Lenton Firs estate, the 95 acres of which also included a substantial proportion of sharply undulating surface which survives as a green setting for large new University buildings. Although the Lenton Firs estate purchased by the University was much the same as the Lenton Hall park of the early 19th century it is useful to recognize its sub-division into the former Lenton Firs Farm and Lenton Hurst Farm. Each brought with it a large house - Lenton Firs and Lenton Hurst, both rented by the University College soon after the end of the war.

Lenton Hurst, with its 8 acres of gardens and lawn, was rented in 1945, and used from 1947 to 1955 to house residential courses for H.M. Forces by the Department of Adult Education. After these courses moved to Shakespeare Street in 1955 the house, by now owned by the University, became for nearly a decade a dormitory annexe of Wortley Hall (at Lenton Firs), its adaptation being completed in the summer of 1956. When Lenton Hall opened in 1965 closely alongside it, Lenton Hurst was taken over by the new Hall, and it is appropriate that the closure of Wortley Hall in 1986 should have been followed by the absorption of its students into a re-named Lenton-and-Wortley Hall.

Lenton Firs House was rented, with 9 acres adjoining it, at the same time as Lenton Hurst, and in February 1946 a small Lenton Firs Hall of Residence for women was opened there with Professor Arthur Radford and his wife as Wardens. In 1950 the estate was purchased by the University, and Florence Nightingale Hall was completed: and so, in January 1951, the Lenton Firs women became the first Nightingale women, and Wortley Hall for men opened at Lenton Firs. The original outbuildings at Lenton Firs, used in wartime to house an emergency regional Civil Defence headquarters, were adapted for temporary use for Geology Department research work and as a library book store. The 90-year-old East Lodge, a gardener's cottage, was adapted to house eight students in 1952, and West Lodge followed in 1954. Both lodges were closed in 1981.

Despite the inability of Wortley Hall to attract much conference income in vacations and thus maintain independent financial viability in accountancy terms, and recurrent debate about whether further expenditure to improve or extend the facilities of the Hall could be justified, Wortley Hall thrived for 30 more years as one of the most successful Halls on the campus, for all its many physical disabilities - if not, indeed, because of them. It was closed in 1986, and the house and residential blocks radically altered and adapted for use by the Department of Architecture, which did not wish to remain in the upper floors of the tower block to which it had reluctantly returned in 1976 after replacement of the lifts there. Conveniently the Department of Architecture now adjoins the Institute of Planning at Paton House. The five

Figure 126: The originally men's Halls of Residence on the northern campus viewed from the south-west.
Includes, west to east , Sherwood, Rutland, Derby, Lincoln and Lenton (-and- Wortley) Halls: and, alongside Derby Road: Lenton Eaves Lodge (opposite to 'Beeston Tower' entrance to Wollaton Park) Lenton Hurst , Redcourt and Paton House (earlier West Hill House and The Cedars).

staff houses of Wortley Hall Close were built in 1953-54, and the five tenants and their wives formed the resident Senior Common Room of Wortley Hall. Their successors are now some distance from the students at Lenton-and-Wortley Hall to whom they act as tutors.

The first major new building constructed on the former Lenton Firs Farm was Cripps Hall, started in September 1957, funded by the Cripps family and designed by Donald McMorran. The first Warden of Wortley Hall, Harry Lucas, became the founding Warden of Cripps Hall, the first of the new men's Halls. It set high standards of provision and construction. It was occupied in September 1959 by 200 men students and tutors, and formally opened by Mr. C.T.Cripps (later Sir Cyril Cripps) on 15 October 1959. Lenton Close, a modern house built in 1934 for H.B.Fletcher on land bought from Sir Thomas Shipstone opposite to Cripps Hall main entrance across Lenton Hall Drive was purchased by the University in 1958 and taken over by Cripps Hall as an annexe to house 25 additional students. Cripps Hall was extended to the design of Gordon Woollatt in 1967-68, and as part of the same operation, with the same architect, contractor and benefactor, the closely adjoining Cripps Health Centre was built. The Hall extension was occupied in autumn 1968 and the Student Health Centre opened in January 1969. Near to Cripps Hall, on what was regarded as a 'hidden' site, three squash courts designed by McMorran were built in 1961.

Apart from the buildings of the Pure Science Faculty (now including one outside the Science precinct) there was only one other major new building on the former Lenton Firs Farm. Although the new McMorran building for Social Sciences and Education north of Highfield House had been first occupied only in 1961, a second new building for Social Sciences, allowing Education to expand to fill the earlier shared building, was under discussion in 1964, planned by Colin Gray. The site eventually chosen was south of Hugh Stewart Hall, overlooking eastwards the old (1838) quarry below Lenton Firs farmstead, which was filled to provide a large car park shared with Cripps and Hugh Stewart Hall. The building was planned urgently with a view to a joint building contract, for which tenders were put in June 1965 and agreed with contractors John Laing in July for an autumn start. Building actually began in April 1966 and was completed in summer 1967. The Psychology Department was not now included, and moved into a new complex that included Geology and Cell Biology on the western margin of the Science area near to the Biology building.

On Lenton Hurst Farm, the western part of the Lenton Firs estate, the new development was entirely residential in the form of five new men's Halls, though Lenton Hall (now Lenton-and-Wortley), the fifth and latest Hall of this group, was built partly on the adjoining garden of Redcourt. The five Halls were built in rapid succession, the first four under paired contracts. Lincoln Hall, designed by F.E.Woolley, was started in March 1961 and occupied in September 1962, while Derby Hall, designed by Brian O'Rorke, was started in May 1961 and occupied in January 1963. They were built by the same contractor 'in tandem'. They were quickly followed by Sherwood Hall (March 1963-October 1964), and Rutland Hall (May 1963-January 1965) (Figure 126) both designed by J. Fletcher Watson and again built in tandem. Derby Hall was expanded by 100 places to 310 by the addition of an L-shaped wing extending southwards towards the 'downland', opened in September 1974 as Derby became a mixed hall in collaboration with Willoughby Hall. Sherwood Hall's 49 new places were built in 1978 and opened in January 1979, when it, too, became mixed. An extension to Lincoln Hall proposed in 1972 was cancelled after disagreement over its siting between the Warden and Mrs. Haywood, the consultant landscape architect for this part of the campus. Lenton (-and-Wortley) Hall (September 1963-October 1965) is discussed below in connection with Redcourt.

The eastern campus - Science and Engineering

The Science area which dominates the eastern part of the main campus, though forming a unified precinct architecturally and academically, comprises two distinct, unequal halves in

Figure 127: Site of Rutland Hall viewed from west of Derby Hall Warden's House in Spring 1963.
Lenton Hurst Farm buildings east of the farm house are already largely demolished. The old Sawley turnpike ran along the post fence in the left middle distance.

physical character. It is more closely built up than any other part of the campus, a condition that has doubtless been determined by the extent of the available level surface shared by the two halves. The old line of Cut Through Lane along the foot of the valleyside slope marks the approximate boundary between the former quarry floor produced in 1838, occupied by buildings of Science Faculty departments, and the river gravels of the Trent valley occupied mainly by Engineering departments, but shared with some other departments and institutes. The Science Library and the Tower Block stand in positions between the two halves.

Although the so-called Clifton Boulevard site of single storey office buildings on the valley floor, extending to 17 acres, was purchased from the city of Nottingham as early as 1949, its major development was deferred for a decade. It was leased back to the Ministry of Works, although one block was released and adapted for use by the Pharmacy Department by 1955, and another for Biochemistry and Metallurgy in 1956. The layout of buildings for the Faculty of Applied Science as it was then called, on the site demarcated by Jellicoe's plan of the mid-1950s, was proposed in 1957 by (Sir) Basil Spence, who had been appointed in 1955, and his proposals were continually modified in detail over the succeeding years in the light of Faculty criticism and suggestions.

A research laboratory for the Mining Department provided in 1955-56 (taken over by Metallurgy in 1972) was followed in 1958-60 by a Mining and Fluid Mechanics laboratory building, the first new building on the site and the first 'spur' of a series of five. A Year I Engineering Teaching Block started in July 1958 was occupied in December 1960, and was extended in 1964-65. The Second and Third Year Teaching Block begun in 1960 was occupied in October 1962, and this was also extended in 1964-65 to its full length. It was linked by an Exhibition Hall with the Year I building to the north of it, and by bridges to two laboratory blocks to the south. Meanwhile other Spence buildings were constructed: Civil, Mechanical and Electrical Engineering laboratories in 1960-62, the Science Library (1962-64), extended to cater for the needs of the Medical Faculty in 1968-69) and the Tower Block started in September 1962.

On the former quarry floor to the north, earlier part of the Lenton Firs estate, buildings were being constructed for Science departments, designed by Basil Spence, Andrew Renton and their colleagues. The Chemistry building was erected in 1958-60, a period of extensive earth moving, road building and intensive construction on the campus. Spence's sketch plans for the Chemistry building had been approved in 1957, and the building was finally occupied in the summer of 1961 with the completion of the radio-chemistry laboratory. The Physics and Mathematics building followed, started in summer 1960 and occupied at Easter 1963. The latest building of this Science group on the quarry floor is that for Computing Science constructed in 1986-88.

The Tower Block was to be 190 feet high, and Sir Basil Spence insisted that it was an architectural imperative - the 'vertical feature' required to set off the profile of the whole complex, though no University department wanted to occupy it. Building started in September 1962, a year late because of uncertainty as to whether the School of Architecture would be joining the University and leaving the city to occupy part of the proposed tower. The building was reduced by one storey for financial reasons, possibly caused by the delay. The contractor was Simms, Son and Cooke. The ten lowest storeys were occupied by Electrical Engineering in August 1964, and the six floors above by Architecture in January 1965.

Other buildings on the Clifton Boulevard site include a laboratory for Cancer Research near to Pharmacy, formed in 1960-61; a Chemical Engineering building (1962-65); Production Engineering (1963-65); new workshop buildings for Production Engineering and Production Management (1984-85); a building technology laboratory for Architecture (1963-64); the Wolfson Institute of Interfacial Technology occupied in early 1971; and the adjacent Institute of Hearing Research (1978-79). The final transfers of then existing departments to the Clifton Boulevard site were made in the summer vacation of 1965. In the same summer two new buildings designed by Andrew Renton were begun, one to provide accommodation for the Geology and Psychology Departments and the other for Cell Biology. Although they were sited on part of the original campus - a narrow strip of land between the East Drive north of the lido and the Clifton Boulevard site, geographically they too formed part of the Science precinct. Building was completed in late 1967. Finally, a new permanent building for Pharmacy was constructed between the Cell Biology and the Geology-Psychology buildings on a northward extension of the latter's foundations that had already been prepared for this possibility. It was begun in February 1969 and occupied in October 1970 - but by the infant Medical School on a temporary basis, and it was 1976 before the long-suffering itinerant Department of Pharmacy, one of the first departments to be expelled from the Trent Building, finally took over its own building after many years of banishment to temporary quarters.

A northern outlier

Before returning to the Central Area to complete this review of the developed precincts of the main campus, a small outlier alongside Derby Road on the northern margin of the campus should be identified. Each of the four old houses included, from Lenton Hurst to Lenton Firs, has been involved in separate combinations of academic and residential use outside the broadscale structure and plan of the University. Lenton Hurst, a centre for Adult Education from 1945 under the aegis of the Delegacy for Extra-Mural Studies, providing short residential courses, mainly for personnel of H.M.Forces, lost its academic character when it became a detached annexe of Wortley Hall and subsequently an integral part of Lenton Hall. Lenton Firs, having functioned as an early Hall of Residence for women, and then for men as Wortley Hall, took an opposite course, and in 1986 became the Department of Architecture, and combined with the Institute of Planning Studies located in the adjacent Paton House as the Department of Architecture and Planning.

Redcourt, with its three acres of gardens, was the University College's earliest 'postwar' purchase of property, in January 1945, and it may have been bought simply because it came on to the market when Lady Cahn moved to the south coast and also sold Stanford Hall near Loughborough (to become a Cooperative College). Redcourt has proved to be an excellent investment. At first it provided a home for the newly established Institute of Education, which occupied it in late 1947 and remained until 1961, when it moved to the new Social Sciences and Education building. This was convenient timing. The five new men's Halls planned in 1959 for part of Lenton Hurst Farm were later allocated an expanded area after the individual architects had presented their proposals, and related considerations of landscape and physical autonomy for the Halls had been taken into account. A small modification of the line of the new road to link with Beeston Lane made space for one of the new Halls to be built north of it, and Lenton (and-Wortley) Hall was constructed between Lenton Hurst and Redcourt, to incorporate both. The new building was mainly on Redcourt grounds, to the plans of Donald McMorran presented in 1961. Building started in September 1963, and the Hall was occupied in October 1965. Redcourt house itself provides excellent accommodation for the Warden and other senior members of the Hall.

Paton House, Redcourt's neighbour and contemporary, earlier called West Hill House, then The Cedars, and then Paton College, was only acquired by the University 23 years after it had first negotiated for its purchase, for it was bought by Paton College in 1949 when the new University could not raise the purchase price, and it came to the University only after Paton College removed to Manchester, as described in Chapter XII. It was then adapted in the summer of 1968 for planning courses of the Department of Architecture and Civic Planning, and later became the Institute of Planning Studies. Like Lenton Hurst, then, its University

Figure 128: Site of the Hallward Library on part of the garden of Lenton Mount.
The view, from the house, includes the bowling green formed after the University bought the property, seen beyond part of the original croquet lawn.

history began with a residential/academic function, but it became exclusively academic instead of fully residential, and now, with Architecture at the former Wortley hall, forms an academic outlier at the northern extremity of the campus.

The Central Area

The Central Area of the University will be expected to contain the premises of the central administration, facilities for congregation, general social and cultural activities and refreshment, and the main general library, together with the chief academic departments most likely to need to use it, and teaching rooms required by them - the Faculties of Arts, and Law and Social Sciences - either within the Central Area or nearby. This is, indeed the case, although Hugh Stewart Hall must also be included in the central precinct, but only on account of historical precedence - it was already there, part of a pre-existing institution but still viable in its original function and probably impossible to convert to another.

The Trent Building originally contained within itself all the facilities listed above in the University College, and the departments of all the Faculties except Engineering, located in the buildings behind it, and the departments of Mining, and Dyeing and Textiles which had remained at the old College on Shakespeare Street. The building has undergone great internal changes, in many stages, in the course of its adaptation to cater for the re-use of space vacated by the exodus of departments to their own purpose-built accommodation elsewhere on the campus, and the expansion of the space requirements of those functions remaining as the University grew. By the end of 1963 Geology was the only science department still housed in the Trent Building, and its final departure in 1968 freed accommodation for English, Slavonic Studies and German. The movement of departments, in fact, cannot be regarded simply as a centrifugal process since the dispersal of departments of the Faculties of Pure Science and Law and Social Sciences, as well as some Arts departments, and later the move of the Library was countered by a centripetal movement of returning Arts Faculty departments and the Law Department after earlier banishment in whole or part to temporary buildings.

Throughout the 1950s it was intended that much vacated space in the building would be taken over by the expanding University Library, and alterations were made to implement the plan. With the opening of the Portland Building in 1956 the Library was able to expand downwards into the former refectory, and from that eastwards into the former kitchens as well as westwards into the former Senior Common Room and the 'Lower Corridor', earlier the hub of student social life. However, as mentioned earlier, a report commissioned in 1961 and presented to the University Council in 1962, recommended that the plan for the Library to remain in the Trent Building should be abandoned and a new library building constructed elsewhere. This was accepted and approved by the U.G.C.. It required a re-planning of the Central Area as a whole, including its roads, to replace the now obsolete McMorran plan of 1958 (Figures 120 and 121) a task for Sir William Holford who succeeded Sir Percy Thomas as consultant architect. The long delay of almost eleven years from 1962 to the end of 1973 when the new Hallward Library opened made planning for the Trent Building during those years difficult.

The decision about the Library meant that the Law Department could eventually transfer its departmental library to the former University Library, and move back to the Trent Building after a period in The Orchard. The Orchard had been bought in 1950, three years earlier than neighbouring Lenton Mount, and was adapted for use by Law and Slavonic Languages. Extensions to it were provided for the expanding Law Department in 1962, and for the Law Library in 1966, followed by a Derwent-type extension in 1969 before the whole Law Department moved to the Trent Building in 1974, and Politics took its place in The Orchard.

Lenton Mount, although one of the University's smaller purchases, is seen in retrospect to have been especially important because of its central location and its large garden, which later provided the site for the new Hallward Library (Figure 128). The sale was negotiated in the summer of 1952 and completed in 1953. The house was adapted to become the University Staff Club, and was occupied in February 1954. It has since been extended, especially by the construction of the present dining room in 1961. Its grass tennis court was incorporated into a bowling green, and its hard court and croquet lawn were useful and popular amenities, but swept away by the building of the library on the garden site, a decision deplored at the time by many members of the University who had become accustomed to regard the site as part of a 'green heart' for the Central Area. An early proposal had been that the new library should be situated behind the Portland Building, and the choice of the Lenton Mount site meant that the 'cowsheds' were reprieved - not for the first or the last time. The site decision was made in 1963, and the building planned by H.Faulkner Brown and Partners; but a start was delayed, mainly for financial reasons, until October 1970, and the new library was not occupied and finally opened until December 1973. This was the last major new building completed in the Central Area, though in 1988-89 an important new Institute for German, Austrian and Swiss Affairs, donated by J.H.Gunn, a graduate of the University's German Department, was constructed on the higher ground between the Trent and Portland Buildings and opened by Mrs. Margaret Thatcher in September 1989.

Meantime, also on the original campus, large changes took place in the group of old Engineering Faculty buildings behind the Trent Building. Initially growth of the departments led to a building extension for Civil and Mechanical Engineering started in 1950, finished in 1952 and opened by Lord Hives in 1953, but the whole area was progressively adapted for other uses as the new buildings alongside Clifton Boulevard came into use. The abandonment of the central area plan of 1958, and the decision to build the new library on Lenton Mount land, confirmed the relative permanence of these older buildings, and Cut Through Lane, which had been shifted to the north side of the copse between it and the site of the new library in anticipation of the redevelopment, was restored to its original line. The new uses were varied. The museum in 1966 took in the former armoury and indoor rifle range which had passed to Electrical Engineering in 1957 when the headquarters of the University O.T.C. and W.R.A.C. moved to the Territorial Army premises on Broadgate, Beeston , near to the University Air Squadron at Broadgate House. The R.E.M.E. lecture huts, workshops and store were erected in the grounds of Broadgate House in 1950 when removed from their position alongside the Vice-Chancellor's garden wall fronting Cut Through Lane, where a large cowshed had earlier stood. In 1955 University maintenance staff transferred from former farm buildings behind Highfield House to outbuildings at Lenton Grove. More recently other parts of the old Engineering buildings have been taken over by Works Directorate staff, and for a student theatre and other purposes, and in 1976 premises were provided for Building Science. Thus, like the 'Cow-sheds', the old Engineering complex has been converted to uses other than academic teaching which benefit from a central position on the campus - a process that is still very active today.

Hugh Stewart Hall, the first men's Hall on the campus, now geographically part of the Central Area but not easily adaptable to uses other than residence, links the Central Area with the residential arc round the open downland. It was greatly extended in the late 1960s, with J.G.Woollatt appointed architect for the extensions in 1964. The large extension enclosing an extended quadrangle on the north-east side was built in two stages, and involved the final demolition of Lenton Firs Farm (originally Lenton Hall Farm) discussed in Chapter VII. Stage II was completed in the spring term of 1969.

Florence Boot Hall, the first and nearest women's Hall, remains separated from the Central Area . It, too, has been extended in two stages. In the summer vacation of 1960 the dining facilities were expanded to accommodate 200 so that the students in the several old houses used as annexes of the Hall could dine with all the residents of the Hall itself. A decade later, in the summer and autumn of 1971, 98 study bedrooms and two tutors' flats were added to the Hall. The Warden's house, designed by Colin Gray, was built in 1966.

It will be apparent that care has been taken from the beginning not to pack buildings into the original campus, and to segregate the Central Area as a recognizable precinct by preserving open surroundings. In addition to the steep slopes running down to the University Park lake, which would have been hazardous sites for large buildings, two particularly important areas of the original campus remain open and 'undeveloped', preserving the green park setting of the University. These are, first, the site of the 'lost village' of Keighton, which separates the Portland Building and the 'Cowsheds' in the Central Area from the Biology building - the outpost of the Science area - with the Botany garden, now no more than a quiet amenity area, along its upper margin; and second, the long slope westwards from the Trent Building and Highfield House down to Florence Boot Hall, the old Stonehouse Wong.

Additions to the main campus

Brief reference to several additions to the University estate which were not part of the plans of the late 1940s forms the concluding paragraphs of this review. Four of the sites are actually physically contiguous with the 'primary' campus - the University Hospital and Medical School, called the Queen's Medical Centre since it was formally opened by the Queen in 1976; the Jesse Boot Conference Centre; the Beeston Flats 'off-campus' residential development; and Lenton Abbey house and grounds. Scattered properties acquired by the University in Dunkirk are very near. Two sites are more distant - Bramcote and Grove Farm.

The events leading to the replacement of the industrial premises and the remnants of the 'village' of Spring Close and the hamlet of Hillside by the Medical School-Hospital complex between Clifton Boulevard and the river Leen (flowing now in the channel of the Nottingham Canal) have been outlined in Chapter XI and will not be repeated here. The Q.M.C., with its ancillary residential and other buildings mainly occupies land that formed part of the dairy farm of Lenton Priory down to the 16th century, and was thus part of its demesne like the adjoining main campus; but the site of the Q.M.C. extends northwards across the line of the former Spring Close road to include a strip of land that formed the southern end of the former Beck Field, one of the open common arable fields of Lenton until its inclosure in 1769 (Figure 129).

Alternative sites considered for the hospital included Ruddington Hall, Clifton, Bramcote and University Park, and even Wollaton Park was mentioned. Preliminary physical and academic planning of the Q.M.C. began in 1965 with the Pickering Report to the University Council submitted in May, and the establishment of a planning office in the 'cowsheds' in October, accommodation that was extended in 1966. The outline development plan was approved by the Ministry of Health in January 1967. Temporary buildings becoming vacant in the summer of 1967 were taken over with the intention of using them for teaching the first intake of students before Phase I of the permanent buildings was completed in early 1971. Session 1969-70 began with six viable medical departments in the temporary buildings, but the protracted public inquiries and appeals through 1967 to summer 1969, and a further period of inaction caused by the allowance of time to minimize the disruption of the ousted businesses which needed to find new premises, impeded entry to the Spring Close site and delayed completion of the stages of the Phase I contract to dates ranging from June 1974 to January 1976. In the event completion and first entry was delayed until early 1975, four years later than originally planned, and the final stage was handed over in May 1976. During these years the Medical School had left the temporary buildings and taken possession of the new permanent building constructed for the unfortunate Pharmacy Department. Clinical teaching relied on the City and General hospitals. The Phase II contract, for the Teaching Hospital, was let in October 1975 for a start in early 1976, and the buildings were handed over during the summer of 1980, though the start of operation of the buildings was delayed by financial problems.

Two of the six residential estates of the early 19th century had not been acquired by the

Figure 129: The Queen's Medical Centre from the north-west
The site of the former Lenton Priory is central in the upper part of the picture, bounded by the former channel of the river Leen (concentric with the bend of the Nottingham Canal); Abbey Street to the White Hart; and Wilford Road. The Hillside row occupied a strip of land between the hospital chimney stacks and the canal near the left margin of the view. The converted surviving buildings of Bayleys' leather works are seen alongside Leen-gate beyond the canal bridge.

University by the 1950s. These were the Lenton Abbey and Lenton House estates, the former mostly covered by council and private housing of the 1920s and 1930s, and the latter still operated by the Boots Company as a horticultural research station, with its chairman and managing director Lord Trent occupying the house. Lenton Abbey house in about 1½ acres of gardens was purchased by the University in 1976, but as an investment only for the time being, the tenants of the flats remaining undisturbed. In the late 1970s the Boots experimental station on the Lenton House estate was run down, but Lenton House itself, now a company house used for purposes of hospitality after the death of Lord Trent, continued in the same role.

The largest University building project of the 1980s began in December 1981 with a gift from Boots of nearly ten acres on the north side of the Lenton House estate adjoining the 'downland' and Rutland Hall, together with £250,000, half the expected cost of building on the land a conference centre and assembly hall which had featured in the University's Centenary Appeal brochure. In 1982 plans were agreed for a scheme costing £700,000 - partly a loan to be repaid from the conference centre's income - a sum that had risen to £800,000 by March 1983. In July 1983 the main contractor went into liquidation, and another tender had to be negotiated for the completion of the partly built centre. Later an external terrace or platform to carry an exhibition marquee was added. The project was completed by September 1984 and was named the Jesse Boot Conference Centre.

The University's residential developments in Beeston (Figure 123) really began in 1953-54 with the building of two Professors' houses on land acquired on Salthouse Lane, where Dagfa House was bought in 1968 but re-leased to the Dorothy Grant High School, already long established there, and later resold to the school's owner. Three large houses in the same vicinity north of Broadgate, Beeston were purchased, The Oaks and Broadwood in 1958 and The Pines in 1959, and adapted as annexes for a total of 49 women, members of Florence Boot Hall. It will be recalled that the same Hall's first annexe was Broadgate House, opposite, in 1930-33. More recent developments have been of a different nature - the construction of 'off-campus' accommodation for students, blocks of flats built in the grounds of these houses, including Broadgate House, and financed by loans for which the buildings themselves, being outside the campus, represent acceptable collateral. After the completion of Woodside Road through the old Lenton Grove estate the Corporation of Nottingham sold their unused land to the University. Thirteen acres east of the road were to be preserved as open space fronting the women's Halls (though now already encroached upon by extensions of Willoughby and Ancaster Halls). In 1959 the University acquired the land west of the new road, surrendering a piece of land west of Nightingale Hall in an exchange arrangement, and on this land, twenty years later, blocks of flats and a communal building were constructed, as described below.

In 1971 it was decided to build blocks of flats on both sides of Broadgate, Beeston providing 450 student places, and in March 1972 a contract was let for 300 places on the north side of Broadgate. Local objections delayed a start, and later one planned 3-storey block had to be reduced to 2 storeys; but work was begun in early March on The Oaks and The Pines sites. In October 1972 the contract was extended to include a further 150 places on the site near Broadgate House, on the south side of Broadgate, and by 1 October 1973 440 places were occupied in the flats developments that began in April 1972. In the summer of 1977 a block to house 54 students called Broadwood Court, situated near to Broadwood House was designed and built with the aid of a grant from the Wolfson Foundation, and was completed in late 1978. The Broadwood Court post-graduate flats project, financed largely from the sale of Bramcote House, was completed in 1984. In 1979, encouraged by the U.G.C. to plan for a further 750 residential places the University decided to start phased flats developments on the Woodside Road site mentioned above, aiming to provide 90 places by October 1980, and thereafter 188 places a year to completion. By the summer of 1980 141 places in three blocks had been completed on the Woodside Road site, and the amenity building was under way, to be completed in 1985. Further blocks of flats have since been constructed on this site. One other small early development in Beeston may be mentioned - the purchase in 1965 of No. 87 Broadgate and its adaptation for occupation by 12 post-graduate women students as a self-catering experiment.

Much of the builtup area of Dunkirk west of Montpelier Road and Clifton Boulevard was designated by the City of Nottingham's development plan for eventual use by the University. This is an important area to the University of the future in view of its contiguity to the fully occupied Science precinct and now to the Queen's Medical Centre, and the University therefore took every opportunity to acquire property there in anticipation of future needs. Houses were bought as they came on to the market, and were let to University employees and to students on an ad hoc basis. In the 1970s the U.G.C. severely pressed the University to sell off its property in Dunkirk and return the proceeds to the Exchequer. The University resisted the pressure in 1974, but in July 1978 it decided to 'divest itself of property' in Dunkirk that had been bought with Treasury funds. However, finally, in June 1979 the University 'bought' its own property there as an investment for the Appeal Fund since it had become feasible at District Valuer's prices. Although in 1951 nine acres of poorly drained land fronting Montpelier Road had been bought with an intention, never realized, to use it as a sports ground, the only new development in Dunkirk has been the Highfields Science Park, in which Nottingham City Council played a leading role. The first building of this project, on land south-east of Beeston Road, almost opposite to the University's south entrance and the former lido, was designed by William Saunders and Partners, and built by H. and E. Loach Ltd. of Colwick. It housed 14 companies, with communal facilities and near proximity to the University's Pure and Applied Science departments, and was occupied in late 1984. A second building planned in 1987 followed.

The residential developments at Bramcote village began with the purchase in August 1959 of Bramcote House, with 9 acres, and its occupation by 33 men students in October 1959. In 1960 more land was being sought near to Bramcote House for a block of 100 flat places, and in 1963 Grove House was leased from the Church, with the intention of joining it with Bramcote House to form the basis of a graduate college. Although Grove House was used briefly as a post-graduate residence the scheme was put in abeyance when it was agreed that Grove House should be taken over by the London College of Divinity, which moved there in 1969, and constructed a new building in 1970. In 1965, however, the University had bought Bramcote Hall Preparatory School with its grounds and playing fields, and then had 62 acres at the Bramcote site with 40 post-graduate men in residence. In 1967 the John Player company made a gift to further the Bramcote development in the form of Player House, a block of flats for 18 to 20 married and unmarried postgraduates on former Bramcote School land, begun in summer 1968 and occupied in March 1969, the first of an intended series for which planning permission was obtained. In January 1983 Bramcote House was sold and the net proceeds applied to the Broadgate post-graduate flats project at Broadwood, Beeston, mentioned above.

The other 'distant' development, the Grove Farm sports grounds, has been discussed in Chapter X above.

Aborted plans and concluding remarks

Mention of some proposals for physical development that failed to materialize will form a suitable corrective ending to this chronicle of seemingly incessant building and inexorable expansion. The failure of negotiations with the city for the establishment of a Physical Education complex based on the lido has been mentioned earlier, and there is an irony in the construction now proceeding of a cultural/arts centre on the site of the derelict buildings of Sir Jesse Boot's lido and its car park, after several unworthy private projects had been canvassed and considered by the City Council. In 1961, when the earlier plans for the central area were beginning to be questioned, it was proposed to demolish the 'cowsheds' behind the Portland Building to make way for an Assembly Hall/Theatre for 750, scheduled for building in 1965 when the Electrical Engineering Department would have moved to the new tower block in the Science precinct. A University Health Centre was to have been incorporated in the scheme. But by 1963 the U.G.C. was having doubts about the project, and it was cancelled. The same site was immediately proposed for the new University Library, but this idea soon lapsed when the Lenton Mount garden site was chosen for the library. Thus, after two reprieves and over 40 years of highly useful, flexible service, the 'temporary buildings' begin to look more and more permanent, while a University Theatre now appears fanciful in view of developments in the city.

A proposed University chapel, which figured in the early plans for development, was eventually considered and approved in principle by Senate and Council in 1962, and in 1963 a benefactor offered funds for building a chapel to hold 1,200, situated on the commanding site west of Hugh Stewart Hall, overlooking the downland and on the north-western margin of the Central Area, as originally proposed. A 1965 start was suggested. However, this project was abandoned, not on account of lack of funds but, it is said, through rejection of a 'traditional' design in keeping with the dominant architectural styles of the campus buildings, and acceptable to the prospective donor, by a Building Committee which appears to have placed aesthetic self-indulgence before the larger advantage of the University community. Such a rebuff to a would-be donor will not have escaped the notice of other potential benefactors.

Undoubtedly mistakes have been made in the course of the University's development of its campus. But bearing in mind the bewildering combination of rapid and surging growth, largely unpredictable; the uncertainties of the availability of public funds, and the academic politics involved in their allocation; the need to sustain continuously all the elements of the University's structure in full operation; and the responsibility of incorporating desirable legacies of the past and of preserving the attractive setting, it must be agreed that the University's governing bodies and their professional officers and advisers, most notably the first Vice-Chancellor, Bertrand Hallward, a man of vision, dedication, drive and charisma have served it outstandingly well.

Frequent change must be expected on a University campus near the end of the 20th century, but most of the University has been built to last. After some 430 years as part of a priory demesne, 260 years of agrarian stagnation as landed estate of absentee owners, and 150 years as primarily ornamental residential parkland, a new era in the topographic history of the campus began 70 years ago and promises to continue indefinitely into the future. It may be hoped that the vision of the University authorities in their future planning will continue to range beyond immediate considerations of academic convenience, and that the legacies of the past, which contribute so much to the beauty and interest of the campus will be jealously defended and preserved. The latest developments are not entirely encouraging. The interesting MRI building erected recently near the head of the slope south of Cripps Hall on a highly conspicuous and important site is wholly detached from the congested Science area. It seriously breaches the principle of academic precincts that has been adhered to from the earliest days of comprehensive development on the campus, a principle that has been highly successful in preserving the essential parkland environment of the University, and it is particularly regrettable that the green collar of the campus has been invaded here at its narrowest point.

NOTES

1. *Dictionary of National Biography 1931-40* (Oxford 1948). Also The Times 15 June 1931.
2. Stanley Chapman, *Jesse Boot of Boots the Chemists: a study in business history* (1974) Hodder and Stoughton. This can be regarded as the definitive work on Sir Jesse Boot and the Boots Company. See also H.J.Davis, *The Honoured Name* (1931) Boots Pure Drug Company.
3. R.Iliffe and W.Baguley, 'Boots the Chemists', *Victorian Nottingham* 18 (1977) 53-87.
4. The conveyance was intended to be from 'Sir Jesse Boot and others to University College, Nottingham', but was abortive because for 20 years the property of the College had been vested in the Corporation of Nottingham as trustee.
5. Jesse Boot built a pavilion of stone and timber and laid out a recreation ground with tennis courts, summer house and children's amusements a few hundred yards above Trent Bridge, and called it Plaisaunce. He and his family used it at weekends in summer, together with senior staff with their families and other friends such as the Armitages.
6. According to Chapman [1974 185] Sir Jesse telephoned not from St. Helier, his house in The Park, Nottingham, but from The Grove, overlooking St. Aubin Bay, recently purchased.
7. It is puzzling to read [Chapman 1974] that Sir Jesse spent £32,745 acquiring 'the house and site' (that is, Highfield House) only to find that Lady Boot 'would not move to Lenton House': and that [p. 155] 'when Sir Jesse Boot appointed (Hedley) Jessop he had invited him to Lenton House and divulged his ambition to develop Highfields as a factory and residential estate ...' since Lenton House had been purchased by John Boot, not by his father.
8. S.Zaleski in *Lenton Times* No. 1 (October 1988), (Lenton Local History Society) following Strauss [1978].
9. J.E.Greenwood [1977] has described Boots' acquisition of the site of their Beeston factories, including the part played by Hedley Jessop, the chief engineer, in obtaining additional land. Although the first concrete-and-glass building was opened only in 1933, five years after the College buildings, the 300-acre site was bought and the soap factory built in 1928-29. See Townroe [1928].
10. *The Lenton Listener* No. 18 (May-June 1982) (Lenton Local History Society) contains an excellent account of the history of the lido.
11. N.U.M.D., Accession 423.
12. The map attached to the void conveyance of November 1923 does not show land specifically assigned for College playing fields on the Hassocks, but by 1924-25 they were laid out and ready for use. Wood [1953 163-4] records that in 1919 the College's athletic ground at Sherwood was wanted for housing development, so in 1920 a field on Holme Road, West Bridgford was bought by the College and the students' union was granted £250 to build pavilions. Aid was offered by the Board of Education in 1921. But in 1922, when Sir Jesse offered the Highfield campus in place of the riverside site the location was inconvenient: so Sir Jesse bought the Lady Bay grounds, which are still the athletic grounds of Boots, and provided the land on University Boulevard. The pavilion there was opened in 1925, and the grounds were in use several years before the College actually moved out from the city to Highfields. It should be noted that the rugby football ground and running track, originally part of the Lenton Grove estate and not the Highfield estate, were on land purchased by Nottingham City Council in connection with its by-pass plans, and are still rented by the University from the Corporation.
13. For the verse see *Ten Years a University* (pamphlet), University of Nottingham (1958) 32-33.
14. Wood's own opinion was very favourable. His pages 96-98 offer a good review of opposing impressions and judgments.
15. See also the Obituary of Percy Richard Morley Horder, *Journ. Royal Inst. British Architects* November 1941.
16. *Nottingham Civic Society Newsletter* 70 (April 1986)
17. The letter, dated 16 February 1928 from Cannes, is printed in full in the University College Nottingham Endowment Appeal brochure of 1928. [Hallward Library, Special Collections, Not 5 E 6 (pamphlet)
18. *Nottingham Civic Society Newsletter* 77 (September 1988) 26. The flats were renovated in 1988 by the City Engineer's and Surveyor's Departments. See also S.Zaleski, 'The road to Penn Avenue', *The Lenton Listener* June-July 1984.

BIBLIOGRAPHY

A list of printed books, articles and maps referred to in the text by the Harvard system of reference (author's name and date of publication, with page where appropriate).

[For references to manuscript and other unprinted documentary sources see the Notes at the end of each chapter.]

Abbreviations			
	EMG	-	East Midland Geographer
	NCSN	-	Nottingham Civic Society Newsletter
	TTS	-	Transactions of the Thoroton Society of Notts.
	TNH	-	The Nottinghamshire Historian
	NAO	-	Nottinghamshire Archives Office
	LAO	-	Lincolnshire Archives Office
	N.U.M.D.	-	Nottingham University Manuscripts Department
	Rotheras	-	Document in the care of Messrs. Rotheras

ANON.	1952	'Francis Wright: Public School Founder'. *Ad Rem* (Butterley Company's House Mag.) Summer 1952
ABLETT, Dave	1980	*A Guide to Old Sneinton* (Nottingham, Sneinton Environmental Society) Reissued 1986
ALLEN, Richard	1839	*The Nottingham and Derby Railway Companion* (London, Hamilton Adams) Compiled by R.Allen
	1840	*The Midland Counties Railway Companion* (Nottingham, R.Allen: Leicester, E.Allen)
	1866	*Allen's Illustrated Handbook and Guide to all the places of interest in Nottingham and its Environs* (Nottingham, R.Allen and Son: London, W.Kent and Co.) Compiled and edited by R.Allen.
	c.1870	*Rambles and rides round Nottingham* (Nottingham R.Allen and Son, Caxton House) No date
	1893	*Illustrated Guide to Nottingham and its neighbourhood* (Nottingham)
ALLIBONE, Jill	1987	*Anthony Salvin: pioneer of Gothic Revival architecture* (Cambridge, Lutterworth Press)
ANDERSON, P.H.	1973	*Forgotten railways: the East Midlands (2).* (Newton Abbot, David and Charles) Includes (p. 116) 'The Suburban Railway, City of Nottingham'
A.T.C.		'The new University building'. *Gong* XVIII, 1, 5-6. Union of Students, Univ. Coll. Nottingham.
AVELINE, W.T.	1880	*The Geology of the country around Nottingham.* Memoir Geol. Survey, HMSO (2nd edn.- 1st edn. 1861). For O.S. sheet 71 NE.
AVERY, B.W.	1956	'A classification of British soils'. *Trans. Sixth Intl. Congr. Soil Science* 5, 279-285
BAILEY, Thomas	1853	*Annals of Nottinghamshire.* History of the county of Nottingham, including the borough. (1852-55) 4 volumes in two. (London, Simpkin Marshall)
BARKER, M.H.('A WANDERER')	1835	*Walks round Nottingham* (Nottingham, T. Kirk and S. Bennett)
BARLEY, M.W. and TRAIN, K.S.S.	1972	See THROSBY below.

BARLEY, M.W. and CULLEN, R.	1975	*Nottingham Now* (Nottingham Civic Society)
BARLEY, M.W.	1987	'Aspley Hall, Nottingham and its fifteenth century tower'. *TTS* 91, 74-78
BARNES, E.G.	1966	*The rise of the Midland Railway, 1844-1874* (London, Allen and Unwin)
BARNES, F.A.	1960	'Meteorological records at Nottingham'. *EMG* 14, 60-61
	1962	'The cold Spring of 1962'. *EMG* 17, 53-55
	1962	'Climatological station at Nottingham Univ.' *EMG* 17, 52-53
	1963	'The hard winter of 1962-63 at Nottingham' *EMG* 19, 139-147
	1966	'Climate and weather'. Chapter 3 in K.C.EDWARDS (ed.) *Nottingham and its Region: a Scientific Survey* 60-102: also Appendix I, pp. 521-527. (Nottingham, British Association for the Advancement of Science)
	1975	'The mild winter of 1974-75 at Nottingham: the anatomy of an exceptional season'. *EMG* 3 (No.43) 153-167
	1987	'Lenton Priory after the Dissolution: its buildings and fair grounds'. *TTS* 91, 79-95
	1989	'The Hillside malting'. *Lenton Times* 3 (Nov. 1989) 14-15
	1989	'Cut off ! James Green and Francis Evans involvement with the Nottingham Canal'. *Lenton Times* 3 (Nov. 1989) 20-22
	1990	'The Dunkirk railway embankment and the 1838 quarries'. *Lenton Times* 4 (June 1990) 4-6
BAYLIS, Ebernezer & Son (Publishers)	1935	*Who's Who in Nottinghamshire*
BECKET, E.M.	1928	*The University College of Nottingham* (Nottm., Saxton)
BEYNON, Robin (ed)	1978	*The Theatre Royal, Nottingham, 1865-1978*: a theatrical and architectural history. (Nottingham, Nottingham City Council)
BINFIELD, Clyde	1988	'Holy murder at Cheshunt College: the formation of an English architect: P.R.Morley Horder, 1870-1944'. *Journ. United Reform Church History Society*, 4, No. 2 (May 1988) 103-134.
BITTENER, John LOWE, David	1990	*Nottingham General Hospital: Personal Reflections* (Special Trustees for Nottingham University Hospitals)
BLACKNER, J.	1816	*The History of Nottingham* Republished 1985
BLAGG, T.M.(ed.)		Parish Register transcripts of the 17th century
BRAND, K.	1983a	'The Nottingham Mechanics' *NCSN* 61 (April 1983) 22-23
	1983b	'Turneys'. *NCSN* 62 (Sept. 1983) 16-20

	1985	'The Strettons of Lenton'. *The Lenton Listener* 35 (Aug-Sept 1985) Lenton Local History Society
	1986	'Richard Charles Sutton'. *NCSN* 69 (Jan 1986) 4-6
	1986-7	'An introduction to Mapperley Park'. In 4 parts *NCSN* 71, 10-14: 72, 4-12: 73, 13-20: 74, 14-19.
	1988	'Thurland Hall'. *NCSN* 75 (Jan 1988) 8-13
	1988	'The Strettons of Lenton'. *NCSN* 76 (Apr 1988) 13-18
BRAUNSDORFF Otto-William	1896	*Some account of the family of Lowe* (Dresden)
BRIDGES, E.M.	1966	'Soils'. Chapter 4 in K.C.EDWARDS (ed) *Nottingham and its Region: a Scientific Survey* 103-109 (Nottingham, Derrys, for the British Association for the Advancement of Science)
BRISCOE, J.P.(ed)	1881	*Old Nottinghamshire* (Nottingham, Norris and Cokayne). Includes papers by J.T.GODFREY (17-25) and A.E.L.LOWE (25-26 and 130-138)
(ed)	1884	*Old Nottinghamshire* - Second Series. Includes A.E.L. LOWE on the Byron vault at Hucknall.
BRISCOE, J.P. and WYLIE, W.H.	1893	*A Popular History of Nottinghamshire* (Nottingham Murray)
BRISCOE, J.P.	1901	*Nottinghamshire and Derbyshire at the opening of the Twentieth Century.* Pike's New Century Series No. 5 (387 pp.) Contemporary Biographies, ed. W.T.Pike (Brighton)
	1908	*Chapters of Nottinghamshire History from the Norman Conquest to 1882* (Nottingham, Derry and Sons)
BROWN, Cornelius	1882	*Lives of Nottinghamshire Worthies* (London and Nottingham)
	1888-90	'About Nottinghamshire, its places and people' Articles from the Nottinghamshire Guardian (book of cuttings.
	1891	*A History of Nottinghamshire* (London, Eliot Stock)
CAMERON, Alan	1975	'Some social consequences of the Dissolution of the monasteries in Nottinghamshire'. *TTS* 79, 50-59
	1976	'The deserted medieval village of Sutton Passeys'. *TTS* 80, 47-59
CAMPION, G.F.(ed)	1938/9	'Roman relics found at Broxtowe'. *Thoroton Society, Excavation Section; Annual Reports for 1937 and 1938* 11-13, 6-18
(ed)	1939	'The Clifton pile dwellings and canoe site'. *Thoroton Society, Excavation Section, Annual Report for 1938* 19-23
CARR, J.W.	1896	*A contribution to the Geology and Natural History of Nottinghamshire* British Assoc. Adv. Science, Nottingham Meeting 1893. James Bell Nottingham.

CARTER James	1866	*A visit to Sherwood Forest* (London, Longmans Green)
CASSANDRA, Duchess of Chandos -		see A.C.WOOD (1958)
CHAMBERS, J.D.	1945	*Modern Nottinghamshire in the making* (Nottm., Nottingham Journal Limited)
	1951	'A century of change'. in *The People of Nottingham* (A souvenir of the Exhibition in the Albert Hall Institute, 25-29 September 1951) p.5
CHAPMAN, John	1774/1785	*Map of Nottinghamshire*, scale 1 inch to 1 mile. Surveyed 1774, printed 1785 for W. Faden
CHAPMAN, S.D.	1967	*The early factory masters* (Newton Abbot, David and Charles)
	1974	*Jesse Boot of Boots the Chemists: a study in business history.* (London, Hodder & Stoughton)
CHARLTON C. (ed)	1978	*Burton Joyce and Bulcote* (Burton Joyce Local History Group)
CHARSLEY, T.J. RATHBONE, P.A.	1990	*Nottingham:a geological background for planning and development.* Technical Report WA/90/1, British Geological Survey, Keyworth, Nottingham.
CHRISTIAN, Roy	1990	*Butterley Brick 200 years in the making* (Henry Melland London)
CLAYTON, K.M.	1953a	'The glacial chronology of part of the Middle Trent basin'. *Proc. Geologists Association* 64, 198-207
	1953b	'The denudation chronology of part of the Middle Trent basin'. *Institute of British Geographers, Transactions and Papers 1953* Publ. No. 19 (1954) 25-36
	1955	'The geomorphology of the area around Notting ham and Derby'. *EMG* 1, No. 3, 16-20
COOPE, Rosalys	1991	'The Wildman family and Colonel Thomas Wildman of Newstead Abbey, Nottinghamshire'. *TTS* 95, 50-66
COPINGER, W.A.	1907	*History and records of the Smith-Carrington family*
COPPACK, Glyn	1968	'A medieval well and associated pottery from Keighton'. *TTS* 72, 51-58
	1971	'The deserted medieval village of Keighton'. *TTS* 75, 41-58
COSSONS, Arthur	1929	'East Chilwell and Keighton'. *TTS* 33, 1-9
	1934	*The turnpike roads of Nottinghamshire* Historical Association Leaflet No. 97, 42 pp. (London, G.Bell and Sons)
	1937	'Out of the past: the turnpike roads of Nottinghamshire'. *The Nottinghamshire Countryside* 1, 1 (July 1937) 10
CROMFORD CANAL COMPANY	1981	*The Cromford Canal Company, 1789-1812*

CURTIS, John 1843-4 *A topographic history of Nottingham and Nottinghamshire from actual survey* (London, W. Strange: Nottingham, Allen, Mercer and Dearden) ix-lxxx + 208 pp. Only parts 1 to 8 of the 15 parts planned were actually published.

DAVIS, H.J. 1931 *The Honoured Name* (Nottingham, Boots Pure Drug Co.)

DEACON C.W. & Co 1908 *The Court Guide and County Blue Book* of Derbyshire, Nottinghamshire [etc]

DEARDEN publ 1839-40 *Dearden's Miscellany* 4 volumes

DEELEY, R.M. 1886 The Pleistocene succession in the Trent Basin *Q J Geol Soc.* xlii, 437-480; and *Science Papers* Vol. 2.

DODD, C. 1963 'Portland Ho !'. *Gong* Autumn 1963, 19-21 (Univ. of Nottm. Students' Union)

DUCHAUFOUR, P. 1958 *Pedologie* (Nancy, Ecole Nationale des Eaux et Forêts)

DUGDALE, Sir WM. 1817-30 *Monasticon Anglicanum* 6 volumes (1846 edition)

EASTON, H.T. 1903 *History of a Banking House* (Smith, Payne and Smith's) (London Blades)

EDWARDS, K.C.(ed) 1966 *Nottingham and its Region: a Scientific Survey* (Nottingham, Derry and Sons: for British Association for the Advancement of Science)

1944 'Nottinghamshire'. Part 60 of *The Land of Britain* ed. L.D.STAMP, 449-460

1962 'The site and setting of the University'. *Northern Universities Geographical Journal* 3, 5-10

ELLIOTT, R.E. 1961 'The stratigraphy of the Keuper Series in southern Nottinghamshire'. *Proc. Yorkshire Geol. Soc.* 33, 197-234

ELTRINGHAM, G. and SCOTT, N. 1964 *A Civic University* (Nottingham: University Careers and Appointments Board and Nottingham Chamber of Commerce)

ENFIELD, Mrs. W. 1854 *Nottingham Sketches* (née Anne Needham)

EVANS, J.T. 1939 'Trent Navigation'. *The Nottinghamshire Countryside* 3, No. 1 (July 1939) 15-19

FAREY, J. 1827 *A treatise on the steam engine , historical, practical and descriptive* (David and Charles reprints, 2 volumes: Newton Abbot 1971)

FELLOWS, G. 1895 *History of the South Notts. Yeomanry Cavalry, 1794-1894* (Nottingham, Forman)

1917 'The family of Hanley or Handley of Bramcote' *TTS* 21, 95-113

FIRTH, J.B. 1916 *Highways and Byways in Nottinghamshire* (MacMillan)

FRY, Terry 1989 *The History of Sherwood a Nottingham Suburb* (Nottingham, private print)

1991 'A portrait of Ichabod Wright from his diaries' *TNH* 46, 23-29.

FYFE, W.W.	1856	*Rambles round Nottingham* Vol. 1 (only one volume published) (Nottingham, F.Gibson: London, Simpkin and Marshall)
GILBERT, Ann	1904	*Recollections of Old Nottingham* (Nottingham)
GINEVER, E.D.	1930	*The parish and priory of Lenton* (Nottingham, R. Milward and Son) xi + 91 pp.
GODFREY, J.T.	1881	See J.P.BRISCOE above
	1884	*The history of the parish and priory of Lenton* (London and Derby, Bemrose and Sons) 499 pp.
GODFREY J.T. & WARD, James	1908	*The Homes and Haunts of Henry Kirke White* (London and Nottingham Simpkin, Marshall)
GOODWIN, W.E.	1913	*The soils of Nottinghamshire* (Kingston) Pamph.
GRAHAM, G.	1959	'University architecture at Nottingham'. *Gong* X, 2 (Spring 1959) 35-40. Supplement. (Nottm. Univ. Union of Students)
GRANGER, Frank	1928a	*Memorials of University College, Nottingham* Pamphlet (Nottingham; Jenkins, James and Lowe)
	1928b	*University College, Nottingham, July Tenth 1928* Pamphlet. (Nottingham, Jenkins James and Lowe)
GRANGER, J.	1904	*Old Nottingham Notes* 2
GRAY, H.L.	1915	*The English field systems* Harvard Historical Studies 22 (Cambridge Mass., Harvard U.P.)
GREEN, Herbert	1936	'Lenton as an open-field village'. *TTS* 40, 97-105
GREEN, J.A.H. et al	1887	*History of the Nottingham Mechanics Institution 1837-1887* (Nottingham)
GREENWOOD, J.E.	1977	*A Cap for Boots: an autobiography* (London, Hutchinson Benham)
GRISENTHWAITE, W.	1830	*A New Theory of Agriculture....on Scientific Principles* 2nd edition, enlarged (Nottingham, S.Bennett)
GUARDIAN, THE Newspaper	1961	'A Dunkirk fights for its survival: claims University "wants to destroy us"'. 17 Aug 1961, 3
GUILFORD, E.L.(ed)	1912	*Memorials of Old Nottinghamshire* (London)
	1924	'Nottinghamshire in 1676'. *TTS* 28, 106-113
HABERLEY, Lloyd	1937	*Medieval English paving tiles* (Oxford)
HADFIELD, C.	1966	*The canals of the East Midlands* Canals of the British Isles - 5. (Newton Abbot, David and Charles)
HADFIELD, C. and SKEMPTON, A.W.	1979	*William Jessop, Engineer* (Newton Abbot, David and Charles)
HAINS, B. and HORTON, A.	1969	*Central England* Geological Survey, HMSO. Also 1975
HAMMOND, T.W.	1926	*Nottingham, Past and Present* 50 crayon drawings (Nottingham, J. and H.Bell for Nottingham Civic Society)
HEATHCOTE, P.F.	1985	'Arthur Marshall'. *NCSN* 66 (Jan 1985) 11-15
HEELEY, Suzanne	1988	'Nottingham General Hospital'.*TNH* 41, 15-21
HEMINGWAY, G.	n.d.	*East Midland canals* Typescript (copy in Univ. of Nottingham, Hallward Library)

HIGGINSON, Mark	1989	*The Midland Counties Railway, 1839-1989: a Pictorial Survey* (Midland Railway Trust)
HIGH PAVEMENT CHAPEL	1930s	'A biographical catalogue of portraits etc. in the custody of the Chapel trustees'.
HOGARTH, A.G.	n.d., c. 1949	*The Trent and I go wandering by*
HUGHES, Samuel	1844	*Quarterly Papers in Engineering ....*
HUNTER, J.M.	1961	'Sources of capital in the industrial development of Nottingham'. *EMG* 16, 35
HUNTSMAN, E. et al	1931	*Jesse, 1st Baron Trent of Nottingham, 1850-1931* Pamphlet containing three obituaries: E. HUNTSMAN, 'Lord Trent as I knew him' (from Nottingham Journal, 15.6.1931) PRINCIPAL HUGH STEWART, 'Benefactor and friend' PROF.F.S.GRANGER, 'Lord Trent' (from The Times, 16.6.1931)
HUSKINSON, G.N.B.	1952	'The Howe family and Langar Hall, 1650-1800'. *TTS* 56, 54-59
ILIFFE, R. and BAGULEY, W.	1970-83	*Victorian Nottingham* (20 volumes) 'A story in pictures'. (Nottingham: The Nottingham Historical Film Unit)
	1978-83	*Edwardian Nottingham* (3 volumes)
INKSTER, I.	1978	'Scientific culture and education in Nottingham, 1800-1843'. *TTS* 82, 45-50
JACKS, Leonard	1881	*The great houses of Nottinghamshire and the county families* (Nottingham, Bradshaw)
JACOB, F.H.	1951	*A history of the General Hospital, Nottingham* (Bristol John Wright & Sons)
JELLICOE, G.A.	1955a	'Development of Nottingham University: landscape design on the grand scale'. *Manchester Guardian* 21 Apr 1955, 5
	1955b	'Landscape design for Nottingham University'. *Architect* 5 May 1955, 231-233
	1955c	*University of Nottingham: a landscape plan* (Nottingham) Pamphlet. Map.
	1955d	*A report accompanying a landscape design for the University of Nottingham* (London, private print)
JESSOP, W.	1786	*A state of the depths of water upon the shallows in the river Trent....*' by W.Jessop and J.Smith. (Nottingham, George Burbage)
JOHNSON, Arthur	1905	*The Nottingham Sacred Harmonic Society: a Retrospect* (Nottingham, Caxton Press)
JONES, W.L.	1980	*Mapperley Hospital centenary*, 1880-1980
KEEBLE, Iris	1990	'We have a cowboy in our family tree'. *Notts. Family History Society* 6, 7 (Apr 1990) 20-24
KERRIDGE, D.H.	n.d.	'A report of the excavations of the medieval site in University Park'. Unpublished manuscript report.
	1954	'University Park in the Middle Ages'. *Survey* 4, 3, 43-48 (Univ. of Nottm. Students' Union)

KING, C.A.M.	1966	'Geomorphology'. Chapter 2 in K.C.EDWARDS (ed) *Nottingham and its Region: a Scientific Survey* (Nottingham: Derrys, for British Association for the Advancement of Science) 41-59
	1972	'The Trent trench'. (East Midland Landforms III) *EMG* 5, pt 5, No. 37, 272-273
LAIRD, F.C.	1810	*A topographical and historical description of Nottinghamshire* (London: Sherwood, Neely and Jones)
LEAF, Violet	1964	'How Osmaston came to be built'. Article in the *Derbyshire Observer* 12 June 1964
LEEMAN, F.W.	1944	*Cooperation in Nottingham: a history of the 100 years of the Nottingham Cooperative Society Limited, 1863-1944* (Nottingham: Nottingham Co-op. Soc. Ltd.)
LEIGHTON-BOYCE,	1958	*Smiths the Bankers, 1658-1958* (London: National Provincial Bank) See pp. 5-65
LINSTRUM, Dick	1972	*Sir Jeffrey Wyattville* (Oxford, Clarendon Press)
LOWE, A.E.L.	c.1871	*The Genealogical and Topographical History of the Hundred of Broxtowe* 40pp. (Nottingham, Richard Allen) The only published part (Lenton) of a planned 15 parts. Foreword dated 25 Jan 1871.
	1872	*Historical Record of the Royal Sherwood Foresters or Notts. Regiment of Militia* (London: Mitchell)
(ed)	1876	*Black's Guide to Nottinghamshire* (Edinburgh: Adam and Charles Black) 286 pp.
	1877	'Wollaton and the Willoughby monuments', in *The Genealogist* O.S., 1 (London)
	1880	*Pedigree of the family of Otter of Welham in the Co. of Nottingham and elsewhere, with notes* (London: Private print)
	1881	'Descent of the site of Lenton Priory since the Dissolution'. In J.P.BRISCOE, *Old Nottinghamshire* 25-26
	1882	'The Strelley monuments in Strelley church'. *Nottinghamshire Guardian* 19 Apr 1882
LOWE. E.J.	1846	*A treatise on atmospheric phenomena* 376 pp. (Nottingham, Renals: London, Longmans)
	1849	*Prognostications of the weather, or signs of atmospheric changes* 48pp. (Nottingham, Renals: London, Longmans)
	1853	*The Conchology of Nottingham* or a popular history of recent land and freshwater mollusca found in the neighbourhood. 172pp. (Nottingham, R.Sutton: London, G.A.Bartlett)

	1853	*The climate of Nottingham during the year 1852* together with descriptions of the atmospheric phenomena which occurred in that year as recorded at Highfield House observatory near Nottingham. (London, Longmans)
	1856	*A natural history of ferns, exotic and British* (London, Groombridge and Sons) Published in monthly parts. 8 volumes 1864
	1858	*A natural history of British grasses* (London, Longmans) Also 1871
	1860	*Practical Meteorology* Orr's Circle of the Sciences [with JOHN B. SCOFFERN] (London)
	1861	*Beautiful leaved plants* (London, Groombridge)
	1862	*A natural history of new and rare ferns* Also in 1868, 1871. (London, Groombridge)
	1862b	*Chronology of the seasons*
	1874	*Our native ferns* or a history of the British species and their varieties. 2 volumes. Also in 1880
	1880	*The coming drought or the Cycle of the Seasons* (London, Bemrose)
	1891	*British ferns and where found* Young Collectors Series (London, Sonnenschein)

The above list of E.J.Lowe's publications is not exhaustive.

MACDONALD, C.J.D.	1927	'The Nottinghamshire royal farm'. *Journ.Royal Agric. Soc. of England* 88, 1-2
MARSHALL, C.E.(ed)	1948	*Guide to the geology of the East Midlands* (University of Nottingham)
MARTINEAU, M.C.	1910	*Memories and reminiscences of Lenton* (Letchworth, The Alden Press) 104pp. For private circulation.
MASON, Michael	1969	*Willoughby, the Immortal* A biography of Sir Nesbit Willoughby. (Oxford: private print)
MASON, Sheila	1981	'Tobacco and Lace: the growth of John Player and Sons, 1881-1903'. *TTS* 85, 102-110.
MEABY, K.T.	1947	*Nottinghamshire County Records of the 18th century* (Nottingham: Forman) For private circulation.
MELLORS, Robert	1908	*In and about Nottinghamshire* (Nottingham: Bell)
	1912	*Lenton, Then and Now* (Nottingham, J. and H.Bell)
	1913	*Mapperley and Carrington, Then and Now* (Nottingham)
	1914	*Old Nottingham Suburbs, Then and Now*
	1916	*Beeston, Then and Now* (Nottingham: Bell)
	1924	*Men of Nottingham and Nottinghamshire* (Nottingham: J. and H.Bell) viii + 351pp. [500 biographies]

	1925	Supplement to the above, pp. 353-368
MEYNELL, Rosemary	1952	'The Story of Francis Wright'. in *Derbyshire Advertiser* Sept. 1952
MIDDLETON, Lady	1905	'Sir Nesbit Willoughby, Admiral of the Blue'. *TTS* 9, 57-78
MILTON, William	1874	*Religion and business: Memorials of Thomas Adams J.P. of Nottingham, lace merchant* (London: Hamilton and Adams) 192 pp.
MOOMAN, Sylvia	1958	'The Library, 1959-1979'. *Gong* (Univ. of Nottm.) Autumn 1958, 45-47
MORRIS, John (ed)	1977	*Domesday Book: 28 - Nottinghamshire* Edited from a draft transcript prepared by C.PARKER and S.WOOD. (Chichester)
MOTTRAM, R.H. and COOTE, C.R.	1950	*Through Five Generations: a history of the Butterley Company* (London: Faber and Faber)
NORTH, Allan	c. 1910	*Nottinghamshire and some neighbouring records* n.d. (London: Published for subscribers)
NOTTINGHAM Borough	1875 1900	Records
NOTTINGHAM City	1980	*Lenton District Plan.* (Planning Dept.) 2 volumes and a map.
	1985	*Nottingham's Heritage* A view of conservation in the city. (Nottingham, May 1985)
NOTTINGHAM CIVIC SOCIETY	1974	*A report on the Nottingham and Beeston Canal* Pamphlet. Nottingham Civic Society Newsletter. Four issues a year. References under authors' names.
NOTTINGHAMSHIRE COUNTY COUNCIL	1972	*Buildings of special architectural interest*
NOTTINGHAM PUBLIC LIBRARIES STAFF	1937	*The Roe-Byron Collection, Newstead Abbey*
OLDFIELD, G.	1980	'The Carringtons and the Smiths'. *TNH* 24 (Spring 1980) 10-12
OLDRINI, T.J.	1873	*Gleanings; or something about Beeston in olden times*
ORANGE, James	1840	*History and Antiquities of Nottingham* [also a Directory] (London) 2 volumes
OUTRAM, Benjamin	1801	'Minutes to be observed in the construction of railways' *Recreations in Agriculture....[etc,]* 4. 473pp
OUTRAM, M.F.	1932	*Margaret Outram, 1778-1863: mother of the Bayard of India*
OXLEY, Alan and RICHMOND, Vernon	1989	*A nostalgic look at Beeston* (Attenborough, Notts.: Robin Hood Publishing). A collection of photographs, mainly of 1920-40.
PAGE, W. (ed)	1906-10	*Victoria County History of the County of Nottingham* 2 volumes
PARKER, Alfred	1932	'Nottingham pottery'. *TTS* 35, 90-97

	1936	'Note on pottery and tiles discovered during the Lenton Priory excavations'. *TTS* 40, 91-96
PHILLIMORE, W.P.W.	1898-1905	Inquisitions Post Mortem (abstracts)
	1894	'Deserted villages of Nottinghamshire'. *Notts. and Derbys. Notes and Queries* ii, 128-135, 150-152, 161-168.
(ed)	1910	*County Pedigrees - Nottinghamshire* Vol.1:-4 Bayleys of Lenton p. 269: Enfields of Nottingham p. 111: Fellows of Beeston Fields p.55 (London, Phillimore & Co.)
PHILLIMORE, W.P.W. and FELLOWS, G.	1904	*Nottinghamshire Parish Registers* 6 (Broxtowe Wapentake)
PIGOTT, S.C.	1949	*Hollins: a study of industry, 1784-1949* 151pp. (Nottingham: Hollins)
PIKE, W.T. (ed)	1901	*Contemporary Biographies* (Pike's New Century Series, No.5). See J.P. BRISCOE above
POSNANSKY, Merrick	1960	'The Pleistocene succession in the Middle Trent basin'. *Proc. Geologists' Association* 71, 285-311.
RENSHAW, M.A.	1956	*Inquisitions Post Mortem,* 1437-1485 - Nottinghamshire. Thoroton Society Record Series, 7.
RICHMOND, Sir I.	1977	'Assessment of site planning' in J.K.S.ST. JOSEPH (ed) *The uses of air photography* (London: John Baker) 2nd edition.
RICHMOND, Lewis	n.d.	*Rambles round Nottingham* (Nottingham Journal)
RIDEN, P.J.	1973	*The Butterley Company, 1790-1832.* A Derbyshire ironworks in the Industrial Revolution. (Oxford, Parchment Printers)
	1990	*The Butterley Company 1790-1820.* Derbyshire Record Society, XVI 199 pp.
ROBERTSON, G.C.(ed)	1910	*The Stretton Manuscripts* (Nottingham, Murrays) [Documents of William Stretton of Lenton, d.1828]
ST. JOSEPH, J.K.(ed)	1977	*The uses of air photography* (London: John Baker) 2nd edition.
SANDERSON, G.	1835	*Map of the country XXX miles round Mansfield* (Mansfield: Sanderson, 10 July 1835) Surveyed 1830-34. Scale 2 inches to 1 mile. Engraved by J. and C. Walker, London.
	1836	*Map of the County of Nottingham* 15 Feb 1836. Scale 1 inch to 1 mile.
SAVAGE, J.P. (ed)	1956	*LordTrent:tributes to a great leader* pamphlet
SEVERN, John	1986	'Lamberts' Factory, Talbot Street, Nottingham'. *NCSN* 69 (Jan 1986) 24-26
SEYMOUR, D.	1981	'University College, Nottingham, 1928-31'. *Univ. of Nottm. Newsletter* 13 (June 1981) 4-7
SHEPHERD, G.H. & Co.	n.d.	(Publ.) *Visitors' Guide Book to Nottingham* (Nottingham: Shepherd, Angel Row)
SHIPMAN, James	1877	'Conglomerate at the base of the lower Keuper'. *Geol. Mag.* IV (2 Dec 1877) 497

	1880	'Notes on the alluvial and drift deposits of the Trent valley near Nottingham'. 20pp. Reprinted from *Annual Report, Nottingham Naturalists' Society* with additions. Also *Science Papers* I
	1883	'Alluvial and drift deposits of the Leen valley' *Midland Naturalist* VI, 76 et seq. *Science Papers* IV
	1884	'Geology'. Section XVII, pp. 408-458 in J.T. GODFREY, *History of the parish and priory of Lenton* (London and Derby: Bemrose and Sons)
	1889	'Notes on the geology of Nottingham: where and how to see it'. *Trans. Nottingham Naturalists' Society 1889* (37th Annual Report) 26-36
SMITH, A.	1861	*A true and faithful history of the family of Smith* (Includes two maps and a large pedigree)
SMITH, Bernard	1910	'The Upper Keuper sandstones of East Nottinghamshire'. *Geol. Mag.* Decade V, Vol. VII, No. 553 (July 1910) 302-311
	1913	'The geology of the Nottingham district'. *Proc. Geologists' Association*, London 24, 205-240
SMITH, P.	1966	'Campus architecture'. *Opus* 1 (Spring 1966) 8-9 (Union of Students, Univ. of Nottingham)
SMITH, R.J.	1979	*Byron Country* (Derby)
SMITH, R.S.	1960	'England's first rails: a reconsideration'. *Renaissance and Modern Studies* 4, 119-134 (Univ. of Nottingham)
	1988	*Sir Francis Willoughby of Wollaton Hall* 52 pp. (City of Nottingham, Arts Department)
	1989	*Early coal mining around Nottingham, 1500-1650* 126 pp.(University of Nottingham, Department of Adult Education)
SMYTHE, Richard	1632	'A Mappe of ye Lorrdshippe of Lenton and Radford taken the tenthe daye of Julye anno 1632 by me Richard Smythe surveyor' (Ms.Nottingham Archives Office, RD 3 L)
SNELL, A.E.	1969	*The Velvet Years* (Autobiography: published privately)
STENTON, F.M.	1906	'The text of the Nottinghamshire Domesday'. in *Victoria County History of.... Nottingham* Vol 1
STEVENSON, P.H.	1901	'The early history of the University College'. *Gong* 6, 5 (May 1901) 64-67, and 6, 6 (June 1901) 81-83 (U.C.N., Union of Students)
STEVENSON, W.H.	1912	*Report on the Manuscripts of Lord Middleton* (Historical Manuscripts Commission)
STEVENSON, Wm.	1893	*Bygone Nottinghamshire* (Nottingham, London and Hull)
STEVENSON, W.	1866	'The building materials of Nottinghamshire' pht.
STITT, F.B.	1959	*Lenton Priory Estate Accounts, 1296-98* Thoroton Society Record Series, XIX

STRAUSS, S.M.	1978	*A short history of Wollaton and Wollaton Hall* 51 pp. (Notts. County Council Leisure Services/ Libraries)
STRAW, A.	1963	'The Quaternary evolution of the lower and middle Trent'. *EMG* 3, 4, (No.20) 171-189
SUMNER, W.L.	1961	'Beeston Observatory'. *Survey* (Univ. of Nottm.) 12, No. 3, 5-12
SUTTON, C.(publ)	1827	*Strangers' guide through the town of Nottingham* (Nottingham)
SUTTON, J.F.	1852	*The Date Book of....Nottingham and its neighbourhood* (Nottingham: R.Sutton) Covers the years 1750-1850.
SWINNERTON, H.H.	1910	'The Bunter Sandstone of Nottinghamshire'. *Trans. Nottingham Naturalists Society* 1910,17-28
	1914	'Periods of dreikanter formation in southern Nottinghamshire'. *Geol. Mag.* Decade VI, 1, (51) No. 594, 208-211
	1918	'The Keuper Basement Beds near Nottingham'. *Proc. Geologists Association* 29, 16-28
	1935	'The denudation of the East Midlands' (Nottingham: British Association Meeting)
	1948	'Permo-Trias'. Chapter 6 : 'Pleistocene and later deposits'. Chapter 8 in C.E.MARSHALL (ed) *Guide to the geology of the East Midlands* (Univ. of Nottm.) 53-59 and 76-79
	1949	'Man as a maker of landscape'. Abbott Memorial Lecture 1948-49. Pamphlet. Appendix by H.H. Swinnerton and John Cawley.(Univ. Coll. Nottm.)
	1955	'The medieval tile works of Lenton Priory' *TTS* LIX, 84-97 (with W.R.CHALMERS and MERRICK POSNANSKY)
SYLVESTER-BRADLEY, P.C. and FORD, T.D. (ed)	1968	*Geology of the East Midlands* (Leicester)
TAYLOR, F.M.	1965	'The Upper Permian and Lower Trias formations in southern Nottinghamshire'. *Mercian Geologist* 2, 181-196
	1966	'Geology'. Chapter 1 in K.C.EDWARDS (ed) *Nottingham and its Region: a Scientific Survey* (Nottingham: Derry, for British Assocn. Adv. Science) 11-40
	1988	*A Lexicon of New Red Sandstone stratigraphy.* Published as two parts of the *Mercian Geologist* 11, parts 1 and 2 (Jan 1958)
THOMIS, M.I.	1968	*Old Nottingham* (Newton Abbot: David and Charles)
THOROTON, R.	1677	*The Antiquities of Nottinghamshire* the descent of lands in each parish from Domesday.

THROSBY, J.		1790	*Thoroton's History of Nottinghamshire* with additional text, and additions for 1690 to about 1790.
		1972	Republished in 3 volumes, with Index in Vol. 3. With a new Introduction by M.W.BARLEY and K.S.S. TRAIN (East Ardsley)
TINN, A.B.		1938	'Local temperature variations in the Nottingham district'. *Quart. Journ. Royal Meteorological Society* 64, 391-405
		1940	'The distribution of thunder rains around Nottingham'. *Quart. Journ. Royal Meteorological Society* 66, 47-65
TOLLEY, Brian		1990	'Lessons from the past'. *Univ. of Nottingham Newsletter* New Series, No. 59 (Dec 1990) 4-5
TOWNROE, B.S.		1928	*Nottingham University College; a record of its history and an appreciation of the new buildings* (Nottingham: privately printed)
TRAIN, K.S.S.	(ed)	1949	*Abstracts of Inquisitions Post Mortem, 1350-1436 - Nottinghamshire* Thoroton Society Record Series, 12
	(ed)	1950	*The Visitation of Nottinghamshire, 1662-64* Thoroton Society Record Series. 13
		1969	*Twenty Nottinghamshire Families* (Notts. Local History Council) Revised 1973
		n.d.	*Lenton House, its owners and occupiers* c.1973 (Nottingham: Boots) Pamphlet
TRUMAN, Nevil		1946	*Sneinton parish church history* (Gloucester)
TRUMAN, P. and HUNT, D.		1989	*Midland Railway Portrait* (Sheffield)
TURNER, A.R. and WALLACE, I.H.		n.d.	*Materials for the history of Paton College, Nottingham* (c. 1968) Typescript. (Copy in Hallward Library, Univ. of Nottingham)
THE VILLAGE PRESS		1990	*The Village Atlas: the growth of Derbys, Notts. and Leics., 1834-1904.* (The Alderman Press) Extracts from O.S. published maps.
WARRINGTON, G. and 8 others		1980	*A correlation of Triassic rocks in the British Isles* Geological Society, London: Special Report 13.
WEBSTER, W.F.	(ed)	1980	*The Protestation Returns, 1641-42 - Nottinghamshire/Derbyshire*
'W.E.D.'		1943	'Nottinghamshire villages'. Book of cuttings from the Nottinghamshire Guardian. (Hallward Library)
WEEKLY, E.	(ed)	1939	*Hugh Stewart, 1884-1934* Some memories of his friends and colleagues. xi + 83pp. (London: John Murray)
WELLS, F.A.		1968	*Hollins and Viyella: a study in business history* (Newton Abbot: David and Charles) 264 pp.
WELLS, Ian		1986	*NCSN* 70 (April 1986) 19

WESTON WEBB, W.F.M.	1929	*The autobiography of a British yarn merchant* (London: Grant Richards & Humphrey Toulmin)
WILLIAMS, F.S.	c.1883	*Nottingham, past and present* (Nottingham: R. Allen)
WOOD, A.C.	1953	*A history of the University College, Nottingham, 1881-1948* 181pp. (Oxford: Blackwell)
	1958	*The Willoughby family* by CASSANDRA, DUCHESS OF CHANDOS
WYLIE, W.H.	1853	*Old and New Nottingham* (Nottingham: J.Bradshaw, Journal Office. London: Longman, Brown, Green and Longman)
WILSON, E. and SHIPMAN, J.	1879	'On the occurrence of Keuper Basement Beds in the neighbourhood of Nottingham'. *Geol. Mag* 532
ZALESKI, S., BERRY, L. and HILL, J.	1989	'The story of the Nottingham Canal'. *Lenton Times* (Lenton Local History Society) 2 (May 1989) 4-9, 12-15, 16-17, 19-20.
ANON	1924	'Opening of the Highfields Baths'. *Gong* XIV, 1 (Christmas 1924) 48
	1925	'Opening of the pavilion at Highfields'. *Gong* XIV, 3 (N.S.) (Summer 1925) 41-42.
	1952	'Francis Wright, Public School Founder'. *Ad Rem.* (Butterley Company's House Magazine) Summer 1952
UNIVERSITY OF NOTTINGHAM	1949	*The University of Nottingham, the youngest English University* 12pp, map. Pamphlet
	1958	*Plans for Development* (2nd edn. 1960). Pamphlet

SOME LOCAL DIRECTORIES

Listed in chronological order of the year of their first appearance. Dates within brackets are those of issues not known to be available at either Nottingham City Local Studies Library (C) or Nottingham University Hallward Library (U).

C		BAILEY	1783	Western and Midland Directory (printed in Birmingham: Pearson and Rollason)
C			1784	British Directory (4 volumes) - Nottinghamshire in Vol. 2, the Western Directory. (London, printer Andrews)
		UNIVERSAL	1790	British Directory...for trade and commerce ...(London, C.Stalker). Five volumes and editions between 1790 and 1798.
C	U		1793	
C			1798	
C	U	WILLOUGHBY	1799	The Northern Directory, compiled by E.Willoughby, Nottingham. (Sold by E. Willoughby, printer C.Sutton).
C	U	HOLDEN	1805	Holden's Triennial Directory, 4th edn. Vol. 11 (London, printer Glindinning)
C			1807	Reprinted
C	U		1809	Reprinted
C	U		1811	Holden's Annual and Country Directory of the U.K. and Wales, in 3 volumes. W.Holden. Also (1814) and (1816).
C		HODSON	1814	The Nottingham Directory (Nottingham, printed and sold by E.Hodson)
C	U	SUTTON	1815	The Nottingham Directory (Nottingham, Sutton and Sons at the Review Office)
			1818	do.
C		PIGOT AND SLATER	1818	Commercial Directory (James Pigot, publisher) Also (1819) and (1820).
C		PIGOT	1822	London and Provincial Directory
C	U		1828	National Commercial Directory Also 1841, 1842, 1844.
C	U		1831	Directory of Nottinghamshire
C	U		1835	National Commercial Directory
C		SLATER	1847	Nottingham and its suburbs.
C	U		1850	As for Pigot 1828
C	U		1857	Major towns and villages only
C	U	GLOVER	1825	Nottingham Directory (S.Glover printer and publisher)
C	U		1844	The History and Directory of ... Nottingham (Nottingham, Stephen Glover publisher J.Howitt)

C	U	WHITE	1832	History, Gazetteer and Directory of Nottinghamshire by William White. (Sheffield, printer Robert Leader)
C	U		1844	History, Directory and Gazetteer for the County of Nottingham, by Francis and John White. (Sheffield, printer John Blurton, sold by F.White and Co.)
C	U		1853	and 1854 - same title and printer: by Francis White and Co.
C	U		1864	Nottinghamshire: History, Directory and Gazetteer. (Production as in 1844)
C	U		1883	History, Gazetteer and Directory of the Borough of Derby and of the town and county of Nottingham (Sheffield)
C	U		1885-6	History, Gazetteer and Directory of Nottinghamshire. 2nd edn. (Sheffield William White)
C	U		1894	Second edition of the above
C	U	DEARDEN	1834	History, Topography and Directory of... Nottingham and the adjacent villages. (Nottingham, W.Dearden)
C	U	ORANGE	1840	The Nottingham Annual Register ... and corrected Directory for 1840, by James Orange. (London, Hamilton, Adams and Co: Nottingham, J.Howitt).
C		KELLY	1848	Post Office Directory of Derbyshire, Leicestershire, Nottinghamshire and Rutlandshire. (London, Kelly and Co.)
C	U		1855-1956	Kelly's Directories of Nottinghamshire for 1855, 1864, 1876, 1881, 1895, 1900, 1904, 1908, 1912, 1916, 1922, 1925, 1928, 1932, 1936, 1941, 1950, 1953, 1956.
C	U	LASCELLES AND HAGAR	1848	Commercial Directory of the town and county of Nottingham. (Nottingham, Stevenson and Co.)
C	U	WRIGHT	1854	Wright's Nottingham Directory (Nottingham, C and N.Wright)
C			1858	Nottingham and suburbs Also 1862, 1864 and 1866.
C			1868	Nottingham and 12 miles around. Also 1871, 1874, 1885, 1887, 1889, 1891, 1892-2, 1894-5, 1896-7, 1898-9.
C			1879	Nottinghamshire
C			1881	Nottingham and 6 miles around. Also 1883
C			1900	Nottingham and surrounding villages
C			1901	Nottingham and neighbourhood Also 1902-3, 1905-6, 1907-8, 1910-11, 1913-14, 1915-16, 1920.

C	U	DRAKE	1860	Directory of the Town and County of the Town of Nottingham. (Sheffield, E.S.Drake and Co.)
C	U	MORRIS	1869	Commercial Directory and Gazetteer of Nottingham and District. (Nottingham, Morris and Co.) Also 1877
C	U	ALLEN	1895	Allen's Red Book, Almanac and Annual Register. Published annually from 1867. Edited by J.T.Godfrey. (Nottingham, R.Allen and Son: London, E.W.Allen) Also 1901, 1902, 1903, 1907, 1914.
		DEACON	1908	The Court Guide and County Blue Book of Derbyshire, Nottinghamshire [etc.]. A fashionable record, professional register and general survey. (London, Charles William Deacon and Co.).
C		BENNETT	1912	Bennett's Business Directory for Nottinghamshire, 1911-12. (Birmingham, Bennett and Co.). Also 1913.
C		TOWN AND COUNTRY	1904	(Trades only). Nottingham and District Trades Directory, (Edinburgh, Town and Country Directories Ltd.)
C				Also 1906-7, 1915-16, 1921-22, 1924, 1930-31
	U			1928-29 (1933-34),(1936-37),(1938-39),(1940-41) (1948-51)
	U	SAXTON	1910	The Nottingham Grey Book. (Nottingham, edited by H.B.Saxton) Also 1911
		COPE	(1930)	Cope's Nottingham Directory and Buyers' Guide. (Walsall) Also (1934), (1936)
		AUBREY	(1931)	Nottingham Directory. (Walsall, Aubrey and Co.) Also(1937), (1941).

APPENDIX 1

VALUATIONS OF LENTON PRIORY IN 1291, 1387 and 1535

1291 - Taxation of Pope Nicholas

Temporalities		*Spiritualities*	
York diocese	£ 92.12s. 6d.	York diocese	£ 108.12s.10d.
Lincoln diocese	37. 3s.10½d.	Coventry and Lichfield	66.13s. 4d.
Coventry and Lichfield	17. 6s. 0d	Lincoln diocese	15.19s. 4d.
Salisbury diocese	13s. 4d.		
Total	£ 147.15s. 8½d.	Total	£191.19s. 4d.

Total income £ 339. 1s. 2½d.

1387 - Valuation (in part)

Temporalities	
Site, in herbage and pasture beyond outgoings	£ 4. 0s. 0d.
3 carucates demesne arable land at 20s. beyond outgoings	3. 0s. 0d.
3 carucates demesne land neglected (uncultivated) at 10s.	1.10s. 0d.
Demesne meadow 80 acres at 2s. 6d. [Trent Wong]	10. 0s. 0d.
A spinney wood	33s. 4d.
Fair	35. 0s. 0d.
Divers free and native tenants, lands and tenements (in Lenton, Kyrkton, Radford and Newthorpe)	40. 4s. 4d.
Perquisites of manorial courts	3. 0s. 8d.
Water mill	3.17s. 6d.
One-third of water mill	10s. 0d.
Place called Le Roche [chapel with closes opposite, south of river Leen]	3.11s. 8d.
Fixed rents of tenants in various parishes in Notts.	15.15s. 2d.
do. do. in Stanton-on-the-Wolds	13s. 4d.
Tithe of corn of rectories of Lenton, Kyrkton, Radford and Sutton	20. 0s. 0d.
Various tithes and pensions, rents etc. in Derbyshire, including, for the rectory of Bakewell	54.13s. 0d.

1535 - Valor Ecclesiasticus (27 Henry VIII)

Temporalities		
Demesne lands, rents, farm of mills,	Lenton	£ 54.10s.0d.
do.	Newthorpe	6. 9s 0d.
do.	Nottingham	1.17s. 2d.
do.	Radford	15.17s. 6d.
do.	Derbyshire	20. 3s. 0d.
do.	Leicestershire	4. 7s. 8d.
do.	Northamptonshire	29. 2s. 8d.
Other rents		17. 4s. 3d.
		149.11s. 3d.

Spiritualities		
Nottinghamshire, tithes of corn and hay:	Beeston	8. 0s. 0d.
	Lenton	6.13s. 4d.
St. Mary's,	Nottingham	18. 0s. 0d.
	Radford	6.13s. 4d.
St. Mary's oblations		9. 0s. 0d.
Other tithes, portions etc.		32. 3s. 2d.
Pensions		5. 6s. 4d.

Derbyshire, tithes etc.		13. 6s. 8d.
portions		37. 9s. 3½d.
Leicestershire, tithes etc.		19. 6s. 8d.
Cheshire, tithes etc., Middlewich		30. 0s. 0d.
Lancashire		8. 6s. 8d.
Northamptonshire, Portions		13. 0s. 0d.
Pensions		2.14s. 2d.
Yorkshire, tithes		28. 0s. 0d.
		237.19s. 7½
Total	£387.10s.10½d.	
Payments	30.13s. 4d.	
Alms	16.15s. 0d.	
Fees	4. 6s. 8d.	
Total	£51.15s. 0d.	
Net value	£335.15s.10½d	

APPENDIX 2

LIST OF THE WILLOUGHBYS WHO SUCCESSIVELY OWNED THE WOLLATON ESTATE

	Held the estate in:	
Ralph Bugge	-c.1240	
Richard Bugge of Willoughby	-c.1283	Younger son
Sir Richard de Willoughby	-1325	Bought land in Wollaton
Sir Richard de Willoughby	1325-1363	Judge. Married Isabella Morteyn, Sutton Passeys.
Edmund Willoughby		Son of Joana, Sir Richard's second wife
Hugh Willoughby	-1448	M.P. 1427-28
Richard Willoughby (eldest son)	1448-1471	M.P. 1434-35. The first Willoughby at Wollaton
Robert Willoughby (half brother)	1471-1474	
Henry Willoughby (son)	1474-1528	Inherited much property through grandmother, including Middleton Manor, Warwicks. Rich and able: coal pits profitable.
John Willoughby	1528-1548	Son by third wife was Sir Hugh the navigator, who froze to death in a fiord in Lapland when on an expedition with three ships to look for the Northern Passage' in 1552-3.
Henry Willoughby (nephew)	1548-1549	Killed at Norwich in Kitt's rebellion: sons were then children. Willoughbys left Wollaton for some years.
Thomas Willoughby (son)	1549-1558	Died aged 16.
(Sir) Francis Willoughby (younger brother)	1558-1596 (1580-88):	Built the new Wollaton Hall made new park. Married (2nd) Dorothy Tamworth, widow, later Lady Wharton. Declining coal mines: debts.
Bridget (eldest daughter) had married her second cousin - (Sir) Percival Willoughby of Bore Place, Kent	1596-1643	Lived mainly at Wollaton, but not before 1599. Knighted 1603: imprisoned in The Fleet for debt. Leased priory lands 1608-29
Francis Willoughby (son)	1643-1665	Married Cassandra Ridgeway, daughter of Treasurer of Ireland. Cleared debts. Lived at Middleton.

Francis Willoughby (son)	1665-1672	Scholar naturalist: an original FRS. Lived mainly at Middleton, occasionally at Wollaton.
Sir Francis Willoughby (son)	1672-1688	Went to live at Wollaton with sister Cassandra: died aged 20. Began repairs and alterations to house and gardens. Cassandra d. 1735.
Thomas Willoughby (younger brother)	1688-1729	First Lord Middleton. Built Wollaton park wall. Bought the Sixty Acres in 1698.
Francis Willoughby (eldest son)	1729-1758	2nd Lord Middleton. Married Elizabeth Southern of Birdsall, Yorkshire, which became the family's main residence.
Francis Willoughby (son)	1758-1774	3rd Lord Middleton
Thomas Willoughby (brother)	1774-1781	4th Lord Middleton. Left Middleton and contents of Wollaton Hall to widow Georgiana (later Mundy) of Shipley Hall - 'the pillager'.
Henry Willoughby (son of Thomas the 1st Lord M.)	1781-1787	5th Lord Middleton
Henry Willoughby	1787-1835	6th Lord Middleton. Built the gate houses and the Camellia House: diverted Derby Road. Bought Lenton Firs and Lenton Abbey.
Digby Willoughby (cousin)	1835-1856	7th Lord Middleton. Bought Lenton Hall.
Henry Willoughby (second cousin)	1856-1877	8th Lord Middleton. Sold the Lenton property
Digby Willoughby (son)	1877-1922	9th Lord Middleton. Wollaton Hall vacant or let
Godfrey Willoughby (brother)	1922-1924	10th Lord Middleton
	In 1925	Wollaton Hall and estate sold to the City of Nottingham

---

APPENDIX 3

DATA FOR CONSTRUCTING A MAP OF FORMER FIELD NAMES

Source A - undated survey notes of the early 17th century

[N.U.M.D., Mi 1/38/41 i-vii]

Name of land	*Adjoining in these directions; length in perches*				
	North	*South*	*East*	*West*	*Area*
Brome Close	No directions given: five parts				
	Sides - 80 and 70: gore head - 52				12a.1r.16p
	Sides - 44 and 68: ends - 80 and 52				23a.0r.16p
	Part sides - 44 and 68: other end - 30				8a.1r.00
	Gore sides - 31 and 24: head - 18				1a.2r.07p
	Sides - 48 and 36: ends - 28 and 18				6a.0r.06p
	All five parts				51a.1r.05p
Cunningre	Wollaton - 104 and 88: ends - 92 and 96				56a.2r.04p deleted 62a.2r.14p
Piece out of Cunningre					1a.1r.29p
Abbey Field	124	120	Sides 60 and 100		61a.0r.00p
	Gores: Sides next highway 24: other 22: head 8				2r.12p
	Middle - 22: head - 8				2a.3r.08p
	Sides - 52 and 40: head - 16				1r.08p
	Total				64a.2r.28p

Sixty Acres	Town field (Cow Close) 120	Lenton 128	Wollaton Cunningre 100	Beeston Field 44	55a.3r.08
	Sides - 60 and 44: Ends - 44 and 36				13a.
	Gore - 70 and 20				2a.3r.00p
	Total				71a.2r.08p
[Another Sixty Acres]	78	120	84	64	45a.3r.06p
W end same	40	40	36	28	8a.
	Total				53a.3r.06p
Highfield	Abbey Field - 84 and 86; Gore - sides 20 and 20:		Cidgie 33 head 6	Ye Lane 25	15a.1r.25p. 1r.20p.
Stonehouse Wong (3 closes)	Other side 103	Next meadow 114	End 15	Beeston end 24	13a.0r.35p.
Stonehouse Meadow	Both sides - 87: ends - 6 and 12				4a.3r.23p,
Little Ffatt Pasture	No directions given: 52 and 62: 54 and 27				14a.3r.05p,
Great Ffatt Pasture	No directions given. Sides 66, 63: ends 44, 60				20a.3r.08p.
	Sides 57 and 66: On ye Round 39 and 25				12a.0r.32p.
	Total				33a.0r.00p.
Low piece of Calfe Close	Calfe Close 18	Tamworth 30	E. end 6	W. end 12	1a.1r.16p.
Higher part of Calfe Close	Borders Rushie Close 32: opposite side 30: head 25				4a.1r.16p.
Ley Close (2 parts)	Quarrel Close 13	Tamworth 35	Calfe Close and Rushy Close 48	Bacon Close 36	6a.1r.08p.
Little Brome Close	Cunningre 30	Russhe Close 24	Highway 36	Quarrel Close 31	5a.
Priors Meadow	Highway 15	23	Ye barne 28	Priors Pingle 18	2a.2r.14p.
Priors Pingle	Priors Meadow 18	The Orchard 14	Highway 6	Bullimires 1 15	a.0r.14p.
Trent Wong	Horsedoles 126	R.Trent 123	Lenton Holmes 66	Beeston Medo 65	50a.2r.14p.
Little Rye Croft	The Greens 8	Great Rye-croft 58	Blotoft 72	Cow Pasture 68	14a.1r.30p.
Great Rye Croft	Little Rye Croft 56	Littling Hook 28	Lyttling 90	Cow Pasture 66	20a.1r.36p.
Lyttling Meadow	Little Rye Croft 5	Grimston Park 32	The Holmes 134	Ryecroft 106	14a.0r.10p.
Legett Wong	Great Leget Wong 24	Cheynye Lane 24	Holme Lane 48	Great Myer Close 44	6a.0r.04p.
Carlholme	48	48	King's Meadow 15	The Lane 17	4a.3r.08p.
Parcel of same	50	50	4	4	1a.1r.00p.

Carlholme	41	35	King's Meadow 12	Highway 10	2a.0r.18p.
Dayhouse Close	Matthews Close 15	The Day House 11	Bushy Close 28	Brome Lane 30	2a.1r.18p.
Cowe Pasture	— ends 54 and 72 —		36	Ye Fatt Pasture 78	22a.0r.17p.
	Half acre allowed for piece 50 x 8				2r.00p.
		Total			25a.3r.31p.
Wheat Croft	Tamworth	Greens	Greens	Ye Mare Close 30	11a.0r.04p.
Tamworth	Sides 84	Wheatcroft 84	Other end 8	Ye Mare Closes 38	12a.0r.12p.

Source B - summary of details from 'Particulars for Concealed Lands in Notts.' [Mi 1/38/40(ii) undated, late 16th century] See Appendix 4 below.

Name of land					
The Rounds	Otherwise Roundabout Water - 3 parcels of Crown wooded land				
1.	Little Mare Close		Cow Pasture	Beeston Hassocks	
2.	Hassocks	Feeding Pasture			
3.	Feeding Pasture	Beeston open field			
Grimston Park	Littling Meadow	Lesser Jervis Close	Great Jervis Close	Entry to Feeding Pastures	2a. Wood, lately waste
Great Jervis Close	Littling Meadow	Horse Doles	Horse Doles	Angle of Little Jervis Close/ Grimston Park	5a. Close of land
Littling Hook	Rye Croft	Feeding Pastures	Littling Meadow	Feeding Pastures	2a. Little close
Blotoft (marsh and island)	Chaunters Close	Littling Meadow	Lenton Commmon Meadow	Ryecroft	
The Greens (Swine Green in small parts)	Starts at a granary - towards -	Cow Pasture from N	E part leads to Priors Close and Miry Close		
Assheholt and Great Doars Park (2 pinghills)	Cause Close	The Greens	Plantation	The Greens Nether Tamworth	1a.1r.00p. Woodland
Doar Park pinghill	Brome Lane	Rushhe Close	Cause Close	Russhe Close	1r.00p. Woodland
Russhe Close	Brome Lane and Dowes Park	Cause Close	Ditch	Lower part of Lees Close: Little Brome Close	

APPENDIX 4

EXTRACT FROM : 'A COPY OF YE PARTICULARS FOR CONCEALED LANDS IN NOTTS.'

['N.U.M.D., Mi 1/38/40(ii). No date.] (Mainly in Latin).

County of Nottingham: Parcels of demesne lands formerly in the possession of the Prior of Lenton, attainted of high treason.

Farm of three narrow parcels of wooded land, formerly and still called The Rowndes, otherwise Roundaboute Water, starting under the southern angle of the Little Maire Close, and going between one of the Feedings called Cowe Pastures and a common called Beeston Hassocks as far as the second [parcel], continuing southwards between another of the Feeding pastures and the said Hassocks, and returning eastwards between the said pasture and the open field of Beeston as far as the third [parcel of wooded land] which extends likewise from the southern part of the third of the Feeding pastures between the same pasture and the said open field of Beeston. 2s. 0d.

Farm of one parcel of wooded land, lately waste, anciently and still called Grimston Park, bordering east on Great Jervis Close, south on Lesser Jervis Close, west on the Feeding pastures, north on Lytling Meadow, and containing two acres of measured woodland 16d.

Farm of a close of land, formerly and still called Greate, otherwise Greater Jervis Close, bordering east and south on the Horse Doles, west on a pingle belonging to the Crown in the tenure of Alexander Wright or assigns, called Little Jervis Close, and Grimston Park, north on Litling Meadow, containing 5 acres 2s. 6d.

Farm of a little close of land, formerly and still called Litling Hooke, bordering east on Litlyng Meadow, south and west on the Feeding pastures and north on Rie Crofte, containing 2 acres 16d.

Farm of a strip of marsh, flooding by running water, formerly and still called Blotoff, with .... two small islands in the same, starting at Litling Meadow and leading between Rye Croft and the common meadow of Lenton as far as a ditch of water which divides one of the said islands from a close called Chaunters Close 6d.

Farm of a parcel of land, now in a number of small parts [divided] by water ditches and hedges, formerly and still called The Grene, otherwise the Swine Grenes, starting at a granary and leading towards the Feeding called Cowe Pasture from the north, the east part bordering on a certain close called Prior's Close and Myry Close as far as a road, part of which touches The Grenes, and afterwards by Chaunters Close and Rye Croft south on the Cowe pasture, and west on Wheatcroft, Tamworthe, Ashehole and the Cawse Close valued at 7s. 0d. and the herbage of the said Grenes will fetch 20d.

Farm of two pinghills, of old and still called the Asheholt, otherwise Great Doars Parke, divided by ancient ditches and hedges and a plantation: east bordering on the Grenes, south bordered by Nether Tamworth, west and north by a close called Cawse Close...the pinghills were formerly flooded ....containing in all 1 acre, 1 rood of measured woodland 8d.

Farm of a close, formerly and still called the Rushe, otherwise Rushie Close, divided by ancient hedges and ditches east from Cawse Close, south and west from the lower part of Lee Close and Little Brome Close, north Brome Lane and Doars Parke. 2s. 6d.

Farm of a pinghill, formerly and still called Dore Park, otherwise Little Doers parke, bordering east on the Cause Close, south and west on the Bushe Close and north on Brome Lane, containing 3 roods of measured woodland 6d.

Farm of a roadway, and herbage of the same, extending from the site of the former priory of Lenton as far as the common called The Grenes, and west as far as the Cuningre, and a barn, a dovecote, a cowhouse, a house called Day House and a garden in the farther part of the said roadway next to the said common, and situated next to a close called Dayhouse Close 12d.

Farm of a little pinghill, formerly and still called the Pinfoulde, bordering east on the said road, south on the Dayhouse Close, west on a close of the Queen in the tenure of Robert Burton or his assigns 2d.

Farm of a small pinghill, formerly and still called the Kiln House Close....the Kilne House 4d.

Farm of a pasture close, formerly and still called the Glassehouse Close, bordered east by other closes....the water of the lyne [Leen], south by the site of the former Priory and Tantony Close, north by the wall ....parish of Lenton and the public road 18d.

Farm of a parcel of land, formerly and still called Tantonie Close, otherwise Tantonie House Yard, bordering east on the aforesaid Glasshouse Close and west on the foundations of ancient walls and the wall of Lenton cemetery.

Sum total 16s. 4d.

Farm of a parcel of wooded land, formerly and still called Bilborowe wood, otherwise Aspley Wood, situated in the parish of Bilborowe.

Parcel of land and possessions of the former monasterie otherwise priory of Dale in the county of Derby.

Farm of a parcel of wooded land lying at Shortwood, containing 15 acres 7s.6d.

Sum total for the premises 29s.10d.

Whereas the said lytle pece of grounde called Grimstone Parke was wood grounde, the tymber and wood felled and soulde out of yt since the Dissolution of the priorie to the king's use, and after during the time that the spring was meinteined because it answered in rent to the Prince, certaine under the colour of challenginge yt for concealed lande have cut downe the yonge wood and afterwards wasted and stacked up the grounde.

Item: None of the premises were ever in record, but parcels of theme claimed by the Inhabitants and occupiers as their Inheritance; other parcels by the occupiers by other colours withheld from the prince without answering to the Queene any rent for the same.

Item: The parcels above named are founde out by the travale of the procurer hereof, who will answer for theme the rente above said and will defende the Quene's title if it will please your Honours to grant him a lease of the premisses.

APPENDIX 5

EXTRACT FROM : 'THE GRANT OF MICHAEL STANHOPE, KNIGHT, FOR DIVERS LANDS, MEADOWS AND PARCELS OF PASTURE, LATE OF THE MONASTERY OF LENTON'.

[N.U.M.D., Mi 1/38/2]. (English)

Letters Patent 'witnessed myself at Westminster, 11 March in the second year of our reign'. The parchment appears to be a copy, and the correct date is almost certainly 'the thirty second year of our reign'. Free transcription below. The values given are to be found in the second part of the document, which is not transcribed here.

Henry VIII by the grace of God of England and France King, etc. etc.: Unto all to whom these patent letters shall come sendeth greetings. Know ye that we, of the advice and assent of our well-beloved council, John Dance Kt., Richard Pollard Esq. and Thomas Moyle Esq., general supervisor of our lands, have granted, given and to farm letten and by these presents granteth, give and to farm let to our well beloved servant Michael Stannop esquire, divers parcels of land, meadow and pasture within our lordship or manor of Lenton in the county of Nottingham as be underwritten, that is to say:

40s. 8d	One parcel, of meadow of the demesne lands that [were] late in the occupation of William Mason, John Standley, Thomas Mason's wife, widow, and John Delapeze [a].
26s. 8d.	Two meadow closes lying nigh the monastery of Lenton aforesaid containing by estimation 8 acres, late in the occupation of John Delapeze, physician.
26s. 8d.	Two other closes called Little Kyeghton containing by estimation 8 acres late in the occupation of John Jepson
20s. 0d.	One pasture close called Great Mare Close containing by estimation 6 acres, late in the occupation of the aforesaid John Jepson.
£3.6s. 8d.	Two other closes whereof one is called Bacon Close and the other Quarrel Close, late in the occupation of Thomas Landisvale.
10s. 0d.	One pasture called Little Mare Close containing 3 acres, late in the occupation of John Thorne.
30s. 4d.	One meadow called Jervis Close [b] containing by estimation 3 acres, late in the occupation of Raff Butler.
33s. 4d.	Another meadow called Edmundson's Close containing 6 acres, late in the occupation of William Edmundson.
14s. 0d.	One close called Great Bolynds and 4 acres of land with one parcel of meadow lying to the same, containing 1 acre, late in the occupation of Robert Jackman.
20s. 0d.	One meadow containing by estimation 2 acres and a half, [lying nigh] the walls of the monastery aforesaid.
£8.0s.0d.	Another meadow called Trent Wong containing by estimation 56 acres (..illegible..[c]) the tenants there: also
20d.	One pasture close within the manor of Radford in the county aforesaid called Plumptre Orchard, late in the occupation of William Sendon [?].
13s.8d.	in addition to the above.

The which said lands, meadows and pastures and other premises aforesaid are parcel of the lands late pertaining to the said late monastery of Lenton aforesaid, and now being in our hands by the attenture of Nicholas Heath, late prior then attainted of other treason. Except and always reserved to us and our heirs all and any woods, underwood ....mines and quarrells and all other royalties whatever ....

The lease was for 21 years

Notes

a] The meadow was almost certainly part of Legett Wong. Only John Delapeze was named as the 'late occupier' later in the document.

b] This will be Little or Lesser Jervis Close - see Appendix 4.

c] It is thought that the missing words were probably 'let among'.

APPENDIX 6

EXTRACT TRANSCRIBED FROM THE 'RENTAL' OF THE FORMER PRIORY DEMESNE DATED c.1554, INCLUDING DETAILS OF LAND USE AND TREE GROWTH

(P.R.O., Rentals and Surveys, Portfolio 24, No. 12: 'Lenton Monastery - Rental (Eliz.?)'

Item	*Area acres*	*No. of trees*	*Land use*
The Roundes which conteyn - [no figure given] - hath growinge uppon it in good indifferent tymber		200	Pasture
The Stonehouse Medowe conteyning	10 ac.		
hathe growinge in the hedge rowes		9	Meadow
The Lytle Kyghton, parcel of my Lady Stanhope's lease containing	5 ac.		
hath in the same		60	Meadow
The Ley Close (c Tamworth) conteyninge	16 ac.		
hathe in the same		7	Pasture
The Lytleynge conteynyth	12 ac.		
and hathe in the same		3	Meadow
The Dayehouse Close conteyns	2 ac.		
and hath in the same		11	Meadow
One close callyd Leget Wonge upper end	8 ac.		
hath in and about the same		3	Meadow
The Calfe Close, parcel of my lady Stannops lease in the tenure of Anne Allen wydow hath in the same		3	Meadow
There ys a pece of severall ground in-closed callyd Grymston Pk wherein are growinge in yonge spyers, some bigger, some lesser asshes		200	Pasture
The Great Mare Close containing	8 ac.	-	Meadow
The Little Brome Close in the tenure of William Nics [Nixe] containing	8 ac.	-	Meadow
One close in the tenure of Robert Bell callyd the Upper End of Litling conteyning parcel,of Lytleynge aforesaid	3 ac.		Pasture
One close called the Lesser Litleynge	2 ac.		Meadow
A close callyd the Jervis Close, parcell of Alexander Wright's lease containing	2 ac.		Meadow, was pasture
First a great felde callyd Syxtie Acre [area not given] conteyning		10	Was arable now pasture
The feyld callyd Marlepit [no area given]		-	Arable
The Warren, otherwise Conningry [no area given]		5	Was arable, now pasture
In the field called the Newe Close up to the Coningry, otherwise the Great Brome Close, conteyning	50 ac.		
hath in the hedgerows		12	Pasture
One close called Newe Close and formerly Short Dunston containing	30 ac.		Formerly arable, now
wherein are the number of		-?	pasture
In one other close called Stonehouse Wong containing	40 ac.		Formerly arable, part
wherein about the hedgerowes are		30	pasture
In one other close called the Wheatcroft Lees conteyning	14ac.		Formerly arable, part
wherein about the hedgerowes		22	pasture

One other close called the Fer [Far] Rye-			Part arable and
croft conteyning	16 ac.		pasture,
and the Near Ryecroft conteyning	8 ac.		part parcel
in the hedgerowes hathe		2	of meadow
One other close next on the south syde			
the Far Rye Crofte nighe unto Grimston			
Park containing	1 ac.		
wherein are in the hedges		9	Pasture
The close called The Kighton, parcel of			
Alexander Wright's lease, in the tenure			
of ..... Rose of Sneynton contains	8 ac.	60	Pasture
The Little Mare Close, parcel of the said			
Alexander's Lease, conteyninge	3 ac.		
wherein are		-?	Pasture
The Quarrell Close and the Bacon Close,			
parcel of the said Alex. lease, cont.	10 ac.		
wherein are		30	Pasture
The Nere Cowe Pasture	14 ac.		
and the Far Cowe Pastures	50 ac.		
otherwise The Fedings, cont. in both	64 ac.		
in the hedges of the fields		6	Pasture
The Grenes in the tenure of Robert Bell			
and Edward Epperston, containing	3 ac.		Pasture
One close called Flaggye Close, otherwise			
Cheyneys Close in Alex Wright's lease	1 ac.		Meadow
One close called Bullmyer in tenure of			
Richard More, pcl of Alexander Wright's			
lease	4 ac.		Meadow
One other close in the holding of William			
Nixt [Nixe] callyd Crabbe Close, cont.	3 ac.		Meadow
One other close callyd The Pryors Medo	3 ac.		Meadow
One other close called the Pond Close			
behind the Orchard, containing	1 ac.		Meadow
One close in the holding of Jac[k]sons			
wyfe, meadow called the Nether Leget Wong	10 ac.		Meadow
One close called Morton, otherwise Edmund-			
son's Close, containing	6 ac.		Meadow
One close in the holdinge of Nicholas			
Easton called Wall Close, containing	2 ac.		Meadow
Robert Bell certeyne chambers of the scite			
decayed and 3 other parcels of the same			Building
parcel of my Lady Stanops lease			decayed
The Little Doore Parke containing	1 ac.		
in tenure of Brian S			Pasture
One other close in the tenure of Anthony			
Weston called Bullmyer, containing	3 ac.		Meadow
In Carleholme in the holding of Len			
Huesby	15 ac.		Meadow
One close called the Hill Close, late in			
the tenure of Richard More	3 ac.		Meadow
('neither parcel of my Lady Stannop nor Alex.			
but in a lease before recit. the rent.....)			
A meadow called Trent Wong, parcel of			
Alex. Wright's lease, containing	96 ac.		Meadow
The heirs of Willowby [Willoughby] hath			
a close called Willowe Home containing	6 ac.		Meadow
and pays yerely at St. Michael 30s.			
(In doubt whether it is severally lett or			
parcel of my Lady Stannop's lease).			

APPENDIX 7

ARRANGEMENTS FOR COMMONING IN LENTON, 1545

[Transcription of N.U.M.D., Mi 1/38/3 36 Henry VIII]

This Award, indented and made the first day of Marche in the year of the Reign of our Sovereign Lord Kyng Henry th'eight by the grace of God Kyng of Yngland France and Yerland, Defender of the Faithe and on yrth of this church of Yngland and Yerland the [supreme head] xxxvi, betwixt the husbands and cotagers of Lenton and Radford by Mr. Henry Willoughby Esquire and Sir Hugh Willoughby knight, by the assent and agreament of the sayd husbands and cotagers there.

Yt ys fyrst awarded by the above named Henry and Hugh that every husband for every oxgang of land shall have their be[a]st pastures free, and every husband at his pleasure to thake one of anothers catell unto his nomber for his pasture but not to be thaken of any stranger or forryner. In consyderation whereof the said husbands as they been accostomed afore tymes shall carry and load at all tymes necessarie stone, gravell and tymber for the reparations of the bryggs, causeys and heyway car[ry]ing free.

We have further ordered and awarded that the cotagers shall have for every cottage 120 beeste pastures and are to thake in of anothers catell but not to thake in of any forrin, paying for every beest 4d. by yere, the one halfe to be payd at Mayday at the putting in of the catell and the other halfe to be payd at Michaelmas, and that all the money so gathered by the byrleymen wyche shalbe elected by the homage of the township yt is to say too [2] of the husbands and one of the cotagers, after the Kyngs Rent and other lords rents payde dew and accostomed yt then all yt in the birleymens hands remeaneth shalbe bestowed to the common welth of the towne as to the mentenance of the hyways bryggs causes and scouryng of dychys by the calling to of other too honest men to the sayd birleymen wyche shalbe elected by the township to se the bestowyng of ye same and also ye laborars be founde of the said monewy to lod[e] and unlode the caryage for the reyporations of stone for hywayes causeys bryggs and dycheys.

Wereof .... we have sette our hands and sealls the day and yere above wrytten.

Thomas De la Peze Ph.
James Thurland
Robertus May, Vicar of Lenton
John Hemffrey
Anthony Weston
John W. Sheppard

APPENDIX 8

SIR MICHAEL HICKS' ESTATE IN LENTON IN 1608

Extracted from the 1608 survey of Crown lands [P.R.O., SC 12/24/12 6591, Exchequer Queen's Remembrancer. P.R.O. LR 2/211 CP 2940, ff.106-158]

All areas given are estimated.

Michael Hicks mil. claims to hold in fee farm demesne land in Lenton, viz. :

Site of the manor, mansion house of 3 bays, an orchard, with the backside and etc. (now in occupation of Jervase Eyre) — 4a.
One other house called the Brickhouse, 1 bay; another house, 1 bay; one other house decayed.
[These two items appear to have been inserted after the schedule had been written. They represent parts of the decaying buildings of the former priory, or cottages built of their materials (Barnes 1987)]. [a]
A close of meadow called Greate Ledgett Wonge, occupied by Richard Hurte, Alderman of the town of Nottingham [b] — 15a. 1r.
A close of meadow called Little Tamworth, now in occupation of the said Richard Hurte, — 6a.
A parcel of land called The Abbey Pinfold, now in occupation of the said Richard Hurte, — 1 perch
A close called Cowe Close, now in occupation of Robert Nixe, — 30a.
A close of arable land and pasture called Rye Close, now in occupation of the said Robert, — 30a.
A close of meadow called Little J... [which should probably read Littling] now in occupation of the said Robert, containing — 28 a.
A close of meadow called Doe Parke, now in occupation of the said Robert, — 1a. 1r.
A close called Ashoulte, now in occupation of the said Robert, — 1a. 1r.
One Agua [water] called Blotofte Poole, now in occupation of the said Robert — [no area given]
A close called Greate Jervis Close, now in occupation of Richard Jonson and Robert Nixe, — 6 a.
A close of pasture called Littlinge Hooke, now in occupation of Jacob Leycester, — 2 a.
A closure of meadow called Carleholme, by estimation now in occupation of Lodovic Oxley. — 7 a.
One other close of meadow called Carleholme, by estimation in occupation of the said Lodovic — 5 a.
A close of arable land called Stanhouse Wonge, now in occupation of Emery Waplington, — 6 a.
A close of pasture called Rushey Close, now in occupation of Sara Ffoster, — 6 a.
A water mill, now in occupation of William Stampe, with adjoining close called Kilneyard,
[A mansion house, 3 bays, stable 3 bays] — 1a. 2r.
One other close called Pryor Meadowe, now in occupation of the said William Stampe, [c] — 2a. 1r.
A close of pasture called Abbey Field and Conygre, now in occupation of Roger Howton, — 80 a.
A close of pasture called Ryeclose, now in occupation of the said Roger, — 12 a.
A close of pasture called Tamworth Close, now in occupation of the said Roger, [d] — 16 a.
A close of pasture called Sixty Acre Close, now in occupation of Brockett, widow, [e] — 60 a.
A close called Brome Close, now in occupation of Roland Dan, — 20 a.
One other close called Stanhouse Wonge, now in occupation of William Kirke, — 10 a.
One other close called Stanhouse Wonge, now in occupation of the said William, containing by estimation [no area given] [f]
A close of pasture called Little Brome Close, now in occupation of ..... [Thomas ?] Markham, — 8 a.
One other close of meadow called Calfe Close, now in occupation of the said ..... Markham, — 6 a.
One dovecote containing 2 bays, and a barn, 9 bays, occupied by Christopher Sprintall. [g]
Two closes called Lea Closes, now in occupation of Jervase Eyre, [h] — 4 a.
A close called Wheate Crofte, now in occupation of the said Christopher Sprintall, — 20 a.
Two closes called Greate Fatt Pasture, with certain parcels of land called The Rounds adjoining, now in occupation of Richard Cawton, — 35 a.
One other close called Little Fatt Pasture, with certain parcels of land called The Rounds adjoining, now in occupation of the said Richard, — 16 a.
A close called Highfield, now in occupation of Christopher Sprintall, — 20 a.
A close called Dewhouse Close, now in occupation of Gervase Eyre, [i] — 2a. 2r.
One house called a Daye house, 2 bays; 1 stable, 2 bays.
A piece of land called The Greens, now in occupation of Alic[e] Sturton and William Davye, — 4 a.
Trent Wonge:
    A piece of meadow called The Trent Wonge, now in occupation of Robert Nixe, held for rent per annum £ 8. — 100 a.

Notes on the above schedule

a) The manor is the former priory and the mansion house a surviving conventual building, thought to have been demolished in 1609 [Barnes 1987]

b) Richard Hurte was mayor of Nottingham in 1595, 1602 and 1609 [Bailey 1853 524, 540, 571].

c) This was the Prior's Mill, situated on the left bank of the river Leen, near to the Abbey Bridge carrying Abbey Street across the stream. The mill was rebuilt in about 1611 under the terms of a lease to Sir Percival Willoughby which allowed a change of site. It is not known whether the mill was moved.

d) The survey records four score acres, but this is a large under-estimate for this land, and may have been an error for 120 acres, if it had been copied from CC/VI. Alternatively the former New Close may be missing, since the large Brome Close is not in the schedule.

e) The Sixty Acres was given 90 acres in other surveys, and 60 acres may have been the area of the open arable field there.

f) The repetition of this item is probably a copyist's error.

g) This entry has been added at the bottom of a manuscript folio.

h) The name Christopher Sprintall was erased and replaced with Jervase Eyre - in the context probably a copyist's correction.

i) This is Dayhouse Close, a name deriving from the priory's dairy house. This reading is confirmed by a corresponding entry in a document of the following year, in which the name is Dayrie House Close.

APPENDIX 9

HARLAXTON, AND THE EXTINCTION OF THE GREGORYS

The third George Gregory and his wife Anne (Orton) moved to Harlaxton Manor, which she had inherited, in about 1748, and both were buried there in the 1750s. Their eldest son, the fourth George - George de Ligne Gregory (1733-1823) JP - High Sheriff of Nottinghamshire in 1791, succeeded to the Harlaxton estate and property in London, Nottingham, Radford and Lenton. Apparently he disliked the Harlaxton Manor house of the time, and in 1785 built Hungerford Hall as a base near to the Harlaxton estate. He died unmarried, having been in possession of the estates, now considerably extended, particularly by inclosures (including that of Lenton in 1758), for some 64 years. 'His character as a landlord and master will long be the theme of praise....' [Sutton 1852].

George de Ligne Gregory died at Rempstone Cottage and left his estates in 1823 to his nephew Gregory Williams. George's brother, William Gregory (1742-1814), the second son of George (III) and Anne, High Sheriff in 1800, had married Olivia Preston of Flasby, Yorkshire in 1783. He was 'of Rempstone Hall', which had been the property of the parents of his grandmother, nee Susanna Williams, and he assumed the additional name and arms of Williams for that reason. William Gregory Wiliams and Olivia had a daughter, Anne, who died unmarried, and an only son, Gregory Gregory-Williams (1786-1854), who inherited the Rempstone, Lenton and Denton (Lincolnshire) estates (respectively of about 1,300, 2,000 and 1,000 acres) from his father in 1814. Eight years later, on inheriting the Harlaxton estate of about 2,500 acres from his uncle George (IV) in 1823, he assumed the name Gregory and dropped that of Williams. The eight years 1814-23, when Gregory travelled and collected objects and ideas in post-Napoleonic Europe were important in determining the character of the new Harlaxton Manor.

The old manor house at Harlaxton, unoccupied since his grandmother's death in the 1750s, had fallen into disrepair, and two ranges of it had collapsed. Gregory Gregory replaced it with an idiosyncratic but palatial new mansion, begun in 1832 and completed in 1844 - a project he had decided upon in 1822. Anthony Salvin, a celebrated pioneer of Gothic Revival architecture, responsible for designing or rebuilding many castles, mansions and country houses - for example, the new Thoresby Hall and Keele Hall - was engaged in 1832 to work to a specific brief by Gregory Gregory. The work was financed by land sales, especially from the Lenton estate, where industrial and housing development had greatly increased land values.

Jill Allibone [1987 40-52] has provided an excellent illustrated account of the architectural history of Harlaxton Manor, and the influences on Gregory and Salvin which produced it - a melange of architectural styles dating from the late 16th and 17th centuries, from Tudor to Baroque, mixed with features copied from French, Italian and Austrian mansions - comparing Gregory at Harlaxton with Horace Walpole's work at Strawberry Hill in the Gothic style.

Gregory Gregory let Rempstone Hall and lived at Hungerton Hall while Harlaxton was being built on a site selected for its views. He was certainly living in his new house at the 1851 census, served by a housekeeper, seven maids, a butler, three footmen and two grooms. He died only three years later, in 1854, and as he too was unmarried the estates passed into the ownership of his cousin, yet another George Gregory (1775-1860). This fifth George was the elder son of Captain Daniel Gregory (d. 1819), the fourth son of George (III) and Anne Gregory, who had married Catherine Beckingham of Bourne Place in Kent. But George (V) enjoyed only six years in possession of Harlaxton Manor and died in 1860. He was yet another unmarried Gregory, and so were his brother Edward and his uncle Edward (1744-1824), the third son of George (III) and for 49 years the rector of Langar (1776 to 1824). The latter seems to have been an interesting character, 'a gentleman whose astronomical pursuits are spoken of with much respect. He has lately erected an observatory near his house, which has order and embellishments without as well as usefulness within' [Throsby 1790/1972 I 208].

In striking contrast to the fecundity of the earlier Gregorys the whole of this final generation of the large Gregory family failed to produce a male heir, and the fifth George Gregory, who died in 1860, was the last of the line. John Sherwin Sherwin of Bramcote Hills, to whom the Manor of Lenton and the Harlaxton Manor estate devolved in 1860, was only a distant relative, but was vested as next in succession under the entail of the will of George de Ligne Gregory, and he assumed the name and arms of Gregory by royal licence. His claim to succession arose from the marriage of Barbara, one of the dozen children (8 sons and 4 daughters at least) of the first George Gregory in the 1660s and 1670s, to George Needham of Little Wymondley, Hertfordshire. One of the three daughters of this marriage became the wife of John Sherwin, High Sheriff of Nottinghamshire in 1721, and he became the maternal grandfather of John Sherwin Sherwin, the Gregorys' family lawyer who succeeded to the estates.

This John Sherwin Sherwin Gregory died in 1869, again without issue, and the Manor of Lenton passed by devise to his widow, Mrs. Catherine Sherwin Gregory, who continued to live at Bramcote Hills until her death in 1892. The main estates, including Harlaxton, then passed to John's cousin, Thomas Sherwin Pearson, who added Gregory to his name. He sold off further parts of the estate in Lenton, including the Keighton Closes, which in 1920 were bought by Frederick Mitchell [1] and soon afterwards re-sold to Sir Jesse Boot, to be incorporated into the original campus of the University College and the associated park and playing field development of the next few years. Thomas Sherwin Pearson Gregory died in 1935, and in 1937 it was his son, Major Philip John Sherwin Pearson Gregory who was selling off remnants of the estate in Lenton [2]. The somewhat ridiculous accretion of family names reflects the tortuous lines of devolution of ownership in a family of diminished fertility. The Bramcote estate passed to Henry Holden, and followed a different course of devolution (Appendix 17).

Finally, although the devolution of Harlaxton manor is not directly relevant to the topographic history of Lenton, its later history is of some interest. Many of the contents were left by the last George Gregory to his friend and distant relative Sir Glynne Welby, for whom Welby Avenue in Lenton is named. But it was Philip Pearson Gregory who put up Harlaxton Manor for sale. The estate sold readily, but the house did not. It was rescued from demolition in 1937, and restored by Mrs. Violet Van der Elst, second wife of a deceased Belgian artist, John Van der Elst. Her fortune came from toilet preparations, notably 'Shavex'. She was a well-known campaigner for the abolition of capital punishment, and a believer in the occult. She sold Harlaxton manor in 1948 to the Society of Jesus. The Jesuits used it as a seminary, but allowed its fabric to deteriorate so much that it had to be sold. It was said that 'with religious zeal they destroyed classical figures, and with financial acumen plundered the woodland' before leaving the estate [3]. In 1966 Harlaxton Manor was leased to Stanford University, California, who passed it on to the present occupants, the University of Evansville, Indiana for use as their British campus, and they have painstakingly restored the building, which is now 'a credit to its owners'.

Notes

1. L.A.O., 4 PG 7 January 1920 - Conveyance of 8a.2.00 in Spring Close and Abbey Lane, occupied by Mr. Henry Woodhouse: T.S.Pearson Gregory to Mr. Herbert Coates, rope and twine manufacturer.
L.A.O., 4 PG 108, 31 March 1920 - Conveyance of 48a.1.15 of land in Lenton: T.S.Pearson Gregory to Mr. Frederick Mitchell. This land comprised mainly the Keighton Closes.
2. Conveyance of $7^3/_4$ acres of land abutting Spring Close and Abbey Street.
L.A.O., 4 PG 222, 14 December 1937.
3. Nottingham Civic Society Newsletter

APPENDIX 10

THE HANDLEYS OF BRAMCOTE AND WILFORD

In 1684 Huntin (Huntington) Handley held 33 acres of the priory demesne estate, all in the Trent vale. He lived at Wilford, so that Nether Wheatcroft and Tamworth would have been accessible via the ford near to the present Clifton bridge, the Holmes and Chain Lane. The Handley family, originally from Yorkshire, was one of those which became prominent after the Dissolution. It was said that a Thomas Handley bought Sempringham Priory's manor of Bramcote at the Dissolution, and added Lenton Priory's property there. The historian Bailey's version [1853 477] was that the manor was granted in 1564 by Letters Patent to Charles Jackson and William Mason, and Richard Handley bought it from them. In either case the Handleys built and lived in the house called Bramcote Manor from the time of James I. This house is not to be confused with Bramcote Hall, described by Lawson Lowe [1876] as 'a fine modern mansion in the Elizabethan style, now the seat of Frederick Chatfield Smith, M.P.', or with Bramcote Hills.

Richard Handley left his son Henry (d. 1603) at Bramcote, and his second son Gervase at Wilford Manor. Henry's son, also Henry, succeeded his father in 1608 and he enlarged the patrimony; but in 1650 he died without an immediate heir, both his son Percival and daughter Mary having died in childhood. In 1645 he had granted a rent charge of £ 40 a year out of his estate at Bramcote, Chilwell and Attenborough for 12 poor persons in almshouses he was about to build on Stoney Street, Nottingham. Curtis [1844 xxxvii] noted that the four centre houses were still 'in the gift of Captain Sherwin of Bramcote, as representative of the Longdon family', by then the owners of the estate at Bramcote. The Sherwin-Gregory family lived at Bramcote Hills, built by John Longdon in the early 19th century (see Appendix 17). This was an outcome of a scandalous story of the descent of the Handley estate and the betrayal of Henry Handley after his many benefactions to the poor, in which an executor, Robert Harding, sold Bramcote Manor to John Sherwin of Nottingham. The chief sufferer was Gervase Handley of Wilford, Henry's cousin, and brother of Huntin' Handley according to Fellows [1917].

At Wilford the Handleys lived in a stuccoed house on the Green, where 'Huntington

Handley in the 18th century seems to have had a large family' which perhaps 'lost its position through impoverishment' - a striking statement of the obvious [Lowe 1876: W.E.D. 1943 139]. M.H.Barker [1835] described a large white house 'across the village green from Wilford churchyard and left of the village school', occupied by Mr. R. Leeson, which was 'little more than a cottage when occupied by the Handleys'. The Handleys sold it to William Lee, grandfather of Matthew Needham (who built Lenton House), and after Lee's death in 1792 Matthew's mother lived there and enlarged and improved it, as did the subsequent owners Samuel Newham and W.S.Burnside before it was sold to Leeson. Huntington Handley was there in the late 17th century. This was not the Manor House, of which Iliffe and Baguley [6 1971 45] published a photograph taken in 1900, with the statement that it was built in 1724, and was 'reputed to have once been the residence of the Clifton family'. This seems unlikely, even if it refers to the Markhams.

With the status of the Handleys much reduced in Bramcote, too, the old gabled Manor House there was occupied by tenant farmers in the 19th century.

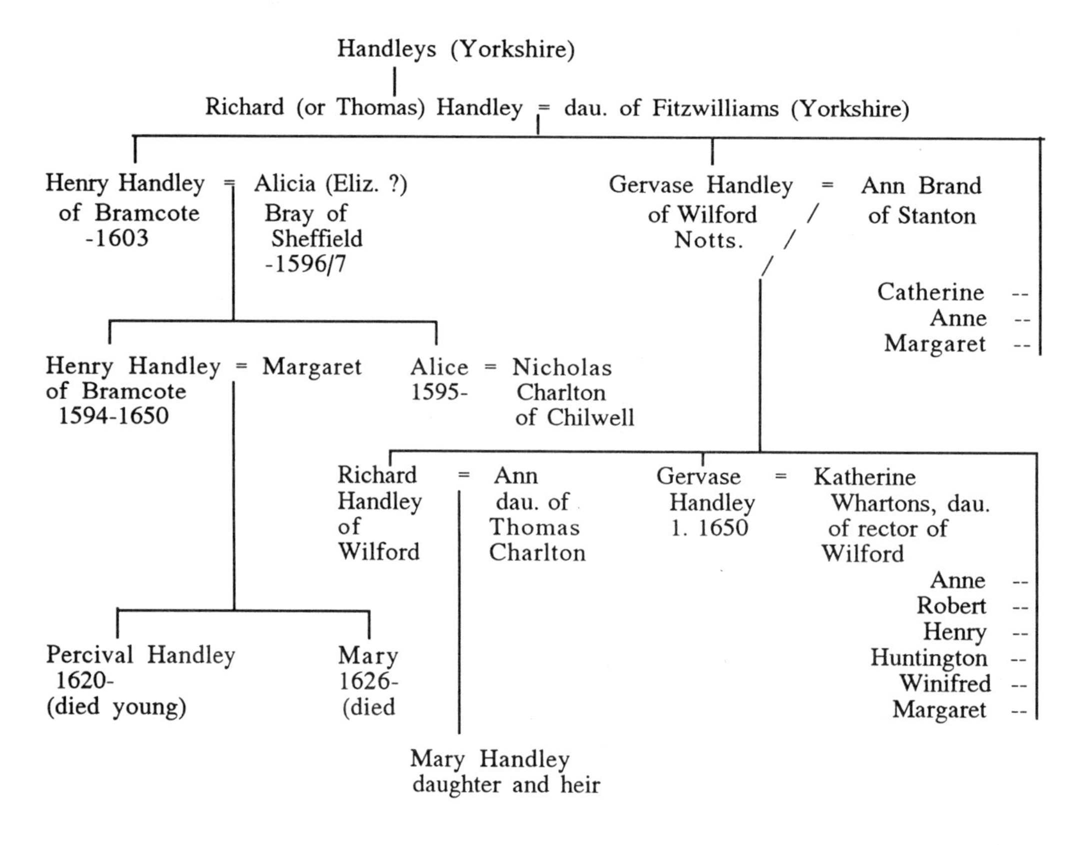

APPENDIX 11

A TERRIER OF THE PRIORY DEMESNE ESTATE MADE FOR THE 1684 SALE

[N.U.M.D., Mi 3 E4. N.U.M.D. Wadsworth 50]

Indenture of 25 and 26 January 1684

All those several closes or parcels of meadow ground commonly called the Rie Close, the Cow Close and Littling, cont. together by estimation then or late in occupation of Christopher Hall or his assigns.	127 acres
Piece or parcel of pasture ground, part of a close commonly called the Broom Close, cont. by estimation occupied by John Moore or his assigns	12 a. [a]
Piece or parcel of meadow ground...Ledgett Wonge....occupied by Josh. Marsh or his assigns	13 a.
Part of a field or close of pasture....the Highfield Close occupied by Rose Parker or her assigns	16 a. [b]
Part of a close or parcel of meadow ground....Rushie Close occupied by George Puggson or his assigns	3 a.
Piece or parcel of meadow ground....the Pryer Meadow occupied by Francis Medeam or his assigns	5 a.
Piece or parcel of meadow ground....the Nether Wheat Croft occupied by Huntin Handley or his assigns	12 a.
Piece or parcel of meadow ground....Greasones Close occupied by William Simpson or his assigns	4 a.
Piece or parcel of meadow ground....Wards Close occupied by John Lee or his assigns	4 a.
Piece or parcel of meadow ground, part of a close called Temes Close, occupied by Jane Ross, widow, or her assigns	4 a.
Close or piece of pasture ground....Hilley Close occupied by Thomas Henson or his assigns	7 a. [c]
Close or piece of park ground....Tomworth occupied by Huntin Handley or his assigns	16 a. [d]
Piece of pasture ground, part of a piece of ground...The Rounds, in the several occupations of Robert Wright and .... Wild, widow, or their assigns	14 a.
Close, piece or parcel of meadow ground....Barleys Close occupied by Robert Barley or his assigns	6 a.
Piece of pasture ground, part of the Highfield Close occupied by William Smith or his assigns	10 a. [e]
Close or parcel of meadow ground....Clarkes Close occupied by .... Clarke, widow, or her assigns	6 a. [f]
Close or parcel of meadow ground....Pares Close occupied by William Pare or his assigns	4 a. [g]
Piece of meadow, parcel of a close called Partable Close occupied by Edward Attenborow or his assigns	5 a.
Close, piece or parcel of pasture ground....the Gorsey Close occupied by Christopher Hall or his assigns	20 a.[h]
Two pieces or parcels of pasture ground....Dovecote Close and Salter Close, together occupied by John Drewry or his assigns	10 a.
Piece or parcel of meadow ground....Little Broom Close in the several occupation of John Scattergood and .... Alcock or their assigns	9 a.
Piece of meadow ground, part of the Rushie Close occupied by Christopher Rest or his assigns	4 a.
Piece of meadow ground being the nether part of Highfield Close next Beeston occupied by Thomas Henson or his assigns	10 a.
Piece or parcel of the Highfield Close next the Field occupied by Rose Parker or her assigns	12 a. [i]
All those fields, pieces or parcels of pasture ground called the Abbey Fields	200 a. [j]
Piece or parcel of meadow ground....the Abbey Orchard occupied by William Birdsey or his assigns	3 a.

Together with all ways etc.

The leases forming 'incumbrances' were:

A lease granted to William Smith of a Highfield Close for 21 years from Lady Day 1670 at a yearly rent of £ 9.

Another lease granted to....Wild of 2 closes called The Rounds, for 21 years from Lady Day 1670 at yearly rent of £13.10s 0d.

Another lease granted to John Scattergood and [Robert] Alcock of the Abbey Fields for 13 years from Lady Day 1682 at a yearly rent of £ 41.

Another lease granted to Rose Parker of 3 closes, part of Highfield Closes, for 21 years from Lady Day 1681 at a yearly rent of £16.10s.0d.

Indenture of 27 and 28 January 1684

The site, circuit and precinct of the late dissolved Priory of Lenton

All that piece or parcel of pasture ground....Trent Wong occupied by ....[John] Garland or his assigns	100 a. [k]
Paper mill and yard belonging occupied by Samuel Smith or his assigns	1 a.
Piece or parcel of pasture ground .... the Sixty Acres occupied by Jno. Sherwin or his assigns	90 a.
Close or parcel of meadow ground....the Oxhouse Close occupied by Jno. Scattergood or his assigns	3 a.
Another close or parcel of meadow ground....the Davye Close occupied by Jno. Leusey or his assigns	2 a. [l]

Piece or parcel of meadow ground, part of the close called Teme Close, occupied by Thomas Vickers or his assigns 3 a.
A little piece of meadow, parcel of Duck Meadow occupied by ....Garner or his assigns
Piece or parcel of meadow ground....The Littling occupied by Hugh Ellenor or his assigns 3 a. [m]
Piece or parcel of meadow ground....the Calfe Close occupied by Thomas Anny or his assigns 2 a.
Piece or parcel of meadow ground....the Five Acres occupied by William Davis, Jervas Davie or their assigns 5 a.
All that other piece or parcel of meadow ground....the Great Broom Close occupied by....Garland or his assigns. 20 a.
Those other pieces or parcels of meadow ground....the Broom Close next Abbey Lane and Carleholme, together occupied by Josh. Marsh or his assigns 10 a.
Piece or parcel of meadow ground....the Over Wheate Crofte occupied by Robert Caulshaw or his assigns 12 a.
Piece or parcel of meadow ground....the Seven Acres occupied by Jno. Tuffin or his assigns 7 a.
Piece or parcel of pasture ground....The Greens occupied by John Scattergood and....Alcock or their assigns 5 a. [n]
Piece or parcel of meadow ground....the Churchyard Close occupied by Huntin Handley or his assigns 5 a.
Messuage or tenement with the garden thereunto belonging, now or late in the tenure or occupation of....Walter, widow, or her assigns
Another messuage or tenement with garden occupied by Jno. Dubleday or his assigns
Messuage or tenement with garden, occupied by Rd. France or his assigns [o].

Notes

a) It is believed that this is the land purchased by Francis Evans in 1791. He later built Lenton Grove on it (see Chapter XI). It appears to have been alienated from the demesne estate at some date in the earlier 18th century (cp. the Sixty Acres).

b) This was probably the nucleus of the later Lenton House estate (see Chapter VIII).

c) This appears to be written as 'Lilley Close' on the dorse of N.U.M.D., Mi 3 E 4, p. 1: but this would be incorrect.

d) The name Tomworth, or Tamworth, was wrongly transcribed by Godfrey [1884] as Farnsworth. For Huntin' Handley see Appendix 10.

e) William Smith's lease was of this close only, a 'Highfield Close'.

f) Widow Clarke lived in Beeston.

g) This close has not been identified, and probably had a different name later.

h) This is the close that 75 years earlier had been assigned by Sir Michael Hicks to his courier, Palmer. It is now part of the Boots factory site.

i) 'The Field' must be the Abbey Field, which bordered the later Lenton House estate on the north side.

j) With an area of 200 acres this item must represent the whole tract on the northern side of the campus from Sandy Lane (Clifton Boulevard) west to the Tottle Brook (Woodside Road) including both the former Warren and the Great Broom Close (Lenton Abbey estate). John Scattergood probably lived at the former priory dairyhouse, later called Abbey House. Robert Alcock was probably the father of Thomas Allicock of Nottingham, 'butcher and grazier', aged 22 when he married Catherine Bellond of Lenton on 26 October 1700 [Phillimore and Fellows 1904 139]. Both Robert Alcock and his co-tenant John Scattergood would also be graziers, and the Abbey Fields provided excellent, healthy sheep pasture.

k) Although the name appears to read Parland there is no doubt that it refers to John Garland, who occupied the largest of the Gregory estate farm holdings in Lenton and lived at The Hall, identified as No. 3 Gregory Street, recently known as the Old Manor House for no good historical reason.

l) This close has not been identified on the ground, but it was almost certainly one of the Abbey Closes. In 1731 it was called Davye Meadow, of 2 acres.

m) This should probably read Littling Hook, which adjoined the large meadow called Littling at its south-west end.

n) The Greens was an irregularly shaped common through which the road from Dunkirk to the Wilford ford ran. As the road became 'fixed' and fenced parts of the former common were enclosed. The exact location of this particular close is not known

o) The last three items here must refer to the 'Brickhouse cottages' on the site of the former priory, probably surviving parts of the priory buildings or constructed from their materials [Barnes 1987].

APPENDIX 12

FARM HOLDINGS THAT INCLUDED LAND ON THE PRESENT UNIVERSITY CAMPUS IN THE EARLY 18TH CENTURY

[Arranged in the order of the 1743 terrier of the Winford-Milward estate]

Occupier ***Winford-Milward estate*** *Property*	*Rent in 1743*	*Area in 1731*	***Gregory estate*** *Property and area in 1738*	*Area in 1725*	*Rent in 1725*
BENJAMIN DEVERALL [a]					
Trent Wong	£61.00	100 ac			
HUGH STANDLEY [b]					
MESSUAGE (Odd House)	£24.10	Part of	HOUSE, croft		£7.00
Middle Broom Close		Abbey	and 3 closes in		
Next Broom Close		Fields	1725: none in 1738		
Broom Meadow					
MR. FIELD					
MESSUAGE (Mill House)	£23.13		A 'workhouse' and		£0.00
			several shops in		
Paper mill & yard			1725		
2 pond yards		1 ac			
5-acre Close (mead.)		5 ac			
David Close (= Davey Meadow)		2 ac			
THOMAS TRIGG					
Duck Meadow	3s/4d				
MR. LOWE					
Near Broom Close	£14.05	10 ac			
Dayhouse Close					
Ox Close (meadow)		3 ac			
WILLIAM NORRIS (Richard Norris in 1725)					
The Hill Close (=	£23.00		MESSUAGE ('his old		
Hilly Cl. pasture)		7 ac	house and homestead')		
Hill Close Gutt			2 COTTAGES (1725)		
Little Tims Cl. (=			Hill Close	2a.3.18	
pt Teem Cl. mead.)		4 ac	2 Reedy Closes		
The other Little Tims			and Home Closes	6a.1.25	
Cl.= Tame Meadow		3 ac	Commons		
Churchyard Close		5 ac		9a.+	Commons
Round Close					

Also WILLIAM NORRIS (Penington in 1725)			HOUSE, orchard,		
			4 COTTAGES		£6.00
			Meadow and a swath	5a.2.0	£4.00
			In Thackholmes	2r.0	5s.
			Wm. Norris in 1738		
			2 tithe barns		
			Tithes of corn and hay		
THOMAS WOOD					
Seven Acres Meadow	£ 6.10s.				
THOMAS PARTRIDGE [c]					
The Cow Close	£54.10s.				
The Gossey Close (Gossey Pasture)		20 ac			
Upper Wheatcroft (Over Wheatcroft Meadow)		12 ac			
Little Littling					
MR. FRANCIS ALLGOOD [d]					
Near Abbey Field	£82.05.				
Far Abbey Field					
Higher Hill Close					
Lower Hill Close		200 ac			
Little Broom Close		9 ac			
Dovecote Close		10 ac			
Abbey Orchard		3 ac			
HOUSE, barn and garden with Wards Close (Wards Meadow)	£9.00.	4 ac			
MR. JNO. CHAMBERLAIN					
The Rye Close	£76.00.		MESSUAGE, croft,		
Great and Middle Littling			4 COTTAGES		£4.00
Rounds Close (= Barleys Meadow)		6 ac	Lands etc. in all		
2 Highfields Closes			Six open fields	53a.1.0	£15.6.6
			Meadows	9a.3.0	7.5.6
			Thackholmes	3.0	7.6
			Formfoot Lane Cl.	2a.2.0	2.10.0
			Bullmires	1a.2.26	3.10.0
			Keeton Meadow	8a.3.31	13.0.0
			Mare Close	5a.3.31	6.0.0
			Mortons	12a.1.04	13.0.0
			Townsend Close	1a.0.12	1.10
			Total	96a.0.24	£66.9.6
MR. JNO. CHAMBERLAIN WITH HUMPHREY HOPKINS (Stephen Western in 1725)					
			HOUSE, homestead		
			3 COTTAGES		£10.
			2 Home Closes (in 1738 only)		

			Lands etc. in all six open fields	66a.1.0	21.12.6
			Meadows	11a.3.0	8.15.6
			Thackholmes	1a.2.0	15.0
			Bacon's Closes	6a.2.0	8.00.0
			Total	86a.0.0	£49.3.0
MR. BEARDSLEY					
Leggitt Wong	£21.10s.	13 ac			
The Greens		5 ac			
ARTHUR BEARDSLEY (1725 only)					
			HOUSE, backside,		£8.00.0
			A cottage		
			In Thackholme	1r.0	
THOMAS FIRTH (Arthur Beardsley in 1725)					
			His (Beardsley's) old HOUSE, homestead and close adjoining		£9.00.0
			Lands in four of the open fields	2a.2.0	12s.6
			Spring Close		4.00.0
			Stanhope Close		5.00.0
			Total		£18.12.6
MR. HAWKESLY					
Priors Meadow	£5.5.0	5 ac			
MR. JNO. DEVERALL & MR. HANDLEY (both of Wilford)					
Tamworth pasture	£23.10.0	16 ac			
Nether Tamworth					
Nether Wheatcroft (meadow)		12 ac			
THOMAS HANSON					
Lower Highfield Cl.	£25.10.0				
Nether Highfield					
Great Rounds Close					
BRIDGETT HOOLEY (Matthew Hooley in 1738)					
Rushy Close	£3.14.0				
Part Rushy Close meadow		3 ac	COTTAGE and garden		
THOMAS NEWHAM					
Lesser Rushy Close	£3.10.0	4 ac	MESSUAGE or farm house		
Part Rushy Meadow			Close adjoining (4 ac)		
			Whitemoor Close		
			Stanhope Close (8 ac)		

			Land etc. in 3 open fields	9a.3.1	
			Meadow	1a.0.0	
WILLIAM COMMINS					
Calf Close (= Geesons Meadow)	£4.0.0	4 ac	COTTAGE and croft adjoining		
JNO. MOORE of Beeston					
Far Broom Close (= Broom Close pasture)	£12.10.0	12 ac			
Rounds Close					
EDWARD ATTENBOROUGH of Beeston					
A Rounds Close	£4.0.0				
WILLIAM BLACK					
Doe Park (meadow)	£2.0.0	1 ac	COTTAGE HOUSE and orchard		
			Land in Sandfield	1 ac	£2.5.0
MATTHEW WELSH (William Welsh in 1725)					
Great Timms	£4.0.0		COTTAGE		
WILLIAM SHELTON					
COTTAGE and garden	10s.0		COTTAGE and croft adjoining		£3.0.0
EDWARD CROWCROFT					
COTTAGE and garden	8s.0				
JNO. ALLING					
COTTAGE and garden	8s.0				
ELIZABETH SHAW (WIDOW) (Richard Beasley in 1725)			HOUSE, homestead		
			6 COTTAGES		£5.0.0
			Lands in all six open fields	61a.1.0	18.12.0
			in Meadows	16a.2.0	12.07.6
			in Thackholme	1a.1.0	10.0
			Upper Keetons	9a.3.17	12.00.0
			Leen Close		4.00.0
			Saffron Close	3a.1.20	6.00.0
			Reedy Closes	8a.0.10	8.00.0
			Willowholme	11a.2.24	17.00.0
			Total	111a.3.31	£83.09.6
WILLIAM DICKINSON (John Swinscow in 1725)			HOUSE and back-side	1a.	£1.0.0
			Lands in all six open fields	52a.3.0	£15.19.0
			in Meadows	10a.	7.10.0
			in Thackholmes	2r.	5.0
			Robinson's Close	3a.1.28	4.00.0

Owner	Property	Area	Value
	Hanging Close	1a.1.36	2.00.0
	Mare Close	4a.3.10	5.00.0
	Briging Close	2a.3.04	3.05.0
	Total	75a.2.38	£38.19s.
JOHN MOSELEY (in 1725)	HOUSE, homestead		£3.00.0
	Piece in Leen croft and 2 COTTAGES in Thackholmes	1a.	10.0
	Nether Keetons	7a.2.39	12.00.0
	Total		£15.10.0
JOHN MOSELEY in 1738 (Hugh Stanley in 1725)	HOUSE, croft and 3 closes		£7.00.0
BENJAMIN ALT (Samuel Cooper in 1725)	MESSUAGE or Inn, Nag's Head (1738) (HOUSE, COTTAGE & backside in 1725)		£6.00.0
	Leget Wong	5a.2.00	8.00.0
	Carlsholme		4.00.0
	Paper Mill Close		3.00.0
	Total	18a.	£21.00.0
JOHN CLARKE	MESSUAGE or farm house		
	Whitemore Close		
	Briggin Close		
	Spring Close	12a.	
WILLIAM BURTON (Widow Colshaw in 1725)	HOUSE, homestead and 1 COTTAGE		£2.00.0
	Lands in five open fields	51a.	£14.17.6
	Carleholmes	2a.1.00	2.15.0
	in Meadows	10a.2.00	7.17.6
	in Thackholme	1a.	10.0
	Bacon Close	5a.3.20	7.10.0
	Lea Close	4a.2.19	5.00.0
	Mare Close	5a.3.13	6.00.0
	Parkside Close		2.00.0
	Total	81a.0.12	£48.10.0.
HUMPHREY HOPKINS - see above - (John Hopkins in 1725)	HOUSE, homestead and 6 COTTAGES		£7.00.0
	Lands in all six open fields	30a.0.00	11.09.0
	in Meadows	9a.2.06	7.02.6
	in Thackholmes	1a.	10.0
	Upper Bullmires	1a.2.13	3.00.0

Stonewall Close	2a.2.16	4.00.0
A COTTAGE of John Wheatley		2.00.0
A COTTAGE of Joseph Taylor at Radford		2.00.0
Total	45a.1.29	£39.01.6

Notes on the above schedule

The last seven entries in the table are included because they held, under the Gregory estate, former 'Alexander Wright closes' or others on the campus, though not land of the Winford-Milward estate.

a) Benjamin Deverall was a Wilford grazier. Trent Wong, because of its proximity to the ford over the river Trent at the end of Trent Lane, Lenton, usually had Wilford tenants.

b) Hugh Standley, who was living in Lenton village on a Gregory estate small holding with a cottage in 1725, and probably in 1731 but not in 1738, appears to have moved to the Odd House, the precursor of Lenton Abbey, and may have built it in the mid 1730s, when the farm there was probably established. The house was first mentioned in the terrier of 1743. The land had earlier been part of the 'Abbey Fields'. Whether the house was new or a barn conversion is not known.

c) A Thomas Partridge was a sheriff of Nottingham in 1686 [Bailey 1853 1077] and a coroner for Nottingham had the same name [Bailey 1853 1077] and may have been the same person or his son, and the tenant of 1743. They were not residents of Lenton; nor was Thomas Wood or Thomas Hanson.

d) Francis Allgood probably lived at Abbey House (the former Dayhouse) but this is not certain.

APPENDIX 13

FARM HOLDINGS THAT INCLUDED LAND ON THE PRESENT UNIVERSITY CAMPUS IN THE LATER 18TH CENTURY

Occupier *Milward estate in 1780*	*Land tax*	*Gregory estate in 1780 (tax) and 1768-9*	*Area 1768-9*	*Tax 1780 (Rent in 1768-69)*
WILLIAM NORRIS				
'Abbey lands'	£4.03.0			£3.12.0
Cummins Close (= Calf Close)	16.0	Keightons		2.00.0
		HOMESTEAD and 6 COTTAGES	1a.0.00	
		Reedy Close	6a.2.08	(4.10.0)
		Keetons Close	8a.0.28	(9.00.0)
		Tithe Barn Croft	1a.0.00	
		Red Field and Moor Field Close	38a.3.26	
		Sand Field Close	17a.0.00	
		Pasture Close	31a.2.09	
		Total	103a.0.31	(£108.05.0)

THOMAS WRIGHT				
'Abbey land' (=	8s.0			8s.0
Little Rushy Close				
or Doe Park)				
		HOUSE and garden		
		Meadow	1a.1.00	
		Cowgate	1a.1.00	
		Total	2a.1.00	(£3.15.0)
WIDOW WELSH				
'Abbey land'	16s.0.			£1.01.4
(Coalhouse Close)				
Newhams Close	12s.0			
		MATTHEW WELSH		
		HOUSE, homestead		£2.00.0
		Stanhope Close	3a.1.36	
		Cowgate	1a.1.00	
		Total	4a.2.36	(£7.05.0)
MRS. WOOD				
'Abbey lands'				
(Seven Acres Close)	18s.8			
MESSRS. ROBERTS of Nottingham				
Leather mills	£3.14.8			
THOMAS STEVENSON				
Abbey House etc.	£14.19.4			
Greens	16.0			
WILLIAM WILKINSON				
Odd House etc.	£10.16.8			
MR. HALL	£5.07.8			
MR. D. DRAKE	£1.00.0			
Late Deveralls	4.07.8			
Nether grounds	23.05.4			
The Rounds	12.0			
Ledgett Wong	3.01.4			
JOSEPH NEWTON	8.0			
JOSEPH BLACK	12.8			
HAGUE AND JAMES	£4.18.8			
MR. JOHN CHAMBERLAIN				£11.09.4
		Upper Farm		2.13.4
		HOMESTEAD	3a.0.00	
		DO. to Lower house	1a.0.00	

	Mortons Meadow	11a.3.16	
	Keetons meadow	9a.0.16	
	Meer Close	5a.3.00	
	Beeston Close	2a.0.00	
	Brickwall Close	2a.2.08	
	Sandfield Close	17a.0.00	
	Beck Field Close	25a.1.15	
	Pasture land	32a.0.00	
	Total	109a.2.17	(£104.13.9)
WILLIAM SHAW (Widow Shaw in 1768)|			£11.18.4
	HOMESTEAD	1a.0.00	
	Reedy Close	9a.1.06	
	Keetons Close	10a.1.20	
	Alwell Field Close	13a.3.02	
	Moor Field and		
	Red Field Close	30a.3.33	
	Meadow Close	19a.2.28	
	Total	98a.0.06	(£90.00.0)
JNO. BRADSHAW			£7.18.0
	HOMESTEAD	1a.0.00	
	Carlholmes	1a.3.34	
	Meer Close	5a.3.23	
	Bacon Close	6a.1.15	
	Lee Close	4a.2.07	
	Bull Piece	2.24	
	Beck field Close	18a.0.19	
	Red Field Close	11a.0.16	
	Pasture Close	14a.3.30	
	Total	64a.2.08	(£49.14.0)
MR. JOHN HOPKINS			£7.01.4
	Upper Farm		2.13.4
	HOMESTEAD	2a.0.00	
	Bullmires	4a.1.31	
	Bacon Close	6a.3.26	
	Stonewall Close	2a.3.07	
	Beck Field Close	16a.0.00	
	Red Field Close	11a.1.08	
	Sand Field Close	10a.0.00	
	Meadow and		
	Pasture Close	27a.3.20	
	Total	81a.1.12	(£72.6.6)
JACOB DOBBS	HOUSE and croft		
	Quarrel Close	4a.0.00	
	Cowgate	1a.1.00	
	Total	5a.1.00	(£6.10.0)

GEORGE WOMBWELL (Widow Wombwell in 1768-69)	HOUSE and garden		
	Bullmires Close	1a.3.29	
	Cowgate	1a.1.00	
	Total	3a.0.29	(£1.03.4)
HENRY BROWN			8s.8d
	HOUSE and croft		
	Spring Close	2a.3.32	
	Cowgate	1a.1.00	
	Total	4a.0.32	(£5.10.0)
STEPHEN WESTON	HOMESTEAD	1a.0.00	
	Spring Close	3a.3.30	
	Briging Close	2a.2.34	
	Cheney Lane Close	3a.0.14	
	Paper Mill Close	1a.1.27	
	Leen Moor Close	3.10	
	Beck Field Close	24a.0.00	
	Meadow Close	15a.0.00	
	Total	51a.3.35	(£39.07.0)
WIDOW PORTER	HOMESTEAD	1a.0.00	
	Robinson Close	3a.2.32	
	Mare Close	5a.0.21	
	Hanging Close	1a.1.21	
	Alwell Field Close	8a.1.04	
	Beck Field Close	20a.2.26	
	Red Field Close	12a.0.00	
	Meadow Close	22a.0.00	
	Total	74a.0.24	(£63.10.0)

Tenants of the Gregory estate are included above only if they held land of that estate in the area of the University campus, or if they also occupied land of the Milward estate.

In the last column above the sums in parenthesis are rents in 1768-69, and those not in parenthesis are Land Tax assessments for 1780.

Other land

Occupier	*Owner*	*Land Tax 1780*	
JOHN MOORE gent.	John Moore	£ 2.09.4	Hill Closes and Far Broom Close
WILLIAM LOWE gent.	William Lowe	10.4	Far Field Close
ELIAS ROBERTS	Thomas Brentnall	1.17.4	
WILLIAM HODGES	William Hodges	18.0	

APPENDIX 14

NOTES IN EXTENSION OF FIGURE 29

1. **Thomas Wright** held land of both Milward and Gregory estates - from Gregorys a cottage with a garden in Lenton, with an acre of meadow and a cowgate, and from Milward a small close of 1½ acres called Little Rushy Close in 1780, but which had been Doe Park in 1684. There was no change between 1780 and 1797.

2. **Widow Welsh**, widow of Matthew Welsh, also held of both estates in 1780. In 1769 Matthew held of the Gregory estate a small holding with a cottage, a cowgate and Stanhope Close of 3½acres. In 1780 Widow Welsh held of the Milward estate 'Abbey land' taxed at 16s. 0d., and Newhams Close. In 1743 the 'Abbey land' was Great Tims, rented for £4. Thomas Newham then occupied the Lesser Rushy Close for £3.10s.0d. a year, and in 1731 this was a part of Rushy Meadow, and 4 acres in area. In 1684 a piece of meadow ground of 4 acres, part of Rushie Close, had been occupied by Christopher Rest, while Teme Close, also 4 acres, was held by Widow Jane Ross. Widow Welsh's Milward estate land passed to Thomas Rowe in 1783, and he was still the occupier in 1798, though the land had been bought by the Gregory estate: but the tax had been reduced from £1.8s.0d. to £1.1s.4d. for reasons unknown.

3. **Mrs. Wood's** land tax of 1780 was transferred unchanged in 1792-94 to Miss Hannah Wood, and in 1795 and 1796 it was due from the executors of Mrs. Wood. But the land cannot be identified in the 1797 land tax schedule, and it was probably re-let by the estate after Mrs. Wood's death to form part of the holding of Messrs. Killingley and Green, a hosiery and bleaching firm, who were taxed first in 1796, paying £1.8s.0d., and were listed in 1797 as occupying the Seven Acres Meadow. W. and S. Stretton built a bleach yard there in 1797, but Green became bankrupt in the same year, and the land was put up for auction in December 1797 by Miss Milward, but appears to have been unsold.

4. Messrs. **Roberts** of Nottingham in 1780 had become Messrs. Ellis, Roberts and Co. by 1794, and were given a 21-year lease. The property was industrial land alongside the river Leen and the Nottingham canal, used by the early leather industry that later developed into Thomas Bayley and Co. of Leengate. The area was about 4 acres, and is detailed in the 1798 survey.

5. **Thomas Stevenson** paid land tax of £15.7s.4d. from 1780 to 1797 for his farm land which was mainly formed into Lenton Hall park in the early 19th century, with some additions and subtractions. Stevenson lived at the old Abbey House, and occupied the farm from 1775 to 1799, He paid land tax of £18.18s.0d. in his last year because additional land bought by John Wright (who had not yet built Lenton Hall) - the triangular Hind and Far Abbey Field - was added to the farm, while the Lenton Firs land had not yet been sold to T.W.Watson, and was therefore included. The area of the farm in 1797-98 was about 135 acres, of which 90 acres a century earlier were parts of the 'Far and Near Abbey Fields'. The farm formed a consolidated block of land extending south-west from the old Beck Field boundary, but not as far as the Sawley turnpike until Wright bought more land. The land tax schedule of 1780 to 1782 distinguished 16s. a year paid in tax by Stevenson in respect of The Greens in Dunkirk - land called in the 1798 survey the Lane Close (2a.2.34) - and the Rounds Close or Barley's Close, which had been occupied by Robert Barley in 1684.

6. **William Norris** rented substantial areas of land from both Milward and Gregory estates in 1780. His farmstead in Lenton village was in the Gregory estate, and the land attached to it included some 56 acres in the former open arable fields and a 31-acre pasture in the Holmes, east of Trent Lane (also enclosed in 1768) which became a large allotment site in the 19th century. In 1743 Norris had held Milward estate lands for an annual rent of £23 - the Hill Close, Hill Close Gutt, two closes, both called Little Tims Close, Churchyard Close and Rounds close. By 1798 the two Little Tims closes were occupied by Thomas Stevenson,

the two Hill Closes, Hill Close Gutt and Rounds Close by William Wigley of Dunkirk Farm, and Churchyard Close by Richard Nutt: but the land tax did not change, so this redistribution dates from before 1780. Between 1789 and 1791 William Norris's land in the Milward estate was taken over by David Drake, and added to his large Dunkirk farm occupied by William Wigley in 1794.

7. **Mr. David Drake** was charged £32.6s.4d. for land tax on his Milward estate land holding in 1780 - over one-third of the total tax on the whole estate. His lands included most of the Trent valley area that had been priory demesne - essentially the 'Dunkirk Farms'. From 1782 onwards most was held in two 21-year leases dated 15 March and 5 April 1782, at annual rents respectively of £94.12s.0d. and £88. Drake's tax in 1782 was £32.14.4d, but subsequently only £20.9s.8d., the difference being accounted for by the farm occupied by James White. In 1791 William Wigley replaced Drake as occupier of the major part of the latter's leaseholding, together with the Milward estate land that had been occupied earlier by William Norris. White's farmhouse, described with his lands (exactly half Drake's 'Nether grounds' holding) was probably built in 1783 on the tax evidence. It is described together with his land holding in the pre-sale terrier of 1798.

The 1780 tax return breaks down Drake's holding into five items.

a) Lands called 'late Deverals' were probably those occupied in 1743 by Mr. John Deverall and Mr. Handley at a rent of £23.10s.0d., and called Tamworth, Nether Tamworth and Nether Wheatcroft. In 1731 Tamworth pasture occupied 16 acres and Nether Wheatcroft Meadow 12 acres. They were then part of the jointure of the widowed Dame Sarah Winford. In 1684 Nether Wheatcroft, 12 acres, had been meadow occupied by Huntin' Handley, who also had the 16 acres of Tamworth, described as a close 'or piece of Park ground'. In 1798 this compact area of about 37 acres comprised: Nether Tamworth (4a.3.20), East Tamworth (6a.2.26), West Tamworth (6a.1.34) and South Tamworth (4a.1.3), together with a farmhouse (Dunkirk Farm) and The Wheatcroft or Nether Wheatcroft in two parts, with buildings (14a.2.9). In 1798 this area was combined with half the 'Nether grounds' discussed below to form the major part of William Wigley's farm.

b) Ledgett Wong lay beyond the Blotoff or Blotah Dyke (followed later by the Beeston canal) in the north-west angle of the junction of Chain Lane with Trent Lane. In 1684 it was 13 acres of meadow ground occupied by Joseph Marsh, and in 1743 it was occupied by a Mr.Beardsley together with The Greens at a rent of £21.10s.0d.. The £3.1s.4d. land tax probably covered also the 5-acre Priors Meadow.

c) The Rounds were not included in the two leases of 1782, but were occupied in 1798 by William Wigley as tenant-at-will.

d) 'Nether grounds' occupied the whole area between Beeston Hassocks and Blotoff Dyke from the Beeston boundary to The Greens and beyond, with the exception of some land along the boundary with Beeston. Divided in 1798 equally between William Wigley and James White, with about 87 acres each, the former with a new cottage and the latter with a new farmhouse and an 'ancient cott', they appear to have been recently created holdings. White's land had been shared in 1743 between Thomas Partridge and Mr. Chamberlain.

e) There was a land tax of £1 on unidentified land, possibly Prior's Meadow.

In 1783 all these lands of David Drake, together with a small holding of Joseph Newton, were taxed a total of £32.16s.4d.. By 1784 James White's farm was detached and taxed at £12.4s.8d., and the remainder, augmented in 1789-90 by land earlier held by William Norris, was by 1794, when William Wigley took over, taxed at £25.8s.8d..

8. **Joseph Newton's** small holding of 1780 (tax 8s.0d.) appears to have been absorbed into David Drake's holding in 1782, when Drake's tax increased from £32.6s.4d. to £32.14s.4d.. Newton was not included in the land tax schedules thereafter.

9) **William Wilkinson** in 1780 was said to hold Milward land taxed at £10.16s.8d.

a year, but this appears to have been an error, and his true tax was £5.7s.8d., which was for the farm attached to the Odd House (later Lenton Abbey). Wilkinson was actually born at this farm in 1759 when his father was the tenant, and returned there as a worker in 1774. John Clayton replaced him as tenant in 1790. Clayton died a few weeks before the 1798 survey, which showed him to have held just over 100 acres.

10) A **Mr. Hall** occupied Trent Wong (now Grove Farm sports grounds) in 1780, taxed at £10.16s.8d. a year, and was replaced as tenant in 1787 by Abel Smith of Wilford; he by Robert Smith in 1796; and he by Samuel Smith in 1797. Though high quality meadow it is surprising to find this area of flooding washland taxed more than twice as heavily as Lenton Abbey farm.

11) The tax of 12s.8d. on **Joseph Black** in 1780 and on William Black from 1782 to 1797 was for a field that was put up for auction in 1797. It was bought by Black himself, though whether at the auction of 27 December 1797 or from Pares and Paget on Lady Day 1798 is not clear. In 1798 Black was charged tax of £1.5s.0d. and in 1799 of £1.5s.0d. for the Five Acre Close (area 6a.0.20) and a meadow of 6 acres in two parts later containing the site of Poplar Farm.

12) **Messrs. Hague and James** were succeeded in 1782 by Messrs. Hopkin and Hooton (or Houghton) as occupiers of land that extended to some 72 acres in early 1798, carrying a land tax of £4.18s.8d.. Richard Hooton was a Nottingham innkeeper, and William Hopkin the elder of Lenton is not to be confused with his brother John, a Lenton farmer who had no 'Abbey land' and whose son kept the White Hart inn at Lenton, or with his son William Hopkin the younger, also an innkeeper, but only 12 years old when Hopkin and Hooton first held the land. Their holding extended from Derby Road near Lenton Hurst southwards in a widening tract to Cut Through Lane, and included much of the area now commonly called 'the downland', east of the old line of the Sawley turnpike, together with the Lenton House estate. There was a small farmstead alongside Beeston Lane, recently demolished, and some evidence to suggest that Hopkin and Hooton may have been primarily horse breeders.

APPENDIX 15

MISS MILWARD'S ESTATE IN 1798

[N.U.M.D. Mi 3 E 4 (1867)]

Occupier	*Premises*	*Area* a.r.p.	*Notes about 1684*
Richard NUTT	The Church Yard Close	4.1.26	Wherein the priory of Lenton formerly stood.
	S. part of the Mill or Great Pond Yard	3.14	
Francis CROSSLAND	N. part of the Mill Close	3.15	Parcel of a close called the Abbey Orchard in 1684, since divided by the Nottm. canal.
William BLACK of Nottingham	The Five Acres Close,## a meadow	6.0.02	In two parts

Thomas ELLIS Thos.ROBERTS Isaac BAYLEY Samuel ROBERTS (under 21-yr. lease from 25 March 1797 at £50 a year)	*Messuage or tenement* with the croft or close in which it stands, being the N. of the Mill or Great Pond Yard	3.04	
	Water mill on R.Leen, now a leather mill, in the Mill or Great Pond Yard		Formerly a corn mill, heretofore a paper afterwards a thimble mill, now used as a leather mill.
	Messuage or tenement with croft or close in which it stands, called Little Pond Yard, together	1.24	
	Water mill or leather mill on the R.Leen in Little Yard		Near or adjoining to the leather mill in the N. part of the Great Pond Yard.
	Davit's Close and southern, remaining part of Mill Close called Abbey Orchard in 1684	2.2.33	
William WIGLEY (under 21-yr. lease to David Drake from 5 April 1782 at £88 a year)	*Messuage, tenement or farm house* (later Dunkirk Farm)		
	The Nether Tamworth	4.3.20	In 1684 the 4 closes were in 2 closes - Tamworth Close and Nether Tamworth Close.
	The East Tamworth	6.2.26	
	The West Tamworth	6.1.34	
	The South Tamworth	4.1.03	
	The Wheatcroft or Nether Wheatcroft with buildings	14.2.09	Now in 2 parts
	The Leget or Ledgett Wong	11.3.04	
	The Prior's Meadow	5.0.07	
The same Wm. WIGLEY (under 21-yr. lease to David Drake from March 1782 at £94.12.0 a year)	Newly erected *Cott or tenement*		
	The Barn Close	19.3.12	In 2 parts
	The Rye Close	22.1.11	In 2 parts: in one close in 1684
	The Great Littling Meadow	11.3.31	All part of the Great Littling Meadow or The Littling in 1684
	The Littling Meadow or Littling Hook	2.3.39	
	South Littling Meadow or Jervas Meadow	6.1.06	
	SW. part of Cow Close	11.2.10	All part of Cow Close in 1684
	Southern alder plantation	3.27	
	SE. part of Cow Close	10.3.00	
	Small part of Cow Close adjoining	1.20	
The same Wm. Wigley (as tenant at will.)	The Rounds or Rounds Close or Barley's Close	8.1.13	In 1684 the south part of a close called The Greens
	The Lane Close	3.2.00	

James WHITE	*New message, tenement or farm house and ancient cotte*		
	North Gorsey Close	13.0.22	In 1684 together
	South Gorsey Close	10.1.17	called Gossie Close
	Nether Littling Meadow or Littling	3.0.07	In 1684 all residue
	Middle Littling Meadow or Littling	8.0.09	of Great Littling Meadow or Littling
	Great Littling Meadow or Littling	8.3.10	
	North Cow Close	7.3.07	In 1684 residue
	Second part of Cow Close	15.0.23	of the
	Northern alder plantation	3.26	Cow Close
	West Round Close	6.2.26	in 2 parts
	Middle Round Close	6.3.33	In 1684 all in 3
	East Round Close	5.3.23	closes called The Round Close together
NOTTINGHAM CANAL CO.	Parcels used for canal and towing paths	1.0.09	
TRENT CANAL CO.	Parcels used for canal and tow path		
MR. BLACK	*Ancient cotte and garden*	36	
JNO.BEARDSLEY	*Ancient cotte and garden*	06	
Philip WHEATLEY	*Ancient cotte and garden*	03	
The late John CLAYTON	*Message, tenement or farm## house* [The Odd House]		
	The Far Fan Broom Close	9.0.12	In 1684 in 5 closes
	The Near Fan Broom Close	10.0.22	called:
	The Middle Broom Close with stackyard and lane	12.2.00	Far Broom Close Broom Close (2)
	The Near Broom Close or Home Close with yard, garden and buildings	6.2.33	Little Broom Close Broom Meadow
	The Four Acres or Broom	4.1.00	
	The Long Meadow or Broom Meadow	8.1.04	
	The Eight Acres or Broom Close	8.0.22	
	The Home Abbey Field	11.1.09	In 1684 parts of
	The Second Abbey Field	12.1.18	Near Abbey Field
Thomas STEVENSON	*The Farm or Barn Yard* and Home Parcel	1.1.11	
	The Oxhouse and Dog or Dayhouse Closes, now laid together	4.2 25	In 1684 the N and remaining part of a close, The Greens

	The Lane Close	2.2.34	
	The Broom Close or Meadow	10.0.13	
	The Calf Close	4.2.28	In 1684 called Greesons Close
	Wards Close	5.0.20	
	The Dove House Close or Home Pasture	10.3.11	In 1684 called Dovecote Close and Salter Close
	The pasture of Great Tims Tines or Ternes	2.3.24	
	The Little Tines or Ternes Close	1.0.00	
	Ternes Meadow or Close	1.1.10	
	The Abbey Field in 2 parts	13.0.11	Next the Turnpike Close or Little Abbey Field
	The Abbey Field or	22.2.20	in 2 parts
	The Lodge Field	17.2.10	against Derby Road
	The Sand Hill and Sand Hill Field together	19.2.22	
	The Pitt Field	11.0.00	in 2 parts
	The Six Acres Close	6.2.17	In 1684 all the six closes above were parts of the Far and Near Abbey Fields.
The late John CLAYTON	Close called the Hind and Far Abbey Fields ##	17.2.12	In 1684 part of the Far Abbey Field
William BLACK of Nottingham	The Rushy Meadow or Close	4.1.24	
	*The two High Field Closes	13.1.15	
	*The Highfield Meadow	3.0.02	in 3 parts
Thomas ROWE	The Little Rushy Close	3.0.32	
	Coal house Close, near the Bridge	2.0.00	In 1684 called Carl-holme or Calf Close
Thomas WRIGHT	The Little Rushy Park	1.2.03	In 1684 called Doe Park
Messrs.HOPKIN and HOOTON	*Cotte* [Lenton House farm]		
	The Turnpike Close or Little Abbey Field	6.2.24	In 1684 part of Far Abbey Field
	The Fourteen Acres	14.3.03	In 1684 called High Hill Close
	Fourteen Acres Meadow	14.0.29	In 1684 called Lower Hill Close
	The Lower High Field or Barn ground	7.0.22	In 1684 in one close and called
	The Home Field	8.2.23	Hill Field Close
	The South High Field	7.2.31	adjoining the Home Field
	The North High Field	7.3.25	In 1684 one close called the Lower High Field

William WIGLEY	The North High Close	4.2.29	In 1684 one close
	The South High Close	4.2.00	called Hill Close
	*The Duck or Gutt Meadow	3.3.11	
Messrs. HOPKIN and HOOTON	*The Turnpike Close or Gutt	7.2.00	
J.W.KILLINGLEY	The Seven Acres Close or Meadow ##	7.2.01	in 2 parts

Notes

* These four closes in 1684 were in three closes called Hill Close or Gutt Meadow, High Field Close and the Nether High Close.

Items included in the auction of 27 December 1797.

Most of the notes referring to 1684 are taken from N.U.M.D., Wadsworth Ms. 52, where they are more numerous than those printed in Godfrey's transcript [Godfrey 1884]. Some appear to be dubious when compared with versions of the 1684 terrier given in N.U.M.D., Mi 3 E 4 and N.U.M.D., Wadsworth 50.

APPENDIX 16

SOME CHANGES IN LAND OWNERSHIP AND OCCUPATION, 1802-1832

Details are derived mainly from the annual land tax assessments

In the second column the owner's name is printed in CAPITALS and the occupier's in lower case.

Holding or estate	*1802*	*Land Tax*	*Changes 1802-1832*
Dunkirk Farm (White's)	JOHN WRIGHT Himself	£9.14.9 9.18.4 9.14.9 9.11.0	Unchanged to 1809. Then 1810-11 Robert Cheetham: 1812 late Robt. Cheetham: 1813-20 Alice Wood: 1821-32 Alice Wood and Cheetham
Dunkirk Farm (Wigley's)	JOHN WRIGHT Wm. Wigley	13.17.1 13.17.3 13.07.0	Unchanged to 1808. Then 1809-11 occupier J.Wright 1813-18 Thomas Robinson 1819 1820-21 T.Robinson, J.Hawley and Mr. Swain 1823 Hawley replaced by MacHage
Lenton Hall	JOHN WRIGHT Himself	15.02.9	Unchanged to 1832(record ends) but in 1808 part of Abbey Field Close added, occupied from 1812 by Thomas Robinson (see above).
The 'downland'	JOHN WRIGHT Himself	5.01.8	Unchanged to 1815. 1816-25 F. Cheetham 1826-32 S. Cheetham This was the 14-Acre Close and 14-Acre Meadow. Cheethams farmed Lenton Abbey.
Lenton Firs	ELIZABETH WATSON Herself	4.02.0 3.04.0	1803-13 unchanged: then LORD MIDDLETON 1819-23 Alexander Foxcroft 1828 (or earlier) to 1832 Dr. John Storer. Part to Wollaton Park.
Lenton House	MATTHEW NEEDHAM Himself	3.13.0	1803-32 unchanged. 1805 - tax redeemed
Lenton Fields	MATTHEW NEEDHAM Himself	- 10.4½	Part of James Green's land bought 1808-09. Redeemed 1810.
Lenton Grove	FRANCIS EVANS Himself	2.18.8	£1.10.0 for his Far Broom Close plus £1.08.8 for Milward land added in 1798. 1803 redeemed. 1803-15 unchanged 1816-32 F.EVANS' EXECUTORS

Highfield	JOSEPH LOWE Himself	4.08.0 19.0	1803 tax redeemed. 1803-13 no change 1814-17 J.H.Lowe 1818-20 his executors 1821-32 Alfred Lowe 1828-32 Alfred Lowe for additional land, probably the four Hill Closes
Lenton Abbey	JAMES GREEN Himself	8.12.2 6.17.3	1803-07 unchanged 1808-13 . Balance of £1.4.5½ for Abbey Field Close and 10s.4½ due from J.Wright and M.Needham. 1818 still James Green 1819-20 T.Ray, T.Hall and J. Cheetham 1821 T.Ray, Mr. Roberts, J. Cheetham 1823 Cheetham, Ray, Roberts and Hall. 1824 tax redeemed 1821-31 Ray held by lease 1832 LORD MIDDLETON bought, Isaac Fisher occupied house
Trent Wong	SAMUEL SMITH Himself	10.16.8	1803 redeemed tax 1803-09 no change 1810 Messrs. Breedon, Facon and Williamson 1811-21 Edward Facon 1822-23 John Williamson and Robert Gregory 1823-32 John Wilkinson
Five Acre Close	WILLIAM BLACK Himself	1.05.0	1803-05 unchanged 1806 bought and occupied by WM. SURPLICE until 1829 1829 Widow Surplice. Passed Gregory estate in exchange
Seven Acre Close	MR. LOCK J.W.Killingley	1.05.7	1803 tax redeemed 1804-08 unchanged 1809-15 LOCK'S EXECUTORS 1818 James Nutt replaced Killingley 1819 James Nutt and M.Nixon 1820 approx. NUTT bought and occupied himself
Leather mill	PARES AND PAGET Ellis and Roberts	1.02.6	1803 tax redeemed 1803-19 unchanged. Then Thos. Turner, Ellis, Roberts and Co.
The Priory (Abbey Orchard)	WM. STRETTON Himself	4s.8	1803 tax redeemed 1803-21 unchanged 1822 James Lee senior 1823-32 William Stretton
Mill Close	WM. STRETTON Himself	15s.0	1803 tax redeemed 1803-15 unchanged

Additions to John Wright's estate

'Late Longdon's' See Appendix 17	Purchased 1803	8s.8	1803-08 unchanged, W.Wigley 1808-19 Wrights 1820-27 T.B.Milnes
'Late Upton's' See Appendix 18	Purchased 1804	£5.16.0	1804-19 Richard Price 1819 J.B.Milnes, I.Armitage et al. 1820 tax redeemed Sold for building
'Late Green's'	Acquired by exchange 1808-09 by Beeston Inclosure Award	£1.04.5½	1812-16 Thomas Robinson 1822 onwards Robert Taylor

APPENDIX 17

'LATE LONGDON'S PROPERTY' ADDED TO JOHN WRIGHT'S ESTATE IN 1803.

Bramcote Manor was purchased by John Sherwin of Nottingham in the 17th century, and the last of his male descendants was a John Sherwin who owned and lived in a house at the end of Pilcher-gate, Nottingham, 'a person of very retired and somewhat penurious habits'. When he died without issue his estate devolved to John Longdon, his eldest sister's son, who took the name of Sherwin, and built Bramcote Hills house in the early 19th century. It was from this John Longdon (alias Sherwin) that John Wright acquired the land in question.

He married Charlotte Mettam daughter of a wealthy Nottingham mercer and draper, 'and by her had John Sherwin Sherwin, the present lord of the manor of Bramcote' according to Bailey's History of 1853. In 1854 John Sherwin Sherwin inherited the Gregory estates of Harlaxton and Lenton and took the name of Gregory, being a distant relative of the last generation of Gregorys, who all died without issue - as did John Sherwin Sherwin Gregory himself in 1869 (see Chapter IV and Appendix 9). John Sherwin Gregory therefore left his estate to his wife Catherine for life. She was described as 'of Bramcote Hills and Harlaxton' in 1883 [Wright] and 1885 [White]. She remained at Bramcote Hills until her death in 1892. She was a daughter of Robert Holden of Nuthall Temple, and from her the property in Bramcote passed on similar terms to her brother, Captain Henry Holden. Captain Holden was Chief Constable of Nottinghamshire from 1856 to 1892, and lived at Lenton House from 1862 to 1865 before moving to Bramcote (see Chapter VIII), where he lived at Bramcote Grove (earlier purchased by Alfred Lowe and briefly occupied by his son Alfred Hurst Lowe in 1841, and by 1844 owned and occupied by Laurence Hall). Henry lived at Bramcote Hills in 1894 [White] and 1897 [Wright]. Later tenants included Horace Arthur Fisher [1904], and Ernest Wentworth Claye in 1908 and 1912 [Kelly] before moving to Lenton House. The third surviving son of Captain Holden, Major E.Frank Holden - of Bramcote Grove in 1912 (Kelly) but Bramcote Hills in 1922 [Kelly] - held the Bramcote estate in 1917 on a life interest. An interesting occupier in 1936 was Fitzherbert Wright.

Miss Longdon, sister of John Sherwin Gregory, inherited the old Handley properties, and herself built and endowed an almshouse for four poor women in 1852.

APPENDIX 18

PROPERTY PURCHASED BY JOHN WRIGHT IN 1804, CALLED 'LATE UPTON'S'

John Wright paid £1.8s.8d. in land tax from 1804 for property in Lenton purchased from Charles Upton, a Derby attorney. The area was between 20 and 30 acres, and although none was part of the present University campus its tenurial origins are of some interest.

In the first decade of the 17th century, before William Gregory purchased the Crown manor of Lenton, a number of small, but long Crown leases of cottages and land in Lenton were granted by Letters Patent to several persons. After each had passed through the hands of several owners very rapidly they were purchased between 1613 and 1617 by Leonard Nixe, a Nottingham merchant. Godfrey [1884 210-11] gave details of six such properties, but wrongly described them as parts of the priory demesne. Leonard Nixe, who was Sheriff of Nottingham in 1591 and Mayor in 1617, 1624 and 1631, conveyed all his tenements and lands in Lenton on 1 January 1633 to William Nixe, merchant, and Richard Hardmeat, skinner, both of Nottingham, for £200. Alderman William Nixe (Sheriff in 1619 and Mayor in 1636,1643, 1644 and 1649), son of Robert Nixe of Wilford, the 'old Mr. Nixe' referred to in 1630 by Sir Wiliam Hicks, (see Chapter IV) married Mrs. Millicent Sacheverill in 1615/16, and lived in an old mansion on Bridlesmith-gate, later the site of the post office. They had several daughters but only one son, Robert, who left as his heir only a daughter, Sarah, and when Alderman William Nixe died in September 1650 all his Lenton property 'passed under settlement' to his eldest daughter, Tabitha.

Tabitha Nixe married Thomas Charlton of Chilwell. Their grandson, also Thomas, died unmarried in 1703, and barred entail of part of the Chilwell estate, settling it on his half-brother, Nicholas Charlton (the last male Charlton of Chilwell Hall) and his heirs, with the remainder in default of issue to his four sisters and their heirs. But Nicholas died in 1748 also unmarried. One of the four sisters of Thomas, Lucy, was married to John Garland of the Hall in Lenton village, who had inherited a small estate in Lenton from his father. John died in 1721, and the heirs to the Lenton property in 1748 were the two surviving daughters of John and Lucy Garland - Rebecca Garland, unmarried, and Lucy, wife of George Brentnall, gentleman, of Derby. Rebecca died in 1769, so the whole property passed to the Brentnalls. This was immediately after it had qualified for an allotment totalling about 41 acres in the Lenton inclosure award of 1768. In the next generation Thomas Brentnall of Spondon sold a share of the property in 1794 for an annuity to Charles Upton of Derby, and soon after 1800 he sold it off in detached lots, mainly to John Wright and Lord Middleton. Wright bought about 16 acres of the lower part of the former Alwell Field, enclosed in 1768. He resold much of this land for building development in 1815 at ten times the price he paid for it, and New Lenton was built upon it. On the rest Francis Wright provided the sites for the church, schools and recreation ground. John Wright also bought enclosed meadow called Morton Nook Meadow in Dunkirk as part of the transaction of 1804.

APPENDIX 19

ALLOTMENTS TO FRANCIS EVANS, JOSEPH LOWE AND JOHN WRIGHT IN BEESTON 1809

Land description	*Ref.*	*Area*	*Exchanged with*
FRANCIS EVANS			
Plot in Tottle Brook Field	35	17a.0.16	[Surrounds 2 Brook Closes: new University flats now on it]
do.	112	13a.2.26	[F.B. playing field, University Boulevard. Hassocks Closes NE.]
Plot of meadow	223	4a.3.14	[Alongside canal]
do.	227	13a.0.13	
Hassocks Close	140	1a.2.19	Richard Sheldon
Brook Close	34	2.18	Richard Sheldon
Total		**50a.3.26**	

For his lands and rights of common and two ancient enclosures, the GleadWongs, exchanged to John Fellows.

Land description	*Ref.*	*Area*	*Exchanged with*
JOSEPH LOWE			
(Plot in Far Field	22	7a.0.00	Exchanged for —)
Far Field Close	235	3a.3.21	William Lowe of Nottingham
JOHN WRIGHT			
(Plot in Tuttle Brook Field	31	6a.3.38	Exchanged for —)
The Brook Close	32	3a.3.33	Adjoining: purchased earlier.
Abbey Field Close	236	10a.2.17	James Green
Hassocks Close	115	5a.0.23	P.S.Broughton
do.	116	5a.0.35	do.
do.	117	5a.0.02	do.
do.	118	3a.0.16	do.
(Hassock Close	151	5a.2.32	Exchanged for —)
(Pasture allotment	161a	1a.0.12	119-120)
Hassocks Close	119	6a.2.09	Trustees of the Poor
do.	120		of Beeston
do.	123	2a.2.07	John Hodges
do.	125	4a.0.26	do.
do.	128	3a.1.33	Henry Attenborough
do.	129	1a.2.07	Thomas Gelsthorpe
do.	130	1a.2.12	John Fellows
do.	131	1a.1.34	Thomas Gelsthorpe
do.	132	3.04	do.
do.	135	6a.0.24	William Lowe
Rounds Close	233	8a.3.18	P.S.Broughton
Pasture allotment	161	2.30	Purchased from Jos. Barker

Total 57a.0.11 in 16 parcels

For lands, rights of common and 5 closes - the Thorndike Closes - exchanged to P.S.Broughton.

APPENDIX 20

EDWARD LOWE AND THE PROPOSED LAWSON OBSERVATORY

Nottingham has never had a public Observatory, so it is of some interest to record how nearly Edward Lowe came to founding one. He was a great admirer of Henry Lawson of Bath, and named his elder son after him. Lawson was a pioneer in the field of instrumental meteorology, the inventor of the Lawson thermometer stand - later replaced by the Stevenson screen - to provide a standard exposure for thermometers measuring air temperature and humidity, and a successful experimenter with self-recording instruments.

Lowe's original scheme envisaged an observatory on high ground north of the city. The Borough Records for 1851 (22 December, p.87) noted that a collection of meteorological and astronomical instruments, together with 1,000 guineas was offered to the Corporation by Henry Lawson, through E.J.Lowe, on condition that £10,000 was raised to provide a house and an income of about £200 a year for an observer, to be administered by trustees. A committee was set up with the Duke of Newcastle as chairman. The Records of 1853 (1 October, p.98) show that the Council agreed to sell land to the Lawson Observatory Committee, either at the south-west end of the Forest, or on Coppice Farm adjoining Mapperley Plains, for £500.

On 1 May 1854 [Records 1854, 102-03] the Chamber Committee reported approval of the Observatory Committee's selection of 6 acres on Coppice Farm, and had submitted a memorial to the Treasury for approval of the sale for £100, which was given.Although a Directory for 1854 [Wright 1854 369] indicated that a government grant of £2,000, a grant of £500 from Nottingham Town Council and an endowment of £2,000 for an observer's salary from a public collection organized by the Duke of Newcastle's committee had been arranged, this was sadly premature, and from reports in the Nottingham Review of 7 August and 1 September it is apparent that government support was refused because Nottingham could not raise sufficient money, while two expert witnesses condemned the proposed site for the purposes of astronomy, and considered that the instruments were over-valued. On 29 September 1854 an advertisement appeared in the press offering subscribers their money back, less 4 per cent for expenses.

After this set-back Henry Lawson, in poor health, proposed to present his instruments to E.J.Lowe, the secretary of the Committee, who had recently built his house on Broadgate, Beeston (Broadgate House) with astronomical and meteorological observation in mind, and had called it The Observatory. Lowe declined to accept the gift because he still hoped and thought that the Lawson Observatory would be established: but a dispute over the money value of the instruments led to the decision to return the subscriptions to the public, and Lowe then accepted the instruments from the Bath observatory, with other objects and books. All were installed at Broadgate House between February and June 1855. Henry Lawson died in the same year. Fyfe described the instruments in his book 'Rambles round Nottingham' in 1856.

APPENDIX 21

THE STRETTONS AND 'THE PRIORY'

William Stretton was the architect and builder of Lenton Hall [Blackner 1815 (1985): Barley and Cullen 1975 38: Brand 1985]. A member of a talented and versatile family associated particularly with Lenton, he was the son, and the partner and successor in business of Samuel Stretton, who was born at Longdon near Lichfield in 1731/32, moved to Nottingham as a bricklayer in about 1750, and in 1754 married at Lenton Elizabeth Wombwell of Lenton. William, the eldest of their three sons and three daughters, was born in 1755. In due course he became his father's assistant in what had become a thriving building business, and in 1788-89 it was 'Messrs. Stretton' who tendered plans and specifications for the town gaol at Weekday Cross. In 1791, when William would have been 36, they were formally partners as S. and W.Stretton.

By 1799 Samuel Stretton, 'gentleman' had retired and lived at Pannier Row [Willoughby 1799]. He died in 1811, but William continued to work, probably until about 1825, when he was 70. For some 60 years, from about 1765, when Samuel leased waste ground on Carter-gate, until 1825, together or individually, Samuel and William were responsible for a wide variety of building work in the Nottingham area - houses, factories, public buildings including churches, bridges and roads - and William was even involved in building the first boat on the Nottingham canal, the 'Nottingham Castle' (1796), 67 feet long and carrying 70 tons. Especially in the 1790s it is difficult to know whether both were involved in their projects. Lengthy lists of their most noteworthy works, especially in the late 1780 and the 1790s were given by Godfrey [1884] and Brand [1985, 1988].

Samuel Stretton lived and operated his business on Long Row where by 1799 William had replaced him. In 1802 however William bought and built his house called The Priory on part of the site of the former Lenton Priory called the Abbey Orchard north of the Nottingham canal which had been in Miss Milward's estate (see Chapter V, Figure 31). In 1801 he already owned land occupied by Richard Nutt and taxed at 4s. 8d. a year. After living at 'The Priory' for some years he moved on 25 June 1814 to Standard Hill, Nottingham, where he was supervising development on the Duke of Newcastle's estate, but returned later to The Priory, where he died in 1828 aged 83.

As early as 1769 Samuel Stretton constructed at the bottom of Goose-gate what William believed to be the first purpose-built cotton mill in the country. He was able to tender, with others, for the new County Hall on High Pavement. Also in 1769 he was assessing plans for the repair of East Bridgford church. It could be said that Samuel Stretton was primarily a builder, working to the design of others. For example, Colwick Hall (1776), the grandstand on the (Forest) racecourse (1777) and alterations to the Assembly Room on Low Pavement (1790) were all for the architect John Carr of York, and Wilford Hall (1781) was designed for Samuel Smith the banker by William Henderson of Loughborough. Samuel took on work for the town and county authorities, for example on the Town Hall at Weekday Cross (1777) and on Stapleford bridge (1786) and Keyworth bridge (1789). His work on churches and bridges, including a number of 'assessments' of building estimates, testify to his abilities as civil engineer and quantity surveyor; but particularly after Samuel's retirement the Strettons' work was mainly to the designs of William Stretton himself.

William was an accomplished artist with an eye for detail accurately observed, and a map maker, and he acted as surveyor for the Newcastle family. He surveyed Nottingham Castle in 1800, and produced his 'Original plan of Nottingham' at 50 inches to 1 mile in about 1803-04 (now in the Nottinghamshire Archives Office) and a map of Nottingham Castle and its grounds with Nottingham Park and King's Meadow in 1805. He also took on the role of civic planner, controlling the 'superior' housing development on Standard Hill from the lease of 1807 onwards. His architectural work was very varied, and included renovation, for example on the front of the old Exchange building in 1815, in which masonry and carving was said to have been executed by Stretton himself. Some of his work as a monumental mason was to be found in the churchyard of St. Peter's, Oxton, and St. Andrew's, Skegby. His stoneyard was in Cow Lane (Clumber Street) at the corner with Parliament Street, on land leased from the Duke of Newcastle. He designed and built St. James' church, Standard Hill (1807-08), and three of the first houses built there between 1810 and 1814, the year in which he moved to Standard Hill from Lenton. He worked on several city inns including the Milton's Head , renovated and leased in 1781, and the New Inn on Long Row, rebuilt in 1797. In the 1790s he became, in effect, an unofficial borough surveyor, and in 1792-93, for example, prepared 31 plans and surveys for the borough council, to which he acted as consultant [Brand 1988].

The Strettons were innovators in the use of materials. They were the first Nottingham builders to import the thin blue slates of the Penrhyn quarries, Caernarvonshire - it is said in 1790 [Stretton Mss. 32 21; Brand 1988] although the route followed by the shipment would be interesting, some six years before the Nottingham canal opened. They also introduced the use of Mountsorrel 'granite' setts from Charnwood Forest for road making when the Hollowstone entrance to the town was widened in 1796-97 having earlier, in 1890, paved Sheep Lane which later became Market Street. Not surprisingly the versatile and innovative William Stretton was a member of the committee appointed to carry out the installations of the new Gas Light Company in 1818.

William Stretton became noted as an antiquarian, especially after he unearthed many medieval artifacts, particularly tiles (see Chapter II) associated with Lenton Priory when building his house on its site. His finds included seven pillars and the fine mid-12th century font now in Holy Trinity church, Lenton. Whether his interest was quickened by his excavations or whether he bought the site because of its historical interest is not known, but the present-day historian can only regret that he destroyed so much by his activities at the priory site. Brand [1988] describes his 'intense life-long passion for antiquities' and suggests that around 1800 William Stretton was 'probably the only serious antiquarian in the county', consulted by John Throsby in preparing his new edition of Thoroton's 'Antiquities of Nottinghamshire' [1790-96]. Although his reputed plan of the priory has not been found William left many papers and notebooks illustrated with his own sketches, relating particularly to the years 1800 to 1824, and now in Nottinghamshire Archives Office, after spending much of his leisure time in his last years 'in the collection of materials for a work on the history and antiquities of Nottinghamshire' which was never published. Some of his notes were edited and printed in 1910 [Robertson 1910]. He 'had a taste in articles of *vertu* of which, at the time of his death, he possessed an extensive museum, at all times open to the inspection of persons of kindred taste' [Godfrey 1884 205]. The notice of William Stretton's death in the Nottingham Journal of 15 March 1828 added that 'In him antiquarians have lost a fund of general and useful knowledge and the poor a warm and benevolent friend'.

But William Stretton was apparently much more than a successful architect, surveyor and builder, and amateur archaeologist and historian. In common with many other enterprising, able and ambitious men in the decades around 1800 he had business interests that extended well outside his professional field. Chapman [1967 150] described him as 'architect and cotton spinner', and he was also one of the four partners in the Cossall Foundry Company, with premises on the Erewash canal, a venture parallel to that of Butterley in which John Wright was involved. The two men would undoubtedly be acquainted for that reason, apart from the fact that both had premises on Long Row. 'The cotton spinners and ironmasters moved in the same social circles, and, indeed, a few outstanding entrepreneurs, notably Joseph Wilkes, William Stretton and the Evanses were active in both industries' [Chapman 1967 150-51].

William Stretton held several parish offices in Lenton - Overseer of the Poor and Surveyor of Highways in 1806 and churchwarden in 1810-16. In 1815 he was an Overseer of the Poor for Standard Hill, to which he had moved. He was closely associated with the churches of central Nottingham, especially as churchwarden at St. Mary's from Easter 1802 to Easter 1806. He put in tower vaulting there in 1812 and refaced the south aisle in 1818-20. He also altered the interior of St. Peter's church in 1812-13.

Susanna Lynham of Eakring (1757-1815) married William Stretton in June 1778. Their six children were given pseudo-classical names beginning with 'S'; Stella (1779-1818), Sempronius (1781-1842), Severus (1783-85), Salacia (b. 1784), Sabina (b. 1787) and Severus William Lynham (1793-1884). Their two surviving sons both had distinguished military careers and married into the aristocracy. Their careers were described by Godfrey [1884 206-209]. Lieut.Col. Sempronius Stretton, C.B., the elder, saw military service in Quebec (1801) and then, after some years in England, in Portugal from 1812. After the Peninsular War he was in the disastrous expedition to New Orleans (1814-15) and then in Flanders for Waterloo, after which he administered part of Paris. After service in Scotland and Ireland he retired, and travelled the continent for some years, though 'returning occasionaly to his residence in Lenton'. During his absences The Priory was let - for example, in 1832 (Glover 1832) and 1833 (Sutton: Poll Book 1833) to Thomas Jerram, though it was unoccupied in 1834. In 1821 Sempronius married the Hon. Catherine Jane Massey, daughter of General Lord Clarina, and after her early death the Hon. Anne Handcock, daughter of the second Viscount Castlemaine, but had no children. He died, aged 62, on 6 February 1842 and was buried at Bromley, Kent [Bailey 1853 iv 431]. The Priory was then unoccupied. It was inherited by his younger brother.

Lieut.Col. Severus Stretton, after joining the Notts. Militia in 1810 served with the 68th Light Infantry in Iberia from 1812, and was severely wounded at the battle of Vittoria in 1813. After recuperating at The Priory he saw further service in Ireland, and from 1812 in Canada; went to Gibraltar in 1825 with the 64th Regiment; and subsequently served in the West Indies and in Nova Scotia until 1843, being given command of his regiment in 1842. From 1848 to 1852 he commanded the 40th, his brother's old regiment. In 1851, the year before his retirement, he married the Hon. Catherine Adela de Courcy, youngest daughter of the 28th Lord Kinsale [Bailey 1853 iv 433]. He was still living in 1884 - with a musket ball still in his body; but he never lived at The Priory.

The Priory was occupied in the 1850s by John and Richard Place, cotton agents; from about 1860 to 1869 by John Bayley, until he emigrated to New Zealand (see Chapter X); and from 1869 until his death in 1879 by Benjamin Walker senior, founder of the Spring Close lace firm, father of the builder of Lenton Eaves, and collaborator with Thomas and John Bayley in educational and social work in Lenton. By 1884, after Walker's death, it was occupied by the Sisters of Nazareth as 'a house of refuge for the aged, sick and infantine poor of the neighbourhood'. More than a century later, and with large building extensions which now envelop it, The Priory still performs much the same function under the name of Nazareth House.

Ken Brand [1988] may be given the last word on William Stretton in the context of the University campus. 'The taste or spirit of William Stretton is most likely to be understood when one examines the 'Gothick' part of Hugh Stewart Hall, Nottingham University, built with its seven castellated bays as Lenton Hall for John Wright (1804)'.

APPENDIX 22

ICHABOD WRIGHT, ICHABOD CHARLES WRIGHT, CHARLES ICHABOD WRIGHT AND MAPPERLEY HALL

Lenton and Mapperley Halls, the only two residences for men of the University College through the 1930s, were the two major homes of the Wright family in the Nottingham area. Their size reflected the affluence of the family by the late 1790s through the growth of their banking business. Their eventual sale by members of the same family within a few months of each other in 1903 seems to have been the outcome of financial problems following the incorporation of Wrights' Bank into what is now Lloyds Bank in the later 1890s, and indicates a continuing close connection between the houses through the bank in a way that is not fully understood. The connection was to be revived in another form through their University College function.

The Mapperley estate of the 18th century, a consolidated holding with two messuage houses and about 100 acres of land plus extensive grazing rights, was advertised for sale by auction in the Nottingham Journal of 14 November 1772. Its 88 acres of meadow and pasture in 18 closes, together with 12 acres of arable land, were bought on 7 January 1773 by John Smith, the banker. He died in 1776, and his daughter Mary and her husband Thomas Wright were apportioned his Mapperley and Basford estates by a deed of partition among his heirs dated 20 May 1777.

Thomas Wright and his family lived in Nottingham town. In August 1790, just before his death, Thomas bought Mrs. Newdigate's house (now called Newdigate House) in Castle-gate and Hounds-gate, together with the paddock between Hounds-gate and Friars Lane upon which there was then only a barn. Newdigate House, a handsome late 17th century town house with a fashionable formal garden, had been bought in 1714 by Francis Newdigate, who died in 1723. A few years earlier it had been occupied by Marshal Talland, a French commander captured at Blenheim in 1704. Thomas Wright had the house substantially rebuilt by the Strettons - according to William Stretton - but he died in the same year. The house was resold in 1817 when his widow Mary died.

Thomas Wright was succeeded in ownership of the Mapperley estate in 1790 by his 23-year-old eldest son, Ichabod. Soon afterwards, in 1792, Ichabod obtained much additional land by the Basford Inclosure Act in Mapperley Park and Carrington, and he immediately began to build Mapperley Hall before he had any thought of marriage.

After unhappy schooldays, especially when aged 8 to 12 (in 1775-79) at Quorn (where Matthew Needham of Lenton House was a boarder from 1777 to 1782), 'kept in constraint and dread of a pedantic Master and a vulgar old woman, his wife', Ichabod entered the bank at the age of 15, and hated this too, working there from 9 a.m. to 7 p.m., 'confined like a prisoner'. He had been anxious to become a classical scholar, but his father wanted him in the bank, which he had to carry on after his father's death when he was 23. He read much, and made sure that his own sons had the classical education at Eton and Oxbridge that he had been denied.

Ichabod received half his father's share in the bank at an opportune time, and married Harriet Maria Day on his birthday, 28 January 1794. In his words Harriet was 'a woman who possessed every charm that could fascinate and delight a Lover, and every virtue that could adorn the character of a Wife'. They had 14 children, all born at Mapperley Hall between 1795 (Ichabod Charles) and 1810 (Lydia Sophia), including three pairs of twins, with only one child (Henry Horatio) dying in infancy. Later Harriet suffered from chronic ill-health, including rheumatism, and she died in 1843. Until about 1824 Ichabod did much to improve his estate, and planted many trees. In 1824 the family stayed in London in a rented house in Harley Street; Ichabod's daughter Henrietta (b.1806) married Henry Howard, son of Lord Carlisle of Castle Howard; and Ichabod began his diaries, which continued until 1860, two years before his death [Fry 1991]. The diaries provide interesting details of the family's life style, their holidays, usually by coach, stays at spas, the minutiae of family life and Ichabod's opinions and prejudices.

Ichabod Wright was a complicated and in some ways contradictory character. Fry [1991] wrote 'Perhaps his successes as a banker, landed squire and soldier need to be set beside his reactionary views on society'- such as his disapproval of education for the masses. He was physically tough, surviving many illnesses and quack doctors in his long life. At 65 he still enjoyed hunting; he recovered from English cholera aged 81 in 1848; and he continued to ride in all weathers despite severe falls at 88 and 90 years of age. He commanded a troop of the Yeomanry cavalry from 1794 to 1807, and later became Lieut. Colonel of the Nottingham Volunteers, dealing with riots. In 1831 he felt particularly threatened by the Reform movement, and the laxity of the authorities in dealing with it. He was a devoted patriarch, a great supporter of local charities, especially Nottingham General Hospital and Carrington village and church. His devoted and admiring youngest daughter, Sophia, who looked after him in his later years, wrote of her 'excellent and kind father', who had a humble opinion of himself, and was respected and loved by all who knew him'. But he was also a reactionary who deplored mass education, including the establishment of the Mechanics Institution, which led to serious disagreement with his brother, John Smith Wright, who was largely responsible for its successful establishment.

In 1830 Ichabod became involved in serious disagreement also with his cousin John Wright of Lenton Hall, who he regarded as selfish, and with an 'ungentlemanly domineering manner'. It led to the dissolution of the partnership at Wrights' bank in the year in which John Wright retired and his son Francis took over the direction of the Butterley Company. This was a crucial event which inevitably led to Francis Wright's sale of the Lenton Hall estate to Lord Middleton in 1845, and migration to Derbyshire.

Ichabod Wright was aged 95 when he died at Mapperley Hall in 1862. Frederick Jackson's map of the estate in 1863, 'the property of I.C.Wright Esq.', suggests an inventory made for inheritance purposes. Ichabod's eldest son, Ichabod Charles Wright, had moved from Watnall Hall to Bramcote, and then in about 1860 to Stapleford Hall. He moved again, to Mapperley Hall after his father's death, and remained there until about 1869. On 25 August 1869 he agreed, with co-leasers Henry Smith Wright (who had just moved to Lenton Hall) and his brother Frederick (who later sold Lenton Hall) to lease Mapperley Hall and part of the estate for 7 years to Edward Manlove of Ruddington, a member of the very well-known machine manufacturing and engineering firm of Manlove, Alliott, of Bloomsgrove Works, Ilkeston Road, Nottingham. Manlove had use of the Hall, its 8 acres of gardens and pleasure grounds, and 14 acres of pasture - only a lesser part of the estate - and with two bedrooms 'reserved for leasers' storages'. Ichabod Charles, still (wrongly) named at Mapperley Hall by Wright's Directory, died in 1871 aged 76 at Heathfield Hall, Sussex, then a home of his son Col. Charles Ichabod Wright of Stapleford Hall.

Ichabod Charles Wright (1795-1871) was one of the brightest, and in later life one of the most eccentric members of the Wright family. He was educated at Eton (1808-14) and Christchurch College Oxford (1814-17), and was a Fellow of Magdalen College from 1819 until 1825, when he married Theodosia, daughter of Lord Denman (afterwards Lord Chief Justice) and joined his father Ichabod in the banking business as joint manager and later partner. As a scholar he was interested in classical literature, and is known from his publications in that field and also in banking. Jacks [1881] described him as 'not only a ripe scholar, but a thoroughly practical man' who 'combined with a cultivated intellect and the possession ,of high scholastic acquirements a genuine spirit of business. Such a combination is rare ...'.

The University's Hallward Library holds copies of several of the books of Ichabod Charles Wright:

> Dante Alighieri, *The Inferno.* (London 1833)
> Dante Alighieri, *The Divine Comedy.* 3 volumes, New Edition (Longmans, London, 1845)
> Dante Alighieri, *The Divine Comedy* translated into English verse: illustrated....after....Flaxman. (4th Edition, London 1861; 5th Edition, London 1867)
> *A letter to the Dean of Canterbury on the Homeric lectures of Matthew Arnold* (London, 1864) pamphlet.

In later life he published a translation of the first part of the *Iliad* of Homer in blank verse, and a selection from the Psalms in verse, written when he was partially blind. The *Dictionary of National Biography* XXI 1020-21 includes a critique of his published work. In addition to his versions of Dante and Homer, his interest in the theory as well as the practice of banking led to his publication of:

> *Thoughts on the Currency*(1841)
> *The Evils of the Currency*(1847), an exposition of Sir Robert Peel's Bank Charter Act of 1844, a work which had reached a 6th edition by 1855.
> *The War and our Resources* (1855)

In addition to his partnership in Wrights' Bank, Ichabod Charles Wright was President of the Trustees Savings Bank on Low Pavement from 1852 to 1871, and was followed in this office by his eldest son, Charles Ichabod Wright from 1871 to 1899. He was also a director of the Midland Railway. His wife Theodosia survived him by twenty-five years, and died in 1895. In later life Ichabod Charles was regarded as a great eccentric, and one of his idiosyncrasies was a habit of using an umbrella when riding on horseback in wet weather.

Charles Ichabod Wright, a colonel of the Robin Hoods, was elected M.P. for Nottingham in November 1868, but after little more than a year he applied for the Chiltern Hundreds through ill-health. In 1876 he was recorded at Radcliffe Hall and Watcombe Park, Torquay, which he bought for £23,000 from I.K.Brunel. He had been living at Stapleford Hall from 1869, his father having then moved to Mapperley Hall. It may be noted that one of his younger brothers, Henry Smith Wright, bought Lenton Hall in 1868, and that another younger brother, Frederick, moved from Radcliffe Hall to take his place at Lenton in 1878. But Charles Ichabod was still said to be at Stapleford Hall on 16 February 1877 when he leased Mapperley Hall to William Lambert for 19 years at £560 a year (though Lambert stayed for only about ten years before moving to Lenton Firs). Although it has been stated that Henry Smith Wright 'sold' Lenton Hall and part of that estate to his brother Fred, these moves suggest that the properties were held as portions of common bank property, with a kind of musical chairs among the Halls of Mapperley, Lenton, Radcliffe, and Stapleford. This view is supported by the fact that Henry and Frederick were co-leasers with Charles Ichabod of Mapperley Hall to William Lambert, and by the events of 1903 detailed in Chapter VII. Meantime, starting in 1873, land began to be released for building development in the southern part of the Mapperley estate which was excluded from the Manlove and Lambert leases.

Mapperley Hall was already a large house; but in 1889-90, after William Lambert left it, the Hall was further extended and altered by the architects Robert Evans and William Jolley (who designed the entrance lodge of 1885 which survives on the corner of Mapperley Hall

Drive and Mansfield Road) and Colonel Wright and his son Charles Bingham Wright returned to live there for a time. The latter was still there in 1900, but in March 1903, shortly before the sale of Lenton Hall, the remaining unsold portions of the Mapperley estate, including the Hall, were sold by court order (see Chapter VII). The property was bought by a syndicate, mainly for building development planned by the architect W.B.Starr: but the Hall itself was an embarrassment, and on 12 July 1904 Starr and the Derbyshire brothers released their claims on it, leaving John Ashworth to make an agreement with Nottingham Corporation on 17 January 1905 whereby the Corporation agreed to buy the Hall and 13,000 square yards of grounds for use as a men's hostel for students of the University College. The purchase price was a derisory £3,400 - even less than the £4,000 that was paid for Lenton Hall. With its large reception rooms - for example a dining room measuring 45 by 20 feet - and many other rooms, together with 20 bedrooms and 3 dressing rooms, and other indoor and outdoor accommodation to scale, it was well suited for the purpose at that time. During the first world war it was commandeered as a VAD hospital for 60 patients. The College recovered it in 1919, and it remained a hostel for men until late October 1939, though after 1928, with the removal of the College from Shakespeare Street to Highfields the location was very inconvenient, while the quality of the residential provision was barely acceptable.

Mapperley Hall was closed as a student residence in October 1939. An article contributed by the College itself to 'The Nottinghamshire Countryside' magazine issue published in January 1940 stated that 'When the autumn term opened attendance proved to be larger than had been anticipated in view of the abnormal circumstances' - war having been declared on 3 September. 'Over 500 fulltime students came up' together with 45 overseas students. 'In addition to the College's own students, accommodation has been found in the College buildings for the Institute of Education and Goldsmiths College from the University of London. This has involved housing a further 500 students.... The Hugh Stewart and F.B.Halls of residence have both been given over to women students', the former to 220 Goldsmiths College women and the latter to 153 women from the three Colleges.

A.C.Wood's history of the University College [1953 136] stated that 'At the beginning of the war, when it was seen that there would be a heavy shrinkage in the number of men students, the College Council decided to close Mapperley Hall as a hostel. The building was taken over in April 1940 to serve as the headquarters of Number 3 (North Midland) Region for Civil Defence, and a special war room....was erected in the grounds'. The implications are palpably contradictory, and the real reason for closure is more likely to relate to the announcement by the College in 'The Nottinghamshire Countryside' of July 1939 that '...Lord Trent, Vice-President and Chairman of the [College] Council, had been appointed Regional Commissioner for the North Midlands in the case of National Emergency, and that Principal Wortley had been appointed Deputy Commissioner' than to any expected shortfall of students needing accommodation. As one of the displaced students from Hugh Stewart Hall, and one of the last to be evicted from Mapperley Hall after living there for little more than a fortnight, the writer can testify that at that juncture any sort of satisfactory student lodging was impossible to find. Fractious students advised, or even provoked by an anarchic Warden, would be a more credible reason for the sudden closure of the Hall, with no prior warning to students, than the bland official version.

After its wartime role as the nerve centre of the regional Civil Defence organization, Mapperley Hall was not wanted further as a hostel by the University College, and it was let to the Electricity Board. In 1974 the Severn-Trent water authority began to share it and from 1976 it was occupied wholly as the headquarters of the Lower Trent Division of the Severn-Trent company.

APPENDIX 23

JOHN WRIGHT AND THE FOUNDERS OF THE BUTTERLEY COMPANY

The four founders of Butterley were Benjamin Outram, Francis Beresford, William Jessop sen. and John Wright, who formed a balanced team of two civil engineers, a prosperous banker with commercial knowledge of the iron trade, and an experienced and influential solicitor. Outram and Beresford established the firm of Outram and Co. in 1790, with Outram the driving force - as he was in the building of the Cromford Canal on which Butterley depended in its early days. They were joined by William Jessop and John Wright in the following year, and it was the Wrights and Jessops who were the proprietors two decades later.

Benjamin Outram

Benjamin Outram dominated the enterprise for the first 15 years, when he was virtually the only active partner, and his memory dominated the next ten. A member of a local professional family, with a somewhat precocious reputation as a surveyor and then a canal engineer, he represented 'entrepreneurial talent in need of financial backing'. He obtained this backing first from Francis Beresford, a wealthy Ashbourne solicitor, and subsequently from John Wright of Lenton Hall. He was a man of great and many-sided ability. His father, Joseph Outram (b.1732), son of an Alfreton gardener, became a modest landowner, and was a commissioner for about 20 inclosure awards and trustee of at least three turnpike trusts. As a boy Benjamin Outram engaged the attention of Francis Beresford and of Francis Fitzherbert, an attorney. He made an early survey of the line of the Cromford canal and was an energetic lobbyist for it. By the age of 25 he was in sole charge of its construction (1789-93). He then set up an engineering practice in Derby and Lancashire, and built the Derby Canal (1793-95), Nutbrook Canal ((1793), Huddersfield Narrow Canal (1794) (which included the remarkable Standridge Tunnel, 5698 yards long) and the Peak Forest Canal (to 1801) with the Marple acqueduct over 100 feet high.

Outram and Co. was established in 1790 by Outram and Beresford specifically to exploit the coal and iron reserves of the Butterley Hall estate which Beresford bought in that year, and at the age of 28 Benjamin Outram was living in Butterley Hall and calling himself 'gentleman'. He was perhaps best known as a pioneer of 'railways' (tramways) and realizing their value as feeders for the canals he became a consultant for 'canals with rail branches', usually from collieries, and an enthusiastic promoter of the 'plate rail'. Following the first use of iron rails at Coalbrookdale in 1767, John Carr of Sheffield in 1787 introduced a cast iron rail with a flat tread and vertical inside flange, and in the 1790s 'plate rails' quickly became widespread, with Outram their leading exponent and the works at Butterley a leading producer. In 1801 Outram published 'Minutes to be observed in the construction of rail ways', but eventually he lost the technical argument to William Jessop, a proponent of flanged wheels, and the builder of the Loughborough and Nanpanton railway in 1792. Meanwhile Outram totally dominated the company at Butterley. His untimely sudden death while visiting London in 1805, aged only 37, after having given up outside work to manage Butterley after his marriage to Margaret Anderson in 1800, cut short a highly charged, versatile career that could have made him a towering figure in the history of the country in the first quarter of the 19th century.

Francis Marcus Beresford

While Francis Beresford, the Ashbourne solicitor and owner of Osmaston, played only a brief and mainly indirect part in the establishment and early growth of the Butterley Company, he may have been crucially responsible for drawing John Wright into the enterprise, and ultimately for the migration of Francis Wright from Lenton to Derbyshire. Beresford's role was to provide early capital, and act as trustee for most of the company's real estate. He had sponsored Benjamin Outram even before they were both involved with the Cromford Canal. The wealthy country attorney in June 1790 bought the 200-acre Butterley Hall estate from the Home family. Perhaps even more significantly in the following year, aged 55, he became John Wright's father-in-law on the marriage of his beautiful youngest daughter Elizabeth to John. Only two months later John Wright joined Beresford and Outram. Francis Beresford died in 1801, leaving his quarter share in Butterley and the trusteeship to his son John, who sold the share to John Wright in 1806 but retained the trusteeship until 1830.

The Christian names Fitzherbert and Beresford - and Francis and Marcus - so common among the Lenton Wrights for the past two centuries - derive from the Derbyshire families into which John Wright and his son Francis married - to Elizabeth Beresford in 1791 and Selina Fitzherbert in 1830 respectively. The Fitzherberts were in Derbyshire in the 12th century. The Royalist Colonel Sir John Fitzherbert died without issue in 1649, and left Norbury Manor to William, son of William Fitzherbert of Swynnerton Hall, Staffordshire, who remained there. He had a great, great grandson, Francis Fitzherbert, who succeeded his maternal uncle as the 12th Baron Stafford. His great, great aunt Maria Smythe was the Mrs. Fitzherbert who enjoyed a liaison with King George IV, and went through a form of marriage in 1785. A daughter and eventual co-heiress of John Fitzherbert of Somersal Herbert was the mother of Francis Marcus Beresford, who married Frances Reynolds. Of their four daughters the eldest, Selina, married Samuel Martin, and Marcus Stapleton Martin, the eccentric bachelor who bought and restored Norbury Manor (now occupied by Charles Wright and his family) was one of their descendants. Elizabeth, who married John Wright was the youngest of the four daughters of Francis and Frances Beresford. John Wright's second son and eventual heir and successor, Francis, married Selina the eldest daughter of Sir Henry Fitzherbert of Tissington. The Beresford-Fitzherbert element remained prominent in the names of the heads of the Butterley Company even after it was incorporated in 1888. Thus, of the 12 directors from 1888 to complete their service before 1945 (and nationalization) all but one were surnamed Wright, and seven had the Christian name Beresford or Fitzherbert or both.

William Jessop (1745-1814)

The Jessops, an able but modest family, were associated with the management of Butterley for 90 years. William Jessop senior was one of the great engineers of the industrial revolution - though unaccountably overlooked by the Dictionary of National Biography. Mentor and adviser to the younger Telford, he made an immense contribution to the development of canals, railways, river navigation and drainage, and was in his time 'the great standing counsel of his profession' (Hughes 1844). Born the son of a Devonport shipwright in 1745, he became in 1759 apprenticed to John Smeaton who rebuilt Eddystone lighthouse, improved canals in Yorkshire in the 1770s and worked on the Grand Canal in Ireland. He then worked for the Pinkerton brothers, contractors for the Erewash Canal, opened in 1779, and afterwards on his own account. In 1782-83 Jessop surveyed the river Trent for the promoters of a Bill for its improvement (see Chapter XIII). He settled in Newark in 1786 as the first resident engineer to the Trent Navigation Company, was immediately made alderman and was mayor in 1797. His work on the Trent finished in 1787. Through the 1780s he had been engaged mainly in river improvement , drainage and harbour works, and thereafter he 'kept many balls in the air' By now in his 40s, and recognized as a very conscientious, talented and established engineer, he presented a report of a survey of the proposed route of the Cromford Canal to its promoters in 1788, and in the following year was appointed its engineer at the same time as Francis Beresford was appointed its solicitor. It was here that Jessop first worked with Benjamin Outram, who was appointed his assistant, and 'superintendent' of the project under Jessop.

The difficult and expensive Cromford Canal, with a 1½-mile tunnel and aqueducts over the Amber and the Derwent, was not completed until 1793, but already in 1791 Jessop, together with John Wright, had joined the partnership of Outram and Company. Indeed the seeds of the idea of the Butterley works were probably sown by Jessop in his Cromwell canal report of December 1788, when he commented on the ironmaking potential of the Butterley site. This probably led directly to the purchase of the 200-acre Butterley Hall estate in June 1790 by Francis Beresford, and the establishment of Outram and Company in the same year to exploit the potentialities of the coal, first, and the ironstone, timber and clay, which would be easy to market by the new canal, when completed.

Jessop's greatest direct practical contribution in the early years of Butterley was as a clear-headed adviser of experience, wisdom and integrity. Indirectly it was his practical work, notably on the Cromford Canal, that really set the business going, and which gave rise to the title of 'Golden Valley' applied to the Butterley district; but his work also brought business directly. In particular large contracts for structural cast iron pipes coincided closely with the distribution of Jessop's professional activities. Cromford was his first canal, but he continued to work as a canal engineer through the 1790s, especially on a series of waterways that transformed the East Midlands coalfields, including the Cromford, Nottingham, Grantham and Ashby canals, and the Leicester navigation (river Soar). While engineer to the Trent Navigation Company and both the Nottingham and Cromford Canals he was actively involved with some ten waterways linked with the river Trent as well as various drainage schemes in the eastern counties, waterways problems in Ireland, and other projects, mainly canals, elsewhere in Britain. These included the Barnsley Canal, and later the Grand Junction Canal and the Caledonian Canal in collaboration with Thomas Telford, the West India Docks, London, and the port of Bristol.

About the turn of the century Jessop's interest turned more to railways. Called in to survey an inadequate water supply for a proposed canal in Surrey in 1799 Jessop suggested instead a railway - the 18-mile long Surrey Iron Railway, the first railway company in Britain, for which he acted as principal engineer in 1801-03. An extension was later surveyed by Jessop's son Josias, co-engineer with Benjamin Outram. The technical dispute between Jessop and his partner Outram on the relative merits of plate rails and flanged wheels has been mentioned above. The flanged wheel of the more experienced Jessop, which eliminated awkwardness at a junction, prevailed to become standard. So too did the gauge of 4 feet 8½ inches - the traditional width between the wheels of the Derbyshire wagon or 'corve' - originally chosen for Outram's plate rails.

After 15 years residence at Newark William Jessop, at the age of 60, took Butterley Hall, expensively renovated, but vacant after the death of Benjamin Outram in 1805. He remained there until his death in November 1814 and burial at Pentrich church, where his wife Sarah, 13 years his junior, followed him two years later. In these later years, suffering from a form of paralysis, he lived in retirement and took only occasional consultancies, despite his eminence. He had seven sons. The eldest, Major John Jessop, C.B. (c.1777-1869), a professional army officer severely wounded at Waterloo, renounced his succession to the Butterley partnership in 1839. Josias (1779-1826), also an engineer, assisted his father on the Croydon railway until February 1804, and then became engineer to the Bristol Docks company. Later he was engineer to the first two railway companies in the East Midlands, the Mansfield and Pinxton (1817) and Cromford and High Peak (1825). He died in 1826 aged 45.

The third son, William the younger (c.1781-1852) first took overall control at Butterley after Benjamin Outram's death when only 22 years old, but aided by George Goodwin, called variously 'managing clerk', 'agent' or 'manager', who died in 1848 as 'superintendent' after 51 years with the Company. William was nominated by his father to succeed him as partner in 1814, and under the new partnership of 1815 he had one-third of the capital of £30,000. He was active and able and succeeded his father 'alike in his interests and in his talents'. He followed his father in residence at Butterley Hall. He was, in his way, a character as remarkable as his father, and when he died in 1852, a year after his retirement, his 'friends and workmen' erected the monumental column in Codnor park 'as a tribute to his private work, great talents and public excellence'. He was in charge at Butterley for 46 years, for 37 of them as junior partner to John and then Francis Wright, but made an immense contribution to the development of the company. Henry and George, younger brothers of William Jessop the younger, (there was also Charles, born in 1786) went to India for the Company, the former being appointed by the East India Company to supervise the construction of a bridge over the Gomptee at Lucknow.

The position as 'working partner' and the major part of the shares of the second William Jessop who held one-third of the capital, went to his nephew, a third William Jessop, son of Major John, though 32/80ths of the Jessop share allocation went to George.

APPENDIX 24

RETAIL BUSINESSES AT SPRING CLOSE, LENTON

9 Spring Close

-1864-65- John Stafford butcher
1869-1886: John Smith grocer, earthenware
1887-91- Arthur Tinkler shopkeeper
-1894-97- Samuel A. Tinkler, shopkeeper
-1900-1910- G.H.Twigg shopkeeper
-1912-20- Lester Sykes shopkeeper
1922- Mrs. Florence Lindley
-1925-56- Mrs. S.A. Foottit

11 Spring Close ('The Travellers Rest')

-1840-61: Joseph Hull plumber and glazier
1862-65- Frederick Thorneley
-1869-86 John North
1887-97- A.Keetley
-1900-13- William Pell
-1915 Mrs. Rebecca Cass
1916-20- George Lomas
-1922-28- Herbert Thorpe
-1932- Albert Alford
-1936- Archie Severn
-1941- A.E.Yeomans

13 Spring Close (1 Snowton Terrace)

-1848-54- Matthew Hadden lace-maker and shopk.
-1858- Wm. Whitehouse, shopkeeper
-1862-65- Thomas Harston shopkeeper
-1871- James Beresford fishmonger/greengrocer
-1876-87- John Shaw, skinner, grocer
-1889-91- George Osborne, shopkeeper
-1894-1928- J.E. Griffiths, grocer/coal
-1932- Frederick Stedham, shopkeeper
-1936-John Coleman shopkeeper
-1950-56- Wm. Hopkinson grocer

10 Commercial Street

-1864-97- George Selby grocer, shopkeeper
1900 Henry Wale
1900- Alfred Henry Bott shopkeeper
-1904-05 Wm. Tomlinson fish frier
1905-10- Thomas Brooks greengrocer
-1915-1936 Robert Brooks, greengrocer

15 Commercial Street

-1869- Thomas Beresford, shopkeeper
-1876- Henry Wormall haberdasher
-1881- Mrs. Mary Ann Wormall, widow,grocer
-1887-89- Thomas Fox small ware dealer
-1891- Henry Brooks joiner, cabinet mkr.
-1894-1900- Mrs. Mary Brooks, small ware then haberdasher and milliner
-1904-08- Henry Brooks haberdasher
-1910-28- Mrs. Mary Brooks haberdasher
-1932-41- Wm. Garner, shopk.
-1950-56- Mrs. Rosetta Garner

25 Commercial Street

-1894 George Thompson shopkeeper
1895-97 Mervill Israel shopkeeper
-1900-05- Joseph Buttery shopkeeper
-1908-13- Mrs. Anne Hemstock, shopkeeper
-1915-16- Mrs. Jane Clarke, shopkeeper
-1920-50- Charles A.Roe shopkeeper
-1956- Mrs.Rebecca Roe shopkeeper

Note: Hyphens before and after dates indicate that terminal dates might be earlier or later respectively than the years given.

APPENDIX 25

OCCUPIERS OF THE HOUSES AT HILLSIDE BETWEEN THE MALTING AND LYNDALE HOUSE, 1841 TO 1881 AND 1928 TO 1956.

Nos. 6 and 7 Hillside (northern cottage)	Nos. 4 and 5 Hillside (southern cottage)
1841	
John Pearson (60), agric. labourer Sarah his wife (56), a daughter, sons William (19) maltster and James (17) also a maltster.	William Smith (35) maltster and wife
John Pearson (40), agric. labourer his wife and 3 children	John Kirkham (59) shoemaker.(In Lascelles and Hagar[1848] called 'cart owner' of Canal Side)
1851	
Sarah Pearson (67) widow, with 3 adult children, Mary, William and James.	Mary Bingham (28), her brothers William (21) and John (18) and Mary's daughter.
John Pearson (52) agric. labourer his wife Ann and 3 sons	John Kirkham (70) widower, agric. labourer. George Kirkham (38), labr. (Sarah Radford (38) and 4 children - visitors). George Kirkham was fishmonger in 1858 [Wright 1858].
1861	
Mary Pearson (44), her unmarried brothers William and James, both agric. labourers.	William Bingham, unmarried, warper. His sister Mary Bingham (39) brother John and niece Sarah.
John Pearson, agric. labr., wife Ann (65), son Thomas (22) agric. labr., grandson Joseph (7).	John Kirkham, agric. labr.(was shoemaker) George Kirkham, labourer and pig feed dealer, wife Sarah, 3 children and general servant Hannah Flint.
1871	
Mary Pearson (59) washer woman, her brothers William (49) and James (45), both gardeners.	William Bingham (38) unmarried, warper, Mary Bingham (46), retired housekeeper, niece Sarah Ann (24) unmarried lace worker.
John Pearson (75) labourer, Joseph Pearson his grandson (18) gardener	Sarah Kirkham (44) widow of George, laundress: son-in-law John Kirkham, boatman, George Kirkham (16) boatman. 3 children
1881	
Mary Pearson (66) unmarried, market stall keeper. Brothers James (55), William (59) gardeners.	Sarah Kirkham (54) widow, washer woman, son Charles (19) daughter Hannah (17). Boarder John Tickwell (61) cordwainer
William Smith (77) widower retired	

The house numbers given above are those quoted in the 1881 census books. Lyndale House was No. 8. The house numbering was changed after the building of the terrace in 1902-03. It is not known who owned these cottages, but it may have been members of the Pearson and Kirkham families.

RESIDENTS OF HILLSIDE NORTH OF THE TERRACE, IN THE 'NEW' HOUSES

1928	*1932*	*1936*
6. James Norris	6. James Norris	6. James Norris
8. Rd. Bernard Berry	8. Percy Bealby	
10. Joseph Frank Hammersley	10. J.F.Hammersley	10. J.F.Hammersley
12. Robert Smith	12. Robert Smith	12. Robert Owen Smith
14. Wm. Albert Norris Wm. Archibald Norris	14. Wm. Albert Norris Wm. Archibald Norris	14. Wm. Archibald Norris

1941	*1950*	*1956*
6. James Norris	6. R. Owen	6. Joseph Lunn
8. George War	8. Miss Nellie M. Holmes	8. Miss N.M.Holmes
10. J.F.Hammersley	10. Lewis Reynolds	10. Lewis Reynolds
12. Robert O.Smith	12. John W.Ross	12. John W. Ross
14. Wm. Archibald Norris	14. Wm. Archibald Norris	14. Wm. Archibald Norris

---

APPENDIX 26

HOUSEHOLDERS OF THE HILLSIDE TERRACE, 1936-1956

Source - Kellys Directories

1936	*1941*	*1950*
18 Mrs. Fanny Lings	18 Mrs. Fanny Lings	18 Harold G.Weaver
20 Percy William Brown	20 Miss Annie G.Brown	20 - -
22 Albert Jarvis (driller)	22 Albert Jarvis	22 Mrs. Louisa F.Jarvis
	24 Isaiah Gregory (miner)	24 Isaiah Gregory
26 Arthur Knight (fitter)	26 Arthur Knight	26 Arthur Knight
28 Sidney Watson (cycle hand)	28 Sidney Watson	28 Herbert Mason
30 Mrs. Annie Hardy	30 Mrs. Annie Hardy	30 Frederick Nutts
32 Harry Mayo	32 Harry Mayo	32 Joseph Troop
34 James Hilton (compositor)	34 Elijah Twigg (labourer)	34 Elijah Twigg
36 Albert Kirchin (fitter)	36 Albert Kirchin	36 Mrs. Ada Kirchin
38 Leslie Wynn (bus conductor)	38 Leslie Wynn	38 Mrs. Gertrude Wynn
40 Ernest Topley (carter)	40 Ernest Topley	40 Ernest Topley
42 Mrs.Laura Miller(shop)	42 Mrs.L.Miller(shop)	42 Mrs.L.Miller(shop)
44 Wm.W.Kenyon (builder)	44 Wilfred Naylor (butcher)	44 Arthur P.Hill
46 Henry Hill (haulage contractor)	46 Harry Hill (transport driver)	46 Harry Hill
48 Horace Pratten (porter)	48 Horace Pratten	48 Horace Pratten

50 Ernest Henshaw (millwright)	50 Cyril Arthur Hawkes (textile worker)	50 Cyril A.Hawkes
52 Frank Lyon (labr.)	52 Frederick Lyon	52 Frederick Lyon
54 Arthur Stevenson (railway checker)	54 Arthur Stevenson	54 George H.Key
56 James Denny (bricklayer)	56 Frederick Westhorpe (cutter)	56 Frederick Westhorpe
58 Albert Keeting	58 Alfred Keeting	58 Alfred Keeting
60 Christopher Smith (fish salesman)	60 - -	60 Miss Annie Woolley
62 Hugh W.Brown (labourer)	62 Samuel E Goodwin (motor driver)	62 Samuel E.Goodwin
64 Harry Hart (bus driver)	64 Harry Hart (bus driver)	64 Mrs. Betsy K.L.Hart
66 Herbert Luglan(miner)	66 John Dudley (labr.)	66 - -
68 Miss Louisa Hart	68 Miss Louisa Hart	68 Miss Louisa Hart
70 Wm. Buckingham (gardener)	70 Mrs. Edith Buckingham	70 Alan Fowles
72 Mrs. Clara Priest	72 Mrs.Florence Laverack	72 Arthur J.Hopewell
Thos. F.Suffolk	Thos. F.Suffolk (moulding sand merchant)	

Different occupiers in 1956: No. 60 - Mrs. Helena L.Booth: No.66 - Frederick A.Brown: No. 68 - Mrs. Nellie Grant. Otherwise as 1950.

SUBSCRIBERS

1 Mrs. Sue Drury
2 Jan Perrett
3 Mrs. P.A. Hill
4 J. Roy
5 F.E. Ritter
6 Mrs. D.E. Summers
7 Helen Struthers
8 Mrs. Pat Thorpe
9 Dr. John Goldingay
10 Roberta Lloyd
11 Dr. Michael D. Steven
12 Rosemary Gower
13 David & Thalia Crossland
14 Judge T.R. Heald
15 Prof. Paul M. Mather
16 Betty Wright
17 Dr. Charles Watkins
18-19 Mary Foley
20 Dr. M.J. McCullagh
21 Peter Hoare
22 Helen Phillips
23 Keith Williams
24 Nicholas & Elaine Barnes
25 Prof. John P. Cole
26 Dr. Peter R. Mounfield
27 Rev. Prof. Douglas J. Davies
28 Derby Hall Library
29 Dr. R.E. Gilbert
30 Dr. J.R. Moon
31 Dr. R.R. Laxton
32 Mark Dale
33 Ian R. Brothwell
34 Dr. Harold Booth
35 Meryl & Alan Aldridge
36 Dr. C.D. Litton
37 P.J. Holland
38 Prof. Monica Partridge
39 Mrs. Mary Lucas
40 Dr. J.C Horton
41 Dr. V. van der Lande
42 Dr. P.R. Seddon
43 D.R. Ringer
44 Carol J. Foster
45 Diana Barley
46 Mrs. Mary Glodkowski
47 Prof. Sir John Smith
48 Dr. Nigel H. Day
49 Dr. Kathleen Collard
50 Audrey & Bernard Lowe
51 Dr. R.I. Winton
52 Glenys M.P. Wortley
53-55 Mrs. K.E. Willoughby
56 D.K. Whynes
57 Dr. Dennis R. Mills
58 Dr. M. Siriol Colley
59 Sir John Anstey
60 Prof. Peter G. Morris
61 Prof. Hinrich Siefken
62 Peter J.D. Preston
63 Mrs. Margaret E. Pykett
64 Dr. Catherine Delano-Smith
65 Brian Loughbrough
66 Dr. R.J. Godfrey
67 Dr. P.T. Wheeler
68 Prof. G.B. Warburton
69 Dr. & Mrs. Donald Rutherford
70 Dr. D.B. Sowerby
71 Howard Taylor & Clare Stewart
72 Dr. John & Mrs. Gillian Farina
73 Walter R. Chalmers
74-75 Dr. M.E. Sprackling
76 Prof. R.H. Osborne
77 Prof. Michael Jones
78 Prof. E.M. Rawstron
79 David C. Griffin
80 Ron Hodges
81 Mrs. W. G. Eltringham
82 William C. Bell
83 David & Mary Alcock
84 John Hollick Frisby
85 Mary F. Robertson
86 Harry & Felicity Rose
87 Djeet & Mitter Bedi
88 Ann Melly
89 Christopher Lewis
90 Mrs. B.M. Parsons
91 Peter Yoong-Pin Lee
92 G. Oldfield
93 Mrs. Lynn Phillips
94 Prof. S.D. Chapman
95 Peter B. Dodson
96 Dr. David W. Bullard
97 Mrs. Myrtle Shaw
98 Robert Frazier
99 Ian M. Conway
100 Dr. & Mrs. R.J. Grout
101 Prof. M.J. Owen
102 Alan E. West
103 Guy & Dallas Barnes
104 Dr. R.E. Dugdale
105 Sandra & Ray Shipp
106 Roger J. Hawkins
107 Roger & Jennie Mansfield
108 Ancaster Hall
109 Dr. Duncan Martin
110 Dr. Stephen Hibberd
111 Greta Stone
112 Prof. Lawrie & Mrs. Jennifer Challis
113 John Paul Dixon Waine
114 David W. Guest
115 Kenneth R. Marshall
116 John Bonell
117 D. Ford
118 Rachel Lindley
119 Dr. E.J. Slater
120 J.M. Hounsfield
121 Philip & Christine Ward
122 Thomas Yat-chan Ng

123 Pete Ross
124 Mrs. Ellen Litman
125 R.D. Sells
126 Claire Wells
127 J.B. & Mrs. J.M. Mowbray
128 T.K. Shaw
129 Dr. G.A. Roberts
130 Prof. M. & Dr. J.F. Poliakoff
131 Gertrude M. Watson
132 Michael Brook
133 Mark J. Kimber
134 Douglas A. Turner
135 Norman Turner
136 Ian T. Radmore
137 Nottingham Subscription Library Ltd.
138 Graham Nannery
139 Dr. Peter Morris
140 Marcus & Jill Oakland
141 Lenton Local History Society
142 C.M. & M.M. Voisey
143 Leonard Taylor
144 Mrs. J.M. Bamford
145 Prof. & Mrs. R.L. Storey
146 W. Grauberg
147 A.E. Lewin
148 Prof. Harold Mattingly
149 Grace M. Beurle
150 Alan H. Wood
151 Dr. Dorothy Johnston
152 Dr. Alan Wint
153 Lincoln Hall Library
154 Dr. S.C. Wallwork
155 P.J. Robinson
156 Prof. E.N. & Mrs. B.E. Corlett
157 Michele Godley
158 Dr. J.H. Molyneux
159 Dr. E. Andrew Boyd
160 Peter & Margaret Crampton
161 Dr. Maurice Caplan
162 Miss S.M. Jones
163 Dr. Philip Baker
164 M.S. Goodman
165 Dr. Roy Bradshaw
166 Sheila O'Connor
167 K.R. Osborn
168 P.A. Neaverson
169 Mr. & Mrs. J.G. Caine
170 Colin A. Hobday
171 Mary & Malcolm Stacey
172 Valerie Rampton
173 Beryl Robinson
174 Christine Ashbee
175 V.H. Taylor
176 Prof. Jane Robinson
177 Jean Russell-Gebbett
178 Dr. S. Seymour
179 Jean Reid
180 Prof. David & Mrs. Peggy Greenfield
181-182 Mrs. Mary Hampshire
183 Stewart Buckthorp
184 Prof. H. Fessler
185 J.R. Haylock
186 S. Zaleski
187 Keith Atherton
188 Mrs. Pam Summers
189 Mrs. Margaret Litchfield
190 Dr. B.H. Tolley
191 Elizabeth M. Steel
192 Alison Stuart
193 Steve & Fiona Rowntree
194 Mrs. Christine Eberlin
195 Prof. Arthur J. Willcocks
196 Dr. J.C. Doornkamp
197 Lenton & Wortley Hall
198-199 Ian Hooker
200 Mrs. Muriel Mitchell
201 Mrs. Monica Stokes
202 Oliver Kingdon
203 Mavis Withnall
204 Linda Shaw
205 Prof. A.T. Birmingham
206 Hallward Library
207 David Gray
208 Brian L. Jones
209 Sheila A. Chambers
210 Janet G. Jones
211 Mrs. G. Wraith
212 A.G. Hammond
213 John Davies
214 M.G. Standeven
215 Robin & Barbara Phillips
216 Veronica Smith
217 John Elliott
218 Arnold E. Teager
219 Glenna & Donald Ager
220 Dr. C.J. Timmons
221 D.N. & J.E. Robinson
222 Nicola Lukes
223 Tony Storey
224 G.V. Reed
225 H.J. Penfold
226 Adam Russell
227 Julian Beck
228 Peter Reeve
229 Denis Vernon Tamplin
230 Charlotte Elizabeth Riggs
231 Mrs. Janet P. Blest
232 Daphne C. Williams
233 Neil Scott
234 R. Cooke

235 Linda Caller
236 Godfrey Hare
237 Roger Davy
238-240 Notts. County Library (Local Studies Library)
241-243 Dr. John Giggs
244 Mrs. Barbara Edwards
245 Dr. David J. Brown
246 V.P. Williams
247 T. Bowmer
248 John M. Bates
249 Mrs. B.E. Bloor
250 Prof. & Mrs. Malcolm Woodbine
251 Steven & Catherine Stead
252 Trevor Buck
253 Blackwells University Bookshop
254 Elaine Watts
255 Dr. R.B. Waterhouse
256 Victoria E. Barnes

Remaining names unlisted